COMPUTER LAW

Other books in *Essentials of Canadian Law* Series

ESSENTIALS OF CANADIAN LAW

COMPUTER LAW

GEORGE S. TAKACH

Partner, McCarthy Tétrault
Special Lecturer in Computers,
Information, and the Law
Osgoode Hall Law School,
York University

COMPUTER LAW
© George S. Takach, 1998

Published in 1998 by
Irwin Law
325 Humber College Blvd.
Toronto, Ontario
M9W 7C3

ISBN: 1-55221-016-2

Canadian Cataloguing in Publication Data

Takach, George S. (George Steven)
    Computer law

(Essentials of Canadian law)
Includes bibliographical references and index.
ISBN 1-55221-016-2

1. Computers – Law and legislation – Canada.
I. Title.   II. Series.

KE452.C6T34 1997   343.7109'99   C97-932646-X
KF390.5.C6T34 1997

Printed and bound in Canada.

1   2   3   4   5   02   01   00   99   98

SUMMARY
TABLE OF CONTENTS

DETAILED
TABLE OF CONTENTS

CHAPTER 7:
COMPUTER LAW: DYNAMICS, THEMES, AND SKILL SETS   *429*

FOREWORD

This book is a gem. It is published in the Irwin Essentials of Canadian Law series. It is essential for anyone — lawyer or non-lawyer — interested, intrigued, or impaled by the challenge modern information technology poses for the rule of law. It is Canadian in the sense that much of its data is Canadian-based. But it will be read with profit by anyone, in any jurisdiction, who must deal with the information revolution and the necessary adjustments in private and public law.

The book is a judicious, well-tempered balance of theory and practice. It gives enough technological background to understand the problem and challenge of the computer and communications transformation. It selects legal puzzles drawn from a kaleidoscope of fact patterns from a busy and rapidly changing law practice. It explains and expounds the law, its adaptability, its limits, and then advances reforms concisely and clearly. It will be valuable to specialized, as well as general, lawyers and law students and to non-lawyers interested in these technological changes and the law's response. It is organized elegantly and written eloquently — in short, a joy to read. Choice, selection, focus, and synthesis are precious gifts in crafting the knowledge society from the Information Age. The author displays these gifts splendidly.

The author has practised computer law for a dozen years and taught it for half that time at two eminent Canadian law schools. The book reflects the distilled wisdom of that experience. The author wrestles with practical, urgent, and endlessly novel problems by imaginatively conceptualizing them in an intellectual framework that takes one back to first principles. The book also demonstrates a scholar's love of history. It skilfully compares the law's response to other related technologies from the printing press forward. And, in one especially intriguing analysis of the evolution of the "signature" for contractual authentication, he reaches back to the Old Testament book of Ruth to describe the giving over of one of a pair of sandals to a contracting party trader in a commercial transaction. The one sandal would be measured for equivalent wear against the other when the contract was to be executed. Thus, in the author's words we are now striving not for the electronic signature but the electronic "sandal," or perhaps its footprint. Reaching forward, he then anticipates new biomedical technologies for authentication by retinal scan or the reading of a fingerprint finely calibrated to ensure it is live and not severed from its owner.

The book comprehensively canvasses Canadian reported — and some unreported — law. But it also navigates confidently among leading and novel U.S. and U.K. precedents with occasional excursions into the European Community. It carefully distinguishes between situations that are genuinely new — a qualitative change — and those that simply represent modest enhancements on the technological scale as viewed through the law's eye. In making those distinctions it insists on a rigorous functional analysis of novelty and an avoidance of the dangerous and loosely applied metaphors that mask the change.

Canada is in an enviable position to lead the information technology revolution. One test of this leadership is whether we have the human resource and human science skills — law, finance, accounting, entrepreneurship — to undergird and enhance impressive scientific and technological accomplishment. This book is a telling testimony that we do in law.

David Johnston
Faculty of Law
McGill University
Chair, Canadian Information Highway Advisory Council

To the two women in my life —
Janis for your unending support and
Natalie for the daily wonder and joy

PREFACE

The computer is the defining technological device of the last quarter of the twentieth century. Encircling the globe with high-capacity computer networks, the Internet included, will be the major technological feat of the first quarter of the twenty-first century. These computer and communications developments have made information the critical asset of our time, surpassing in importance the traditional assets of land and physical goods. Such technological, economic, and social trends have brought into focus the importance of computer law. Therefore, after practising it for the last dozen years and teaching it at law schools for the last half-dozen years, it gives me great pleasure to discuss the principal features of computer law and to canvass its primary controversies and challenges. As part of the Essentials of Canadian Law series, this book does not purport to be comprehensive, but it does throw its light widely, illuminating the peaks and even some of the valleys of computer law.

The Theory and Practice of Computer Law

Although some readers may question whether computer law should be considered a separate jurisdiction on the legal map, I believe that well before reaching the final chapter, they will agree with me that there is indeed a discernible legal subdiscipline worthy of this title. This cannot be surprising given the enormous impact of the computer and information industries on the economy and on society at large. Law is a reflection of the human environment from which it emanates. Therefore, how could there not be a computer law, given that we are witnessing the computer revolution usher in the Information Age? Moreover, the diverse subtopics that constitute computer law are united by common dynamics and themes. This book, by proposing the four dynamics of computer law, makes a particularly strong case for the legal subdiscipline of computer law. Such an approach — a theory of computer law — has important ramifications both from an academic perspective, as well as from the point of view of the day-to-day practice of law.

This book is accessible to the newcomer to computer law, as well as interesting to the expert, and useful to both. The time-starved practitioner will use it most as a quick reference guide, entering it by means of the index, or table of cases, or table of contents, in a non-linear manner, as if it were a website. And such use is to be welcomed; if the book helps a harried lawyer meet a deadline or assists an articling student find a case just on point, well that is wonderful. I should, however, alert practitioners to the fact that there are a number of cross-references in the text, and I hope they will follow up on these when considering a particular issue. As a reference work, the usefulness of this book can be enhanced by a cover-to-cover read. Understanding the dynamics and themes that recur and animate the different areas of computer law can help the busy practitioner solve day-to-day problems. By the same token, legislators, academics, and regulators need to learn about the specific cases in order to make good law and policy. Macro and micro. Forest and trees. In this book I have tried to fuse theory with practice, as each illuminates, informs, and improves the other.

The importance of mastering and integrating theory *and* practice in the computer law field is a principle I teach my law students. Theory and practice, so often two solitudes in other subdisciplines of the law, simply must converge in the computer law area if the law hopes to remain relevant in this hugely important realm of human endeavour. Thus, when teaching computer law, law school must act as both a social science faculty and a professional school preparing students for the practice of law. And computer law is an ideal course for teaching substantive law and legal method. Most law school courses focus on an area of law, like contracts, and draw on examples from a range of industries, activities, and fact patterns. This is a valuable pedagogical approach, but so is one that focusses on an industry and then draws on the various subareas in the law that apply to the technologies and business practices within it. At the level of theory, this teaching method allows for comparative learning, as the nature and effect of different legal subfields are compared and contrasted. And with respect to legal practice, this method of education is indispensable because, of course, clients rarely prepackage their problems into neat, tidy, legal pigeonholes; instead, the file comes in the door as a mess of facts that cuts across a wide swath of potential legal (and extralegal) remedies. Former students of mine who never intended to practise computer law — they took the course because it sounded interesting in the law school syllabus – have commented that even though they now practise family law, general corporate-commercial law, or what have you, they very much appreciated the skill sets they acquired during the computer law course. In a similar vein, but at another level, before delving into an analysis of the law, this book begins with a first chapter that canvasses the key elements and societal implications of computer-based technologies, thus firmly grounding the theoretical law in the practical technolgy.

How did I choose the particular topics covered by this book? Partly, the selection is intended to reflect what computer lawyers do. This should please those of my partners at McCarthy Tétrault who still ask me from time to time what my law practice is all about. And my practice does touch all the topics covered in this book, though some with more frequency than others.[1] Also, the book covers many of the topics that are included in the computer law courses I have taught over the last six years at Osgoode Hall Law School, York University, and the Faculty of Law, University of Toronto. In short, the topics covered by this book are the ones of most relevance and interest to my clients and students, and to me. It should be noted, however, that this book does not discuss the impact of computers on lawyers and their practice of law. This is an interesting and important area, but is simply a different topic from the substantive legal issues that I consider to make up computer law, and thus is not treated here.[2]

A word is perhaps in order about the title of this work. I have chosen *Computer Law*, notwithstanding that other works in the field are appearing under the titles of *Information Technology Law*, *Droit d'Informatique* (in France), *Internet Law*, and a host of other names. Indeed, I added the word "Information" to my law school course title a few years ago, so that it now reads "Computers, Information, and the Law." And I was tempted to call this work *Computer and Internet Law* because the Internet features prominently in its pages. Although all these monikers are

---

1 One aspect of my practice, however, that is not reflected here is the mergers, acquisitions, and financing legal work I do for technology companies and their investors. More precisely, the discussion does not extend to share and asset purchase agreements, or shareholders and lending arrangements, but in other respects the material in this book is very relevant to high-tech M&A/financing legal work. For a useful book covering these and other business law topics related to technology companies, see George S. Takach, *The Software Business in Canada: Financing, Protecting and Marketing Software*, 2d ed. (Toronto: McGraw-Hill, 1997), and for a book focussing on the venture capital financing business from a U.S. perspective (venture capital and related financing being such an important driver of computer businesses), see Joseph W. Bartlett, *Venture Capital: Law, Business Strategies, and Investment Planning* (New York: John Wiley & Sons, 1988).

2 For a perceptive study of the profound impact that computers, and particularly computer networks, will have on the legal profession, their place in society, and on the nature of legal practice, see M. Ethan Katsh, *Law in a Digital World* (New York: Oxford University Press, 1995).

valuable, in the end I have settled on *Computer Law* because it is short, pithy, and, when all is said and done, the computer is still the glue that connects the many facets of law discussed in the following pages.

Inevitable Obsolescence

All books about the law become dated rather quickly, as new statutes are passed, new court decisions are rendered, and new issues make their way onto the legal radar screen. This occupational hazard of the legal writer is perhaps most acute in the computer law field, given the breakneck pace of change within the technological and business spheres that underpin this area of law. Some would even question the utility of a book in such an environment. Obviously, I strongly disagree. Of course, there will be new technical and legal developments — in the computer law field, they are a daily occurrence. It is, however, precisely the daily avalanche of new legal precedents and conundrums that makes it necessary to stand back and take stock from time to time. Canadian computer law practitioners can be forgiven for sometimes feeling overwhelmed at the daunting task of staying current with new developments. In addition to keeping abreast of Canadian happenings, the global nature of the computer business and of their clients' activities requires them to at least have a passing knowledge of developments in the United States, Europe, and increasingly in Asia as well. And while the Internet assists in this endeavour, it also compounds the challenge by bringing to the Canadian lawyer's desktop yet another stream of digital information to be reviewed and digested.

Thus, there is a need for a framework of analysis — a user interface — by which to manage this huge amount of legal information. While this book attempts to state the law as at May 1998, it equally strives to provide a conceptual architecture within which lawyers, judges, law students, computer business and technical people, legislators, regulators, and policy analysts can make sense of the vast mass of computer-related legal material that buffets them daily. What follows is an astrolabe for legally navigating the digital seas. As well, it discusses a set of skill sets that people involved in the computer and network industries can use to weather the next information-based storm. Of course, even these tools will need to be recalibrated from time to time; and the new cases and statutes will need to be chronicled, so there will be a second edition of this book, probably early in the new millennium. Accordingly, I would be obliged if you would send me your comments on the following discussion, including references to cases and developments you think are important that have been left out, and other matters (or unreported cases, etc.) you think should be mentioned in the next edition. A truly meaningful legal text is like a living tree: it needs nourishment from its readers. Or, drawing on a computer analogy, the second edition of a book is like a successful new release of a software product — both require active input from their users. I look forward to hearing from you, and you can contact me at:

George S. Takach
McCarthy Tétrault
Suite 4700, Toronto Dominion Bank Tower
Toronto-Dominion Centre
Toronto, Ontario
Canada
M5K 1E6

phone: (416) 601-7662
fax: (416) 868-1891
e-mail: gtakach@mccarthy.ca

Quality versus Quantity

A word is required about the depth of treatment of the subjects covered by this book. Some will wonder why a particular issue was not expanded upon, or why a subtopic was not worthy of an entire chapter, and so on. Clearly, this book could be twice as long (and still these same questions could be reasonably asked). In keeping with the mandate of the Essentials of Canadian Law series, however, I have endeavoured to focus on that which is essential, just as an artist might try to capture the "essence" of a bowl of fruit in a still life painting. When the law school course I teach was a small seminar and students had to write term papers, I purposely limited these essays to a rather short length, and not because I had to read them all. When students first learned of the brief paper length they were elated. It was only later, as they got into the research and writing, that they learned the hard truth that it is easier (by far) to write a long paper than a short paper. And so it is, I think, with a book. The reason I limited the length of the papers was to force the students to think and, most importantly, to exercise judgment. In a seventy-page student paper even the least inspired author will eventually stumble across all the relevant points, but in the meantime may force the reader through forty-five pages of unnecessary chaff. To write a good paper that does not exceed twenty pages, now that is a skill.

I learned this lesson from two people. One was a university professor who had every student in his course write a five-page paper every week; I have never been as intellectually challenged, and I have never learned so much, before or since. In a legal context the point was brought home to me early in my career by John J. Robinette, perhaps the greatest legal advocate this country has ever known. I was just back from the bar admission course as a junior lawyer at McCarthy Tétrault (then still McCarthy & McCarthy) when I had to research and draft a legal opinion that was to be signed (and liberally revised) by Mr. Robinette. In my first draft of the opinion I cited three cases as authority for a particular point. I'll never forget Mr. Robinette looking up from the draft and asking, gently but firmly, "Which of these three decisions is *the* leading case?" I pointed to it. He then smiled and in a manner that endeared him to his colleagues, he put a thin pencil line through the other two and said, "Then we won't be needing these." I tried to remember this advice as I wrote each paragraph of this book.

A sentiment similar to the one expressed by Mr. Robinette came frequently to mind as I read many of the older cases that I cite in this book. The cases that date from the last century and the early part of this one are so much shorter than today's decisions, but without any appreciable diminution in quality. As a junior lawyer some years ago I asked a secretary at McCarthy's who was close to retirement how lawyers managed to prepare complex legal documents before the advent of word processing, when adding or subtracting something meant a lengthy manual retyping of the whole document. I said this to the secretary as I returned a draft for what must have been its sixth rewrite, and I added, "You must be delighted with this new technology that makes revisions so much simpler and faster." The secretary thought for a moment, smiled, and replied: "Not really, I actually work more on a document now because of all the changes the young lawyers make. You see, in the days of the manual typewriter, lawyers simply got it right the first time, and they managed to close deals with a lot less paper." Again, I have taken the advice to heart; I have tried to get it right, succinctly.

Foreign Judicial Decisions

The judicial decisions referred to in the following pages are, not surprisingly, primarily Canadian. There is, however, a liberal sprinkling of American, British, and even Australian case law in this book. Some will find this startling, but it really should not raise eyebrows. The simple truth is it is an extremely common practice for Canadian judges to cite judicial authorities from other countries.[3] In literally every subarea of

---

3   The compliment is also repaid: see, for example, *Howley v. Whipple*, 48 N.H. 487 (1869), an early U.S. telegraph case that cites an even earlier Upper Canada telegraph case, *Kinghorne v. The Montreal Telegraph Co.* (1859), 18 U.C.Q.B.R. 60. The English also pay the same compliment to the Americans: consider the hundred-year-old U.K. copyright case, *Hollinrake v. Truswell*, [1894] 3 Ch. 420 (C.A.) that draws upon U.S. copyright jurisprudence.

the law covered by this book — from intellectual property, to criminal law/constitutional law, to privacy/data protection, to commercial law, to electronic commerce and Internet-related issues — courts in this country have made use of the thinking of members of the bench in other countries.[4] Bora Laskin, the former Chief Justice of the Supreme Court of Canada, wrote about this phenomenon some thirty years ago while he was a justice of the Ontario Court of Appeal and concluded that "Canadian courts are hospitable to cases from other common law jurisdictions, and that, English cases apart, American decisions are the most frequently cited from such other jurisdictions."[5] Laskin also foresaw the day when the use of U.S. case law would exceed that from England.

Of course, great care must be exercised when utilizing foreign decisions to interpret Canadian statutes or in determining the next phase of development of the common law in a particular subarea of the law.[6] Thus, Canadian courts in a number of contexts have warned against an

---

4   For example, the three leading cases in Canada (from courts in British Columbia, Ontario, and Quebec, respectively) on the scope of copyright protection for computer software all cite U.S. case law at length: *Prism Hospital Software Inc.* v. *Hospital Medical Records Institute* (1994), 57 C.P.R. (3d) 129 (B.C.S.C.); *Delrina Corp.* v. *Triolet Systems Inc.* (1993), 47 C.P.R. (3d) 1 (Ont. Gen. Div.); and *Matrox Electronic Systems Ltd.* v. *Gaudreau*, [1993] R.J.Q. 2449 (Que. Sup. Ct.). For instance, in the latter case the court stated at 2455: "With respect to the definition of 'computer program,' American copyright law is quite similar to Canadian law, and reference to American jurisprudence in this area is helpful."

5   Bora Laskin, *The British Tradition in Canadian Law* (London: Stevens & Sons, 1969) at 104–5 [*Tradition*].

6   In this regard, the degree of reliance by some Canadian courts on foreign jurisprudence can be quite disconcerting. Consider the following passage from *R.* v. *Crane and Walsh* (1985), 45 C.R. (3d) 368 at 373 (Nfld. Dist. Ct.), a decision that had to consider the privacy issues surrounding a traditional letter (and cited later in this book in the context of e-mail/Internet privacy issues) and where apparently access to U.S. legal sources was unavailable: "Neither counsel cited any case referring to search and seizure of personal mail. Further, by not having access to American case law I am left in a rather disadvantageous position when considering this novel legal point. When considering the application of s. 8 of the *Charter* it is helpful to consider the experience of the American courts in applying the Fourth Amendment to the American Constitution."

unthinking deference to foreign legal decisions.[7] This is particularly true in the intellectual property area where, although Canada shares a common legal heritage with, for example, the United Kingdom, the United States, and Australia, there now exist numerous important differences in the statutes in these respective jurisdictions. Recent international initiatives such as the *1996 WIPO Copyright Treaty*, however, generally have the effect of increasingly harmonizing the intellectual property laws of different countries.[8] Where the underlying statutory or common law principle is similar in Canada to another jurisdiction, Canadian courts have not hesitated to at least consider the jurisprudence in that other jurisdiction when coming to a resolution on a novel or thorny problem. And this is to be encouraged, particularly with respect to the law related to an industry as global in its outlook as the computer industry. The litmus test, however, for determining whether to use a foreign case should not be the decision's jurisdiction or author, but rather the quality of the reasoning and its applicability to Canadian conditions.[9]

---

7   *Compo Company Limited* v. *Blue Crest Music Inc.*, [1980] 1 S.C.R. 357 [*Compo*]; *Cie. Générale des Établissements Michelin-Michelin & Cie.* v. *C.A.W.-Canada* (1996), 71 C.P.R. (3d) 348 (F.C.T.D.). In the *Compo* case, however, after stating at 367 that U.S. copyright cases "must be scrutinized very carefully because of some fundamental differences in copyright concepts which have been adopted in the legislation of that country," the court goes on to cite liberally from a number of U.S. decisions. An English court has also warned against the unthinking use of American computer law decisions involving copyright matters: *Ibcos Computers Ltd.* v. *Barclays Mercantile Highland Finance Ltd.*, [1994] FSR 275 (H.Ct.); but see also *John Richardson Computers Limited* v. *Flanders*, [1993] FSR 497 (H.Ct.), a decision involving the first full hearing of a software copyright case in the United Kingdom that cited liberally American case law.

8   The *1996 WIPO Copyright Treaty* is available from the WIPO website: <www.wipo.org/>.

9   Or, as Bora Laskin stated in *Tradition*, above note 5 at 105, "*Stare decisis* apart, it is the fitness of the solutions to legal issues offered by the cases and not their source that should be the moving consideration of their value." Seven years later, the same writer (then Chief Justice of the Supreme Court of Canada) expressed a similar view in *Morgentaler* v. *R.*, [1976] 1 S.C.R. 616 at 629 when he commented on the use by Canadian judges of U.S. constitutional law authorities when considering the then Canadian Bill of Rights: "This Court has found such decisions to be helpful in the past and remains receptive to their citation, but they do not carry any authority beyond persuasiveness according to their relevance in the light of context."

ACKNOWLEDGMENTS

Although the writing of a book is an intensely solitary experience, books like this one simply do not get written in a vacuum. I therefore wish to acknowledge, first and foremost, the primary debt I incurred while working on this project to my wife, Janis, and my daughter, Natalie, who continue to provide a constant source of encouragement and solace throughout my working, writing, and teaching endeavours. Family is so important. I also want to give a heartfelt thanks to my extended family at McCarthy Tétrault, the firm where I practise law. There is simply no doubt in my mind that I practise law at the finest law firm in the country; for the stimulating intellectual and professional environment created by my partners and our firm's associates I am truly grateful. A number of my partners will recognize elements of their intellectual handiwork in the following pages and to them I am particularly indebted. Yet another part of the McCarthy Tétrault family are the clients of the firm that I work with; thank you for the constant stream of interesting files. And as for Fonda Chau, my secretary, who tamed the ungainly manuscript with her cool professionalism and word processing magic, I simply could not have done it (and run a busy law practice at the same time) without her. Thank you very much.

I should also like to acknowledge my gratitude to the two great law schools in Toronto, Osgoode Hall Law School at York University and the Faculty of Law, University of Toronto, where I have taught computer law courses over the past half-dozen years. Teaching serves to sharpen my thinking about legal issues and allows me periodically to take stock and assess the big picture. It also pushes me to stay current with legal developments, lest I be embarrassed by a particularly bright student who stays up half the night surfing Internet legal sites in New Zealand for the latest Kiwi computer law case (this has happened). A great pleasure that I derive from my students is the symbiotic relationship we share: they tell me about the latest technology gizmos (and neat

New Zealand legal websites) and I help them make sense of computer law. It's a wonderful arrangement. Finally, I would like to thank Irwin Law, and particularly William Kaplan, Jeffrey Miller, Pamela Erlichman, and Maraya Raduha for allowing me to aggregate and focus my thinking into a single work that they have published with such professionalism.

George S. Takach
Toronto, May 1998

LAW IN THE INFORMATION AGE

Law is the set of rules created by governments to order social and economic behaviour and to mediate and resolve conflicts among people. Law (which includes publicly sanctioned force) may be contrasted with private force. There was a time, for example, when a person who felt aggrieved by another's malicious statements would resort to the sabre or pistol for a duel, and a bloody family feud might have erupted. Today, the maligned person would commence a lawsuit. And lawsuits have multiplied because the fabric of society has become complex, with many more interests and entities and many more situations where interests collide than in the past. Thus, the areas of law have multiplied beyond the traditional subjects of property, contract, and criminal law, to include negligence (tort), commercial, corporate, family, securities, environmental, labour, and tax. Although some bemoan the number of laws, lawyers, and legislators in Canada, consider what our country would be like without the rule of law. It is not such a hard thing to imagine; one only has to look at the evening television news to see agonizing, bloodstained reports of communities that refuse to adopt, or for some unfathomable reason decide to jettison, the rule of law, and replace it with the arbitrary, capricious, and violent rule of private force.

Computer law is the body of legal rules related to the broad spectrum of activities and transactions involving computing technologies. Drawing upon the general concept of law noted above, computer law strives to order relations among people who create and use computer and information-based assets, to manage the conflicts that invariably

1

arise among them. If this conceptualization seems somewhat "authority-heavy," an equally valid view would be that computer law is the grease that makes the interconnected wheels and sprockets of the computer and information industries operate more efficiently. Under either approach, computer law encompasses a wide variety of subdisciplines of the law, including intellectual property, criminal law, regulatory regimes, and commercial law, as well as legal issues related to doing business electronically, including contract and evidence law, and libel and jurisdiction.

A. COMPUTER LAW: DYNAMICS, THEMES, AND SKILL SETS

As this book surveys a diverse landscape of subdisciplines in the law and examines how each area applies to computer and networking technologies, and software and information-based products, four principal dynamics — referred to in this book as the four dynamics of computer law — emerge. Most important is the rapid, almost torrid, pace of technological change, not only in terms of the development and release of new high-technology products, but also in terms of the new delivery systems of traditional content, such as the Internet. A second dynamic is the elusive nature of information and the fact that it derives its economic value from its context; as well, most information is never complete, but is in a continual state of becoming. A third dynamic is the melding of the two spheres that hitherto were distinctly private or public, as technological developments blur the line between them; the ultimate example is the Internet, which brings the world's largest communications network directly into a person's home through a personal computer or laptop. The final dynamic is the erosion of the borders between matters national and international. The computer industry is probably the most globally oriented business; the Internet has since confirmed high technology's contempt for geographic frontiers.

Each of these dynamics presents computer law and its practitioners with several fundamental challenges. In meeting these challenges, the legal system can consider four themes, the elements of which weave themselves through this book. First, there is the goal of consistency; that is, the legal rules related to the computer industry should be consistent with the best jurisprudence related to earlier technologies, and should also be consistent today around the world, as well as across the different subdisciplines of computer law. A second theme relates to control points and the roles played by geography, identity, and paper as regulatory control points; the corollary is that in an electronic world the traditional control points are under pressure, and new ones have to be devised. A third theme involves the liability regimes applicable to intermediaries. Entities that do not themselves initiate infringing, or criminal, or libellous conduct, but that propagate or facilitate it, pose some difficult questions for the law. And finally, one must consider the dangers of mischievous metaphors. Lawyers, judges, and legislators all tend to analyse current activities and persons or entities associated with them in terms of categories developed in the past. This is a useful approach but must be carried out carefully, as there is a serious danger of remaining trapped in outdated and ill-fitting legal paradigms.

Bolstered by the analytical tools offered by these dynamics and themes, the legal practitioner can approach any legal challenge posed by new technology and related business practices by employing one or more of the following skill sets. The common law entails assisting a judge to learn thoroughly the technological bases for a particular problem, and then bringing the tremendously flexible common law to bear by adapting and shaping it as required. Time and again, courts have shown a receptiveness to understand the new technology, a keen ability to tackle the various dynamics and themes of computer law, and a willingness to use their significant latitude to craft appropriate rules for a specific technologically driven problem. Where the common law falls short, contracts can be harnessed, in effect, to create private law between the contracting parties. Contracts can be particularly helpful in responding to the dynamics and themes of computer law. Similarly, technological skills can be employed to the same end; for example, technology can be used to prevent unauthorized use of intellectual properties. Technology drives the dynamics and themes of computer law, so it is not surprising that technology can also be used to address a number of the issues it raised in the first place. Contracts and technology, however, are not without their limitations, including concerns about uniformity of treatment (i.e., different contracting parties can be treated unequally), cost of access, lack of transparency (i.e., contracts can be kept confidential), and transaction costs. Hence, the fourth skill set, law reform, is important. Changing statute-based law often remedies a shortcoming in the previous state of statute- or judge-made law and is the desirable method for responding to a particular challenge posed by technology. To be efficient and effective, however, law reform in the computer law area must exhibit a sustained ability to stay abreast of technological developments and to effect statutory change in smaller but more regular increments than has traditionally been the case in Canada.

B. TECHNOLOGY TRENDS, SOCIETAL IMPACT, AND THE LAW

Before turning to a discussion of substantive questions of computer law, it is worth describing, however briefly, a few key aspects of the technology that underpins the computer revolution and that has brought us into the Information Age. Thus, it is important to understand what hardware, semiconductor chips, and software do, what data and databases are, how communications technologies and networks work, and what the primary features of the Internet are. More important, however, is to appreciate the dramatic and continuing drop in the price of computing power and telecommunications services and the enormous social and economic impact of this. The discussion of technology in this book centres not on technical questions such as how many bits or bytes can be — or even will be — compressed onto the head of a pin, but rather on the legal aspects of the technology and its trends and applications. And central to this is an understanding of the fantastic speed with which technological change occurs in this area. The first dynamic of computer law, namely, the rapid pace of technological change, figures prominently in the discussion in chapter 1.

With respect to technology applications, an understanding of the key principles of computer law, let alone its more subtle nuances, requires some familiarity with the powers that have been unleashed by the digitization, manipulation, mass storage, and communication of information. It is also important to appreciate the trend toward increasingly smaller and more intelligent computers. The collective result is an Information Age in which distance has been eliminated, mass customization has been enabled, and all businesses and organizations have become dependent on computers and networks. The discussion of these issues in chapter 1 serves as the technical, societal, and economic backdrop for a host of legal issues that are the subject of the book.

C. INTELLECTUAL PROPERTY LAWS

Intellectual property laws provide legal protection for products emanating from the minds of people. In order to understand intellectual property laws, it is necessary to appreciate the economics of information, which differ radically from the economics for traditional property such as real estate and tangible goods. These traditional assets operate in a world of natural scarcity, but information does not, given the second dynamic of computer law, namely, the elusive nature of information.

Information can be reproduced (and transmitted) at virtually no cost (particularly over the Internet), and is also capable of universal possession. Thus, the rationale for intellectual property law regimes is to bring various degrees of artificial scarcity to bear on information-based assets, thereby creating protection for the works of authors and inventors in order to encourage the production of these works and ultimately their dissemination for the benefit of all people. Accordingly, trade secrets/breach of confidence protects information that is not publicly known. Patents protect novel ideas that are not kept secret. Copyrights afford protection not for ideas but for the form of expression of ideas. Chip protection covers certain elements of the designs used to develop semiconductor chips. Trade-mark law prevents unfair competition by prohibiting competitors from using confusing marks and symbols to sell their goods or services. This book looks at intellectual property as its first substantive topic because the issues surrounding the economics of information will animate a number of other areas of the book.

With technological change advancing quickly, the intellectual property regimes face a number of challenges. Indeed, all four of the dynamics of computer law are being felt very acutely in the intellectual property area. Moreover, the intellectual property statutes emanate from the Industrial Revolution and will be hard-pressed to remain current in the Information Age. How, and indeed whether, patents should apply to software are burning questions in the computer industry. Similarly, copyright protection for software has yielded a number of judicial answers over the last few years. The application of traditional intellectual property laws to new information-based products, such as electronic databases, and to new technologies, such as multimedia works and the Internet, also raises a host of questions. Should there be other means of legal protection for information-based products? Besides these substantive issues, there are process-related questions regarding the way intellectual property issues are posed and resolved in our current legal system.

D. CRIMINAL LAW

Criminal law is another means that can be employed to protect information-based assets, but, of course, the criminal law does much more in its attempt to safeguard a number of other interests important to people, businesses, organizations, and governments. Unfortunately, a society dependent on computers, telecommunications, networks, and information is extremely vulnerable to computer crime. Indeed, computers and networks can figure in criminal activity in a multitude of ways. They can be the subject of crime, as when a computer is stolen or when one is accessed without authorization. As well, computers and networks can be the means by which other crimes are perpetrated. The exact amount of computer crime is difficult to measure because much harmful computer-related activity cannot be detected, and many organizations are reluctant to report themselves being victimized by computer criminals. Computer crime is a significant and growing problem, however, and it manifests itself in the following guises: unauthorized gain (including theft, software piracy, stealing computing or telecommunications resources, high-tech forgery, and unauthorized computer-based gambling including via the Internet); unauthorized destruction (including the deletion of data and the implantation in software, computers, and networks of "viruses," "worms," and other malicious software-based devices); unauthorized manipulation (including "hacking"); unauthorized intrusion (including wire-tapping and other means of scanning electronic-based communications, and surveillance with miniature cameras, microphones, and other intelligent but very small devices); illegal images (such as obscene pornography and child pornography); and illegal speech (such as racist and hateful messages, and libel).

The criminal law, prescribed in Canada primarily by the *Criminal Code*, delineates the behaviour that society, acting through Parliament, has deemed to be socially unacceptable. In combatting persons who engage in harmful computer-related activity, law enforcement authorities use mainly the following offences of the *Criminal Code*: theft, fraud, computer abuse, data abuse, obscenity and child pornography, hate propaganda, and interception of communications. A number of other offences in the *Criminal Code* may also be relevant from time to time, particularly where a computer is used to facilitate a crime. The criminal law has been traditionally concerned with protecting the integrity of the individual and tangible property. Thus, the four dynamics of computer law — the rapid pace of technological change, the elusive nature of information, the blurring of private/public and of national/international — coupled with the general rule of criminal law interpretation that *Criminal Code* provisions be construed strictly and in favour of the accused in the event of doubt as to the applicability of the particular provision, have challenged the ability of the *Criminal Code* to stay current with the new mischiefs possible with the widespread use of computers and networks. The result has been the amendment of the *Criminal Code* to include several new computer-related provisions. The Internet and other computer-based technologies and business practices raise many questions under these and the older provisions of the *Criminal Code* and highlight the challenges of enforcing a national criminal law in an increasingly global computer crime environment.

E. THE REGULATORY ENVIRONMENT

Governments regulate information in order to achieve a number of objectives. They institute and administer data protection laws in an effort to protect the privacy of individuals. Privacy has been expressed as the fourfold right to control intrusion into a person's seclusion; control the disclosure of private facts about a person; prevent a person being put into a false light in the public eye; and control the exploitation of a person's image and likeness. It is increasingly difficult for individuals to protect these rights in the Information Age. Computers, databases, and telecommunications networks, not to mention current developments in photography and other surveillance technologies, present significant threats to people's privacy. Most observers view this as an unfortunate byproduct of modern technology, and accordingly many look to the law to offer a bulwark against the various technologies and business practices that threaten privacy. The four dynamics of computer law, however, conspire to make the law's task in this regard a difficult one indeed.

Information is power, particularly in the Information Age, so it is not surprising that many governments attempt to control the export of strategically important technologies and information that might, in the hands of a country's enemies, prove to be extremely detrimental to the country's security interests. Thus, the Canadian government regulates the export from Canada of powerful computers and related technologies (such as software) that could be used in military applications. Also subject to export control are encryption technologies that interfere with the ability of law enforcement and intelligence agencies to eavesdrop on the communications of our adversaries. Given the technology trends enumerated in chapter 1, particularly to increased miniaturization and to the development of the Internet for transmitting software as well as data, the enforcement of export controls in the area of high technology is becoming more problematic.

The federal government has for many decades regulated the telecommunications and broadcasting industries in Canada. The traditional rationale for doing so with respect to the former related to protecting the public interest in the context of an important utility and transportation-like service provided by monopolists and quasi-monopolists. Subsequently, protecting the indigenous Canadian participants in the telecommunications industry also became an important foundation for regulation. On the broadcasting side, scarcity on the radio wave spectrum was an initial driver for regulation. Today, with the 500-channel universe upon us, protection of Canadian sovereignty through cultural policies is much more important. These and other reasons have led to the development of an extensive regulatory regime for telecommunications and broadcasting overseen primarily by the Canadian Radio-television and Telecommunications Commission. The four dynamics of computer law — the rapid pace of technological change, the elusive nature of information, and the blurring of both private/public and national/international — make the tasks of the gatekeepers and conduits of the Information Age daunting. The Internet, in particular, raises questions about whether the government can regulate the information highway effectively, assuming it decides to do so for policy and political reasons.

F. COMMERCIAL LAW

The business of selling computers, software, and information-based products differs from other enterprises in a number of legally important ways. To understand these differences, it is first necessary to appreciate that the computer industry is driven by three interrelated phenomena. Perhaps the most fundamental and far-reaching of these is the incredibly short product cycles; that is, hardware, software, and information-based products and services are developed, marketed to customers, and then overtaken by new products, in ever decreasing timespans. This trend is closely linked to the first dynamic of computer law, namely, the torrid pace of technological change.

Short product cycles also influence a unique aspect of software, namely, that it invariably has errors, or "bugs" in it. It is important to understand for legal purposes that software cannot be made to be perfect. For example, the year 2000 problem looms darkly over the industry. Another result of short product cycles is the fact that distribution channels for much hardware, and most software and information-based products, are typically multitiered and variegated.

Short product cycles and complicated product distribution channels have implications under competition law. Canada's *Competition Act* provides for a number of criminal offences and reviewable practices provisions that, although they apply to the economy generally, are particularly germane to the high-tech business. Also relevant to a discussion of commercial law issues is the fact that information-based products in electronic form are licensed, rather than sold, to end users.

Copies of books are sold; copies of software are licensed. There are a number of historic reasons for licensing software, as well as certain contemporary rationales for the practice. A particularly common vehicle for licensing mass market software is the shrinkwrap licence, a form of agreement whose enforceability has been questioned by a number of courts, though recent cases suggest some countries seem to be more amenable to the vehicle. Another area of licensing controversy involves the particular scope of rights granted to licensees, and whether the rights granted are broad enough to cover new technical delivery mechanisms and media. These cases illustrate some of the difficulties inherent in the field of technology licensing given the first dynamic of computer law, namely, the rapid pace of technological change.

Computer products also present several questions under negligence law. Some relate to the creation of software, particularly in light of the fact that bug-free software is an unattainable goal. As well, computers can be used in a variety of ways that are negligent. The year 2000 problem encompasses a virtual hornet's nest of negligence issues, for the creator as well as the user of computers. Ironically, negligence can also arise when computers are not used. The applicability of sales legislation to computer products raises a series of questions. Is software a "good" in order to come under the auspices of sale of goods statutes? How are the implied warranties and conditions of merchantable quality and fitness for a particular purpose to be applied to computer-based products? Can suppliers of these products exclude these warranties and conditions, and limit other liabilities, through contract? Questions regarding the application of bankruptcy legislation are also germane. Upon the bankruptcy of the licensor of software, can the trustee in bankruptcy disclaim previously granted licence agreements? Conversely, what are the rights of the licensor of technology if its licensee goes bankrupt?

As in all areas of commercial endeavour, tax questions can pose intriguing problems for the suppliers and users of computers, software, and information-based products. Somewhat reminiscent of the discussion in the area of sales legislation, a threshold question for sales tax regimes is whether software is a good or a service. Similarly, Canada's withholding tax on software has experienced several bouts of uncertainty over the years. The Internet creates some intriguing international tax questions. The application of certain international trade rules to the high-tech sector is also noteworthy. Categorizing computer-based goods for tariff classification raises yet another challenge for public authorities, different in substance but similar in terms of process to those of sales and tax legislation. Although (like competition law) applicable to most industries, government procurement rules have particular poignancy to the computer sector, since governments are major purchasers of high-tech products and their procurement practices in this area can be unfairly skewed against certain suppliers of computers, software products, and related services. Given the impact of technology on the workplace, whether in the office or on the factory floor, it is worth noting several kinds of labour and employment law ramifications related to information technology.

G. ELECTRONIC COMMERCE

The sale of goods and services, and related activities such as the transport, insurance, and financing of goods, is accompanied by the generation and movement of information. For the past few hundred years, paper-based documents — contracts, purchase orders, invoices, bills of lading — have served as the predominant means to record and share commercial information. With the advent of the telegraph, commercial information began to be communicated electronically without paper. The telex and fax continued this trend, as did direct computer-to-computer communications, often referred to as electronic data interchange (EDI), an important means for transmitting commercial information in certain industries. Today, the Internet is poised to become the central means of doing business electronically, both for one-on-one transactions like those consummated by early electronic communication technologies, as well as for the new open environment of many-on-many ushered in by computer networks. As well, once data are received, they are also often stored electronically; increasingly, even paper-based documents are scanned and their contents stored electronically through imaging systems, both to save money and to improve accessibility to such information. This shift from a paper-based to an electronic-based commercial information environment raises numerous legal issues, particularly given the buffeting effect of the first two dynamics of computer law, namely, the rapid pace of technological change and the elusive nature of information.

Contract law has developed a number of principles and doctrines to promote certainty among business people in their commercial relations; these include the requirement that various contracts be in writing and be signed in order to be enforceable and other rules related to when and where a contract comes into existence. These rules are quite elaborate and well developed for contracts arising in a paper context, but their application to agreements concluded in an electronic environment can be ambiguous and uncertain. Nevertheless, courts have been adept at understanding the new technologies and business processes and at assisting business people in adopting them by recognizing their legal legitimacy. In a manner reminiscent of contract law, evidence law strives to ensure the predictable and fair ordering of relations among business entities, individuals, governments, and others by ensuring that only reliable evidence is permitted to be provided to judicial and other decision makers in legal, administrative, and related proceedings. Again, as with contract law, a number of evidence law rules were developed in a paper-based environment, such as those that make admissible records that were created in the normal course of business. The application of these common law and statutory rules, where express computer-related evidence law rules have not been enacted, raises some questions, but for the most part — again as with contract law — courts have endeavoured to understand the particular technology confronting them, and then have sensibly applied the relevant legal rule, almost invariably with the result that the computer-generated record has been admitted into evidence. Notwithstanding the positive track record, there are uncertainties in the law of evidence as it relates to computer-generated records that probably warrant some law reform initiatives. Similarly, certain records retention rules are too closely aligned with paper-based forms of recording and storage and require changes in statutory language to accommodate electronic formats.

H. INTERNET LEGAL ISSUES

In the history of computer law, the development and inexorable growth of the Internet has raised complex legal issues. This book, however, does not treat the Internet as a unique phenomenon. Rather, it views the Internet as another step in the steady evolution of computers and networks and integrates the analysis of Internet issues into the technologies and business processes of its predecessors, such as telegraphy, telephony, and broadcasting. Indeed, the four dynamics of computer law that have driven these industries are currently buffeting the Internet as well; moreover, the Internet may well be the phenomenon that best exemplifies the active and sustained operation of the rapid pace of technological change, the elusive nature of information, and the blurring of private/public and national/international. Accordingly, although there are some revolutionary characteristics of the Internet (such as framing, linking, and caching), for the most part the legal issues presented by it are best understood by carefully drawing on appropriate existing and historical analogies. Thus, intellectual property issues relating to the Internet are canvassed in the intellectual property chapter; its impact on criminal law is discussed in the criminal law chapter; regulation of it by the CRTC is addressed in the regulatory environment chapter; licensing and tax issues germane to it are covered in the commercial law chapter; and business practices and consumer protection regulation with respect to it are considered in the electronic commerce chapter. This is in addition to numerous other references to the Internet peppered throughout the book.

Three other Internet issues are particularly noteworthy. The Internet, as explained at the outset of the book, provides unprecedented opportunities for local, regional, national, and global communications of text and other content. Some of these messages will be defamatory. A pressing question is what liability should be visited upon intermediary disseminators of libellous electronic messages? The same question is asked in the context of copyright and criminal law. In addressing these questions, courts must be wary of adopting mischievous metaphors and instead must thoroughly understand how much knowledge and control was exercised by the Internet participant regarding the alleged harm. Jurisdiction is also a fascinating Internet issue. The jurisdiction of a government to pass and enforce laws is generally limited in terms of the physical geography under the control of that government. The Internet, of course, allows users to cross borders instantaneously. Thus, the fourth dynamic of computer law talks in terms of a blurring of national and international. Courts must determine when to take jurisdiction over a person or legal entity physically resident outside the court's jurisdiction because of that person's Internet-based activity having some effect on people who are resident within the court's jurisdiction. Although it is still early days on this point, the trend in the United States seems to be that an electronic presence in the United States effected over the Internet, particularly when it leads to follow-on commercial activity, is sufficient for a finding of jurisdiction by most U.S. courts. This has important ramifications for Canadians doing business on the Internet. Finally, it is also worth noting several of the issues involved in applying consumer protection legislation, including securities law and banking rules, to the Internet.

CHAPTER 1

TECHNOLOGY TRENDS, SOCIETAL IMPACT, AND THE LAW

An understanding of the key principles of computer law, and its more subtle nuances, requires some appreciation of the technology that underpins the computer revolution and that has brought us into the Information Age. Accordingly, there follows a brief exposition of some of the principal technical aspects of computers, software, data, and the networks that are increasingly linking computers.[1] More importantly, several key technological trends and applications are also highlighted. In this discussion the emphasis is not on technical questions. Rather, the focus is on the legal aspects of the technology. This chapter also

---

1   There are numerous texts and journals where detailed information can be found regarding all the different aspects of computer and related technologies. A good, comprehensive and yet accessible volume for the non-technical reader is Anthony Ralston & Edwin D. Reilly, eds., *Encyclopedia of Computer Science*, 3d ed. (New York: Van Nostrand Reinhold, 1993). For an entry-level work with many helpful pictures consider Sherry Kinkoph, Jennifer Fulton & Kelly Oliver, *Computers: A Visual Encyclopedia* (Indianapolis: Alpha Books, Macmillan, 1994). For works that offer succinct descriptions of technical terms used in computing and networking, the following are recommended: George McDaniel, ed., *IBM Dictionary of Computing* (New York: McGraw-Hill, 1994); and Bryan Pfaffenberger, *Internet in Plain English* (New York: MIS Press, 1994) [*Plain English*]. Of course, the rapid pace of technological change makes books on computers and related technologies out of date quite quickly, and so journals can be an invaluable source of information. *Scientific American* and *Communications of the ACM* are journals with particularly strong and timely articles on various technical subjects related to computers and communications.

discusses the impact the technology and the technological trends are having on society. The law, with certain limited exceptions, is a reflection and outgrowth of the society in which it is rooted. To understand the main elements of computer law, therefore, it becomes important to grasp how computer-based technologies are shaping the world. The emphasis here will not be on the sociological, psychological, or political aspects of these transformations (though these are many and far-reaching), but on their legal significance.[2] This chapter will also begin to illuminate the contours of the four dynamics of computer law, namely, the rapid pace of technological change, the elusive nature of information, the blurring of public and private, and the blurring of national and international.

Although an overview of the technology and its trends and applications is useful — and so this chapter is particularly germane for those who are not technically proficient — the reader is cautioned that what follows is very general. In fact, the technologies involved in computers and networks can be exceedingly complex. Moreover, the rapid pace of change in the computer and related industries quickly outdates even a sophisticated, detailed explanation of the technologies currently underpinning the Information Age. These two factors — startling complexity and a breathtaking pace of change — have important ramifications for the legal process. They mean, for example, that lawyers must spend a significant amount of time and energy educating themselves, as well as judges and legislators, in technical matters and the new business processes engendered by groundbreaking technologies when they are involved in cases and law reform initiatives relating to computing and network technologies. It also means the law is presented with a supremely difficult task when attempting to remain relevant and meaningful in the complicated and ever changing world of computers and networks.

---

2   This is not to say the sociological, psychological, or political dimensions of the computer revolution are not important or fascinating, as they are certainly both. For example, for a penetrating study, from a sociologist's perspective, of computers and the Internet and their roles in redefining human identity and community through a culture of simulation and computer-based interaction, see Sherry Turkle, *Life on the Screen: Identity in the Age of the Internet* (New York: Simon & Schuster, 1995).

A. THE BASE TECHNOLOGY

Computers can be described in a variety of ways. One approach is to break down the computer into several distinct components, namely hardware, software, and chips (semiconductor integrated circuits). It is also useful, however, to understand a computer purposefully, as in the following definition: "A digital computer is a machine that will accept data and information presented to it in its required form, carry out arithmetic and logical operations on this raw material, and then supply the required results in an acceptable form."[3] In short, computers process data and are used increasingly to communicate data as well. And most importantly for the purposes of the analysis in this book, computers are continually improving their ability to perform these functions, in terms of speed and ease of use, all the while dropping in price.[4] The performance–price ratio of computers is improving at a dizzying rate. The price of computer-processing power has declined by about 30 percent a year over the last twenty years; it is estimated that the cost of information processing is only 1/100 of 1 percent of what it was in the early 1970s.[5] This trend will likely continue and therefore bring to the marketplace a host of new computer applications, as well as a wide array of new ways of performing the current functionality of computers. Thus, the first dynamic of computer law — the rapid pace of technological change — requires the reader to constantly update the discussion that follows.[6]

---

3   Ralston & Reilly, *Encyclopedia of Computer Science*, above note 1.

4   For a concise but extremely readable account of the history of the development of computers, see Maurice Estabrooks, *Electronic Technology, Corporate Strategy, and World Transformation* (Westport, Conn.: Quorum Books, 1995) [*Electronic Technology*].

5   These figures are taken from "A Survey of the World Economy: The Hitchhiker's Guide to Cybernomics," *The Economist*, 28 September 1996 ["Cybernomics"]. This survey also notes that, compared to the declines in prices in other industrial inputs, the fall in prices of computing power has been dramatic indeed. For example, between 1890 and 1930, the price of electricity declined only 65 percent, roughly a 2 to 3 percent decrease a year.

6   For an overview of the devices and technologies being developed by the world's leading computer product laboratories that will make much of the following discussion dated within the next five to ten years, see Neil Gross, "Into the Wild Frontier," *Business Week*, 23 June 1997.

1) Hardware

As its name suggests, hardware is the collection of tangible components of the computer consisting of plastic, metal, glass, and other physical items. Each computer requires an input device in order that data be entered into the computer. A common hardware device to accomplish this task is the keyboard, which permits a user to type data into the computer. Other hardware input devices include monitors that permit users to indicate choices by touching different parts of the screen and tablets that allow users to write data on them, then transform the handwriting into electronic equivalents. Another form of data entry device is a voice recognition system that can transform speech into electronically stored data. However data are entered into the computer, they are processed in a central processing unit, which contains chips and other devices that perform the mathematical or other desired functions on the inputted data. Both before and after being processed, the data are stored on a memory device, another hardware component, that is able to maintain the data in electronic form. The data also have to be presented to the human user by means of another hardware item, typically involving a terminal, by which a user can see representations of the data on a screen, and a printer that can transform the electronically stored data into printed words, figures, and images. There are then a myriad of hardware devices used to transmit data, such as modems, controllers, and routers. There are a number of companies furiously developing so-called "network computers," which likely will do little processing, because they will be intended primarily for sending and receiving data over the Internet and other networks.[7]

Hardware devices, and computers generally, are categorized by the amount of data they can process and the speed with which they operate. At one end of the spectrum are very powerful mainframe computers that are used by large companies, governments, and other organizations to process vast amounts of data quickly. At the other end of the spectrum is the personal computer that, as its name suggests, can be used by a single user, often in the home. Between the mainframe and the personal computer is the mini computer, often powerful enough to serve the data processing needs of the mid-sized company. There are numerous other types of computers, as well as various configurations of computers. For example, super computers, as well as numerous personal computers

---

7   See the articles contained in the "Annual Report on Information Technology: The Information Appliance," *Business Week*, 24 June 1996; and "The Network Computer: How Bill Became Larry," *The Economist*, 24 May 1997.

and slightly more powerful workstations connected together, can provide huge amounts of computing power. At the level of the personal computer, increasingly powerful and miniature semiconductor chips and other hardware components have spawned the lightweight and mobile laptop computer, as well as even smaller palmtops (personal digital assistants, as they are sometimes called) and some computerized personal organizers not much bigger than a pocket calculator. This is to say nothing of the tiny, special purpose computers that are increasingly imbedded in devices such as television sets, microwaves, and automobiles. As for the future, researchers are working at fusing computing technologies with materials science to produce intelligent construction materials, such as bridges that will be able to monitor a number of aspects of themselves.[8] Other researchers are working on computers that, because of the miracle of miniaturization, will be sewn into clothing.[9] In short, hardware (and computers generally) are becoming smaller, better, and cheaper.

2) Chips

The central hardware component is the semiconductor integrated circuit or *chip* as it is commonly called. Chips are very small pieces of semiconductor material, such as silicon, that contain miniaturized electronic circuits consisting of transistors, resistors, capacitors, and diodes, all electronically connected and packaged to form a fully functioning circuit with a specific set of functions.[10] Chips are made by a painstaking and expensive process of placing photolithographic patterns — or masks — on a pure substrate, such as a silicon wafer, and then treating and etching the wafer with a conductive substance so that, at the conclusion of the process, extremely compact circuits are left on the wafer. Transistors, invented just after the end of the Second World War, are the forerunner of the current chip and began to replace vacuum tubes in various electronic devices by the mid-1950s. The modern chip was invented in the early 1970s and came to prominence as a critical building

---

8   Geoffrey Rowan, "Visionaries See Invisible Computing" *The [Toronto] Globe and Mail* (1 April 1997).

9   Victoria Griffith, "Wearable Computers: Prêt à Portables" *Financial Times* (18 December 1996). See also Robert Everett-Green, "Joystick On Your Collar: Computers Get Ready-to-Wear" *The [Toronto] Globe and Mail* (28 February 1998).

10   For a comprehensive discussion of chip fabrication technologies and methodologies, as well as the business of chipmaking, see Richard H. Stern, *Semiconductor Chip Protection* (New York: Harcourt Brace Jovanovich, 1986–1991).

block component of the first personal computer in the early 1980s. Ever since, chips have become smaller, cheaper, and more powerful at an astonishing rate. The processing power of chips generally has doubled every eighteen months to two years, a trend likely to continue for the foreseeable future.[11] It is not an overstatement that chip technology is the foundation of the computer revolution and a key driver of the Information Age.[12]

To fully appreciate the miracle of chip technology, and its other worldly rate of technical improvement, consider that in 1971 the Intel 4004 chip contained 2300 transistors and was able to process at a speed of 0.06 MIPS (millions of instructions per second) (i.e., 60,000 instructions per second). By contrast, today's Intel Pentium Pro chip contains 5.5 million transistors and operates at speeds of 400 MIPS (i.e., 400,000,000 instructions per second). And by the year 2011, Intel believes chips will contain one billion transistors and operate at 100,000 MIPS.[13] As for prices, if the automobile industry were able to produce the same performance–price improvements as the chip industry, a car today would cost under five dollars and would get 250,000 miles to a gallon of gasoline.[14]

3) Software

Software, or computer programs, are the statements and instructions that operate the computer and perform the various functions useful to the user of the computer. Operating system software runs the computer by, among other things, coordinating the operation of the different hardware components of the computer. Application software, such as a word processing computer program, carries out the various functions on the data inputted into the computer by the user. Although resident

---

11   This is often referred to as Moore's Law, after Gordon Moore, a founder and Chairman of Intel Corp. Moore said the power and complexity of the silicon chip would double every eighteen months: see Mary Gooderham, "Microchip at 25: More Power To It" *The [Toronto] Globe and Mail* (15 November 1996). See also Tim Jackson, *Inside Intel: Andy Grove and the Rise of the World's Most Powerful Chip Company* (New York: Dutton, 1997).

12   Bill Gates, one of the co-founders of Microsoft, pays appropriate homage to the chip in his extremely readable account of the rise to prominence of the personal computer industry and its inexorable extension through the Internet over the next few years: Bill Gates, *The Road Ahead* (New York: Viking, 1995) [*Road Ahead*].

13   Otis Port, "The Silicon Age? It's Just Dawning," *Business Week*, 9 December 1996.

14   "Cybernomics," above note 5.

on a diskette or a computer's hard drive memory device, or embedded right into a chip, the actual software instructions executed on a computer are intangible, having been converted from a high-level, almost written language (the source code of the program) into electronic bits (which are further described below). Software is typically developed in a multistage process beginning with a high-level design of what the software is intended to do and what specific requirements of the user it will fulfil.[15] These functional specifications are then translated into a series of design specifications that plot and outline the various processes and procedures to be carried out by the software within the computer. Only after a great deal of time and effort has gone into the design of the program is the writing — or coding — of the specific computer-sensitive instructions and statements undertaken. Once the code is written, it is tested, and various errors corrected, in a painstaking process of making the software stable enough for commercial use. This traditional process of software creation is being supplemented — and in some cases supplanted — by newer techniques where prewritten modules of code, sometimes called objects, are woven together to produce commercial quality software programs in much shorter time.[16]

However software is developed, it is a fact of life in the software world that software cannot be made perfect. The imperfections in software can take many forms. If the software is custom-developed for a particular user, the developer of the software may have failed to include all the functionality requested by the user. Or the user may have failed to adequately convey its requirements to the software developer. In either case, the software in such a circumstance will contain design deficiencies. Or, the software, including prewritten software, can have bugs, or errors, in it. These can be attributable to coding flaws, or to higher-level problems in the logic design or architecture of the computer program. A spectacular example of a design flaw is the so-called millennium bug, a problem attributable to the fact that much software has been programmed with two-digit date fields, and therefore will process incorrectly commencing in the year 2000; this problem is discussed in detail in section D(1), "Negligence in Creation: The Y2K Problem," in chapter 5. In short, perfect software simply does

---

15   For a classic description of the process, first published in 1975, detailing the trials and tribulations involved from the software developer's perspective, see Frederick P. Brooks, Jr., *The Mythical Man-Month: Essays on Software Engineering, Anniversary Edition* (Reading, Mass.: Addison-Wesley, 1995).

16   Peter M.D. Gray, Krishnarao G. Kulkarni & Norman W. Paton, *Object-Oriented Databases: A Semantic Data Model Approach* (New York: Prentice Hall, 1992).

not exist. As a result, most software developers offer ongoing support and maintenance programs for their products so that users can receive corrections to periodic problems.

4) Data and Databases

Data are the elements of information put into, processed by, stored, and then outputted and/or communicated by the computer. They might be the addresses on a mailing list, photographs from a gallery, excerpts of music from a digital jukebox, the words in a word processor, the figures on an electronic spreadsheet, or the prices of shares on a computerized stock ticker.[17] To be processed, stored, and transmitted electronically, data are digitized, or transformed in the computer into an electronic format, namely into 1s and 0s represented inside the computer by two electronic states: 1s are on (high-voltage electronic current), and 0s are off (low-voltage). Each binary value is one "bit," and eight bits make one byte, which in turn makes one character (such as a single letter or number). Data can also be stored optically, by means of little variegated bumps on a CD-ROM; these bumps can then be read by a laser in the CD-ROM machine; a CD-ROM is like a music CD and has read-only-memory. Although such bit-based technology, whether in electronic or optical form, seems quite cumbersome, what makes it all work in a cost-effective manner is the lightning speed of the computer.

The predecessor of the computerized database is the paper-based directory, a book listing names, addresses, or other information about a specific group of persons or organizations. There are, of course, several important differences between the computerized database and the paper-based directory, the most obvious being the space limitation inherent in the paper-based work; as discussed below, much more data

---

17   Although any material stored in a computer is generally referred to as data, it is sometimes useful for legal purposes to think of data as being one point along a longer continuum that includes: symbols — the individual digits or letters; data — the aggregation of digits into numbers and letters into words; information — the aggregation of data into useful portions of meaning, such as sentences and paragraphs; knowledge — the distillation from information of ideas, concepts, and techniques; and wisdom — an advanced state of knowledge implying understanding. This typology is illustrated in Thomas A. Stewart, *Intellectual Capital: The New Wealth of Organizations* (New York: Doubleday, 1997) [*Intellectual Capital*] at 69 as follows: "*data*: The temperature is 77 degrees [Fahrenheit]. . . . *information* . . . That's hot for this time of year. . . . *knowledge* . . . We should postpone the ski trip. . . . *wisdom*: Everybody talks about the weather, but nobody does anything about it."

can be stored electronically on, say, a CD-ROM disk than in even a thick paper-based directory. However, the paper-based directory, given its static medium, does not permit the user to select or edit the data; rather, the data are presented precisely how the compiler of the directory intended them to be presented. This can be as a listing of raw data, such as in a telephone white pages, where all the people with phones in a given geographic area are included in alphabetical order. Or, in some cases, the compiler selects or edits the raw data for presentation in the way the editor feels will be the most useful to the reader; indeed, often space limitations of the paper-based medium force compilers to edit and present only a limited selection of the total data. The computerized database is a collection of data organized for storage in a computer and designed for easy retrieval of the data, or components thereof, by users of the computer.[18] In a computer-based, electronic environment, where storage capacity is increasingly less of an issue, vast quantities of data can be made available to the user. Moreover, if the data are contained in a relational database, the compiler of the data can empower the user to be the one who selects and edits the data in precisely the manner desired by the user. A relational database is a database management system that stores information in tables and conducts searches by using data in specified columns of one table to find additional data in another table. For example, consider the data in the human resources program of a large organization which contains information regarding all employees. If data regarding these people were stored in a relational database, then one table might, for example, contain fields for employee name, employer department, and hire date. Another table might contain the person's name, salary, and age. Another table might contain the person's name and educational qualifications. By accessing such a database, a user could extract data in a number of different ways: for example, to determine how many persons earning over $80,000 are under the age of fifty, or how many have at least one graduate degree. The relational database performs this extremely useful, time-saving work by matching values in two or more tables to relate information in one to the others.

---

18   For a good introduction to database technology, see Fred R. McFadden & Jeffrey A. Hoffer, *Modern Database Management*, 4th ed. (Redwood City, Calif.: Benjamin/ Cummings, 1994).

5) Networks

Computers do more than just process data, they also transmit them. The business of transmitting data, however, pre-dates computers by about one hundred years, given that the telegraph first entered into widespread use in the 1850s. The telegraph was a seminal technology; from the time that Gutenberg developed the moveable type printing press in 1485 until the telegraph almost four hundred years later, information moved only as fast as goods and people, given that the mail was carried by horse-drawn carriage or sailing ship. The telegraph was the first technology to disengage the transmission of information from general transportation, thereby commencing the collapse of geographic distance in human affairs.[19] By the 1880s voice communication by telephone was beginning to challenge the telegraph's supremacy as the primary means of communications.[20] As for broadcasting, in the early 1900s radio technology came into use, twenty-five years later the first crude television was demonstrated, and in the mid-1960s cable television was beginning to rapidly penetrate the market in Canada. At the same time as cable television appeared in Canada, early efforts of data communications between computers were being perfected. By the beginning of the 1970s computers were being linked into local and wide area networks. In the early 1990s cellular radiotelephone, as well as satellite transmission data services, were introduced. Today, the Internet, a network of networks, brings together many of the disparate elements of the computer and telecommunications revolutions.

Information can be transmitted by a number of different technologies, including traditional copper wire, still the basis for most telephone lines, and more recent vehicles such as fibre optics, coaxial cable (for cable television transmission), cellular radio telephone, and satellite.[21] Each of these technologies can transmit digital signals at different rates, thus making some technologies more or less appropri-

---

19   For a discussion of the development of the current information highway, and its antecedents such as the telegraph, see W.T. Stanbury & Ilan B. Vertinsky, "Assessing the Impact of New Information Technologies on Interest Group Behaviour and Policymaking," in *Technology, Information and Public Policy*, ed. Thomas J. Courchene (Kingston, Ont.: John Deutsch Institute, Queen's University, 1995) [*Technology*].

20   For a fascinating study of the telephone, see Ithiel de Sola Pool, ed., *The Social Impact of the Telephone* (Cambridge, Mass.: MIT Press, 1977).

21   For a good discussion of the key technological and business aspects of each method, see Robert K. Heldman, *The Telecommunications Information Millennium: A Vision and Plan for the Global Information Society* (New York: McGraw-Hill, 1995).

ate for carrying various transmissions; for example, full motion video transmission needs significant transmission capacity or bandwidth, which currently fibre optics can satisfy, but which traditional copper wire cannot, although new digital data compression technologies (such as ADSL — asymmetric digital subscriber line) are on the horizon that may be able to pump more bits through copper wire. The foreseeable future will witness a great deal of competition between various service providers — the telephone companies, the cable companies, intermediate service providers, satellite companies, cellular companies — in terms of technologies and in the regulatory arena.[22] Regardless of the short- and long-term outcomes of this competition, the trend, of course, is toward the implementation of better, faster, and smaller means of communication.[23] And again, massive price declines have already been experienced in the latest communications technologies; the increased competition will only continue the downward spiral in global telecommunications costs.[24]

6) The Internet

The Internet is an extremely important phenomenon, both for computer law and for society.[25] Begun in the early 1970s as a means of linking various U.S. military, industrial, and academic research partners by computers hooked up over telephone lines, the Internet has over the past few years expanded — indeed exploded — astonishingly to include

---

22   Geoffrey Rowan, "Let the Internet Access Wars Begin" *The [Toronto] Globe and Mail* (14 May 1997).

23   Consider that a wire cable 3.25 inches in diameter contains 1300 pairs of copper wire, and each pair carries one telephone conversation; a 0.75 inch in diameter coaxial cable, used by the cable companies, carries 78 video channels, expandable to 500 with compression technologies; a fibre optic bundle .5 inch in diameter can carry 500,000 telephone calls or 5000 video channels over 32 hairlike strands. From Andrew Kupfer, "The Race to Rewire America," *Fortune*, 19 April 1993.

24   In today's dollars, the cost of sending a single word in a transatlantic telegram in the 1860s would be US$60, and such high costs stunted the use of the telegram for many decades. By contrast, a three-minute telephone call in the fall of 1996 between New York and London was about US$2; in 1930 the same call would have cost more than US$200. By the year 2005 the cost of a transatlantic videophone call could drop to a few cents an hour. See "Cybernomics," above note 5.

25   For an accessible account of the implications of the Internet for business, education, and home use, see Gates, *Road Ahead*, above note 12. See also Information Highway Advisory Council, *Preparing Canada for a Digital Future* (Final Report) (Ottawa: Industry Canada, 1997).

millions of businesses and individual users.[26] For many people, a personal computer linked to the Internet is primarily a communications device, and only secondarily a data processor. With the advent of telephony on the Internet, the computer and communications industries will be merged, at least outwardly to users. As well, some argue that the Internet has moved beyond being a communications infrastructure to becoming a new software platform.[27] Most profound, however, is the Internet's role as a platform for the new "networked intelligence" that results from millions of people being able to communicate as never before with like-minded counterparts.[28] Given the importance of the Internet, it is worth describing, briefly, some of the services and features of the Internet, as well as several of its principal participants.[29]

---

26   No one really knows, at any one time, precisely how many users there are of the Internet. Vinton G. Cerf, one of the pioneers of the Internet, indicated in 1995 that the number of host computers (which is much smaller in number than the number of users) on the Internet increased from 200 to 5,000,000 between 1983 and 1995, a factor of 25,000: Vinton G. Cerf, *Computer Networking: Global Infrastructure for the 21st Century*, <http://www.cs.Washington.edu/homes/lazowska/cra/networks. html>. In 1995, an estimate, based on a survey, put the number of e-mail users on the Internet at 27.5 million: Federation of American Scientists, FAS Cyberstrategy Project, *Cybersats*, <http://www.fas.org/cp/netstats.htm>. A survey in the spring of 1997 put the estimate of the number of users of the Internet in the United States and Canada at 50.6 million, more than double the number shown in a similar survey done eighteen months before: "Internet Users Double" *The [Toronto] Globe and Mail* (1 April 1997).

27   "A World Gone Soft: A Survey of the Software Industry," *The Economist*, 25 May 1996. See also Amy Cortese, "The Software Revolution," *Business Week*, 4 December 1995, which discusses how small software programs called "applets" written in Java and other new object-oriented programming environments, might be marketed and distributed over the Internet, thereby presenting an alternative to the current distribution model for software products.

28   See Derrick de Kerckhove, *Connected Intelligence: The Arrival of the Web Society* (Toronto: Somerville House, 1997) [*Connected Intelligence*]. De Kerckhove, the Director of the McLuhan Program in Culture and Technology at the University of Toronto, highlights the importance of interactivity and hypertextuality in the context of the Internet.

29   For a perceptive analysis of the Internet by a court, including how it differs from earlier communications technologies such as books, newspapers, radio, and television, see generally *American Civil Liberties Union v. Reno*, 929 F. Supp. 824 (E.D. Pa. 1996) [*ACLU*]; in this decision, at 844, the court labelled the Internet a "unique and wholly new medium of worldwide human communication." This decision was essentially confirmed by the U.S. Supreme Court: see *Reno v. American Civil Liberties Union*, 117 S. Ct. 2329 (1997).

The Internet is a fascinating exercise in symbiotic anarchy. Technically, it is a network of computer networks.[30] Thousands of host computers serve as electronic repositories for huge volumes of data, stored according to an address system that gives each site, and "mailboxes" within sites, a residency within cyberspace. Untold and growing numbers of router computers serve as relay stations for the information travelling between host computers. The Internet is an intricate web of computers and networking infrastructure, able to operate by means of a series of non-proprietary standards — called data transfer protocols — for the naming of sites and for the sending of data. While no single entity owns or controls the Internet, the Internet Society provides technical leadership in terms of planning its long-term architecture and engineering.[31] Other groups are responsible for handing out network registrations so that an Internet address, such as < gtakach@mccarthy.ca >, continues to mean only a single place on the Internet.

There is a wide and varied range of services on the Internet. At one end of the spectrum is electronic mail, or e-mail, whereby electronic messages can be sent to specific electronic mailboxes registered to individuals. E-mail is a store and forward system, and it can take a few minutes for a message to pass through the various computers on its possibly roundabout way to its destination. E-mail can also be routed to multiple recipients. A very different group-based feature is the usenet, or usegroup, a discussion forum where participants can post messages and commentary about certain subjects or current interest topics. Sites that agree to carry a usegroup will then be sent all new postings, thus creating a propagation system whereby one posting becomes replicated thousands of times as it is sent to computers around the world. Some of these discussion forums operate in real time, such as MUDS (Multi-User Dungeons) and MUSES (Multi-User Simulation Environments). Perhaps the fastest growing dimension of the Internet is the World Wide Web, which allows organizations to create websites of information at a specific address — such as < www.mccarthy.ca > for the McCarthy Tétrault

---

30   In the *ACLU* decision, *ibid.* at 830, the court stated that "[t]he Internet is not a physical or tangible entity, but rather a giant network which interconnects innumerable smaller groups of linked computer networks. It is thus a network of networks." For a good overview of various technological and other aspects of the Internet, see Pfaffenberger, *Plain English*, above note 1.

31   In the *ACLU* decision, *ibid.* at 832, the court stated that "[t]here is no centralized storage location, control point, or communication channel for the Internet, and it would not be technically feasible for a single entity to control all of the information conveyed on the Internet."

law firm — which can then be accessed by users from any point along the Internet. An incredibly powerful aspect of the "Web," as it is colloquially called, is the ability to link between different pages on a site — or to link between different sites half a world away — simply by clicking on highlighted words. This hypertext feature has allowed the Internet to become an invaluable resource of discovery for a whole population of only semi–computer-literate users.

There are a number of participants on the Internet who facilitate access to it. Online service providers may be viewed as the full service alternative, offering, through their own computers, a number of in-house services to their subscribers only, in addition to offering access to the Internet. These companies will typically aggregate various types of content, services, and features for a variety of pricing schemes, depending on what the user finds most attractive. A much scaled-down variation on the online service provider is the bulletin board system (BBS) operator, who might even be an individual, who runs a computer with some group messaging software that allows the BBS operator to serve as a discussion moderator. At the other end of the spectrum is the Internet service provider that, in most cases, simply offers access to the Internet for a flat monthly fee, regardless of the amount of use. In between these two are the services springing up from telephone and cable companies that offer greater or fewer customer services and the all-important Internet access. A variation on all of these facilitators is the "freenet," typically a community-based organization that provides access to the Internet as well as to some of its own services. And then, of course, there are the multitude of content providers, ranging from the entities noted above to libraries, universities, corporations, governments, and individuals who, for a small investment, can create their own presence on the Internet through a custom home page. All these persons and entities are also users of the Internet as well, given that the Internet blurs the distinction between listeners and speakers, namely, the consumers and producers of information.

B. TECHNOLOGY TRENDS AND THE LAW

Having discussed some of the basics of computer and networking technologies, it is worth describing, briefly, how these technologies are being put to use today, and how some of the current technological trends and applications might unfold over the next few years. In doing so, it should be kept in mind that people often overestimate the short-term impact of technology — just as they underestimate its long-term impact! When the telephone first appeared, it was widely believed that although it might be useful for calls of a personal nature, surely nobody would do business over the telephone.[32] Those who think the Internet is a lot of hype are, in the short term, partly right — but in the long run will be woefully wrong, and they will fail to understand the enormous impact that the Internet will have on the development of computer law. This is not to say that the Internet will soon replace all forms of human communications, particularly because it is quite rare for a new communications medium to obliterate a predecessor entirely — witness how well radio and the cinema have held up against television and the videocassette player (but there are not many telegraphs in use today!).[33] The Internet is, however, steadily becoming embedded in the social and economic fabric of the world. Nonetheless, specific predictions made about this new communications infrastructure even three short years ago are proving incorrect, as certain anticipated uses for the Internet have not materialized — while unforeseen uses grow exponentially.[34] In any event, the point in the following discussion is not to gaze into a predictive crystal ball simply for the sake of such gazing, or for the psychic income that such gazing might generate, but rather to highlight the legally relevant aspects of some of the key trends and applications of computing and network technologies.

1) Digitization

A fundamental application for computing technologies is digitization, which entails reducing all the different forms of representations of information into numeric-based electronic signals that can then be recorded electronically or on an optical medium. Of course, with new documents it will not be a case of transforming them into a digital format, but of keeping them as such because they were created inside computers as

---

32 Indeed, the operator of the U.S. telegraph system at the time, Western Union, did not think anyone would want to talk to one another over great distances, so they declined an offer to buy the telephone patents for $100,000, a decision they later came to regret; see Estabrooks, *Electronic Technology*, above note 4 at 23.

33 For example, box office receipts of cinemas in the United States were up 8 percent in 1996, reversing a decline in recent years: see *The Economist*, 4 January 1997.

34 See the insightful "A Survey of Electronic Commerce: In Search of the Perfect Market," *The Economist*, 10 May 1997, which points out that, for example, consumer sales on the Internet are still in an embryonic stage, but that business-to-business Internet commerce is booming, as witnessed by General Electric currently buying one billion dollars' worth of goods from suppliers online annually, and Cisco Systems (the leading supplier of internetworking technology) selling a similar dollar amount of products from its website.

digital word processing documents or some other files. Thus, scanning technologies, which allow for easy transformation of paper-based documents into electronic, digital form, will be used to input only the previous generation of books, images, and other paper-based materials.[35] The ability to store all information, including text, images (moving as well as still), and sound, in a digital format is as revolutionary a development as the invention of the first printing press with movable type. The first CDs that fused all the types of content — text, graphics, photos, music, narration, videos, animation, etc. — present as clear a core step in history as Gutenberg's first books printed with his movable type innovation.[36] And this is perhaps more so, because with digitization people have freed themselves from the shackles of the printed medium, the primary platform for the preservation and presentation of information over the last five hundred years. Once digitized, information is in its most fluid form. Reduced to electronic bits and bytes, information can be stored, changed, adapted, transmitted, reproduced, all with impunity, and at extremely low cost. Elusive, ephemeral, amorphous digital information veritably dances. Digitization, therefore, highlights the second dynamic of computer law — namely, the elusive nature of information — and will have an enormous impact on the law. Previously, the fixation of infor-

---

35   This is done ingeniously by the scanner changing light reflected from an image into electrical current, then using a chip that changes the electrical current into a digital signal by using a series of mathematical formulas: see Kinkoph *et al.*, *Computers: A Visual Encyclopedia*, above note 1 at 297.

36   As to the impact of Gutenberg's revolutionary invention, see Marshall McLuhan, *The Gutenberg Galaxy: The Making of Typographic Man* (Toronto: University of Toronto Press, 1962). Although McLuhan was critical of much that was wrought by Gutenberg, he was much more hopeful for the electronic age; see Marshall McLuhan & Bruce R. Powers, *The Global Village: Transformations in World Life and Media in the 21st Century* (New York: Oxford University Press, 1989). From a legal perspective, Gutenberg's printing press kicked off the long development of copyright law, which continues to this day: see Benjamin Kaplan, *An Unhurried View of Copyright* (New York: Columbia University Press, 1967); Simon Nowell-Smith, *International Copyright Law and the Publisher in the Reign of Queen Victoria* (Oxford: Clarendon Press, 1968); and George A. Gipe, *Nearer to the Dust: Copyright and the Machine* (Baltimore: Williams & Wilkins, 1967). For an exploration of the impact of various media, from print to electronic, on the development of law, see M. Ethan Katsh, *The Electronic Media and the Transformation of Law* (New York: Oxford University Press, 1989). Ethan Katsh, in this book at 11, also gives due recognition to another great Canadian scholar, Harold Innis who, more than a decade before McLuhan became popular, stressed that the "materials on which words were written down have often counted for more than the words themselves," which is a more accurate statement than McLuhan's famous dictum that "the medium is the message."

mation in a physical medium like paper dictated a number of key rules in areas as diverse as intellectual property law, and especially copyright, to contract/commercial law, where legal rules have for several hundred years been devised with a paper-based business information environment in mind. As society travels the information highway from "papersville" to "electronicsville," a number of legal potholes will have to be attended to if the ride is to be a smooth and successful one.[37]

Digitization, of course, does not mean the end of books or other paper-based documents. Much electronic mail is printed out so that a paper-based copy can be maintained as a record. And bookstores continue to do a brisk business selling books. Nonetheless, huge amounts of data never appear on paper, and over time this trend will continue. The powers unleashed by digitization are compelling. For example, text that is in digital form can be searched and linked by keywords.[38] Thus, an encyclopedia on a CD-ROM allows the user to navigate various articles all related to the user's principal topic simply by clicking from one article to another connected by common keywords. While the traditional index in a paper-based encyclopedia serves a similar function, the ease with which the exercise is performed in an electronic environment makes the CD-ROM version of the work a revolutionary improvement.[39] Such keyword-based searching of digital-based content, through the use of HTML hypertext linking technology, is driving the explosive growth of the World Wide Web portion of the Internet.[40] This new ability to search, browse, and navigate documents by keywords is as far reaching a technological step forward as the development of movable type five hundred years ago.

Such linking technology also raises numerous legal issues. Consider a securities prospectus that has been put online and is available to

---

37 See George S. Takach, "Preventing Ambulance-Chasing on the Info Highway" *The [Toronto] Globe and Mail* (11 February 1994). One of the shortcomings of Ontario's laws noted in this article has since been remedied by the repeal of the previous s. 5 of the *Sale of Goods Act* (Ontario), as discussed in section A(1)(e), "Law Reform," in chapter 6.

38 See Cristina Brandao, "Rewiring the Ivory Tower," *Canadian Business Technology,* Winter 1996. This piece observes that an increasing number of academic journals are going online, and incorporating hyperlink features when they do.

39 The paper-based book, however, remains an excellent format for presenting a linear story, such as a novel, where the reader proceeds page by page from the beginning, to the middle, and finally to the end of a story. For non-linear searching of fact-intensive sources, such as databases, the electronic environment is clearly superior to its paper-based predecessor.

40 See de Kerckhove, *Connected Intelligence,* above note 28, for an insightful discussion of the societal ramifications of hypertext linking technology.

potential investors instead of the traditional paper-based one. The use of hypertext links in such a document might mean that investors never see important warning sentences in the prospectus as they link from key passages describing the business to the financial statements later on. Or what if the prospectus has within it links to other documents, or even to other websites that might contain explanatory or supplemental material? Does that other document now become part of the prospectus? Or is a hypertext link to another website an endorsement of that other site, which might give rise to liability in a legal sense?

2) Manipulation

Once digitized, the electronically stored information, be it a picture, music, video, drawing, text, or what have you, can be easily altered. Black and white movies can be coloured. Music can be sampled and manipulated. Text can be edited.[41] Photos can be digitally retouched to remove or add subjects.[42] The adage "a photo never lies" is no longer true.[43] Cameras are available that take digital pictures so that the photos do not even have to be scanned into the computer, rather, the "digital film" is played back on the computer; then pictures can be printed out in hard copy or sent out over the Internet — after they are modified as required by the photographer.[44] The ability to manipulate digitized content without any degradation of quality is without precedent. As a

---

41   To understand the impact of the digital revolution on the presentation and communication of the written word, see Roger E. Levien, "The Civilizing Currency: Documents and Their Revolutionary Technologies," in *Technology 2001: The Future of Computing and Communications*, ed. Derek Leebaert (Cambridge, Mass.: MIT Press, 1991).

42   See Kenneth Kidd, "Frontlines: Snap Judgments" *The [Toronto] Globe and Mail, Report on Business Magazine*, February 1995, about the business in Vancouver that specializes in digitally altering photographs to remove, for example, former spouses from vacation pictures.

43   For an arresting example, see the two pictures of Pope John Paul II in *Computerworld*, 16 October 1995. On the left is the standard papal image, with the Pope wearing white robes, a gold cross, and a tall white and gold mitre on his head. On the right is a digitally retouched derivative of this image to make the Pope look like a leader of the Jewish faith, and has him dressed in black, with a Star of David, a black yarmulka, and a moustache and beard. A visitor from Mars would not be able to tell which is the "real" picture.

44   See Peter Burrows, "HP Pictures the Future," *Business Week*, 7 July 1997, which chronicles the strategy of Hewlett-Packard, a computer manufacturer, to compete in the photography market against companies such as Kodak; both companies have a range of digital photography products.

result, in the digital world, artists and creators are challenging the old rules that dictated what is creative, what is original, and what is derivative. Advertisers are struggling to determine how much digital modification of a photo for use in an advertisement constitutes a misleading change in the representation of information.

Not surprisingly, digitization and manipulation of data, which underpin the second computer law dynamic — the elusive nature of information — have triggered a host of moral, ethical, and legal issues. The ease with which electronic data can be manipulated raises a wide array of legal challenges. In regard to intellectual property, numerous questions pertain to a creator's "moral rights" in a work and in its digitally produced and metamorphosed progeny. The criminal law relating to forgery and counterfeiting will be put to the test. In the areas of contract law and evidence law, there will be questions surrounding proof and authentication; for example, in an environment where digital-based material is manipulated regularly, what, if anything, constitutes the legal "original," and how is the existence of it proven in court? Given that copyright exists only in original works, manipulation of digital-based materials will also raise issues surrounding the ownership of copyright in such works. Further, the legal rules pertaining to misleading advertising will also need to be reassessed given that photographs can now be digitally altered without any degradation in the quality of the images.

3) Mass Storage

Once digitized, information is stored electronically or on an optical disk. Data storage is not a new human activity — the library at ancient Alexandria some three thousand years ago was said to store thousands of volumes of manuscripts. What has changed is the scale on which data storage can be effected. All the paper-based white pages telephone directories for all the cities in Canada take up half a dozen long book shelves; such a display can still be seen at some local reference libraries. The same amount of data can be stored on a few CDs. All the information in Alexandria's library could be stored on a few more CDs. Computers allow us to record, store, and retrieve information in ways simply not possible in a paper-based environment. And so, not surprisingly, huge databases have been developed, and more are being created each day. For example, the technological trend of mass storage permits retailers to record and store in "data warehouses" every individual's purchasing history — recorded down to the last intimate item bought at a pharmacy. And while the terms *storage* and *warehouse* have passive connotations in the world of physical objects, the data in electronic databases are anything but quiescent. They can be sorted and filtered, and merged with other databases, to provide "profiles" of data subjects, or to strategically link seemingly unrelated raw data into a meaningful whole.

The legal issues engendered by mass storage, and related activities and capabilities, are legion and novel. The ability to store vast quantities of personal information raises a host of privacy law issues. These concerns are heightened when the data are transmitted and stored outside of a data subject's domestic jurisdiction, possibly denying any effective legal recourse to the affected person. As such, mass storage brings sharply into focus the third and fourth dynamics of computer law, namely the blurring of both private/public and that of national/international. Criminal law concerns will also come to the fore as electronic mischief makers — as well as hard-core felons — gain remote access to these huge repositories of information. There are also novel legal uncertainties that touch on the second dynamic of computer law: Who owns these mountains of data? Can data be bought and sold like traditional, tangible assets?

4) Communications

Computers have always been used to store and manipulate information; indeed, they have traditionally been called "data processing" devices. An enormously important current technology trend is the development of the computer into a communications device as well — computation, processing, and now communication. In the first phase of computing, roughly from 1960 to 1980, mainframe computers automated large batch-based data calculating activities, as in running a payroll or keeping track of financial information. In the 1980s, the second phase of computing saw personal computers appear on desks and on factory floors, but still primarily oriented to processing data on a stand-alone basis. Since the early 1990s, we have witnessed the rise of the third phase of computing, namely networking, whereby the personal computers on desks have been exchanging e-mail and sharing documents through various groupware applications. And hence there follows the rise of ubiquitous computer networks, where the previously stand-alone personal computer now becomes a gateway to access a vast array of other computers belonging to individuals, corporations, and organizations, all of them also hooked up to the network, including the mother of all networks, the vast Internet.

Of course, networks are not entirely new. The telephone system is a network, as is cable television. To date, however, these two types of networks have been very different from computer networks. The telephone has been essentially single point to single point interactive communication, while cable television (and its predecessor off-air broadcast) has been single point to multipoint non-interactive communication. Computer networks facilitate single point to multipoint, and increasingly multipoint to multipoint, interactive communications.[45] This particular dynamic has never been seen before, and its impact will be profound, with huge ramifications for our educational, retail, financial, and political systems, to mention but a few areas that will be changed radically by the Internet.[46] Elizabeth Eisenstein has chronicled the far-reaching social changes precipitated in Europe around 1500 as a result of the shift from scribe processes (monks and other persons copying manuscripts) to Gutenberg's print technology, including the fundamental and irreversible impact on education, language, religion, science, and on social trends such as the growth in censorship, intellectual property, and national cultures.[47] The shifts and accelerations resulting from the displacement of print by electronic media centred on the Internet will be as basic and far-reaching in their own right.

Not surprisingly, the Internet also presents the legal system with fundamental challenges. From a narrow, regulatory perspective, how and where — or even whether — to slot the Internet into the current framework of telecommunications and broadcasting regulation raises some real conundrums. The growth in international telecommunications will eliminate distance as a legal fact, thereby illustrating the fourth computer law dynamic, namely the blurring of the national and the international. However, laws are stubbornly national in scope, with nationalism being understood primarily as a geographic concept. Thus, core jurisdictional questions will need to be revisited in all legal areas — including contract, criminal, intellectual property, commercial, and tort.

---

45   De Kerckhove, *Connected Intelligence*, above note 28, gives a penetrating analysis of how the interactivity of the Internet makes it a radical departure from any other communications medium.

46   See, for example, Patrick Butler *et al.*, "A Revolution in Interaction," *The McKinsey Quarterly* 1 (1997): 4, which argues that the new networking technologies, including the Internet, are decreasing transaction costs related to searching and contracting with partners, and that this will have widespread beneficial effects for the global economy.

47   Elizabeth L. Eisenstein, *The Printing Revolution in Early Modern Europe* (Cambridge: Cambridge University Press, 1983).

5) Miniaturization

If all of the above is not already reason enough to gape in awe at the computer revolution and the Information Age that it has spawned, consider that the computer on today's desk (and everywhere else) and its software is a "Model T" compared to what is coming in the next few years. This is largely because of the continued miniaturization of the computer, which in turn has been made possible by stunning advances in the design and fabrication of the semiconductor chip, the fundamental building block of computers and the foundation technology of the Information Age. As computers, and chips, get smaller and more powerful, they will insinuate themselves into every last nook and cranny of society. For good or ill, no part of human endeavour will be free from the effects of the computer. Already, it is the rare corporation or government entity that has not automated its financial/accounting systems with computers. In most computing environments, however, this is only the beginning. Computers have spread to the factory floor, and onto every desktop, and lately lap, in the organization. Consider any business, government department, school, university or other place of learning, any store, place of amusement, hospital or other medical facility, any hotel, airplane, or army unit — all have become increasingly dependent on the compact computer.

A key legal outcome of the ubiquitous computer will likely be a rise in lawsuits dealing with a wide array of liability issues as computers — as small as the size of a wristwatch — infiltrate every crevice of human endeavour. Notwithstanding their uncontestable success as a base technology — clearly the defining technological device of the last quarter of the twentieth century — computers are nevertheless risky devices. Custom software often cannot be built because of the limits of the current technology. Even computer systems that can be built usually arrive overbudget and well after the initially scheduled completion date. And computers and networks have a nasty habit of failing. When they do, chaos follows. An important question is whether our liability regimes, both contract- and tort-based, are up to the challenge posed by computers. The widespread adoption of computing technology will also have an impact on the rate of computer crime, as the number of potential victims increases exponentially. And the pervasive spread of computers and networks will mean overall that many more cases involving the other legal issues discussed in this book will arise as the number of computer law incidents multiplies exponentially. One has difficulty envisaging unemployed practitioners of computer law.

6) Intelligent Computers

Computers will also become smarter, meaning easier to use and more efficient. Already we are witnessing the growing use of *expert systems* and *artificial intelligence*, software that has the capacity to learn over time based on the data fed into it.[48] A decade ago, a thoughtful report prepared by Canada's National Research Council included a précis of a number of artificial intelligence/expert systems being worked on by computer scientists around the world at that time.[49] The titles of articles of some of these initiatives are revealing, and one can only imagine what has transpired in this field in the interim: "REGWASTE: An Expert System for Regulating Hazardous Wastes"; "Air Traffic Control Using AI [artificial intelligence] Techniques"; "Potential Defence Applications of Expert Systems"; and "Expert Systems for University Admissions." Today, there is even talk of intelligent legal software.[50] Another development worth noting is *neural network* technology that apparently mimics the stimulus and response action of the human brain, resulting in computers that are able to analyse extremely complex situations in a matter of minutes rather than days as is the case with conventional computing technology.[51] And to deal with information overload, the fact that there is *too much* information available on the Internet, there will soon be intelligent *agent software* that learns, over time, what interests the user, and then goes out on the Internet and retrieves information of particular relevance to the user, while the user enjoys a vigorous tennis game.[52]

---

48   For an overview of expert systems, see Frank Puppe, *Systematic Introduction to Expert Systems: Knowledge Representations and Problem Solving Methods* (Berlin: Springer-Verlag, 1993); and Amar Gupta & Bandreddi E. Prasad, eds., *Principles of Expert Systems* (New York: The Institute of Electrical and Electronics Engineers, 1988). See also Frederick Hayes-Roth & Neil Jacobstein, "The State of Knowledge-Based Systems," *Communications of the ACM* 37(3) (March 1994): 27.

49   National Research Council Canada, Associate Committee on Artificial Intelligence, *The Social Context of Artificial Intelligence: Guideline and Discussion Paper* (Ottawa: The Committee, 1989).

50   Adam Szweras, "Expert Computer Systems Could Give Legal Opinions, Make Administrative Decisions, Law Prof. Predicts" *The Lawyers Weekly* (14 January 1994).

51   Geoffrey Rowan, "'Unique' Software Thinks like a Human" *The [Toronto] Globe and Mail* (31 December 1996).

52   For a discussion of intelligent agents, and one possible scenario for the unfolding of the computer revolution over the coming years, see Nicholas Negroponte, *Being Digital* (New York: Vintage Books, 1995). See also *Communications of the ACM* 37(7) (July 1994), an issue devoted to intelligent agents.

Such agent software devices, and artificial intelligence/expert systems/neural network technology in general, raise some fundamental ethical questions. Immanuel Kant, the brilliant eighteenth-century German philosopher, believed that the quality that set humans apart from all other species was our ability to make moral, autonomous judgments throughout our lives; in a sense, our ability to decide makes us humans.[53] One wonders, if Kant were alive today, whether he would be distressed by the development of thinking machines that, in many areas of human endeavour, displace the need for human judgment and decision making. In effect, prior to the advent of the computer, humans possessed a monopoly on information-processing tasks. Now that is no longer the case. Perhaps Kantian philosophy would be willing to draw a distinction between those computing and networking technologies that are tools to assist humans make better decisions, and those that represent a wholesale abdication of what is essential to the human condition. As for the legal issues surrounding these systems, again liability will be a major focus. Consider a medical expert system that misdiagnoses a patient. Who is responsible? The doctor using it? The software company that created it? The eminent doctors who contributed to the knowledge base within the product? Or some combination of all three? And what should be the negligence standard by which such products are judged?

C. SOCIETAL IMPACT AND LEGAL ISSUES

Having considered, briefly, several key technologies and technological trends and applications, it is worth asking what their impact has been, and will continue to be, on society at large. In a word, immense.[54] The computer revolution, by which is meant the widespread, sustained, and irreversible use of the computer in every area of economic and social activity, ushered in the Information Age. Understanding several of the

---

53 Immanuel Kant, *Groundwork of the Metaphysic of Morals*, trans. H.J. Paton (New York: Harper & Row, 1964).

54 For an overview of the pervasive and fundamental societal changes wrought by the information highway and related technological developments, see Gilles Paquet, "Institutional Evolution in an Information Age," in Courchene, *Technology*, above note 19. For a management guru's perspective on the profound changes occurring in our computer-networked world, see Don Tapscott, *The Digital Economy: Promise and Peril in the Age of Networked Intelligence* (New York: McGraw-Hill, 1996).

key dynamics of this information era is critical to a discussion of computer law. Accordingly, the remainder of this chapter reviews the phenomena of elimination of distance and mass customization, both brought about by the computer-network technological developments discussed above. To understand these aspects of the Information Age, it is useful to consider the underpinnings of two earlier eras in history, the agrarian and the industrial. And again, the interplay of the four dynamics of computer law — rapid pace of technological development, the elusive nature of information, and the blurring of private/public and national/international — can be identified throughout the remaining pages of this chapter.

1) The Information Age

A comparative, analytical approach clarifies the defining indicia of the Information Age. During the Agricultural Revolution, land was the prime asset in the economy, the source of most wealth, and the vehicle that determined many social and power relationships. The defining assets of the Industrial Revolution were the physical goods first produced in mass production factories in England and other industrialized countries in the mid 1800s. In 1860, agriculture accounted for about 45 percent of Canada's gross domestic product.[55] By 1920, this figure was at about 15 percent, and manufacturing, the product of industrialization, was at its peak as a percentage of GDP, at about 25 percent.

The Information Age should not be viewed as displacing the two previous eras. Land is still an important component of the economy — people still need to eat food, for which land is necessary — and the economy still produces and uses vast amounts of factory-produced goods. Rather, information must be seen as an additional layer, important itself, but also incredibly strategic in the agriculture[56] and manufac-

---

55   These and the following GDP statistics on Canada have been compiled by Statistics Canada and John Kettle: see *The [Toronto] Globe and Mail* (2 August 1996).

56   See Alanna Mitchell, "Cattle Left Home on the Range in Satellite Auction" *The [Toronto] Globe and Mail* (3 October 1996), which describes the use of video, satellite, and Internet technologies to replace face-to-face cattle auctions, with the positive results of saving costs and increasing prices due to the ability to reach a larger number of buyers. See also Alexander Wooley, "Harvesting High Tech" *The [Toronto] Globe and Mail* (15 March 1997), which discusses how farmers are using satellite-based global positioning systems and computers on board combines to obtain valuable data on soil moisture and past chemical use patterns in order to optimize crop yields.

turing sectors.[57] Today, the information services sector of the Canadian economy — comprising publishing, television, communications, advertising, banking, research, education, government, etc. — accounts for about 30 percent of GDP. This includes those entities whose final product comes in the form of information. If entities that make information machines, such as computers and telephones, are included, as well as service organizations where information is the lifeblood but not the primary product, the percentage of the economy based on information can comfortably be put at 60 percent; agriculture, industry, and general services make up the remainder.

For over twenty years social scientists have chronicled the growing importance of the information sector in the economy, by measuring either GDP statistics or the percentage of people engaged in the generation and transmission of information.[58] In a seminal work in the mid-1970s, Daniel Bell concluded that the United States was undergoing a profound shift to a "post-industrial" stage of development.[59] More recently, another scholar in this field concluded that the production, processing, and distribution of information accounts for 40 percent of the world's industrial production.[60] Although criticism has been levelled at the methodology used in some of these studies,[61] it is difficult to dispute that information has attained a pre-eminent role in the economy

---

57   For a discussion of how various advanced computer-based information technologies, because of their cheap processing power, large storage capacities, and efficient networking capabilities, have infiltrated and changed key aspects of the Canadian manufacturing sector, see John Baldwin, Brent Diverty & David Sabourin, "Technology Use and Industrial Transformation: Empirical Perspectives," in Courchene, *Technology*, above note 19. See also Gene Bylinsky, "The Digital Factory," *Fortune*, 14 November 1994, which analyses the role of software and computer networks in profoundly transforming the factory floor, with superb economic results.

58   For a review of how economists have handled the information economy, see D. McL. Lamberton, "The Information Economy Revisited," and Robert E. Babe, "The Place of Information in Economics," both in *Information and Communication in Economics*, ed. Robert E. Babe (Boston: Kluwer, 1994).

59   Daniel Bell, *The Coming of Post-Industrial Society: A Venture in Social Forecasting* (New York: Basic Books, 1973; 1976).

60   Herbert S. Dordick, *The Information Society: A Retrospective View* (Newbury Park, Calif.: Sage, 1993).

61   For a critical analysis of the key Information Age theorists, see Frank Webster, *Theories of the Information Society* (London: Routledge, 1995).

and society, thereby justly earning for the current era the label Information Age.[62] In fact, some economists, led by Paul Romer at Stanford University, have recognized in what is called New Growth Theory that knowledge, ideas, and information are as important — if not more so — as labour, capital, and natural resources, in fueling economic growth.[63]

The Information Age title, however, is deserved not merely as a result of economic theory or statistics related to GDP and employment. As relevant is the fact that computers are embedded in every activity undertaken in the economy and society. Today, businesses could not operate, schools could not educate, professionals and other service providers could not provide services, governments could not govern, and the military could not fight wars, if they did not have computers and the huge volumes of information stored, processed, and disseminated by computers.[64] For confirmation of this, consider the immense angst and cost being expended on the year 2000 problem. Many older software programs work on the basis of two-digit date fields (e.g., 1997 is 97) and are not able to recognize the new millennium's date of 2000, given that 00 will either not register on these computers, or perhaps even worse, will register as 1900.[65] Of course, a positive view is that businesses, schools, professionals, the military, service providers, and governments can now achieve ambitious new goals in the Information Age because of computers and computer networks. Regardless of one's assessment of

---

62   For an excellent overview of the economic, technological, and sociological implications of the Information Age, see Jorge Reina Schement & Terry Curtis, *Tendencies and Tensions of the Information Age: The Production and Distribution of Information in the United States* (New Brunswick, N.J.: Transaction, 1995).

63   See Paul M. Romer, "Endogenous Technological Change," *Journal of Political Economy* 98 (1990): S71. Romer believes that technological change, namely the improvement in the instructions for mixing together raw materials, lies at the heart of economic growth and at S72 states that: "One hundred years ago, all we could do to get visual stimulation from iron oxide was to use it as a pigment. Now we put it on plastic tape and use it to make videocassette recordings." For a similar perspective, but focussing on the critical role of information and knowledge at the level of the individual firm, see Stewart, *Intellectual Capital*, above note 17.

64   For a compelling analysis of the digitization of the military, both during and since the 1991 Gulf War, see "Defence Technology: The Information Advantage," *The Economist*, 10 June 1995, and "The Future of Warfare: Select Enemy, Delete," *The Economist*, 8 March 1997. Apparently the Pentagon also has plans to develop high-tech weapons to attack the domestic computer systems of its adversaries: see Gary H. Anthes, "Info Warfare Risk Growing," *Computerworld*, 22 May 1995.

65   For various materials on the year 2000 problem, see: <http://www.year2000.com/>. The legal implications of the year 2000 date problem are discussed in section D(1), "Negligence in Creation: The Y2K Problem," in chapter 5.

the prospects for a society where information is the defining asset, it simply cannot be denied that this is the Information Age. This has even been recognized in a recent judicial decision, where the court stated: "Information is the currency of modern life. This has been properly called the information age."[66]

Law is a reflection of the economy and the society from which it emanates. Thus, it is not surprising that land-related laws first developed with the ascendancy of the role of land as the principal asset in the agrarian era. It is for this reason that mortgage legal principles, and related documents, still contain a healthy dose of "olde English," given that the legal rules for mortgages date from several hundred years ago. Similarly, the enactment of the *Sale of Goods Act* in England in the 1880s is the quintessential legal development in the industrial era, which was so concerned with the production and distribution of physical goods. Therefore, living as we are in the Information Age, it is appropriate to ask if our laws have stayed current with the rise to prominence of information as a valuable asset. Put another way, do we need to develop new laws and legal principles for the new era, or can we make do relying, for the most part, on laws intended for a previous era? These questions form a constant theme throughout this book.

2) Elimination of Distance

Almost by definition, geography played an important role in the agrarian era. In the industrial era, geographic space was still important because it was (and still is) expensive to send physical goods to distant customers. In contrast, a central feature of the Information Age is how computers linked to electronic networks eliminate physical distance. Current telephony, broadcast, and cable systems have already caused the world to shrink. Full electronic networks that can transmit all forms of digital information and content will eliminate geographic distance as a factor in a number of areas of human endeavour, including education, medicine, engineering, most business services, finance, and entertainment. Consider the growing area of telemedicine. Arthroscopic surgery involves inserting compact medical instruments into a patient and having a doctor perform the operative procedure by viewing a monitor that displays the images conveyed by the instruments and by manipulating dials on a computer that in turn control the instruments in the patient.

---

66   *Vancouver Regional FreeNet Assn. v. M.N.R.* (1996), 137 D.L.R. (4th) 206 at 213 (F.C.A.).

With this sort of procedure it no longer matters whether the doctor is in the same room as the patient or half a continent away. Indeed, access to medical expertise may increase dramatically as specialists are able to ply their trade around the world over networks. This is not science fiction; there are currently numerous telemedicine facilities up and running.[67] Activities capitalizing on the same technological dynamics that are driving telemedicine include the rapidly growing phenomena of Internet banking and distance education by universities that offer courses through a combination of satellite, broadcast, and Internet facilities.

The legal impact of the elimination of distance will be enormous. Computer networks are a prime exponent of the fourth dynamic of computer law, namely, the blurring of the national with the international. Hence, novel legal questions abound when a person or organization is able to convey a presence in another jurisdiction electronically, or when someone in one jurisdiction accesses a website located on a computer resident in another jurisdiction. When is a company legally carrying on business in another jurisdiction, such that it is subject to that other jurisdiction's laws, simply because people in that other jurisdiction can access its website? Or, in the telemedicine example, is a doctor who is physically present in Toronto, operating remotely on her patient resident in a hospital in Denver, Colorado (the patient broke his leg skiing), required to be licensed in Colorado to practise medicine in Colorado? Is the doctor in fact practising medicine in Colorado? Does the Canadian doctor's malpractice insurance cover the doctor for procedures effected on patients who are physically outside of Canada at the time? These questions will multiply exponentially as new and intriguing applications are found to help eliminate the concept of geography as a factor in human endeavours.[68]

3) Mass Customization

With information exchange becoming such an important activity in our society, and with data capture, storage, and manipulation becoming less and less expensive, businesses, public sector agencies, and governments are getting to know individuals as never before. In one sense, this is not

---

67 See Joanne Sommers, "Nortel, Bell Linking Doctors, Patients in Different Cities" *The [Toronto] Globe and Mail, Report on Telecommunications* (6 May 1997).

68 For a discussion of some legal and non-legal obstacles confronting telemedicine in certain jurisdictions, such as the unwillingness of medical insurance companies to pay for non–face-to-face consultations, see Mitch Betts, "Network Medicine Offers Its Share of Headaches," *Computerworld*, 26 September 1994.

an entirely new phenomenon. In the agrarian era, the local butcher, for example, knew intimately what each of his hundred customers in the village preferred by way of types and cuts of meat, and the appropriate item would be waiting on the relevant day of the week because the butcher knew each customer personally. The quality and selection may not have been very exciting, and products were quite expensive because economies of scale were hard to come by in such an environment. In other words, the benefits of mass production could not be realized, but at least the customer received what the customer desired, and when the customer wanted it, from the limited selection. In the industrial era the production of goods – and services — moved into factories. Economies of scale were realized in factories that produced goods, as well as services such as education (i.e., the "factory" is the school), culture (opera house, concert hall, cinema), medicine (hospital), information (library), and government (Parliament, city hall). These factories were marvels of efficiency, and they caused costs to drop dramatically, thereby ushering in the era of mass consumption. Knowledge of the individual customer, however, and of that customer's preferences — the dual hallmarks of the earlier era — were lost. More consumers were able to buy a car, but all Model Ts were black. The defining benefit of mass production, a dramatic decrease in prices, was able to be realized, but the benefits of customization became elusive.

The technology trends noted above today permit *mass customization*, the result obtained from fusing the intimacy of the customized agrarian era with the mass production efficiency of the industrial era. Networked computers running huge databases can now recreate the detailed knowledge that the butcher had of each of his customers; today each retailer, or government, or school can know each customer or citizen or constituent.[69] The fundamental difference, of course, is that while the medieval butcher's geographic term of reference was the village, the modern database creator's field of activity is literally the world, thereby permitting large economies of scale to result in lower unit prices. This is both an exhilarating prospect (for the retailer), and possibly an uncomfortable one too (for the data subject)! Contributing to the phenomenon of mass customization is the ability of computers and networks to divide a product or service into its information and physical delivery components. Currently, a patient goes to a hospital both for information and the delivery of the requisite service. Similarly, a con-

---

69   For a treatment of mass customization from the perspective of the management guru, see Don Peppers & Martha Rogers, *The One to One Future: Building Relationships One Customer at a Time* (New York: Doubleday, 1993).

sumer goes to a retail store for information (i.e., to find out price, quality, availability, colour, etc.) and to take physical delivery of the product. Increasingly, these two functions are being separated, and performance of the former will no longer require physical attendance at the site of delivery of the latter. Instead, information will be provided in advance to the prospective user of the service or product.

This is already occurring in a number of areas, for example, in the low-tech environments of direct mail catalogues or ordering pizzas by telephone. With full digitization of content, where product catalogues or medical information or customer information is online, the bifurcation process will be complete. Moreover, the information delivery component will be by far the more valuable of the two parts of the system. It is the primary value-added activity, while shipping product will become a commodity-like function with relatively low margins. Airlines, for example, make more profit from moving information over their computer-based reservation networks than from moving people in their planes. And as the consumer learns about a particular product or service in an online or networked environment, the provider of this information will be learning about the consumer, adding yet more personal information to the already burgeoning database.

The collection, aggregation, and especially dissemination to third parties of such data of course brings to light a set of legal issues involving privacy, data protection, and even a raft of commercial issues. It is not surprising that such a fundamental shift in the way that much of business will be done will result in an important re-evaluation of many of the legal principles in effect today, all with a view to bringing into the Information Age those laws that are currently completely out of date or in need of partial upgrading. The third dynamic of computer law — involving the blurring of the private and public spheres — will bring to the fore a number of legal questions. Data protection and surveillance laws will have to be updated (where they exist) or enacted (where none exists). For example, so-called cookies can be embedded in the software that users employ to access the various websites of the Internet. This cookie software can tell its creator what websites were visited by the user, and eventually will be able to convey information on the actual purchases made, money spent, etc. All this can be done without the user having any knowledge of the cookie. The law of privacy will likely be called upon to address this type of technology.

4) Dependency on Computers

As computers become pervasive, our dependency on them grows.[70] The ability to store all the key financial and operating data of a business on a single CD, permitting an executive to access it on a laptop computer while she is at her summer cottage, illustrates the power and benefits of the new technology.[71] Powerful and beneficial indeed, until the executive has it stolen from her car. Then an ugly Achilles' heel of the Information Age is revealed. Some thieves may only think about fencing the laptop for a few hundred dollars; more sophisticated felons, however, are beginning to realize that the data in the laptop are far more valuable. They can be used for extortion through a slow sale of individual files back to the executive or for industrial espionage through a quick sale to the executive's competitor. Obviously, these risks to security must be addressed by all users of the new technology. Another risk presented by dependency involves malfunction or breakdown of the computer infrastructure of the organization.[72] Soon all businesses and organizations will be unable to function if their computers are not operating properly.

---

70   Though at least one court has determined that a household is not as dependent on the computer as it is on the television. In *Re Larsen*, 203 B.R. 176 (Bankr. W.D. Okl. 1996), an American bankruptcy court concluded that the personal computer in 1996 is where the television was in the mid-1950s, an intriguing and entertaining device, but not yet critical enough to be excluded from a secured party's lien as a necessary household item in a personal bankruptcy, though the judge conceded that one day it may well attain such an important status. The court noted that the television has gone from an expensive curiosity to a necessity as a family's relatively inexpensive primary source of information and entertainment, but that the personal computer is not yet at this stage. Persons exhibiting symptoms of Internet addiction may disagree with this court's assessment: see Ed Susman, "Studies Identify Internet Addiction" *The [Toronto] Globe and Mail* (16 August 1997). These symptoms include: having an inability to control Internet use; lying to family members or friends to conceal the extent of involvement with the Internet; and going through withdrawal when not online. See also *Re Ratliff*, Guide to Computer Law (CCH) ¶47,745 at 70,529 (Bankr. E.D. Okla. 1997), where a bankruptcy court did find that in view of the computer's role as a key resource for gathering information, the debtors' use of the computer for school purposes, and the importance of learning computer skills, the personal computer was exempt from a lien as being protected household goods.

71   Unless one takes the view that laptops have no place in a cottage. On the other hand, busy people would use the cottage a lot less if they could not remain connected to the rest of the world while at the cottage.

72   For a discussion of a number of risks posed by computers, particularly in the health sector, see Jacques Berleur, Colin Beardon & Romain Laufer, eds., *Facing the Challenge of Risk and Vulnerability in an Information Society* (Amsterdam: North-Holland, 1993).

As well, huge costs in financial and operational terms can occur if a proposed new system was simply too complicated and could not be built.[73] An insatiable appetite has been created for ever more powerful computers, software, and networks to perform more Herculean tasks: a computer-based expert system to run part of Canada's air traffic control regime; a gargantuan automated baggage handling system at Denver's new international airport; a revolutionary computerized stock trading system for the Toronto Stock Exchange, just to name a few examples. Incidentally, these three (and many other large software development projects) all experienced huge technical problems, commensurate delays in completion, and mountainous cost overruns.[74] More recent examples of high-profile high-tech heartburn include the one-day outage experienced by America Online, a leading Internet service provider, IBM's trials and tribulations with its computer systems at the 1996 Atlanta Olympic Games, and the crashing of the Toronto Stock Exchange's computer because of unusually heavy trading loads as a result of the Bre-X fiasco.[75]

A dispassionate observer of these trends could be forgiven for having the uneasy feeling that our mastery of the technology has not kept pace with our stratospheric expectations. Many computer programmers are working well outside their comfort zone, a situation with profound

---

73   For a discussion of a number of famous, as well as lesser-known, computer meltdowns, see Lauren Ruth Wiener, *Digital Woes* (Reading, Mass.: Addison-Wesley, 1993). A 1994 study of large computer software development projects reported that only 9 percent are concluded on time and on budget, and fully one-third are abandoned prior to completion: see Barrie McKenna, "Cancelled Contracts Cost Ottawa Millions" *The [Toronto] Globe and Mail* (4 September 1996). For some wise yet practical advice on how to avoid disappointments in the implementation of information technology projects, see Alistair Davidson, Harvey Gellman & Mary Chung, *Riding the Tiger* (Toronto: HarperCollins, 1997).

74   High-profile failures caused by errors in software are also not new: in 1962, a single character error in the control software for the Mariner I Venus probe sent the rocket booster off course, leading mission control to destroy it, and in 1990 the AT&T long distance network was knocked out for nine hours due to a problem with the routing software: see Ralston & Reilly, *Encyclopedia of Computer Science*, above note 1. Closer to home, a news report attributed to software glitches several deaths and injuries related to overdoses of radiation therapy: see Barbara Wade Rose, "Fatal Dose," *Saturday Night*, June 1994.

75   Mitch Wagner, "AOL Unplugged," *Computerworld*, 12 August 1996; Mindy Blodgett, "IBM Misses Chance for the Gold," *Computerworld*, 29 July 1996; and Janet McFarland, "Latest TSE Computer Crash Angers Investors, Members" *The [Toronto] Globe and Mail* (2 April 1997). See also the brief story in *The Economist*, 8 June 1996, regarding the destruction of $500 million worth of uninsured spacecraft and scientific satellite when apparently a software failure made the launch rocket go off course just after lift-off.

legal implications. Of course, many software development projects can fail because of problems caused by the customer as well. In any event, the dependency that society has developed on computers brings to the forefront questions about legal liability. How should negligence be assessed with respect to software programmers, given the lack of software programming standards? Should society contemplate some form of licensing regime to help ensure the competence of persons working in the software field? A university degree in engineering and an engineer's licence is required of someone designing a bridge for our concrete highways, yet no such accreditation or licensure is required of the persons constructing our information superhighways. Is insurance available to either the developer or the user to cover computer-related risks? Can contracts be used to allocate risks, and in some cases completely limit one party's liability? In short, how well have our legal liability regimes, both in contract and tort/negligence, kept pace with developments driven by the first dynamic of computer law, the torrid pace of technological change?

5) Legal Implications

The societal trends discussed above have important legal ramifications, and a number of these have already been alluded to in the previous paragraphs. Other questions can be contemplated. With an increasing proportion of society's wealth linked to the generation and dissemination of computer and information-based assets, are traditional intellectual property laws appropriate to ensure optimum levels of production of information? With ubiquitous networks presenting criminals with untold new opportunities to cause harm, is the criminal law adequate to ensure public safety? Should the government regulate the content flowing over these networks, and if they do so, how can they do so effectively? Should laws regulate the massive databases that collect copious amounts of personal data? A government's jurisdiction to regulate has traditionally been geographically oriented (e.g., the government of British Columbia can only make laws in the province of British Columbia); how will governments exercise jurisdiction over a network like the Internet that ignores geographic boundaries? How should traditional principles of contract, evidence, and tort law be customized to deal with the challenges posed by the computer revolution? It is to these and a host of similar questions that we turn in the remainder of this book.

When approaching these questions, it is worth being mindful of how uncontrolled and unruly it all is. Primarily contributing to this sense of anarchy is the speed with which all these developments are unfolding. It was three hundred and fifty years before the first major improvement was made to Gutenberg's original printing press — replacing human power with steam. In contrast, the commercial use of the Internet is only a few years old, but rarely a month passes without the announcement of some new Internet technology! Technological advances occur at breakneck speed, but law reform moves at a much slower pace. Contributing to the difficulties surrounding the development of sensible legal rules for computer and network technologies is the fiendishly elusive nature of information itself — it is a hard asset to pin down. Adding to the feeling of anarchy is the profoundly democratic nature of much of the new technology; for example, a personal computer and a handheld scanner can make a computer user a budding publisher on the Internet. In other words, even if the legal system could craft the rules necessary for the Information Age, how will they be implemented and enforced locally and in each home? And how will all this be done in foreign jurisdictions, given the global nature of the computer revolution, but the parochial domestic reach of national laws? These factors — what this book refers to as the four dynamics of computer law — and how lawyers, judges, and legislators come to understand and master them, will have an important effect on how the legal questions raised in this book are ultimately answered.

FURTHER READINGS

Books

BELL, Daniel, *The Coming of Post-Industrial Society: A Venture in Social Forecasting* (New York: Basic Books, 1973; 1976)

DE KERCKHOVE, Derrick, *Connected Intelligence: The Arrival of the Web Society* (Toronto: Somerville House, 1997)

ESTABROOKS, Maurice, *Electronic Technology, Corporate Strategy, and World Transformation* (Westport, Conn.: Quorum Books, 1995)

GATES, Bill, *The Road Ahead* (New York: Viking, 1995)

JOHNSTON, David, Deborah JOHNSTON & Sunny HANDA, *Getting Canada OnLine: Understanding the Information Highway* (Toronto: Stoddart, 1995)

NEGROPONTE, Nicholas, *Being Digital* (New York: Vintage Books, 1995)

PFAFFENBERGER, Bryan, *Internet in Plain English* (New York: MIS Press, 1994)

STEWART, Thomas A., *Intellectual Capital: The New Wealth of Organizations* (New York: Doubleday, 1997)

TAPSCOTT, Don, *The Digital Economy: Promise and Peril in the Age of Networked Intelligence* (New York: McGraw-Hill, 1996)

Internet Sites

Canadian Legal Information Centre
<http://www.schober.com/~wwlia/ca-home.htm>

Decisions of the Supreme Court of Canada
<http://www.droit.umontreal.ca/doc/csc-scc/en/index.html>

Department of Justice (Canada)
<http://canada.justice.gc.ca/>

Wired
<http://www.wired.com>

INTELLECTUAL PROPERTY LAWS

Intellectual property laws provide legal protection for products emanating from the minds of people and, accordingly, cover a variety of computer and information-based technologies and products. The rationale for intellectual property laws lies in the peculiar economics associated with intellectual properties. This chapter begins by discussing several important economic differences between intellectual properties, on the one hand, and real property and tangible physical, movable property (goods), on the other hand. Understanding these differences will bring into focus the core principles and more subtle nuances of the various intellectual property law regimes. The chapter then discusses how the core intellectual property law regimes of trade secrets/breach of confidence, patents, copyrights, and semiconductor chip protection apply to information-based products. Of course, not all questions regarding intellectual property laws and their application to information-based products are settled. The four dynamics of computer law, namely, the rapid pace of technological change, the elusive nature of information, and the blurring of private/public and national/international, conspire to ensure that the application of intellectual property laws to software and other information-based assets is in a constant flux. Accordingly, the last part of the chapter discusses how these laws apply (or may not apply) to software, multimedia content, databases, and to activities on the Internet. Finally, in addition to covering the substantive aspects of intellectual property law regimes, the material in this chapter explores the process-related question of how well, or poorly, the current civil procedure system is wrestling with these complicated matters.

A. THE ECONOMICS OF INFORMATION

In chapter 1, a number of differences between the agrarian and industrial eras, on the one hand, and the Information Age, on the other hand,
were highlighted. Similarly, economic differences exist between the
principal assets of these three epochs. Illustrative of the second dynamic
of computer law — the elusive nature of information — information-
based assets differ radically from those of tangible assets, such as land
and goods. Understanding these differences is vital to an appreciation of
the rationale and role of intellectual property laws, as well as the specific
substantive provisions of these legal regimes. Although the following
discussion is not comprehensive, a brief overview of the key concepts
will assist the reader to become comfortable with the discussion of legal
issues that follows.

1) Tangible Assets

The central economic fact governing the traditional assets of land
(including buildings) and goods (such as tables, chairs, and automobiles) is natural scarcity. There is a finite amount of land in the world.
Similarly, notwithstanding recycling efforts, natural resources such as
minerals are inherently scarce commodities. Equally, the energy sources
required to transform natural resources into finished goods are also, for
the most part, non-renewable. In a world characterized by finite physical assets, economics can be understood as the study of the allocation
within society of scarce resources. As for the legal system, an economy
based on land and goods and that recognizes private property need only
have a criminal law prohibiting trespass (for land) and theft (for goods).
Once the law provides that non-owners cannot occupy the land and
cannot take goods of others, the economic rules of supply and demand
will operate to determine how much of a particular asset is sold and purchased, and at what price.[1] It is easy to determine if a non-owner is
squatting on someone else's land or is occupying someone else's premises. It is also easy to ascertain whether a car owner has been deprived
of that good; if she wakes up in the morning, and the car is not in the
driveway, it has been stolen. Tangible, physical goods lend themselves
to simple property ownership regimes. Further, they are not subject to

---

1   For a seminal elaboration of these concepts by one of the pioneers of the law and
    economics school of thought, see Richard A. Posner, *Economic Analysis of Law*, 4th
    ed. (Boston: Little, Brown, 1992).

the four dynamics of computer law. They are not nearly as susceptible to technological change, they are not elusive, and their delimitation both within the private/public and national/international spheres is simple and constant. Tangible goods are static, and hence the legal system for their protection can be quite straightforward.

Of course, ownership of even the traditional assets of land and goods has become more complicated over time. Real property rights are now hemmed in and overlaid by a host of public and quasi-public rights, such as easements in favour of utilities, and zoning restrictions in favour of the common good.[2] Through condominium law we have created owner-ship rights in a type of real property that, in a sense, is disassociated from the underlying earth; for units on the second and subsequent floors, these real property rights literally hang in mid-air. Laws governing rela-tionships also permit security interests and other contingent ownership rights to be granted in movable goods, such as automobiles. Nonethe-less, we have in our real property and personal property security regis-tration systems relatively simple and efficient mechanisms by which these various interests can be ordered and recorded. Thus, when a per-son buys a house (or a condominium), a lawyer can give a very mean-ingful opinion as to who owns title to the property and what third party interests affect such title. In contrast, a lawyer's opinion to a purchaser of the intellectual property in a computer program would be so full of qualifications as to be meaningless. The four dynamics of computer law raise all sorts of questions as to the ownership of the intellectual prop-erty in the software. Who, exactly, contributed what to the software, so as to have had an ownership interest in it? Were aspects of it created by programmers at their homes, and does this mean they might own parts of it personally even if they were employees at the time? Were there international contributors to the software, perhaps collaborating over the Internet? Which intellectual property laws apply to them? The lack of an effective ownership registration system compounds these ques-tions. Tangible assets raise few of these questions.

2) Information-based Assets

Information-based assets differ radically from land and goods. The funda-mental difference is that today information can be reproduced at virtually

---

2   For analysis of property as a cluster of rights, and not as a thing, see C.B. Macpherson, ed., *Property: Mainstream and Critical Positions* (Toronto: University of Toronto Press, 1978); and Arnold S. Weinrib, "Information and Property" (1988) 38 U.T.L.J. 117.

no cost.[3] This was not always true. Prior to the printing press, copying a book by hand in monasteries in Europe in the Middle Ages was as laborious a task as writing the original copy. Gutenberg changed all this with his invention of the movable type printing press, which dramatically reduced the time, effort, and cost involved in producing copies. More recently, the photocopier has driven the marginal cost of reproduction even lower.[4] The printing press and the photocopier did not, however, reduce the still significant cost of transporting books, newspapers, and other paper-based media on which information has traditionally resided. Today, digital-based content can be reproduced by computers *and* transmitted around the world by telecommunication networks at no cost and with no degradation in the quality of the work. In many respects, it is no longer appropriate to talk about scarcity of information in the current technological environment. To illustrate this point, several commentators make reference to the story in The Gospel According to Matthew of the fishes and loaves, where the disciples fed the crowds from a few baskets that miraculously replenished themselves with fish and bread; apparently after everyone ate, twelve baskets were still filled with food.[5] This is a rare situation in which physical, tangible goods behaved like information. What was truly a miracle in the corporeal world, however, is an everyday occurrence in the incorporeal sphere of information-based assets. Just like the adage says, in the physical world cake cannot be held after it is eaten. By contrast, in the world of information, you can eat your cake and still have it, too.

The fact that information can be copied and transmitted at no incremental cost leads to the second fundamental aspect of information, that it is capable of universal possession. A touchstone of traditional, physical assets is that at any one time only one person is capable of possessing a particular table, chair, or automobile. Indeed, exclusive possession, and the ability to exclude others from the asset, are the hallmarks of ownership for traditional assets like land and goods. An ownership regime based on exclusion gave rise to the old legal adage that "possession is nine-tenths of the law," which is a pithy way of say-

---

3   For a perceptive analysis of the legal ramifications of this fact and other related indicia of information, see R. Grant Hammond, "Quantum Physics, Econometric Models and Property Rights to Information" (1982) 27 McGill L.J. 47. See also R.J. Roberts, "Is Information Property?" (1987) 3 I.P.J. 209.

4   An early discussion of the legal impact of the photocopier is provided in George A. Gipe, *Nearer to the Dust: Copyright and the Machine* (Baltimore: Williams & Wilkins, 1967).

5   Matt. 14:17-20.

ing that with traditional assets ownership and possession are synonymous, because possession of tangible assets is exclusive. This turn-of-phrase clearly pre-dates the Information Age. Given the second dynamic of computer law, exclusive possession becomes fiendishly difficult with information-based assets, where multiple, simultaneous or near-simultaneous possession is the norm. Put another way, because we can physically see and experience fences, doors, and locks, it is easy to forget that ownership of real and tangible property is about relationships. Perhaps it is also important that all real estate has been claimed and is owned by someone. An exception is the land under the oceans, and this fact, along with the fluid nature of water and the migratory habits of fish, actually brings to mind other fish examples that somewhat approximate the information world: the salmon, cod, and other fish disputes that break out between Canada, the United States, and (on the east coast) other countries. Another example is air, also generally not owned, and migratory, and the cause of crossborder disputes because of airborne pollution. Intellectual property constantly has to be carved out of the ether, or like nomadic fish, pulled from the ocean. Information is diffusive, it leaks, it spreads, it ebbs and flows. Historically, we used a physical net to catch it — paper — but after the invention of the printing press and the photocopier this net began to tear. And once information is stored, aggregated, processed, and disseminated electronically, leaving all physical carriers behind, the analogy with water and air is complete. The evanescent nature of information combined with the ability to reproduce and transmit it at extremely low cost seriously affects the legal ownership regimes applicable to information-based assets.

3) The Rationale for Intellectual Property Laws

Given the ease with which information can be reproduced and transmitted, how should society implement a private property ownership regime for elusive information-based assets? This question assumes, of course, that a system of private property protection is both desirable and required in order that sufficient amounts of information be created. If cars were not protected by the criminal offence of theft, they would likely not be produced because they would be stolen from factories, thus denying the manufacturer a return on effort; for markets to operate efficiently, a private property regime is required in order that producers be able to recoup economic rewards for their work. Put another way, laws impose barriers to free consumption so that manufacturers and distributors can earn a return for their efforts. It is no different for information and intellectual property.[6] If there were no means of capturing some economic returns for investing in the human and other capital required to create, say, software, a great deal less software would be produced. This point is particularly salient for creators of information-based assets, like software or movies, because these assets typically are extremely expensive to produce but, once created, are incredibly inexpensive to reproduce. There are, of course, other economic models that might result in sufficient production of intellectual properties. For example, several hundred years ago rich patrons, rather than copyright, were responsible for underwriting the creation of most artistic works, and more recently the state has been an important patron of the arts. These alternatives to the market system, however, are not without their own disadvantages as the many angst-filled relationships between composer and patron, between cash-strapped government and state-subsidized artist, can attest.

One option for protecting information in a free market system is simply to draw on the legal regime associated with goods, and make the theft of information a criminal offence. The problem with this approach, however, is that the criminal law is too blunt an instrument to apply to information. Consider the theft of a book. If someone physically removes a book from a store without paying for it, that person has stolen the book, the physical medium on which the information resides, and the person would be guilty of the offence of theft but only of the paper-based good that is the book. Thus, the criminal law works well enough for the physical containers into which information is poured, the units of tangible media on which information is imprinted or electronically stored. Matters become more complicated, however, when that which is taken is not the physical medium. For example, what if the thief reads the book, with the intention of writing her own book on a similar subject? If the thief copies each sentence, word for word, so that her book is the same as the author's book, and the thief sells multiple copies of "her" resulting book, one may still envisage a role for the criminal law. What should happen,

---

6   This view has had proponents in the economic literature since the time of Adam Smith, who wrote that while monopoly was hurtful to society, a temporary monopoly granted to an inventor was a good way of rewarding risk and expense: Adam Smith, *An Inquiry into the Nature and Causes of the Wealth of Nations,* book V, chapter I, part III (London: W. Strahan and T. Cadell, 1776, [New York: A.M. Kelley, 1966]). For a study that canvasses the views of pro-patent and anti-patent economists, see Fritz Machlup, *An Economic Review of the Patent System* (Washington: U.S. Government Printing Office, 1958).

however, if the thief merely copies a few sentences from the existing book into her own manuscript? Or what if she merely writes, in her own work, about ideas also articulated in the first book? And what if the thief had not stolen the first book, but bought it from a retailer who in turn acquired it from the authorized publisher of the work? These questions are more problematic from a legal perspective, and they raise a host of additional issues. Is it clear the author of the previous book was the first to describe a particular idea, or even use the particular words he used to describe it? Many ideas and information-based works and the form of expression found in them are, to a greater or lesser degree, derivative in their form and/or content.[7] The great scientific thinker, Sir Isaac Newton, articulated this concept well when, in paying homage to the authors of the great scientific works that preceded him and their influence upon his own thinking, exclaimed: "If I have seen further it is by standing on ye sholders of Giants."[8] Could there have been a Mozart without a Haydn to precede him, or a Brahms, Bruckner, or Mahler without a Beethoven? The stylistic similarities among the paintings of the Group of Seven Canadian landscape artists (and Tom Thomson) are uncanny. Of course, each *bona fide* painter, author, composer, or other creator adds new and different elements, but what exactly is old and what is new is often difficult to separate. The criminal law is not well suited to this enquiry with information-based assets because the parameters of criminal offences should be very well delineated, given the serious consequences that flow from a conviction. The certainty of the physical parameters of tangible goods permits the criminal law to determine the ownership of such assets; the ephemeral nature of information requires the legal system to look beyond the criminal law for a regime to perform the same function.

Given the shortcomings of applying the criminal law of theft to information the way it is applied to physical assets, but cognizant of the need to protect at least certain aspects of information-based assets, the legal system has devised several specific regimes in order to afford protection to the creators and owners of intellectual properties, assets that

---

7   For a short, but incisive, discussion of this point, see Rick Salutin, "Intelligent Theft is a Pillar of Artistic Creation" *The [Toronto] Globe and Mail* (29 November 1996).

8   This passage is cited in *Lotus Development Corporation* v. *Paperback Software International*, 740 F. Supp. 37 at 77 (D. Mass. 1990) [*Paperback*], where the court, rightfully, points out that in a copyright law context the tricky exercise is to determine just how broad these shoulders are and just how much a subsequent creator can step on them.

emanate from the mind. The major regimes are: trade secrecy/breach of confidence — to protect secret information; patents — to protect certain non-secret ideas that are implemented in inventions; and copyrights — to protect the expression of ideas. Each of these regimes, in its own particular manner, affords creators the right to limit the copying, use, and economic exploitation of specific aspects of information created by them. In economic terms, these intellectual property legal regimes exist to maintain artificial scarcity in information assets, thereby compensating for the lack of natural scarcity in information. To counteract the second dynamic of computer law — the elusive nature of information — intellectual property regimes have been crafted to give legal substance and form to certain aspects of information; that is, they cut down certain trees from the forest of ideas and with these trees build legal fences around certain creative content and inventions. The exercise is more daunting, though, because the better analogy is trying to carve chunks of air out of the atmosphere. Once this difficult task is accomplished — once the forest of ideas is subdued — the regimes that relate to publicly available information, namely patent and copyright, also recognize that the legal scarcity they establish should not continue indefinitely because society has a long-term interest in the wide dissemination and use of information. Therefore, these regimes protect for periods of time that are considered sufficient to provide adequate economic returns to creators, after which the protection ceases. In some cases, there are even limited exceptions to the exclusivity during the term of protection, as in the case of fair dealing with a copyright work for private study or research; to return to the forest metaphor, having cleared the land and given most of it over to private ownership, some parks and other public spaces are created for the betterment of all people. In short, ensuring that adequate amounts of information are created, and guaranteeing the appropriate allocation of information resources within the economy and society at large, given their critical importance to the economy and society, require the establishment of sophisticated intellectual property law regimes that carefully regulate the exploitation and disclosure of information so as to balance the needs of creators and users of these important assets.[9] This involves a delicate balancing act among diverse and competing interests, an exercise the criminal law simply is incapable of fulfilling, and that the intellectual property law regimes strive to achieve.

B. THE ESSENTIALS OF INTELLECTUAL PROPERTY LAW REGIMES

Having discussed, briefly, the rationale for intellectual property laws, this section describes, concisely, the key parameters of the principal intellectual property law regimes — trade secrecy, patents, copyright, semiconductor chip protection, and trade-marks. There are additional regimes, but they are of lesser importance, such as industrial design registration and plant breeders rights.[10] Some would also view the personality rights conferred by tort law as a species of intellectual property law, or at least affording intellectual property type protection, but in this work they are dealt with in the context of privacy rights.[11] As for the regimes that are covered, the intent is to give a useful overview that focusses on the computer industry. Trade secrets/breach of confidence

---

9   Nonetheless, there are cases that state that the sole purpose of copyright is the protection of authors: see, for example, *Canadian Assn. of Broadcasters* v. *Society of Composers, Authors and Music Publishers of Canada* (1994), 58 C.P.R. (3d) 190 (F.C.A.). But see also *Apple Computer Inc.* v. *MacKintosh Computers Ltd.* (1986), 10 C.P.R. (3d) 1 (F.C.T.D.) [*Apple Computer*], where one of the purposes of the *Copyright Act* was said to be to encourage disclosure of works for the advancement of learning. Indeed, very early on in English copyright law the requirement for a balance between private and public interests was recognized: see *Sayre* v. *Moore* (1785) 1 East's Reports 361 at 362 (K.B.), in which the court, in deciding the scope of copyright protection in a map, stated:

> The rule of decision in this case is a matter of great consequence to the country. In deciding it we must take care to guard against two extremes equally prejudicial; the one, that men of ability, who have employed their time for the service of the community, may not be deprived of their just merits, and the reward of their ingenuity and labour; the other, that the world may not be deprived of improvements, nor the progress of the arts be retarded.

A contemporary articulation of this dual role of copyright law can be seen in the following two recitals in the Preamble of the *1996 World Intellectual Property Organization (WIPO) Copyright Treaty*:

> The Contracting Parties,
>
> . . .
>
> Emphasizing the outstanding significance of copyright protection as an incentive for literary and artistic creation,
> Recognizing the need to maintain a balance between the rights of authors and the larger public interest, particularly education, research and access to information, as reflected in the Berne Convention,
> Have agreed as follows:
>
> . . .

This treaty is available from the WIPO website: <http://www.wipo.org/>.

10   See *Industrial Design Act*, R.S.C. 1985, c. I-9; and *Plant Breeders' Rights Act*, S.C. 1990, c. 20.

11   See section A(1), "Privacy Laws," in chapter 4.

protects information that is not publicly known. Patents protect novel and inventive ideas that are not kept secret. Copyrights afford protection not for ideas but for the form of expression of ideas. Chip protection covers certain elements of the designs used to develop semiconductor chips. Trade-mark law prevents unfair competition by prohibiting competitors from using confusing marks and symbols to sell their goods or services. After discussing the core parameters of these intellectual property regimes, this section also explains a number of ownership issues and the principal remedial measures (such as injunctions and damages) common to them. The section ends with an overview of several of the international aspects of intellectual property law systems.

1) Trade Secrets/Breach of Confidence

The law of trade secrets and breach of confidence affords important protection for a wide range of information-based assets that are not publicly known, by prohibiting someone from using or disclosing, or otherwise misappropriating, another person's trade secret or confidential information. Based on judge-made common law in Canada,[12] trade secrets/ breach of confidence protection is particularly attractive to many creators of information because no administrative formalities are required to obtain a trade secret and the protection extends indefinitely for so long as the information remains confidential.[13] The leading Canadian breach of confidence case, the decision of the Supreme Court of Canada in *LAC Minerals*, articulates a three-part test for a breach of confidence to be actionable: first, the information must have the necessary quality of confidence; second, the information must be imparted in circumstances giving rise to an obligation of confidence; and third, there must be a misuse or unauthorized use of that information.[14] Prior to this decision, the doctrinal basis for trade secrets/breach of confidence protection in Canada was unclear, in some cases being based on property

---

12   This is as compared with the United States, where all states have adopted a trade secrets statute: see Roger M. Milgrim, *Milgrim on Trade Secrets* (New York: Matthew Bender, 1986) (looseleaf, updated).

13   While persons in the computer industry often agree contractually that they can disclose each other's trade secrets after a certain period of time, such a limitation on the term of trade secrets is not required by law; indeed, for example, the *North American Free Trade Agreement*, in Article 1711(3), confirms that trade secret protection is to extend indefinitely (so long as the information maintains its confidential quality).

14   *LAC Minerals Ltd. v. International Corona Resources Ltd.* (1989), 26 C.P.R. (3d) 97 (S.C.C.) [*LAC Minerals*].

rights, in others on contract, and in yet others on equitable principles, including unjust enrichment.[15] The court in *LAC Minerals* concluded the right of action is *sui generis*, and is essentially a reflection of the policy that disclosures made in confidence between business people should be protected.[16] Essentially the same rationale has underpinned the law of breach of confidence in a non-commercial setting as well, as can be seen in the English "privacy" cases.[17]

A broad spectrum of information and information-based assets in the computer industry can come within the ambit of trade secrets/confidential information, including software, as well as the designs and specifications for software.[18] To appreciate the breadth of coverage of this branch of intellectual property protection, consider the following definition of a trade secret found in the Alberta law reform commission report on trade secrets: "information including but not limited to a formula, pattern, compilation, programme, method, technique, or process, or information contained or embodied in a product device or mechanism which (i) is, or may be used in a trade or business, (ii) is not generally known in that trade or business, (iii) has economic value from not being generally known, and (iv) is the subject of efforts that are reasonable under the circumstances to maintain its secrecy."[19] A trade secret, therefore, could include a plan for a new information-based product or service, before it was disclosed to the marketplace. Even an amalgam of

---

15 For a good discussion of the doctrinal underpinnings of trade secret law prior to the decision in *LAC Minerals*, above note 14, see Institute of Law Research and Reform (Edmonton, Alberta) and A Federal Provincial Working Party, *Trade Secrets* (Report No. 46, July 1986) [*Trade Secrets*].

16 This same sentiment has animated U.S. trade secret law: see *Burten* v. *Milton Bradley Company*, 763 F.2d 461 at 467 (1st Cir. 1985), where the court expounded a dual rationale for trade secret law; first, to encourage the formulation and promulgation of ideas by ensuring that creators benefit from their creations; second, the "public has a manifest interest . . . in the maintenance of standards of commercial ethics."

17 See section A(1), "Privacy Laws," in chapter 4.

18 *Software Solutions Associates Inc.* v. *Depow* (1989), 25 C.P.R. (3d) 129 (N.B.Q.B.); *Matrox Electronic Systems Ltd.* v. *Gaudreau*, [1993] R.J.Q. 2449 (Que. Sup. Ct.) [*Matrox*]; and *Ticketnet Corp.* v. *Air Canada* (1987), 21 C.P.C. (2d) 38 (Ont. H.C.J.) [*Ticketnet*]. In a recent U.S. case, the architecture, organization, and structure of a computer program were protected as trade secrets: *Fabkom, Inc.* v. *R.W. Smith & Associates, Inc.*, 1997 Copyright Law Decisions (CCH) ¶27,590 at 29,476 (C.D. Cal. 1996) [*Fabkom*].

19 *Trade Secrets*, above note 15 at 256. The idea, however, must be original and have some concreteness: see *Promotivate International Inc.* v. *Toronto Star Newspapers Ltd.* (1986), 8 C.P.R. (3d) 546 (Ont. S.C.).

several publicly available elements of information is susceptible of protection where the final collection results in a unique composite of information.[20] The key is that the information not be available generally, and that the discloser take reasonable steps to keep the information confidential.[21] A recent case found that the following protective measures taken by a software company were adequate to establish a trade secret: confidentiality issues were discussed with employees; employees signed confidentiality agreements; confidential documents were kept in locked filing cabinets; employees used passwords and confidential "login" numbers to ensure computer security; employees and visitors wore identification badges; the premises were secured by an alarm system and patrolled by a security guard twenty-four hours a day; and access to every section of the premises was regulated by a "Cardkey" reader.[22]

Just as a wide variety of information is capable of being protected under the doctrine of trade secrets/breach of confidence, so there are numerous circumstances in which a duty of confidence can arise. Probably the most common problematic confidee — if the volume of litigation is any indicator — is the employee of the knowledge-based business. Many judicial decisions have found former employees liable under trade secret law for disclosing the former employer's trade secrets to the new employer, an entity often owned by the departing employees.[23] In these employee-related cases, courts have the fiendishly difficult task of distinguishing between the general skill and knowledge of the employee,

20   See, for example, *ICAM Technologies Corp.* v. *EBCO Industries Ltd.* (1991), 36 C.P.R. (3d) 504 (B.C.S.C.) [*ICAM*], where a business plan for a new venture involving several high-technology elements and government procurement opportunities, none of which was secret in itself, were held to be confidential when considered as a whole. See also *Telex Corporation* v. *International Business Machines Corporation*, 367 F. Supp. 258 (N.D. Okla. 1973) in which a combination of material that was not new, novel, secretive, or innovative was protected as a trade secret because together they formed a valuable "design composite."

21   Milgrim, *Milgrim on Trade Secrets*, above note 12, cites a U.S. case, *Management Science America, Inc.* v. *Cyborg Systems, Inc.*, 1977-1 Trade Cases (CCH) ¶61,472 (N.D. Ill. 1977), in which a software program was still considered to be a trade secret after 600 copies of it were distributed because each was accompanied by a restrictive software licence. See also *Data General Corporation* v. *Digital Computer Controls, Inc.*, 188 U.S.P.Q. 276 (Del. Cir. Ct. 1975), where the court upheld the secrecy of multiple copies of documentation distributed with computers because of, among other reasons, the proprietary rights notice contained on them.

22   *Matrox*, above note 18. Similar measures were held to support the finding of trade secrets in a recent American software-related case in *Vermont Microsystems, Inc.* v. *Autodesk, Inc.*, 5 Computer Cases (CCH) ¶47,210 at 67,224 (D. Vt. 1994).

23   For example, see *Matrox*, above note 18.

which the employee is able to exercise after leaving the employer, as compared with the proprietary information of the former employer, which may not be so used by the former employee.[24] Information, however, is an elusive asset, and drawing the line between that which is owned by an employer and that which is owned by the employer's former employee can be an almost Sisyphean exercise. In a recent case, for example, portions of a plaintiff's statement of claim were struck out for not describing with sufficient particularity the specific confidential information that was allegedly taken by the former employees.[25] Given the difficulty of differentiating between the two, employers often address the issue in a contract with the employee, sometimes adding a non-competition provision to help ensure, prophylactically, the protection of the employer's trade secrets. Such agreements must be drafted with great care, as the restrictions in them must be reasonable from the perspective of the term of the restriction, the actual activity being restricted, and the geographic scope of the restriction. In a recent case, a six-month non-competition period for a software programmer that covered North America and the United Kingdom was upheld, the court concluding that such non-competition covenants are "about the only efficacious means that an employer has to gain some measure of protection [over its trade secrets]."[26]

Beyond employees, courts have been prepared to impress a duty of confidence on a number of recipients of trade secrets. For example, in one case an interim injunction was granted against an entity that had been previously negotiating a potential joint venture arrangement in the high-technology industry when this company apparently threatened to

---

24 This conundrum pre-dates the computer age: see *Amber Size and Chemical Company, Limited* v. *Menzel*, [1913] 2 Ch. 239.

25 *SLM Software Inc.* v. *Dimitri* (1996), 65 C.P.R. (3d) 330 (Ont. Gen. Div.).

26 *Teleride Sage Ltd.* v. *Ventures West Management Inc.* (1996), 67 C.P.R. (3d) 361 at 362 (Ont. Gen. Div.). In this case the court stated at 361–62:

> It is obvious in an industry based on innovation, inspiration, rapid obsolescence, shared information and group dynamics that it will always be exceedingly difficult to determine what skills and information fall within the definition of confidential information, that it will be difficult for the most honest employee to know what skills and knowledge he can share with his new employer and that it will be exceedingly difficult for the former employer to determine what the former employee is, in fact, sharing with the new employer. What is not sophisticated, difficult of interpretation, or difficult to police is the non-competition clause of reasonable length and geographical scope.

For a good text covering restrictive covenants, including those found in an employment context, see Michael J. Trebilcock, *The Common Law of Restraint of Trade: A Legal and Economic Analysis* (Toronto: Carswell, 1986).

launch a competing business on its own, thereby possibly misappropriating trade secrets of the plaintiff.[27] In another case, a partner in a high-technology initiative was stopped from having business discussions with another potential partner, as this could cause a leak of information.[28] In another case, a supplier of computer services was prohibited from possibly disclosing one customer's information to another client.[29] In a recent case, a purchaser of high-technology equipment was held liable for disclosing one supplier's trade secrets to another supplier.[30] In a recent U.S. case, a user was held to have violated a software supplier's trade secrets when the user conveyed to a third party specifications for a bond trading system, the court finding that the user's list of specifications was influenced by the plaintiff's software that the user had been operating for years.[31] This case, as well as others, illustrates with poignancy the second dynamic of computer law, the elusive nature of information, and should teach recipients of trade secrets/confidential information to be extremely circumspect in respect of what they have access to in order to avoid contaminating themselves.[32] Given that the parameters of confidential information are difficult to determine in advance — judges often even have difficulty in hindsight — parties should through contract, technology, and by minimizing exposure attempt to reduce the likelihood of a breach of trade secrets/confidence claim.

---

27   *Alphanet Telecom Inc.* v. *Delrina Corp.* (1994), 53 C.P.R. (3d) 156 (Ont. Gen. Div.) [*Alphanet*].

28   *Ticketnet*, above note 18.

29   *Computer Workshops Ltd.* v. *Banner Capital Market Brokers Ltd.* (1990), 74 D.L.R. (4th) 767 (Ont. C.A.).

30   *Wil-Can Electronics Can. Ltd.* v. *Ontario (Ministry of the Solicitor General)*, [1992] O.J. No. 2537 (Gen. Div.) (QL) [*Wil-Can Electronics*].

31   *Fabkom*, above note 18.

32   For example, in *TDS Healthcare Systems Corporation* v. *Humana Hospital Illinois, Inc.*, 880 F. Supp. 1572 (N.D. Ga. 1995) the defendant acquired a hospital that used the plaintiff's software. When an affiliate of the defendant that developed software competitive with the plaintiff's software obtained access to the plaintiff's software, the defendant was found liable for, among other reasons, not using best efforts to prevent the unauthorized disclosure of the plaintiff's software, as required by the relevant software licence agreement.

2) Patents

The *Patent Act*[33] grants the holder of a patent the exclusive right within Canada to make, use, or sell the invention covered by the patent for a period of twenty years from the date the application for the patent was filed.[34] Inventions that can be patented comprise processes, machines, manufactures, and composition of matter; by contrast, scientific formulae cannot be patented. Trade secrets, then, are secret ideas; patents cover applied ideas. As a result, patents have been issued for a wide range of devices associated with computers and their predecessors, including the telegraph, the telephone, many components of the computer, and the semiconductor chip. Today patents cover a variety of devices, such as the writing heads in computer hard drives, and more controversially, numerous software programs and specific features in computer programs.[35] It is not surprising that IBM applied for the most number of patents at the U.S. Patent Office in 1996. IBM and other like-minded companies find patents attractive because, notwithstanding that their duration is quite short relative to copyright protection, a patent is the most powerful form of intellectual property protection. A patent is effective against everyone, not just a copier or someone who misappropriates, as is the case with copyrights and trade secrets; in other words, truly independent creation, which is a defence to a copyright or trade secret claim, is not a defence to a patent infringement claim. Given this high level of protection, several important tests must be met before a patent is issued, and indeed, even after a patent is issued a third party can attack the patent on the grounds that one of these tests was not in fact met at the time the application was filed, notwithstanding that the patent office was of a different view when it issued the patent.

The first requirement is that the invention be "useful," that is, that it work and have utility in an industrial sense. Most computer and software-related inventions have little difficulty meeting this test. Also, the invention must be novel, meaning that it cannot have been known or disclosed more than twelve months prior to the filing of the application for the patent. Given Canada's "first to file system," where the first person

---

33 R.S.C. 1985, c. P-4. The *Patent Act* is federal legislation, as the subject matter of "Patents of Invention and Discovery" is a federal power under the *Constitution Act, 1867* (U.K.), 30 & 31 Vict., c. 3, s. 91(22). The *Constitution Act, 1867* can be found in R.S.C. 1985, Appendix II, No. 5.

34 For patents granted with respect to applications filed in Canada and the United States prior to 1 October 1989 and 8 June 1995, respectively, the term of protection is seventeen years from the date of issuance of the patent.

35 See section C(2), "Patent Protection for Software," in this chapter.

to lodge the patent application with the Patent Office has priority even if someone else may have invented it earlier, prudence dictates filing the application before any public disclosure is made of the invention. This practice of early, predisclosure filing is reinforced by the fact that some countries consider any disclosure prior to filing to invalidate the patent. Thus, in the fast-paced computer business one must be extremely vigilant not to disclose the invention prematurely, perhaps at a trade show or user group meeting or some other venue, where a description of the invention before a filing of a patent application can be fatal to the hopes for the patent. Equally, in a university environment, where the doctrine of "publish or perish" often leads professors to disclose patentable material before a patent filing, professors and administrators involved with software (and other) patentable technologies and research must realize that early publication may cause the patent to perish. Notwithstanding the importance of the novelty requirement, perhaps the most difficult test that an invention must meet in order to be patented is that it not be obvious; in other words, courts have long required the invention to exhibit a certain degree of inventiveness beyond that which would be considered average in the industry.[36] A leading case summarizes this test as whether an unimaginative technician (and not a competent expert) skilled in the art would have come upon the solution taught by the patent; if so, then the invention is not deserving of a patent.[37] Put another way, the invention or the improvement, to be patentable, must go beyond what was common knowledge at the time of the filing of the application.

---

36 Traditionally, the requirement for inventiveness was judicially inferred from the term *invention*; since October 1996, the *Patent Act* has contained a specific provision requiring an invention to be non-obvious.

37 See *Beloit Canada Ltd.* v. *Valmet Oy* (1986), 8 C.P.R. (3d) 289 at 294 (F.C.A.) in which the court stated:

> The test for obviousness is not to ask what competent inventors did or would have done to solve the problem. Inventors are by definition inventive. The classical touchstone for obviousness is the technician skilled in the art but having no scintilla of inventiveness or imagination; a paragon of deduction and dexterity, wholly devoid of intuition; a triumph of the left hemisphere over the right. The question to be asked is whether this mythical creature (the man in the Clapham omnibus of patent law) would, in the light of the state of the art and of common general knowledge as at the claimed date of invention, have come directly and without difficulty to the solution taught by the patent. It is a very difficult test to satisfy.

See also *Xerox of Canada Ltd.* v. *IBM Canada Ltd.* (1977), 33 C.P.R. (2d) 24 (F.C.T.D.) in which the court reviewed a number of English cases that have considered the obviousness test.

The patent application, and, if it issues, the patent itself, contains a rather detailed description of the invention and its proposed application, including a disclosure of prior art related to the invention as well as the best mode of working the patent. This detailed disclosure represents a key public policy rationale for patents, namely, that in return for what is often an extremely strong monopoly position, albeit for a limited time, the patent holder disclose the invention to the public. This disclosure then allows others to learn the workings of the patent, and to prepare to work it after the patent expires, as well as possibly to work around it during its term. Following the detailed description will be the specific claims, which set out the particular parameters of the monopoly by describing the precise features that the patent holder claims are new and inventive and for which the monopoly is granted. It is these claims that are examined to determine if the impugned device infringes upon the patent, either because the infringer's product clearly comes within the purview of the patent claims, or because the invention has been taken in terms of its substance, or "pith and marrow," as some judges refer to the essence of the patented invention.[38] It takes significant skill to draft patent claims well, particularly in the area of software patents, and in Canada expert patent agents perform this task. Patent agents, who alone can prosecute a patent application before the Patent Office other than the inventor, are also able to perform searches of existing patents at various patent offices to obtain a preliminary sense of whether a proposed patent will be permitted.

Companies in the computer industry are well advised to consult with a patent agent in order to gauge the opportunities for achieving competitive advantage through filing for patents. Equally important is reviewing the patent filings of competitors to ensure, from a defensive perspective, that all necessary precautions in terms of product design are being taken to avoid infringing the rights of others. At a minimum this would involve searching for patents and patent applications filed under the name of competitors. More extensive searches would include infringement searches, and even prior art searches in some situations, to gauge the state of patents and patentability generally vis-à-vis an inventor's handiwork. In short, patents should be thought of both offensively and defensively. It should be noted, however, that

38   *Cutter (Canada) Ltd. v. Baxter Travenol Laboratories of Canada Ltd.* (1983), 68 C.P.R. (2d) 179 (F.C.A.).

currently a patent search cannot reveal all filings submitted to the Patent Office because patent applications are kept confidential for eighteen months after they are filed. Therefore, it can happen that a patent search result comes up clear, a person relies on this result to start marketing their particular product, only to be confronted subsequently by a patent the filing date of which pre-dates the commencement of the person's marketing, and hence is enforceable against the person. This is a particularly dangerous problem in the fast-paced computer industry.

3) Copyright

Where trade secrets protect ideas and patents protect applied ideas implemented in an invention, copyright protects only the form of expression of ideas.[39] The *Copyright Act*[40] grants this protection for expression by reserving to the copyright owner the exclusive right to reproduce the copyright work, and to exercise certain other rights including publication and translation of the copyright work, the right to perform the work in public, and the right to communicate the work to the public by telecommunication, as well as the right to authorize any of the foregoing. The *Copyright Act* also prohibits the rental, for a motive of gain, of computer software and sound recordings that are capable of being reproduced. Recent amendments to the *Copyright Act* also give performers (such as actors, singers, and musicians), the makers of sound recordings and broadcasters copyright in the reproduction of their respective performances, sound recordings, and communication signals, as well as the right of sound recording performers and makers to receive royalties for public and broadcasting performances of such works (previously only composers and lyricists were entitled to such royalties). The most recent amendments to the *Copyright Act* also

---

39   See *Matrox*, above note 18 at 2455: "It is fundamental that copyright can
     protect the form of expression of computer programs, but not the ideas
     embodied therein." See also *Delrina Corp.* v. *Triolet Systems Inc.* (1993), 47
     C.P.R. (3d) 1 (Ont. Gen. Div.) [*Delrina*]. See also Article 2 of the *1996 WIPO
     Copyright Treaty*, available from the **WIPO** website: <http://www.wipo.org/> that
     provides: "**Scope of Copyright Protection**. Copyright protection extends to
     expressions and not to ideas, procedures, methods of operation or
     mathematical concepts as such."
40   R.S.C. 1985, c. C-42. The *Copyright Act*, like the *Patent Act*, is federal legislation
     as copyrights are a federal power under the *Constitution Act, 1867* (U.K.), 30 & 31
     Vict., c. 3, subs. 91(23), found in R.S.C. 1985, Appendix II, No. 5.

establish a compensation regime whereby performers, producers, and composers are to be paid the proceeds of a new tax to be levied on blank audio recording media, such as cassettes, in return for private copying of musical works no longer being an infringement of copyright.[41] These new provisions recognize the third dynamic of computer law, namely that the boundary between the private and public realms is blurring, and that enforcement of the law against copying for private use is very difficult but of increasing concern because of the improved quality of copies made with digital technologies; hence this radically different approach to compensation for creators of copyright materials.[42] The *Copyright Act* also prohibits what may be termed "secondary infringement," namely, where a person sells, leases, distributes, exhibits, or imports into Canada any work that to the person's knowledge is infringing copyright or would infringe copyright if it had been made in Canada.

Creators of software, multimedia products and other information-based assets find copyright protection attractive because of its relatively long term; in Canada, the copyright in a work generally subsists for the lifetime of the author of the work plus 50 years, though certain rights, such as the rights of performers and sound recording makers, are only 50 years in duration. In the case of works of joint authorship, which would include most software and other information-based assets, the 50-year period begins to run from the death of the last joint author to die, and therefore protection for software is afforded for between 80 and 100 years, given the relative youthfulness of many software programmers. A further attraction is the lack of formalities involved in obtaining copyright protection, as copyright arises automatically upon creation of the work, unlike the case with patents

---

41   The most recent amendments to the *Copyright Act*, contained in Bill C-32, *An Act to Amend the Copyright Act*, S.C. 1997, c. 24, amending R.S.C. 1985, c. C-42, were passed by Parliament in April 1997 (and are referred to herein as the "Bill C-32 amendments" or "Bill C-32").

42   A government background document to Bill C-32 cites a report of the Task Force on the Future of the Canadian Music Industry that notes that nearly 44 million blank tapes were sold in Canada in 1995, of which it is estimated 39 million were used by consumers to copy sound recordings: "Legislative Highlights" available at <http://www.pch.gc.ca/main/c32/back.htm>. Nonetheless, criticism has been levelled at the new private copying exemption/blank tape levy on the basis that it is a blunt instrument and legitimizes a free copying mentality that may well spill over to other works. It is interesting to speculate if the blank tape levy will, over time, be the model for compensation regimes in other areas such as home movies and computer software.

which must be registered.[43] There is a registry of copyrights maintained in Ottawa, but registration is voluntary, though particularly with the new statutory damages provision added to the *Copyright Act* by Bill C-32, copyright owners should be registering their copyrights even if they did not do so previously. While it is easier to obtain a copyright than a patent, the protection afforded by copyright is weaker than patent. While a patent holder's rights are effective against all others in the jurisdiction, even persons who have had no previous contact with the patent holder or the patented invention, truly independent creation is a defence to a copyright claim. To attract copyright, a work must be an "original" literary, dramatic, musical, or artistic work fixed in some material form.[44] Originality in a copyright context is not at all similar to the patent standards of novelty or inventiveness; rather, an original copyright work is merely one that is not copied from another source.[45]

A wide range of information-based assets can come within the scope of original literary works, including books, reports, and other written material. Multimedia products on, for example, a CD-ROM, will often contain literary, artistic, and musical works thus touching three of the four protected categories.[46] For the most part, the *Copyright Act* is rela-

---

43   *Fletcher v. Polka Dot Fabrics Ltd.* (1993), 51 C.P.R. (3d) 241 (Ont. Gen. Div.) [*Fletcher*]. While not mandatory, it is advisable to place on the work the "c" in a circle copyright symbol "©" and the word "copyright," as these give notice to potential infringers and hence more favourable remedies to the copyright owner. The *Copyright Act* limits a copyright owner's remedies to an injunction if the defendant can prove it was unaware and had no reasonable ground for suspecting that copyright subsisted in the work; it should also be noted that this provision does not apply if the copyright is registered. As well, it is extremely useful to register early on in respect of a work that may be the subject of criminal copyright remedies given that a certificate of copyright ownership obtained after the alleged offence occurred will not be acceptable to show that someone other than the accused owned the copyright: see *R. v. Laurier Office Mart Inc.* (1995), 63 C.P.R. (3d) 229 (Ont. Gen. Div.)

44   See *Canadian Admiral Corporation Ltd. v. Rediffusion, Inc.* (1954), 20 C.P.R. 75 (Ex. Ct.) [*Canadian Admiral*] where the fixation requirement is referred to. In the context of software, there is American authority for the proposition that even transitory fixation in RAM-type memory suffices: *MAI Systems Corporation v. Peak Computer, Inc.*, 991 F.2d 511 (9th Cir. 1993). This issue has not been definitely determined yet in Canada, although see *International Business Machines Corporation v. Ordinateurs Spirales Inc./Spirales Computers Inc.* (1984), 80 C.P.R. (2d) 187 (F.C.T.D.) [*Spirales*].

45   *Fletcher*, above note 43.

46   See, for example, the U.S. case of *Playboy Enterprises, Inc. v. Starware Publishing Corp.*, 900 F. Supp. 433 (S.D. Fla. 1995), where the defendant was found to have infringed *Playboy*'s copyright in photographs by reproducing digitized versions of them on 10,000 CD-ROM disks.

tively technology-neutral, concentrating on acts (such as reproduction) and types of works (such as a literary work) rather than on particular technology-based content delivery mechanisms. Every now and then, however, the statute is usefully updated to remove doubt in respect of new technologies. For example, the 1909 U.S. copyright statute was updated expressly to accommodate perforated rolls in player pianos (sometimes called pianola rolls) after the U.S. Supreme Court held these were not protected by the predecessor statute.[47] In a similar vein, the Canadian *Copyright Act* was amended to cover a live telecast of a sporting or similar event if it is simultaneously taped. This was a result of an earlier case that held that televised live sporting events do not qualify for copyright protection given that they did not come within the then existing categories of photography or films.[48] As well, prior to 1988 the *Copyright Act* did not expressly mention computer software, and thus there was uncertainty as to whether copyright protection extended to computer programs.[49] This uncertainty was resolved in the 1988 amendments to the *Copyright Act* by expanding the definition of literary work to cover "computer programs," and providing a definition for computer programs.[50] The scope of protection of software under copyright law, beyond the literal statements of source code, has generated vigorous debate over the past decade.[51]

The *Copyright Act* prohibits anyone from copying or exercising the other rights granted under the statute without the permission of the copyright owner. A person or entity infringes the rights of the copyright owner by doing something only the owner has the right to do under the *Copyright Act*. With respect to infringement by copying, a qualitative as well as quantitative analysis is undertaken, with the result that the

---

47 *White-Smith Music Publishing Company* v. *Apollo Company*, 209 U.S. 1 (2d Cir. 1908). Two years later, the English (and by implication the Canadian) *Copyright Act* was similarly revised to cover pianola rolls, to counteract the decision in *Boosey* v. *Whight*, [1900] 1 Ch. 122 (C.A.).

48 *Canadian Admiral*, above note 44.

49 See, for example, the decision in *Apple Computer, Inc.* v. *MacKintosh Computers Ltd.* (1987), 18 C.P.R. (3d) 129 (F.C.A.), aff'g *Apple Computer*, above note 9, where judges disagreed as to whether software embedded on a chip was protected as a "translation" or "reproduction" of the original software.

50 The *Copyright Act*, above note 40, s. 2, defines *computer program* as a set of instructions or statements expressed, fixed, embodied, or stored in any manner that is to be used directly or indirectly in a computer in order to bring about a specific result.

51 For a further discussion of the scope of protection of software under copyright law, see section C(3), "Copyright Protection for Software," in this chapter.

reproduction of relatively small, but qualitatively important, parts of a copyright work can lead to a finding of infringement.[52] For larger scale unauthorized commercial copying, the *Copyright Act* contains criminal sanctions against piracy, which can range from a fine of $25,000 and/or imprisonment of up to six months for a summary offence conviction, to a fine of $1 million and/or imprisonment of up to five years, for an indictable offence conviction, as well as destruction or other disposition of the copies and plates used to make the infringing copies.[53] This provision may be relevant when, as in the *Rexcan Circuits* case, an organization acquires some software legally but then makes unauthorized copies of it.[54] Such activity, euphemistically dubbed "corporate overuse" of software, or more pointedly "non-commercial piracy," continues to be a serious concern to software developers, as many users of software continue to refuse to acknowledge the illegality of making unauthorized copies of software.[55] The criminal provisions of the *Copyright Act* have been used to convict illegal copiers of videotapes and sound recordings,[56] and more recently the operator of a bulletin board that made illegal copies of software available from it.[57] It should be noted that while

---

52   *Prism Hospital Software Inc.* v. *Hospital Medical Records Institute* (1994), 57 C.P.R. (3d) 129 (B.C.S.C.) [*Prism*]. See also *University of London Press, Limited* v. *University Tutorial Press, Limited,* [1916] 2 Ch. 601, where the court at 610 put forward the arguably questionable proposition that "what is worth copying is prima facie worth protecting," though the court did note this was a "rough practical test."

53   The term *plate* is broadly defined in the Canadian *Copyright Act.* In *R.* v. *Ghnaim* (1988), 28 C.P.R. (3d) 463 (Alta. Prov. Ct.) [*Ghnaim*], the court concluded that the term *plate* was broad enough to cover videocassette recorders used to make unauthorized videotapes, such that thirty-three of them were ordered forfeited to the Crown. Arguably, a similar result would follow where computers are used to make illegal copies of software.

54   *R.* v. *Rexcan Circuits Inc.,* [1993] O.J. No. 1896 (Prov. Ct.) (QL). In this case a company was fined $50,000 for making unauthorized copies of software for its use within the company.

55   See Mitch Betts, "Dirty Rotten Scoundrels?" *Computerworld,* 22 May 1995, which reports the results of an ethics survey conducted among information systems professionals and found, among other things, that 47 percent of respondents admitted to making unauthorized copies of software, even though 78 percent of respondents agreed this should not be done.

56   *Re Adelphi Book Store Ltd. and The Queen* (1972), 7 C.P.R. (2d) 166 (Sask. C.A.); *Ghnaim,* above note 53; *Photo Centre Inc.* v. *R.* (1986), 9 C.P.R. (3d) 425 (Que. Sup. Ct.); *R.* v. *Miles of Music Ltd.* (1989), 24 C.P.R. (3d) 301 (Ont. C.A.).

57   *R.* v. *M. (J.P.)* (1996), 107 C.C.C. (3d) 380 (N.S.C.A.) [*M. (J.P.)*]. The accused in this case was a young offender (age seventeen); he was sentenced to eighteen months' probation and 150 hours of community service.

the *Copyright Act* contains a limitation period of three years for civil remedies, summary conviction proceedings (but not indictable offence ones) must be brought within six months.[58]

The *Copyright Act* also includes, however, several specific exceptions to infringement by providing that certain acts do not constitute unlawful copying. An important defence is the right of fair dealing with any work for private study or research.[59] The fair dealing provisions may be an important element of any defence related to a claim of reverse engineering, though the legalities of reverse engineering software and related products have not yet been addressed by a Canadian court; in a couple of U.S. decisions,[60] the American "fair use" defence was found to be important by both courts, though it should be noted that American fair use is somewhat broader than its Canadian fair dealing counterpart.[61] The Bill C-32 amendments added several limited exceptions relevant to educational institutions, such as the use of copyright materials for testing purposes, and by libraries and archives in order, for example, to maintain their permanent collections. Bill C-32 also added the exception for the private copying of sound recordings, the trade-off for the levy on blank audio recording tapes mentioned earlier. Two specific defences in the *Copyright Act* which date from 1988, the year computer software was expressly added to the statute, permit owners of a copy of a computer program to make back-up copies of the program, and to make modifications to the program necessary for the interoperability of the program with other programs, but both of these defences are of little practical use because the vast majority of software is licensed and not sold,[62] and hence it is the rare user of a computer program that owns the copy of the software being used.[63] It should also be noted that once a copy of a copyright work is sold with the permission of the copyright

---

58   R. v. *Shimming* (1991), 35 C.P.R. (3d) 397 (Sask. Prov. Ct.); *Ghnaim*, above note 53.

59   Also important is the defence of fair dealing for the purpose of criticism, review, or newspaper summary: see *Allen* v. *Toronto Star Newspaper Ltd.* (1995), 26 O.R. (3d) 308 (Gen. Div.), rev'd (1997), 36 O.R. (3d) 201 (Div. Ct.) [*Allen*].

60   *Sega Enterprises Ltd.* v. *Accolade, Inc.*, 977 F.2d 1510 (9th Cir. 1992); *Atari Games Corp.* v. *Nintendo of America Inc.*, 975 F.2d 832 (Fed. Cir. 1992).

61   See, for example, *Cie Générale des Établissements Michelin-Michelin & Cie* v. *C.A.W.-Canada* (1996), 71 C.P.R. (3d) 348 (F.C.T.D.), where the court concluded that use of a copyright for purposes of "parody" is not fair dealing under Canada's *Copyright Act* the way it is a fair use under American copyright legislation.

62   See section C, "Licences for Software and Content," in chapter 5.

63   By contrast, for example, the similar defences under the U.K. copyright law apply to "lawful users" of a computer program: see *Copyright, Designs and Patents Act, 1988* (U.K.), 1988, c. 48, ss. 50A, 50B, & 50C.

owner, the copyright owner cannot control any further resale of such copy (so long as no further copies are made) because the right to distribute or resell a work is not included in the bundle of rights afforded the holder of a copyright under the current version of the Canadian *Copyright Act*. Mention should also be made of the fact that in addition to giving copyright owners the right to control the copying and the other protected uses of their copyright works, the *Copyright Act* also gives to creators so-called moral rights, which permit the creator to protect the integrity of the work, namely, to prevent it from being distorted or mutilated, and to have the author's name remain associated with the work.[64] Moral rights, which prohibit anyone other than the creator from modifying or altering the work in a manner that would dishonour the creator's reputation, are particularly germane in respect of multimedia works where images, among other elements, can be easily manipulated and modified once they are in digital form.

4) Semiconductor Chip Protection

The *Integrated Circuit Topography Act*[65] protects registered chip topographies, which are the stencil-like designs that lay out the various interconnections for the electronic elements embedded on a semiconductor chip. While the *ICT Act* has a much narrower application than the three other intellectual property regimes reviewed above, there are a number of chip manufacturers in Canada who stand to benefit from it. It should be noted, however, that there have been relatively few registrations under the *ICT Act*, and apparently no proceedings brought to date under it (and only one case under the equivalent U.S. statute[66]), probably because of developments in the technologies used to design chips and the basic economic fact that the immensely expensive, intricate process technologies used to fabricate chips may afford sufficient practical protection to this industry. Nevertheless, it is still worth considering the *ICT Act*, even if only briefly, because it might represent an example of the type of *sui generis* solution that could be applied to software (and possibly other technologies or information-based assets), given that a

---

64   See *Snow* v. *The Eaton Centre Ltd.* (1982), 70 C.P.R. (2d) 105 (Ont. H.C.J.).

65   S.C. 1990, c. 37, referred to herein as the *ICT Act*. Like the *Patent Act* and the *Copyright Act*, the *ICT Act* is federal legislation. The *ICT Act* is quite recent legislation, having come into force only in May 1993.

66   *Brooktree Corporation* v. *Advanced Micro Devices, Inc.*, 757 F. Supp. 1088 (S.D. Cal. 1990), aff'd 977 F.2d 1555 (Fed. Cir. 1992).

number of commentators are uncomfortable with software being protected by both copyright and patent.[67] In essence, the *ICT Act* is a unique amalgamation of copyright and patent concepts, following largely the U.S. semiconductor chip protection statute to respond to the seeming inappropriateness of trying to protect chip topographies under either patent or copyright; topographies were considered too machinelike to come within the copyright regime, and yet were too much like a writing to come within the patent system; put another way, topographies are too functional for copyright and not inventive enough for patent. Therefore, in this area the rapid pace of technological change was addressed by a statutory solution rather than piecemeal development of existing intellectual property laws applied to a new technology. Nonetheless, the *ICT Act* should not be viewed as a panacea, as it contains several concepts that are by no means self-defining and these raise a number of new questions.

The *ICT Act* gives the owner of a registered topography the exclusive right to reproduce, make, import, or commercially exploit the topography or any substantial part thereof. The *ICT Act* shows its hybrid nature by providing that only "original" topographies may be registered and then defining as an original topography one that has not been copied from another topography *and* is not "commonplace" within the chip industry. Thus, the standard of originality lies somewhere above the copyright test, but arguably below the patent test of absolute novelty. There is no decided case yet as to what commonplace means, and this will be one area of uncertainty regarding the *ICT Act* that will require judicial determination before an accurate assessment of the test can be made. Other hybrid elements of the *ICT Act* include a term of protection for registered topographies that is quite short, at least by copyright standards, being ten years from the earlier of the filing date in Canada or first use in Canada or anywhere else in the world. In order to be protected, the topography must be registered. While these aspects of the *ICT Act* are patentlike, the *ICT Act*'s relatively broad "fair dealing" provisions for purpose of analysis, education, research, or teaching, coupled with a reverse engineering exception that permits third parties to strip away and study the various layers of the topography so long as they do not use any copies in their subsequent product, are conceptually derived from the fair dealing provisions of the *Copyright Act*, though are arguably broader in scope. The *ICT Act* also provides, in a copyrightlike manner, that no infringement of a registered topography can occur where the second topography is "independently created." The

---

67 See section C(3), "Copyright Protection for Software," in this chapter.

provision of the *ICT Act* that states that no rights are granted under it for "any idea, concept, process, system, technique or information that may be embodied in a topography" is also derivative of the black letter copyright law principle that copyright does not protect ideas and concepts, and specifically is reminiscent of section 102(b) of the U.S. copyright law that articulates this copyright principle expressly by providing that copyright does not extend to any "idea, procedure, process, system, method of operation, concept, principle, or discovery."[68] While the Canadian *Copyright Act* does not currently contain such a statutory provision, there are cases under the *Copyright Act* that articulate the same principles.[69]

5) Trade-marks

A trade-mark is a word or symbol that is used to distinguish the products or services of one supplier from those of another. Trade-marks are widely used in the computer and information industries to permit suppliers to differentiate themselves in an increasingly crowded and international marketplace. Trade-mark law is as much about consumer protection as it is about intellectual property, given that trade-marks do not protect information itself or its expression, but rather serve to prevent fraud and confusion by giving purchasers guarantees of quality regarding the many different goods and services in the marketplace. As an indication of this purpose, it is worth noting that the *Criminal Code* contains several provisions making it a criminal offence to forge or deface a trade-mark or to take a number of other steps regarding trade-marks or passing off goods that have the effect of misleading the purchasers of such goods.[70] These criminal provisions are not utilized very often, and instead owners of trade-marks tend to rely on the civil law to protect their interests.[71] Under the common law tort doctrine of passing-off, the owner of an unregistered trade-mark can stop another supplier from using a confus-

---

68   *Copyright Act of 1976*, as amended and codified, 17 U.S.C. §102(b).

69   See, for example, *Moreau v. St. Vincent*, [1950] Ex. C.R. 198 at 204 [*Moreau*], wherein the court concluded that copyright does not extend to a "system or scheme or method for doing a particular thing"; and *Hollinrake v. Truswell*, [1894] 3 Ch. 420 at 427 (C.A.) [*Hollinrake*], where the court held that copyright does not extend to "ideas, or schemes, or systems, or methods." See also Article 2 of the *1996 WIPO Copyright Treaty*, above note 39, that has been adopted by Canada, and, therefore, will require Canada to adopt a similar statutory provision.

70   See ss. 406 to 412 of the *Criminal Code*, R.S.C. 1985, c. C-46, as amended.

71   See, however, *R. v. Locquet* (1985), 5 C.P.R. (3d) 173 (Que. Sess. Ct.) where an accused was convicted under the *Criminal Code's* trade-mark provisions for falsifying a trade-mark on a computer program.

ingly similar trade-mark to pass off its goods or services as those of the original trade-mark owner.[72] The essence of the tort of passing-off is to prevent unfair competition by which one supplier sells his goods or services as being those of another supplier. In order to make out a passing-off claim, however, the plaintiff must show actual confusion in the relevant geographic marketplace, which in turn requires that the supplier bringing the action prove that it has built up a sufficient reputation in its trade-mark in the relevant marketplace. Given these difficulties with unregistered trade-marks, suppliers of computer and information-based goods and services are well advised to register their trade marks under the *Trade-Marks Act*,[73] particularly given that registration under this statute affords nationwide protection, even if the product or service has not been sold from coast to coast. A registered trade-mark gives its owner the exclusive right to its use throughout Canada in respect of the wares and services for which it is registered. Thus a third party infringes the registered owner's exclusive rights in the trade-mark if the third party uses the trade-mark, or a confusingly similar mark, in association with similar products and services. The *Trade-Marks Act* also prohibits the use by a third party of a registered trade-mark in a manner that depreciates the goodwill in the trade-mark. Once products bearing registered trade-marks are sold with the consent of the owner of the registered trade-mark, however, the owner cannot restrict or control further sales of the goods bearing the mark.

A further limitation to the protection afforded by registered trade-marks is that not all use of a trade-mark attracts liability under the *Trade-Marks Act*. Rather, in respect of goods, a trade-mark is only deemed to be used if, at the time title to the goods, or possession of them, is transferred, the trade-mark is affixed to the goods or related packaging. In respect of services a trade-mark is used if it is displayed or used in conjunction with the advertising of those services. In other words, persons other than the registered owner of the trade-mark may make use of the mark where it is not being used in a trade-mark manner,

---

72 *Enterprise Rent-A-Car Co.* v. *Singer* (1996), 66 C.P.R. (3d) 453 (F.C.T.D.). See also *Consumers Distributing Company Limited* v. *Seiko Time Canada Ltd.*, [1984] 1 S.C.R. 583 [*Seiko*], where adequate notice posted to buyers at the point of sale regarding the differences in services offered with a product precluded a finding of passing-off; and George S. Takach, "Passing Off, Trade Mark Protection and Parallel Imports After *Consumers Distributing* v. *Seiko*" (1985) 63 Can. Bar Rev. 645. The *Seiko* case may be of important precedential value to certain suppliers in the computer industry.

73 R.S.C. 1985 c. T-13. Like the other intellectual property statutes, the *Trade-Marks Act* is federal legislation.

subject to such use not constituting dilution of the value of the registered trade-mark. A variation on this point can be seen in an American case where the defendant computer company created a small computer to calculate golfing handicaps based on a formula of the plaintiff, the United States Golf Association (USGA).[74] When the defendant publicly referred to the fact that its device used the USGA handicapping algorithm, the plaintiff argued that it had protection in the handicapping system on a trade-mark–related basis, but the court did not agree, concluding that the formula was functional. The court also found that there was no misappropriation by the defendant under the *INS* doctrine[75] because the plaintiff and the defendant did not compete directly with one another.

In order to be registered under the *Trade-Marks Act*, the trade-mark must meet several tests, the two principal ones being that it must be distinctive of a single supplier or source of products and that it not be clearly descriptive. Distinctiveness is important given that the very purpose of a trade-mark is to distinguish one supplier's products or services from those of all other suppliers. Accordingly, a trade-mark that is not distinctive will not be registrable, though it is possible for a trade-mark to acquire a secondary meaning in Canada over time, and thus become distinctive and registrable; but a trade-mark will not be registrable if it is confusing with an existing registered trade-mark.[76] Also, a trade-mark must not be clearly descriptive. This test often poses a challenge to suppliers of computer and information-based products because of their tendency to choose product names that do indicate something essential about the nature of the product. Thus, IBM was refused registration of

---

74   *United States Golf Association v. St. Andrews Systems, Data-Max, Inc.*, 749 F.2d 1028 (3d Cir. 1984).

75   For a discussion of the *INS* doctrine, see section C(8), "Other Measures of Protection," in this chapter.

76   For example, in *Cognos Inc. v. Cognisys Consultants Inc.* (1994), 53 C.P.R. (3d) 552 (T.M. Opp. Bd.) [*Cognos*], the applicant's proposed trade-mark "Cognisys" was refused registration on the ground of being confusing with the opponent's trade-mark "Cognos," particularly in light of the aural and visual resemblance between the trade-marks. See also *Motorola Inc. v. Fonorola Inc.* (1996), 66 C.P.R. (3d) 537 (T.M. Opp. Bd.), where the applicant's proposed trade-mark registration for "Fonorola" was refused in light of the opponent's trade-mark "Motorola"; *Ready Systems Corp. v. Financial Models Co.* (1993), 52 C.P.R. (3d) 125 (T.M. Opp. Bd.), where the applicant's proposed trade-mark registration "Vertex" for software was refused in light of opponent's trade-mark "VRTX"; and *Dialog Information Services, Inc. v. PMS Communications Ltd.* (1995), 62 C.P.R. (3d) 406 (T.M. Opp. Bd.), where the applicant's proposed trade-mark registration for "Dialnet" for software and data communication services was refused in light of opponent's registered trade-mark "Dialog."

"Business Solution Centre" for use in association with services for providing pre-installation planning, user education, technical support, and installation assistance,[77] "Money Machine" was found to be too descriptive for automated teller machines,[78] and "The Complete Networking Solution" was found to be too descriptive for computer, hardware, and local area network hardware.[79] In the United States, the term "CD Creator" was held to be too descriptive of a product used to develop CD-ROM titles.[80] In contrast, the federal court, on appeal from the Registrar of Trade-marks, permitted the registration of "AuditComputer" for use in association with the services of examining and testing bookkeeping records by computer and related consulting services.[81] Relatively innocent distinctiveness and descriptiveness problems can also arise in the computer industry because of the habit of using contractions for tradenames and trade-marks, as in the *Cognos* case[82] and as in *Digicom, Inc.* v. *Digicon, Inc.*,[83] where the plaintiff's name was a contraction of "digital communications" and the defendant's was a contraction of "digital consultants." The court found the two names confusing, as the parties operated in the same industry, and found for the company that had adopted its name first in time. This case illustrates well that the best trade-marks and trade-names are those that are not descriptive, but rather are completely new and coined words, or words that may have a common meaning but are not related to the business of the entity.

The registration process involves submitting an application that includes the trade-mark and a description of the specific wares or services in respect of which the trade-mark is being or proposed to be used. The Trade-marks Office reviews the application as to form and substance, and if the registrar finds the trade-mark registrable and not confusing

---

77   *Computer Innovations Distribution Inc.* v. *International Business Machines Corp.* (1988), 23 C.P.R. (3d) 530 (T.M. Opp. Bd.).
78   *Canada Trustco Mortgage Co.* v. *Guaranty Trust Co. of Canada* (1987), 15 C.P.R. (3d) 86 (T.M. Opp. Bd.).
79   *IBM Canada Ltd.* v. *Cabletron Systems, Inc.* (1995), 66 C.P.R. (3d) 343 (T.M. Opp. Bd.). See also *Mitel Corporation* v. *Registrar of Trade Marks* (1984), 79 C.P.R. (2d) 202 (F.C.T.D.), where Mitel was refused registration for the trade-mark "Superset" for telephone instruments as the term was laudatory and descriptive.
80   *Lewis Management Company, Inc.* v. *Corel Corporation*, 6 Computer Cases (CCH) ¶47,472 at 68,863 (S.D. Cal. 1995).
81   See *Clarkson Gordon* v. *Registrar of Trade Marks* (1985), 5 C.P.R. (3d) 252 (F.C.T.D.), where the court at 255 allowed this application because in order to get from the trade-mark to its meaning, "one has to separate the two words of which it is formed, reverse them and add a verb between."
82   *Cognos*, above note 76.
83   328 F. Supp. 631 (S.D. Texas 1991).

with other prior applications or registrations, the application is advertised in the *Trade-marks Journal* to allow third parties to object to the proposed registration. If the application is unopposed, or if the opposition is unsuccessful, a certificate of registration will issue upon payment of the registration fee. The registration is effective for fifteen years, and may be renewed indefinitely. The indefinite term is defensible because a trade-mark does not really protect information *per se*, the way a patent or even a copyright does; rather, a trade-mark serves a consumer protection function by designating a single source for a particular good or service. If at some point the trade-mark ceases to be used, or is otherwise challenged for non-registrability or lack of distinctiveness, a party may bring expungement proceedings to remove the trade-mark from the register. Once it is registered, the trade-mark must be used in association with the wares or services for which it is registered, unless the application was based on proposed use, in which case the applicant must also file a declaration of use indicating that the applicant has actually begun to use the trade-mark in Canada. This typically means being attached to the good, as in the case of hardware, or used in marketing literature in the case of services, but in the case of software it may also be shown in the screens of the computer program.[84] The trade-mark must also be used in the form it is registered; in one case the registered trade-mark "Bull" was stricken from the register because the owner never used it as such, but rather only as part of the composite mark "CII Honeywell Bull," the name of a French computer company.[85]

6) Ownership Issues

Given the elusive nature of information-based assets, and the fact that most information is the product of some form of collaboration, it is not surprising that a number of complicated issues arise in respect of the ownership of these assets. Generally, the creator of the intellectual property is the first owner of it, subject to an important exception where the creator is an employee and creates the intellectual property in the course of employment, in which case the employer usually is the first

---

84   *BMB Compuscience Canada Ltd.* v. *Bramalea Ltd.* (1988), 20 C.I.P.R. 310 (F.C.T.D.)
      In a similar vein, in *Riches, McKenzie & Herbert* v. *Source Telecomputing Corp.*
      (1992), 46 C.P.R. (3d) 563 (T. M. Opp. Bd.), a trade-mark registration for an
      online information service was permitted on the basis of showing the trade-mark
      on the screens accessed by subscribers to the service.
85   *Registrar of Trade Marks* v. *Compagnie internationale pour l'informatique CII
      Honeywell Bull, Société Anonyme* (1985), 4 C.P.R. (3d) 523 (F.C.A.).

owner of the work.[86] An author, for copyright purposes, is the individual(s) who actually writes the work — it is not enough merely to contribute ideas to the project to become an author (or co-author) of the work — and similarly, someone does not obtain a copyright interest in a work merely because they participated in a conversation.[87] Moreover, under the Canadian *Copyright Act* the author has to be a human being, thus raising interesting questions in respect of the ownership of computer-generated output — such as written, musical, or artistic material — where the bulk of "creativity" was generated by the advanced computer rather than any human.[88] It is also worth noting that the Crown can own copyright in information-based materials produced by or for it, and it is not contrary to the constitutional freedom of expression to limit exploitation of the Crown's copyright.[89]

The *Copyright Act* provides that the author of the copyright work is the first owner of the copyright, and that any transfer of copyright must be in writing. These two rules, however, are subject to the important exception that where an author is an employee who creates copyright works in the course of his or her employment, the employee is deemed to transfer his or her copyright to the employer unless there is a written agreement between the employee and the employer to the contrary.[90] Taken together, these rules can often frustrate the intention of a party

---

86   For operation of this rule in the context of patents, see *Spiroll Corp. Ltd.* v. *Putti* (1975), 64 D.L.R. (3d) 280 (B.C.S.C.); and *Seanix Technology Inc.* v. *Ircha*, [1998] B.C.J. No. 179 (S.C.) (QL).

87   *Hanis* v. *Teevan* (17 March 1995), No. 2063/87 (Ont. Gen. Div.) [unreported] [*Hanis*]; *Gould Estate* v. *Stoddart Publishing Co.* (1996), 30 O.R. (3d) 520 (Gen. Div.).

88   In the United Kingdom's 1988 copyright law amendments, and in several government reports in Europe and Canada, this question is being answered on the basis that the computer/software is merely a tool, and the copyright rests with the person manipulating the tool to actually produce the output: *Copyright, Designs and Patents Act, 1988*, (U.K.), 1988, c. 48, subs. 9(3).

89   *R.* v. *James Lorimer & Co. Ltd.* (1984), 77 C.P.R. (2d) 262 (F.C.A.).

90   In the *Hanis* case, above note 87, it was held that the "agreement to the contrary" must be between the employees and their employer, and thus a professor was unsuccessful in arguing that the software written by employees of the university was owned by the professor as a result of agreement between the employees and the professor. See also *Canavest House Ltd.* v. *Lett* (1984), 2 C.P.R. (3d) 386 (Ont. H.C.J.), where the court gave ownership of copyright in certain software to an employer in the absence of a written agreement to the contrary. Similarly in the patent context, the employer is generally held to be the owner of a device invented by an employee (on the basis of an implied term in the employment contract), or at least the employer has a licence to work the invention: see *W. J. Gage Ltd.* v. *Sugden*, [1967] 2 O.R. 151 (H.C.J.).

commissioning the creation of a knowledge-based asset, as was the case in the *Mainville* case where an independent contractor, hired to do some programming work, ended up owning the software he wrote because he did not assign in writing his intellectual property rights to the company.[91] As software and other knowledge-based companies increasingly allow employees to work at home and connect to the office and co-workers electronically, another example of the blurring of private/public (the third dynamic of computer law), ownership disputes are also arising where employees claim to have developed a particular information-based item at home and not on company time.[92] In order to avoid doubt, and lengthy and costly disputes, it is prudent for organizations in any way involved in the development of software and other information-based works to clarify and confirm in writing with their staff, meaning employees and literally anyone else who works on the particular project, which of them will own the work product emanating from the relationship. Failure to do so results in cases such as *Allen* v. *Toronto Star Newspapers Ltd.*, where a freelance photographer was held to be the owner of a photograph taken for a magazine cover, given the custom in the relevant industry and the absence of an agreement to the contrary.[93] It should also be noted that while moral rights cannot be assigned, they can be waived by the author. In short, it is advisable to counteract the four dynamics of computer law by addressing through a written agreement who will own the resulting intellectual property rights regardless of what new technologies may be worked on, regardless of how evanescent these work products emanating from these technologies may be, and whether they are developed in a private or international setting.

Joint creators of information-based assets will often agree to be co-owners of the intellectual property in the work or invention. Such an

---

91   *Amusements Wiltron Inc.* v. *Mainville* (1991), 40 C.P.R. (3d) 521 (Que. Sup. Ct.). For an opposite conclusion, see *Massine* v. *de Basil*, [1936–45] M.C.C. 223 (cited in *John Richardson Computers Limited* v. *Flanders*, [1993] FSR 497 at 499 (H.Ct.)), where the court concluded that it was an implied term of a retainer arrangement for an independent contractor that the copyright in the work developed by the independent contractor, which was one component of a larger work, would rest with the commissioning party.

92   See the U.S. case *Avtec Systems, Inc.* v. *Jeffrey G. Peiffer*, 1995 Copyright Law Decisions (CCH) ¶27,432, at 28,477 (4th Cir. 1995), where the copyright in a software program written by an employee software developer was held to be owned by the employee personally, rather than the employer company. Notwithstanding his employee status, the court concluded he developed the software at home and not in the course of his employment.

93   *Allen*, above note 59.

ownership arrangement means that, in the absence of an agreement to the contrary, neither co-owner can exploit the work without the consent of the other, and where there is such exploitation each co-owner must remit to the other one-half of the profit generated by such exploitation.[94] For many joint venturers this is not a desired state of affairs, and the parties would be better off to have ownership vest in a single entity with the other obtaining adequate licence rights to it. In any event, to achieve maximum certainty co-owners are also usually well advised to agree contractually as to the scope of use and exploitation that each of them can make of the particular intellectual property. Another area of uncertainty relates to the granting of enforceable security interests in patents, copyrights, and trade-marks. As the statutes governing these properties do not expressly provide for the registration of security interests, there is some question as to how to perfect a security interest in these assets. It is a common practice to record in the relevant registry the applicable security agreement, though it is not clear what the legal effect of doing so is. As a result, some secured lenders insist on obtaining a written assignment of the intellectual property, which assignment is then registered in the relevant intellectual property office. This assignment is coupled with a grant back to the borrower of exclusive distribution rights, which grant includes collateral security language indicating that the secured lender cannot exercise any effective rights with or over the intellectual property until the borrower is in default. Such a security arrangement may cause problems under trade-marks and even copyrights, and therefore in some cases lenders merely require the initial delivery of unsigned and undated assignments, which only become effective upon the borrower's default. The risk with this sort of arrangement is that such an assignment, when ultimately completed, may not be good against a previously registered assignment if the borrower takes the unscrupulous step of assigning the same intellectual property interest twice to two different people.[95]

---

94 For application of the consent requirement in a patent context, see *Forget* v. *Specialty Tools of Canada Inc.* (1995), 62 C.P.R. (3d) 537 (B.C.C.A.).

95 See, for example, the discussion in Michel Racicot & George S. Takach, "Agaguk — Un Nouveau Conflit Fédéral-Provincial" (1992) 4 Les Cahiers de Propriété Intellectuelle 401. As for a U.S. discussion of perfecting a security interest in software/copyright, see *Re Avalon Software, Inc.*, 209 B.R. 517 (Bankr. D. Ariz. 1997).

7) Remedies for Infringement

The copyright, patent, chip protection, and trade-marks statutes, and the common law of trade secrecy and breach of confidence, together with the rules of civil procedure of Canada's various courts, provide a wide range of remedies where the creator of an information-based asset believes its intellectual property rights have been infringed. These remedies are extremely important because protecting information-based assets can be particularly difficult, given their intangible, elusive nature. If the creator has a strong *prima facie* case that infringement has occurred, and where serious damage is occurring or about to occur to the creator as a result, and where there is clear and compelling evidence that the infringer has incriminating material in its possession or control that the infringer would destroy if he or she were served with a regular infringement claim, the creator may apply *ex parte* to a court for an "Anton Piller order."[96] Such an order serves essentially as a civil search warrant, permitting the creator to attend unannounced at the premises of the alleged infringer to protect vital evidence from being destroyed, and thus responds to the second dynamic of computer law.[97] Given the draconian effect such an order can have on an unsuspecting defendant, the plaintiff must make full and complete disclosure of all relevant information in the application for the order.[98] Moreover, the court invariably requires the plaintiff to give several undertakings, including that the plaintiff will compensate the defendant for any damages as a result of the order, and the order must be carried out in good faith and in strict com-

---

96   *Capitanescu v. Universal Weld Overlays Inc.* (1996), 71 C.P.R. (3d) 37 (Alta. Q.B.). This remedial measure takes its name from *Anton Piller K.G. v. Manufacturing Processes Ltd.*, [1976] 1 All E.R. 779 (C.A.), the English case that first granted this powerful order.

97   The rationale for the Anton Piller order was well expressed by the English House of Lords as follows in *Rank Film Distributors Ltd. v. Video Information Centre*, [1982] A.C. 380 at 439 [*Rank Film*]:

>They are designed to deal with situations created by infringements of patents, trade marks and copyright or more correctly with acts of piracy which have become a large and profitable business in recent years. They are intended to provide a quick and efficient means of recovering infringing articles and of discovering the sources from which these articles have been supplied and the persons to whom they are distributed before those concerned have had time to destroy or conceal them. Their essence is surprise. . . . They are an illustration of the adaptability of equitable remedies to new situations.

98   In *Pulse Microsystems Ltd. v. SafeSoft Systems Inc.* (1996), 67 C.P.R. (3d) 202 (Man. C.A.), an Anton Piller order was set aside because the plaintiffs failed to provide the court with full and fair disclosure of all material facts.

pliance with all undertakings.[99] Notwithstanding the requirement to give these safeguards, the Anton Piller order is an important procedural remedy to creators of information-based assets, given the ease and speed with which digitally stored information on computer disks and computers containing the incriminating evidence can be wiped clean.

Another strong remedy for software developers, manufacturers of computer products, and content creators, is the interlocutory injunction (as well as the related interim injunction), which prohibits the defendant from continuing any alleged acts of infringement from the time the injunction is granted until trial.[100] Three conditions generally need to be met before a court will grant an interlocutory (or interim) injunction. First, the plaintiff must show that there is a "serious question" or a "fair question" to be tried,[101] and therefore the court, on an interlocutory injunction application will generally not enquire as to whether the defendant has in fact copied or misappropriated the relevant intellectual property. An exception to this rule may come into play where the granting of the order will effectively bring the matter to an end because the defendant will be unable to survive until trial, or where the interlocutory injunction would impact on the employment plans of individuals, in which cases the court is entitled to pay closer attention to the likely outcome of the merits of the case.[102] Second, the plaintiff must show that it will suffer irreparable harm not compensable in damages if the injunction is not granted.[103]

---

99 In *Rank Film*, above note 97 at 439, the court stated: "Because they operate drastically and because they are made, necessarily, ex parte - i.e., before the persons affected have been heard, they are closely controlled by the court. . . . They are only granted upon clear and compelling evidence, and a number of safeguards in the interest of preserving essential rights are introduced."

100 *Omega Digital Data Inc.* v. *Airos Technology Inc.* (1996), 32 O.R. (3d) 21 (Gen. Div.) [*Omega*]; *Kamengo Systems Inc.* v. *Seabulk Systems Inc.* (1996), 26 B.L.R. (2d) 43 (B.C.S.C.) [*Kamengo*]. But see also *Digital Equipment Corporation* v. *C. Itoh & Co. (Canada) Ltd.* (1985), 6 C.P.R. (3d) 511 at 512 (F.C.T.D.), where, in refusing an interlocutory injunction because the plaintiff could not demonstrate that it would suffer irreparable harm, the court noted that an injunction is an "extraordinary remedy" and "ought not to be lightly granted." Equally, an application for an interlocutory injunction must be brought promptly or the plaintiff will lose the ability to enjoin conduct that has been ongoing for some time: see *Amdahl Canada Ltd.* v. *Circle Computer Services Inc.* (4 December 1994), 92CQ- 30531 (Ont. H.C.J.) [unreported].

101 *Omega*, above note 100 ("serious question"); *Kamengo*, above note 100 ("fair question").

102 *Omega*, above note 100; see also *RJR-MacDonald Inc.* v. *Canada (A.G.)* (1994), 54 C.P.R. (3d) 114 (S.C.C.).

103 See *ITV Technologies, Inc.* v. *WIC Television Ltd.*, [1997] F.C.J. No. 1645 (T.D.) (QL) (interim injunction granted); and *ITV Technologies, Inc.* v. *WIC Television Ltd.*, [1997] F.C.J. No. 1803 (T.D.) (QL) (interlocutory injunction denied) [*ITV*].

Third, the balance of convenience must favour the plaintiff. As an example of this latter factor, courts will sometimes seek to preserve the status quo, for example, by granting the plaintiff's motion for an interlocutory injunction if the defendant has not entered the market with the allegedly infringing product, while often refusing the motion if the defendant has entered the market, particularly if the defendant will be able to satisfy any damages ultimately awarded at trial.[104] It should be noted there is a line of case law in Canada supporting the proposition that once a clear violation of intellectual property rights has been established, the balance of convenience need not be considered, with the result that an injunction is granted,[105] though where the validity of the claim of the copyright or trade-mark is put into question this approach is not followed.[106] In a recent case, a court granted a temporary injunction, mindful of the fact that the actual trial was to be brought on extremely quickly.[107]

If infringement or misappropriation of an intellectual property right is proven at trial, the owner of the relevant copyright, patent, trade secret, chip topography, or trade-mark will be entitled to enjoin any further infringing activity by the defendant through a permanent injunction. The term of the injunction if issued in respect of a trade secret may extend beyond the time that the information becomes generally known, in order that the misappropriator not be entitled to use the information as a "springboard," even after honest competitors have access to the information.[108] In some cases the injunctive order is cast in extremely broad terms. In one case the defendants were ordered to cease using the plaintiff's product, which is understandable, as well as *any* other software product that performed a similar function, which constitutes an incredibly broad prohibition.[109] The order granting the permanent injunction may even provide for the return to the plaintiff of copies of the infringing work that have been provided to third parties.[110] The

---

104   *Nintendo of America Inc. v. Camerica Corp.* (1991), 36 C.P.R. (3d) 352 (F.C.A.).

105   *Jeffrey Rogers Knitwear Productions Ltd. v. R.D. International Style Collections Ltd.* (1985), 6 C.P.R. (3d) 409 (F.C.T.D.). See also *Spirales*, above note 44, where reference is made to the principle that courts are more willing to grant interlocutory injunctions in copyright infringement actions when the copying by the defendant is very clear.

106   *Upjohn Co. v. Apotex Inc.* (1993), 51 C.P.R. (3d) 292 (F.C.T.D.); *ITV*, above note 103.

107   *Alphanet*, above note 27.

108   *Kamengo*, above note 100; *Matrox*, above note 18.

109   *Gemologists International Inc. v. Gem Scan International Inc.* (1986), 7 C.I.P.R. 225 (Ont. H.C.J.) [*Gemologists*].

110   *Prism*, above note 52.

Copyright Act provides that in a copyright case, a permanent injunction may be all the plaintiff is entitled to if the defendant did not have knowledge that copyright subsisted in the work.

Damages based on a wide variety of measures can be awarded when infringement of an intellectual property right is proven. With respect to a violation of trade secrecy or misappropriation of confidential information, compensation has been based on the lost profits of the plaintiff,[111] as well as the development costs of the information.[112] Compensating the plaintiff for foreseeable damages is a common copyright measure of damages.[113] Yet another approach is to determine fair compensation for the right to use the information.[114] The *Copyright Act* also permits a plaintiff to recover conversion damages if the defendant destroys the infringing copies without the copyright owner's permission.[115] This remedy is linked to another provision of the *Copyright Act*, which deems the copyright owner to be the owner of the infringing copies as well, and requires the defendant to deliver up the infringing copies to the copyright owner. A court may award damages for copyright infringement even where the infringer made no profits.[116] With enactment of the recent Bill C-32 amendments, the *Copyright Act* now also contains a statutory damages provision that permits a court to award monetary damages between $500 and $20,000. Punitive or exemplary damages for copyright infringement can also be awarded where the defendant's conduct is egregious and shows virtual contempt for the intellectual property rights of the plaintiff.[117] An infringer of another person's patent is liable for all damages sustained by the patent holder, and such damages may be expressed as a payment of reasonable or generous royalties in such a manner as is considered to be fair in all of the circumstances of the case.[118] A court may also award punitive damages in a patent infringement suit.[119] A patent holder may choose to order an accounting of the infringer's profits in lieu of damages in appropriate

---

111 *Kamengo*, above note 100; *Wil-Can Electronics*, above note 30.

112 *ICAM*, above note 20.

113 *Prism*, above note 52. This case illustrates well the practice of granting multiple damage claims in appropriate circumstances.

114 *Pharand Ski Corp. v. Alberta* (1991), 37 C.P.R. (3d) 288 (Alta Q.B.).

115 *91439 Canada Ltée v. Editions JCL Inc.* (1994), 58 C.P.R. (3d) 38 (F.C.A.)

116 *Fletcher*, above note 43.

117 See *Wil-Can Electronics*, above note 30; see also *Prism*, above note 52, where an employee of the defendant was also found personally jointly liable for copyright infringement.

118 *Unilever PLC v. Procter & Gamble Inc.* (1995), 61 C.P.R. (3d) 499 (F.C.A.).

119 *Lubrizol Corp. v. Imperial Oil Ltd.* (1996), 67 C.P.R. (3d) 1 (F.C.A.).

circumstances.[120] These remedies are all in addition to the criminal offence of piracy provided in the *Copyright Act*.[121] Finally, with traditional copyrights and other intellectual properties, an owner could often press the Canadian customs authority to stop the offending goods at the border.[122] Such a useful "control point" is more problematic in the Internet era where copyright material is being copied and uploaded and downloaded from machine to machine.

8) International Aspects

The computer and information industries are extremely global in nature. This fact, highlighting the fourth dynamic of computer law (the blurring of national/international), was true even before the advent of the Internet. With Canadian suppliers of computer and information-based products exploiting their wares around the world, it is important that they be able to obtain intellectual property protection in foreign countries. This is done through a variety of international treaties and conventions. In the copyright field, Canada is a signatory to the *Berne Convention*[123] and the *Universal Copyright Convention*.[124] Most recently, Canada has become a party to the *Rome Convention*,[125] with many of the amendments to the Canadian *Copyright Act* effected through Bill C-32 aimed at implementing Canada's obligations under this convention. These treaties grant the nationals of signatory countries reciprocal protection based on the principle of national treatment, as well as establishing certain minimum substantive requirements, such as the term of

---

120   In a case that an appellate court (in *Beloit Canada Ltée* v. *Valmet Oy* (1995), 61 C.P.R. (3d) 271 at 274 (F.C.A.)) termed "almost Dickensian in its length and complexity," a judge commented on the "pitfalls of granting the remedy of an accounting of profits other than in exceptional and appropriate circumstances and after due deliberation by the court": *Beloit Canada Ltée* v. *Valmet Oy* (1994), 55 C.P.R. (3d) 433 at 435 (F.C.T.D.).

121   See section B(3), "Copyright," in this chapter.

122   See, for example, *Dennison Manufacturing Co.* v. *M.N.R.* (1987), 15 C.P.R. (3d) 67 (F.C.T.D.), where a copyright owner tried to compel the minister responsible for customs to stop allegedly infringing materials at the border.

123   *Berne Convention for the Protection of Literary and Artistic Works*, 9 September 1886, as revised, CTS 1948/22. The general current version of this convention, and the one to which Canada has adhered, is the one done in Paris in July, 1971. For a list of signatory countries to this convention, see the WIPO website: <http://www.wipo.org/>.

124   The *Universal Copyright Convention*, 6 September 1952, as revised, UNTS 216/132, T.I.A.S. 3324 was adopted by UNESCO in 1952.

125   *International Convention for the Protection of Performers, Producers of Phonograms and Broadcasting Organisations* (1961), done in Rome on 26 October 1961, UNTS 496/43.

copyright not being shorter than the life of the author plus fifty years. Thus, a copyright work by a Canadian is automatically granted the same protection in, for example, the United States (another signatory to the *Berne Convention*) as a work by an American, which protection may be different than that afforded the work in Canada. With respect to patents and trade-marks, Canadians must file applications in foreign jurisdictions in order to obtain protection there and vice versa.[126] This is assisted somewhat by the *Paris Convention*, to which Canada and currently over 110 countries are a party.[127] The *Paris Convention* provides that if a filing is made in one *Paris Convention* country, the filing date in any other *Paris Convention* country is the earliest filing date in a *Paris Convention* country so long as the subsequent filing is effected within six and twelve months in the case of trade-marks and patents, respectively. For example, if a Canadian files in Canada for a trade-mark on January 1, and if it files for a U.S. trade-mark registration any time before June 30 of the same year, the filing date in the United States will be deemed to be January 1. Canada and some sixty other countries are also parties to the *Patent Cooperation Treaty,* which allows patent applications filed in one treaty country to be deemed applications in other treaty countries, thereby greatly assisting the international patent filing process.[128]

There is no international treaty covering chip protection. Rather, the *ICT Act* provides for bilateral reciprocity by allowing Canada to extend protection for those nationals whose countries provide similar protection to Canadians. Currently, Canada has such reciprocal arrangements with the United States and most countries in Europe.[129] The World Intellectual Property Organization (WIPO) is advocating an international treaty for chip protection, but to date this effort has not been successful.[130] WIPO is particularly active in encouraging a number of countries to improve the level of intellectual property protection

---

126 See *Vanity Fair Mills, Inc. v. T. Eaton Co. Limited,* 234 F.2d 633 (2d Cir. 1956) [*Vanity Fair*].

127 *Paris Convention for the Protection of Industrial Property,* 20 March 1883, as revised, CTS 1928/3. For a list of signatory countries, see the WIPO website: <http://www.wipo.org/>.

128 *Patent Cooperation Treaty (1970),* done in Washington on 19 June 1970, as amended, CTS 1990/22.

129 See SOR/93-282, 28 May 1993, for the United States, Australia, and Japan, and SOR/94-677, 1 November 1994, for most European countries.

130 WIPO is a Geneva-based specialized agency of the United Nations. Canada is one of the currently 161 countries that are members of WIPO. WIPO undertakes numerous efforts to promote the protection of intellectual property around the globe, including by administering various international treaties related to intellectual property. WIPO's website is at <http://www.wipo.org/>.

provided by their domestic laws, especially in developing countries. This process has also become a part of multilateral trade agreements. The *North American Free Trade Agreement* contains a chapter on intellectual property that sets out minimum requirements for copyright, patent, trade-mark, and trade secrecy protection that must be adopted by each signatory country.[131] The World Trade Organization, the successor to the GATT, also has an agreement on intellectual property which, as with the earlier NAFTA, requires a number of countries to update their intellectual property laws.[132] Most recently, WIPO was instrumental in effecting the conclusion in December 1996 of two treaties, the *WIPO Copyright Treaty* and the *WIPO Performances and Phonograms Treaty*. These treaties became effective when thirty countries adopted them, and like other international intellectual property conventions, they are only binding on the signatory countries.[133] Of course, having laws in the statute books that provide, in writing, adequate substantive protection for intellectual property are not worth much if these laws cannot be practically enforced through the country's judicial system. In this regard, a number of organizations, such as the Business Software Alliance (BSA) and the Software Publishers Association (SPA), groups of largely American-based producers of mass market software products, expend significant financial and human resources in tracking down pirates of intellec-

---

131   The NAFTA, to which Canada, the United States, and Mexico are parties, was implemented in Canada by the *North American Free Trade Agreement Implementation Act*, S.C. 1993, c. 44. Chapter 17 of the NAFTA is devoted to intellectual property issues.

132   The WTO's new regime on intellectual property is contained in the *Agreement on Trade-Related Aspects of Intellectual Property Rights, Including Trade in Counterfeit Goods*, one of the subsidiary agreements to result from the Uruguay Round of international trade negotiations. The text of this Agreement can be found at <http://itl.irv.uit.no/trade_law/documents/freetrade/wta-94/art/iia1c.html>. Canada made a number of WTO-related amendments to its intellectual property statutes through the *World Trade Organization Agreement Implementation Act*, S.C. 1994, c. 47, including the adoption of performers' rights. For a good overview of the WTO's new intellectual property agreement, see Klaus Stegemann, "Uruguay Round Results for New Issues," in *Technology, Information and Public Policy*, ed. Thomas J. Courchene (Kingston, Ont.: John Deutsch Institute, Queen's University, 1995).

133   As of 15 January 1998, fifty-one countries, including Canada, have signed the *WIPO Copyright Treaty* and fifty countries, including Canada, have signed the *WIPO Performances and Phonograms Treaty*; the WIPO website <http://www.wipo.org/> can be used to review up-to-date lists of signatories.

tual property and trying to convince local authorities to bring legal action against them.[134]

These international efforts of adopting stronger intellectual property laws around the world are particularly welcome in the age of the Internet. Indeed, the territorial basis of patent, copyright, and other intellectual property laws will probably have to be modified to adequately cope with a number of challenges posed by the Internet's ability to facilitate sustained crossborder remote access activities. In effect, the fourth dynamic of computer law is sorely testing the current global intellectual property legal regime that is still stubbornly nationalist in orientation. For example, the Canadian *Patent Act* prohibits the making, selling, or using in Canada of a device, say a patented software-based process, for which a Canadian patent has been granted. A determined infringer may be able to operate the patented process in an off-shore haven that does not recognize patent protection for the particular item, and the required data would be transmitted to Canada. It is open to question whether the rule of patent law that allows products to be stopped at the border if they are produced abroad by processes that infringe a Canadian patent would apply to such data. Or, in the copyright context, current copyright statutes generally presume that the creation and publication of a copyright work will all take place in the same jurisdiction. The Internet, and related networks such as corporate intranets, permit intense collaboration among the nationals of multiple countries. This sort of scenario creates serious uncertainties under current copyright regimes. Accordingly, to deal with these sorts of patent and copyright issues engendered by the Internet, amendments to national intellectual property laws will likely be required, in addition to requiring global adoption of such statutes.

---

134 These groups have their work cut out for them. In 1996 the BSA compared the number of personal computers sold to the number of software packages sold, and using a ratio of 1:3 (every PC uses roughly three software programs), the BSA estimated that half the software programs in use are pirated, illegal copies: "Intellectual Property: The Property of the Mind," *The Economist*, 27 July 1996. In 1995 the SPA estimated that in 1994 the software industry lost $8 billion in revenues to piracy: Stuart J. Johnston, "Microsoft Pilot Helps Firms Pinpoint Piracy," *Computerworld*, 12 June 1995.

C. CONTENTIOUS ISSUES

With technological changes advancing at a fast pace, the intellectual property regimes face a number of challenges. Indeed, all four of the dynamics of computer law are being felt acutely in the intellectual property area. Moreover, the intellectual property statutes emanate from the Industrial Age, and will be hard-pressed to remain current in the Information Age. How, and indeed whether, patents should apply to software are burning questions in the computer industry. Similarly, copyright protection for software has yielded a number of judicial answers over the last few years. The application of traditional intellectual property laws to new information-based products, such as electronic databases, and to new technologies, such as multimedia works and the Internet, also raises a host of questions. Are there other means of legal protection available for information-based products? Besides these substantive issues, there are process-related questions regarding the way intellectual property questions are posed and resolved in our current legal system.

1) Legal Dispute Resolution

Before turning to the substantive topics, it is worth looking at the difficulties inherent in legal decision making in the high-technology intellectual property arena. First, there is the need for the legal system, including lawyers, judges, and legislators, to be able to understand the new technologies. This is not a trivial exercise, as noted by an American judge in an early computer law case:

> [I]n the computer age, lawyers and courts need no longer feel ashamed or even sensitive about the charge, often made, that they confuse the issue by resort to legal "jargon", law Latin or Norman French. By comparison, the misnomers and industrial shorthand of the computer world make the most esoteric legal writing seem as clear and lucid as the Ten Commandments or the Gettysburg Address; and to add to this Babel, the experts in the computer field, while using exactly the same words, uniformly disagree as to precisely what they mean.[135]

---

135   *Honeywell, Inc. v. Lithonia Lighting, Inc.,* 317 F. Supp. 406 at 408 (N.D. Ga. 1970).

This language barrier between technologists and the legal community means that legislators must be extremely careful to draft laws in this area without using jargon, and in as technology-neutral a fashion as possible. In the contractual area, lawyers should also strive to describe technological concepts in functional, objective terms, rather than in techno-speak (or as some would argue, techno-babble) shorthand.

The complexity of the subject matter, coupled with the first dynamic of computer law, might be taxing the traditional adversarial system of civil litigation to the limit. Consider the following passage from the decision of an American judge presiding over a lengthy, complicated patent lawsuit involving semiconductor chip technologies developed by Hitachi and Motorola, the parties to the litigation:

> For reasons stated above, the Court is constrained to find damages both for infringements by Hitachi and by Motorola. It is both in making the initial infringement determination and in fashioning the remedy that this Court is made acutely aware of the travesty of justice cases such as this pose upon courts. The subject matter of this suit is extremely complex and delicate; not the sort of thing the lay person should be put in a position of judging. The intricacies of the patents and devices involved is clear only to the engineer. The far-reaching effects of infringement is known only to the business persons and marketing specialists involved with Motorola and Hitachi. What is more perplexing to this Court is these two parties have dealt personally with each other for years. They have negotiated their differences with the skill and expertise only they can possess. Yet suddenly they left behind their prior relationship and expected this Court to ferret out the wrongdoings of which each is accused. Even worse, they hired lawyers to compound and exponentially increase their disputes and damages. This court has seen more than ninety motions filed in this case, replete with bickering and petty insults. The parties would have saved time, money, feelings, and relations had they curbed their emotions and sat down to settle their difference out of court. In short, this suit is not the sort of thing Federal Courts should spend time and energy upon. The parties present this Court not with legal questions, but with questions related to engineering and electronic technology more suitably determined by those intimately familiar with the art.
>
> With that, the Court shall begin its bewildering foray into the issue of damages.[136]

---

136 *Motorola, Inc. v. Hitachi, Ltd.*, 2 Computer Cases (CCH) ¶46,280 at 62,103, quote at 62,118–19 (W.D. Texas 1990).

A similar admission was made by a judge in a Canadian case involving technical subject matter:

> The matter of a serious question to be tried is doubtful. The plaintiff avers that the defendant's device infringes the plaintiff's patent, because as it seems, the defendant's device is capable of the basic functions claimed for the plaintiff's patented device. The defendant's counsel says it is clear and obvious that his client's device, because of its functions, does not infringe. Quite simply, the parties' respective technologies and the comparison between them are unintelligible to this judge, as presented by the parties' respective counsel. This judge is just unable to form an opinion on the basis of the parties' respective submissions, involving as they do, functions of electromagnetic formulae.
>
> One often hears complaints by members of the so-called "patent bar" or "intellectual property bar" that Federal Court judges lack the scientific and technical formations for easy understanding of patent cases involving electrical and chemical and other scientific inventions. That complaint is probably true, and this judge openly admits it. On the other hand, it is said that members of those bars from which the complaint arises, will never accept an appointment to this bench, because they already earn from their generally affluent clients, incomes which significantly surpass judicial salaries. Present-day Canadian society does not seem to be imbued with the ideal of sacrifice in order to give service to the country and its institutions and the truth of that observation may well lie at the root of the lack of judges of a scientific or technical background, such as this judge.[137]

Finally, consider the following passage from a recent Canadian case involving a technical subject matter, in this case chemical compounds; the court had to determine whether a particular fabric softener infringed the patents that protected another brand of fabric softener:

> The trial of these actions on the claim and counterclaim was not ordinary in its duration. The public litigation extended over 35 long (early until late) days, from October 16, 1990 until February 8, 1991, in both Toronto and Ottawa. No doubt because of the high incidence of unfilled vacancies, and some illness among the judges of the Trial Division, no sufficient duration of uninterrupted reflexion and writing time could be accorded to this judge until October 1992. Given the mind-boggling volume of documentary evidence, conflicting scientific and other testimony, and written and oral argument, it is admittedly diffi-

---

137   *Geonics Ltd.* v. *Geoprobe Ltd.* (1991), 37 C.P.R. (3d) 346 at 348 (F.C.T.D.).

cult for this judge now to sort out the evidence, especially the chemistry which was all new to the judge upon reading over the file prior to the opening of the trial in Toronto. Expert witnesses — called because, one supposes, of their eminence in the chemical science in which they proudly purport to be expert — are a large hindrance rather than much help because, of course, they are paid to contradict the eminent scientists on the opposite side. They remind one of another ancient profession (law, or soldiery) rather than learned experts of technical precision seeking to find and to explain scientific verities.

When one considers the apparent silliness of trial by a judge who is utterly unschooled in the scientific substance of a patent, hearing conflicting testimony of so-called experts to speak the antithesis of scientific verity, and lawyers who have been engaged in the particular case for years before the trial, one knows that this field cries out for reform. It wastes the scarce resources of the court, which is not configured for getting at the truth of arcane scientific contradictions. A judge unschooled in the arcane subject is at difficulty to know which of the disparate, solemnly mouthed and hotly contended "scientific verities" is, or are, plausible. Is the eminent scientific expert with the shifty eyes and poor demeanour the one whose "scientific verities" are not credible? Cross-examination is said to be the great engine for getting at the truth, but when the unschooled judge cannot perceive the truth, if he or she ever hears it, among all the chemical or other scientific baffle-gab, is it not a solemn exercise in silliness? Reform is much needed in the field of non-mechanical patents' litigation.[138]

These judicial pronouncements are disturbing. They raise a number of questions about the capacity of the traditional civil litigation system to deal with highly technical subject matter. In essence, is the first dynamic of computer law — namely, the rapid pace of technological change — presenting a material obstacle to effective judicial dispute resolution? Several remedial measures are possible. One remedy is to remove intellectual property disputes from the standard judicial system and submit these cases to alternative dispute resolution processes such as mediation and, in particular, arbitration. Arbitration is a legal dispute process where the parties to the dispute choose their own decision maker. For a case involving a software-related patent or a software copyright issue, arbitration permits the parties to choose an arbitrator who has experience in the software field, or who has technology/business or

---

138 *Unilever PLC v. Procter & Gamble Inc.* (1993), 47 C.P.R. (3d) 479 at 488–89 (F.C.T.D.) [*Unilever*].

technology/legal experience. Or if the case merits the additional expense, a panel of three arbitrators could be chosen, with each member having a technical, business, and legal background. This was done in the arbitration between IBM and Fujitsu in the mid-1980s.[139] In addition to allowing parties to choose their own expert "judge," arbitration has the further advantage of permitting the parties to keep confidential their dispute; of course, in some cases a party to a dispute does not want to keep matters quiet, and indeed wants the glare of publicity to pressure the other party into a settlement. In regular court proceedings there are means by which certain sensitive evidence can be ordered sealed by the court in envelopes that the public does not have access to. This can be very important in an intellectual property case where disclosure of the trade secret or other information would defeat the very relief sought by the plaintiff. Nonetheless, the existence of the litigation in court will be a matter of public record, as will certain papers filed with the court. By contrast, at least in theory, an arbitration and all documents related to it, can be kept private, though depending on the parties and the facts of the case, rumours may begin to circulate regarding the arbitration. Indeed, in the case of a major arbitration where the parties have agreed contractually to keep the matter confidential, an invidious situation can arise where inaccurate and highly speculative stories surface in the trade press regarding the arbitration, and the underlying positions and claims made by the two parties, but these cannot be rectified or even rebutted because of the non-disclosure rules, thereby potentially causing damage to at least one of the parties' relationships with third parties.

A further advantage often touted for arbitration is the greater speed with which the matter can be brought to a determination in an arbitral setting. In many Canadian cities the courts are so clogged that it can take months, if not years in some cases, before the substantive merits of the case can be heard, as opposed to motions for interim or interlocutory relief which can generally be heard within a matter of weeks; the ability to obtain interim relief in a rather timely fashion, and usually in less time than it takes to appoint the arbitrator, argues for the practice of reserving the right to resort to the regular judicial system for such relief even if the substantive merits of the case are subject to arbitration. And in the computer industry, with its short and ever shrinking product cycles, justice delayed is truly justice denied. Moreover, prompt decisions can also result in cost savings. Full-blown court-based litigation can be extremely expen-

---

139   The "clean room procedure" established by this arbitration for the creation of non-infringing software is referred to in Richard A. Brait, "The Unauthorized Use of Confidential Information" (1991) 18 C.B.L.J. 323.

sive, primarily because of the protracted nature of the pretrial skirmishing. Therefore, a short arbitration, even with the parties paying the fees and expenses of the arbitrator, can be cheaper than litigation. Of course, sometimes parties to an arbitration get what they pay for, particularly given the preference of a number of arbitrators who are business people to achieve "justice" by merely splitting the difference between the two protagonists. High-quality dispute resolution determination, which often entails finding completely in favour of one of the parties, is an art honed through long experience, precisely the expertise that seasoned judges bring to any dispute. This is why retired judges are in such demand as arbitrators.

Parties not resident in the same jurisdiction and affected by the fourth dynamic of computer law — the blurring of national and international — will often resort to arbitration in a neutral third country as a means of not giving the appearance of advantage to one party by using its legal system for disputes. Again, this is an example of resorting to a contractual solution to address one of the four dynamics of computer law. One further benefit to arbitration is the ability of parties to an arbitration to craft the procedural rules that will apply to their dispute resolution process.[140] For example, the parties may wish to provide for intensive education of the arbitrator(s) in the relevant technical subject matter, perhaps even by having a neutral instructor provide at least certain background material. Of course, a critical objective for every advocate in an intellectual property case is to educate the judge by distilling the essence of the technologies or science involved and then imparting this in a manner that is both intellectually honest but easily understandable — no mean feat! Arbitration can arguably assist this process by allowing a greater panoply of teaching and demonstrative aids, given the generally more relaxed approach to the rules of evidence in an arbitration setting than those found in the court room.

In this regard it should be noted that judges will sometimes attempt to bridge the technology knowledge gap by appointing a technical expert (nominally) to assist the judge. As noted above in the passage from the *Unilever* case,[141] typically in each intellectual property case the plaintiff and defendant each retain a subject matter expert to explain why the position of the party retaining the expert is firmly buttressed by

---

140 To the extent the parties are silent on a procedural point, the relevant provincial arbitration statute will apply; for example, in Ontario the *Arbitration Act, 1991*, S.O. 1991, c. 17 for arbitrations among Ontario entities, and the *International Commercial Arbitration Act*, R.S.O. 1990, c. I.9 for arbitrations with a party that is outside of Ontario.

141 *Unilever*, above note 138.

the technical evidence. Given, however, that these experts invariably vehemently disagree, a judge will on occasion recruit an "independent" expert to assist the judge in sorting through the technical evidence and the respective experts' reports of the parties. For example, such an expert was appointed by the trial judge in the *Altai* case.[142] Indeed, in this decision the influence of the court-appointed expert was so great as to raise the question whether the judge overly deferred to the views of the expert. For instance, the expert developed a mechanistic formula for weighing certain aspects of the two software programs in issue in the litigation (i.e., source code counted for 1000 points, organization of the program counted for 100 points, etc.) that would only result in a finding of copyright infringement if there was copying by the defendant of the source code of the plaintiff's program. Interestingly, while the trial decision, concluding that there was no copyright infringement by the defendant, was upheld on appeal, the appeal court made no mention of this formula and instead devised a very different legal test for copyright infringement, which is discussed below. There is, then, the danger that a judicial decision maker overly defers to a court-appointed expert. Interestingly, this concern is not evident in an arbitration setting where the technical expert is the decision maker because the parties can engage in a dialogue directly with the expert, a key concern with the court-appointed expert being that the parties neither appoint the expert nor have any direct interaction with him or her. Nonetheless, there may well be a place for court-appointed technical experts in intellectual property cases provided suitable respect for due process principles can be guaranteed the parties. In short, the regular judicial system continually needs to take advantage of new means by which the distance between the technical and legal worlds can be abridged.

2) Patent Protection for Software

Whether computer software should be able to be patented has engendered significant debate in Canada, the United States, and other countries, notably in Europe and Japan. The *Patent Act* provides that mere scientific principles or abstract theorems are not patentable subject matter. In the *Schlumberger* decision, the leading Canadian software patent case, it was held that the particular computer program before the court was not patentable because the program merely performed a series of

---

142   *Computer Associates International, Inc.* v. *Altai, Inc.*, 3 Computer Cases (CCH) ¶46,505 at 63,357 (E.D.N.Y. 1991), aff'd 982 F.2d 693 (2d Cir. 1992).

mathematical calculations in order to extract useful information.[143] Accordingly, in the mid-1980s, the Canadian Patent Office issued guidelines (which have since been superseded) on the patentability of computer-related subject matter that included the statement that computer programs *per se* are not patentable. The *Schlumberger* case, however, did not preclude a computer program or a data processing system from being proper patentable subject matter. Indeed, over the past decade the Canadian[144] and U.S.[145] Patent Offices have been allowing patent applications that consist largely of, and in many cases entirely of, computer software, particularly where they are artfully and skilfully drafted to include some hardware elements in the claims and so long as they do not focus overly on stand-alone algorithms but rather refer to systems, processes, or methods to achieve a concrete solution to a specific problem. As a result, the current guidelines for the patentability of computer-related subject matter issued by the Canadian Patent Office no longer contain the statement that computer programs *per se* are unpatentable.[146] Similarly, the lengthier U.S. guidelines regarding computer-related inventions are also quite amenable to appropriately drafted software-related patents.[147]

The U.S. guidelines give a useful discussion of the criteria for patent protection for software-related inventions. Processes will be found to be non-patentable if, for example, they consist solely of mathematical operations or simply manipulate abstract ideas without some practical application. Thus, the guidelines indicate that patent claims that define a "data structure" *per se* will be considered to relate to information

---

143   *Schlumberger Canada Ltd.* v. *Commissioner of Patents* (1981), 56 C.P.R. (2d) 204 (F.C.A.).

144   See *Re Honeywell Information Systems Inc.* (1986), 11 C.I.P.R. 81 (Pat. Appeal Bd.); *Re Application of Fujitsu Ltd.* (1985), 9 C.P.R. (3d) 475 (Pat. Appeal Bd.). See also *Re Application of Vapor Canada Ltd.* (1985), 9 C.P.R. (3d) 524 (Pat. Appeal Bd.), where, in allowing some claims, the decision denied other claims that were directed only to the extraction of information from recorded data or which describe a computer performing the kinds of steps for which computers were invented. Or consider *Re Application For Patent of General Electric Co.* (1984), 6 C.P.R. (3d) 191 (Pat. Appeal Board), where a software program was held patentable as part of a large engine control system.

145   See *Re Alappat*, 33 F.3d 1526 (Fed. Cir. 1994); and *Arrhythmia Research Technology, Inc.* v. *Corazonix Corporation*, 958 F.2d 1053 (Fed. Cir. 1992) [*Arrhythmia*].

146   Canadian Intellectual Property Office, The Patent Office Record, "Notice 16," Vol. 123, No. 8, 21 February 1995.

147   United States Department of Commerce, Patent and Trademark Office, "Examination Guidelines for Computer-Related Inventions," 61 Fed. Reg. 7478, 29 March 1996 (also reproduced in Guide to Computer Law (CCH) ¶60,530 at 82,103).

rather than a computer-implemented process, and hence will not be patentable. By contrast, algorithms implemented by a computerized process that actually manipulate data to achieve a specific result are patentable. In this regard, the U.S. guidelines cite the *Arrhythmia* case, where the patent, based on complex algorithms, was allowed as it was found directed to the analysis of electrocardiographic signals in order to determine certain characteristics of heart function.[148] That is, the output from the patented system was not an abstract number but signals related to a patient's heart activity.

A number of commentators have criticized the issuance by the U.S. Patent Office of software-oriented patents. The criticism stems from several arguments, including: software is too mathematical and scientific; software is not embodied in a physical device; changes to software programs are effected too incrementally to be inventive; the difficulties of searching the Patent Office for software patents, particularly given that the search will not reveal current applications, are particularly onerous for individual software developers and smaller companies; the Patent Office has issued a number of patents that would not have been issued had the relevant state of prior art been brought to the Patent Office's attention; the Patent Office's staff are inexpert in matters related to software; and for many years the software industry got along fine relying solely on copyright and trade secrets.[149] The contrary view is that applications for software patents should be treated no differently than other patent applications.[150] Thus, if the patent application reveals only a scientific formula, or if it is not novel or inventive, it should not issue. The U.S. and Canadian Patent Offices have also upgraded their skills in the software area so that they are better able to analyse the prior art and inventiveness questions. Accordingly, software patents seem firmly embedded in the intellectual property landscape, as illustrated by the successful patent infringement claim brought by Stac Electronics in 1994 against Microsoft in respect of the unauthorized use of certain data compression technologies for which the former owned several

---

148   *Arrhythmia*, above note 145.

149   For a canvassing of these and other criticisms of software patents, see Richard Stallman, "Against Software Patents: The League for Programming Freedom" (1992) 14 Hastings Comm. & Ent. L.J. 295; and Pamela Samuelson, "*Benson* Revisited: The Case Against Patent Protection for Algorithms and Other Computer Program-Related Inventions" (1990) 39 Emory L.J. 1025.

150   See David Bender, "The Case for Software Patents" (1989) 6:5 The Computer Lawyer 2.

patents.[151] Even in Europe, where the *European Patent Convention*[152] expressly states that computer software is not patentable material, the European Patent Office and some national courts have been willing to grant patent protection for certain software-related inventions.[153] The U.S. Patent Office, however, has recognized that the controversial patent it had issued for a multimedia interface device was issued in error and has taken the unusual step of revoking it.[154] These sorts of controversies will always be with us as the various patent offices, and the courts, delineate on a case-by-case basis the particular parameters of software-oriented patents.[155] And as the Internet continues to grow in size and importance, patents related to it will also engender such debate. This is currently the case with the Freeny patent, which purports to cover a method of doing electronic commerce on the Internet.[156]

---

151   The suit resulted in a jury awarding Stac $120 million for patent infringement, though the parties ultimately settled on the basis of Microsoft paying Stac $40 million in royalties and $40 million for an equity investment. The importance of this litigation in highlighting the strategic value of patents in the computer industry prompted a number of stories about it in the general press: see Anthony Aarons, "Software Giant Dealt Big Loss in Patent Fight" *Los Angeles Daily Journal* (24 February 1994); Lawrence M. Fisher, "Judge Rules Microsoft Must Recall DOS Software" *New York Times* (11 June 1994); and Lawrence M. Fisher, "Microsoft in Accord on Patent: Agrees to Pay Stac in Data Storage Case" *New York Times* (22 June 1994).

152   The *EPC Convention on the Grant of European Patents (European Patent Convention)* of 5 October 1973, as amended, is available at <http://www.epo.co.at/epo/>.

153   See Laurence Tellier-Loniewski and Alain Bensoussan, "Europe Extends Patent Protection to Software" *The National Law Journal* (September/October 1996) available at <http://www.ljx.com/practice/ computer/p6europe.html>. In this piece the authors note Japan is also actively issuing software patents, given that in 1994 the Japan Patent Office received 335,000 patent applications, of which 24,000 (7 percent) were software-related.

154   The U.S. Patent Office took this step after much criticism had been levelled at the broad scope of the patent: see Michael D. Bednarek, "Comptons New Media's Patent Saga: Lesson for the Software Industry and Others in Emerging Technologies" (1995) 69 Patent World 29.

155   For example, in a recent U.S. case a court refused to uphold a patent for a software product that expanded abbreviations into proper words as it did not meet the test of non-obviousness and other existing programs were already employed for similar purposes: *Productivity Software International, Inc. v. Healthcare Technologies, Inc.*, 5 Computer Cases (CCH) ¶47,258 at 67,584 (S.D. N.Y. 1995).

156   The Freeny patent (U.S. Pat. No. 4,528,643, 9 July 1985), currently owned by E-Data Corp., describes a method of doing business whereby users select a digitally distributed product from an online catalogue and then have it transmitted electronically to their personal computer. For a sense of the controversy in the computer and network industries surrounding this patent, see Neil Gross, "E-Commerce: Who Owns the Rights," *Business Week*, 29 July 1996.

3) Copyright Protection for Software

The *Copyright Act* has always been an uncomfortable home for software. Affording copyright protection to computer programs by calling them literary works has been an effective and efficient way of combatting wholesale piracy, the practice of reproducing all or almost all of a computer program and selling the illegal copy on a bootleg basis. By amending the definition of literary work in the *Copyright Act* to cover computer programs in 1988, software developers were given quick protection in Canada and abroad through Canada's participation in the *Berne Convention*. The alternative of crafting a separate legal regime for software, as has been done with chip topography technology, would have resulted in a much slower pace of protection both domestically and globally. It is, nonetheless, something of a fiction to call software a "literary work." Novels, plays, art, and music, the traditional core copyright works, are communicative vehicles intended to express artistic or aesthetic values. The real genius in these types of works is their expressive flair. Of course Shakespeare crafted intriguing plots and created notorious characters, but his really profound contribution to English literature is his dialogue, the actual words he chose to express and give life to his eternal themes. There is no "correct" or best way to write about a love between two young people whose families stand in the way. Shakespeare expressed it one way in *Romeo and Juliet*, but Leonard Bernstein expressed it another way in *West Side Story*. Monet and Cézanne both painted the French countryside, but with much different styles — each with his own expressive imprint; the same can be said of Emily Carr and Tom Thomson with respect to Canadian landscape painting.

In contrast, a computer program that runs a company's payroll is a utilitarian device that controls a machine to perform certain predetermined functions.[157] Other software processes documents, sorts data, performs calculations; these are very different activities than the purpose of a book, which is simply to convey information. Even maps and charts, which have long been covered by copyright, merely convey information — they do not operate machines. Thus, in a case some one hundred years ago, a British court refused to recognize copyright in a cardboard pattern with writing and scales on it that was used for making sleeves for clothes. The court concluded that the item did not convey information or pleasure but rather was for practical use, and therefore its protection should be sought in the bailiwick of patent; the court was particularly concerned about giving the long term of copyright protection to such an industrial device.[158] A similar unease and ambivalence towards software can be seen in three reports that addressed intellectual property protection for software prior to the 1988 addition to the *Copyright Act* of computer programs. In 1971 the Economic Council of Canada argued against extending copyright protection to software, lest it grant protection to ideas.[159] In 1984, a government white paper responded to the same concern by proposing that software be divided into two categories, that which is human readable and that which is

---

157   Some would argue computer program statements do not even look very literary; consider the following sampling of source code, in a mixture of English and French computer commands, reproduced in an early Canadian software infringement case, *Dynabec Ltée* v. *La Société d'Informatique R.D.G. Inc.* (1985), 6 C.P.R. (3d) 322 at 327 (Que. C.A.):

Ok
LIST

```
10    LPRINT<La Compagnie d'Informatique ABC>:
      LPRINT:LPRINT:LPRINT:LPRINT
20    LPRINT TAB (31) <MON CLIENT LTEE>
30    LPRINT:LPRINT:LPRINT
40    LPRINT TAB (29) <LISTE DU SALAIRE BRUT>:
      LPRINT:LPRINT:LPRINT
50    LPRINT TAB (10) <NOM DE L'EMPLOYE>,
      TAB (30) <TAUX>, TAB (45) <HEURES>,TAB (60)
      <BRUT>
60    LPRINT:LPRINT:LPRINT
70    CLS LPRINT<La Compagnie d'Informatique
      ABC>: LOCATE 10,25
80    INPUT >Entrez le nom de l'employé>;
      NOM: LOCATE 12,25
90    INPUT <Entrez son taux horaire>;
      TAUX :LOCATE 14,25
100   INPUT <Entrez le nombre d'heures>;
      HEURES
```
      . . .

158   *Hollinrake*, above note 69. In coming to its conclusion, the court stated at 428:
      [A] literary work is intended to afford either information and instruction, or pleasure, in the form of literary enjoyment. The sleeve chart before us gives no information or instruction. It does not add to the stock of human knowledge or give, and is not designed to give, any instruction by way of description or otherwise; and it certainly is not calculated to afford literary enjoyment or pleasure. It is a representation of the shape of a lady's arm, or more probably of a sleeve designed for a lady's arm, with certain scales for measurement upon it. It is intended, not for the purpose of giving information or pleasure, but for practical use in the art of dressmaking. It is, in fact, a mechanical contrivance, appliance or tool.
      But see also the discussion of this case in *Apple Computer*, above note 9.

159   Economic Council of Canada, *Report on Intellectual and Industrial Property* (Ottawa: Information Canada, 1971).

executed on a computer, and that the former should have the same term of protection as other copyright works, but protection for the latter be limited to five years.[160] This highly controversial and much criticized proposal was not adopted by a subsequent Parliamentary report, which nonetheless had its own strange suggestion, namely, that using part of one program as a non-substantial part of another program be a permitted exception to copyright protection as a form of fair dealing.[161] The government rejected all these concerns and proposals when it amended the *Copyright Act* in 1988 to provide express protection for computer programs as literary works, much in keeping with the trend of other industrialized countries.[162] Nevertheless, given the differences between software and traditional copyright works, a number of respected commentators have called for software to be protected under its own statute, a *sui generis* solution that is capable of responding to the unique attributes of software.[163] One common theme in these proposals is to reduce the term of protection for software. Given the relative youthfulness of many software programmers, the copyright term of protection of life of the author plus 50 years effectively gives software 80 to 100 years of copyright protection, a term that many consider too lengthy in light of the rapid pace of technological change in the industry and the related short, and ever shortening, product life cycles. In effect, the spirit of concern that animated the court in the *Hollinrake* case[164] continues to find expression in these proposals.

---

160   Consumer and Corporate Affairs Canada, Department of Communications, *From Gutenberg to Telidon, A White Paper on Copyright: Proposals for the Revision of the Canadian Copyright Act* (Ottawa: Supply and Services Canada, 1984).

161   House of Commons, Standing Committee on Communications and Culture, *Report of the Sub-Committee on the Revision of Copyright: A Charter of Rights for Creators* (Ottawa: Supply and Services Canada, 1985).

162   For example, the *1996 WIPO Copyright Treaty*, available from the WIPO website: <http://www.wipo.org/>, provides in Article 4 that computer programs are to be given copyright protection as literary works.

163   See, for example, Pamela Samuelson *et al.*, "A Manifesto Concerning the Legal Protection of Computer Programs" (1994) 94 Colum. L. Rev. 2308; and Robert A. Arena, "A Proposal for the International Intellectual Property Protection of Computer Software" (1993) 14 U. of Pa. J. Int'l Bus. L. 213.

164   *Hollinrake*, above note 69.

In light of the foregoing discussion, it is not surprising that determining the appropriate scope of protection for software within the parameters of the *Copyright Act* — except when presented with the case of wholesale copying — has proven to be an extremely difficult and controversial exercise, indicative of the first two dynamics of computer law, namely, the rapid pace of technological change and the elusive nature of information. Put another way, separating non-protectable idea from protectable expression in software presents courts with a daunting task. In the *Whelan* case, the leading U.S. case of the 1980s, the court determined that the purpose or function of a computer program would be its idea, and that everything not necessary to that purpose would be protectable expression.[165] Therefore, in that case, copyright protected not just the actual computer statements and instructions that made up the program, but extended as well to the "sequence, structure and organization" of the program, thus providing the initial creator of the program with a very strong level of protection for the software through copyright. In Canada the *Gemologists* case exhibited a similarly broad scope of protection by finding that the defendants had copied the "overall logical structure" and "sequence of menus" of the plaintiff.[166]

Partly in response to a torrent of scholarly and industry criticism levelled at the decision in *Whelan*, a new standard has emerged for separating idea from expression in software copyright cases. Expressed in the *Altai* decision at the appellate level,[167] the current American leading case, as the "abstraction-filtration-comparison test," a key element of the new approach is to recognize that computer programs, rather than having a single overriding idea or purpose, comprise numerous sub-ideas, and thus the initial step in the test requires a dissection of the software into these constituent ideas. Then, in the all-important filtration stage, a number of elements of the software are identified that are not afforded copyright protection, such as those portions of software code that are in the public domain or those aspects of the software that are dictated by the external computing environment or simply by efficiency, as is the case where there is only one way, or a very limited number of ways, in which to program a particular idea. In this latter situation it is sometimes said that there is a "merger" of idea and expression; low-tech examples of this are the silhouettes of a man and a woman on the

---

165   *Whelan Associates, Inc. v. Jaslow Dental Laboratory, Inc.*, 797 F.2d 1222 (3d Cir. 1986) [*Whelan*].

166   *Gemologists*, above note 109.

167   *Computer Associates International, Inc. v. Altai, Inc.*, 982 F.2d 693 (2d Cir. 1992) [*Altai*].

respective washroom doors, as these symbols are classic examples of the merger of idea with expression. After applying the two steps of abstraction and filtration, the court is left with a smaller number of kernels of protectable software, which are then compared with the defendant's product to see if they have been copied.[168] This abstraction-filtration-comparison standard results in a lower level of copyright protection for software than resulted from the test articulated in the *Whelan* case.[169] The concept of filtering out unprotectable elements of a software program as part of the infringement analysis has been adopted in the important *Delrina* case in Canada.[170] After a lengthy review of the *Altai* case, the court concluded that whether or not the U.S. "abstraction-filtration-comparison" method should be followed by a Canadian judge, some filtering process should be undertaken under the Canadian *Copyright Act* as well, when separating protectable expression from unprotectable idea in a software case. In *Delrina*, as in the *Altai* case, there was no finding of infringement, the court having concluded that the significant similarities in the two programs were attributable largely to the fact that both programs had to correspond to the same external programming constraints given that they were both used to monitor the performance of a particular computer system.[171] In contrast, in the Canadian *Prism* case, while the *Altai* standard of infringement is preferred over that articulated in *Whelan*, infringement was found because the court concluded

---

168   Since the decision in *Altai*, some nuances have been added to the test by various U.S. circuit appellate courts. For example, in *Gates Rubber Company* v. *Bando Chemical Industries, Limited*, 9 F.3d 823 at 834 (10th Cir. 1993), the court, in a footnote, indicated that in some cases the order in which the components of the test are applied may be different; for example, it might be in a certain case that the comparison step should come before filtration as even unprotectable elements are useful to consider in carrying out the evidentiary analysis as to whether there has been copying.

169   Copyright infringement, however, will still be found in the United States under even the *Altai* standard if the two programs' similarities are not dictated by external constraints or the use of common programming techniques, but rather are attributable only to copying, as was the case in *CMAX/Cleveland, Inc.* v. *UCR, Inc.*, 804 F. Supp. 337 (M.D. Ga. 1992).

170   *Delrina*, above note 39. See also *Matrox*, above note 18, where the court reviews the *Whelan* and *Altai* decisions and decides to adopt the approach found in the latter case.

171   See also *Systèmes informatisés Solartronix* v. *Cégep de Jonquière* (1990), 38 C.P.R. (3d) 143 (Que. Sup. Ct.), where the defendant's program that automated the operation of a cement plant was found not to copy or plagiarize the plaintiff's program that performed the same function because the design and methodology of the two programs were based on factors common to cement plants, and therefore the court found it not surprising that the two programs were very similar.

that the similarities in the two programs were not driven by external constraints, but were simply the product of copying.[172]

The reduction of the scope of protection for software represented by the *Altai*, *Delrina*, and *Matrox* cases has a counterpart in the degree of protection afforded by copyright to a program's "user interface," which are the various aspects of the program's screen layout, including the use of particular words in menu commands. In the area of user interfaces, the highwater mark for U.S. copyright protection came in the *Softklone* case, in which the court determined that the particular words, such as "speed" and "data," used in a status screen were protected such that the defendant had to select alternative words in its functionally equivalent product.[173] A similar result was arrived at in the trial decisions in various cases brought by Lotus against other developers of spreadsheet programs who imitated the menu commands in the Lotus 1-2-3 product.[174] In the *Lotus* cases, the defendants felt it important to recreate the same "look and feel" of the plaintiff's products given the leading position in the marketplace of the Lotus products, and the need to be able to sell the defendants' products without having to retrain users. In an important reversal, the appeal court in the *Lotus* case denied protection for the user interface, concluding that the series of commands were a method of operation, and hence expressly precluded copyright protection under subsection 102(b) of the U.S. copyright law.[175] The First Circuit Appeals court in *Lotus* analogized the Lotus software's user interface to the symbols and words on the display panel of a videocassette recorder machine, another method of operation and system the court found to be incapable of protection under copyright law. Although the Canadian *Copyright Act* does not contain a provision equivalent to subsection 102(b) of the U.S. statute, the Canadian decision in *Moreau*[176] states that copyright does not extend to a "system or scheme or method for doing a particular thing," thus the door is open for a Canadian court to adopt

---

172   *Prism*, above note 52.

173   *Digital Communications Associates, Inc.* v. *Softklone Distributing Corporation*, 659 F. Supp. 449 (N.D. Ga. 1987).

174   *Paperback*, above note 8; *Lotus Development Corporation* v. *Borland International, Inc.*, 799 F. Supp. 203 (D. Mass. 1992), 831 F. Supp. 223 (D. Mass. 1993). Together with the cases referred to below in note 175, these cases are collectively referred to as the *Lotus* cases.

175   *Lotus Development Corporation* v. *Borland International, Inc.*, 49 F.3d 807 (1st Cir. 1995), aff'd 116 S.Ct. 804 (1996). The decision of the U.S. Court of Appeals for the First Circuit was affirmed by the U.S. Supreme Court on 16 January 1996 by a 4:4 deadlock vote; one Supreme Court justice had earlier recused himself, and upon such a tie, the lower court decision is affirmed.

176   *Moreau*, above note 69. See also *Hollinrake*, above note 69 at 427, which held that copyright does not protect "ideas, or schemes, or systems, or methods."

the First Circuit Appeals court's reasoning in *Lotus* in an appropriate Canadian case involving user interfaces.

4) Copyright Protection for Electronic Databases

Computers are able to collect, aggregate, process, store, and transmit huge volumes of data.[177] These technological and business trends have resulted in many compilers of facts, who traditionally made available the fruits of their effort in a paper-based directory (i.e., a telephone book or a business directory), now providing customers with two computer disks: one containing the raw data and one containing search software to access the data. It is clear that under copyright law the compiler has protection for the software contained on the latter disk. More problematic is the scope of protection for the data residing on the former disk; in other words, could the compiler use copyright to prevent someone from making unauthorized copies of the data? This question is emblematic of the second dynamic of computer law, namely, the elusive nature of information. In order to be protected under the *Copyright Act*, an electronic database would have to come within the *Act*'s definition of a *compilation*.[178] Interestingly, prior to 1994 the *Copyright Act* did not contain a definition of compilation, and it was left up to courts to determine what scope of protection would be provided for compilations of data and other works.[179] In the pre-1994 compi-

---

177   See section A(4), "Data and Databases," in chapter 1.

178   Subsection 5(1) of the *Copyright Act* provides protection to "every original literary, dramatic, musical and artistic work," and the definition of literary work in s. 2 includes "tables . . . and *compilations* of literary works" (italics added).

179   The following are the primary pre-1994 compilation cases, together with a description of the particular type of compilation that was protected: *Stevenson v. Crook*, [1938] 4 D.L.R. 294 (Ex. Ct.) — bridge tallies; *Deeks v. Wells*, [1931] 4 D.L.R. 533 (Ont. C.A.) — *Underwriters Survey Bureau Ltd. v. American Home Fire Ass'ce Co.*, [1939] 4 D.L.R. 89 (Ex. Ct.) — instruction manual; *National Film Board v. Bier* (1970), 63 C.P.R. 164 (Ex. Ct.) — glossary of terms; *British Columbia Jockey Club v. Standen* (1985), 8 C.P.R. (3d) 283 (B.C.C.A.) — horse racing form; *Horn Abbot Ltd. v. W.B. Coulter Sales Ltd.* (1984), 77 C.P.R. (2d) 145 (F.C.T.D.) — game of questions and answers; *Slumber-Magic Adjustable Bed Co. Ltd. v. Sleep-King Adjustable Bed Co. Ltd.* (1984), 3 C.P.R. (3d) 81 (B.C.S.C.) — advertising brochure; *École de conduite tecnic Aube Inc. v. 15098858 Québec Inc.* (1986), 12 C.I.P.R. 284 (Que. Sup. Ct.) — driver training manual; *L'Index téléphonique (N.L.) de notre localité v. Imprimerie Garceau Ltée* (1987), 18 C.I.P.R. 133 (Que. Sup. Ct.) — telephone directory; *Euclid Industries Can. Ltd. v. Reg Holloway Sales Inc.* (1989), 25 C.I.P.R. 290 (F.C.T.D.) — catalogues; *Éditions Hurtubise HMH Ltée v. Cégep André-Laurendeau* (1989), 24 C.I.P.R. 248 (Que. Sup. Ct.); *Caron v. Assoc. des Pompiers de Montréal Inc.* (1992), 42 C.P.R. (3d) 292 (F.C.T.D.) — charts in a calendar; *Pool v. Pawar* (1993), 50 C.P.R. (3d) 396 (B.C.S.C.) — foreclosure listings; *U & R Tax Services Ltd. v. H&R Block Canada Inc.* (1995), 62 C.P.R. (3d) 257 (F.C.T.D.) — an income tax form.

lation cases, Canadian courts applied a "sweat of the brow" approach and afforded copyright protection to compilers that expended either (a) intellectual effort, in the sense of selecting or arranging the material comprising the compilation, or (b) labour or menial effort in compiling the material. Unfortunately, the pre-1994 cases do not take pains to distinguish between these two types of effort, and regularly intersperse words such as *selection, skill, taste, judgment, thought,* and *arrangement*, which connote the intellectual activity of selection or arrangement, with words such as *work, industry,* and *labour*, which denote the task of physically compiling material. This distinction is important because since 1994 the *Copyright Act* has included the following definition of compilation: "'compilation' means (a) a work resulting from the selection or arrangement of literary, dramatic, musical, or artistic works or of parts thereof; or (b) a work resulting from the selection or arrangement of data."[180] Part (b) of this definition, which would apply to the raw data contained in electronic databases, is noteworthy because of its emphasis on "selection or arrangement" of data. Does this mean that since 1994 Parliament intended to no longer extend protection to compilers who expend effort in compiling data but who present it in a straightforward, unoriginal manner?

This is precisely the state of the law in the United States as a result of the *Feist* case, in which the U.S. Supreme Court held that copyright does not protect a white pages telephone directory because it consisted of facts presented in a completely ordinary, uncreative way.[181] Moreover, the court in *Feist*, clearly repudiating a line of case law based on the "sweat of the brow" approach that had developed in the United States, concluded that facts and raw data are not copyrightable in any event, even where they are arranged or selected in an original manner. Thus, in the United States copyright protection for factual compilations is quite thin, given that the second compiler can copy facts from even a compilation whose selection and arrangement is protected by copyright so long as the facts, as presented by the second comer, are selected or arranged differently.[182] The *Feist* decision makes extremely problematic the protection of certain electronic databases through copyright.[183]

---

180 *Copyright Act*, above note 40, s. 2.
181 *Feist Publications, Inc. v. Rural Telephone Service Co., Inc.*, 499 U.S. 340 (1991) [*Feist*].
182 There have been, however, a number of U.S. cases decided after *Feist* where paper-based directories have been protected under copyright because of the selection and arrangement of facts within them. See, for example, *CCC Information Services, Inc. v. Maclean Hunter Market Reports, Inc.*, 44 F.3d 61 (2d Cir. 1994). In this case the infringing work was resident in electronic form.
183 See John F. Hayden, "Copyright Protection of Computer Databases after *Feist*" (1991) 5 Harv. J.L. & Tech. 215.

In the most recent Canadian case to address the scope of protection for fact-intensive works, the trial court, after clearly being briefed on the point by both sides, declined to decide on the express question of whether to follow the reasoning in *Feist*.[184] Nonetheless, the decision, involving the scope of protection for headings and other materials in a yellow pages business directory, in many important respects resembles a Feistian analysis by not extending copyright to cover such elements of a yellow pages directory. Moreover, it should also be noted that in a leading Canadian copyright case involving software, *Feist* was cited for the proposition that an author's original literary work does not cover underlying facts.[185] As well, the CRTC has also taken a rather Feistian approach to the protection — or rather lack of protection — afforded basic telephone directory listing information.[186] Finally, it should also be pointed out that only two of the pre-1994 Canadian compilation cases involved fact-intensive works of the "data" variety; for the most part these cases would be ones that would fall into subsection 2(a) of the compilation definition. Thus, Canadian courts have simply not had a great deal of experience with fact-intensive, let alone data-related, compilations in the pre-1994 *Copyright Act* era, and this should make courts less inclined to maintain a sweat of the brow approach to protecting electronic databases in the face of a clear alternative in the *Feist* case.

Thus it came as no surprise that the Federal Court of Appeal in the *Tele-Direct* case,[187] in upholding the trial decision, went beyond the trial decision to expressly approve of the U.S. *Feist* approach to protecting compilations and to unequivocally jettison in Canada the sweat of the

---

184   *Tele-Direct (Publications) Inc.* v. *American Business Information Inc.* (1996), 27 B.L.R. (2d) 1 (F.C.T.D.). This decision was upheld by the Federal Court of Appeal, which latter court did expressly consider the *Feist* case: see below note 187.

185   *Prism*, above note 52.

186   Telecom Decision CRTC 92-1, *Bell Canada-Directory File Service*, (3 March 1992). In this decision the CRTC concluded at 8 that: "In the Commission's view, copyright could attach to a compilation of basic non-confidential listing information as a result of the sorting, arrangement or classification of that information. However, in the Commission's opinion, basic non-confidential listing information cannot attract a claim of copyright in and of itself. Thus, while it may be possible to claim copyright for a directory, either in hard copy or in electronic form, the raw listing information contained in the directory is not subject to being copyrighted." In a subsequent decision the CRTC seemed more ambivalent about the scope of copyright protection for such information: see Telecom Decision CRTC 95-3, *Provision of Directory Database Information and Real-Time Access to Directory Assistance Databases*, (8 March 1995).

187   *Tele-Direct (Publications) Inc.* v. *American Business Information, Inc.* (1997), 76 C.P.R. (3d) 296 (F.C.A.).

brow theory of copyright protection for databases and other fact-intensive works. The Federal Court of Appeal confirmed that some amount of creativity must exist for a creator to obtain copyright protection in a fact-intensive work, and that the in-column listings of a yellow pages directory were too obvious and commonplace to satisfy this test. The Canadian court, echoing the sentiments of the *Feist* case and its U.S. progeny, concluded that certain compilations of routine data are so mechanical as to be denied copyright protection.

Given the decision of the Federal Court of Appeal in the *Tele-Direct* case, it could be argued that too little protection is afforded compilers of fact-intensive works, particularly where they are provided to users in an electronic form. In this regard, it is interesting to note that the European Union has adopted a directive, which member states are required to implement into national law, that will offer specialized protection to databases.[188] The directive provides that copyright laws only protect databases where there is originality in the selection or arrangement of their contents. This approach follows *Feist*. On the other hand, the directive would establish a new form of right which protects the factual contents of the database. This *sui generis* right will prevent the unauthorized extraction of all or a substantial part of the contents of a database, and prevent such contents from being made available to the public. The new right would be shorter in duration than copyright — only fifteen years — though a new term would begin to run whenever the database is significantly changed. In light of the appellate decision in the *Tele-Direct* case, the adoption in Canada of a right of data extraction similar to the new right created by the European Union's database directive should be strongly considered, though it would be preferable if such a new right were adopted in the United States at the same time it were made law in Canada. In this regard it should be noted that a bill was introduced in the 104th U.S. Congress in 1996 that would have given protection to databases along the lines of the European directive, albeit the new right of extraction would have been for a period of twenty-five years (rather than fifteen years as under the European directive), but primarily because of intense opposition from a number of users and disseminators of online services, this bill was not enacted into

---

188   *Directive 96/9/EC of the European Parliament and of the Council of 11 March 1996 on the legal protection of databases.* This directive was required to be implemented into national law by the members of the European Union by 1 January 1998 and can be found in the *Official Journal of the European Communities* of 27/3/96 No. L77 at page 20 or at <http://www2.echo.lu/legal/en/ipr/database/ database.html>.

law.[189] Similarly, in December 1996, WIPO had proposed the adoption of an international treaty regarding the protection of databases together with two other proposed treaties (one dealing with copyright and the other with performers' rights), but again due to vociferous opposition only the latter two treaties were adopted and the database treaty was dropped.[190] Of course, it can be expected that database protection initiatives will appear again on the U.S. and WIPO agendas, and in Ottawa as well when the next round of amendments to the *Copyright Act* are contemplated. In the meantime, in the absence of intellectual property protection for the facts in a database, it may be possible, in appropriate circumstances, for creators and distributors of databases to protect their fact-intensive, information-based products by contract.[191]

5) Multimedia Works

The ability to digitize all the different traditional forms of copyright content and to fuse the resulting material into digital compilations presents copyright law with a number of challenges. Until recently, most copyright content was made available in a single format. A book was sold to the public on paper. Music was supplied on a vinyl record, or more recently on a cassette tape. In effect, content was presented to the public as one of the four categories of works recognized by the *Copyright Act*, namely, artistic, musical, dramatic, or literary works. There was some co-mingling of the categories — as when a movie contained a musical soundtrack — but not much. In the digital era, all this is changing rapidly. A current good example is the CD-ROM multimedia product that contains, on a single disk, text, photographs, music, animation, and video clips. Moreover, these different content elements can be altered and melded, so that the result is a seamless, single product rather than discreet portions of pre-existing content. One legal question that

---

189 *Database Investment and Intellectual Property Antipiracy Act of 1996*, H.R. 3531. See Julius J. Marke, "Database Protection Acts and the 105th Congress" *The New York Law Journal* (18 March 1997); also found on the Web at <http://www.ljx.com/copyright/0318 dbase.html.>.

190 See Pamela Samuelson, "Confab Clips Copyright Cartel: Big Media Beaten Back," *Wired*, March 1997 ["Big Media"], and John Browning, "Confab Clips Copyright Cartel: Africa 1, Hollywood 0," *Wired*, March 1997 ["Africa 1"]. Ostensibly another reason why the database treaty did not pass is the conflicting views of the Europeans and the Americans that the data extraction right should last fifteen and twenty-five years, respectively.

191 See section C(8), "Other Measures of Protection," in this chapter.

arises from such a CD-ROM product is how to categorize it under the *Copyright Act*'s four categories of works. Is it a literary, dramatic, artistic, or musical work? This can be an important question because while many of the *Copyright Act*'s rules apply to all these works in the same way, there are some differences in treatment depending on the nature of the work. To help resolve this problem, the 1994 amendments to the *Copyright Act* included a definition of compilation, the first part of which provides that a compilation means a work resulting from the selection or arrangement of literary, dramatic, musical, or artistic work or of parts thereof.[192] Equally important, the statute provides that where a work contains two or more of these elements, the work will be considered of the type whichever of which there is the most. Although this is helpful, it is not a self-defining concept in all cases. There are many CD-ROM products where it will not be a simple task to determine what type of copyright work it is. Accordingly, it can usefully be asked whether the distinctions in the *Copyright Act* between the treatment afforded different works is still sensible. Perhaps it is time to recognize that the artificial differences perpetuated in the *Copyright Act* are anachronistic and should be abolished. For example, why the compulsory licensing regime only applies to books and mechanical sound recordings is puzzling, when these have become intermingled in the marketplace with so many other types of media.

Another legal challenge posed by CD-ROM and other multimedia works is how difficult and time-consuming it is for a creator or distributor of such a work to obtain the permission from the holders of the copyright and other proprietary rights. For example, the publisher of the paper-based version of a book may not have the electronic rights to the book, in which case the creator of a CD-ROM product wishing to use all or part of the book would have to deal directly with the author or his or her estate. Similarly, whoever holds the copyright in a film — perhaps the film studio, director, or producer — may not have the electronic rights in the underlying book where the film is based on a story from a book. As well, the copyright in the soundtrack may be held by another entity. Or the actors may not have signed releases covering multimedia rights. In a similar vein, the publisher of a magazine that contains a photo usually does not have the copyright, let alone electronic rights, in the photo. And again, if there are people in the photo, releases should be obtained from them. Music rights are also complicated. First, there

---

192   See section C(4), "Copyright Protection for Electronic Databases," in this
      chapter.

is the need for a synchronization license if the music is to be used in conjunction with video or other images. Then, if the music is to be put on a separate, stand-alone soundtrack release, either on CD or cassette, a mechanical licence would also be required. And if use of a particular recording is required, then a further recording licence is required. Finally, if the resulting multimedia product were to be shown in public, then a performance licence would also be required. No wonder clearing the various rights for use of a work in a CD-ROM or other product, perhaps on the Internet, can be a fiendishly difficult exercise.

To assist in this process there are various collectives and rights administration groups that have been sanctioned and facilitated by the *Copyright Act*. Perhaps the best known is SOCAN (Society of Composers, Authors and Music Publishers, in Canada), which tracks the number of times certain songs are played, and then obtains payment from the radio stations and other broadcasters and distributes this money to the composers and performers.[193] Given that music can be transmitted over the Internet, SOCAN has proposed a tariff for musical works accessed over this medium.[194] As for synchronization rights, these can be cleared in Canada through the CMRRA (Canadian Musical Reproduction Rights Agency). Yet another copyright collective is CANCOPY, which administers the rights to photocopy pages of literary works. CANCOPY facilitates large users of photocopy materials, such as universities and governments, in reproducing such materials with the permission of the relevant authors/publishers. One current shortcoming of CANCOPY is that it has not yet obtained the electronic rights for most of the works it represents, and thus for these rights users must continue to go to individual authors or publishers, which is an extremely laborious process.

With these various copyright collectives as the precedential backdrop, several commentators have called upon the establishment of a similar rights clearance organization for multimedia works purposes. These proposed schemes would still require, however, voluntary partic-

---

193   For an explanation of how SOCAN's rates are set by the Copyright Board under the *Copyright Act*, see *SOCAN (Re)* (1991), 37 C.P.R. (3d) 385 (Copyright Board).

194   See proposed tariff No. 22 in *Transmission of Musical Works to Subscribers Via a Telecommunications Service Not Covered Under Tariff Nos. 16 or 17*, Canada Gazette, Supplement, Part I, 19 October 1996. This tariff is being opposed by Internet service providers who argue that the Internet is not a broadcast medium and therefore does not require a "per subscriber-type tariff"; rather, the Internet allows people to contract for the right to use intellectual property rights: see Canadian Association of Internet Providers, *Report on Political and Regulatory Activities for 1996-1997*, 23 April 1997, available at the CAIP website: <http://caip.ca/>.

ipation by the copyright holder; that is, they do not include a proposal for compulsory licensing of copyright works for use by others, as there currently exists for books after a period of time and for mechanical musical recordings at all times. Of course, a compulsory licence regime for multimedia works would raise numerous questions about the protection afforded the integrity of the copyright work through the exercise of moral rights, and much resistance to such a scheme could be expected from artists and their representative organizations.

6) Copyright and the Internet

Copyright owners view the Internet and the other networks encircling the globe with great hope and, at the same time, immense trepidation. The former sentiment derives from the Internet representing a new and extremely cost-efficient mechanism for distributing copyright content to vast numbers of users. Ironically, it is these same features that make the Internet the ultimate copyright infringement technology. Not only can the computers on the Internet reproduce copyright content at extremely low cost and without a degradation of quality, but also these unauthorized copies can be transmitted over the myriad of telecommunications networks that comprise the Internet — all in a matter of seconds. The Internet can be used in a number of other ways to reproduce and disseminate copyright works. There is, for instance, the phenomenon of fans of movies, television shows, rock bands, and other elements of modern culture who create websites using copyright material in the form of images, photos, and music without permission of the copyright owners.[195] All of the abovementioned technological facts have prompted some commentators to conclude that the Internet has sounded the death knell of copyright. For example, John Perry Barlow has argued that the copyright law system, which he believes is intrinsically connected to paper-based media, simply no longer works in a digital, networked environment.[196] Barlow does not believe incremental change in copyright law will do the trick; he advocates a wholesale jettisoning of the copyright system. In effect, Barlow would argue that the four dynamics of computer law — the rapid pace of technological change, the elusive nature of information, and the blurring of private/public and national/international — make an anachronism of copyright law. However, the rejoinder to Barlow, drawing on a highway analogy, would be

---

195   See Constance Sommer, "Hollywood Readies for Fight over Internet Ownership" *The [Toronto] Globe and Mail* (11 January 1997).

196   John Perry Barlow, "The Economy of Ideas: A Framework for Rethinking Patents and Copyrights in the Digital Age (Everything You Know about Intellectual Property is Wrong)," *Wired*, March 1994.

that it is precisely because automobiles can reach speeds of 200 kilometres an hour that we need speed limits. It is because the Internet permits copying and transmission capabilities never before witnessed that copyright law must rise to the new challenge.

In short, Barlow's exhortation that the Internet heralds the demise of copyright law is too extreme. Copyright law is flexible and resilient and very much able to adapt to technological challenges, just as it has over the last hundred years when confronted with new reproduction and transmission technologies — photographs, pianola rolls, sound recordings, broadcasting, cable transmissions, cassette recordings, and photocopies. Nonetheless, there are aspects of the Internet that will require careful thought and creative law reform from a copyright law perspective. One issue related to the mechanics of Internet transmission is that sending content in a digital format requires the making of at least one additional copy at the user's computer terminal, but often at an intermediate server and other computers as well. This presents an interesting dilemma. If someone in Vancouver buys an authorized copy of a book, this person may send this book to a friend in Halifax by courier or mail. If the person has an electronic version of the text of the book, the electronic version cannot be sent over the Internet without making a copy of it. Similarly, a person can today go into a bookstore or a library and browse through the books before deciding to buy or borrow one (and the principle noted above permits the library to lend out the book assuming the library bought an authorized copy of it in the first place). Such browsing in the case of a physical work like a book does not require a copy of the work to be made; but, in an electronic, online environment, it would entail making one or more copies of the digital-based work.

Issues such as these have prompted the American, and subsequently, the Canadian governments to appoint experts to consider whether the copyright laws of their respective countries need modification in light of the Internet.[197] The resulting study in the United

---

197   Governments outside of North America have also commissioned studies of the intellectual property and other questions related to the Internet. These studies include: Commission of the European Communities, *Copyright and Related Rights in the Information Society* (Luxembourg: Office for Official Publications of the European Communities, July 1995); Ministère de la Culture et de la Francophonie, *Industries Culturelles et Nouvelles Techniques* (Paris: 1994); Australia, Report of the Copyright Convergence Group, *Highways to Change: Copyright in the New Communications Environment* (August 1994). These studies are referred to in the study commissioned by the Canadian government of the state of the law in Canada regarding the liability of participants in the Internet content distribution chain for liability under copyright, trade-mark, criminal, privacy, and civil laws: see Michel Racicot *et al., The Cyberspace is Not a "No Law Land": A Study of the Issues of Liability for Content Circulating on the Internet* (Ottawa: Industry Canada, 1997).

States, the *Lehman Report*, advocated a number of changes to copyright law to bolster protection on the Internet, including: making clear that digital transmissions fall within the U.S. distribution right; abolishing the "first sale" rule for digital transmissions; eliminating "fair-use rights" where digital copies could be licensed; and promoting digital licensing and "metering" technologies by making it illegal to circumvent technological means used to prevent unauthorized copying.[198] The Canadian report echoed many of the positions in its American counterpart, deriving its basic outlook from the premise that any access of copyright content on the Internet requires the making of one or more additional copies on intermediate computers or on an end user's terminal, and that any such copying, to be legal, must be done with the permission of the copyright owner.[199] Hence, the Canadian report concludes that online browsing would constitute an infringement unless expressly authorized.[200] With respect to the liability of online service providers, the Canadian report recommends that BBS operators be liable for infringement and not be treated as common carriers, but that this rule should be subject to a defence if they did not have actual or constructive knowledge of the offending material and they acted reasonably to limit potential abuses.

The *Lehman Report* has been criticized for being overly concerned with the rights of copyright owners, while ignoring the legitimate

---

198   United States, Information Infrastructure Task Force, *Intellectual Property and the National Information Infrastructure: The Report of the Working Group on Intellectual Property Rights* (Bruce A. Lehman, Chairman) (September 1995).

199   Canada, Information Highway Advisory Council (IHAC), Copyright Subcommittee, *Copyright and the Information Highway: Final Report of the Copyright Subcommittee* (Ottawa: The Council, March 1995) available on the Web at <http://xinfo.ic.gc.ca/info-highway/reports/copyright/copy_e.txt>. The final phase 1 IHAC report, *Connection, Community, Content: The Challenge of the Information Highway: Final Report of the Information Highway Advisory Council* (Ottawa: The Council, 1995) incorporated most of the copyright subcommittee recommendations: <http://strategis.ic.gc.ca/IHAC> and also at <http://xinfo.ic.gc.ca/info-highway/final.report/eng/>.

200   The report of the Copyright Subcommittee referred to above in note 199 points out that the Canadian *Copyright Act* does not require the addition of an electronic transmission right because the statute already includes the right in para. 3(1)(f) "to transmit the work by telecommunication." Similarly, Canada does not require the "first sale" doctrine, as is the case in the United States, because the Canadian *Copyright Act* does not control distribution of copyright works, and hence a Canadian copyright owner ceases to be able to control distribution of the work once it is published with authorization, in effect giving rise to the same result as the first sale doctrine.

requirements of users, including individuals and libraries.[201] For example, critics of the *Lehman Report* suggest that consideration should be given to creating a first sale provision in the digital environment that would allow someone to transmit to someone else a digital work provided that upon completion of the transmission the originator deleted its copy of the work.[202] There is also a concern that technology tracking and metering devices will apply to all available copyright content, thereby effectively eliminating the fair use provisions of the *Copyright Act* in the digital Internet environment, a result that will cause serious hardship to innumerable users and destroy an important aspect of the copyright law regime.[203] These and other critical views are based on the premise that copyright law represents a delicate balance between the creators and users of copyright works, and that as each new reproduction and transmission technology comes to the fore this balance has to be carefully recalibrated to ensure that the fundamental objectives of the statute continue to be achieved. Those critical of the *Lehman Report* argue that by ignoring the needs of the first sale doctrine, browsing, and fair use/fair dealing, the prospect for a digital environment that is overly weighted to creators looms as a real threat to the preferred balance in copyright matters. It would appear these criticisms have not fallen on deaf ears. In the United States, a bill that was introduced in the 104th Congress in 1996 to implement many of the recommendations proposed by the *Lehman Report* was ultimately not approved by the U.S. Congress. Similarly, while the *1996 WIPO Copyright Treaty*[204] reflects some of the intellectual spade work of the *Lehman Report* by, for example, making it a copyright infringement in Article 8 merely to make available a work in an on-demand mode before any reproduction or communication of the work is made, several of the portions of the draft treaty that were particularly opposed by critics of the *Lehman Report* were removed during the vigorous negotiations in Geneva in December 1996.[205]

---

201   Pamela Samuelson, "The Copyright Grab," *Wired*, January 1996 ["Copyright Grab"].

202   See James V. Mahon, "A Commentary on Proposals for Copyright Protection on the National Information Infrastructure" (1996) 22 Rutgers Computer and Technology Law Journal 233.

203   Pamela Samuelson talks ominously about the transformation of the "information superhighway into a publisher-dominated toll road": Samuelson, "Copyright Grab," above note 201.

204   The *1996 WIPO Copyright Treaty* is available from the WIPO website: <http://www.wipo.org/>.

205   See Samuelson, "Big Media," above note 190; and Browning, "Africa 1," above note 190.

The recent amendments to the *Copyright Act* effected by Bill C-32[206] do not include Internet-related provisions, whether proposed by the Canadian Information Highway Advisory Council (IHAC) report or otherwise. There likely will be, at some point in the future, such amendments, and Canada has not yet implemented into domestic legislation the *1996 WIPO Copyright Treaty*. Until these events come to pass, however, it is useful to consider what activities on the Internet conducted by which parties might constitute an infringement of copyright under the current *Copyright Act*. In undertaking such an analysis, each fact situation must be considered on its own merits. There are so many different participants on the Internet, and they each engage in a multitude of activities. Fact-specific, function-oriented determinations must be made, and generalized phrases — such as "common carrier" or "bulletin board service provider — must be avoided, given that with the wide range of "push" and "pull" technologies available today, various types of end users and service providers can participate in a plethora of posting, transmission, and receipt activities. For example, the term *common carrier*, particularly in the context of a "common carrier defence for copyright infringement," is no longer useful. With respect to some of their activities the telephone companies (the traditional common carriers) do have knowledge (real and constructive based on negligence) and the ability to control passage of the content, while some non-telephone–company entities should be counted among common carriers for activities where they serve as passive conduits of transmission. The same point is made in this book in the discussions regarding intermediary liability under criminal law[207] and libel law.[208] It must be determined what knowledge the Internet participant had of the infringing or harmful activity, in terms of both actual knowledge and "constructive knowledge" through either negligence or related criminal law concepts. As well, it must be made clear what control the Internet participant could exercise over the offensive activity, involving either directly or indirectly its ongoing storage or electronic distribution.

The three rights in the *Copyright Act* most relevant to the Internet are the rights of reproduction, transmission to the public by telecommunication, and the secondary distribution rights. An end user that posts or initiates the transmission of content by sending an e-mail or putting content on a website will likely violate the reproduction right, and often the transmission and distribution rights as well. Thus, bulletin

---

206   See above note 41.
207   See section B(5)(b), "Intermediary Liability," in chapter 3.
208   See section C(1), "Cyber Libel," in chapter 6.

board operators on the Internet will be liable for copyright infringement when they make copies of software available to third parties via the bulletin board service.[209] Entities that make other copyright content available by means of websites and bulletin boards will also be liable.[210] If, however, the end user is small and relatively judgment-proof, as many are on the Internet, then a key question is when might larger, more solvent service providers also be liable for transmitting content that they did not initiate?

This question has been asked by courts in a number of copyright contexts involving a range of pre-Internet environments. The fact patterns are usually the same: the infringer is an individual of modest financial means who carries out or sets in motion the infringement and then disappears (or if caught is not worth suing). And so courts have turned their attention to others involved, directly or indirectly, in the infringing activity. Thus, in an American case involving bootleg musical recordings, the "bad guy" made the master bootleg recordings without paying relevant royalties, then effected distribution and marketing through a fulfilment house (which made, packaged, and mailed the records) and through radio stations and an advertising agency.[211] In this decision, the court dismissed the threshold claims of the three latter entities that they could not be liable; the court concluded that the excessively low sales price of the records was so suspiciously below the usual market price that they either deliberately closed their eyes or were recklessly indiffer-

---

209   See M. (J.P.), above note 57. See also "Computer Bulletin Board Raided as Companies Allege Software Piracy" *The Lawyers Weekly* (30 August 1996); and a press release of CAAST (the Canadian Alliance Against Software Theft) "Vancouver based Bulletin Board Faces Charges for Software Theft," dated 20 June 1994, announcing a raid by the RCMP against a Vancouver-based bulletin board operator that resulted in charges involving sixteen counts of copyright infringement for unauthorized software copying.

210   See *Playboy Enterprises Inc. v. Webbworld Inc.* (N.D. Texas, 27 June 1997), mentioned in *Computer & Online Industry Litigation Reporter*, 15 July 1997, at 24,433 where a judge found a website operator liable for illegally copying *Playboy's* adult photographs and assessing $310,000 in damages ($5,000 for each of the sixty-two photos). In an earlier case, *Playboy* brought suit against Event Horizons, a bulletin board operator that also scanned *Playboy* pictures, and settled for $500,000: see *Computer Industry Litigation Reporter*, 15 October 1992 at 15,710. Interestingly, this report of this case and settlement indicated that *Playboy* has also decided to sponsor its own electronic bulletin board system; thus, in 1992, one could ask whether Event Horizons did not in fact provide *Playboy* with valuable market testing services!

211   *Screen Gems-Columbia Music, Inc. v. Mark-FI Records, Inc.*, 256 F. Supp. 399 (S.D.N.Y. 1966).

ent to it. Going even further back in a number of U.S. cases, proprietors of dance halls were held to be liable for copyright infringements committed by the musical bands they hired, even where the musicians were independent contractors who selected the actual compositions played by them without any input from the dance hall owner.[212] A landlord, however was held not to be liable for copyright infringement committed by a tenant where the landlord had no power or control over the tenant and did not benefit financially beyond receipt of the usual rent.[213]

In the United States, several cases have addressed the issue of copyright infringement liability by third parties in an Internet context. In *Sega Enterprises Ltd.* v. *MAPHIA*, a BBS operator was held liable for soliciting users to upload video games for use by other subscribers of the service.[214] In this case, and others like it, the third party is not merely a passive conduit but rather actively encourages subscribers to disseminate bootleg copies. In the subsequent *Netcom* case, however, it was held that where an online service provider's computer merely copies content as part of the automatic and natural functioning of the Internet, the service provider will not be directly liable for infringement.[215] The *Netcom* court, however, concluded that the service provider may be liable under a theory of contributory infringement once the service provider is put on notice of the existence of the infringing material on the service provider's computer. These cases are of limited jurisprudential value in Canada, given that Canadian copyright law does not have a doctrine of contributory infringement. In pre-Internet cases, the question has arisen whether the supplier of equipment, services, or facilities can infringe the right to authorize the exercise of the reproduction and other substantive rights in the *Copyright Act*.[216] In these cases, suppliers

---

212   *Irving Berlin, Inc.* v. *Daigle*, 26 F.2d 149 (E.D. La. 1928). For a similar result in Canada, see *Canadian Performing Right Society Ltd.* v. *Canadian National Exhibition Assn.*, [1938] 2 D.L.R. 621 (Ont. S.C.).

213   *Deutsch* v. *Arnold*, 98 F.2d 686 (2d Cir. 1938). Similarly, in Canada in *de Tervagne* v. *Beloeil (Town)* (1993), 50 C.P.R. (3d) 419 (F.C.T.D.) [*de Tervagne*], a municipality and a cultural centre were not liable when they merely rented a hall to the infringer.

214   857 F. Supp. 679 (N.D. Cal. 1994). See also *Playboy Enterprises, Inc.* v. *Frena*, 839 F. Supp. 1552 (M.D. Fla. 1993) [*Frena*], where a BBS operator was found responsible for facilitating the distribution of unauthorized copies of content over the BBS.

215   *Religious Technology Center* v. *Netcom On-Line Communication Services, Inc.*, 907 F. Supp. 1361 (N.D. Cal. 1995).

216   See, for example, *de Tervagne*, above note 213; and *Vigneux* v. *Canadian Performing Right Society Ltd.* (1945), 4 C.P.R. 65 (P.C.). See also *CBS Songs Ltd.* v. *Amstrad Consumer Electronics plc.*, [1988] 2 All E.R. 484 (H.L.).

of equipment and related items have not been found liable in situations where they do not exercise effective ongoing control of the equipment in a manner sufficient to influence the use to which the equipment is put by its immediate user (i.e., the principal infringer). Moreover, if the equipment supplier were to have such control, and the commensurate knowledge, then in Canada the basis for liability would not likely be the authorization right, but rather by finding the equipment supplier a co-infringer in its own right.

In some situations, the service provider may be able to argue certain defences available under the *Copyright Act* or otherwise. In the case of the transmission right, the question can arise as to who is the "public" in the context of the Internet because the transmission right applies only to "transmissions by telecommunication to the public." This issue raises squarely the third dynamic of computer law, namely, the blurring of private/public. In this regard, one Canadian decision took the position that radio or television broadcasts are not performances in public when received in private homes.[217] A more recent decision expresses the better view that a broadcasting signal beamed into private homes either off air or over cable transmission is to the public, given that it is much more in keeping with the plain and usual meaning of the words "in public," namely, "openly, without concealment and to the knowledge of all."[218] Moreover, there is authority in the United Kingdom for the proposition that even a part of the public, such as a group or club, can constitute the public.[219] Under such an approach the concept of "private" is essentially limited to activities that take place wholly within the confines of a private dwelling house for the occupants of such house and their relatives and close friends. A not dissimilar concept of public can be derived from the criminal cases referred to in section B(6), "Illegal Speech," in chapter 3, with perhaps the added nuance that a domestic unit can retain its quality of privateness even if it undertakes an activity outside of the home (i.e., there can be a private showing of a movie in a community hall normally open to the public where only members of a family and their private invitees have access to the hall). Following this line of reasoning, it may be possible to have circumstances on the Internet where the concept of "private" is recreated in an electronic, networked environment, such as through the transmission of material to a

---

217   *Canadian Admiral*, above note 44.

218   *Canadian Cable Television Assn. v. Canada (Copyright Board)* (1993), 46 C.P.R. (3d) 359 at 370 (F.C.A.).

219   *Jennings v. Stephens*, [1936] 1 All E.R. 409 (C.A.). See also *R. v. Continental Cablevision Inc.* (1974), 5 O.R. (2d) 523 (Prov. Ct.).

small e-mail list of family members who otherwise meet the necessary criteria of the term as it is understood in a physical, pre-Internet context. In other words, the law should countenance a degree of privateness on the Internet where the functional rationales for such a state are duplicated in an Internet environment (i.e., the transmission is by a non-commercial entity to a reasonable number of relatives or acquaintances without charge such that it does not take away sales of copies of the relevant work by the copyright holder, etc.).[220] Support for this position can be found in a case that held that the transmissions of programs from a television network head office to its affiliates did not constitute a communication to the public.[221]

Also with respect to the transmission right, section 3(1.3) of the *Copyright Act* provides: "For the purpose of paragraph [3](1)(f), a person whose only act in respect of the communication of a work to the public consists of providing the means of telecommunication necessary for another person to so communicate the work does not communicate that work to the public." This exemption would apply, for example, where the service provider merely transmitted the content between two other participants in the Internet chain and without making a further copy of it in the process of transmission. It is not yet clear, however, how courts will approach this provision, and certain other sections of the *Copyright Act*, in light of the Internet activity known as "caching." So-called "local caching" occurs when the content of a website is stored on a personal computer of an Internet user to get quicker access to the site. "Proxy caching" is essentially the same process, but is done by an Internet service provider. All caching consists of the making of a copy and therefore is arguably prohibited by the *Copyright Act*, unless the service provider can support a defence along the lines of "implied consent." The likelihood of success of such an argument is diminished in light of the decision in *Bishop* v. *Stevens*, where the Supreme Court of Canada concluded that a broadcaster's right to broadcast a work was not broad enough to permit a recording of the work, even though the recording was an ephemeral recording used only in the broadcasting of the work.[222] In this case, the court noted that there are complex issues bound up in the question of ephemeral recording rights for broadcasters, and that Parliament, rather than the courts, should sort these out. Similarly, caching raises a series of issues for content providers, including quality

---

220 See section B(6), "Illegal Speech," in chapter 3.
221 *CTV Television Network Ltd.* v. *Canada (Copyright Board)* (1993), 99 D.L.R. (4th) 216 (F.C.A.).
222 [1990] 2 S.C.R. 467.

control questions relating to keeping the website (and all its cached versions) up to date, as well as a host of economic issues that approximate, in some respects, the debate in Canada almost a decade ago regarding the payment of royalties by cable companies for the retransmission of distant signals. Internet service providers will argue, however, that caching is simply part and parcel of the technological structure of the Internet. Parliament would do well to address this contentious issue when it entertains the next set of amendments to the *Copyright Act*.

7) Trade-marks and the Internet

When a customer walks into a bank branch, she will be confronted, and comforted, by various items of proof that indicate she is dealing with a particular financial institution. In cyberspace, there are no physical storefronts or buildings to provide authentication to the consumer. Recreating such a sense of security is difficult in an online environment such as the Internet (though the use of passwords and encryption can go a long way in certain electronic circumstances). Hence, trade-marks are important to designate sources of origin and ensure quality control on the global Internet. Moreover, improper use of trade-marks can cause serious confusion and inefficiency in the international electronic marketplace.

A second important aspect of trade-marks on the Internet relates to the domain names that are used as addresses in cyberspace. The domain name of one entity, such as <Stellar> in the full international top-level domain name <Stellar.com>, can conflict with a registered or even unregistered trade-mark of another entity, again leading to possible confusion and dispute in an online environment. In Canada, whether one party's use of a trade-mark in an electronic environment infringes another party's trade-mark — on a Web page or in a domain name — will generally turn on whether trade-mark use is being made of the trade-mark. Such trade-mark use will often be made out where the trade-mark is used in respect of services, as the Canadian *Trade-Marks Act* provides that advertising constitutes such use in respect of services. A liability finding is also likely where digital-based goods, such as software or other information-based assets, are being supplied directly from the website, inasmuch as trade-mark use in respect of goods requires the use to be made at the time of transfer of their title or possession. Thus, liability would be harder to prove where the trade-mark appears in respect of goods to be supplied at a later date. Nevertheless, if the use of the trade-mark in a website or in a domain name is such as to depreciate or dilute the goodwill in a trade-mark, then it is possible to find liability even if goods and services are not being marketed from the site.

With respect to the trade-mark enforcement question, although no cases have yet been reported in Canada involving the substantive merits between a holder of a registered trade-mark and an alleged infringer of the trade-mark in an Internet environment, in one case the court held that the defendant's domain name "pei.net" was not confusing with, and therefore should be allowed to coexist with, the plaintiff's domain name "PEINET".[223] This is a surprising decision, and possibly was influenced by the fact that the defendant had agreed to change his domain name; there is also an intimation in the decision that the court may not have been adequately briefed on the issues, thus contributing to the unusual finding. In the United States, a number of courts have found identical domain names to be infringing of previously registered trade-marks. Illustrative of these cases is a pair brought against an entity that was in the business of registering a number of domain names (including air-canada.com, eddiebauer.com, and yankeestadium.com) in the hopes of selling them to business users of such names at a subsequent date for a tidy profit. Thus, in *Panavision International, L.P.* v. *Toeppen*, the plaintiff owned the registered trade-mark "Panavision" and "Panaflex" for motion picture cameras, but the defendant registered the domain names "panavision.com" and "panaflex.com".[224] Similarly, in *Intermatic Incorporated* v. *Toeppen*, the defendant's only intended use for the domain name "intermatic.com" was to eventually sell it to the plaintiff for a healthy profit.[225] In this case, however, the court found for the plaintiff under trade-mark dilution laws and ordered the defendant to cease use of the domain names in issue. The court in the *Intermatic* case noted that some commentators take a dim view of "cybersquatters,"[226] the name given to those who hoard domain names as the defendant did; however, the court also made the point that "[s]peculation and arbitrage have a long history in this country."[227] A similar result to that in the *Intermatic* case was achieved in a case where the defendant used the problematic

223   *PEINET Inc.* v. *O'Brien* (1995), 61 C.P.R. (3d) 334 (P.E.I. S.C.T.D.). See also *ITV*, above note 103, for a Canadian interlocutory injunction decision involving a registered trade-mark and a domain name.

224   938 F. Supp. 616 (C.D. Cal. 1996) [*Panavision*].

225   7 Computer Cases (CCH) ¶47,570 at 69,470 (E.D. Ill. 1996) [*Intermatic*].

226   *Ibid.* at 69,474.

227   *Ibid.* at 69,475. See also Patrick Brethour, "Firms Cash in on Web Addresses" *The [Toronto] Globe and Mail* (4 December 1996). In effect, wherever markets create get-rich-quick opportunities, it is to be expected that legal friction will follow: Elizabeth Raymer, "Battles over Domain Names on the Rise" *The Lawyers Weekly* (21 February 1997). See also Paul M. Eng, "Get Your Hands Off My .COM," *Business Week*, 28 July 1997.

trade-mark in a *bona fide* business. In *Toys "R" Us* v. *Akkaoui*, an injunction was granted against a sex website operated under "Adults 'R' Us" on the basis that such use dilutes the value of the plaintiff's registered trade-mark.[228] This U.S. theory is similar to the depreciation of goodwill cause of action provided in the Canadian *Trade-Marks Act* based on the dilution negatively affecting the name and reputation of the holder of the registered trade-mark and its ability to use it.[229] Also in the United States, outside the context of domain name-related disputes, it should be noted that a bulletin board service operator was found liable for trade-mark dilution for facilitating use of the plaintiff's registered trade-mark, thereby illustrating that third parties can also be visited with liability in appropriate circumstances.[230] A similar result could be expected in Canada under appropriate facts if the third party had knowledge of the infringing activity and could have taken steps to curtail it.

The domain name-related cases noted in the previous paragraph illustrate that conflicts can arise on the Internet by virtue of the manner in which domain names are assigned. In Canada, the ".ca" domain names have been administered in a fashion that takes some cognizance of whether the proposed registrant owns a registered Canadian trademark, and so there are not nearly the same number of disputes in Canada as in the United States, where InterNIC (the Internet Network Information Center established by the National Science Foundation) has delegated the administration of the popular ".com" domain names to Network Solutions, Inc. (NSI). In the early days of commercial use of the Internet, NSI simply distributed domain names on a first come, first served basis without any regard to ownership of related U.S. or foreign registered trade-marks. Now, NSI requires applicants to certify that to their knowledge the use of the proposed domain name does not violate rights granted under trade-mark or other statutes. As well, NSI has instituted a domain name dispute policy under which, among other things, a domain name registrant must relinquish the rights in the registration if another party's trade-mark registration pre-dates the domain name registration. Notwithstanding these more recent policies, several problems still bedevil the domain name registration pro-

---

228   40 U.S.P.Q. 2d 1836 (N.D. Cal. 1996).

229   See also *Inset Systems, Inc.* v. *Instruction Set, Inc.*, 937 F. Supp. 161 (D. Conn. 1996); and *Bensusan Restaurant Corporation* v. *King*, 937 F. Supp. 295 (S.D.N.Y. 1996), aff'd 126 F. 3d 25 (2d Cir. 1997) for examples of owners of registered trade-marks clashing with non-cybersquatter users of conflicting domain names; these cases are discussed in section C(2), "Jurisdiction," in chapter 6.

230   *Frena*, above note 214.

cess. One is a function of the fact that there can only be one registration for, say, "Stellar.com", even though "Stellar Books" and "Stellar Financial", to use fictitious examples, and possibly a number of other companies using "Stellar" as a trade-mark, use the trade-mark for their respective goods or services; that is, there can be, and often are, multiple registrations of trade-marks in the same country so long as they relate to uses in different, non-overlapping channels of business. In this sense, the Internet domain naming system is not as robust as the trade-mark system because the domain name, in addition to serving as a marketing vehicle like a trade-mark, also plays the key function of being an address.[231] In other words, the Internet domain naming system has created, in its present guise, too much scarcity, to put the issue in terms of the analysis set out in section A, "The Economics of Information," in this chapter. By the same token, however, although only one "Stellar" can exist on the ".com" registry, another "Stellar" can be registered under the Canadian registry of ".ca", and similarly in other national registries around the world, even for the same types of goods and services. In this sense, the international domain naming system does not create enough scarcity.

The Internet trade-mark and domain name problems, particularly in the context of national trade-mark registration regimes, have precursors in the pre-Internet era. For example, in the *Vanity Fair* case, a U.S. court had to wrestle with the Canadian retailer and a U.S. clothing manufacturer, each owning trade-mark registrations for their respective countries and coming into conflict when they made crossborder sales and distributions of catalogues.[232] In other words, the increase in international trade in goods over the decades has pointed out the shortcomings of national-based trade-mark registration regimes. But, given the fourth dynamic of computer law — namely, the blurring of national/international — what was an inconvenience in the physical world has become a major deficiency in the Internet system where success depends on the ability to connect users across borders. Accordingly, numerous initiatives are under way to study and alleviate the problems associated with the international Internet domain name system. For

---

231 For example, the domain name "whitehouse.org" is the mnemonic form for the following digital address: 198.137.240.91. Apparently, the Professional Golfers Association of America (whose acronym is "pga") paid $25,000 to the Potato Growers Association of Alberta (whose acronym is also "pga") for the name "pga.com". Whether this is true or merely apocryphal, it illustrates the limitations of the domain naming system.

232 *Vanity Fair*, above note 126.

example, a WIPO group is studying the problem,[233] and an international *ad hoc* group appointed by a number of international organizations has produced a report and agreement addressing a few aspects of the problem.[234] The various solutions proposed include expanding the number of top-level domains, expanding domain names themselves to accommodate trade-mark and country references, creation of single global databases and directories to assist in the screening and selection of domain names and trade-marks, and even a proposal for a *sui generis* system of intellectual property protection for domain names. Whichever of these solutions, or combinations of them, come to be widely accepted by the Internet community, it is clear that only through a coordinated, fully international response will the pressing Internet-related trade-mark issues be settled.

8) Other Measures of Protection

A creator or owner of information-based assets can look to three means to protect them: intellectual property legal regimes; contract, whereby a user of the asset agrees not to make certain use of the asset; and technology, by which the owner of the asset, through technical means, restricts what users can do with the asset.

It should be noted that within the intellectual property area new rights can be created from time to time, typically by the legislative branch, as when the European directive on databases created the right of data extraction for a fifteen-year term. Such a new right, however, can also be created by judges exercising their prerogative under the common law, as exemplified in the famous *INS* case in the United States.[235] In this decision, the court created a "quasi-property" right in "hot news" when it prevented the defendant news wire service from transmitting to its subscribers news stories that it learned of by reading the newspapers that used the plaintiff's news wire service. The majority of the court concluded there is no copyright in news, but felt it necessary to give a remedy to the plaintiff, given that the defendant:

---

233   See the memoranda prepared by WIPO entitled *Issues Relating to Trademarks and Internet Domain Names* prepared for the consultative meetings on trade-marks and Internet domain names held in May 1997, at<http://www.wipo.org/>.

234   See the *Final Report of the International Ad Hoc Committee: Recommendations for Administration and Management of gTLDs*, 4 February 1997, and the related *Establishment of a Memorandum of Understanding on the Generic Top Level Domain Name Space of the Internet Domain Name System*, 28 February 1997, both available at <http://www.iahc.org/>.

235   *International News Service v. Associated Press*, 248 U.S. 215 (2d Cir. 1918) [*INS*].

admits that it is taking material that has been acquired by complainant as the result of organization and the expenditure of labor, skill, and money, and which is salable by complainant for money, and that defendant in appropriating it and selling it as its own is endeavoring to reap where it has not sown, and by disposing of it to newspapers that are competitors of complainant's members is appropriating to itself the harvest of those who have sown. Stripped of all disguises, the process amounts to an unauthorized interference with the normal operation of complainant's legitimate business precisely at the point where the profit is to be reaped, in order to divert a material portion of the profit from those who have earned it to those who have not; with special advantage to defendant in the competition because of the fact that it is not burdened with any part of the expense of gathering the news. The transaction speaks for itself, and a court of equity ought not to hesitate long in characterizing it as unfair competition in business.[236]

A recent decision in the United States stated that the "hot news" misappropriation doctrine can be invoked when: the plaintiff expends resources generating or collecting information; the value of the information is time-sensitive; the defendant's use of the information constitutes free riding on the plaintiff's costly efforts; the defendant's use is in direct competition with the product offered by the plaintiff; and this ability to free ride reduces the incentive to produce the product or service such that its continued existence may be threatened.[237] Thus, in the INS case, the court concluded that if the plaintiff collector of news was not protected, they would cease to collect it, to the detriment of the news-reading public.

Justice Brandeis registered a strong dissent in the INS case, largely on the basis of a review of the previous British cases that, Brandeis concluded, did not afford protection for a quasi-property right in information outside of the known parameters of copyright and the other intellectual property regimes.[238] Brandeis was of the view that:

---

236   *Ibid.* at 239–40.

237   *National Basketball Association* v. *Motorola, Inc.*, 105 F.3d 841 (2d Cir. 1997) [*Basketball*].

238   For example, in *INS*, above note 235, Justice Brandeis at 255 cited *Sports and General Press Agency, Limited* v. *"Our Dogs" Publishing Company, Limited*, [1916] 2 K.B. 880, where the court held that the "official photographer" of a dog show could not prohibit others from making and publishing photos of the show where there was no condition to entry to the show not to take photographs. The court added that even if there were such a condition on entry, it would not restrict someone who, from a high roof, could take photos without buying a ticket to the show; that is, the plaintiff would have had to have built a high wall if it wanted to keep out unwanted photographers.

The general rule of law is, that the noblest of human productions
— knowledge, truths ascertained, conceptions, and ideas —
become, after voluntary communication to others, free as the air to
common use.[239]

Brandeis was not blind to the free-rider problem encountered by the
plaintiff; he simply thought that a common law creation of a property
right in news was a dangerous remedy that did not take into account all
the relevant factors. Thus, Brandeis thought the legislature was the
appropriate place to consider such issues as: If a property right is
extended to the plaintiff, what happens to the newspapers dependent on
the defendant? Is the plaintiff required to give them access to the news
wire service at a reasonable price? Should the property right sound in
damages alone, or should injunctive relief be available? Brandeis
believed it was dangerous for the court to venture into these areas:

> The injustice of [the defendant's] action is obvious. But to give relief
> against it would involve more than the application of existing rules
> of law to new facts. It would require the making of a new rule in anal-
> ogy to existing ones. The unwritten law possesses capacity for
> growth; and has often satisfied new demands for justice by invoking
> analogies or by expanding a rule or principle. This process has been
> in the main wisely applied and should not be discontinued. Where
> the problem is relatively simple, as it is apt to be when private inter-
> ests only are involved, it generally proves adequate. But with the
> increasing complexity of society, the public interest tends to become
> omnipresent; and the problems presented by new demands for justice
> cease to be simple. Then the creation or recognition by courts of a
> new private right may work serious injury to the general public,
> unless the boundaries of the right are definitely established and
> wisely guarded. In order to reconcile the new private right with the
> public interest, it may be necessary to prescribe limitations and rules
> for its enjoyment; and also to provide administrative machinery for
> enforcing the rules. It is largely for this reason that, in the effort to
> meet the many new demands for justice incident to a rapidly chang-
> ing civilization, resort to legislation has latterly been had with
> increasing frequency.[240]

---

239   *INS*, above note 235 at 250.
240   *Ibid.* at 262.

The admonition of the majority judgment in *INS* that it was wrong, and constituted "unfair competition," for the defendant to "reap where it had not sown," has become a very difficult test to operationalize in subsequent cases because it just begs the questions: what was sown, what was reaped, and on what basis should the decision be made to protect any particular element of what was sown. Thus, while in the United States a number of cases have found protection for a plaintiff on the basis of *INS*, others have declined. For example, in one case, the court granted protection to a person that recorded and sold copies of a tape of animal sounds used by hunters and photographers to attract animals when the defendant copied these sounds for a competing product.[241] By contrast, in a recent case the National Basketball Association was unsuccessful in using the *INS* doctrine against the defendants who operated a pager service that provided subscribers with simultaneous key data about NBA basketball games by utilizing modern information processing and communications.[242] The defendants' staff watched telecasts of the games and transmitted the facts of the game to subscribers by means of the pagers. As in the *INS* and other related cases, there was no violation of copyright because only facts were being disseminated, and there is no copyright in the underlying facts. The appellate court in the *Basketball* case, however, concluded that the *INS* doctrine did not apply because at the time the NBA did not have a service competitive with that of the defendants. Even if the NBA did, the court stated, it would still not apply the *INS* case so long as the defendants continued to collect the facts as they had done previously and did not derive them from the NBA pager service.

The American *INS* doctrine of "hot news quasi-property" has not been welcomed into Commonwealth jurisdictions. Juxtaposed against the *INS* case, for example, is the *Victoria Park Raceway* decision of Australia's highest court.[243] In this case, the operator of a horse racing track wanted to prevent a radio station from broadcasting coverage of the horse races. A platform had been built by the radio station adjacent to the horse track for just such purpose. The court considered the *INS* decision, but refused to adopt the approach of the majority, opting instead for reasoning that approximated closely the Brandeis dissent, which the

---

241   *United States Sporting Products, Inc.* v. *Johnny Stewart Game Calls, Inc.*, 865 S.W.2d 214 (Tex. App. 1993).

242   *Basketball*, above note 237.

243   *Victoria Park Racing and Recreation Grounds Company Limited* v. *Taylor* (1937), 58 C.L.R. 479 (Austl. H.C.). [*Victoria Park Raceway*].

court stated represented the "English view."[244] The approach in *Victoria Park Raceway* was reconfirmed in Australia in a decision almost fifty years later, in which the High Court of Australia unequivocally stated that the doctrine of misappropriation of information in which someone has a quasi-property right is simply not a part of Australian law.[245] It should be noted, however, that the court in *Victoria Park Raceway* stated that if the plaintiff did not want the defendant seeing what went on on its land, it should build a higher fence. Similarly, the court also noted that had the broadcasts originated from within the race track from patrons who were granted entry to it, it would have been open for the plaintiff to impose a condition on the entry of such persons that they not communicate to anyone outside the race track the knowledge they obtained inside it, and such a covenant could be enforced against both the patron as well as any person who induces the patron to breach this contract. In support of this proposition the court cited one of the *Exchange Telegraph* cases.[246]

The latter points raised by the court in *Victoria Park Raceway* illustrate the ability of creators and owners of information-based assets to protect them through contractual means in certain circumstances. An *Exchange Telegraph* case a year before the one cited by the Australian court gives a good example.[247] In this case the London Stock Exchange had given to the plaintiff the exclusive right to disseminate the stock ticker and other time-sensitive information related to the activities of the stock exchange, subject to the condition that it not be provided to certain brokers. The plaintiff, therefore, in turn made the financial information available to subscribers only on the basis of a written con-

---

244 In refusing to accede to the argument that the races should be protected as quasi-property given the enterprise and labour of the plaintiffs in establishing the race course and conducting the races, the court in *Victoria Park Raceway*, above note 243, stated at 509:

[C]ourts of equity have not in British jurisdictions thrown the protection of an injunction around all the intangible elements of value, that is, value in exchange, which may flow from the exercise by an individual of his powers or resources whether in the organization of a business or undertaking or the use of ingenuity, knowledge, skill or labour. This is sufficiently evidenced by the history of the law of copyright and by the fact that the exclusive right to invention, trade marks, designs, trade name and reputation are dealt with in English law as special heads of protected interests and not under a wide generalization.

245 *Moorgate Tobacco Co. Ltd.* v. *Philip Morris Ltd.* (1984), 56 A.L.R. 193 (Austl. H.C.).

246 *Exchange Telegraph Company Limited* v. *Central News, Limited*, [1897] 2 Ch. 48. See also *Exchange Telegraph Company Limited* v. *Giulianotti*, [1959] Scots Law Times 293 (O.H.).

247 *Exchange Telegraph Company* v. *Gregory & Co.*, [1896] 1 Q.B. 147.

tract that prohibited the subscriber from conveying the information to any third party. The defendant induced a subscriber to breach this restriction so that it could obtain the information, and the court upheld an injunction issued against the defendant prohibiting such conduct. In the subsequent *Exchange Telegraph* case cited in *Victoria Park Raceway* involving the same plaintiff's horse racing information, a similar result was achieved even in circumstances where the race results transmitted to subscribers had already become relatively widely available through other means.

These *Exchange Telegraph* cases stand for the proposition that disseminators of information can utilize contractual means to limit the use and further distribution or disclosure of that information.[248] The usefulness of these cases may also be enhanced in a mass market environment if Canadian courts adopt the reasoning of a recent U.S. case in upholding so-called shrinkwrap licences.[249] In the *Exchange Telegraph* cases, the courts imply that in addition to the plaintiff protecting its information-based assets through contract, it could also protect them under a common law property right prior to their publication, after which they would be protected by copyright. Although the courts in these cases did not use the now familiar terms of *trade secret* or *confidential information*, in all likelihood these are the kinds of information-based legal rights they were defining, rather than the broader property right referred to in the majority in *INS*. Confirmation of this view can be seen in the references in the *Stewart*[250] decisions at both the Ontario Court of Appeal and the Supreme Court of Canada to the *Exchange Telegraph* cases as authority for a property-based trade secret right.

Where the owner of an information-based asset is unable to bring the item under one or another intellectual property law regime, or where use of a contract is awkward or impractical, or where an intellectual property or contract is available but the owner is concerned about the practical ability to enforce either, the owner may turn to one of several

---

248   A similar result was obtained in a U.S. Supreme Court case, *Board of Trade of the City of Chicago v. Christie Grain and Stock Company,* 198 U.S. 236 (1905), where the distribution of commodity price quotes was protected by contract.

249   *ProCD, Incorporated v. Zeidenberg,* 86 F.3d 1447 (7th Cir. 1996). For a discussion of this case and shrinkwrap licences, see section C(2), "Shrinkwrap Licences," in chapter 5.

250   *R. v. Stewart* (1983), 5 C.C.C. (3d) 481 (Ont. C.A.), rev'd (1988), 41 C.C.C. (3d) 481 (S.C.C.). This property-based approach has been superseded by understanding trade secrecy/breach of confidence protection in Canada as being a *sui generis* form of protection, as noted in the *LAC Minerals* case discussed in section B(1), "Trade Secrets/Breach of Confidence," in this chapter.

technical devices to thwart the unauthorized use or copying of the asset. For some time, copy protect technology has been available for use on diskettes in order to prohibit the making of extra copies of mass marketed software, but the inconvenience of these devices largely stunted their acceptance and widespread use by software suppliers. With respect to the transmission of information in the broadcasting environment, encoding techniques are used to scramble signals so that only paying subscribers can access the broadcast. And for shipping digital assets over the Internet, various technological mechanisms are being considered and tested to code and tag specific digital documents or files with so-called rights management information (information that identifies the work, the owner, and author of it and information about the terms and conditions of its use) so that use of the work can be limited in accordance with the respective payment made by the user.[251] The law supports these technical efforts in several ways. For example, the *Radio-communication Act*[252] makes it an offence for anyone but an authorized subscriber to decode encrypted subscription programming signals or to retransmit such illegally obtained signals.[253] In a similar vein, the U.S. *Lehman Report* on the Internet recommended the establishment of civil and criminal penalties for removing copyright management information contained in digital files. While this recommendation has not yet been implemented into U.S. law, the *1996 WIPO Copyright Treaty* requires signatory countries to provide adequate and effective legal remedies against people removing or altering any electronic rights management information or from distributing works where such information has been removed.

9) Internet Linking and Framing

To end this survey of contentious intellectual property issues, it is fitting to discuss two practices that have developed on the Internet, namely, linking and framing, as these have given rise to several legal

---

251   See, for example, Art Kramer, "Web Becoming World's Biggest Juke Box" *The [Toronto] Globe and Mail* (2 August 1997).

252   R.S.C. 1985, Chap. R-2, as amended.

253   This and related provisions in the *Radiocommunication Act* have been used in several cases against entities importing into Canada devices for descrambling U.S. direct to home satellite television services: *Expressvu Inc. v. NII Norsat International Inc.*, [1997] F.C.J. No. 1004 (T.D.) (QL), aff'd [1997] F.C.J. No. 1563 (C.A.) (QL); *R. v. Knibb* (1997), 198 A.R. 161 (Prov. Ct.); but see also *R. v. Ereiser* (1997), 156 Sask. R. 71 (Q.B.) for a contrary view.

proceedings that may have an impact on further development of the Internet. As discussed in section A(6), "The Internet," in chapter 1, linking is a core feature of the Internet, perhaps its single most important dimension in terms of attracting millions upon millions of non-technical users to the medium. A link (sometimes called a hyperlink or hypertext link) is an area on a computer screen that, when activated, transports the user to another website. Links are often in bold blue lettering; by clicking on the blue letters, the user can travel around the world, seamlessly and effortlessly, from site to site. It is one of the features of the Web that is truly magic. Most links simply connect a user to the first page of another website. Some entities, however, have devised rather clever uses for linking.

In one case, an online news service in Scotland linked to the stories of the Scottish *Shetland Times* newspaper's website; that is, the link did not deposit the user at the electronic doorstep of the online newspaper, but took the user well inside, by-passing advertising and other content the online newspaper wanted its users to see.[254] In another case, a Microsoft Internet city guide website linked to a site operated by Ticketmaster for online ordering of tickets to live events; again, the Microsoft link allegedly took the user beyond the screens that Ticketmaster would have liked users to visit.[255] Another clever variation of linking is *framing,* which was the subject of a lawsuit commenced by *The Washington Post,* CNN, and a number of other media companies with news websites, against a defendant that linked to these sites, but in a novel manner.[256] When a user from the defendant's website clicked on the link space, say of CNN, rather than being a regular link the CNN site was displayed in

---

254   *Shetland Times Co. Ltd.* v. *Wills* (Scotland Court of Session, 24 October 1996) [*Shetland Times*], reported in *Computer & Online Industry Litigation Reporter,* 21 January 1997 at 23,534. See <http://www.shetland-times.co.uk/> for materials from the plaintiff's perspective.

255   *Ticketmaster Corporation* v. *Microsoft Corporation,* No. CV97-3055 RAP (C.D. Ca.), reported in *Computer & Online Industry Litigation Reporter,* 6 May 1997 at 24,087 and complaint reproduced at 24,144 [*Ticketmaster*]. For a copy of the complaint, see "Web Suit" *The National Law Journal* (12 May 1997) and also available at <http://www.ljx.com/internet/tktmaster.html>. See also Larry Armstrong, "Ticketmaster vs. Microsoft," *Business Week,* 12 May 1997.

256   *Washington Post Co.* v. *Total News Inc.,* No. 97 Civ. 1190 (S.D.N.Y., complaint filed 20 February 1997) [*Washington Post*], reported in *Computer & Online Industry Litigation Reporter,* 6 May 1997 at 24,091 and complaint reproduced at 24,148ff. Another novel web-based activity is "meta tagging," where a third party's trademarks are inserted into web pages in order to have web-based search services index a website under an unrelated heading: see *Oppedahl & Larson* v. *Advanced Concepts,* No. 97-Z-1592 (D. Colo., complaint filed 23 July 1997), reported in *Computer & Online Industry Litigation Reporter,* 16 September 1997 at E1.

a *window frame* that contained the defendant's logo and advertising. A similar phenomenon is often seen on television when, at the end of a program, the screen splits and additional information or content (perhaps about the next show) is broadcast on one side of the screen as the credits from the previous program are scrolling in another window.

In both of these Internet framing cases the company whose site was linked took exception to the practice and commenced legal proceedings claiming a wide array of infringements. In the *Shetland Times* case, the plaintiff argued copyright infringement and was successful in securing an injunction. In the *Ticketmaster* case, Ticketmaster has claimed trademark dilution, misleading representation, and unfair competition, among other heads of liability. In the *Washington Post* case, the plaintiffs argued misappropriation along the lines of the *INS* case,[257] trade-mark dilution, trade-mark infringement, copyright infringement, false advertising, and unfair competition. The tenor of these claims is similar to that which animated the majority in the *INS* case; namely, the persons linking and framing in these particular ways are trying to reap where they did not sow. Thus, Ticketmaster claims that Microsoft was "feathering its own nest at Ticketmaster's expense."[258] *The Washington Post* labelled the defendant's website "parasitic."[259] The defendants are accused of "pirating" copyrighted materials.[260] Of course, moral outrage (real or feigned) does not a recognized legal claim make. The *Shetland Times* injunction case is not very helpful, given that its main finding was centred on the copyright that the court concluded the plaintiff had in the titles to its news stories (and which appeared on the defendant's site for purposes of effecting the link). The *Washington Post* case settled rather quickly, and therefore there will not be a judgment forthcoming from that proceeding. Microsoft initially contested the Ticketmaster claim, arguing fair use and news reporting as defences, and that being linked is simply part of the operation of the Internet; therefore, Ticketmaster should not be able to complain about Microsoft's links.[261] This case, however, has now also settled, so again we will have to wait for another dispute to have a court decide these issues..

---

257   *INS*, above note 235.

258   See "Web Suit," above note 255 at 3.

259   *Washington Post*, above note 256 at 24,148.

260   *Ibid.* at 24,150.

261   "Microsoft Answers Ticketmaster's Charges of Electronic Piracy," *Computer & Online Industry Litigation Reporter*, 1 July 1997 at 24,421.

Nevertheless, several observations can already be made at this point about these sorts of cases. First, they illustrate clearly the first dynamic of computer law. As well, they show the multifaceted legal response that accompanies new perceived mischiefs; that is, although the discussion in this chapter has segmented the analysis of intellectual property into its constituent categories, fact patterns often involve two or more of the intellectual property regimes at the same time. Indeed, in the *Washington Post* and *Ticketmaster* cases, there were also technical responses offered by the plaintiffs as they tried to neutralize the linking by programming countermeasures to the links, which of course were met by further linking measures. In terms of the law, the *Washington Post* case raised some particularly interesting issues; whereas a straight link to a website's first page should not be problematic under copyright law since the link does not copy any material and serves only as an address to another location, in Canada questions such as moral rights may be raised in addition to those listed in the plaintiffs' claim. Moreover, in some framing cases in the United States the concept of derivative work may also arise; that is, in the United States the right to make derivative works rests with the copyright holder of the original material. This concept, for example, was used in a U.S. case to enjoin someone from taking the pages of an art book that contained pictures on each page and remounting the pages/pictures on tiles, and selling the tile product.[262] Although no copy was made of the page from the art book, the court held that an unauthorized derivative work was made, and found for the owner of the copyright in the book. Interestingly, a diametrically different result was obtained in a Canadian case where the defendant was permitted to transfer pictures from a magazine and mount and resell them in a different medium where no copies were made of them.[263] These sorts of analogies may play a role in sorting out the controversies surrounding linking and framing.

---

262   *Mirage Editions, Inc.* v. *Albuquerque A.R.T. Co.*, 856 F.2d 1341 (9th Cir. 1988) [*Mirage Editions*].

263   *Fetherling* v. *Boughner* (1978), 40 C.P.R. (2d) 253 (Ont. H.C.J.). See also *Lee* v. *A.R.T. Company*, 125 F.3d 580 (7th Cir. 1997), where the appellate court disagreed with the approach in the *Mirage Editions* case, above note 262, and found that mounting art on tiles did not infringe the artist's copyright.

FURTHER READINGS

Books

CHROMECEK, Milan, & Stuart C. MCCORMACK, *World Intellectual Property Guidebook: Canada* (New York: Matthew Bender, 1991)

DOWNING, Robbie, *EC Information Technology Law* (Chichester: John Wiley & Sons, 1995)

HUGENHOLTZ, P. Bernt, ed., *The Future of Copyright in a Digital Environment* (The Hague: Kluwer, 1996)

HUGHES, Roger T., ed., *Trade Secrets* (Toronto: Law Society of Upper Canada, 1990)

NIMMER, Raymond T., *The Law of Computer Technology: Rights, Licenses, Liabilities,* 2d ed. (Boston, Mass.: Warren, Gorham & Lamont, 1992) (looseleaf, updated)

SOOKMAN, Barry B., *Sookman Computer Law* (Toronto: Carswell, 1991) (looseleaf, updated)

WARSHOFSKY, Fred, *The Patent Wars: The Battle to Own the World's Technology* (New York: John Wiley & Sons, 1994)

Internet Sites

Canadian Intellectual Property Office
<http://xinfo.ic.gc.ca/opengov/cipo>

European Patent Office
<http://www.epo.co.at/epo/>

United States Copyright Office
<http://lcweb.loc.gov/copyright/>

United States Patent and Trademark Office
<http://www.uspto.gov>

World Intellectual Property Organization
<http://www.wipo.org/>

CHAPTER 3

CRIMINAL LAW

A society dependent on computers, telecommunications, networks, and information is extremely vulnerable to computer crime. Computers can be the subject of crime, as when they are stolen or accessed without authorization. As well, computers and networks can be the means by which other crimes are perpetrated. Computer crime involves some form of unauthorized gain, destruction, manipulation, or intrusion, or some form of illegal image or speech. In combatting computer crime, authorities are squarely faced with the four dynamics of computer law, namely, the rapid pace of technological change, the elusive nature of information, and the blurring of private/public and national/international. These dynamics, together with the general interpretative principle that criminal laws must be construed narrowly, have resulted in the courts in Canada having an uneven track record of convicting persons charged with computer and information-related activities that cause wilful harm and damage to third parties. Nevertheless, and to a large degree because of certain of these cases that resulted in acquittals, the Canadian government has revised the *Criminal Code* on several occasions to give law enforcement agencies additional assistance in fighting computer crime.[1] Today the *Criminal Code* contains a number of different

---

1   R.S.C. 1985, c. C-46. The *Criminal Code* is federal legislation, as the *Constitution Act, 1867* (U.K.), 30 & 31 Vict., c. 3, s. 91(27), gives the federal government power over criminal law. The *Constitution Act, 1867* can be found in R.S.C. 1985, Appendix II, No. 5.

provisions that can be pressed into service against persons who perpe-trate computer-related crime. In other cases, the applicability of the *Criminal Code* to certain harmful behaviour remains in question, requir-ing Parliament to be vigilant as to the adequacy of the criminal law to deal with new computer-related threats and risks, and to protect people, property, and governments in the Information Age.

A. A TYPOLOGY OF HARMFUL CONDUCT

The actual nature and amount of computer crime are not precise. Com-puter crime has been defined as "any illegal, unethical, or unauthorized behaviour involving automatic data processing and/or transmission of data."[2] Canada's Royal Canadian Mounted Police (RCMP) uses the fol-lowing working definition of computer crime: "any criminal activity involving the copying of, use of, removal of, interference with, access to or manipulation of computer systems, computer functions, data or com-puter programs."[3] These definitions cast the net of computer crime broadly indeed. As for the quantum of computer crime, exact and reli-able statistics are hard to come by because much malicious computer-related activity is difficult to detect. Moreover, many organizations do not report themselves as victims of computer crime since this could result in a loss of confidence among customers and investors.[4] At the same time, some observers question whether the actual incidence of computer crime is as great as is popularly thought. For example, a sur-vey conducted by the Ontario Provincial Police in the early 1980s reported that only 4 percent of respondents had been victimized by

---

2   Ulrich Sieber, *The International Emergence of Criminal Information Law* (Koln: Heymanns, 1992) at 5 [*Criminal Information Law*].

3   RCMP, Operational Policy 1992, cited in Donald K. Piragoff, "Computer Crimes and Other Crimes against Information Technology in Canada," in *Information Technology Crime: National Legislations and International Initiatives*, ed. Ulrich Sieber (Koln: Heymanns, 1994) at 86 [*Information Technology Crime*].

4   See Patrick Brethour, "Newbridge Mum on Fraud Charge" *The [Toronto] Globe and Mail* (10 December 1996); and Joe Chidley, "Cracking the Net," *Maclean's*, 22 May 1995. The *Criminal Code* does not require a victim of computer crime to report it. Thus, someone hit by a software "virus" can stay mute; compare this to certain types of public health legislation, such as Ontario's *Health Protection and Promotion Act*, R.S.O. 1990, c. H.7, that requires physicians and certain other persons to report certain "virulent" diseases.

computer crime.[5] Today, however, computer crime is a significant and growing problem.[6] Computer crime manifests itself in a wide variety of guises,[7] most of which fall within one or more of the following broad categories: unauthorized gain, destruction, manipulation and intrusion, and illegal images and speech. These categories are in addition to the many types of situations in which a computer is used to facilitate one of the "traditional" offences set out in the *Criminal Code*.

1) Unauthorized Gain

In this category of damaging conduct falls a broad range of theft and theftlike activities. Stealing computer equipment, and recently, valuable components like chips, is an age-old form of illicit conduct involving new devices. Commercial piracy of software — making multiple copies of a computer program and selling them — is a modern means by which an owner of property can be deprived of the benefits accruing from the property. Benefiting economically from others without paying compensation, and thus "stealing their resources," would include the theft of computer, telecommunications, and cable/satellite services.[8] The Internet is also becoming a popular venue for various scams to bilk unsuspecting and gullible users, such as taking a customer's money but not delivering the agreed upon goods.[9] Another use for computers in this

---

5   See Ulrich Sieber, *The International Handbook on Computer Crime* (New York: Wiley & Sons, 1986) at 33. Interestingly, 46 percent of respondents to the OPP survey thought computer crime to be an important concern, thereby leading some to conclude that the general level of concern expressed vis-à-vis computer crime is not borne out by real crime statistics. For a discussion of survey results reporting much higher rates of computer crime, see Council of Europe, *Computer-Related Crime* (Strasbourg: Council of Europe, 1990).

6   For example, it is estimated that in 1995 losses in the United States from computer viruses alone amounted to $1 billion: Gary H. Anthes, "Old, New Viruses Swarm PC Users," *Computerworld*, 6 May 1996 ["Viruses"].

7   For example, in 1991 German police registered 5004 cases of "computer crime" consisting of: 3963 cases of cash dispenser manipulations, 787 cases of computer fraud, 82 cases of forgery of computer data, 95 cases of alteration of data and computer sabotage, and 77 cases of illegally obtaining computer data (especially hacking): Sieber, *Criminal Information Law*, above note 2 at 6–7.

8   For a good discussion of the types and amount of telecommunications fraud, see chapter 2 of Robert W.K. Davis & Scott C. Hutchison, *Computer Crime in Canada: An Introduction to Technological Crime and Related Legal Issues* (Toronto: Carswell, 1997) [*Computer Crime*].

9   Some of these types of unauthorized gain are discussed in section C(3), "Regulating Cyberspace," in chapter 6.

area is to access payroll, banking, and other records stored on computers to divert monetary amounts to the perpetrator's account.[10] High-tech forgery, manipulation of automated teller machines, and accessing a competitor's industrial secrets resident on computer systems, are three more examples of damage engendered through unauthorized gain. Another activity is gambling. Many Internet sites offer games of chance, ranging from blackjack to roulette to slot machines, all provided in a computerized environment and resident on a computer outside of Canada and the United States to remove themselves from the federal, provincial, and state laws that prohibit or regulate gambling.

Traditional and modern rationales for theft converge in the unauthorized taking of laptop computers. One report indicates that in 1996 the number of laptops stolen in the United States was 265,000, an increase of 27 percent over 1995.[11] The epidemic proportions of this problem indicate that laptop computers are stolen not only for the value of the machines, but also for the value of the data stored on them. Apparently one laptop stolen from a credit card company contained 314,000 credit card numbers. The trends of mass storage and miniaturization highlighted in sections B(3), "Mass Storage," and B(5), "Miniaturization," in chapter 1 and implemented in laptop computers have produced a computing environment that is extremely vulnerable to computer crime. Indeed, all the trends detailed in chapter 1, such as the rise of ubiquitous communication networks, the explosive growth of the Internet, the ability to digitize and manipulate data and other content, and society's increasing dependence on the computer and networks, contribute to a world where the computer criminal can operate more effectively, more internationally, more easily, more surreptitiously, and more dangerously than ever before. Computer crime is the unfortunate Achilles' heel of the Information Age.

---

10   Ulrich Sieber, in *Information Technology Crime*, above note 3 at 9, gives an example of "salary-doubling," a common crime implemented by computer whereby a person, typically an existing employee, enters fictitious employee/salary information into the company's computers in order to have such funds transferred to the perpetrator at a later date.

11   Mindy Blodgett, "Laptop Thefts Escalate: Data Loss, Not Cost of Hardware, Top Concern," *Computerworld*, 31 March 1997; see also Beppi Crosariol, "Lapjacked!" *The [Toronto] Globe and Mail, Report on Business Magazine*, October 1996.

2) Unauthorized Destruction

This category includes criminals who access computer systems remotely in order to destroy data. As well, many malicious computer-related activities are committed by disgruntled company employees.[12] This category also includes "viruses," "worms," and other software-based booby traps that are intended to infiltrate computer systems and cause damage.[13] The most drastic virus deletes data and/or causes a computer program to become completely inoperable. More subtle ones, however, can also take their toll, such as viruses that only change certain letters throughout data resident on a computer. Indeed, often these more circumspect perpetrators can inflict more harm because they can go undetected for so long. Moreover, even viruses that are seemingly benign — some simply display a greeting — take up much time and effort on the part of computer users once they are detected.[14] Viruses are particularly dangerous due to their ability to replicate and transmit themselves over networks, as in the case of the famous one let loose by Robert Morris, which swept across the Internet to infect a large number of computers.[15]

The Internet has increased the virus problem dramatically. In a 1995 survey, 75 percent of respondents indicated that the viruses that attacked them came from diskettes, and 9 percent said the viruses came from e-mail attachments.[16] This latter form of dissemination did not exist the year before. In another survey, 76 percent of respondents at larger companies indicated they had been hit by a computer virus.[17] In a more recent survey, 80 percent of all virus infections were reported to have been transmitted over the Internet.[18] Indicative of the extent of the problem is the most recent phenomenon of the spread, again over Internet e-mail, of virus hoaxes, namely messages that carry warnings about non-existent viruses. These hoax messages, however, cause massive

---

12 A recent survey recorded that 42 percent of larger company respondents indicated offensive computer-related behaviour by "company insiders": Bob Violino, "The Security Facade," *Information Week*, 21 October 1996 ["Security"].

13 For a historical overview of viruses, see David Ferbrache, *A Pathology of Computer Viruses* (London: Springer-Verlag, 1992).

14 For a description of the good, the bad, and the ugly of viruses, see Alan Solomon, *PC Viruses: Detection, Analysis and Cure* (London: Springer-Verlag, 1991).

15 See *United States* v. *Morris*, 928 F.2d 504 (2d Cir. 1991).

16 The National Computer Security Association, "1996 Computer Virus Prevalence Survey," reported in Anthes, "Viruses," above note 6.

17 Violino, "Security," above note 12. See also Geoffrey Rowan, "Computer Viruses Cost Firms: Study" *The [Toronto] Globe and Mail* (17 December 1996).

18 Barb Cole-Gomolski, "Hackers Hitch Ride on E-Mail; Lack of Security Opens Door," *Computerworld*, 28 April 1997.

inconvenience and consume scarce information system personnel resources, and therefore are a scourge in themselves.[19] Of course, a number of public agencies and private companies combat viruses by detecting them and supplying the marketplace with antivirus scanning software, but these efforts and products are invariably reactive in nature and therefore determined perpetrators of viruses can invariably stay one step ahead of these antidote measures; hence, the need to criminalize this antisocial, harmful behaviour.

3) Unauthorized Manipulation

Just as *virus* has entered the modern lexicon, so too has *hacker*, though originally this term was used to denote a computer virtuoso. Hacker has acquired a darker connotation of late, being used to label individuals who spend inordinate amounts of time attempting, often successfully, to gain access to other computers connected to one or more networks.[20] Once inside the victim computer, the motivations of hackers vary, from an intention to commit fraud, theft, or industrial espionage to mere adventurism and egotistical gratification at being able to penetrate a security system implemented for just the purpose of trying to keep hackers out.[21] In a profile on a notorious hacker, he is quoted as explaining his rationale for breaking into computers as "it's neat . . . it's a challenge . . . I love the game."[22] Even where there is no theft or destruction or damage, the very presence of the hacker in a third party's computer causes the third party to expend resources and incur costs. These can sometimes be substantial, as when a Toronto-based hacker gained

---

19   Sharon Machlis, "Virus Hoaxes Make IS Sick: Warnings, Carried by E-Mail, Spread Hysteria and Waste Resources," *Computerworld*, 28 April 1997.

20   In *United States* v. *Riggs*, 739 F. Supp. 414 (N.D. Ill. 1990), a "Legion of Doom" member objected to being referred to as a hacker on the grounds that it was prejudicial, but the court found that it was an appropriate term given his harmful activities. In coming to this conclusion, the court noted the dual use of the term *hacker*, namely to designate those who obtain unauthorized access to computers, as well as those who are computer hobbyists with an intense interest in exploring the capabilities of computers and communications.

21   For a "psychological profile" of various hackers, see Warwick Ford, *Computer Communications Security: Principles, Standard Protocols and Techniques* (Englewood Cliffs, NJ: Prentice Hall, 1994).

22   Jonathan Littman, "In the Mind of 'Most Wanted' Hacker, Kevin Mitnick," *Computerworld*, 15 January 1996.

unauthorized access into fifty university sites around North America.[23] And the hacking mentality has engendered new forms of harmful manipulation of computer resources and information-based assets, as when hackers broke into websites at the U.S. Department of Justice and the Central Intelligence Agency in order to add inflammatory text and messages to these sites.[24] Yet another form of offensive behaviour is the so-called denial of service, illustrated by the bombardment of an Internet access company in September 1996 with electronic requests for services that disabled the service provider for days.[25] The ability to create harm and mischief over the Internet is limited only by the imagination of computer savvy perpetrators.

Society's use of the same term *hacker* to denote both computer criminal and computer expert illustrates a schizophrenic dimension of the modern computer-Internet age that links closely with the third dynamic of computer law, namely, the blurring of private/public. The private activity of sitting in front of one's computer terminal and programming computer codes into the wee hours of the morning or searching the Internet for neat information by uncovering and navigating within cool sites is, in a physical sense, no different from the manipulation required to hack into a secure site in order to perpetrate a criminal offence. The distinction is almost purely in the mental element of the hacker at the time of the two different activities. There are few crimes outside of the non-computer/Internet realm where the *actus reus* of the offence so closely approximates a common, legitimate activity. For example, while driving a car may be said to be very similar to stealing a car, in fact the analogy is inapposite because a person very rarely drives another person's car (the correct analogy), while on the Internet a computer user is always in someone else's site when utilizing the Web. On another plane, withdrawing money from a bank teller is different from robbing the bank teller because one does the former so infrequently. On the other hand, deciphering the various features of a bank's complicated website, and its interface to various merchant sites, does not seem dissimilar to accessing an off-limits portion of the same bank computer. It also matters that in the physical world, to commit a crime one has to physically remove oneself from one's home and enter a new and clearly marked physical space where it is invariably perfectly clear that a crime is being

---

23   Katrina Onstad & Barbara Wade Rose, "Is This Any Way to Run Cyberspace?: Why the Hacker Ethos is Bad for the Net," *Canadian Business Technology*, Summer 1996. See also Joe Chidley, "Cracking the Net," *Maclean's*, 22 May 1995.

24   Violino, "Security," above note 12.

25   *Ibid.*

committed; there is no doubt the bank robber who enters a bank branch with a gun in hand and a ski mask on his face shouting "this is a hold up" knows he is committing a crime. The fellow who accesses the bank's main "electronic vault" by a computer terminal in the privacy of his own home — the computer he just used to visit the same bank's website — does not have the same physical indicia of blameworthiness. This is not offered as an excuse for the criminal activity of unauthorized access to a computer, but it is worth noting because it illustrates the extent of the difficulty in combatting it.

4) Unauthorized Intrusion

Modern technology affords a number of means by which persons can intrude into the private communications of others. Wire-tapping and related technologies were once the sole domain of law enforcement officers. Today, with the proliferation in communication technologies, it is not surprising that some of them lend themselves to intrusion quite readily. In particular, it is notoriously easy to scan and record conversations undertaken by analog cellular telephones. The equivalent of the previous era's wire-tapping equipment can be purchased in many electronics stores for eavesdropping on cellular telephone conversations. Efforts to make mobile phone transmissions more secure are, of course, being undertaken; but in one of the immutable laws of computer technology, for every security-related development "cause" there is the "effect" of the security-breaking counterdevelopment designed, manufactured, and on the market usually within a matter of weeks. For example, at one time digital wireless phones were heralded as the solution to the scanning-based intrusion problem. Digital phones include a chip that encrypts conversations into complex binary computer code. No sooner, however, did this technology appear then a new breed of digital scanners was developed that, in addition to monitoring digital cellular phone calls, could capture faxes and paging messages sent digitally over wireless networks.[26] Prudence, and security, continue to dictate that confidential conversations be reserved for wire-based phones.

Intrusive activities, particularly those practised by governments, pre-date the era of the cellular telephone. In 1591 Queen Elizabeth I effected censorship over international mail by requiring all letters sent out of England to be carried by messengers approved by the Crown; this

---

26   John J. Keller, "Wireless Security Still Way Down the Line" *The [Toronto] Globe and Mail* (21 March 1997).

decree had the effect of shutting down private mail services set up in London by foreign merchants.[27] James I extended the same prohibition to domestic mail in 1609, and Oliver Cromwell emphasized the importance of a centralized post office in 1657 in order to uncover the "many dangerous and wicked designs which have been and are daily contrived against the peace and welfare of this Commonwealth, the intelligence whereof cannot well be communicated but by letter of escript."[28] Subsequently, in England the post office was given a monopoly on the conveyance of telegraphic messages, which monopoly, in the last third of the nineteenth century, was held to cover the fledgling telephone as well.[29] Although one rationale for these actions was to bolster the revenue flowing to the public purse, the ability to eavesdrop on private communications was another. In the twentieth century, for example, postal censorship was not restricted to the two World Wars. In the United States, one infamous case in the late 1970s resulted from the massive mail search activities undertaken by the Central Intelligence Agency, wherein between 1953 and 1973 some 215,000 pieces of mail were opened and 1.5 million names from these letters were entered into government computers.[30] One can only imagine the possibilities for intrusion and recordation in an environment of e-mail messaging, global voice messaging, and huge computer storage capacity.

Another kind of intrusion practised today involves private persons sending to others unsolicited and unwelcome e-mail messages that are harassing or even threatening in tone. Again, there is nothing new in using the mails to send similar missives, or in using the telephone in an offensive manner, particularly given the archaic technology of the telephone that has it ring loudly until it is answered.[31] While not necessarily as audible as the telephone, e-mail can be particularly offensive and threatening because of its immediacy and its ability to be shared with third parties. In a recent Canadian case, a university student was warned that his computer privileges would be curtailed if he continued to send offensive e-mail to another student.[32] In a disturbing American case, a university student sent to an Internet acquaintance in Canada chilling e-mail messages regarding abduction, bondage, torture, humiliation, rape, sodomy, murder, and necrophilia including references to the Paul

---

27 See *Encyclopaedia Britannica*, 1965 ed., s.v. "postal services."

28 *Ibid.* at 306.

29 *A.G. v. The Edison Telephone Company of London (Limited)* (1880), 6 Q.B. 244 (Ex. D.).

30 *Birnbaum v. United States*, 436 F. Supp. 967 (E.D.N.Y. 1977).

31 *Motherwell v. Motherwell* (1976), 73 D.L.R. (3d) 62 (Alta. C.A.).

32 *Blaber v. University of Victoria* (1995), 123 D.L.R. (4th) 255 (B.C.S.C.).

Bernardo murders.[33] When one of these diatribes, consisting of a gruesome story in which the victim had the name of a classmate, was shared with this classmate, the authorities charged the student with transmitting threats to kidnap or injure a person through interstate or foreign commerce. One of three appellate judges was prepared to convict, but the two in the majority acquitted the accused on the ground of there being an insufficient threat; rather, they concluded the communications were an attempt to foster a friendship based on shared sexual fantasies.

5) Illegal Images

Pornography is a huge business on the Internet. The ability of computers to scan, and of networks to transmit, sexually explicit images, has caused sex to become an important commercial Internet activity. The keyword *sex* entered into an Internet search engine in August 1997 produced a response indicating that there are 425,449 sites with the word *sex* in them; the equivalent figures for the terms *museum, art gallery,* and *symphony* were 388,110, 71,125, and 59,893, respectively. It should be noted that the following terms found more sites than *sex: university* — 7,801,043; *education* — 2,051,768; *pet health* — 1,354,091, and *god* — 554,599. *Playboy* estimates it receives 5 million hits a day at its website.[34] Much of the pornography on the Internet, or distributed on CD-ROM, is relatively non-controversial, at least in Canada. Where it involves the undue exploitation of sex, however, it risks being obscene under Canada's *Criminal Code*. It is apparently for this reason that a major Internet service provider in Canada decided to cease carrying certain newsgroups.[35] Similarly, universities in Canada from time to time ban usegroups with sexual content they consider obscene,[36] generally flagged by adjectival monikers such as "alt.sex.bestiality", "alt.sex.stories", and "alt.sex.bondage", though the effectiveness of such bans is often questionable given the ability of users to access these sources through multiple means. Child pornography, which is also illegal under the *Criminal Code*, has seen a resurgence in the last few years as a result

---

33   *United States* v. *Alkhabaz*, 104 F.3d 1492 (6th Cir. 1997).

34   "Cybersex: An Adult Affair," *The Economist*, 4 January 1997 ["Cybersex"].

35   See the advertisement by i.star Internet Inc. in *The [Toronto] Globe and Mail* (13 July 1996), which reads, in part, "With Leadership Comes Responsibility . . . Our recent decision to no longer offer access to Internet newsgroups that blatantly contravene the laws of Canada, . . ."

36   Joe Chidley, "Red-Light District: From S&M to Bestiality, Porn Flourishes on the Internet," *Maclean's*, 22 May 1995.

of computer and network technologies. A decade ago, police forces had virtually won the battle against the domestic production and importation into Canada of child pornography. The Internet has breathed new life into this form of pornography, with digital images crossing national frontiers with impunity.[37] And with a computer on virtually every desk, no organization is immune from the phenomenon of one of its employees downloading such material at the office, as apparently happened recently with a Department of National Defence civilian employee in Ottawa, who was arrested for downloading and storing on his computer a large quantity of child pornography.[38]

The Internet is not the first technology platform to be used so extensively by the sex trade. In a revealing survey, *The Economist* points out that sex-related applications have been in the vanguard of the development of videoconferencing, the cinema, the videocassette, the compact disk, pay-per-view television, and direct-to-home digital satellite technology.[39] This survey points out that "adult entertainment" business activities often lead the way for the embryonic development of technology, including new online payment mechanisms. Development then continues to serve medicine, education, and a range of mainstream commercial and industrial applications. Similarly, the activities of watching and recording sexually explicit material at home gave impetus to the development of the video camera as well as the video rental store.[40] One can go even further back in history, however, for example to the American Civil War, when one of the first widespread uses of the then latest photographic devices was to take pornographic pictures that were sent by mail to the soldiers on the front lines; and, perhaps not surprisingly, the U.S. postal service was pressed into action as a censor to try to stop this flow of pornographic images. Of course stopping it then, and now, will prove to be extremely difficult given the volume of material. A recent survey estimates that about 10,000 adult entertainment sites generate $1 billion

---

37 Jeff Sallot, "Internet Eases Sexual Exploitation" *The [Toronto] Globe and Mail* (27 August 1996). See also Peter Kuitenbrouwer, "A Mountain of Smut: Police Make an Arrest in a Child Porn Ring on the Internet," *Maclean's*, 18 November 1996, which details the seizure by police of 30,000 files containing child pornography belonging to a young man in Kirkland Lake, Ontario, who allegedly participated in an international child pornography swap arrangement.

38 Scott Feschuk & Henry Hess, "Internet Porn Results in Arrest: Ottawa Scientist Faces Charges" *The [Toronto] Globe and Mail* (10 December 1996).

39 "Cybersex," above note 34.

40 Sara Silver, "Virtual Sex Drives On-Line Technology" *The [Toronto] Globe and Mail* (21 June 1997).

a year in revenues.[41] Perhaps most telling is another survey estimate that more than one-quarter of households that own computers visit adult sites each month.[42]

6) Illegal Speech

The Internet is an ideal technology for those people who wish to disseminate messages that are racist or hateful. The same features that make computers and networks attractive to corporations, governments, and others who wish to disseminate their messages make these technologies indispensable to bigots and hatemongers. The Internet is global, provides instant communication, is relatively inexpensive, permits the transmission of text, video, audio, music, and pictures, and allows for feedback by readers. If the pen is mightier than the sword, the Internet is more powerful still. Again, the various features of the Internet, such as its ability to collapse geography, make this communication medium extremely attractive to persons who would spread perverse and problematic propaganda.[43] It is also worth recalling the assessment of the District Court in the *ACLU* case, namely, that there is no single point through which the vast amount of information flowing over the Internet can be controlled.[44] In the Supreme Court decision in the *ACLU* case, the court stated that on the Internet: "Through the use of chat rooms, any person with a phone line can become a town crier with a voice that resonates farther than it could from any soapbox. Through the use of web pages, mail exploders, and newsgroups, the same individual can become a pamphleteer."[45] It is almost as if an unrepentant racist or malicious hate propagator had designed the Internet.

Just as not all pornography is criminally obscene, not all sharp or critical communication is illegal, only that which incites hatred or which wilfully promotes hatred. Assuming one is dealing with the latter, the Internet reveals yet another unfortunate strength, the ability of the hate propagator to attempt to evade arrest by establishing her server in a jurisdiction with laws more lax than Canada's. The United States, for example, takes a more lenient approach to hate speech than Canada,

---

41   *Ibid.*

42   *Ibid.*

43   See section A(6), "The Internet," in chapter 1.

44   *American Civil Liberties Union v. Reno*, 929 F. Supp. 824 (E.D. Pa. 1996), aff'd (*sub nom. Reno v. American Civil Liberties Union*) 117 S. Ct. 2329 (1997) [*ACLU*]. The Supreme court decision is also available on the web at <http://www.ciec.org/SC_appeal/opinion.shtml>.

45   *Ibid.* at 2344.

given the former's strong tradition of upholding freedom of speech through its constitution. Thus, Canada has seen some of its undesirable elements relocate south of the border to establish websites.[46] Of course, prosecuting these persons for their Internet activities poses the same risk as it does for paper-based activities; such prosecutions bring them significant notoriety and many more readers than if they would have been left to peddle their drivel in some Internet cul-de-sac.[47] Nevertheless, even when successful prosecutions are brought against such persons resident outside of Canada, practical questions arise as to what steps can be taken to block their messages from reaching Canadian computer screens, given the anarchic nature of the Internet.

B. *CRIMINAL CODE* OFFENCES

The criminal law, prescribed in Canada primarily by the *Criminal Code*, delineates the behaviour that society, acting through Parliament, has deemed to be socially unacceptable.[48] In combatting persons who seek to achieve in a computer context unauthorized gain, destruction, manipulation or intrusion, or who seek to participate in the dissemination of socially unacceptable images or speech, law enforcement authorities turn mainly to the following provisions of the *Criminal Code*: theft, fraud, computer abuse, data abuse, obscenity and child pornography, hate propaganda, and interception of communications. A number of other offences in the *Criminal Code* may also be relevant from time to time, particularly where a computer is used to facilitate a crime. The criminal law, traditionally, has been largely concerned with protecting the integrity of the individual and tangible property. Thus, the four dynamics of computer law — the rapid pace of technological change, the elusive nature of information, and the blurring of private/public and national/international — coupled with the general rule of criminal law interpretation that *Criminal Code* provisions be construed strictly and

---

46 See Donn Downey, "Rights Panel's Jurisdiction over 'Zundelsite' Disputed" *The [Toronto] Globe and Mail* (27 May 1997).

47 See Anthony Keller, "Patrolling the Internet" *The [Toronto] Globe and Mail* (2 December 1996), pointing out that one of the better-known hate peddlers was given a decade's worth of courtroom platforms in Canada, while in the United States he has become an anonymous crank since he is left alone by the authorities.

48 See Kent Roach, *Criminal Law* (Concord, Ont.: Irwin Law, 1996) at 2: "Criminal laws are primarily designed to denounce and to punish inherently wrongful behaviour, and to deter people from committing crimes or engaging in behaviour that presents a serious risk of harm."

in favour of the accused in the event of doubt or uncertainty as to the applicability of the particular provision, have challenged the ability of the *Criminal Code* to stay current with the new mischiefs possible with the widespread use of computers and networks. The result has been the amendment of the *Criminal Code* to include several new computer-related provisions. The Internet and other computer-based technologies and business practices raise a number of novel questions under these and the older provisions of the *Criminal Code*, and highlight as well the challenges of enforcing a national criminal law in an increasingly global environment.

1) Theft

Given Canada's market-based economy anchored in the institution of private property, it is no surprise that the offence of theft — stealing someone else's property — is a cornerstone of the *Criminal Code*. Thus, if an item of hardware or computer chips are wrongfully taken, the *Criminal Code*'s theft provision in subsection 322(1) could be used to prosecute the thief.[49] The question, however, whether the theft offence should apply to confidential information has confronted a number of courts in Canada and abroad, and in particular was considered in two cases in the mid-1980s by well-respected appellate courts. In *R. v. Stewart*,[50] the Ontario Court of Appeal concluded that information, in this case confidential information regarding employees of a hotel that a labour union wished to obtain for purposes of an organizing drive, could be "property," and therefore the accused was found guilty of counselling theft when he attempted to induce a hotel employee to provide him with

---

49   The theft offence currently reads as follows:

>   322. (1) Every one commits theft who fraudulently and without colour of right takes, or fraudulently and without colour of right converts to his use or to the use of another person, anything whether animate or inanimate, with intent,
>   (a) to deprive, temporarily or absolutely, the owner of it, or a person who has a special property or interest in it, of the thing or of his property or interest in it;
>   (b) to pledge it or deposit it as security;
>   (c) to part with it under a condition with respect to its return that the person who parts with it may be unable to perform; or
>   (d) to deal with it in such a manner that it cannot be restored in the condition in which it was at the time it was taken or converted.
>   (2) A person commits theft when, with intent to steal anything, he moves it or causes it to move or to be moved, or begins to cause it to become movable.
>   . . .

50   (1983), 5 C.C.C. (3d) 481 (Ont. C.A.).

the employee information.[51] By contrast, in R. v. *Offley*, the Alberta Court of Appeal held that information could not be property for purposes of the *Criminal Code*'s theft provision.[52] This divergence was resolved by the Supreme Court of Canada when it held in the *Stewart* case that information, for policy reasons, should not fall within the purview of "property" for purposes of the theft or fraud offences under the *Criminal Code*.[53] The court concluded that the offence required there to be a permanent "taking," and that when information is disclosed it is still available to the victim. The Supreme Court took a very physically oriented view of both property and deprivation, finding that, except in rare circumstances, someone cannot be deprived of information; the court found, by contrast, that someone can be deprived of confidentiality, but it in turn cannot be taken, as one enjoys it but cannot really own it. From a practical perspective, the court was also concerned about the difficulties of defining with adequate precision what constitutes confidential information.[54] The court noted, for example, that a contrary finding to its own would have a severe impact on the mobility of labour, such that the court did not want to criminalize the environment in which employees switched employers. The court recognized that the civil law of trade secrecy and copyright were

---

51 In a similar vein, in R. v. *Scallen* (1974), 15 C.C.C. (2d) 441 (B.C.C.A.), the British Columbia Court of Appeal concluded that a person's credit in a bank account could be subject to the theft offence, noting that the word *anything* in the relevant *Criminal Code* provision is very broad and does not require the subject matter to be tangible or in a material form.

52 (1986), 28 C.C.C. (3d) 1 (Alta. C.A.) [*Offley*]. In an earlier decision, R. v. *Falconi* (1976), 31 C.C.C. (2d) 144 at 148 (Ont. Co. Ct.) [*Falconi*], the court held that a pharmacy prescription cannot be property for purposes of the theft offence, but only after struggling valiantly with the tough questions posed by the case: "One may have little difficulty in conceptualizing a piece of land or a wrist watch, which are characterized by the classical common law terms of real property and personal property respectively. However, when one attempts to similarly characterize the written or spoken words of a person the task, couched as it is in metaphysics, becomes rather more difficult."

53 R. v. *Stewart* (1988), 41 C.C.C. (3d) 481 (S.C.C.) [*Stewart*].

54 The unease of the Supreme Court is captured in the following passage in *ibid.* at 492:

Moreover, because of the inherent nature of information, treating confidential information as property *simpliciter* for the purposes of the law of theft would create a host of practical problems. For instance, what is the precise definition of "confidential information"? Is confidentiality based on the alleged owner's intent or on some objective criteria? At what point does information cease to be confidential and would it therefore fall outside the scope of the criminal law? Should only confidential information be protected under the criminal law, or any type of information deemed to be of some commercial value?

available in appropriate cases to deal with misappropriation of information, and that the court would not criminalize such behaviour unless Parliament clearly amended the *Criminal Code* to capture such conduct.

The Supreme Court in the *Stewart* case was reacting to the second dynamic of computer law — the elusive nature of information — and, utilizing a narrow, strict interpretation approach to criminal law, concluded that the *Criminal Code*'s theft provision, as currently drafted, was inappropriate to handle the evanescent, ephemeral nature of information.[55] The various decisions in the *Stewart* and *Offley* cases were the subject of some commentary.[56] And almost anticipating the Supreme Court's invitation to law reform, Alberta's Institute of Law Research and Reform produced an excellent report on trade secrets that included a proposed model law for both civil and criminal misappropriation of confidential information.[57] To date, however, the federal government has not adopted the recommendations from this report, and thus the theft provision of Canada's *Criminal Code* currently does not extend to the unauthorized disclosure of confidential information. Accordingly, creators and owners of trade secrets and confidential information must find protection for these information-based assets either under the *Criminal Code*'s fraud provision,[58] or under the civil intellectual property protection regimes.[59]

---

55 The principle that penal statutes are subject to rules of strict and narrow interpretation was articulated by Laskin, C.J.C. in the *McLaughlin* case, below note 63 at 335, as follows: "the general rule that in construing criminal statutes they should, where there is uncertainty or ambiguity of meaning, be construed in favour of rather than against an accused. In short, he must be brought fully within the statute and cannot be held guilty of a violation if it is only applicable in part." A few years before the *McLaughlin* case, the Supreme Court of Canada expressed the doctrine of strict interpretation as follows: "It is unnecessary to emphasize the importance of clarity and certainty when freedom is at stake . . . if real ambiguities are found, or doubts of substance arise, in the construction and application of a statute affecting the liberty of a subject, then that statute should be applied in such a manner as to favour the person against whom it is sought to be enforced. If one is to be incarcerated, one should at least know that some Act of Parliament requires it in express terms, and not, at most, by implication": *Marcotte* v. *Canada (Deputy A.G.)* (1975), 19 C.C.C. (2d) 257 at 262 (S.C.C.) [*Marcotte*]. For a recent case that cites *Marcotte* for this proposition, see *R.* v. *McIntosh* (1995), 95 C.C.C. (3d) 481 (S.C.C.).

56 For an article in favour of the Supreme Court's position, see R. Grant Hammond, "Theft of Information" (1984) 100 L.Q. Rev. 252; for a contrary position, see Arnold S. Weinrib, "Information and Property" (1988) 38 U.T.L.J. 117.

57 Institute of Law Research and Reform (Edmonton, Alberta) and A Federal Provincial Working Party, *Trade Secrets* (Report No. 46, July 1986).

58 See section B(2), "Fraud," in this chapter.

59 See section B(1), "Trade Secrets/Breach of Confidence," and B(3), "Copyright," in chapter 2.

If Parliament at some point does decide to update the theft provision to cover confidential information, it should consider the statutory history, and jurisprudential treatment, of the current section 326 of the *Criminal Code*.[60] This provision was initially restricted to electricity when it first came to Canada from England and was implemented through *The Electric Light Inspection Act*, 1894 (Canada) chapter 39, section 10. The provision was brought into the *Criminal Code* in 1906, and in 1934 was extended to include "telephone or telegraph line" and "obtains a telephone or telegraph service" (the current phrase is "telecommunication facility or service"). In 1954 gas was added to the provision and in 1960 "telephone or telegraph line" was changed to "telecommunication wire or cable" in order to capture cable television service. This brief history illustrates that as new utilities and technology-based services come to the marketplace, and as unscrupulous persons abuse them, the provision has been amended to protect such new product offerings and technologies.[61] Given the first dynamic of computer law, however, such amendments can have a difficult time staying current both with new technologies and unanticipated technology-related activities. Thus, in *Maltais v. R.*[62] the Supreme Court had to decide whether the 1960 version of the provision, which covered a "telecommunication wire or cable" was broad enough to capture an accused who had broadcast propaganda over the radio waves when a radio station was overtaken in the course of a labour dispute. The court answered in the negative, and acquitted, on the basis that the phraseology of "wire or cable," while broader than telephone and telegraph line, was not broad enough to cover transmission by Hertzian waves sent through the air.

---

60   326. (1) Every one commits theft who fraudulently, maliciously, or without colour of right,
   (a) abstracts, consumes or uses electricity or gas or causes it to be wasted or diverted; or
   (b) uses any telecommunication facility or obtains any telecommunication service.
   (2) In this section and section 327, "telecommunication" means any transmission, emission or reception of signs, signals, writing, images or sounds or intelligence of any nature by wire, radio, visual, or other electro-magnetic system.
61   It should also be noted that the *Radiocommunication Act*, R.S.C. 1985, c. R-2 as amended contains provisions prohibiting the decoding or use of encrypted broadcasting signals.
62   (1977), 33 C.C.C. (2d) 465 (S.C.C.) [*Maltais*].

Subsequent to the charge being laid in the *Maltais* case, the theft of a telecommunications service provision was updated yet again so that "wire or cable" was replaced by "facility." While this change made it clear that the provision covers radio and television broadcasting, in yet a further decision the current wording was held not to extend to the unauthorized manipulation of a computer.[63] As well, in a case a few years after the *Maltais* decision, a husband and wife were accused of stealing a pay television service when the husband, who had expertise in electronic communications, hooked up a device to his television set to improve regular cable television reception but which also, apparently inadvertently, descrambled the pay-tv signal, with the result that until their arrest, the couple enjoyed a pay-tv service for free.[64] The court believed the accused's statement that the device was not intended to receive pay-tv signals, and therefore concluded that the couple merely enjoyed a windfall in respect of which they should not be held responsible. The Alberta Court of Appeal concluded that ensuring adequate scrambling was up to the pay-tv company, as viewers who receive unscrambled signals through no connivance of their own do not offend paragraph 326(1)(b). Indeed, the court speculated whether "electronic technology has again outpaced the legislation passed for its own protection."[65] In effect, the history of the current section 326 of the *Criminal Code* illustrates how difficult it is for the law to stay current with rampaging technology.

Courts in countries other than Canada have also been confronted with the challenge of applying existing criminal law provisions to new technologies. In many such cases property and theft have been restricted to tangible, physical assets, with acquittals being entered as in the *Stewart* case. For example, in the English case, *R. v. Gold*, the accused, who accessed data in a computer by using another person's access code and password, was acquitted under an antiforgery and counterfeiting statute, which required the making of a false "instrument," because the court concluded that electronic messages do not constitute an instrument.[66] In some cases, however, courts are willing to take a broader view of the criminal law. In one recent American case, the court had to determine whether a CD-ROM disk, containing obscene images, could come within the definition of "obscene material,"

---

63   See the discussion of *R. v. McLaughlin*, [1980] 2 S.C.R. 331 [*McLaughlin*] in section B(3), "Computer Abuse," in this chapter.

64   *R. v. Miller and Miller* (1984), 12 C.C.C. (3d) 466 (Alta. C.A.).

65   *Ibid.* at 470.

66   [1988] 2 All E.R. 186 (H.L.).

which was defined as any "photographic product" in the form of still photographs, undeveloped film, videotape, or a purely photographic product or a reproduction of such product in any book, pamphlet, magazine, or other publication.[67] The court acknowledged that a computer's monitor screen is not a photosensitive surface, such as the silver halide surfaces of traditional photographic film. Nonetheless, the court decided the CD-ROM was a photographic product because "the video capture board and scanner used to record the obscene images produced by these discs reproduced the images — aided by appropriate computer hardware and software — with the exactness of a photograph."[68] In another recent U.S. case,[69] an accused argued that a criminal statute prohibiting the transmission of obscene material by "computer or mails" did not cover the downloading of images over the Internet. The court disagreed and concluded:

> The use of the words "by computer" are sufficient to cover this conduct. Congress was no more required to explain in intricate detail the technology of sending pictures over the Internet than it was to explain the chemical process of developing film into photographs. This court will not indulge in metaphysical hair-splitting to rule that "by computer" does not give constitutionally adequate notice that defendant's alleged activity in this case is prohibited.[70]

In these two U.S. cases a much more purposive approach was taken to the criminal law, with seemingly little heed being paid to the principle of narrow interpretation of criminal law statutes.

2) Fraud

Harmful activity that may not be subject to the theft offence as a result of the *Stewart* decision may nevertheless come within the *Criminal Code*'s fraud provision.[71] For example, in *R. v. Marine Resource Analysts*

---

67 *Anthony Aloysius Davis v. State of Oklahoma*, 7 Computer Cases (CCH) ¶47,533 at 69,232 (Okla. Crim. App. 1996) [*Davis*].
68 *Ibid.* at 69,236.
69 *United States of America v. Michael Lamb*, 7 Computer Cases (CCH) ¶47,622 at 69,719 (N.D.N.Y. 1996) [*Lamb*].
70 *Ibid.* at 69,726.
71 The *Criminal Code*'s fraud provision reads as follows:
    380 (1) Every one who, by deceit, falsehood or other fraudulent means, whether or not it is a false pretence within the meaning of this Act, defrauds the public or any person, whether ascertained or not, of any property, money or valuable security, [is guilty of an offence] . . .

Limited,[72] a former employee of the federal government continued using the government's computer facilities for his consulting business, without paying for such use, after he left the employment of the government. The cost of such usage came to $27.30. Ostensibly because of the principle involved, the Crown charged the accused with theft of a telecommunications service and with fraud. For reasons similar to those given in the *McLaughlin* case,[73] the court acquitted on the former charge (i.e., a computer is not a telecommunications facility), but the court did convict on the fraud charge, finding that the accused defrauded the government of $27.30; that is, in order to make out a fraud case there must be a dishonest deprivation. Where an intangible like information is at issue, however, the deprivation is not in the "taking" of the information because, as with the theft offence, information will not constitute property for purpose of the fraud offence. The deprivation, rather, comes from the accused denying the owner of the information or intellectual property a revenue stream that would otherwise be generated from the information. Thus, in the *Stewart* case no finding of fraud was made both because the information was not property and also because the hotel was not in the business of selling its employee information and hence would lose no revenue from a disclosure of this information. Similarly, there was no finding of fraud in the *Falconi* case because the court found there is no property in a pharmacy prescription and pharmacists do not earn revenue from the mere fact of making out prescriptions.[74]

By contrast, in R. v. *Leahy* the court found that the accused's making of unauthorized copies of software under the guise of a software rental business warranted a finding of fraud because of the economic deprivation this activity visited upon the owners of the intellectual property in the software.[75] In support of this finding, the court stated:

> On this inquiry, a number of highly-placed executive officers of the computer companies alleged to have been victimized testified. All these witnesses spoke of the extremely high cost of producing and marketing computer programs, which they stated involved programmers, writers and other personnel, many man-hours of work over an extended period of years, and an investment in the production of millions of dollars before any returns could be realized at all and thereafter,

---

72   (1980), 41 N.S.R. (2d) 631 (Co. Ct.), leave to appeal refused (1980), 43 N.S.R. (2d) 1 (C.A.).

73   *McLaughlin*, above note 63.

74   *Falconi*, above note 52.

75   (1988), 21 C.P.R. (3d) 422 (Ont. Prov. Ct.).

a similar investment in advertising and marketing the product, including support services. It is clear that these manufacturers have a substantial economic interest in their product to protect. They claim that the unauthorized making and distribution of copies of their software is highly damaging to their own enterprises through loss of sales, increased costs of providing support services and loss of reputation."[76]

In a similar vein, in R. v. *Kirkwood* an accused was convicted of fraud for making, selling, and renting videotapes because the accused was thereby depriving the rightful owner of the videos of revenues that the rightful owner would have earned but for the accused's activities.[77] Thus, in appropriate circumstances, creators and owners of intellectual property can find the *Criminal Code*'s fraud provision helpful in combatting bootleggers, counterfeiters, and others who would unfairly misappropriate the fruits of intellectual labour.

3) Computer Abuse

Hackers, as noted above, compromise the integrity of computers by gaining access remotely, and then typically manipulating data and computer files. Even if they do not take the next step of destroying data, or committing a further act such as stealing money or copying sensitive information, hackers cause great anxiety by merely roaming unwelcome through a computer. A stranger breaking into your house and wandering around in your rooms is quite disconcerting, even if she leaves your VCR as she departs. So it is not surprising that the *Criminal Code* has been used to fight hackers for some time, though the initial skirmish did not end in a conviction for many of the same reasons that led to acquittals in the *Stewart* and *Maltais* cases. In R. v. *McLaughlin*, a student at the University of Alberta hacked his way into the university's computers.[78] The hacker was charged with theft of a telecommunications service because at the time (mid-1970s) that was the closest provision to hacking available in the *Criminal Code*. The Supreme Court of Canada, however, decided it was not close enough. The court concluded that a computer is not a telecommunications facility, holding that the function of a computer is not to channel or transmit information to outside recipients so as to be susceptible to unauthorized use; rather, a computer is a data processing device. The court also noted that the definition of

---

76   *Ibid.* at 430–31.
77   (1983), 35 C.R. (3d) 97 (Ont. C.A.).
78   *McLaughlin*, above note 63.

telecommunications in the *Criminal Code* is the same as that found in Canada's broadcasting legislation, and that broadcasting legislation does not cover computers. Again, in the face of the first dynamic of computer law, the court took a very restrained, circumspect approach to a technology-oriented section of the *Criminal Code* and declined to give an expansive interpretation of the relevant provision, calling on Parliament to undertake this task if the country's legislators so wished. It is interesting to speculate whether the court, if it were to render its decision today, would come to a different conclusion given that now computers are used as much to transmit data as to process it, particularly in light of the development of the Internet. In an ironic sense, the technology may have "caught up" to the law in this instance.

Whereas Parliament declined to change the law in response to the Supreme Court's invitation in the *Stewart* case, in 1985 Canada's law makers responded to the call to action in the *McLaughlin* case by adding to the *Criminal Code* the following section 342.1:

(1) Every one who, fraudulently and without colour of right,

    (a) obtains, directly or indirectly, any computer service,

    (b) by means of an electro-magnetic, acoustic, mechanical or other device, intercepts or causes to be intercepted, directly or indirectly, any function of a computer system,

    (c) uses or causes to be used, directly or indirectly, a computer system with intent to commit an offence under paragraph (a) or (b) or an offence under section 430 in relation to data or a computer system, or

    (d) uses, possesses, traffics in or permits another person to have access to a computer password that would enable a person to commit an offence under paragraph (a), (b) or (c)

is guilty of an indictable offence and liable to imprisonment for a term not exceeding ten years, or is guilty of an offence punishable on summary conviction.

(2) In this section,

"computer password" means any data by which a computer service or computer system is capable of being obtained or used;

"computer program" means data representing instructions or statements that, when executed in a computer system, causes the computer system to perform a function;

"computer service" includes data processing and the storage or retrieval of data;

"computer system" means a device that, or a group of interconnected or related devices one or more of which,

(a) contains computer programs or other data, and
(b) pursuant to computer programs,
    (i) performs logic and control, and
    (ii) may perform any other function;

"data" means representations of information or of concepts that
are being prepared or have been prepared in a form suitable for
use in a computer system;

"electro-magnetic, acoustic, mechanical or other device" means
any device or apparatus that is used or is capable of being used to
intercept any function of a computer system, but does not include
a hearing aid used to correct subnormal hearing of the user to not
better than normal hearing;

"function" includes logic, control, arithmetic, deletion, storage
and retrieval and communication or telecommunication to, from
or within a computer system;

"intercept" includes listen to or record a function of a computer
system, or acquire the substance, meaning or purport thereof;

"traffic" means, in respect of a computer password, to sell,
export from or import into Canada, distribute or deal with in
any other way.[79]

This provision, often referred to as the "computer abuse" offence, is
aimed at several potential harms: paragraph 342.1(1)(a) protects
against the theft of computer services, paragraph 342.1(1)(b) is
intended to protect privacy, and the recently added paragraph
342.1(1)(d) is aimed at persons who trade in computer passwords (such
as personal identification numbers and similar codes) or who crack
encryption systems. Paragraph 342.1(1)(b) is required because the
wiretap provision in section 184 arguably is limited to person-to-person
communications and therefore may not be adequate to cover computer-
to-computer communications.[80] Thus, this provision is continuing the

---

79   While the bulk of s. 342.1 dates from 1985, para. 342.1(1)(d), and the
     corresponding definitions of *computer password* and *traffic* in subs. 342.1(2), were
     enacted in April 1997 by *An Act to Amend the Criminal Code and Certain Other Acts,*
     S.C. 1997, c. 18 ("Bill C-17").

80   For a discussion of s. 184, see section B(10), "Interception of Communications,"
     in this chapter.

concern of the *Criminal Code* with the preservation of privacy and secrecy, just as the *Criminal Code* has provisions making it illegal to open a person's correspondence, the low-tech equivalent to computer-related communications.[81] With respect to paragraph 342.1(1)(d), it should be noted that Bill C-17 also added a new section 342.2 that makes it an offence to make, possess, or distribute any instrument or device primarily used for committing an offence under section 342.1. This new provision is similar to subsections 191(1), 327(1), and 351, which make it an offence to possess a scanning device and instruments used to tap into telecommunications transmissions or break and enter into a house.

The potentially wide breadth of the computer abuse provision can be seen in, among other things, paragraph 342.1(1)(c) that makes it an offence merely to use a computer to *intend* to commit either of the two above offences or to commit mischief in relation to data.[82] The rationale for paragraph 342.1(1)(c) is that the law enforcement authorities, and potential victims, should not be required to wait until actual harm is inflicted before the computer abuse behaviour is considered criminal. In effect, paragraph 342.1(1)(c) creates the equivalent of the offence of trespass for real property, where it is also the case that one does not have to wait for the "real" harm to occur. Several other aspects of this provision make it extremely broad. The definition of *computer system* is quite expansive, covering every device that contains some software-related functionality. With the pervasive diffusion of computers today, a personal organizer, pocket calculator, and even a car or television (which both contain software-based features) can come within the ambit of the section. The definition of *data* is also wide-ranging, including data "in a form suitable for use in a computer system," which would include data in the process of being transmitted, or in offline storage, in addition to data inside a computer. The key limitation on the expansive scope of the abuse of computer section is provided by the *mens rea* required by the provision, namely that the perpetrator effect one of the activities enumerated in paragraphs 342.1(1)(a), (b), or (c) "fraudulently and without colour of right." Interestingly, these words are also found in the definition of *theft* in section 322 of the *Criminal Code*. *Fraudulently* essentially means dishonestly and unscrupulously, and with an intent to cause deprivation to another person.[83] The phrase *without colour of right* means without an honest belief that one had the right to carry out the particular action. To establish a colour of right, one would

---

81   *Criminal Code*, s. 345: "Everyone who stops a mail conveyance with intent to rob or search it is guilty of an indictable offence and liable to imprisonment for life."

82   See section B(4), "Abuse of Data," in this chapter for a discussion of the provisions of the *Criminal Code* relating to mischief in respect of data.

83   *R. v. Zlatic* (1993), 79 C.C.C. (3d) 466 (S.C.C.).

have to have an honest belief in a state of facts that, if they existed, would be a legal justification or excuse. Thus, the computer abuse provision should not apply where a person accidentally did one of the enumerated acts, or mistakenly believed she was authorized to do so.

There have been a number of prosecutions under section 342.1 which have resulted in convictions. In one case, however, an accused was held not to come within paragraph 342.1(1)(a) because he was considered too far removed from the actual activity of accessing the particular computer at issue.[84] In *Forsythe* there was a chain of three accused, a person (Curtis) who accessed the Canadian Police Information Computer, a second accused (Wagner) who previously worked for the Edmonton police department and arranged for Curtis to do the accessing, and the third person (Forsythe) who dealt only with Wagner and employed him in Forsythe's firm of private detectives. The court concluded that Curtis and Wagner came comfortably within the "directly or indirectly" language of paragraph 342.1(1)(a) (and Wagner had pleaded guilty previously), but that Forsythe was too remote to come within the provision. This is perhaps an overly conservative reading of section 342.1, given that the court found that Forsythe knew exactly what Wagner was doing, Forsythe had copies of the computer information in print-out form, and Forsythe billed his clients for the information derived from the computer. Nonetheless, the court's approach again exemplifies the judicial restraint that will be shown when, as in the *McLauglin* and *Maltais* cases, a judge believes an accused does not come squarely within an offence.

4) Abuse of Data

The computer abuse offence created by section 342.1 of the *Criminal Code*, which protects the integrity of computers and computer-related communications, does not address data *per se*. This was left to a companion addition to the *Criminal Code* in 1985, namely the provisions relating to mischief with respect to data which read as follows:

> 430(1.1) Every one commits mischief who wilfully
> (a) destroys or alters data;
> (b) renders data meaningless, useless or ineffective;
> (c) obstructs, interrupts or interferes with the lawful use of data; or
> (d) obstructs, interrupts or interferes with any person in the lawful use of data or denies access to data to any person who is entitled to access thereto.
>
> . . .

---

84   R. v. *Forsythe* (1992), 137 A.R. 321 (Prov. Ct.) [*Forsythe*].

(5) Everyone who commits mischief in relation to data
    (a) is guilty of an indictable offence and liable to imprisonment for a term not exceeding ten years; or
    (b) is guilty of an offence punishable on summary conviction.
(5.1) Everyone who wilfully does an act or wilfully omits to do an act that it is his duty to do, if that act or omission is likely to constitute mischief causing actual danger to life, or to constitute mischief in relation to property or data,
    (a) is guilty of an indictable offence and liable to imprisonment for a term not exceeding five years; or
    (b) is guilty of an offence punishable on summary conviction.

As with the abuse of computer provisions discussed above, the abuse of data offences are drawn in broad terms. Note that the definition of data is found in subsection 342.1(2) and is expansively defined to capture, in addition to information, specific representations of information; that is, in addition to covering information this definition would also apply to individual binary digits as well as letters or numbers that, at a higher level of aggregation, comprise information. This wording attempts to address the second dynamic of computer law, namely, the elusive nature of information. As with section 342.1, the limitation in the scope of section 430(1.1) comes from the *mens rea* requirement, namely, that the accused, to be convicted, must have acted "wilfully." In this regard, it is necessary to note that section 429 of the *Criminal Code* provides (in part):

(1) Every one who causes the occurrence of an event by doing an act or by omitting to do an act that it is his duty to do, knowing that the act or omission will probably cause the occurrence of the event and being reckless whether the event occurs or not, shall be deemed . . . "wilfully" to have caused the occurrence of the event.
(2) No person shall be convicted of an offence . . . where he proves that he acted with legal justification or excuse and with colour of right.

The abuse of data provision in section 430(1.1) is broad enough to encompass most every kind of virus imaginable, particularly where the virus destroys data in some manner. It should be noted, however, that section 430(1.1) requires the accused to have actually interfered with data; thus, mere possession of a virus computer program just before it is disseminated over a network or more generally released into the stream of commerce is not sufficient for a conviction under this section. This may be contrasted with the new section 342.2 implemented in April 1997 by Bill C-17,[85] and subsections 191(1) and 327(1) of the

---

85   See section B(3), "Computer Abuse," in this chapter.

Criminal Code, the companion sections to the provisions that prohibit the interception of private communications and the theft of telecommunications services, that make it, respectively, an offence to possess or deal in any scanning device or any device that can be used to tap into telecommunications transmissions;[86] similarly, section 351 makes it an offence to possess instruments that may be used to break and enter into a house. It should also be noted that section 430(1.1) is aimed at more than just activity that destroys data. Actions that obstruct the use of data are also covered, as was the case in *Re Turner and the Queen*, where the accused, by modifying software operated on the computer of a service bureau, caused a customer of the service bureau to be unable to access its data resident on the service bureau's computer.[87] Considered under subsection 430(1), the general mischief in relation to property section because the data abuse provision had not then been enacted, the court held that the accused's defence that no data were destroyed was immaterial given that obstructing the use of the physical media on which the data were resident was sufficient to constitute the offence. In a recent case, an accused was convicted under subsection 430(5) for deleting what he argued was his own data from a computer owned by someone for whom the accused worked.[88] This case illustrates the second dynamic of computer law; the elusive nature of information led the accused to believe he could deal with "his data" as he pleased, but the company he worked for also believed it had rights in such data. As noted generally in the context of trade secrets in section B(1), "Trade Secrets/Breach of Confidence," in chapter 2, this case also argues for the utility of written agreements between persons to confirm their respective rights in the information that each discloses to the other and that they develop together.

5) Obscenity and Child Pornography

Most criminal law concerns itself with the owner's rights in particular information, and not that much attention is paid in the *Criminal Code*

---

86 In *R. v. Duck* (1985), 21 C.C.C. (3d) 529 (Ont. Dist. Ct.) it was held that the "Telefreak" computer program, when operated on a Commodore computer, is such an instrument given that its purpose is to allow the user to make long distance calls in a manner that does not cause them to be reflected in the telephone company's records. "Phreaking" is hacker lingo for stealing a telecommunications service.

87 (1984), 13 C.C.C. (3d) 430 (Ont. H.C.J.).

88 *R. v. Downs*, [1996] S.J. No. 703 (Prov. Ct.) (QL).

to the content itself of the information; content concerns are much more the purview of the privacy and export control discussions that follow in chapter 4. Nevertheless, there are several *Criminal Code* provisions that contain restrictions on the content of communications, including sedition (section 61), obscene material (section 163), child pornography (section 163.1), criminal harassment (section 264), uttering threats (section 264.1), criminal libel (sections 296–301), hate propaganda (sections 318 and 319) and false messages (section 372). Of these sections, perhaps the most actively enforced by prosecutors are the following provisions that prohibit the creation and distribution of obscene materials:

163.(1) Every one commits an offence who
    (a) makes, prints, publishes, distributes, circulates, or has in his possession for the purpose of publication, distribution or circulation any obscene written matter, picture, model, phonograph record or other thing whatever; or
     . . .
(2) Every one commits an offence who knowingly, without lawful justification or excuse,
    (a) sells, exposes to public view or has in his possession for such a purpose any obscene written matter, picture, model, phonograph record or other thing whatever;
    (b) publicly exhibits a disgusting object or an indecent show; . . .

Also important are the following provisions related to child pornography:

163.1(1) In this section, "Child Pornography" means
    (a) a photographic, film, video or other visual representation, whether or not it was made by electronic or mechanical means,
        (i) [depicting a person under 18 years in sexual activity], or
        (ii) [having its dominant characteristic the depiction of a minor's sexual organs or anal region]; or
    (b) any written material or visual representation that advocates or counsels sexual activity [with a minor that would be an offence under the *Criminal Code*].
(2) Every person who makes, prints, publishes or possesses for the purpose of publication any child pornography [is guilty of an offence].
(3) Every person who imports, distributes, sells or possesses for the purpose of distribution or sale any child pornography [is guilty of an offence].
(4) Every person who possesses any child pornography [is guilty of an offence].

It should be noted that section 163 is subject to the defence that the material was distributed for the public good and section 163.1 is subject to the defences that the material had artistic merit, or an educational, scientific, or medical purpose.

It is useful to note the differences in the kinds of material to which these provisions are directed. The types of media through which child pornography may be depicted are arguably narrower than obscene material under section 163, given that the former would not include sound-based materials or written materials (other than those that advocated or counselled sexual offences under the *Criminal Code*). By contrast, written descriptions involving the undue exploitation of sex could violate section 163. Any visual representation of a minor in a sexual situation would qualify as child pornography, whereas sexually explicit material will be found to violate section 163 of the *Criminal Code* if it involves the undue exploitation of sex, either because of the images involving explicit sex with violence or explicit sex that is degrading or dehumanizing, or other explicit sex where children are used in the production.[89] The determination of whether there is an "undue exploitation of sex" is based on community standards of tolerance; a key question in an obscenity case is whether the Canadian community as a whole would tolerate the impugned materials.

a) Community Standards

Given the vast amount of pornographic material available on the Internet, it is not surprising that this new distribution medium raises some interesting questions in respect of the *Criminal Code*'s obscenity and child pornography provisions. One such question is how the "community standard" under section 163 in respect of obscene material ought to be discerned in an Internet environment. Should the traditional approach continue, or should a narrower community standard evolve that focusses on the Internet and, for example, the specific subscribers to a particular BBS service or newsgroup. While not yet explored in any Canadian case in respect of the Internet, such an argument was offered in the *Thomas* obscenity case in the United States.[90] In this case the San Francisco-based operators of an Internet BBS that disseminated child pornography were charged with obscenity in Tennessee, where the authorities downloaded material from the computer server located in California. The law enforcement authorities consciously sought out a

---

89   *R. v. Butler* (1992), 89 D.L.R. (4th) 449 (S.C.C.); *R. v. Jorgensen*, [1995] 4 S.C.R. 55 [*Jorgensen*].

90   *United States v. Thomas*, 74 F.3d 701 (6th Cir. 1996).

conservative community in which to bring the case in order to improve their chances of success in convicting the service's owners. The co-accused argued that the court should fashion an Internet-based standard for considering the appropriate scope of the community standard by which to judge their material. The court refused to take this approach, and simply followed the long standing obscenity rule in the United States that prosecutions may be brought either where the material is produced or where it is obtained.

In pre-Internet obscenity cases Canadian courts have also expressed the view that they will not carve out narrow communities, such as a university film-viewing audience, for purposes of determining the applicability of section 163.[91] At the same time, however, Canadian courts have recognized that the manner and circumstances of distribution are relevant in determining whether or not a publication is obscene; that is, as one court put it, while distribution of certain magazines to a neighbourhood store accessible to all ages would not be tolerable, distribution to an "adult" bookstore to which children of a certain age are not admitted might not be objectionable, and packaging and pricing of material may be relevant as well.[92] For example, in R. v. O'Reilly, a sexually explicit performance was held not to be obscene when performed in a small theatre with admittance restricted to persons above eighteen years of age, with an admission fee charged and a notice posted near the box office indicating the nature of the performance.[93] In the context of the Internet, it is useful to consider several findings in the ACLU case, namely, that currently no effective technology exists to prevent minors from accessing a particular website but that this may change in the not too distant future;[94] at the same time, however, Internet communications are much less intrusive than broadcasts, in the sense that a user must take active steps to access a particular website, and so users of the Internet cannot be "surprised" the way viewers might be watching television or listening to radio.

---

91   R. v. Goldberg and Reitman (1971), 4 C.C.C. (2d) 187 (Ont. C.A.).

92   This is a summary of a lengthier passage in R. v. Sudbury News Service Limited (1978), 39 C.C.C. (2d) 1 (Ont. C.A.); this passage was cited and adopted by Dickson J. in Towne Cinema Theatres Ltd. v. R. (1985), 18 C.C.C. (3d) 193 (S.C.C.).

93   (1970), 1 C.C.C. (2d) 24 (Ont. Co. Ct.).

94   ACLU, above note 44.

b) Intermediary Liability

An important question in respect of both sections 163 and 163.1 is who is liable under these provisions, given that in the computer industry, and particularly over the Internet, multiple participants can be involved in or facilitate the distribution of material to end users. In the context of the Internet, for example, there are BBS operators, online service providers, information suppliers, telecommunications carriers, website operators, newsgroup moderators, e-mail list distributors, and other distributors of content, as well as governments, corporations, and other users (including individuals) who both access as well as disseminate material. Mindful of the four dynamics of computer law, and the ever changing landscape of the Internet, an analysis of each fact situation must always be undertaken based on its own merits, and on the basis of the particular technology and activities specifically involved in the case. Great care must be taken, as well, in attempting to apply metaphors of the real world to the various actors and activities on the Internet. In some cases, it may be appropriate to think about an Internet service provider that merely provides technical Internet access as a telecommunications carrier, or the moderator of a usegroup as a newspaper publisher, or an online service provider that offers access to third party databases as a bookstore or library. In other cases, however, these analogies may not be helpful, and one must always be vigilant not to fall into the trap of using the easy but ultimately incorrect metaphor in place of independent fact gathering and analysis. Moreover, in some respects the Internet will defy analysis by analogy. Nevertheless, where an individual is responsible for the creation of the obscene material or the child pornography, there is little doubt the person will come within subsections 163(1) and 163.1(2), as was the case in *R. v. Pecciarich*, where the accused was charged under both provisions.[95] In terms of the creation of the offensive materials, this case illustrates all too graphically the blurring of private/public, in that prior to the ascendance of computer and network technology an individual would be hard-pressed to create and disseminate on a large-scale high-quality pornography; that is, the resources and funding of a larger organization would typically be

---

95   (1995), 22 O.R. (3d) 748 (Prov. Ct.) [*Pecciarich*]; see *R. v. Pecciarich* [1995] O.J. No. 2238 (Prov. Ct.) (QL) for the sentencing decision, which resulted in the first-time offender being sentenced to two years probation and 150 hours of community service. Interestingly, the court did not ban the accused from using a computer modem, as requested by the Crown, as this would affect the accused's learning and employment opportunities; the judge did order him not to upload or download any computer material that is erotic, obscene, or pornographic in nature.

required both for production and distribution purposes. By contrast, the accused in the *Pecciarich* case single-handedly scanned pictures of children's bodies from retail store catalogues and then manipulated the images into pornographic contexts using a standard personal computer.[96] The accused then distributed the child pornography over the Internet. The case illustrates how in today's technology environment everyone can become a publisher, distributor, retailer, marketer and seller, with a global reach.

Turning from the creation of pornographic material to its dissemination, it was well established under section 163 that to be found to be a distributor under paragraph 163(1)(a), or to be found to be a seller under paragraph 163(2)(a), the accused had to have knowledge of the obscene nature of the contents of the materials. While subsection 163(1) is a strict liability offence, (i.e., there is no "knowingly" requirement as in subsection 163(2)), an honest and reasonable belief in a state of facts which, if true, would render conduct innocent constitutes a defence.[97] It should be noted, however, that such a mistake cannot be a "mistake of law," as where an accused, knowing of the sexually explicit materials, believes them not to be obscene, for if a court ultimately concludes that the materials are obscene, the accused will be liable even if it had an honest and reasonable belief to the contrary. With respect to a retailer under subsection 163(2), the pre-Internet cases are clear that the person who sells to the ultimate consumer must have knowledge of the obscene material, and thus in a paper-based environment an accused news seller was acquitted because it did not know it had materials that were obscene.[98] Indeed, for the Supreme Court of Canada in the *Jorgensen* case, which dealt with a retailer of pornographic videos charged under section 163, the distinction between producer/distributor and retailer is an important one:

> In my view there are sound reasons for such a distinction. Producers and distributors can be presumed to be familiar with the content of the

---

96   In Paul Knox, "Child Porn Flood Swells: High-Tech Era Creates Nightmare" *The [Toronto] Globe and Mail* (27 August 1996), there is mention of technology soon being able to create computer-generated images of lifelike child pornography without using real children. The definition of *child pornography* in s. 163.1 is arguably broad enough to capture such material, though in one sense such technology is to be welcomed because it avoids one harm to which s. 163 is aimed, namely, the exploitation of minors in the creation of child pornography.

97   *R. v. Metro News Ltd.* (1986), 32 D.L.R. (4th) 321 (Ont. C.A.); *Jorgensen*, above note 89.

98   *R. v. Dorosz* (1971), 4 C.C.C. (2d) 203 (Ont. C.A.) [*Dorosz*].

material that they create or distribute. Furthermore, if the law casts upon them the obligation of being familiar with the material they make or distribute, that can easily be discharged. On the other hand, a seller of pornographic material may include among her merchandise magazines, books and a myriad of other products. Until the materials arrive at the seller's shop, he or she has had nothing to do with the material. It might be suggested that the seller can ask the distributor or producer about content when the material is ordered. This is not likely to produce a helpful response. Anyone in the business of producing or distributing pornographic material for profit is not likely inclined to scare off buyers by telling them his or her product can potentially subject the potential purchaser to criminal liability. It would, therefore, be perfectly reasonable for Parliament to have assumed that the seller would ordinarily not be aware of the specific nature of the contents of the material sold, in which circumstance imposing criminal liability would result in the conviction of many persons who did not possess a blameworthy mind state.

Conversely, the producer or distributor will generally be aware of the contents of the material which may result in its being found to be obscene. The imposition of criminal liability in the absence of knowledge of the contents will be less likely to result in the conviction of those that are mentally blameless. In addition, a producer or distributor who knows that absence of knowledge in default of a reasonable inquiry cannot be relied on can easily find out what the material contains. On the other hand, it would be unreasonable to expect the seller to read every book or magazine and view every video or film to ferret out the portions that may run afoul of the obscenity provisions.[99]

The *Jorgensen* decision also makes it clear that the quality of knowledge on the part of the retailer must be more specific than just knowing of the nature of the material, i.e., that it is generally pornographic. Thus, the operator of a video retail outlet must be aware of the relevant facts that made the material obscene, i.e., the specific parts of a videotape that go beyond legal pornography to illegal obscenity, such as the scene where there are images of explicit sex with violence. This knowledge may be directly acquired, as when the operator views the videotape, and indeed in one case a retail outlet that made copies of videos for sale or rental was assumed to have such knowledge.[100] The requisite knowledge for subsection 163(2), however, may also be acquired indirectly, as

---

99 *Jorgensen*, above note 89 at 96–97.
100 *R. v. Harris and Lighthouse Video Centres Limited* (1987), 35 C.C.C. (3d) 1 (Ont. C.A.).

when the proprietor receives warnings from authorities, or statements from others; and wilful blindness will also suffice if the accused suspects the materials may be obscene but does not review them because he knows that looking would fix him with knowledge. This standard of liability is not unlike the one for disseminators of material under civil libel.[101] Section 163.1 regarding child pornography does not include a "knowledge" requirement on the part of sellers, though we do not yet have a case indicating the precise *mens rea* required under this provision and what, if any, defences might be available.

c) Internet Distribution

The liability of Internet-based BBS operators under section 163 has been considered in several Canadian cases. Where the BBS operator creates the obscene materials, as in the *Pecciarich* case,[102] the court has little difficulty in finding the accused guilty of distribution as well by uploading files containing the obscene material onto bulletin boards, which the public was then able to access through an application process. In another case, however, the BBS operator did not create the obscene material, and argued it should be considered a seller and that it did not have knowledge of the specific files being uploaded by it and subscribers on its BBS, and therefore did not have the requisite knowledge for a seller under subsection 163(2).[103] The court disagreed, finding the accused to be a distributor, based on a number of factors, including the large number of people that could access the BBS, and the ability of the obscene material, in digital form, to be further distributed, in electronic or hard copy form if printed out, once made available electronically on the BBS. The court, after citing from the *Jorgensen* and *Dorosz* cases, concluded that the distinction between retailer and wholesaler drawn in the latter case "makes sense with print material" but "is not one which is necessarily applicable to computer technology."[104] This could be a very important decision. It determines the dichotomy between distributor and retailer not on the basis of whom a party sells to, but rather whether the purchaser can in turn further disseminate copies of the material. Under such an approach, the transmission of digital-based products in electronic form may effectively negate the concept of retailer, thus making a distributor of all participants, including end users, because they in turn can retrans-

---

101   See section C(1), "Cyber Libel," in chapter 6.
102   *Pecciarich*, above note 95.
103   *R. v. Hurtubise*, [1997] B.C.J. No. 40 (S.C.) (QL) [*Hurtubise*].
104   *Ibid.* at para. 11.

mit the obscene materials. In essence, the third dynamic of computer law, namely, the blurring of private/public, appears to have obliterated the previously important distinction between subsections 163(1) and 163(2) of the *Criminal Code* drawn by the Supreme Court of Canada in the *Jorgensen* case.

In addition to distributing and selling obscene material and child pornography, an accused can be convicted under sections 163 and 163.1 for publishing or exposing to public view these materials. These elements raise the beguiling question of how the concept of "public" should be determined in the context of the Internet. In a pre-Internet case, *R. v. Rioux*,[105] a private showing of obscene films in the accused's home was not found to constitute "circulation" for purposes of para- graph 163(1)(a). Further along the private–public continuum, in *R. v. Harrison*[106] it was held that an obscene film was not exposed to public view under paragraph 163(2)(a) where it was shown only to relatives and friends of the groom at a stag party in a community hall that, while generally open to the public, was being used for a private gathering; there was a notice posted on the wall outside the hall indicating that this was a private party and warning even the invited guests that stag films were going to be shown. In concluding that the persons in this case con- stituted a private group, and that the situation was tantamount to show- ing a film in one's home, the court relied, in part, on the definition of *private* in the Oxford dictionary, which includes the phrases: "kept or removed from public view . . . not within the cognizance of people gen- erally . . . not open to the public; intended only for the use of particular and privileged persons," and which were contrasted to the following definitions of *public*: "done or made by or on behalf of the community as a whole . . . generally accessible or available" and *public place*: "A place to which the general public has a right to resort . . . Any place so situated that what passes there can be seen by any considerable number of persons, if they happen to look."[107] By contrast, in *R. v. Vigue*[108] a film was held to be exposed to public view because it was shown to invited guests as well as to two people who paid an admission charge. In coming to this conclusion, however, the court was clearly troubled by the fact that the two paying viewers were not invited by the person organizing the screening; they were simply allowed in the room by the person who was helping to run the film projector (who was not the organizer of the

---

105   (1969), 10 D.L.R. (3d) 196 (S.C.C.).
106   (1973), 12 C.C.C. (2d) 26 (Alta. Dist. Ct.).
107   *Ibid.* at 28–29.
108   (1973), 13 C.C.C. (2d) 381 (B.C. Prov. Ct.) [*Vigue*].

viewing).[109] In the course of the judgment the court struggled with the concept of public and private in the following terms:

> I have been troubled as to what is the test of privacy. Does the invitation have to be extended by the accused or may he delegate one or more people to invite guests? May invited persons invite others? Would it still be a private occasion if the accused stands on the street and invites everybody who comes past? Is a personal invitation the only criterion of privacy? Or is acquaintance with the invited person part of the test?
>
> In addition does the payment of money affect the question of privacy and to what extent? In this case the accused says that he received money which he did not ask for and he used it simply to replace the bulb in the projector.[110]

These sorts of considerations and factors animate the third dynamic of computer law and will likely loom large in analyses of the public/private determinations involving Internet situations.

The *Hurtubise* case addressed both the publication and exposing to public view issues under section 163. In respect of the former, the court held that there was possession of the obscene material for the purpose of publication given the ability of the computer to show material to a number of people and to produce material easily and inexpensively, as discussed above. In respect of the offence of "exposing to public view," the counsel for the accused argued that his clients should have been charged under this provision (for which counsel argued his clients did not have the requisite *mens rea*), and in this regard it is interesting to note that the bulletin board service in *Hurtubise* took active steps to limit access to specific subscribers who were adults; that is, this case is consistent with the trend in other cases involving the "private/public" differentiation, such as in the case of copyright infringement[111] and regulation of broadcasting,[112] namely, that it is increasingly difficult to retain a concept of private in the world of modern communications, at least in respect of those applications where people generally are able to

---

109   The court's willingness to convict in the *Vigue* case may also have been coloured by the nature of the films in issue, and the court's reaction to them at 382: "The films I saw were of poor quality and would, I think, be quite loathsome to many people because of their subject-matter. To have shown them to a pre-wedding party as accused testified he had, would be in execrable taste and destructive, if young people are to commence married life with any respect for their relationship."
110   *Vigue*, above note 108 at 383.
111   See section C(6), "Copyright and the Internet," in chapter 2.
112   See section C(3), "Regulating the Internet," in chapter 4.

participate in or subscribe to the particular activity. In the case of the Internet, this is arguably exacerbated by the fact that solicitation and subscription is far easier in a networked environment than was previously the case. Nonetheless, the application of the provisions in sections 163 and 163.1 to Internet services such as e-mail or usegroups will have to be determined on a case-by-case basis, and may turn on the particular nature of the service involved; for example, a limited and closed e-mail list should be treated differently than a large, open-ended usegroup. Obviously, any material posted to a generally accessible website will be considered to reside in a public place. With certain present and future technologies such as passwords based on biometric features[113] and encryption, however, it should be possible to carve out private enclaves within the broader Internet and to recreate, in a virtual environment, the privacy that courts have accorded a person's own physical house.

Subsection 163.1(4) makes it an offence to "possess" child pornography. Computers, and particularly networks (and especially the Internet), raise some new questions as to the concept of possession. Under subsection 4(3) of the *Criminal Code*, a person possesses something when (a) it is in that person's personal possession; (b) the person knowingly has it in the actual possession of another person; or (c) the person knowingly has the item in a place for use or benefit of himself or another person. Precomputer/Internet cases have held that the key ingredients of possession are knowledge and control, each of which must occur simultaneously. Thus, where a subscriber to a BBS consciously downloads some child pornography to his computer, there is a likely a strong case that he had both the requisite knowledge and control. The many intermediaries on the Internet, however, may be in a different situation if in respect of the particular activity involving the child pornography they lacked the knowledge of its presence. More problematic is the control issue. Does this factor require, for example, an Internet service provider to request a BBS to delete some child pornography of which it has knowledge? Or does it require the wholesale disconnection of the BBS's connection to the Internet, given that the Internet service provider does not exercise editorial control over the particular pornography?

d) Legislative Responses

The foregoing discussion of sections 163 and 163.1 of the *Criminal Code* illustrates that there are a number of uncertainties associated with these provisions when considered in the context of computers and networks,

---

113   See section A(2), "Signatures," in chapter 6.

particularly for intermediaries such as Internet service providers. As a result, some ISPs have ceased to carry a number of pornographic use-groups, both on their own volition or at the suggestion of public authorities. Similarly, a number of Canadian universities have taken steps to restrict access to "alt.sex" newsgroups.[114] Given the amorphous nature of the Internet, such activities may not limit access to people determined to reach these sites, since they can usually find another electronic route.[115]

Not surprisingly, some elements within government wish to go further and legislate certain measures to fight child pornography in particular. For example, Bill C-396, a private member's bill entitled *An Act to Restrict the Use of the Internet to Distribute Pornographic Material Involving Children*, was introduced into Canada's House of Commons on 8 April 1997. This bill, which died on the order paper when the 1997 federal election was called, would have required the licensing of all persons who facilitate access to the Internet, with such licences being refused (or cancelled if previously issued) to anyone who has been convicted under section 163.1 of the *Criminal Code*. The bill would also have made it an offence to knowingly permit the use of its service for the placing of child pornography on the Internet or the viewing, reading, copying, or recovery of child pornography from the Internet. The bill would also have required Internet service providers to check whether subscribers had been convicted under section 163.1, and to refuse service to such persons, and to block access by its subscribers to any material that the government determines to be child pornography. The bill would also have made directors of corporations liable if they were aware of the circumstances giving rise to the offence.

Elements of the broad parameters of Bill C-396 can also be seen in the U.S. *Communications Decency Act of 1996* (CDA), which criminalizes the transmission to minors of obscene or indecent messages and the use of interactive computer services to display to minors sexually explicit material that is patently offensive by contemporary community standards.[116] This legislation is relevant to Canadians for a number of reasons, including the fact that Canadian users acquire much content from U.S. information providers, the statute may have an impact on Canadians providing services to Americans, and the statute may contain elements

---

114   See Richard S. Rosenberg, "Free Speech, Pornography, Sexual Harassment, and Electronic Networks: An Update and Extension," in *The Electronic Superhighway: The Shape of Technology and Law To Come*, eds. Ejan Mackaay, Daniel Poulin & Pierre Trudel (The Hague: Kluwer, 1995).

115   See Warren Caragata, "Crime in Cybercity," *Maclean's*, 22 May 1995.

116   This legislation is Title V of the *Telecommunications Act of 1996*, Pub.L. 104-104, 110 Stat. 56.

that one day might be adopted in Canada. Important provisions in this statute are several affirmative defences on behalf of Internet service providers, including where they take effective technologically feasible actions to prevent minors accessing knowledge of the offending material, or where they restrict access to the sexual material by requiring use of a credit card, debit account, adult access code or adult personal identification number. In the recent ruling by the United States Supreme Court in the *ACLU* case, two of the core provisions of the CDA were held to be unconstitutional for being overly broad.[117] While upholding the provision of the CDA aimed at prohibiting the transmissions of obscene messages, the majority of the court found that the provisions regarding "indecent" and "patently offensive" messages were too vague to pass muster under the First Amendment of the U.S. Constitution (that protects freedom of speech). Drawing upon the extensive findings regarding the Internet made by the lower court,[118] the majority also concluded that the affirmative defences provided by the CDA were not technologically or economically feasible for most content providers on the Internet. In an ironic variation of the first dynamic of computer law, where it is usually the law that cannot keep pace with technology, the *ACLU* case illustrates the problem of a law being ahead of the then available technology! In a perceptive partial minority opinion, Justice Sandra O'Connor noted that in the past the U.S. Supreme Court would uphold a law that regulates pornography by creating an "adult zone" in the physical world because in such an environment geography and identity can enable the owner of an adult establishment to prevent the entry of children. Justice O'Connor noted that effecting the same protection of children through zoning on the Internet in 1997 is not possible because speakers and listeners can mask their identities; she added, however, that content "tagging," screening, and other technologies are being developed that, if they come into widespread use, may permit effective zoning on the Internet in the future.[119] In effect, the *ACLU* case is

---

117   *ACLU*, above note 44.
118   *Ibid.* As noted in section A(6), "The Internet," in chapter 1, this decision gives a very thorough description and analysis of the structure, operations, uses, and nuances of the Internet. Another lower court decision also found the CDA unconstitutional: *Shea v. Reno*, 930 F. Supp. 916 (S.D.N.Y. 1996). This latter decision gives a good discussion of "tagging" and various other measures being developed to permit the private screening of content over the Internet.
119   Private tagging and content categorization schemes have their own critics, particularly as they raise the spectre of censorship by persons not accountable to the public at large: see Lawrence Lessig, "Tyranny in the Infrastructure," *Wired*, July 1997.

required reading for all legislators who wish to regulate the Internet because the case makes it clear how difficult it will be to tame the Internet tiger, given the four dynamics of computer law.

6) Illegal Speech

The *Criminal Code* makes certain types of speech illegal. Subsection 319(1), for example, provides that "[e]very one who, by communicating statements in any public place, incites hatred against any identifiable group where such incitement is likely to lead to a breach of the peace" is guilty of an offence. As well, subsection 319(2) provides that "[e]very one who, by communicating statements other than in private conversation, wilfully promotes hatred against any identifiable group" is guilty of an offence.[120] Significant definitions related to these "hate speech" provisions are contained in subsection 319(7), namely: *communicating* includes communicating by telephone, broadcasting, or other audible or visible means; *public place* includes any place to which the public have access as of right or by invitation, express or implied; and *statements* includes words spoken or written or recorded electronically or electromagnetically or otherwise, and gestures, signs, or other visible representations. These provisions raise a number of particularly interesting and difficult issues in terms of their application in an electronic environment like the Internet. The intention here, therefore, is not to examine the various elements of these offences, such as the meaning of *promote* and other keywords or defences, but rather to review the application of these offences in the context of computer and network technologies.[121]

With respect to subsection 319(1), a key question is whether a networked computer environment, and particularly the Internet, can be considered to be a "public place." A threshold point in this regard is whether the concept of public place, as used in this provision, is limited to physical places, which then begs the question whether the Internet is

---

120   Other provisions of the *Criminal Code* include s. 318, which makes it an offence to advocate or promote genocide, and s. 320, which authorizes the seizure of copies of hate propaganda. Regulations under the *Broadcasting Act* also prohibit licensees from distributing programming that exposes individuals to hatred or contempt on the basis of discrimination: see *Pay Television Regulations, 1990*, SOR/90-105, para. 3(2)(b), 25 January 1990; *Specialty Services Regulations, 1990*, SOR/90-106, subs. 3(b), 25 January 1990; *Television Broadcasting Regulations, 1987*, SOR/87-49, para. 5(1)(b), 9 January 1987; and *Radio Regulations, 1986*, SOR/86-982, subs. 3(b), 18 September 1986.

121   For a discussion of the hate speech offences generally, see *R. v. Keegstra* (1990), 61 C.C.C. (3d) 1 (S.C.C.).

a physical place. When Canadian novelist William Gibson coined the phrase "cyberspace" in the early 1980s, it was intended to describe a space without physical or even temporal dimensions.[122] In many areas, however, the Internet has become a virtual version or alter ego for physical counterparts. Justice Sopinka of the Supreme Court of Canada suggested outside the courtroom, that the message-posting capability of the Internet approximates the ability to hang posters from physical telephone poles; considered in this light, cyberspace is a place for purposes of subsection 319(1).[123] Justice Sopinka made this analogy in the context of a recent Supreme Court of Canada decision that struck down as unconstitutional a municipal bylaw that prohibited posters on public property; the law was held to be an unjustifiable infringement on the freedom of expression, preventing the communication of political, cultural, and artistic messages.[124] In this context, Justice Sopinka stated:

> In many ways, it may be said that electronic media such as Internet are the posters of the late twentieth century providing an invaluable means of expression to a wide audience. Like posters, the cost is relatively inexpensive and therefore it is available to people of modest economic means. In some cities, electronic mail services are entirely free. Just as with posters, we must be cognizant of the tremendous value of electronic mail.[125]

At the same time, however, Justice Sopinka discussed the less positive aspects of the electronic media, and in particular its potential to be used for obscene and hateful expression. In this regard, he noted:

> The freedom of speech over computer networks is no more absolute than for any other means of expression. . . . The ability of computer networks to provide a new and expansive forum for sexual and racial harassment, obscenity and violent messages may in fact demand government attention.[126]

---

122   William Gibson, *Neuromancer* (New York: AceBooks, 1984).

123   Hon. John Sopinka, "Freedom of Speech and Privacy In the Information Age" (Address to the University of Waterloo Symposium on Free Speech and Privacy in the Information Age, 26 November 1994) ["Freedom of Speech"]. See also an updated version of this address delivered at the Faculty of Law, Queen's University, on 21 November 1996. Both versions are available at <http://www.canniff.com/tdenton/sopinka.html>.

124   *Peterborough (City) v. Ramsden* (1993), 106 D.L.R. (4th) 233 (S.C.C.).

125   Sopinka, "Freedom of Speech," above note 123 at 5.

126   *Ibid.* at 6.

Assuming the Internet is a *place* for purposes of subsection 319(1) of the *Criminal Code*, is it a *public* one? Consider that the Internet comprises a multitude of services, features, and participants, and the facts of each scenario would have to be analysed carefully in order to apply subsection 319(1) sensibly. For example, an open bulletin board on a so-called freenet, where no fees are charged to participate and all users have access to all messages posted by all other users, is a good candidate to be considered a public place. By contrast, private e-mail, particularly if encrypted and resident on a personal computer in a private home, may not be a message resident in a public place. There are pre-Internet indecent exposure or prostitution solicitation cases, however, that hold that a person, although physically on private property, can be deemed to be in a public place if the person is in view of the public. Thus, in *Hutt* v. *R.*, an automobile was held not to be a public place because the particular offence occurred wholly within the vehicle.[127] In contrast, in other cases the subject automobile lost its private character because while the indecent or other impugned act was performed in the automobile it was able to be viewed from the public street.[128] After the *Hutt* decision the term *public place* in section 195 of the *Criminal Code* was amended to include *any motor vehicle in a public place* and *any place open to public view*. These cases have some consequences for the Internet. First, by analogy to them it may be possible to argue that someone comfortably ensconced in the seemingly private environs of her own home nevertheless is deemed to be in a public place, depending on the quality and nature of the person's connections with public portions of the Internet. Second, at some point Parliament may take up the challenge and legislate the meaning of public and private on the Internet in an attempt to clarify these blurring definitions in the computer environment.

With respect to the potential liability of Internet intermediaries under section 319, much will turn on the approach taken by courts to the word *communicating* in both provisions. The dictionary meaning of this word is broad enough to encompass mere carriage or transmission of messages initiated by someone else. Nonetheless, it will be interesting to see if courts adopt reasoning analogous to that in *The Electric Despatch*

---

127   (1978), 38 C.C.C. (2d) 418 (S.C.C.) [*Hutt*].

128   *R.* v. *Wise* (1982), 67 C.C.C. (2d) 231 (B.C. Co. Ct.); *R.* v. *Figliuzzi* (1981), 59 C.C.C. (2d) 144 (Alta. Q.B.). See also *R.* v. *Buhay* (1986), 30 C.C.C. (3d) 30 (Man. C.A.), where it was held that a public place includes a doorway in a private house if the accused performs the indecent act in such a way as to be exposed to public view; in essence, the private dwelling takes on a public presence for the narrow purpose of the commission of the offence. See also the discussion of "public" in section B(5), "Obscenity and Child Pornography," in this chapter.

Company of Toronto v. *The Bell Telephone Company of Canada*, which held that a person who transmits a message is the sender of it, and that a telecommunications carrier should not be considered to have transmitted the message where it did not have knowledge of it.[129] Great care, however, must be taken when assessing the jurisprudential value of this century-old case, as it involved two litigants disputing a non-competition covenant in a purchase and sale agreement; moreover, a reading of the trial decision in this case shows that the key concern of the plaintiff was not the transmission of messages but the act of permitting a certain competitor of the plaintiff to connect to the defendant's telephone system. In any event, again a detailed analysis will have to be undertaken of each specific case, including understanding what the particular role of the intermediary was in the particular circumstances. Different considerations will apply to a passive provider of a telecom service than to a moderator of a discussion group that posts inflammatory messages.

Although the term *public place* in section 319 raises questions with respect to the Internet, the definitions of *communicating* and *statements* in subsection 319(7) likely capture every form of message, regardless of its medium. As with the definitions of *data* in section 342.1 discussed earlier, these definitions in subsection 319(7) are technology-neutral and apply regardless of the particular mode of transmission utilized. The same may not necessarily be said of another federal statute that is aimed at prohibiting hate messages. Under subsection 13(1) of the *Canadian Human Rights Act* (CHRA), it is a discriminatory practice to repeatedly communicate telephonically, or cause to be so communicated by means of the facilities of a telecommunications undertaking, any matter that exposes a person to hatred based on prohibited grounds of discrimination.[130] It is clear this provision applies to telephone answering machines, as determined in the *Taylor* case where the subsection also withstood constitutional scrutiny.[131] It is not yet clear how the provision will be interpreted in relation to the Internet. One argument may focus on the concept of *telephonically* within the provision and draw on the case law that stands for the proposition that "telephone" relates to the transmission of sounds or voice, thereby not extending the provision to text-based Internet messages.[132] Several

---

129   (1891), 20 S.C.R. 83.
130   R.S.C. 1985, c. H-6.
131   *Canada (Canadian Human Rights Commission)* v. *Taylor* (1990), 75 D.L.R. (4th) 577 (S.C.C.) [*Taylor*].
132   See, for example, *IBM Canada Ltd.* v. *Deputy M.N.R., Customs and Excise*, [1992] 1 F.C. 663 (C.A.) [*IBM*], though it should be noted that this is a customs case and hence its applicability in a human rights context is questionable.

arguments may be mustered against this approach, including the fact that modems (the devices used by most people to connect to the Internet) transmit sound-based tones in the process of transmitting text and digital content over telephone lines. A somewhat broader approach is that *telephonically* should cover all communications over the Internet, since computing and telephony technologies converge here. Essentially this approach was articulated by a U.S. court in a recent case involving the issue of a person's reasonable expectations of privacy in e-mail transmissions.[133] Such an approach would be consistent with the principle that human rights legislation should be given a liberal and purposive interpretation, and that any doubts are to be resolved in a manner that promotes the goals of the legislation.[134] Support for this approach can be gleaned from the *Taylor* decision where Justice Dickson pointed out that human rights legislation operates differently from the *Criminal Code*. Therefore, the principle of narrow construction of criminal statutory provisions, as articulated in the *Maltais*[135] and *McLaughlin*[136] cases, should not come into play in respect of subsection 13(1) of the CHRA, and indeed the more purposive approach taken in the U.S. *Davis*[137] and *Lamb*[138] cases should be adopted.

Subsection 13(3) of the CHRA provides an exemption from the prohibition in subsection 13(1) for an owner or operator of a telecommunications undertaking that is used by others. This provision is similar to the general principle, seen often in this book, that innocent disseminators of third-party messages should not be liable for the content of those messages, but only so long as the disseminator does not have actual knowledge of the offending nature of the third party's message or fails to have knowledge due to negligence or wilful blindness; the same

---

133   *United States v. Maxwell*, 45 M.J. 406 (U.S. Ct. App. Armed Forces 1996) (Westlaw). In this case the court stated at paras. 416–17: "In answering these questions, we have examined the relationship between appellant and AOL [America Online] from four different perspectives. First, the technology used to communicate via e-mail is extraordinarily analogous to a telephone conversation. Indeed, e-mail is transmitted from one computer to another via telephone communication, either hard line or satellite. We have recognized that '[t]elephone conversations are protected by the Fourth Amendment if there is a reasonable expectation of privacy.'"

134   See Ruth Sullivan, *Driedger on the Construction of Statutes*, 3d ed. (Toronto: Butterworths, 1994).

135   *Maltais*, above note 62.

136   *McLaughlin*, above note 63.

137   *Davis*, above note 67.

138   *Lamb*, above note 69.

general principle is articulated by the law in respect of copyright,[139] libel,[140] obscene material under the *Criminal Code*,[141] criminal libel,[142] and broadcasting.[143] The knowledge elements, however, are lacking in subsection 13(3) of the CHRA, ostensibly because it dates from a time when only telephone companies carried telephonic messages, and did so as true common carriers in a manner that saw them fulfil this role without having any occasion to monitor a customer's conversations. Today, however, over the Internet an owner or, especially, an operator of a network may well have reason to monitor messages. In effect, just as the provision in subsection 13(1) could be drafted more broadly, the exemption in subsection 13(3) is too broad, because it is based on "status" rather than an assessment of function. The real question should be whether the owner or operator of the telecommunications undertaking had knowledge of (actually or through negligence or wilful blindness) and control over the offending message.

7) Criminal Libel

Another form of illegal speech is criminal libel. Under section 301 of the *Criminal Code*, someone convicted of publishing a criminal libel is liable to imprisonment for two years; the sentence can be increased under section 300 to five years if the publisher of the libel knows it to be false. A defamatory libel is defined as a "matter published, without lawful justification or excuse, that is likely to injure the reputation of any person by exposing him to hatred, contempt or ridicule, or that is designed to insult the person of or concerning whom it is published."[144] Perhaps the most interesting provisions relating to criminal libel are the sections addressing the liability of persons who publish newspapers and sell other works. The former, contained in section 303, provides as follows:

> 303.(1) The proprietor of a newspaper shall be deemed to publish defamatory matter that is inserted and published therein, unless he proves that the defamatory matter was inserted in the newspaper without his knowledge and without negligence on his part.

---

139   See section C(6), "Copyright and the Internet," in chapter 2.
140   See section C(1), "Cyber Libel," in chapter 6.
141   See section B(5), "Obscenity and Child Pornography," in this chapter.
142   See section B(7), "Criminal Libel," in this chapter.
143   See section C(2), "Regulating Broadcasting," in chapter 4.
144   *Criminal Code*, subs. 298(1). For a discussion of the criminal libel rules and their historic rationale and development, see *R. v. Stevens* (1995), 96 C.C.C. (3d) 238 (Man. C.A.).

(2) Where the proprietor of a newspaper gives to a person general authority to manage or conduct the newspaper as editor or otherwise, the insertion by that person of defamatory matter in the newspaper shall, for the purposes of subsection (1), be deemed not to be negligence on the part of the proprietor unless it is proved that

    (a) he intended the general authority to include authority to insert defamatory matter in the newspaper; or

    (b) he continued to confer general authority after he knew that it had been exercised by the insertion of defamatory matter in the newspaper.

(3) No person shall be deemed to publish a defamatory libel by reason only that he sells a number or part of a newspaper that contains a defamatory libel, unless he knows that the number or part contains defamatory matter or that defamatory matter is habitually contained in the newspaper.

The definition of newspaper is in section 297, and reads as follows:

any paper, magazine or periodical containing public news, intelligence or reports of events, or any remarks or observations thereon, printed for sale and published periodically or in parts or numbers, at intervals not exceeding thirty-one days between the publication of any two such papers, parts or numbers, and any paper, magazine or periodical printed in order to be dispersed and made public, weekly or more often, or at intervals not exceeding thirty-one days, that contains advertisements, exclusively or principally.

As a threshold matter, it may be asked whether section 303 applies to publications circulated in an electronic environment, given that the definition of newspaper speaks in terms of being "printed." The traditional method of printing is to imprint ink onto paper by mechanical means. A more purposive approach, however, would focus on simply the process of making multiple copies of a document. Thus, in one case unrelated to the *Criminal Code*, there is a suggestion that photocopies should be considered printed.[145] In this regard, the cases in section C(1),

---

145 *Xerox of Canada Ltd.* v. *IBM Canada Ltd.* (1977), 33 C.P.R. (2d) 24 (F.C.T.D.). In this case, one party had to prove, in respect of a patent infringement action, that a particular document had been "printed" given the *Patent Act*'s then requirement for a "printed publication" for this particular purpose. After reviewing the sketchy evidence before it, the court approached the "printed" question by being sensitive to "the state of printing and reproducing methods," and concluded at 85: "Without deciding, I would suggest that today a run of so-called 'photostatic copies,' might well be held to be 'printed.'"

"Cyber Libel," in chapter 6 in the civil libel discussion, that address whether a newspaper or a periodical is only paper-based or could also exist in an Internet context, are indirectly relevant and should be referred to on this point. To avoid doubt, Parliament, in light of the first dynamic of computer law, might consider amending the definition of *newspaper* to make it more technology-neutral. The next noteworthy point about subsection 303(1) is that a proprietor of a newspaper may not avoid responsibility simply because he did not have knowledge of the defamatory material; in addition, he cannot have been negligent in respect of its insertion in the newspaper. This mirrors the standard of liability for "innocent disseminators" under civil libel.[146] Subsection 303(2) addresses the situation where the proprietor has appointed someone else, such as an editor, to manage the editorial content of the newspaper and who serves to relieve the proprietor of responsibility, unless she gave a general permission to the editor to insert libellous material or she does not revoke the editor's responsibility after the proprietor learns of the editor's insertion of libellous material in the newspaper. This particular provision has interesting counterparts in the Internet world, where it is not uncommon for an online service provider to contract out to a third party responsibility for overseeing the editorial aspect of a particular electronic information-based service, as was the case in *Cubby, Inc.* v. *CompuServe Inc.*[147]

With respect to persons who sell newspapers that happen to contain libellous material, such vendors are only liable, as a result of subsection 303(3), if they have knowledge of the defamatory material or if they know that the particular newspaper habitually carries such libellous matter. Interestingly, the second prong of this knowledge test is arguably narrower than the equivalent test for civil libel with respect to news vendors and other innocent disseminators;[148] that is, there are likely circumstances where one could attract liability as a distributor under the civil standard of negligence but not come within subsection 303(3). Similarly, persons who sell books, magazines, or other things (other than newspapers) under subsection 304(1)[149] must have knowledge of

---

146 See section C(1), "Cyber Libel," in chapter 6.
147 776 F. Supp. 135 (S.D.N.Y. 1991). This case is discussed in section C(1), "Cyber Libel," in chapter 6.
148 See section C(1), "Cyber Libel," in chapter 6.
149 "304(1) No person shall be deemed to publish a defamatory libel by reason only that he sells a book, magazine, pamphlet or other thing, other than a newspaper that contains a defamatory matter if, at the time of the sale, he does not know that it contains the defamatory matter."

the defamatory material, and again this seems narrower than the equivalent civil libel standard, which would also include negligence, unless knowledge is interpreted rather broadly as including wilful blindness along the lines articulated in the *Jorgensen* case.[150] Equally, under subsection 304(2),[151] where an employee sells such material, the employer's liability requires actual knowledge or knowledge that defamatory material was habitually contained in the subject material, again establishing a standard arguably narrower than the civil libel one. Moreover, the distinction in these provisions between newspapers and other publications appears to be unjustifiable in an electronic environment where CD-ROMs and online databases blur the definitions.

Although not directly related to the criminal libel provisions, it is worth speculating how another control on the media — the law of contempt of court in the guise of bans on the publications of trial proceedings — will be applied in a computer and networked environment. It was traditionally the law that a newspaper or broadcaster had absolute liability if it published or broadcast any material that was subject to a court-ordered ban.[152] More recently, however, this strict rule in respect of so-called contemptuous publications has been loosened in those circumstances where, for example, a reporter is ignorant of the ban, in which case a due diligence defence might be raised provided the parties involved acted with all reasonable care and had no intention of interfering with the court process.[153] Of course, regardless of the prospects for liability or immunity of an Internet participant in respect of publication bans, the practical question should also be asked to what extent they can be made to work in an Internet environment. Consider the experience with the notorious court-imposed ban on information related to the 1993 legal proceedings involving Karla Homolka, who at the time was alleged to have assisted Paul Bernardo in carrying out the grizzly murders of three young women in St. Catharines, Ontario. Soon after the court-imposed ban, some Internet newsgroups began carrying material from the trial. A number of these were deleted from university

---

150   *Jorgensen*, above note 89.

151   "304(2) Where a servant, in the course of his employment, sells a book, magazine, pamphlet or other thing, other than a newspaper, the employer shall be deemed not to publish any defamatory matter contained therein unless it is proved that the employer authorized the sale knowing that
   (a) defamatory matter was contained therein; or
   (b) defamatory matter was habitually contained therein, in the case of a periodical."

152   *R. v. Odham's Press, Ltd.*, [1956] 3 All E.R. 494 (Q.B.).

153   *R. v. Edge*, [1988] 4 W.W.R. 163 (B.C.C.A.).

access by university administrators, but as an Internet expert stated at the time: "As soon as one news group is closed down, the story shows up somewhere else."[154] In short, although bringing legal action against particular Internet participants is possible, regulating the whole of the Internet is a close to impossible task. It would appear that the judiciary is cognizant of these dynamics of the Internet. In the recent *Dagenais* case, the Supreme Court of Canada, in overturning a publication ban, stated:

> It should also be noted that recent technological advances have brought with them considerable difficulties for those who seek to enforce bans. The efficacy of bans has been reduced by the growth of interprovincial and international television and radio broadcasts available through cable television, satellite dishes and shortwave radios. It has also been reduced by the advent of information exchanges available through computer networks. In this global electronic age, meaningfully restricting the flow of information is becoming increasingly difficult.[155]

Justice Sopinka, in a speech that resonated with the four dynamics of computer law, commented on the *Dagenais* case as follows:

> Those opposing bans express concern about the efficacy of some publication bans. They note that recent technological advances such as satellite dishes and computer networking have created substantial difficulty in enforcing such bans. The fact that it is becoming much more difficult to meaningfully restrict the flow of information must be weighed into the balancing equation. If the efficacy of a ban is minimal due to technology, then it becomes harder to justify its existence. Once again, we see that the courts will have to consider the impact of the information age on the balancing of rights and freedoms under the *Charter*.[156]

8) Gaming and Betting

The proliferation of computers and networks, particularly the Internet, raise a number of novel issues under the *Criminal Code*'s provisions related to gaming and betting.[157] The legal regime for gambling in Canada

---

154 See Mark Nichols, "Wired World," *Maclean's*, 17 January 1994.

155 *Dagenais v. Canadian Broadcasting Corp.*, [1994] 3 S.C.R. 835 at 886.

156 Sopinka, "Freedom of Speech," above note 123 at 7.

157 Even the traditional activity of wagering on horse races is witnessing the application of Internet-related technologies: see Neil A. Campbell, "Tracks Decry Lack of Help with 'Illegal' Betting" *The [Toronto] Globe and Mail* (16 January 1997).

created by sections 201 to 207 of the *Criminal Code* operates on the basis that sections 201 to 206 prohibit gambling and numerous other gaming activities (including lotteries, sports betting, and the like) unless they are regulated by a province. As well, paragraph 207(4)(c) effectively requires that any lottery scheme using a computer or video device be operated by a provincial government (which can include a provincial Crown corporation). Thus, a provincial government (or more likely one of the provincial Crown corporations that operates one of Canada's casinos) could create an Internet-based gaming site, subject to a number of considerations discussed below. One challenge would be to recreate in an online, virtual environment the various regulatory protections that are provided in provincial law with respect to the current casinos. For example, these casinos generally restrict admittance to persons above a certain age, and they prohibit the use of devices such as calculators. These same issues will be difficult to address in an Internet environment,[158] but with the ongoing development of various biometric authentication devices, technology will likely appear in the marketplace to solve these problems.[159]

An interesting constitutional/jurisdiction issue posed by Internet-based casinos is whether such a site offered by one province could accept customers from another province. The *Criminal Code*'s gaming provisions do not expressly contemplate the Internet era where a person physically resident in one province could access the casino website operated by another province.[160] In this regard, it should be noted that a province cannot legislate activities outside its physical boundaries. However, a province whose residents access another province's Internet casino likely could take jurisdiction of the activity within its province, in light of the discussion on Internet jurisdiction in section C(2), "Jurisdiction," in chapter 6, though it is open to question how one province could bring enforcement action against another province as they each enjoy immunity from one another. Equally, in light of the fourth dynamic of computer law — namely, the blurring between national/international — a provincially sanctioned gaming Internet site in Canada may well

---

158   For a discussion of recreating in an Internet environment the same security as provided by geography and identity in a physical environment, see Justice O'Connor's decision in the Supreme Court decision in *ACLU*, above note 44.

159   See section A(2), "Signatures," in chapter 6.

160   Other provisions in the *Criminal Code*'s gaming rules also illustrate their pre-Internet nature. For example, subs. 201(1) makes it an offence to keep a "common gaming house" or "common betting house." Does "house" include an Internet site? What if the server for the website is situated in a house?

run afoul of the laws of another jurisdiction outside of Canada if the site accepted patrons from that jurisdiction, and in this context the Canadian province might not enjoy immunity if its activities were characterized as "commercial" rather than governmental in nature.[161] Similarly, a provincial government could take action against non-Canadian operators of gaming websites, just as the states of Minnesota and Missouri have done, as illustrated by the *Granite Gate*[162] and other cases discussed in chapter 6.

9) Other Offences

The foregoing discussion has focussed on those provisions of the *Criminal Code* most relevant to computer crime. Other offences, however, may also be germane in certain circumstances. There are, for example, a number of provisions that can come into play where a computer or a network facility is used as a means to facilitate an otherwise traditional offence, or where information stored on a computer is the subject of the criminal behaviour. Into these categories of offences fall forgery (section 366), uttering a forged document (section 368), drawing or using a document without authority (section 374), falsification of books and documents (section 397), falsification of employment records (section 398), and the making, circulating, or publishing of a false prospectus (section 400). With respect to those offences that refer to documents, the 1985 amendments to the *Criminal Code* which enacted the computer abuse and abuse of data provisions also implemented a revised definition of *document* in order to cover computer-based materials:

---

161   In this regard it is interesting to note that U.S. concern with gambling on the Internet may be on the increase; see the proposed *Internet Gambling Prohibition Act of 1997*, S 474 IS, 105th Cong. 1st Session (1997), available at <http://www.ljx.com/internet/gamblebill.html>. This bill, if enacted, will make it a federal crime in the United States to operate an Internet gambling site as well as to access a gambling site by means of the Internet: see David Post, "Betting on Cyberspace" (1997) 19(5) American Lawyer 96(2). Even without such a law, the state of Missouri has obtained an injunction against a Pennsylvania corporation that offers gambling over the Internet: see *State of Missouri v. Interactive Gaming & Communications Corp.*, No. 197CF0014(1) (Mo. Cir. Ct., 23 May 1997), reported in *Computer & Online Industry Litigation Reporter*, 15 July 1997 at 24,441. Also on the jurisdictional front, it will be interesting to see how regulators in Canada respond to computerized gambling in aircraft: see Ralph Schoenstein, "The Odds Favour In-Flight Gambling" *The [Toronto] Globe and Mail* (23 August 1997).

162   *State of Minnesota v. Granite Gate Resorts, Inc.*, 1996 WL 767431 (D. Minn.) (Westlaw) [*Granite Gate*].

> "document" means any paper, parchment or other material on which is recorded or marked anything that is capable of being read or understood by a person, computer system or other device, and includes a credit card, but does not include trade-marks on articles of commerce or inscriptions on stone or metal or other like material.[163]

This was a useful amendment since today so much information is stored electronically and the copying, scanning, and other technologies allow non-technical people to engage in counterfeiting and forgery activities.[164] It is also worth noting that sections 406 to 409 contain offences regarding the forging of trade-marks, and in one case these provisions were used to convict an unauthorized distributor of software who had reproduced a third party's trade-mark on the software product to deceive purchasers of the product.[165]

Computers and networks can be used in other *Criminal Code* offences, such as criminal harassment (section 264), uttering threats (section 264), extortion (section 346), obtaining a benefit through false pretences (section 362), fraudulent fortune telling for consideration (section 365), making false messages (sections 371 and 372), and making anything resembling a bank-note (section 457). Some of these provisions, such as those relating to uttering threats, extortion, and fortune telling, are drafted without a specific reference to a particular communications medium and therefore should apply without difficulty in a computer and networked environment. Others, however, use phrases that may be problematic, such as the appearance of "writing" in the false pretences offence, which raises the question whether electronic messages (such as e-mail over the Internet) constitute writings; for a discussion of this issue see section A(1), "The Writing Requirement," in chapter 6. Some provisions are also tied to certain communication vehicles, such as the telegram, cablegram, and radio message in section 371 or the telephone call in subsections 372(2) and (3). Again, the question arises whether either of these provisions would capture text-based messages transmitted over the Internet; in the case of subsections 372(2) and (3) because of the *IBM* case referred to in note 132 above. It should also be noted that the various offences related to the "mails," such as sections 345 (stopping a mail conveyance with intent to rob or search), 356 (theft from mail), and 381 (using mails to defraud) only apply to

---

163   *Criminal Code*, s.321.

164   See *R. v. Sebo* (1988), 42 C.C.C. (3d) 536 (Alta. C.A.), where a photocopier was used to create a forged document.

165   *R. v. Locquet* (1985), 5 C.P.R. (3d) 173 (Que. Sess. Ct.).

"mailable matter" conveyed by Canada Post Corporation, and thus would only apply to e-mails transmitted by or through this corporation.[166] In effect, in order to ensure that the *Criminal Code* is always and consistently relevant to the needs of the computer and network dynamics coursing through the economy and society at large, the statute needs to be constantly reviewed and updated.

It is worth noting that criminal or quasi-criminal provisions are also dealt with in other parts of this book: section B(3), "Copyright," in chapter 2 includes a discussion of the criminal piracy provisions of the *Copyright Act*; section B(1), "Criminal Offences," in chapter 5 discusses the criminal offences under the *Competition Act*; and section C(3), "Regulating Cyberspace," in chapter 6, dealing with regulation, makes mention of the *Criminal Code*'s provisions relating to contests and promotions. Another provision in the *Criminal Code* worthy of brief mention is section 21, the aiding and abetting section, which provides that everyone is a party to an offence who does or omits to do anything for the purpose of aiding any other person to commit the offence. It might be asked, for example, whether certain participants on the Internet might come within the purview of section 21 depending on their activities in disseminating content or facilitating an activity that is otherwise problematic under one of the other provisions discussed in this chapter. In this regard, it should be noted that to be a party to an offence, the aider or abetter must have knowledge that the principal was intending to commit the relevant offence and the aider/abetter must have acted with the intention of assisting in the commission of the offence; that is, the person accused of aiding and abetting must know the circumstances necessary to constitute the

---

166 The *Canada Post Corporation Act*, R.S.C. 1985, c. C-10, subs. 2(1), contains the following definitions:

> "mail" means mailable matter from the time it is posted to the time it is delivered to the addressee thereof;
> "mail conveyance" means any physical, electronic, optical, or other means used to transmit mail;
> "mailable matter" means any message, information, funds, or goods that may be transmitted by post;
> "post" means to leave in a post office or with a person authorized by the Corporation to receive mailable matter;
> "post office" includes any place, receptacle, device, or mail conveyance authorized by the Corporation for the posting, receipt, sorting, handling, transmission, or delivery of mail;
> "transmit" means to send or convey from one place to another place by any physical, electronic, optical, or other means;
> "transmit by post" means to transmit through or by means of the Corporation.

offence the person is accused of aiding, although in certain situations recklessness or wilful blindness may suffice as well.[167] In the context of the Internet, this test appears to be quite close to that set out for intermediary liability for libel on the Internet.[168]

10) Interception of Communications

Since the passage in 1974 of the *Protection of Privacy Act,* Canada's criminal law has concerned itself with countering unauthorized telephone wire-tapping and electronic surveillance.[169] Initially aimed only at police authorities, the *Criminal Code*'s interception of communications provisions has a much wider application as the technological devices that permit electronic eavesdropping have become widely available; thus, the heightened importance of the following:

> 184 (1) Every one who, by means of any electro-magnetic, acoustic, mechanical or other device, wilfully intercepts a private communication is guilty of an indictable offence and liable to imprisonment for a term not exceeding five years.
>
> (2) Subsection (1) does not apply to
>> (a) a person who has the consent to intercept, express or implied, of the originator of the private communication or of the person intended by the originator thereof to receive it;
>> (b) a person who intercepts a private communication in accordance with an authorization or pursuant to section 184.4 or any person who in good faith aids in any way another person who the aiding person believes on reasonable grounds is acting with an authorization or pursuant to section 184.4;
>> (c) a person engaged in providing a telephone, telegraph or other communication service to the public who intercepts a private communication,
>>> (i)   if the interception is necessary for the purpose of providing the service,
>>> (ii) in the course of service observing or random monitoring necessary for the purpose of mechanical or service quality control checks, or

---

167   See, for example, *R. v. Roan* (1985), 17 C.C.C. (3d) 534 (Alta. C.A.); *Dunlop and Sylvester v. R.* (1979), 47 C.C.C. (2d) 93 (S.C.C.); *Director of Public Prosecutions for Northern Ireland v. Maxwell,* [1978] 3 All E.R. 1140 (H.L.).
168   See section C(1), "Cyber Libel," in chapter 6.
169   S.C. 1973-74, c. 50.

(iii) if the interception is necessary to protect the person's rights or property directly related to providing such service; or

(d) an officer or servant of Her Majesty in right of Canada who engages in radio frequency spectrum management, in respect of a private communication intercepted by that officer or servant for the purpose of identifying, isolating or preventing an unauthorized or interfering use of a frequency or of a transmission.

Important definitions related to this prohibition are contained in section 183 and are as follows:

"electro-magnetic, acoustic, mechanical or other device" means any device or apparatus that is used or is capable of being used to intercept a private communication, but does not include a hearing aid used to correct subnormal hearing of the user to not better than normal hearing;

"intercept" includes listen to, record or acquire a communication or acquire the substance, meaning or purport thereof;

"private communication" means any oral communication, or any telecommunication, that is made by an originator in Canada or is intended by the originator to be received by a person who is in Canada and that is made under circumstances in which it is reasonable for the originator to expect that it will not be intercepted by any person other than the person intended by the originator to receive it, and includes any radio-based telephone communication that is treated electronically or otherwise for the purpose of preventing intelligible reception by any person other than the person intended by the originator to receive it;

To complete the picture under the *Criminal Code*, it should be noted that *telecommunications* is defined in the *Interpretation Act* as "any transmission, emission, or reception of signs, signals, writing, images, sounds, or intelligence of any nature by wire, radio, visual, or other electromagnetic system."[170] As well, section 193 of the *Criminal Code* makes it an offence to unlawfully use or disclose an intercepted private communication, and section 193.1 makes it illegal to use or disclose a radio-based telephone communication. Other statutes also have provisions aimed at preserving the confidentiality of communications. Subsection

---

170 R.S.C., c. I-21, subs. 35(1). This is similar to the definition in the *Telecommunications Act*, discussed in section C(1), "Regulating Telecommunications," in chapter 4.

9 (1.1) of the *Radiocommunication Act*, for example, makes it an offence to intercept and make use of, or intercept and divulge, any radiocommunication, which essentially covers any transmission of signals lower than 3,000 Ghz.[171] Certain provincial privacy statutes also contain provisions making it a tort to, among other things, listen to or record a person's conversation, or to listen to or record messages travelling to or coming from that person by telecommunications. This can serve as an important supplement to section 184 of the *Criminal Code*. For example, in *R. v. Dunn*[172] the court held that a policeman listening to a telephone conversation on an extension was not a violation of section 184 because one of the parties to the conversation consented to the policeman's eavesdropping; essentially the same activity, however, was held to be actionable under Manitoba's *Privacy Act* in the *McBee* case.[173] Finally, it should also be noted that, as discussed in the next part of this chapter, with the enactment of the *Canadian Charter of Rights and Freedoms* (*Charter*) in 1982,[174] eavesdropping, surveillance, and related activities carried out by government also come under scrutiny of the *Charter's* various provisions, and specifically section 8 of the *Charter* that provides that "[e]veryone has the right to be secure against unreasonable search or seizure."

Various technologies and business processes have raised questions under section 184 of the *Criminal Code* and section 8 of the *Charter*, largely because of the second dynamic of computer law — the elusive nature of information. For example, a number of cases in Canada have considered whether the signals obtained by a dial number recorder (DNR) (in the United States referred to as a "pen register") constitute a telecommunication for purposes of section 184. A DNR is a device that is used by a telephone company to track the numbers called by a telephone subscriber and the length of those calls, but it does not record the content of the calls. In the *Samson* case,[175] the Newfoundland Court of Appeal concluded that DNR-type information is not covered by section 184, as that provision is aimed at protecting only conversations. In several later cases, the holding in the *Samson* case was not followed, and the courts in these subsequent cases decided that DNR information related to at least

---

171   R.S.C. 1985, c. R-2.

172   (1975), 28 C.C.C. (2d) 538 (N.S. Co. Ct.).

173   *Ferguson v. McBee Technographics Inc.* (1989), 24 C.P.R. (3d) 240 (Man. Q.B.). The various provincial privacy statutes are discussed in section A(1), "Privacy Laws," in chapter 4.

174   The *Charter* is Part I of the *Constitution Act, 1982*, being Schedule B to the *Canada Act 1982* (U.K.), 1982, c. 11. The *Canada Act 1982* can be found in R.S.C. 1985, Appendix II, No. 44.

175   *R. v. Samson* (1983), 45 Nfld. and P.E.I.R. 32 (Nfld. C.A.) [*Samson*].

local calls should be protected as these calls are not normally monitored by DNR technology, as opposed to long-distance calls which are so monitored for billing purposes.[176] More recently, however, the Ontario Court of Appeal in the *Fegan* case followed *Samson*, without any mention of the decisions finding to the contrary.[177] In contrast, the Manitoba Court of Appeal in a decision rendered around the time of the *Fegan* case indicated it believed the police required judicial authorization to obtain information about an individual's utility records.[178] In any event, the *Criminal Code* now contains, in section 492.2, a provision for obtaining a warrant for a number recorder. Interestingly, outside of Canada, courts have been equally divided about DNR information. In a U.S. Supreme Court decision,[179] the majority concluded that such information should not be protected by the U.S. Fourth Amendment (which protects against unreasonable search and seizure). The eloquent dissent in this case, however, was subsequently followed in a decision regarding Colorado's state constitution.[180] In the *Malone* case originating in the United Kingdom, the European Court of Human Rights concluded that providing the police with the telephone numbers and duration of calls made by the accused, but without the contents, was an invasion of the accused's right of privacy and contrary to section 8 of the *European Convention of Human Rights*, which guarantees against unreasonable search and seizure.[181]

---

176   *R. v. Griffith* (1988), 44 C.C.C. (3d) 63 (Ont. Dist. Ct.) [*Griffith*]; *R. v. Mikituk et al.* (1992), 101 Sask. R. 286 (Q.B.); and *R. v. Kutsak (T.L.)* (1993), 108 Sask. R. 241 (Q.B.).

177   *R. v. Fegan* (1993), 80 C.C.C. (3d) 356 (Ont. C.A.) [*Fegan*].

178   *R. v. Makwaychuk* (1993), 81 C.C.C. (3d) 186 (Man. C.A.).

179   *Smith v. Maryland*, 442 U.S. 735 (1979).

180   *People v. Sporleder*, 666 P.2d 135 (Colo. 1983). This case notes and cites the two lines of authority that have developed over this question in the United States. In coming to the conclusion that DNR information should be protected, the court, reminiscent of the decision of Justice McLachlin in the *Plant* case, below note 182, stated at 142: "Knowledge of these facts can often yield inferential knowledge of the content of the conversation itself. In addition, a pen register record holds out the prospect of an even greater intrusion in privacy when the record itself is acquired by the government, which has a technological capacity to convert basic data into a virtual mosaic of a person's life." The reasoning in the *Sporleder* court would also go further than that exhibited by the Canadian decisions in note 176, and hold long-distance call data protected as well; just because these data are recorded by the telephone company as an incidence of the service it provides does not make it fair game for police scrutiny, to paraphrase the conclusion of the court.

181   The *Malone* case is discussed in James Michael, *Privacy and Human Rights: An International and Comparative Study, with Special Reference to Developments in Information Technology* (Aldershot, U.K.: Dartmouth, 1994).

A debate similar to the one in the DNR cases arose in the Supreme Court of Canada decision in *R. v. Plant*.[182] In this case the police, without a warrant, were given access to a suspect's electricity consumption records, which showed roughly quadruple the level of usage compared to neighbours, and which indicated the probable growing of marijuana in a hydroponic environment, a suspicion originally conveyed to the police by an anonymous tip. The majority of the court stated that such electricity consumption records should not be protected under section 8 of the *Charter*, having regard to, among other factors, the type of information (the majority felt they did not reveal personal information about the accused (i.e., the court was only willing to provide protection for a "biographical core of personal data")), the nature of the relationship between the original data collector and the accused (the utility collected this information in the normal course of business), the place where the information was obtained (not in the accused's home or any other place ordinarily considered private), and the manner in which it was obtained (the police had computerized access to the utility's computers, albeit on a password basis, and the majority was under the impression the utility records were made available to the general public upon request). In a spirited separate opinion, Justice McLachlin disagreed with many of these conclusions, stating that the police should have to obtain a warrant to access utility records for a number of reasons, including the following: the records were not public, and there was no evidence that the general public could access them; and the records are capable of telling much about one's personal lifestyle, and that this is precisely why the police wanted access to them. Justice McLachlin also disagreed with the majority on the issue of where the information was found and stated:

> Computers may and should be private places, where the information they contain is subject to the legal protection arising from a reasonable expectation of privacy. Computers may contain a wealth of personal information. Depending on its character, that information may be as private as any found in a dwelling house or hotel room.[183]

The DNR and *Plant* cases illustrate in dramatic fashion the second dynamic of computer law but with an interesting twist. In these cases it is not the content of the communications that is elusive, but rather the inferences that can be drawn from them. Put another way, what is valuable is not the content of the message, but its context.

---

182   [1993] 3 S.C.R. 281 (S.C.C.) [*Plant*].
183   *Ibid.* at 303–4.

Both section 184 of the *Criminal Code* and section 8 of the *Charter* will only afford protection to communications that are made in circumstances where the originator of the communication had a reasonable expectation that the communication will not be intercepted. Numerous cases, therefore, have had to wrestle with the difficult question of which technologies may be said to afford their users a reasonable expectation of privacy. Again, the elusive nature of information has resulted in judicial divergence. For example, courts have disagreed as to whether a sealed letter sent through the mail is a private communication. In *R. v. Newell*, the court concluded that the sender of a letter should not have a reasonable expectation of privacy because, among other things, the recipient of the letter might voluntarily show the letter to others, or it might be misplaced and come into the hands of a third party:

> Letters and mailed tapes are different from a normal telephone call or private discussion. An average person is entitled to expect no one will listen to a telephone call or record a private discussion by a body pack. Unlike a letter, a telephone call or private discussion is not given to others for the purpose of transmission nor is it intended by the originator that the words be preserved for later reference.[184]

In contrast, in *R. v. Crane and Walsh*,[185] the court held that the privacy of the mails is an important and highly confidential element of society, and should be protected just as telephone calls are. Thus, the court concluded that the section 8 *Charter* protection against unreasonable search and seizure applied to mail.

Similar disagreement has accompanied cellular phone technology. In *R. v. Solomon*, a conversation over a cellular phone was held not to be confidential because the radio waves used to transmit cellular messages could be scanned by third parties.[186] By contrast, in *R. v. Cheung* cellular phone messages were held to be confidential because although cellular phone messages could be scanned, the state of scanner technology before the court did not easily permit the use of a scanner to intercept the cellular calls of any particular person.[187] Thus, the police in the

---

184   (1982), 69 C.C.C. (2d) 284 at 286 (B.C.S.C.) [*Newell*].
185   (1985), 45 C.R. (3d) 368 (Nfld. Dist. Ct.).
186   (1992), 77 C.C.C. (3d) 264 (Que. Mun. Ct.). It should be noted, however, that in a subsequent decision ((1993), 85 C.C.C. (3d) 496 (Que. Mun. Ct.)), the court in *Solomon* reversed its earlier ruling by holding that under the *Charter* a person nevertheless expects that the police will not intercept and record his or her conversations made over a cellular phone.
187   (1995), 100 C.C.C. (3d) 441 (B.C.S.C.) [*Cheung*].

Cheung case intercepted the cellular calls of the suspect at the switchboard at the phone company rather than by use of a general scanner device because they would have "little to no chance to intercept communications of the target individuals by using scanners."[188] In coming to this conclusion, the court in *Cheung* was very conscious of having to discern the intricacies of the specific technology before it in order to make a sensible determination, thereby heeding the first dynamic of computer law: "As technological advance and counter-advance leapfrog over each other, I am sure that ease and difficulty of interception will shift from time to time. The state of technology at the time of any disputed interception will be important, because it will bear upon the reasonable expectations of the caller."[189] It should be noted that the definition of *private communications* was amended to include any radio-based communication that is encrypted, and in addition subsection 193(1) has been added to the *Criminal Code* to make it an offence to use or disclose any private communication that has been intercepted.

Another problematic technology that has been considered in the context of section 184 is pager devices. In *R. v. Nin*, the court concluded that a pager communication is not private because the paging unit that receives the message plays the message audibly such that anyone in the vicinity of the recipient would hear the message.[190] The same pager technology was similarly treated in *R. v. Lubovac*.[191] As well, in this case a further ground for not finding privacy was the fact that the person leaving the pager message dictated it on the pager company's tape-recording device, and that this consensual recording broke the chain of confidentiality. In a subsequent American case, it was also held that a pager message was not private because the pager device might be in the possession of someone other than the intended recipient of the message.[192] Interestingly, this specific rationale was considered and not approved in the *Nin* case. Again, one is struck by the diversity of judicial response to a particular technology. In any event, these cases are extremely dependent on the specific types of devices being considered. Thus, a court might come to a different conclusion if presented with a more modern paging technological process where the caller's message is merely forwarded to the

---

188   *Ibid.* at 447.
189   *Ibid.* at 443.
190   (1985), 34 C.C.C. (3d) 89 (Que. Sess. Ct.) [*Nin*].
191   (1989), 52 C.C.C. (3d) 551 (Alta. C.A.).
192   *United States* v. *Meriwether*, 917 F.2d 955 (6th Cir. 1990).

recipient's pager (without being recorded by the paging company) and the pager only displays the message on a small readout screen after being called up by a password.

A number of questions arise when section 184 of the *Criminal Code* and section 8 of the *Charter* are considered in the context of the Internet. Based on the holding in the *Fegan* and *Plant* cases that only the content of conversations is protected, would this imply that Internet service providers or network operators could monitor which websites a user visited, so long as the Internet service provider did not pry into the actual information retrieved? For instance, is "cookie" technology, comprising software that a third party can attach to an Internet browser in order to monitor the websites visited by another person without her knowledge, described in more detail in section A(1), "Privacy Laws," in chapter 4, outside the purview of subsection 184(1) so long as it does not relay the content of messages? And if subsection 184(1) does not apply to cookies, is paragraph 342.1(1)(b) applicable?[193]

Given that the originator of the communication must have a reasonable expectation of privacy in her message for section 184 to apply, how will courts treat e-mail? Some would argue that most users are aware that system and network operators are always able to view e-mail, such that the proper analogy to e-mail is not the sealed envelope but the open-faced postcard (and hence senders of postcards, like e-mail, are more circumspect in what they say in their respective messages). The trial court in the *ACLU* decision observed that unlike mail in the postal system, e-mail sent over the Internet is not sealed or secure and can be accessed or viewed by intermediary computers between sender and recipient unless it is encrypted.[194] As well, e-mail can be easily, and is often, forwarded electronically by the recipient to other users; indeed, this is a prime feature of e-mail and makes it a very powerful and functional service. Focussing on these attributes, and consistent with the *Newell* case, most e-mail over the Internet would arguably not come within the definition of a private communication under subsection 184(1), and neither would messages posted to websites, bulletin boards, newsgroups, discussion forums, and the like. In support of this view is an American case in which a court, considering the privacy rights in an e-mail message sent from one employee to another in a company, concluded that once the employee sent the message over the

---

193 See section B(3), "Computer Abuse," in this chapter.
194 *ACLU*, above note 44.

e-mail system the employee lost any reasonable expectation of privacy.[195] In another American case, however, an appellate military court concluded that an e-mail user did have a reasonable expectation of privacy in those messages stored on computers of an online service which he alone could retrieve by use of a password and which had not yet been forwarded by the user to others.[196] In this case the court usefully differentiated between e-mail sent over the Internet and e-mail transmitted within the much more secure America Online system. Even within the latter, however, the court concluded there was a range of privacy expectations, with no right of privacy, for example, attaching to e-mails once they are forwarded from subscriber to subscriber. In effect, the court carefully dissected the different technologies and message-passing techniques to sensibly arrive at a result appropriate to the circumstances. This case illustrates that it is important to look at e-mail not as a single mode of communication, but rather to consider its various permutations, with the result that some, but not others, of it might meet the test for private communication under subsection 184(1). In such an analysis, for example, it would be important whether the particular type of e-mail is encrypted.

11) Search, Seizure, and Surveillance

In the previous section the issues related to section 184 of the *Criminal Code* were discussed and mention was made of section 8 of the *Charter*, which provides that "[e]veryone has the right to be secure against unreasonable search or seizure." A key question in light of this *Charter* section and the inexorable development of more and more sophisticated electronic and optical devices by which to monitor, track, and probe various aspects of individuals is when should the police require prior judicial authorization, through the means of search warrants, before they can employ these high-tech products and mechanisms. In this

---

195   *Smyth v. Pillsbury Company*, 914 F. Supp. 97 (E.D. Pa. 1996). In this case the court also concluded, at 101, that even if it could be said the employee had a reasonable expectation of privacy in the contents of e-mail messages, the court would not find the interception of e-mail communications to be a substantial or offensive invasion of privacy: "Again, we note that by intercepting such communications, the company is not, as in the case of urinalysis or personal property searches, requiring the employee to disclose any personal information about himself or invading the employee's person or personal effects. Moreover, the company's interest in preventing inappropriate and unprofessional comments or even illegal activity over its e-mail system outweighs any privacy interest the employee may have in those comments."

196   *United States v. Maxwell*, 42 M.J. 568 (U.S. Air Force Ct. of Crim. App. 1995) (Westlaw).

regard it is important to note that the Supreme Court of Canada in the *Dyment*[197] case concluded that section 8 of the *Charter* should be interpreted in a broad and liberal manner so as to secure the citizen's right to a reasonable expectation of privacy against governmental encroachments. In this case the court adopted the views of a leading American proponent of privacy rights by stipulating that "society has come to realize that privacy is at the heart of liberty in a modern state. . . . [G]rounded in man's physical and moral autonomy, privacy is essential for the well-being of the individual."[198] The court then adopted the reasoning in a task force report of the Canadian government titled *Privacy and Computers*, that privacy, in addition to protecting a person's home and person, also should arise in an information context. The court stated:

> Finally, there is privacy in relation to information. This too is based on the notion of the dignity and integrity of the individual. As the Task Force put it (p. 13): "This notion of privacy derives from the assumption that all information about a person is in a fundamental way his own, for him to communicate or retain for himself as he sees fit." In modern society, especially, retention of information about oneself is extremely important. We may, for one reason or another, wish or be compelled to reveal such information, but situations abound where the reasonable expectations of the individual that the information shall remain confidential to the persons to whom, and restricted to the purposes for which it is divulged, must be protected. Governments at all levels have in recent years recognized this and have devised rules and regulations to restrict the uses of information collected by them to those for which it was obtained; see, for example, the *Privacy Act*.[199]

Notwithstanding these sentiments, the Supreme Court's approach to informational privacy in the context of search and seizure does not extend to records related to electricity consumption, given the decision in the *Plant* case.[200]

In a trio of important cases, the Supreme Court of Canada has held that three forms of high-tech surveillance offended section 8 of the *Charter*; though in all of them the evidence obtained was admitted because the court held doing so would not bring the administration of

---

197 *R. v. Dyment*, [1988] 2 S.C.R. 417. In this case a police officer's receipt of a blood sample of the accused taken by a doctor who was administering medical treatment before any charges were laid was held to constitute an unreasonable search and seizure under s. 8 of the *Charter*.

198 *Ibid.* at 427.

199 *Ibid.* at 429–30.

200 *Plant*, above note 182.

justice into disrepute.[201] In *R.* v. *Wise*, the court concluded that the police could not use an electronic tracking device that attached to an automobile without first obtaining a search warrant.[202] In *R.* v. *Wong* the court also believed that judicial oversight was required for use of tiny hidden cameras and microphones in a hotel room setting.[203] In concluding that the *Charter* protects against surreptitious video surveillance conducted by agents of the state, the court noted that "modern methods of electronic surveillance have the potential, if uncontrolled, to annihilate privacy.[204] Finally, in *R.* v. *Duarte* the court concluded that concealed audio surveillance through a small microphone violated section 8 of the *Charter*.[205] These are noteworthy cases for the Information Age, though their impact is somewhat dulled by the fact that the illegally obtained evidence was admitted in any event.

Notwithstanding this trio of Supreme Court cases, police are able to utilize high-tech equipment to conduct warrantless surveillance where the subject matter was in an open space. Thus, in *R.* v. *Elzein*, videotaping and photography by the police were found to be acceptable because the suspect was in a public place.[206] In a similar vein, in a recent case a court held that there was no violation when police conducted surveillance of a computer bulletin board operation by using a false identity to obtain online access to it, and when they kept a verbatim record of communications they had with the operation; again, an important element of the court's reasoning centred on the public nature of this particular bulletin board service.[207] The implications of these rulings could

---

201   Subsection 24(2) of the *Charter* provides that if evidence was obtained in a manner that infringes the freedoms of the *Charter*, the evidence is excluded if its admission would bring the administration of justice into disrepute; thus, evidence can be admitted even if it was obtained in a manner that violates s. 8 of the *Charter* if the court believes its admission will not bring the administration of justice into disrepute.

202   (1992), 70 C.C.C. (3d) 193 (S.C.C.) [*Wise*].

203   (1990), 60 C.C.C. (3d) 460 (S.C.C.) [*Wong*].

204   *Ibid.* at 479.

205   (1990), 53 C.C.C. (3d) 1 (S.C.C.) [*Duarte*].

206   (1993), 82 C.C.C. (3d) 455 (Que. C.A.) [*Elzein*].

207   *R.* v. *Morin*, [1996] R.J.Q. 1758 (Crim. Ct.). The court in this case summarized its view at 1764 as follows: "En somme, l'accusé a lancé des invitations générales de communiquer avec lui, et ce, à plusieurs reprises. Il est impossible de conclure qu'une personne raisonnable, dans la situation de l'accusé, pouvait s'attendre au respect de sa vie privée en de telles circonstances. Une personne raisonnable saurait que, lorsque de telles invitations sont lancées au public en général, elle ne peut pas s'attendre à ce qu'il n'y ait pas d'étrangers, y compris des policiers, qui communiquent avec elle."

become disturbing given that, in respect of the *Elzein* case, more and more high-powered miniature cameras are being used to monitor more and more public areas, such as in some cities in England where whole sections of the downtown are blanketed with cameras.[208] When connected by powerful computer networks and visual image and data processing links, these cameras can produce an environment where there is a conceptual shift from seemingly monitoring a physical place (e.g., a specific lobby of a particular building), to tracking individuals. Similarly, it seems unreasonable that police should be able to conduct electronic surveillance on a bulletin board system operator in a sustained and detailed manner for as long as they please without some judicial oversight in the form of a warrant. Even if not problematic from a criminal search and seizure perspective, such camera-based environments and Internet-related activities raise serious privacy concerns of a more general nature, such as those discussed in section A, "Privacy and Data Protection," in chapter 4.

In response to the *Wise, Wong,* and *Duarte* cases, the search warrant provisions of the *Criminal Code* have been recently augmented. The traditional provision, section 487, is virtually unchanged since the first Canadian *Criminal Code* in 1892, and permits a justice of the peace to issue a warrant for searching a "building, receptacle or place" where there are reasonable grounds to believe that an offence was committed therein and that there is anything that will afford evidence thereof. This provision is arguably limited to physical places, though it is open to question whether the word *place* might not be able to apply to a non-physical place, such as a site on the Internet.[209] As well, the evidence referred to in this provision again seems to contemplate physical items, as one court has concluded that it cannot be used to search for incorporeal items.[210] In the context of data, software, and other intangibles, therefore, this usually meant the police would take the whole computer and the tangible media on which the software resided. To remedy this deficiency, Bill C-17, enacted in April 1997, extended the coverage of section 487 to computers, so that police are now expressly permitted to

---

208 See David Brin, "The Transparent Society," *Wired*, December 1996.

209 One commentator takes this view; see Davis & Hutchison, *Computer Crime*, above note 8.

210 See *Re Banque Royale du Canada and The Queen* (1985), 18 C.C.C. (3d) 98 (Que. C.A.) where a s. 487 warrant was held not to cover monies in a bank account.

search a computer system.[211] These new provisions are similar to section 16 of the *Competition Act*, which since 1986 has permitted the investigating authorities to use the computers on the premises being searched to search any data available to the computer system.[212] This recognizes that in today's networked world an organization's data are often not physically located on its premises, or even in the computer located on its premises, but rather may reside in computers at distant locations. These are good examples of legislation striving to stay current with the new and ever changing data processing and communications environment. In a recent case a court even upheld the ability of the investigating authorities under the *Competition Act* to bring their own software onto the premises to help facilitate a computer search.[213]

In 1993, several other search warrant provisions were added in light of the decisions in the *Wise, Wong,* and *Duarte* cases. Section 492.1 authorizes the issuances of warrants for electronic tracking devices, while section 492.2 does the same for telephone number recorders, the type of device discussed in the previous part in the *Griffith* and *Fegan* cases. In both of these new provisions the standard for issuing the warrant is a reasonable suspicion that an offence has occurred or will occur, which is lower than the reasonable belief standard in the traditional section 487. It should also be noted that the 1993 amendments included the new section 487.01, which permits the issuance of a warrant (on the

---

211   The new additions to section 487 read as follows:

  (2.1) A person authorized under this section to search a computer system in a building or place for data may

  (a) use or cause to be used any computer system at the building or place to search any data contained in or available to the computer system;

  (b) reproduce or cause to be reproduced any data in the form of a print-out or other intelligible output;

  (c) seize the print-out or other output for examination or copying; and

  (d) use or cause to be used any copying equipment at the place to make copies of the data.

  (2.2) Every person who is in possession or control of any building or place in respect of which a search is carried out under this section shall, on presentation of the warrant, permit the person carrying out the search

  (a) to use or cause to be used any computer system at the building or place in order to search any data contained in or available to the computer system for data that the person is authorized by this section to search for;

  (b) to obtain a hard copy of the data and to seize it; and

  (c) to use or cause to be used any copying equipment at the place to make copies of the data.

212   R.S.C. 1985, c. C-34, as amended.

213   *Re United States Pipe and Founding Co.* (1994), 58 C.P.R. (3d) 463 (Ont. Gen. Div.).

reasonable belief standard) where no other provision in the *Criminal Code* or other statute authorizes the search. This latter provision is extremely broad and could conceivably be used to authorize any type of computer or network search imaginable. Section 487.1, also a new provision, establishes a procedure for applying for, and issuing, warrants by telephone, fax, and other telecommunications technologies.

Notwithstanding these new provisions, computer crime often presents investigators with thorny evidentiary problems. For example, given the elusiveness of information, it is common for the computer and Internet-based criminal to deny he had anything to do with the offensive conduct. Thus, in the *Pecciarich* case, the defence counsel argued that the accused should not be convicted because it was possible for someone other than the accused to have uploaded the pornographic material; that is, the defence contended that the connection between the accused and the impugned activity could not be conclusively proved in a computer-based environment.[214] The court did not accept this argument, and held that the accused was responsible for the creation and distribution of the offending materials as a result of circumstantial evidence linking him to the materials. From time to time, accused also challenge the admissibility of computer-generated evidence, but, as explained in section B, "Evidence Law," in chapter 6, these arguments usually fall on deaf ears given that most courts have been favourably disposed to admitting computer-generated evidence in criminal cases either under the *Canada Evidence Act* or the relevant common law rules. Counsel for accused can also propose some novel and intriguing arguments in respect of computer-related evidence. In one instance, the accused in an American first-degree murder case argued that he attempted to destroy completely the electronic version of a ransom note, but that it was retrieved from the computer's hard drive by authorities with the assistance of a software program.[215] The accused did not contest that the search warrant obtained by the police was improper with respect to the seizure of the computer, but argued it was inadequate to obtain the data from the computer that the accused mistakenly believed he had destroyed, and that a subsequent search warrant was required for this material. The court disagreed, and concluded:

> An attempt to destroy evidence is not equivalent to a legally protected expectation of privacy. Appellant's unsuccessful attempt to delete documents or files from his computer did not create a legally protected

---

214 *Pecciarich*, above note 95.
215 *Commonwealth v. Copenhefer*, 587 A.2d 1353 (Pa. 1991).

expectation of privacy which would have required a second warrant before the prosecution applied technology to elicit the content of files buried in the memory of the computer. At best, appellant had the hope of achieving secrecy, but his hope did not prohibit the state from subjecting validly seized physical evidence from any scientific analysis possible within current technology.[216]

12) International Issues

The global nature of the computer business and the transnational reach of computer networks highlight the fourth dynamic of computer law, the blurring of the national and international realms. The ability of computer criminals to easily access computer facilities in other countries through international telecommunications hubs, and the extremely mobile nature of data and information, raise a number of international legal issues in a criminal law context. Given Canada's federal structure, questions of jurisdiction between courts of different provinces are addressed in several provisions of the *Criminal Code*. For example, under paragraph 476(e), an offence committed through the mails can be prosecuted either where the letter was posted, or where it was received, or in any place in between where the letter passed. In the international sphere, notwithstanding subsection 6(2) of the *Criminal Code*, which provides that no one can be convicted in Canada of an offence committed outside the country, courts in Canada, the United States, and elsewhere (including in the United Kingdom) have routinely exercised criminal jurisdiction if the facts underlying the activity have a real and substantial connection to the host country or have an effect upon it.[217]

In addition to the jurisdiction question, transnational computer crime has brought into focus the need for international cooperation in the computer crime field. There is, for example, a need to harmonize computer crime laws because mutual assistance or joint efforts in bringing to justice felons using the Internet, through extradition and other forms of mutual assistance, are only possible if the underlying laws of the two relevant countries are more or less equivalent.[218] The alternative is the development of computer crime havens, countries from which

---

216   *Ibid.* at 1356.
217   For a discussion of these and other jurisdiction-related cases see section C(2), "Jurisdiction," in chapter 6.
218   For example, obtaining evidence in foreign jurisdictions for use in Canadian courtrooms is governed by the *Mutual Legal Assistance in Criminal Matters Act*, R.S.C. 1985, c. 30 (4th Supp.).

computer felons operate with impunity. An example of this can already be seen with gaming on the Internet, as discussed in section B(8), "Gaming and Betting," in this chapter. Canada regulates gaming, as does the United States. As a result, the bulk of the operators of Internet gaming sites operate from Central American or Caribbean countries in an effort to elude North American law enforcement efforts. Nevertheless, in at least one U.S. state a court has taken the position that the government has jurisdiction to prosecute the provider of such a service in the state in which customers of the service access it.[219] One enforcement option if the prosecution is successful is to order all Internet service providers in the jurisdiction to cease to carry access to the offending website. This, of course, will be difficult, because the site likely will reappear again, under a different domain name. Truly effective action against international computer crime will require harmonization of computer crime laws. To this end, the members of the OECD, the Council of Europe, and the United Nations have all undertaken activities to create guidelines for, and to coordinate the implementation of, computer crime legislation. Canada has been extremely active in these efforts,[220] but more needs to be done including the crafting of an international convention that would specifically address the prosecution of computer crime with an international dimension.

219 *Granite Gate*, above note 162; this case is discussed under Internet jurisdiction in section C(2), "Jurisdiction," in chapter 6. The state of Missouri takes a similar view: see above note 161.
220 For example, Canada's Donald Piragoff of the Federal Department of Justice was the primary author of the U.N.'s computer crime handbook.

FURTHER READINGS

Books

DAVIS, Robert W.K. & Scott C. HUTCHISON, *Computer Crime in Canada: An Introduction to Technological Crime and Related Legal Issues* (Toronto: Carswell, 1997)

PIRAGOFF, Donald K., "Computer Crimes and Other Crimes Against Information Technology in Canada," in *Information Technology Crime: National Legislations and International Initiatives*, ed. U. Sieber (Koln: Heymanns, 1994)

SIEBER, Ulrich, *The International Emergence of Criminal Information Law* (Koln: Heymanns, 1992)

Internet Sites

CERT Coordination Center
<http://www.cert.org/>

Electronic Frontier Foundation
<http://www.eff.org/>

Royal Canadian Mounted Police
<http://www.rcmp-grc.gc.ca/>

CHAPTER 4

THE REGULATORY ENVIRONMENT

Governments regulate information in order to achieve a number of objectives. They institute and administer data protection laws in an effort to protect the privacy of individuals. Governments control the export of certain high-tech information in order to protect a nation's security interests. In the area of telecommunications and broadcasting, the Canadian government exercises the regulatory power to preserve and enhance Canadian culture, sovereignty, and a host of other objectives. In each of these areas two important questions can be asked. The initial, threshold level inquiry is whether governments should regulate these areas of endeavour at all. The answer to this question will be based on an amalgam of policy and political considerations. If the decision is made to introduce government regulation, then the analysis shifts to determining the optimum manner in which such regulation may be effected. In this regard it is important to understand that the four dynamics of computer law — the torrid pace of technological change, the elusive nature of information, and the blurring of private/public and national/international — are making it more difficult for governments to regulate computers, networks, and data effectively.

A. PRIVACY AND DATA PROTECTION

Privacy has been expressed as the fourfold right to: control intrusion into a person's seclusion or solitude; control the disclosure of embarrassing private facts about the person; prevent being put into a false light in the public eye; and control the exploitation of a person's image and likeness.[1] It is increasingly difficult for individuals to protect these rights in the Information Age. Computers, databases, and telecommunications networks, not to mention current developments in photography and other surveillance technologies, present significant threats to people's privacy.[2] Each of the four dynamics of computer law presents significant obstacles to the preservation of privacy. Most observers view this as an unfortunate by-product of modern technology, given that privacy is necessary for people's emotional and psychological well-being.[3] Accordingly, many look to the law to offer a bulwark against the various technologies and business practices that threaten privacy, though it should also be stated that technology itself can assist in protecting privacy, as noted by the justice minister of Canada in a recent speech on privacy and data protection.[4] The legal subfield of data protection relates to the various statutory measures that have been implemented, or that are advocated, to control the collection, use, and dissemination of personal data. Before turning to this important area, however, it is worth highlighting several aspects of privacy law.

---

1   William L. Prosser, "Privacy" (1960) 48 Calif. L.R. 383. Each of these rights is the subject of discussion in this book. Controlling intrusion is the subject of sections B(3), "Computer Abuse," B(10), "Interception of Communications," and B(11), "Search, Seizure, and Surveillance," in chapter 3 as well as some discussion in the next section below; the regulation of personal information is dealt with in the bulk of section A, "Privacy and Data Protection," in this chapter; the right to avoid being put in false light is the subject of the libel discussion in section C(1), "Cyber Libel," in chapter 6; and the exploitation of image and likeness is touched upon briefly in the section A(1), "Privacy Laws," in this chapter.

2   See, for example, David Brin, "The Transparent Society," *Wired*, December 1996, for a revealing description of new surveillance techniques engendered by miniature cameras.

3   See Arthur R. Miller, *The Assault on Privacy: Computers, Data Banks, and Dossiers* (Ann Arbor: University of Michigan Press, 1971). Note, however, that not all commentators place such a high value on privacy: see Richard A. Posner, "The Right of Privacy" (1978) 12 Ga. Law Rev. 393, in which the author, an exponent of the law and economics school, concludes at 419 that keeping personal data private in certain circumstances is economically inefficient: "If what is revealed is something the individual has concealed for purposes of misrepresenting himself to others, the fact that disclosure is offensive to him . . . is no better reason for protecting his privacy than if a seller advanced such arguments for being allowed to continue to engage in false advertising of his goods."

4   Hon. Allan Rock, Minister of Justice and Attorney General of Canada, "Notes for an Address to the Eighteenth International Conference on Privacy and Data Protection," 18 September 1996 ["Notes"]. These notes are available at: <http://infoweb@magi.com/~privcan/conf96/se_rock.html>.

1) Privacy Laws

Canadian law,[5] like that of the United Kingdom,[6] does not recognize a general "right of privacy"; there is in Canada, for example, no general tort of invasion of privacy.[7] Nevertheless, there are a number of statutes and judicial principles that have been used by courts in Canada to support various privacy rights. In the constitutional setting, section B(10), "Interception of Communications," and section B(11), "Search, Seizure, and Surveillance," in chapter 3 discussed how the Supreme Court of Canada in several cases has concluded that section 8 of the *Charter*,[8] which provides protection against unreasonable search and seizure, should be interpreted in a broad and liberal manner so as to secure the citizen's right to a reasonable expectation of privacy against governmental encroachments, including in the context of informational privacy. As well, in four provinces there are privacy statutes that establish a tort, actionable without proof of damages, where someone knowingly and unreasonably violates the privacy of another person.[9] These statutes do

---

5   For an overview of Canadian privacy law, see Peter Burns, "The Law and Privacy: The Canadian Experience" (1976) 54 Can. Bar. Rev. 1.

6   *Kaye v. Robertson*, [1991] FSR 62 (C.A.). For an excellent discussion of U.K. privacy law, see Raymond Wacks, *Personal Information: Privacy and the Law* (Oxford: Clarendon Press, 1989) [*Personal Information*].

7   Contrast this to the American tradition of a much stronger support for a right of privacy, dating from at least the famous essay by Samuel Warren and Louis Brandeis, "The Right to Privacy" (1890) 4 Harv. L. Rev. 193. It should be noted, however, that not all American courts have assiduously followed the noble sentiments expressed in this renowned essay: for example, in *Olmstead v. United States*, 277 U.S. 438 (1928) [*Olmstead*], the U.S. Supreme Court held that there was no privacy right against police wire-tapping because there was no physical intrusion; the articulate dissent by Brandeis in *Olmstead* does not carry the day until *Katz v. United States*, 389 U.S. 347 (1967), which held that wire-tapping a public phone booth was unconstitutional under the U.S. Fourth Amendment (which protects against unreasonable search and seizure). Even today, however, the U.S. judiciary's support of informational privacy is not unanimous: see the *Dwyer* decision referred to below in note 30.

8   *Canadian Charter of Rights and Freedoms*, Part I of the *Constitution Act, 1982*, R.S.C. 1985, Appendix II, No. 44, being Schedule B to the *Canada Act 1982* (U.K.), 1982, c. 11.

9   In Newfoundland — *An Act Respecting the Protection of Personal Privacy*, R.S.N. 1990, c. P-22; in Manitoba — *The Privacy Act*, R.S.M. 1987, c. P125; in Saskatchewan — *An Act Respecting the Protection of Privacy*, R.S.S. 1978, c. P-24; and in British Columbia — *Privacy Act*, R.S.B.C. 1979, c. 336. It should be noted that while these statutes are generally animated by the same principles, there are a number of differences between them, and in particular the British Columbia statute differs in several important respects from the other three.

not define *privacy*, but generally set out the following as acts that constitute a violation of privacy: audio or visual surveillance of a person or the person's home by any means, including eavesdropping or spying on the person; except for British Columbia, listening to or recording a person's conversation or listening to or recording messages travelling to or coming from that person by telecommunications;[10] except for British Columbia, use of a person's letters, diaries, or other personal documents without the person's consent; and use of a person's likeness (or in British Columbia, "portrait"), name, or voice for advertising, sales promotion, or other commercial use without the person's consent. These rights are not absolute. Except for Manitoba's statute, these laws provide that the nature and degree of protection of privacy to which a person has a right is that which is reasonable under the circumstances, taking into account the interests of third parties. All statutes provide several defences, including explicit or implicit consent of the targeted individual, investigations by public authorities, news gathering activities, and publications that are in the public interest or constitute fair comment or that are privileged under the rules of the defamation law. Assuming these defences do not apply, the statutes provide for various remedies, including damages, injunctions, an accounting of profits, and delivery up of documents that have resulted from the wrongful act.

These four privacy statutes raise several questions in the context of modern computer and network technologies. For example, how would the audio and visual surveillance provisions apply to the Internet? "Cookie" technology, for instance, comprises a software device that can be attached to a user's Internet browser when the user visits the cookie implanter's website.[11] The cookie can then tell the implanter what pages of the website were visited by the user and in certain circumstances there is also the capability to have the cookie relay back to the implanter what other websites the user visits, and what the user buys there, etc. This information, which effectively tracks someone's "clickstream," is then made available by the cookie implanter to third parties, such as

---

10   See, for example, *Ferguson v. McBee Technographics Inc.* (1989), 24 C.P.R. (3d) 240 (Man. Q.B.), also discussed in section B(10), "Interception of Communications," in chapter 3, where the prohibition against interception of communications in Manitoba's *Privacy Act* was held to be broader than the interception of private communications provision in s. 184 of the *Criminal Code*.

11   For a brief overview of cookie technology, see Stephen H. Wildstrom, "They're Watching You Online," *Business Week*, 11 November 1996, and Stephen H. Wildstrom, "Privacy and the 'Cookie' Monster," *Business Week*, 16 December 1996. For more information on cookies, see <http://illuminatus. com/cookie.fcgi>.

merchants looking for high-quality data on the purchasing preferences of individuals. It is unclear if the antisurveillance provisions of the abovenoted privacy statutes cover cookie and cookielike technologies. As well, in terms of the unauthorized recording of messages provisions, the Newfoundland and Saskatchewan statutes afford protection for messages sent by telecommunications, whereas Manitoba's equivalent provision refers to messages sent over the telephone. This latter formulation is arguably narrower, and may not be broad enough to capture certain Internet-related transmissions if, as in a 1992 decision, matters pertaining to the "telephone" are held to relate to the transmission of sounds and voice only.[12]

With respect to the other provinces, articles 35 and 36 of Quebec's *Civil Code* expressly provide for the right of privacy, and specifically the interception of communications, surveillance, use of personal documents, and appropriation of image are enumerated as constituting invasions of the privacy of a person. In a recent case, a Quebec judge prohibited a literary magazine from using the picture of a woman seated in a public place on the grounds that it violated her right to privacy and specifically her right to remain anonymous.[13] As for the right of publicity in the common law provinces beyond the aforementioned privacy statutes, judges in Canada have found there to be a tort of appropriation of personality where the likeness of a person has been used for commercial gain for purposes of commercial endorsement.[14] In a recent decision the court stressed that this right of publicity is quite different from a right of privacy; for example, the latter, as provided in the abovementioned privacy statutes, ends upon the death of the subject individual, while the right of publicity, which the court characterized as "a form of intangible property akin to copyright or patent," can be inherited by heirs.[15]

---

12 *IBM Canada Ltd.* v. *Deputy M.N.R., Customs and Excise*, [1992] 1 F.C. 663 (C.A.). See, however, the discussion of this case in section B(6), "Illegal Speech," in chapter 3, given that its precedential value in the context of a law such as a privacy statute may be questionable.

13 *Aubry* v. *Duclos* (1996), 141 D.L.R. (4th) 683 (Que. C.A.). This case contains a discussion of a number of earlier Quebec cases involving personality rights, which include, in appropriate circumstances, the right to privacy and anonymity.

14 See *Athans* v. *Canadian Adventure Camps Ltd.* (1977), 17 O.R. (2d) 425 (H.C.J.); *Krouse* v. *Chrysler Canada Ltd.* (1973), 40 D.L.R. (3d) 15 (Ont. C.A.) [*Krouse*].

15 *Gould Estate* v. *Stoddart Publishing Co.* (1996), 30 O.R. (3d) 520 (Gen. Div.). In this case the court stated at 528 that "[r]eputation and fame can be a capital asset that one nurtures and may choose to exploit and it may have a value much greater than any tangible property. There is no reason why such an asset should not be devisable to heirs."

From time to time, the law of nuisance has also been pressed into service in the interests of preserving privacy. In one case, the plaintiffs were granted an injunction and damages against the defendant public authority for following, watching, and besetting the plaintiffs' boat in Toronto harbour.[16] In another case, a plaintiff brought a case against relatives for continual harassment through telephone calls and letters.[17] In this latter decision the court recognized a claim in nuisance by invasion of privacy through the abuse of the telephone system, because of the annoying ringing of the telephone's bell and the fact that the plaintiff had to answer the phone to make it stop ringing. The court did not extend the same legal principle to the letters sent by the defendant, as the court held that the mail is not as intrusive a communications medium as the telephone.[18] As well, in appropriate circumstances, courts will also enjoin the disclosure of personal information, or award damages to the plaintiff after the disclosure, where the information was imparted in confidence and the subsequent disclosure betrays such confidence. For example, in several British cases newspapers have been prohibited from publishing personal information on this basis.[19] The jurisprudential basis for these decisions is not unlike that seen in section B(1), "Trade Secrets/Breach of Confidence," in chapter 2 in the discussion of the protection of trade secrets and confidential information. As Lord Denning stated in the *Fraser* case:

> [T]he court will, in a proper case, restrain the publication of confidential information. The jurisdiction is based, not so much on property or on contract, but rather on the duty to be of good faith. No person is permitted to divulge to the world information which he has received in confidence, unless he has just cause or excuse for doing so. Even if he comes by it innocently, nevertheless, once he gets to know that it was originally given in confidence, he can be restrained from breaking that confidence.[20]

---

16   *Poole and Poole v. Ragen and The Toronto Harbour Commissioners,* [1958] O.W.N. 77 (H.C.J.).

17   *Motherwell v. Motherwell* (1976), 73 D.L.R. (3d) 62 (Alta. C.A.).

18   See, however, *Mather v. Columbia House* (1992), 12 L.W. 1226-004 (Ont. Sm. Claims), where unsolicited mailings that continued despite repeated requests to stop, were held to be a form of trespass.

19   *Duchess of Argyll v. Duke of Argyll,* [1967] 1 Ch. 302; *X. v. Y.,* [1988] 2 All E.R. 648 (Q.B.); *Stephens v. Avery,* [1988] 2 W.L.R. 1280 (Ch. D.) [*Stephens*]; *Fraser v. Evans,* [1969] 1 All E.R. 8 (C.A.) [*Fraser*].

Where, however, the information sought to be protected relates to persons who generally seek publicity, courts are reluctant to enjoin the publishing of confidential information.[21]

In a manner akin to the abovenoted British breach of confidence cases, in Quebec, the Canadian Broadcasting Corporation was found, on the basis of the *Civil Code*, to have caused damage to a viewer critical of a certain show by causing an invasion of that viewer's privacy by the host of the show reading the viewer's critical letter on the air, and in so doing identifying the viewer and encouraging other viewers to contact him, which subsequently resulted in the viewer receiving offensive phone calls and letters.[22] In Ontario, a court awarded damages to a plaintiff when the defendant, without authorization of the plaintiff, played in public a tape of a telephone conversation with the plaintiff; the court called this action an "invasion of privacy," and partly relied on the *Krouse* case for precedent.[23] It should also be noted that a number of statutes also prohibit the interception of electronic communications.[24]

2) Data Protection

In terms of information privacy, a leading definition of privacy conceives of it as the "claim of individuals, groups, or institutions to determine for themselves when, how, and to what extent information about them is communicated to others."[25] Many commentators and the public at large worry that computers and networks are eroding the ability of individuals to make these determinations in respect of their personal information.[26] Although records have been kept about people for hundreds of years, the shift in the storage medium from paper to electronic has raised multiple new concerns. Computers can simply gather and

---

20   *Fraser*, above note 19 at 11. Emphasizing that pre-existing relationships are not critical to this form of protection, the court in *Stephens*, above note 19 at 1286, expressed the legal obligation as follows:

> [the defendant] submits that in the absence of either a legally enforceable contract or a pre-existing relationship — such as that of employer and employee, doctor and patient, or priest and penitent — it is not possible to impose a legal duty of confidence on the recipient of the information merely by saying that the information is given in confidence. In my judgment that is wrong in law. The basis of equitable intervention to protect confidentiality is that it is unconscionable for a person who has received information on the basis that it is confidential subsequently to reveal that information. Although the relationship between the parties is often important in cases where it is said there is an implied as opposed to express obligation of confidence, the relationship between the parties is not the determining factor. It is the acceptance of the information on the basis that it will be kept secret that affects the conscience of the recipient of the information.

21   In *Woodward v. Hutchins*, [1977] 1 W.L.R. 760 (C.A.), pop singers including Tom
     Jones wanted the court to prohibit a former employee of the company that ran the
     singers' tours from divulging stories that occurred on various singing tours. The
     court refused, and Lord Denning stated at 763–64:

> No doubt in some employments there is an obligation of confidence. In a
> proper case the court will be prepared to restrain a servant from disclosing
> confidential information which he has received in the course of his
> employment. But this case is quite out of the ordinary. There is no doubt
> whatever that this pop group sought publicity. They wanted to have themselves
> presented to the public in a favourable light so that audiences would come to
> hear them and support them. Mr. Hutchins was engaged so as to produce, or
> help to produce, this favourable image, not only of their public lives but of
> their private lives also. If a group of this kind seek publicity which is to their
> advantage, it seems to me that they cannot complain if a servant or employee of
> theirs afterwards discloses the truth about them. If the image which they
> fostered was not a true image, it is in the public interest that it should be
> corrected. In these cases of confidential information it is a question of
> balancing the public interest in maintaining the confidence against the public
> interest in knowing the truth. . . . In this case the balance comes down in favour
> of the truth being told, even if it should involve some breach of confidential
> information. As there should be "truth in advertising," so there should be truth
> in publicity. The public should not be misled. So it seems to me that the breach
> of confidential information is not a ground for granting an injunction.

Similarly, in *Lennon v. News Group Newspapers Ltd. and Twist*, [1978] FSR 573
(C.A.), ex-Beatle John Lennon urged the court to block a newspaper from
publishing revelations about Lennon provided to the paper by Lennon's first wife.
Again the court refused, concluding at 574–75:

> It seems to me as plain as can be that the relationship of these parties has
> ceased to be their own private affair. They themselves have put it into the
> public domain. They made it public to all the world themselves, and I do not
> think that one or other of them can obtain an injunction to stop it being
> published. One only has to read these articles all the way through to show that
> each of them is making money by publishing the most intimate details about
> one another and accusing one another of this, that and the other, and so forth.
> It is all in the public domain. I do not regard this as a breach of confidence at
> all. If there is any action it is for libel and, as she says it is true, there is no
> ground for an injunction.

22   *Robbins v. Canadian Broadcasting Corp.* (1957), 12 D.L.R. (2d) 35 (Que. Sup. Ct.).
     The particular provision of the Quebec *Civil Code* relied on by the court at 39 reads
     as follows: "1053. Every person capable of discerning right from wrong is
     responsible for the damage caused by his fault to another, whether by positive act,
     imprudence, neglect or want of skill."

23   *Saccone v. Orr* (1981), 34 O.R. (2d) 317 at 321 (Co. Ct.).

24   See section B(10), "Interception of Communications," in chapter 3.

25   Alan F. Westin, *Privacy and Freedom* (New York: Atheneum, 1967) at 7.

26   "Virtual Privacy," *The Economist*, 10 February 1996.

store much more information. The means for collection are also becoming automated, as when a point of sale system in a store automatically records every purchase made by a consumer. Computers also permit data to be combined from various sources much more readily.[27] And then the data can be reproduced at no cost. These and other factors have resulted in the creation of huge databases within governments and countless private sector companies. In addition to collecting, combining, and storing data, computers and telecommunication networks permit remote access to information in a manner not permitted previously. The paper-based file, kept in a locked filing cabinet in a room with a locked door in a building that limits entry to authorized persons, is a rather secure mechanism for storing sensitive personal information. Polls indicate that the same information, when resident on a computer system to which many users have access, is perceived to be insecure, and indeed these concerns lead many people to view the loss of personal privacy as the chief threat of the Information Age.[28]

---

27 The Privacy Working Group of the U.S. government's Information Policy Committee, Information Infrastructure Task Force, illustrated the phenomenon of computer-based data aggregation in the following manner. In the days before computers,

> in order to build a profile of an individual who had lived in various states, one would have to travel from state to state and search public records for information about the individual. This process would have required filling out forms, paying fees, and waiting in line for record searches at local, state, and federal agencies, such as the departments of motor vehicles, deed record offices, electoral commissions, and county record offices. Although one could manually compile a personal profile in this manner, it would be a time-consuming and costly exercise, one that would not be undertaken unless the offsetting rewards were considerable. In sharp contrast, today, as more and more personal information appears on-line, such a profile can be built in a matter of minutes, at minimal cost.

See *Privacy and the National Information Infrastructure: Principles for Providing and Using Personal Information*, 6 June 1995, at 1–2. This report is available at <http://www.iitf.nist.gov/ipc/ipc/ipc-pubs/niiprivprin_final.html>.

28 See, for example, the results of an attitudinal survey of a group of U.K. respondents that attempted to measure which of thirteen examples of invasion of privacy would most upset them, and whether they thought it should be prohibited. The "central computer" that would have data available to anyone who asks for it, elicited the strongest reaction; 87 percent said it would constitute an invasion of privacy; 71 percent said they would be annoyed; 85 percent said it should be prohibited by law. Similar figures for private detectives were 39 percent, 19 percent, and 30 percent, respectively: reported in Wacks, *Personal Information*, above note 6. See also Ekos Research Associates Inc., *Privacy Revealed: The Canadian Privacy Survey* (Ottawa: Communications Canada, 1993), which, based on a survey of 3000 Canadian households, reported that 81 percent of respondents believed that computers are reducing the level of privacy in Canada.

People have a broad range of concerns with the practices of collecting, aggregating, and disseminating information. There is the frightening, and real, prospect of unsavoury and dangerous people, such as pedophiles and convicts gaining access to such information.[29] At the other end of the spectrum is the use of consumption-related data and mailing lists by credit card companies, retailers, and others. For example, in the case of *Dwyer* v. *American Express Company*, a credit card company ranked cardholders in different categories based on their spending habits, and then rented out its mailing lists of cardholders to merchants who would then target these individuals with marketing and sales programs.[30] The plaintiff cardholder argued that these practices amounted to an intrusion into the cardholders' seclusion, the disclosure of private financial information, and an appropriation of personality rights by trading on the personal spending habits of cardholders, and thereby caused damage to the cardholders. The court disagreed, concluding that the compilation by the card company of mailing data in its own records does not constitute an invasion of privacy, noting that the right to privacy does not extend to the mailbox. As well, the court stated that including names on mailing lists does not disclose financial information about cardholders, particularly given that, as the court put it, "a single random cardholder's name has little or no intrinsic value to defendants (or a merchant)";[31] rather, the credit card company creates value by categorizing and aggregating the names, and therefore, the court concluded, the appropriation claim also failed. In effect, the court said, the only damages the plaintiffs could have suffered was an excess of unwanted mail, and thus the court dismissed the claim. This case illustrates well the second dynamic of computer law, namely, the highly ephemeral nature of information and the fact that information, malleable and plastic asset that it is, often takes its value from its context. It also makes clear why governments have for some time been concerned with data protection matters. The Canadian government first focussed on these issues when it appointed a Task Force on Privacy and Computers in the early 1970s, which resulted in an important report and a series of related studies.[32] Governmental concern continues to this day, as illustrated by the fact that privacy issues were treated by the national Information Highway Advisory Council as an important research topic.[33] This governmental concern has translated

---

29   "Inside Information," *The Economist*, 29 June 1996.
30   652 N.E.2d 1351 (Ill. App. 1995) [*Dwyer*].
31   *Ibid.* at 1356.
32   *Privacy and Computers* (Ottawa: Information Canada, 1972).
33   *Privacy and the Canadian Information Highway* (Ottawa: Industry Canada, 1994).

into a number of statutes in Canada, which are discussed below. As these laws draw their inspiration from recommendations issued by the Organization for Economic Cooperation and Development (OECD) developed in the 1970s, it is worth considering these guidelines first.

3) The OECD Data Protection Guidelines

The OECD, the Paris-based organization dedicated to promoting economic cooperation and growth among its members,[34] promulgated its *Guidelines Governing the Protection of Privacy and Transborder Flows of Personal Data (OECD Guidelines)* in response to the rapid growth of the use of computer and telecommunications technologies in the OECD countries.[35] With respect to data protection, the *OECD Guidelines* set out eight basic principles:[36]

1. **Collection limitation principle.** There should be limits to the collection of personal data and any such data should be obtained by lawful and fair means and, where appropriate, with the knowledge or consent of the data subject.
2. **Data quality principle.** Personal data should be relevant to the purposes for which they are to be used, and, to the extent necessary for those purposes, should be accurate, complete and kept up-to-date.
3. **Purpose specification principle.** The purposes for which personal data are collected should be specified not later than at the time of data collection and the subsequent use limited to the fulfilment of those purposes or such others as are not incompatible with those purposes and as are specified on each occasion of change of purpose.
4. **Use limitation principle.** Personal data should not be disclosed, made available or otherwise used for purposes other than those specified in accordance with paragraph 3 except: (a) with the consent of the data subject; or (b) by the authority of law.
5. **Security safeguards principle.** Personal data should be protected by reasonable security safeguards against such risks as loss or unauthorized access, destruction, use, modification or disclosure of data.

---

34   OECD membership currently consists of the former "Western" European countries, Austria, Iceland, Norway, Finland, Denmark, Turkey, Mexico, the Czech Republic, Hungary, Poland, Korea, the United States, Japan, Canada, Australia, and New Zealand: see <http://www.oecd.org/>.

35   For a copy of the *OECD Guidelines*, see Appendix 1 to James Michael, *Privacy and Human Rights: An International and Comparative Study* (Brookfield, Vt.: Dartmouth, 1994).

36   *OECD Guidelines*, ss. 7 to 14.

6. **Openness principle.** There should be a general policy of openness about developments, practices and policies with respect to personal data. Means should be readily available of establishing the existence and nature of personal data, and the main purposes of their use, as well as the identity and usual residence of the data controller.

7. **Individual participation principle.** An individual should have the right: (a) to obtain from a data controller, or otherwise, confirmation of whether or not the data controller has data relating to him; (b) to have communicated to him, data relating to him (i) within a reasonable time; (ii) at a charge, if any, that is not excessive; (iii) in a reasonable manner; and (iv) in a form that is readily intelligible to him; (c) to be given reasons if a request made under sub-paragraphs (a) and (b) is denied, and to be able to challenge such denial; and (d) to challenge data relating to him and, if the challenge is successful, to have the data erased, rectified, completed or amended.

8. **Accountability principle.** A data controller should be accountable for complying with measures which give effect to the principles stated above.

The *OECD Guidelines* also define *personal data* as "any information relating to an identified or identifiable individual (data subject)."[37]

The *OECD Guidelines* do not have the force of law and are a set of principles that each member country of the OECD is urged to implement in its national law. Nonetheless, the OECD "fair information practices" principles, as they are sometimes called, are important because they have formed the basis for many national data protection legal regimes, as well as numerous voluntary codes of conduct dealing with personal information. With respect to the latter, the Canadian Standards Association has recently adopted a *Model Code for the Protection of Personal Information (CSA Code)*.[38] The *CSA Code*, in its introduction, expressly states that the *OECD Guidelines* were used as the basis for the development of the *CSA Code*, which consists of ten interrelated principles. The *CSA Code* also includes commentary on each principle that elaborates on specific procedures that might be used by an organization to implement the principle. The *CSA Code* represents a marked improvement over other voluntary codes of conduct for data protection, and several financial institutions, for example, have indicated that they will be adopting it. The non-binding nature of the *CSA Code*, however, coupled with the corresponding lack of an effective sanction mecha-

---

37   *OECD Guidelines*, subs. 1(b).
38   CAN/CSA — Q830-96.

nism, has led the federal privacy commissioner to conclude that the *CSA Code* is inadequate and that data protection legislation covering the private sector is required.[39]

4) Data Protection Legislation

The fair information practices contained in the *OECD Guidelines* have been enshrined in a number of federal and provincial statutes. Federally, the *Privacy Act* has regulated the collection and use of personal information by the federal government and a number of federal public agencies since 1982.[40] This statute applies to personal information recorded in any form and not merely that which is computer-based. The *Privacy Act* contains the principles of the *OECD Guidelines*, with some interesting nuances. Usefully, the statute sets out the only grounds on which personal information can be disclosed,[41] though this provision also permits the government to disclose personal information where public interest in the disclosure clearly outweighs any invasion of privacy that could result from the disclosure.[42] The *Privacy Act* establishes the office of the privacy commissioner to receive and investigate complaints. The privacy commissioner acts as an information ombudsman, conducts audits on the government's information-handling practices, and prepares an annual report that serves as a report card on the government's progress in implementing responsible information-handling techniques. The role of the privacy commissioner is essentially advisory, however, given that legal appeals from decisions of the government as to matters pertaining to the statute are to the Federal Court and not to the privacy commissioner.

The *Privacy Act* is coupled and coordinated with the *Access to Information Act*, a statute that gives Canadians the right to access information in records under the control of the federal government.[43] The term *record* is defined very broadly and in a technology-neutral manner, and includes correspondence, photographs, sound recordings, and computer-based material regardless of physical form.[44] The statute does, however, contain a number of exemptions from the right of access, an

---

39 *Privacy Commissioner of Canada*, Annual Report, 1996–97 (Ottawa: The Privacy Commissioner of Canada, 1997) at 30–31.
40 R.S.C. 1985, c. P-21.
41 *Ibid.*, subs. 8(2).
42 *Ibid.*, para. 8(2)(m).
43 R.S.C. 1985, c. A-1.
44 *Ibid.*, s. 3.

important one being that the government is not to disclose a record containing trade secrets of a third party; confidential financial, commercial, scientific, or technical information supplied by a third party that is treated consistently in a confidential manner by the third party; or information the disclosure of which could reasonably be expected to result in material financial loss.[45] The Federal Court, which decides appeals under the *Access to Information Act*, has construed these exemptions narrowly, only rarely finding against disclosure. For example, the court has set a very high onus on an applicant to show the probability of financial loss from disclosure.[46] In another case, the court has held that while aircraft maintenance records supplied by an airline to a government inspector come within the confidential information exemption, notes taken by the government inspector based on these records do not, as these would not have been "supplied" by the airline.[47] This latter case illustrates very well the elusive nature of information. In one of the few cases holding in favour of non-disclosure, the court decided that disclosing information regarding a quota to import cheese would satisfy the economic harm test provided in section 20 of the *Access to Information Act*.[48]

Privacy and access to information statutes covering information held by provincial governments have been enacted in all provinces (except Prince Edward Island).[49] All share the same general structure of implementing the principles found in the *OECD Guidelines*, coupled with an enforcement mechanism. One procedural difference between some of the statutes is in the role of the relevant information/privacy commissioner. For example, Ontario's statute provides for a right of appeal to the Ontario information and privacy commissioner, rather than to a judge. The only really significant difference lies in Quebec, where since 1994 the *Civil Code* and the *Act Respecting the Protection of Personal Information in the Private Sector*,[50]

---

45   *Ibid.*, s. 20.
46   See *Canada Packers Inc.* v. *Canada (Minister of Agriculture)* (1988), 53 D.L.R. (4th) 246 (F.C.A.).
47   *Air Atonabee Ltd.* v. *Canada (Minister of Transport)* (1989), 27 C.P.R. (3d) 180 (F.C.T.D.).
48   *Canada Information Commissioner* v. *Canada (Minister of External Affairs)* (1990), 72 D.L.R. (4th) 113 (F.C.T.D.).
49   For example, in Ontario, see the *Freedom of Information and Protection of Privacy Act*, R.S.O. 1990, c. F.31. This statute covers the ministries and agencies of the Ontario government; the *Municipal Freedom of Information and Protection of Privacy Act*, R.S.O. 1990, c. M.56, extends essentially the same legislative regime to Ontario municipalities and subsidiary bodies, such as municipal hydro-electric commissions.
50   S.Q., 1993, c. 17.

have extended, as the name suggests, data protection rules beyond the Quebec public sector to cover all companies, service providers, and anyone else in the province of Quebec. Quebec's data protection law is the only such statute in Canada of general application to have its coverage extend beyond the public sector. In 1996, however, the federal government announced its intention to enact a privacy law by the year 2000 that would cover the private sector.[51]

5) Other Legislation

While Quebec has been the only province to date to enact a general data protection statute covering the private sector, there are in the various common law provinces a number of other statutes and/or regulations that address data protection issues. It is quite common, for example, to institute fair information practices in the credit reporting industry.[52] Generally, these statutes require consumer credit reporting agencies to be registered with the government, and to adhere to the sound data-handling practices enumerated in the statutes and in related regulations. Given the use to which credit reports are put by financial institutions and others, these statutes also contain provisions regarding the type of information that may be collected on individuals and included in a credit report. For example, Ontario's statute provides that information in a consumer report regarding bankruptcy, court judgments, tax arrears, criminal convictions, and other negative information cannot be more than seven years old.

Statutes regulating or relating to various other industries or sectors of the economy will often have provisions enumerating standards for dealing with personal information. For example, in the financial services field, federal and provincial statutes governing banks, insurance companies, and other entities have been amended over the past few years to give regulators the authority to make regulations in the data

---

51   Rock, "Notes," above note 4. See also Industry Canada and Justice Canada, Task Force on Electronic Commerce, *The Protection of Personal Information: Building Canada's Information Economy and Society,* 13 February 1998, available at <http:// strategis.ic.gc.ca/privacy> and at <http://canada. justice.gc.ca>. The United States is also considering whether to implement a comprehensive data protection regime: see Catherine Yang, "How Do You Police Cyberspace," *Business Week,* 5 February 1996.

52   In Ontario, for example, see the *Consumer Reporting Act,* R.S.O. 1990, c. C.33.

protection area.[53] To date, however, specific regulations have not been passed in this area, with most governments seemingly being satisfied to have financial institutions rely on voluntary codes of conduct, though, as noted above, this likely will change federally in the next few years if Ottawa enacts privacy legislation for the federally regulated private sector. One area where the necessity to protect personal information is particularly acute is the health care field. The Supreme Court of Canada, in the *Dyment* case, recognized this when it spoke of a patient's need to reveal information "of a most intimate character" in order to obtain medical care.[54] Thus, it is not surprising that statutes governing hospitals, such as a regulation under Ontario's *Public Hospitals Act*, stipulate that a hospital may not disclose patient data to a third party except under the circumstances enumerated in the regulation.[55] Similarly, many statutes governing the various health care providers make it professional misconduct to divulge patient data without approval from the patient.[56] Courts in Canada have also held that doctors and other health care providers have a common law duty to keep patient information confidential, notwithstanding that the physician or dentist owns the patient record.[57] These statutory provisions and common law rules are useful, but there is concern that as the practice of medicine moves from the individual doctor–patient relationship in the doctor's office to a medical team-based approach in an institutional setting, with computer-based technologies storing and communicating personal health data among physicians and health care providers, new and broader protections are required.[58] Accordingly, both Alberta[59] and

---

53   For example, see the *Bank Act*, R.S.C. 1985, c. B-1, s. 459. Banks and other financial institutions are also subject to a common law duty of confidentiality that requires banks to hold their customers' data in confidence subject to several exceptions: see *Tournier v. National Provincial and Union Bank of England*, [1924] 1 K.B. 461 (C.A.).

54   *R. v. Dyment*, [1988] 2 S.C.R. 417 at 433. This case is discussed in section B(11), "Search, Seizure, and Surveillance," in chapter 3.

55   Hospital Management, R.R.O. 1990, Reg. 965, as amended.

56   See, for example, in Ontario, subs. 36(1) of the *Regulated Health Professions Act, 1991*, S.O. 1991, c. 18; and s. 1 of Regulation 856/93 under the *Medicine Act, 1991*, S.O. 1991, c. 30.

57   *Wells (Litigation Guardian of) v. Paramsothy* (1996), 32 O.R. (3d) 452 (Div. Ct.); *Axelrod (Re)*, (1994), 20 O.R. (3d) 133 (C.A.).

58   See, for example, Tom Onyshko, "Common-Law Protection for Doctor-Patient Confidentiality Needs Reform, U.S. Expert Says" *The Lawyers Weekly* (24 February 1995).

59   Bill 30, *Health Information Protection Act*, given first reading on 11 June 1997.

Manitoba[60] have recently introduced comprehensive data protection legislation for the health care sector, and Ontario is contemplating doing the same.[61] While the health information privacy statutes resulting from these initiatives likely will resemble one another in terms of general principles, it is unfortunate that they are not based on a standard, model law. With telemedicine across provincial boundaries soon to be a reality, differing regulatory treatment of health information will cause serious compliance problems for health care administrators.

6) International Developments

Many countries, particularly those in Europe, have enacted data protection laws, commencing with the Scandinavian countries in the 1970s. More recently, to try to ensure a harmonization of various national laws dealing with the protection of personal data, the European Union has adopted a *Directive on Data Protection*.[62] The directive and the various existing national laws generally implement the fair information practices found in the *OECD Guidelines*, but sometimes with important nuances. For example, the U.K. *Data Protection Act 1984* requires data users and computer services companies who process personal data for others to register under the statute.[63] Importantly, this statute also provides data subjects with civil remedies, including compensation for damages arising from inaccurate data or the unauthorized disclosure of

---

60 *The Personal Health Information Act*, S.M. c. 51 (assented to 28 June 1997). Apparently part of the rationale for passage of this legislation was to bolster public confidence in light of the creation of a proposed computer network linking Manitoba's entire health care system, the SmartHealth computer project; see David Roberts, "Manitoba Bill Still Flawed, Critics Say" *The [Toronto] Globe and Mail* (25 June 1997).

61 See the Ontario Ministry of Health's consultation paper, *A Legal Framework for Health Information*, June 1996 and Ontario's *Personal Health Information Protection Act, 1997*, a draft bill circulated for consultation in November 1997. See also Neil Seeman, "Focus on Health Law: Ontario Revamping Confidentiality Laws" *The Lawyers Weekly* (14 March 1997).

62 *Directive 95/46/EC of the European Parliament and of the Council of 24 October 1995 on the protection of individuals with regard to the processing of personal data and on the free movement of such data.* This directive can be found in the *Official Journal of the European Communities* of 23 November 1995, No. L281 at page 31 or at <http://www2.echo.lu/legal/en/dataprot/directiv/directiv.html>.

63 *Data Protection Act 1984* (U.K.), 1984, c. 35, subs. 4(1). This statute will likely be superseded by new legislation implementing the European *Directive on Data Protection*: see House of Commons (U.K.) *Data Protection Bill*, session 1997–98, available at <www.parliament.the~stationery~office.co.uk/pa/pabills.htm>.

personal data. Particularly noteworthy for Canadians is the provision in many of these European laws and the European directive, that the export of personal data can be prohibited where the country of the transferee does not provide adequate data protection laws. These "export" rules ostensibly played an important part in Quebec deciding to extend its data protection law to the private sector.

The other major international dimension to data protection relates to the various measures that have been taken by international organizations, and in international treaties and agreements, to reduce national legal and regulatory obstacles to transborder data flows. For example, the *OECD Guidelines*, together with a subsequent OECD declaration,[64] exhort member countries to refrain from creating unjustified barriers to the international exchange of data and information. This sentiment found expression in the *Canada–U.S. Free Trade Agreement*, and now in the *North American Free Trade Agreement* (NAFTA) that includes Mexico.[65] Article 1302 of the NAFTA provides that governments cannot erect barriers to the free flow of information across their borders, subject to the ability to implement *bona fide* security or privacy rules. The free trade approach to transborder data flow, enshrined in the NAFTA, can be seen, for example, in the data processing provisions of the *Bank Act* and other federal financial institutions legislation. For example, while section 245 of the *Bank Act* requires a bank to maintain and process its data in Canada, the same provision, coupled with Guideline No. E-3,[66] allows the Canadian subsidiaries of foreign banks to quite easily obtain an exemption to process their data outside of Canada so long as the Office of the Superintendent of Financial Institutions has adequate access to such records in a timely manner and the business operations of the Canadian entity are not adversely affected.

B. EXPORT CONTROL OF TECHNOLOGY

As information is power — and in the Information Age it surely is — it is not surprising that many governments around the world attempt to control the export of strategically important technologies and information that might, in the hands of a country's actual or potential enemies,

---

64 OECD, *Declaration on Transborder Data Flow*, adopted 11 April 1985.

65 *North American Free Trade Agreement*, implemented in Canada by the *North American Free Trade Agreement Implementation Act*, S.C. 1993, c. 44.

66 Office of the Superintendent of Financial Institutions Canada, *Processing Information Outside Canada*, May 1992, found in *Consolidated Bank Act and Regulations 1998*, 10th ed. (Toronto: Carswell, 1997) at 636.

prove to be extremely detrimental to the country's security interests. Accordingly, the Canadian government enforces a pair of laws that can be used to curtail the export from Canada of relatively powerful computers and related technologies (such as certain software) that could be useful in military applications. Also subject to export control are encryption technologies that interfere with the ability of law enforcement and intelligence agencies from eavesdropping on the communications of our actual and potential adversaries. Given a number of the technology trends enumerated in chapter 1, particularly increased miniaturization and the development of the Internet as a means to transmit software as well as all sorts of data, the enforcement of export controls in the area of high technology is arguably becoming more problematic. The four dynamics of computer law — the rapid pace of technological change, the elusive nature of information, and the blurring of private/ public and national/international — present significant challenges to those government regulators who wish to control the export of certain computer and related products and technologies.

1) The Law of Export Control

The Canadian government controls the export of computers, technology and other products by means of two different statutes, the *Export and Import Permits Act (EIPA)*,[67] and the *United Nations Act*.[68] Under the latter statute, Canada can restrict the export of goods, as well as the movement of people and money, and the provision of services, to any country against which the United Nations has imposed economic sanctions. It was under the *United Nations Act* that Canada implemented economic sanctions against Iraq when it invaded Kuwait in 1991,[69] and more recently against the various former territories of Yugoslavia.[70] The *EIPA* is narrower in scope in that it only applies to the export of goods, including software and technical data. Like the *United Nations Act*, however, under the *EIPA* the export of goods can be controlled on the basis of destination by placing a country on the Area Control List (ACL) kept under the *EIPA*.[71] Under the *EIPA* the export of munitions and certain

---

67   R.S.C. 1985, c. E-19, as amended.

68   R.S.C. 1985, c. U-2, as amended.

69   United Nations Iraq Regulations, SOR/90-531, 7 August 1990, as amended.

70   United Nations Federal Republic of Yugoslavia (Serbia and Montenegro) Regulations, SOR/92-342, 2 June 1992, as amended; United Nations Republic of Bosnia and Hercogovina Regulations, SOR/95-145, 14 March 1995, repealed by SOR/96-222, 23 April 1996.

71   Area Control List, SOR/81-543, 3 July 1981, as amended.

strategic technologies are also controlled by placing such goods on an Export Control List (ECL).[72] An exporter shipping out of Canada any good on the ECL (regardless of its destination, except for most goods shipped to the United States), or shipping any good to an ACL country (regardless of the type of good), requires an export permit from the Canadian government. Since its enactment in 1947 until the fall of the iron curtain in the early 1990s, the primary rationale for the *EIPA*, and similar legislation in the United States and in Canada's other NATO allies and other like-minded democracies such as Japan and Australia, was to prevent the Soviet Union and other Communist states from acquiring military goods, and strategic computer, software, and other dual-use technologies that could be used against the West in a military confrontation. The term *dual-use* illustrates another aspect of the elusive nature of information, namely, that it often assumes its value — in this case strategic and military value — from the context of its use. With the demise of the former East Bloc, there has been a relaxation of certain aspects of export control, such as the disbanding of COCOM, the Coordinating Committee that was based in Paris and that coordinated the implementation of the West's various export control regimes; the COCOM system, since July 1996, has been superseded by the *Wassenaar Arrangement*.[73] Nonetheless, the *EIPA*, and its two lists remain, albeit the ACL, whose list of countries varies over time, has been much shorter since the removal of the countries formerly comprising the East Bloc. By the same token, particularly in response to Iraq's use of missiles in the 1991 Gulf War, the provisions in the ECL related to missiles have been augmented. Thus, it remains an offence under the *EIPA* to export a good from Canada without an export permit where one is required either under the ECL or the ACL. Under the *EIPA* a company may be fined and its employees may be fined or imprisoned or both if they violate the *EIPA*.

The *EIPA*, pursuant to the *Export Permit Regulations*,[74] provides for two types of export permits: the General Export Permit (GEP) and the Individual Export Permit (IEP). Under the former, an exporter is permitted to ship specific goods to certain countries without having to sub-

---

72   Export Control List, SOR/89-202, 13 April 1989, as amended. The current ECL is at SOR/97-131, 4 March 1997, and is contained in *A Guide to Canada's Export Controls*, published in September 1996 by Canada's Department of Foreign Affairs and International Trade.

73   *The Wassenaar Arrangement on Export Controls for Conventional Arms and Dual-Use Goods and Technologies* was established at meetings of thirty-three states in Vienna, Austria, on 11–12 July 1996.

74   Consolidated Regulations of Canada, 1978, c. 602.

mit to the government an individual export permit application. If the particular export of an ECL item is not covered by a GEP, then the exporter may apply for an IEP by completing the requisite form, which includes a detailed description of the product or technology being exported together with its intended destination. The treatment of U.S. origin goods is also worth noting given the large amount of technology exports from the U.S. to Canada. Item 5400 of the ECL provides that all U.S. origin goods intended to be exported from Canada to a third country require a permit, which in most cases will be automatic under General Export Permit No. Ex.12 — United States Origin Goods,[75] as this allows the re-export from Canada of otherwise non–ECL-controlled goods of U.S. origin, except where the intended destination is an ACL country or one of the following: Cuba, North Korea, or Iran. In essence, there is an unfettered Canada–U.S. border from the perspective of export controls. Thus, a Canadian exporter can ship most goods in the ECL to the United States without a permit. Conversely, in order to allow the free flow of goods up to Canada from the United States, the Canadian government has agreed to honour U.S. trading restrictions on certain countries, but only insofar as U.S. origin goods are concerned. For example, goods made in Canada may be exported to Cuba and do not require a Canadian export permit. Indeed, Canada requires, by force of law, that Canadian-based companies do not comply with foreign directives in respect of the U.S. trade embargo of Cuba,[76] but this Canadian law does not apply in the case of U.S. origin goods re-exported from Canada. Particular problems can arise in the definition of *U.S. origin*. The Canadian government takes the position that once a U.S. input component undergoes significant transformation, such that it is shipped out of Canada pursuant to a different tariff classification than upon its importation, it is no longer a U.S. origin product. For its part, the U.S. government takes the view, generally, that any Canadian product that still contains at least 20 percent U.S. content is American for purposes of U.S. export controls, and in some cases, as with encryption products, the U.S. government takes the view that these products are always subject to U.S. rules regardless of how they may be integrated into other items. In these cases, the respective export control laws of Canada and the United States can be in direct conflict, with the unfortunate Canadian exporter caught in the crossfire.

---

75 SOR/97-107, 29 January 1997.
76 See Foreign Extraterritorial Measures (United States) Order, 1992, SOR/92-584, 9 October 1992, as amended, enacted under the *Foreign Extraterritorial Measures Act*, R.S.C. 1985, c. F-29.

2) Regulating High-Technology Exports

It is through the *EIPA*'s ECL that the government controls the export of certain computers, software, and other technologies. The ECL contains eight groups of goods.[77] Certain high-technology products could fall under Group 2, the military list, but most technology items are considered dual-use (i.e., they have both a civilian use and a military use) and thus are included in Group 1, the industrial list of goods. As noted above, a good listed in the ECL requires a permit in order to be exported from Canada, either a GEP or an IEP. Computers are a good example of a dual-use technology found on the ECL. The 1991 Gulf War illustrated just how central sophisticated computers and software programs have become to the military, both for logistics purposes, as well as command, control, and communications, and even integrated into smart bomb and missile technologies. As noted in chapter 1, the waging of war has become an increasingly high-tech exercise. Recognizing, however, that the personal computer and laptop are ubiquitous, the ECL does not attempt to control the export of every single computer. Rather, it controls only those digital computers having a processing power of greater than 260 Mtops, an Mtop being roughly equivalent to one Megahertz (MHz) of a pentium processor;[78] that is, only relatively high-end computers are captured by the permit requirements of the ECL. In terms of structure, format, and approach, the method of regulation found in the ECL for computers is quite reasonable; it is not product-specific; rather, it contains a set of technical specifications that are technology-neutral for the most part and that are functional in their description. Of course, given the first dynamic of computer law, the government must be vigilant in updating these specifications as individual computers become more powerful. As well, exporters of high-tech goods must be aware that multiple personal computers with co-processors, or one computer having more than one processor operating in parallel, could easily exceed the ECL's threshold for computers. It should also be noted that under a GEP a computer that exceeds the 260 Mtop threshold but is below 500 Mtops can be exported provided the destination is not one of a few countries, including currently Iran, Iraq, and North

---

77   The groups are: Group 1 — Dual Use; Group 2 — Munitions; Group 3 — Nuclear Non-Proliferation; Group 4 — Nuclear-Related Dual Use; Group 5 — Miscellaneous Goods; Group 6 — Missile Technology Control Regime; Group 7 — Chemical and Biological Weapons Non-Proliferation; and Group 8 — Chemicals for the Production of Illicit Drugs.

78   See item 1041.3 of the ECL for a description of controlled digital computers.

Korea.[79] As well, under another GEP, a computer not exceeding 1500 Mtops can be exported without an IEP if the destination is Hong Kong, Japan, Australia, New Zealand, Turkey, or one of seventeen countries in Europe.[80] Also, another GEP authorizes travellers to take personal computers and associated software out of Canada to any destination except a country on the ACL for a maximum of three months, provided that no transfer of technology takes place as a result of the exportation and that the computer is used only by the exporter and only for business or education purposes.[81] In short, as computers become more powerful and widespread, these thresholds will be constantly raised and the coverage within them revised; so it is always important to check the most current ECL and GEPs to understand the current export control rules applying to computers.

As for software and technology, each controlled item on the ECL includes an entry for related software and the technology that is used to develop, produce, or use the controlled item. Thus, if an item is on the ECL, it is almost certain that the software and technology designed for its development, production, or use is also covered by the ECL. For example, item 1081 of the ECL controls, among other things, manned, untethered submersible vehicles designed to operate at depths exceeding 1000 metres, while item 1084 controls software specially designed or modified for the development, production, or use of, among other things, equipment controlled by item 1081, and item 1085 controls technology related to these submersible vehicles. With respect to separate, stand-alone software products, item 1044.3 of the ECL covers such products as the source code of operating system software and certain development tools and compilers specially designed for multidata-stream processing equipment, and certain expert system software. As discussed in more detail below, Category 1150 of the ECL also covers certain encryption software. All of the software items in the ECL, however, are subject to the General Software Note that appears at the beginning of Group 1 of the ECL and that provides that the ECL's control rules do not apply to software which is either:

---

79   General Export Permit No. Ex. 29 — Eligible Industrial Goods, SOR/94-735, 24 November 1994 (GEP 29).

80   General Export Permit No. Ex. 30 — Certain Industrial Goods to Eligible Countries and Territories, SOR/94-734, 24 November 1994 (GEP 30).

81   General Export Permit No. Ex. 18 — Portable Personal Computers and Associated Software, SI/89-121, 10 May 1989, as amended.

1. Generally available to the public by being:
   a. Sold from stock at retail selling points, without restriction, by means of:

      1. Over-the-counter transactions;

      2. Mail order transactions; or

      3. Telephone call transactions; and

   b. Designed for installation by the user without further substantial support by the supplier; or

2. In the public domain.[82]

The intent of the General Software Note is to exclude from the coverage of the ECL, and hence to permit the export without a permit, of "off-the-shelf" mass market software and software "in the public domain," unless the software is destined for a country on the ACL, or U.S. origin software in which case the considerations noted above apply. While the General Software Note therefore serves a useful purpose, and again is a reflection of the general recognition that personal computer-based software is now ubiquitous in the world and therefore its export from Canada need not be controlled, the particular provisions of the General Software Note contain some problems. One is that the forms of distribution mentioned in paragraphs 1(a)(1), (2), and (3) do not contemplate distribution of software over the Internet, an increasingly popular way to acquire software program licences. That is, it is unclear whether sales of software from a website by a software developer constitute a selling from stock at a retail selling point. Thus, for greater clarity, the provision should be amended to allow for sales effected electronically, whether or not the seller is a retailer. Another problem is the use of the phrase *without restriction* in subsection 1(a) of the General Software Note to qualify the manner in which the software must be sold from stock at retail selling points. In short, what does *without restriction* mean? As discussed in chapter 5, software invariably is licensed subject to an agreement that does in fact contain restrictions on its use, disclosure, and further dissemination or transfer, though the license restrictions pertaining to certain "shrinkwrapped" software often contain fewer of these restrictions. In effect, it is not clear how the *without restriction* language in the General Software Note is to be applied to software licenses.

---

82   The General Software Note is at the beginning of the list of Group 1 items in the ECL.

A further problem centres on the phrase *public domain* in section 2 of the General Software Note. Use of this wording is confusing. In copyright parlance, a copyright work enters the public domain when it is no longer protected by copyright, typically because the copyright term has expired.[83] Accordingly, the use of the term *public domain* in the General Software Note is unfortunate because the definition of *in the public domain* in the ECL means software (or technology) that has been made available without restrictions upon its further dissemination, and this definition expressly provides that copyright restrictions do not disentitle software (or technology) from being in the public domain. Moreover, given that most software is licensed subject to restrictions on its further dissemination (i.e., as discussed in chapter 5 most software licences restrict the ability to transfer the software to a third party), it is arguably only a relatively small number of commercial software programs that would qualify as being in the public domain under the General Software Note. Perhaps by *in the public domain* the government really means *freeware*, software in which copyright subsists but which is given away without restriction. There is, however, not much of this kind of software in commercial use. In any event, the term *in the public domain* could be more precise to better reflect the policy rationale behind the provision.

In contrast to the relatively problematic language in the General Software Note, the General Technology Note that appears at the beginning of Group 1 of the ECL refers to *technology* as being specific information necessary for the development, production, or use of a product, such information taking the form of *technical assistance* (which includes instruction, training, and consulting services) and *technical data*. In turn, technical data is stated to be able to take many forms such as blueprints, plans, diagrams, models, formulae, tables, engineering designs and specifications, manuals, and instructions written or recorded on other media or devices such as disk, tape, or read-only memories. This broad definition of technical data would cover most information in electronic form, and therefore would encompass the transmission of controlled technology over the Internet. In today's networked environment, where researchers even within the same company may collaborate with

---

83 In the United States, before that country adhered to the *Berne Convention*, a work could also cease to be protected by copyright, and hence fall into the public domain, if it failed to comply with certain formalities, such as the marking of each copy of the work with the "©" copyright symbol. As Canadian copyright law never required such formalities, works in Canada could not enter the public domain for failure to mark the work in a particular manner.

colleagues in other countries via a high-speed, broad bandwidth intranet, organizations must be extremely careful not to violate the export control rules by inadvertently transmitting controlled technical data over the intranet, either directly, or simply by permitting someone outside of Canada to pull down the problematic material from the Canadian site.

3) Regulating Encryption Technologies

Encryption is a critical feature of computers and networks in the Information Age. Maintaining the security of computers and confidentiality of transmissions over networks is seen as a fundamental weakness of the computer-enabled environment. Many users, for example, are uncomfortable sending personal or otherwise sensitive data over the Internet, or conducting commerce by means of it, because of concerns about security and privacy. Encryption is seen by many as the chief means of allaying these fears. There are many cryptography systems now commercially available. Most are based on a system of scrambling messages by means of a mathematical algorithm, transmission of the sensitive message in such scrambled form, and then descrambling the message by means of a second algorithm or device made available only to the authorized recipient.[84] Password-based cryptography systems are also used to secure limited access to computers, including highly mobile (and highly prone to theft) laptop computers. Not surprisingly, encryption systems of all varieties are finding their way into software, computer, and Internet products and services around the world at a very rapid rate. As a result, Category 1150 of the ECL is assuming greater importance.

Category 1150 of the ECL covers encryption technologies and provides as follows:

1150. Information Security

Note:

The control status of "information security" equipment, "software," systems, application specific "electronic assemblies," modules, integrated

---

84   For an overview of encryption systems, see Lorijean G. Oei, "Primer on Cryptography," in *Online Law: The SPA's Guide to Doing Business on the Internet*, ed. Thomas J. Smedinghoff (Reading, Mass.: Addison-Wesley, 1996) [*Online Law*]. See also Deborah Kerr, "Public Key Mystery," *Computerworld*, 9 September 1996; and Industry Canada, Task Force on Electronic Commerce, *A Cryptography Policy Framework for Electronic Commerce: Building Canada's Information Economy and Society* (February 1998) [*Cryptography Policy*] available at <http://strategis.ic. gc.ca/SSG/cy00005e.html>.

circuits, components or functions is determined in this category even if they are components or "electronic assemblies" of other equipment.

1151. Equipment, Assemblies and Components

1. Systems, equipment, application specific "electronic assemblies," modules or integrated circuits for "information security," as follows, and other specially designed components therefor:

   a. Designed or modified to use "cryptography" employing digital techniques to ensure "information security";
   b. Designed or modified to perform cryptanalytic functions;
   c. Designed or modified to use "cryptography" employing analogue techniques to ensure "information security":

Note:

1151.1.c does not control the following:

   1. Equipment using "fixed" band scrambling not exceeding 8 bands and in which the transpositions change not more frequently than once every second;
   2. Equipment using "fixed" band scrambling exceeding 8 bands and in which the transpositions change not more frequently than once every ten seconds;
   3. Equipment using "fixed" frequency inversion and in which the transpositions change not more frequently than once every second;
   4. Facsimile equipment;
   5. Restricted audience broadcast equipment;
   6. Civil television equipment;

   d. Designed or modified to suppress the compromising emanations of information-bearing signals;

Note:

1151.d. does not control equipment specially designed to suppress emanations for reasons of health or safety.

   e. Designed or modified to use cryptographic techniques to generate the spreading code for "spread spectrum" or the hopping code for "frequency agility" systems;
   f. Designed or modified to provide certified or certifiable "multilevel security" or user isolation at a level exceeding Class B2 of the Trusted Computer System Evaluation Criteria (TCSEC) or equivalent;
   g. Communications cable systems designed or modified using mechanical, electrical or electronic means to detect surreptitious intrusion.

Note:

1151. does not control:

a. "Personalized smart cards" or specially designed components therefor, with any of the following characteristics:

  1. Not capable of message traffic encryption or encryption of user-supplied data or related key management functions therefor; or

  2. When restricted for use in equipment or systems excluded from control under entries 1. to 6. of the Note to 1151.1.c. or under entries b. to h. of this Note;

b. Equipment containing "fixed" data compression or coding techniques;

c. Receiving equipment for radio broadcast, pay television or similar restricted audience television of the consumer type, without digital encryption and where digital decryption is limited to the video, audio or management functions;

d. Portable or mobile radiotelephones for civil use, (e.g. for use with commercial civil cellular radiocommunications systems) that are not capable of end-to-end encryption;

e. Decryption functions specially designed to allow the execution of copy-protected "software," provided the decryption functions are not user-accessible;

f. Access control equipment, such as automatic teller machines, self-service statement printers or point of sale terminals, which protects password or personal identification numbers (PIN) or similar data to prevent unauthorized access to facilities but does not allow for encryption of files or text, except as directly related to the password or PIN protection;

g. Data authentication equipment which calculates a Message Authentication Code (MAC) or similar result to ensure no alteration of text has taken place, or to authenticate users, but does not allow for encryption of data, text or other media other than that needed for the authentication;

h. Cryptographic equipment specially designed and limited for use in machines for banking or money transactions, such as automatic teller machines, self-service statement printers, or point of sale terminals.

1152. Test, Inspection and Production Equipment

1. Equipment specially designed for:

  a. The "development" of equipment or functions controlled by Category 1150, including measuring or test equipment;

  b. The "production" of equipment or functions controlled by Category 1150, including measuring, test, repair or production equipment;

2. Measuring equipment specially designed to evaluate and validate the "information security" functions controlled by 1151. or 1154.

1153. Materials
None

1154. Software
1. "Software" specially designed or modified for the "development," "production" or "use" of equipment or "software" controlled by Category 1150.
2. "Software" specially designed or modified to support "technology" controlled by 1155.
3. Specific "software" as follows:
   a. "Software" having the characteristics, or performing or simulating the functions of the equipment controlled by 1151. or 1152.;
   b. "Software" to certify "software" controlled by 1154.3.a.

Note:
1154. does not control:

   a. "Software" required for the "use" of equipment excluded from control under the Note to 1151.;
   b. "Software" providing any of the functions of equipment excluded from control under the Note to 1151.

1155. Technology
"Technology" according to the General Technology Note for the "development," "production" or "use" of equipment or "software" controlled by Category 1150.

It should be noted that words in quotations are defined in the "Definitions for Terms in Groups 1 and 2" section in the ECL. In particular, the following terms are defined in the ECL as follows:

"Cryptography": The discipline which embodies principles, means and methods for the transformation of data in order to hide its information content, prevent its undetected modification or prevent its unauthorized use. "Cryptography" is limited to the transformation of information using one or more secret parameters (e.g. crypto variables) or associated key management.

"Information security": All the means and functions ensuring the accessibility, confidentiality or integrity of information or communications, excluding the means and functions intended to safeguard against malfunctions. This includes "cryptography", cryptanalysis, protection against compromising emanations and computer security.

"Microprogramme": A sequence of elementary instructions maintained in a special storage, the execution of which is initiated by the introduction of its reference instruction register.

"Programme": A sequence of instructions to carry out a process in, or convertible into, a form executable by an electronic computer.

"Software": A collection of one or more "programmes" or "microprogrammes" fixed in any tangible medium of expression.

Category 1150 of the ECL is drafted in very broad terms and covers a wide variety of software and hardware products that implement cryptographic functionality. For example, it covers not only items that perform cryptography functionality, but also items "designed or modified to use cryptography," thus capturing software that includes, for example, an interface for a specific encryption device but does not yet contain it. However, Category 1150 tries to strike a reasonable balance by providing for numerous exceptions. This form of lengthy, but detailed, regulation is to be preferred, so long as the contents of the provision are regularly reviewed and amended to ensure that it stays current with the reality of the global marketplace. It should also be noted that, interestingly, the rationale for the control of encryption technologies is somewhat different than for other high-technology products, given that the concern is not so much that these cryptography products will be "used against the West" in the manner that other dual-use technologies might be turned against us. Rather, the concern is that if foreign governments and other entities are provided with encryption features, they will be able to keep their messages free from eavesdropping by Western intelligence services. Nonetheless, subsection 1(z.4) of the Schedule to GEP 29, and GEP 30, subsection 5(1)[85] contain important exceptions to item 1151, stipulating that, subject to the other provisions of such general export permits, the following may be exported:

(i)   access control equipment, including automatic teller machines, self-service statement printers and point of sale terminals, that protects password or personal identification numbers (PIN) or similar data to prevent unauthorized access to facilities, but that does not allow for encryption of files or text, except as directly related to the protection of the password or PIN,

(ii)   data authentication equipment that calculates a Message Authentication Code (MAC) or similar result to ensure that no alteration of text has taken place or to authenticate users, but that does not

---

85   See above notes 79 and 80, respectively.

allow for encryption of data, text or other media other than that needed for the authentication, and

(iii) cryptographic equipment specially designed, developed or modified for use in machines for banking or money transactions, such as automatic teller machines, self-service statement printers and point of sale terminals.

These exceptions mirror the exemptions contained in paragraphs (f), (g) and (h) in the Note to Item 1151. These provisions are useful, for example, for banks and other financial institutions in Canada that are increasingly providing non-Canadian clients with access to computer systems in Canada, and that wish to implement as much security as possible around these access mechanisms. These exemptions, however, relate essentially to encryption devices that authenticate the identity of users of a particular system, but do not cover technologies that encrypt the underlying data itself.

Category 1150 is subject to the General Software Note discussed above, and therefore encryption devices implemented on off-the-shelf software do not require Canadian export permits, unless they are of U.S. origin. Moreover, the United States government views encryption devices as military goods, and the United States has traditionally imposed a virtual ban on the export (outside of North America) of all products containing cryptography features, even if found in off-the-shelf commercially available products.[86] This is why it has been common for a U.S. software company to have a North American version of a product and a non–North American version, the latter having a lower level of encryption protection built into it because of the U.S. export controls on cryptography technologies. Recently, however, Washington has been considerably loosening its approach to the regulation of encryption technologies permitting, for example, 56-bit encryption products in certain circumstances.[87] Similarly, the Canadian government is currently issuing export permits for 56-bit encryption products, and in some cases even stronger products for certain applications.

---

86 For a discussion of the U.S. controls on the exports of encryption technologies, see Thomas J. Smedinghoff, "Export Controls and Transnational Data Flow," in Smedinghoff, *Online Law*, above note 84.

87 See Wendy R. Leibowitz, "Encryption Takes Center Stage: Is Government a Trusty Neighbour?" *The National Law Journal* (7 July 1997). See also *Bernstein v. United States Department of State*, 945 F. Supp. 1279 (N.D. Cal. 1996) in which it was held that the U.S. government's licensing scheme of cryptographic software was unconstitutional (under the U.S. "free speech" First Amendment) because it failed to meet certain constitutional procedural safeguards.

A few years ago, an intriguing controversy erupted in the United States surrounding the proposed "Clipper chip," a device the government proposed building into each telephone, switching device, and computer.[88] The Clipper chip would encrypt all communications, and would thereby make secure all messages and transmissions, with one fundamental exception, namely, the government and its agencies and law enforcement officials (the police) would be able to access each device once appropriate judicial wire-tapping authority was obtained. The U.S. government proposed this regime because it is rather difficult to tap into fibre optics transmission capacity, and the government wanted to maintain its surveillance capacity in the new networked environment. This is a legitimate concern for the United States (and other) governments as evidence obtained through wire-tapping has been instrumental in prosecuting, for example, drug dealers. However, because of privacy concerns, the Clipper chip proposal engendered a great deal of criticism, and the controversial proposal has since been superseded by a less intrusive, but still controversial alternative whereby private parties can use various encryption technologies so long as a copy of the digital key necessary to decipher the technology is lodged with the U.S. government.[89] This escrow arrangement, argues the government, is necessary to give the government the ability to track criminals in the modern era of telecommunications. Many U.S. civil libertarians remain sceptical and concerned. The United States is not the only country wrestling with these sorts of issues. For example, the French government has for some years banned the use of any private use of encryption technologies. The Canadian government has recently released a discussion paper on cryptography that is engendering heated debate over these issues.[90] The issues are not simple to resolve because they are driven inexorably by all four of the dynamics of computer law.

---

88   For a discussion of the Clipper chip debate, see Lance J. Hoffman, ed., *Building in Big Brother: The Cryptographic Policy Debate* (New York: Springer-Verlag, 1995).

89   See John P. Barlow, "Save the Bill of Rights!: Jackboots on the Infobahn," *Wired*, April 1994. Barlow stated that trusting the government with privacy under the Clipper chip proposal was like having a peeping Tom install window blinds. For a more measured response, see Philip Elmer-Dewitt, "Who Should Keep the Keys?" *Time*, 14 March 1994. For the perspective of U.S. law enforcement agencies, see the transcript of testimony of the director of the FBI, Louis J. Freeh, before the U.S. Senate Judiciary Committee on 4 June 1997, at <http://www.epic.org/crypto/legislation/freeh_6_4_97. html>. See also Todd Lappin, "Clinton's New Clothes: A New Report Lays Bare the Encryption Policy Scam," *Wired*, August 1996.

90   Industry Canada, *Cryptography Policy*, above note 84. See also "Industry Asks: What Price Security? Customer Confidence in Having Safe Internet Runs Up against Need to Control Illegal Activities" *The Ottawa Citizen* (8 April 1998).

C. REGULATING THE INTERNET

The federal government has for many decades regulated the telecommunications and broadcasting industries in Canada. The rationale for doing so with respect to the former related to protecting the public interest in the context of an important utility and transportation-like service provided by monopolists and quasi-monopolists. After 1987, Canadian ownership and control regulation was established, matching similar provisions that had long been in place in the United States and elsewhere. Recently, this form of regulation has come under increasing pressure, as the World Trade Organization and other international organizations press for the removal of barriers to international trade in telecommunications. Broadcasting regulation was initially aimed at creating and promoting the presence of an indigenous Canadian voice to provide to Canadians an alternative to U.S.-based radio (and subsequently television, and more recently satellite) programming. These and other reasons have led to the development of an extensive regulatory regime for telecommunications and broadcasting overseen primarily by the Canadian Radio-television and Telecommunications Commission (CRTC), although Industry Canada regulates radio spectrum allocation and use, as well as some other areas. The four dynamics of computer law — the rapid pace of technological change, the elusive nature of information, and the blurring of private/public and national/international — make the regulation of the gatekeepers and conduits of the Information Age, especially the Internet, a daunting task.

1) Regulating Telecommunications

The federal *Telecommunications Act*[91] regulates "telecommunications common carriers" operating in Canada, which are entities that own or operate transmission facilities used to provide telecommunications services

---

91   S.C. 1993, c. 38, as amended.

to the public for compensation.[92] The *Telecommunications Act* sets out the following telecommunications policy objectives for Canada:

> **Objectives.** – It is hereby affirmed that telecommunication performs an essential role in the maintenance of Canada's identity and sovereignty and that the Canadian telecommunications policy has as its objectives
>
> (a) to facilitate the orderly development throughout Canada of a telecommunications system that serves to safeguard, enrich and strengthen the social and economic fabric of Canada and its regions;
> (b) to render reliable and affordable telecommunications services of high quality accessible to Canadians in both urban and rural areas in all regions of Canada;
> (c) to enhance the efficiency and competitiveness, at the national and international levels, of Canadian telecommunications;
> (d) to promote the ownership and control of Canadian carriers by Canadians;
> (e) to promote the use of Canadian transmission facilities for telecommunications within Canada and between Canada and points outside Canada;
> (f) to foster increased reliance on market forces for the provision of telecommunications services and to ensure that regulation, where required, is efficient and effective;
> (g) to stimulate research and development in Canada in the field of telecommunications services;
> (h) to respond to the economic and social requirements of users of telecommunications services; and
> (i) to contribute to the protection of the privacy of persons.[93]

---

92   *Ibid.*, s. 2. Related definitions are:
"exempt transmission" apparatus means any apparatus whose functions are limited to one or more of the following:
(a) the switching of telecommunications,
(b) the input, capture, storage, organization, modification, retrieval, output or other processing of intelligence, or
(c) control of the speed, code, protocol, content, format, routing, or similar aspects of the transmission of intelligence;
"intelligence" means signs, writing, images, sounds, or intelligence of any nature;
"telecommunications" means the emission, transmission or reception of intelligence by any wire, cable, radio, optical or other electromagnetic system, or by any similar technical system; and
"transmission facility" means any wire, cable, radio, optical, or other electromagnetic system, for the transmission of intelligence between network termination points, but does not include any exempt transmission apparatus.

93   *Ibid.*, s. 7.

Making sense of this policy in the real world is a challenge indeed. Like a multiheaded Hydra, the internal conflicts between the subparts of the policy soon become apparent. For example, it is not a trivial exercise to reconcile the promotion of Canadian ownership (subsection (d)) with fostering greater reliance on market forces (subsection (f)), which latter goal often involves non-Canadian interests. Responsibility for implementing this Sisyphean telecommunications policy rests with the CRTC,[94] and with the federal government, which issues directives that are binding on the CRTC.[95] The CRTC is the present-day successor to a number of other bodies that have regulated telecommunications in Canada since 1906.

The *Telecommunications Act* sets out a number of rules that apply to telecommunications common carriers. As a threshold matter, in order to operate as a telecommunications common carrier, the carrier must be at least 80 percent Canadian owned and controlled in fact by Canadians.[96] As well, the regulated rates charged by a carrier must be just and reasonable, and in some cases are subject to prior approval by the CRTC.[97] In practice, fewer and fewer rates are subject to CRTC approval, as the CRTC "forbears" from regulating the increasingly competitive telecommunications markets under section 34 of the *Telecommunications Act*. More broadly, most aspects of the services provided by the carrier are subject to conditions imposed by the CRTC, contained in "Conditions of Service."[98] It is a criminal offence to contravene any provision of the *Telecommunications Act* or any regulation or decision made under it.[99] The *Telecommunications Act* also provides that no carrier shall

---

94 The CRTC is established under the *Canadian Radio-television and Telecommunications Commission Act*, R.S.C. 1985, c. C-22, as amended.

95 The federal government currently exercises its responsibility for telecommunications through the Minister of Industry.

96 *Telecommunications Act*, subss. 16(1) & (3). This restriction, however, is affected by the provisions of the *Canadian Telecommunications Common Carrier Ownership and Control Regulations*, SOR/94-667, 25 October 1994, which permit, among other things, the indirect foreign ownership of up to 33-1/3 percent of the voting shares of a holding company that controls a Canadian carrier, and an even higher percentage of non-voting shares, provided there is no control-in-fact by a non-Canadian. These Canadian ownership restrictions may be dropped in the future if the on-going negotiations on international telecommunications liberalization at the World Trade Organization bear fruit.

97 *Telecommunications Act*, subss. 25(1) & 27(1). Once approved, such rates are called "tariffs."

98 See *ibid.*, s. 24; however, the CRTC may also forbear from regulating the conditions of services, and has done so in the case of many competitive services.

99 *Ibid.*, s. 73.

unjustly discriminate in respect of the services it provides or the rates it charges, nor shall it give any unreasonable preference to any person, including itself, nor subject anyone to an undue or unreasonable advantage.[100] Since the early 1980s, the duty on carriers to supply services to everyone at reasonable rates and without discrimination has led to a number of CRTC decisions that have fostered increasing competition in the market for telecommunications services and ancillary products. For example, currently there is competition in the attachment and sale of terminal apparatus,[101] the provision of enhanced services (computer-based services provided on top of the core basic telephone service),[102] publication of directory listing information,[103] and long-distance telephony.[104] In a decision in early 1997, the CRTC determined that the provision by Bell Canada and its Stentor partner companies across Canada of the Sympatico Internet connection service did not constitute an unreasonable advantage or undue preference, as was argued by a number of independent Internet service providers.[105] Several years ago the CRTC determined that it will be implementing a policy of local telephony competition as well, once various costing and other mechanisms can be constructed.[106] In a series of decisions released on 1 May 1997, the CRTC established the basic framework for opening local telephony to competition, at the same time announcing that telephone companies can apply for broadcasting licences.[107] The ultimate goal is meaningful convergence, whereby the telephone and broadcast industries are free to offer all services to all consumers in a single competitive environment. Shortly after these decisions, the CRTC gave two telephone companies permission to conduct market trials for broadcasting services, including

---

100   *Ibid.*, s. 27. Again, the CRTC may forbear from regulation under this section.
101   Telecom Decision CRTC 82-14, *Attachment of Subscriber-Provided Terminal Equipment*, 8 C.R.T. 848 (23 November 1982).
102   Telecom Decision CRTC 84-18, *Enhanced Services*, 10 C.R.T. 486 (12 July 1984).
103   Telecom Decision CRTC 95-3, *Provision of Directory Database Information and Real-Time Access to Directory Assistance Databases* (8 March 1995).
104   Telecom Decision CRTC 92-12, *Competition in the Provision of Public Long Distance Voice Telephone Services and Related Resale and Sharing Issues* (12 June 1992).
105   Telecom Decision CRTC 97-1, *Bell Canada and Bell Sygma Inc. — Joint Marketing of Sympatico Internet Services* (13 January 1997).
106   Telecom Decision CRTC 94-19, *Review of Regulatory Framework* (16 September 1994).
107   Telecom Decision CRTC 97-8, *Local Competition* (1 May 1997) and Telecom Decision CRTC 97-9, *Price Cap Regulation and Related Issues* (1 May 1997).

the delivery of pay-per-view movies.[108] Another example of the impact of convergence is telephony over the Internet, a phenomenon that likely will come before the CRTC for greater scrutiny once the technology improves to the point of it becoming a viable alternative to long-distance calling; to date the CRTC has indicated that Internet service providers facilitating voice telephony over the Internet will be treated as telephone service resellers and will have to make contribution charges to the established telephone companies.

2) Regulating Broadcasting

The federal *Broadcasting Act*[109] regulates broadcasting in Canada. This statute in subsection 2.(1) defines *broadcasting* as:

> any transmission of programs, whether or not encrypted, by radio waves or other means of telecommunication for reception by the public by means of broadcasting receiving apparatus, but does not include any such transmission of programs that is made solely for performance or display in a public place.

Integral to this definition of broadcasting is the definition of *program*, which is as follows:

> sounds or visual images, or a combination of sounds and visual images, that are intended to inform, enlighten or entertain, but does not include visual images, whether or not combined with sounds, that consist predominantly of alphanumeric text.

Subsection 4(2) of the *Broadcasting Act* provides that it applies "in respect of broadcasting undertakings carried on in whole or in part within Canada." The *Broadcasting Act* further provides that a *broadcasting undertaking* includes a *distribution undertaking*, a *programming undertaking*, and a *network*, and these are defined as follows:

> "distribution undertaking" means any undertaking for the reception of broadcasting and the retransmission thereof by radio waves or other means of telecommunication to more than one permanent or temporary residence or dwelling unit or to another such undertaking;

---

108 Telecom Decision CRTC 97-11, *Applications Under the Broadcasting Act and the Telecommunications Act for Authority to Conduct Technical and Market Trials* (8 May 1997).
109 S.C. 1991, c. 11.

"programming undertaking" means an undertaking for the transmission of programs, either directly by radio waves or other means of telecommunication or indirectly through a distribution undertaking, for reception by the public by means of broadcasting receiving apparatus;

"network" includes any operation where control over all or any part of the programs or program schedules of one or more broadcasting undertakings is delegated to another undertaking or person.[110]

It should also be noted that the term *other means of telecommunication* in these definitions is in turn defined to mean "any wire, cable, radio, optical or other electromagnetic system, or any similar technical system."[111]

The *Broadcasting Act* sets out a broadcasting policy for Canada. This policy is longer than the policy contained in the *Telecommunications Act*, but it is worth setting out in its entirety because the multitude of often competing demands placed on the Canadian broadcasting system are only evident upon a review of the complete policy, which provides as follows:

3. (1) **Declaration.** – It is hereby declared as the broadcasting policy for Canada that
(a) the Canadian broadcasting system shall be effectively owned and controlled by Canadians;
(b) the Canadian broadcasting system, operating primarily in the English and French languages and comprising public, private and community elements, makes use of radio frequencies that are public property and provides, through its programming, a public service essential to the maintenance and enhancement of national identity and cultural sovereignty;
(c) English and French language broadcasting, while sharing common aspects, operate under different conditions and may have different requirements;
(d) the Canadian broadcasting system should
    (i)   serve to safeguard, enrich and strengthen the cultural, political, social and economic fabric of Canada,
    (ii) encourage the development of Canadian expression by providing a wide range of programming that reflects Canadian attitudes, opinions, ideas, values and artistic creativity, by displaying Canadian talent in entertainment programming and by offering information and analysis concerning Canada and other countries from a Canadian point of view,

---

110   *Ibid.*, subs. 2(1).
111   *Ibid.*, subs. 2(2).

(iii) through its programming and the employment opportunities arising out of its operations, serve the needs and interests, and reflect the circumstances and aspirations, of Canadian men, women and children, including equal rights, the linguistic duality and multicultural and multiracial nature of Canadian society and the special place of aboriginal peoples within that society, and

(iv) be readily adaptable to scientific and technological change;

(e) each element of the Canadian broadcasting system shall contribute in an appropriate manner to the creation and presentation of Canadian programming;

(f) each broadcasting undertaking shall make maximum use, and in no case less than predominant use, of Canadian creative and other resources in the creation and presentation of programming, unless the nature of the service provided by the undertaking, such as specialized content or format or the use of languages other than French and English, renders that use impracticable, in which case the undertaking shall make the greatest practicable use of those resources;

(g) the programming originated by broadcasting undertakings should be of high standard;

(h) all persons who are licensed to carry on broadcasting undertakings have a responsibility for the programs they broadcast;

(i) the programming provided by the Canadian broadcasting system should

(i) be varied and comprehensive, providing a balance of information, enlightenment and entertainment for men, women and children of all ages, interests and tastes,

(ii) be drawn from local, regional, national and international sources,

(iii) include educational programs and community programs,

(iv) provide a reasonable opportunity for the public to be exposed to the expression of differing views on matters of public concern, and

(v) include a significant contribution from the Canadian independent production sector;

(j) educational programming, particularly where provided through the facilities of an independent education authority, is an integral part of the Canadian broadcasting system;

(k) a range of broadcasting services in English and in French shall be extended to all Canadians as resources become available;

(l) the Canadian Broadcasting Corporation, as the national public broadcaster, should provide radio and television services incorporating a wide range of programming that informs, enlightens and entertains;

(m) the programming provided by the Corporation should
   (i)   be predominantly and distinctively Canadian,
   (ii)   reflect Canada and its regions to national and regional audiences, while serving the special needs of those regions,
   (iii)   actively contribute to the flow and exchange of cultural expression,
   (iv)   be in English and in French, reflecting the different needs and circumstances of each official language community, including the particular needs and circumstances of English and French linguistic minorities,
   (v)   strive to be of equivalent quality in English and in French,
   (vi)   contribute to shared national consciousness and identity,
   (vii)   be made available throughout Canada by the most appropriate and efficient means and as resources become available for the purpose, and
   (viii) reflect the multicultural and multiracial nature of Canada;
(n) where any conflict arises between the objectives of the Corporation set out in paragraphs (l) and (m) and the interests of any other broadcasting undertaking of the Canadian broadcasting system, it shall be resolved in the public interest, and where the public interest would be equally served by resolving the conflict in favour of either, it shall be resolved in favour of the objectives set out in paragraphs (l) and (m);
(o) programming that reflects the aboriginal cultures of Canada should be provided within the Canadian broadcasting system as resources become available for the purpose;
(p) programming accessible by disabled persons should be provided within the Canadian broadcasting system as resources become available for the purpose;
(q) without limiting any obligation of a broadcasting undertaking to provide the programming contemplated by paragraph (i), alternative television programming services in English and in French should be provided where necessary to ensure that the full range of programming contemplated by that paragraph is made available through the Canadian broadcasting system;
(r) the programming provided by alternative television programming services should
   (i)   be innovative and be complementary to the programming provided for mass audiences,
   (ii)   cater to tastes and interests not adequately provided for by the programming provided for mass audiences, and include programming devoted to culture and the arts,

(iii) reflect Canada's regions and multicultural nature,

(iv) as far as possible, be acquired rather than produced by those services, and

(v) be made available throughout Canada by the most cost-efficient means;

(s) private networks and programming undertakings should, to an extent consistent with the financial and other resources available to them,

(i) contribute significantly to the creation and presentation of Canadian programming, and

(ii) be responsive to the evolving demands of the public; and

(t) distribution undertakings

(i) should give priority to the carriage of Canadian programming services and, in particular, to the carriage of local Canadian stations,

(ii) should provide efficient delivery of programming at affordable rates, using the most effective technologies available at reasonable cost,

(iii) should, where programming services are supplied to them by broadcasting undertakings pursuant to contractual arrangements, provide reasonable terms for the carriage, packaging and retailing of those programming services, and

(iv) may, where the Commission considers it appropriate, originate programming, including local programming, on such terms as are conducive to the achievement of the objectives of the broadcasting policy set out in this subsection, and in particular provide access for underserved linguistic and cultural minority communities.[112]

As with the telecommunications policy noted above, this broadcasting policy seemingly contains a number of objectives that could easily conflict with each other. Nonetheless, what is clear is that Parliament has declared as Canada's broadcasting policy a series of objectives that go well beyond merely parcelling out space along the finite radio spectrum.

The *Broadcasting Act* mandates the CRTC to "regulate and supervise all aspects of the Canadian broadcasting system with a view to implementing the broadcasting policy."[113] Indeed the *Broadcasting Act* provides in a further declaration that the Canadian broadcasting system constitutes a single system and that the objectives of the broadcasting

112 *Ibid.*, subs. 3(1).
113 *Ibid.*, subs. 5(1).

policy can best be achieved by providing for a single, independent, public regulator — the CRTC.[114] The power of the CRTC in broadcasting matters is subject only to directions of the government, which can be both general[115] and specific,[116] but in both cases are binding on the CRTC.[117] The CRTC carries out its functions under the *Broadcasting Act* primarily through imposing licence conditions on broadcasting undertakings and passing regulations that are binding on them.[118] The CRTC's enforcement powers are bolstered by sections 32 and 33 of the *Broadcasting Act*, which make it a criminal offence to carry on a broadcasting undertaking without a licence or to contravene or fail to comply with the terms of a licence or a regulation made by the CRTC.

The CRTC and the federal government, acting largely through the Department of Heritage, have implemented the broadcasting policy in a myriad of regulations, policies, and licence conditions.[119] To illustrate the breadth of policy tools available to the CRTC and the government, consider the following mechanisms that have been deployed over the past number of years to foster Canadian content in television, which is a prime rationale for CRTC regulation of broadcasting today:

- *Government support for the CBC*: The *Broadcasting Act* proclaims the Canadian Broadcasting Corporation to be "the national public broadcaster,"[120] and notwithstanding recent budget cuts, hundreds of millions of public dollars continue to be contributed to the CBC.
- *Other government subsidies*: Other public monies are used to support Telefilm Canada, and provincial funding agencies, which fund productions that meet Canadian content rules.

---

114   *Ibid.*, subs. 3(2).
115   *Ibid.*, subs. 7(1).
116   *Ibid.*, subss. 26(1) & 27(1).
117   *Ibid.*, subss. 7(3) & 27(2).
118   The licensing and regulation-making powers are contained in subss. 9(1) & 10(1), respectively, of the *Broadcasting Act*.
119   For a useful collection of various CRTC policies, together with an annotated version of the *Broadcasting Act*, see McCarthy Tétrault (Peter S. Grant *et al.*), *1996–97 Canadian Broadcast and Cable Regulatory Handbook* (Toronto: McCarthy Tétrault, 1996). For a comprehensive work on the powers and procedures of the CRTC, together with its experience in regulating telecommunications, see Michael H. Ryan, *Canadian Telecommunications Law and Regulation* (Toronto: Carswell, 1993) (looseleaf, updated).
120   *Broadcasting Act*, para. 3(1)(l). The CBC has played a central role in fostering a Canadian presence on Canada's airwaves since its creation in 1935 when the Prime Minister of the day, R.B. Bennett, apparently quipped, "better the state than the States."

- *Canadian content quotas*: Since 1961, television stations and networks have had to show a minimum amount of Canadian content, currently generally 60 percent during the eighteen-hour broadcast day and 50 percent during prime time. Specific spending quotas are also being imposed to support Canadian drama production. Certain stations are also being required to expend specific amounts on Canadian drama. Canadian-owned pay television and specialty program services on cable television have their own Canadian content rules, as do Canadian-owned pay-per-view undertakings that, for example, must ensure that at least one in twenty of their first-run film titles are Canadian.
- *Restrictions on distribution of U.S. television signals*: The number of U.S. off-air television signals that may be carried by cable companies are generally limited to the four U.S. commercial networks and PBS.[121] Also, the "simultaneous substitution rule" permits Canadian broadcasters to prevent U.S. off-air television signals from being delivered to Canadian cable homes when the Canadian station is showing the same program at the same time.[122] Indirect support for Canadian services is provided under section 19.1 of the *Income Tax Act*, which denies Canadian advertisers from claiming advertising on U.S. border stations as an allowable business expense. The number of U.S. satellite services carried by cable television companies is also limited.[123]
- *Levies on private sector participants*: Cable television companies and other distributors of broadcast programming provide direct financial support for Canadian production through an independently administered fund.[124] As well, 5 percent of gross revenues from pay-per-view undertakings such as direct-to-home satellite, must be spent on funding the development of Canadian programming.[125]

---

121 See *Approval of Cable Distribution of Fox Network Affiliates*, Public Notice CRTC 1994-107, 29 August 1994.

122 See *Cable Television Regulations, 1986*, SOR/86-831, s. 20, 1 August 1986.

123 *Distribution and Linkage Requirements*, Public Notice CRTC 1994-60, 5 June 1994, as amended by the Eligible Satellite Services list issued periodically by the CRTC.

124 *The Production Fund*, Public Notice CRTC 1994-10, 10 February 1994.

125 *Licensing of New Direct-to-Home (DTH) Satellite Distribution Undertakings, and New DTH Pay-Per-View (PPV) Television Programming Undertakings*, Public Notice CRTC 1995-217, 20 December 1995.

It should be noted with respect to "Canadian content" that the CRTC does not define Canadian content by "content," *per se*, but by the origin of the content. The CRTC has adopted the point system developed by the Canadian Audio-Visual Certification Office, the federal agency that determines whether film productions qualify as Canadian for purposes of obtaining the benefits of tax credit regime in the *Income Tax Act*. Under this system, each creative function is given a certain number of points (e.g., director, two points; writer, two points; leading performer, one point, etc.), and a production must earn a minimum of six points (or eight points under the new cable fund) to be considered Canadian, and at least one of the director or writer and one of the two leading performers must be Canadian.[126] In short, to be considered Canadian the program need not be about hockey, or any other Canadian story, but must have a critical mass of Canadians involved in the production.

3) Regulating the Internet

The Internet poses a number of challenges to the regulatory regimes for telecommunications and broadcasting outlined above. Consider an Internet environment of much greater bandwidth than today, where in addition to text, a website could carry and would permit the truly efficient downloading of images, music, and full-motion video. One service that would arise would be video-on-demand (VOD), where customers could rent movies over the Internet instead of trudging to the video rental store. Of course the "full" Internet will offer much more than VOD. Just focussing on videos for a moment, newspapers delivered online will include video clips, rather than just text and fixed images. A company in the travel business will not only provide videos of prospective destinations, but may also provide travel videos supplied by satisfied clients. A hockey league may provide instructional videos, as well as Don Cherry's popular hockey video series. Universities and others will provide courses by distance education over the Internet; in cinema studies, this might entail downloading entire movies. Or book and magazine retailers might add video products to their websites. In a technical environment (which will not be attained for a number of years) comprising digitization and broadband networks, the content will be transmitted from all to all at modest cost, the sources of content will proliferate, and what people see on their information appliance (a computer or an inter-

---

126   See *Recognition for Canadian Programs*, Public Notice CRTC 1984-94, 15 April 1984; for the application of the point system to the cable fund, see 2(c) of *The Production Fund*, Public Notice CRTC 1994-10, 10 February 1994.

active television set) will be determined by them rather than a broadcaster. The technical and business model for the full Internet will be the bookstore, magazine stand, and video rental store — with greater choice and with a great deal of "pull" technology, where the user dictates what she sees, rather than "push" technology, where the broadcaster determines what the viewer sees. But even the pre-Internet examples of bookstore, magazine stand, and video rental store do not really capture the potential of the Internet. One important service for the baseball-crazed business person will enable her to pull down from the Internet a tape of highlights of her favourite team's latest game. Depending on how much time the harried viewer has, she can choose the two-, five-, or ten-minute versions, and she can watch these at any time. Moreover, this content might be available from any number of sources on the Internet. And this model can be multiplied by an almost infinite amount of content delivery operations over the Internet, just as the number of websites proliferate inexorably.

Several questions regarding the *Broadcasting Act* arise from such an Internet environment. The first is whether the federal government has the legislative power to regulate the Internet. Paragraph 92(10)(a) of the *Constitution Act, 1867* gives jurisdiction to the federal government over interprovincial "telegraphs," among other interprovincial works or undertakings.[127] In a consistent line of constitutional decisions, the federal government's jurisdiction over telegraphs has been extended to include telephones,[128] wireless radio communications and broadcasting,[129] and

---

127 The *Constitution Act, 1867* (U.K.), 30 & 31 Vict., c. 3, found in R.S.C. 1985, Appendix II, No. 5, is the old *British North America Act*, renamed by means of the *Canada Act, 1982* (U.K.), 1982, c. 11.

128 *Alberta Government Telephones v. Canada (C.R.T.C.)*, [1989] 2 S.C.R. 225 [*AGT*]. See also *Corporation of the City of Toronto v. Bell Telephone Company of Canada*, [1905] A.C. 52 (P.C.). In *Commission du Salaire Minimum v. The Bell Telephone Company of Canada*, [1966] S.C.R. 767, the federal jurisdiction over the telephone company was held to apply to all matters that are an important part of the operation of the interprovincial business, in this case minimum wage rules.

129 *Re Regulation and Control of Radio Communication in Canada*, [1932] A.C. 304 (P.C.) [*Radio Reference*]; *R. v. Gignac*, [1934] O.R. 195 (H.C.J.) [*Gignac*]. See also *Re C.F.R.B. and Canada (A.G.)*, [1973] 3 O.R. 819 (C.A.), where the jurisdiction of the federal government was held to cover the whole of broadcasting, including matters pertaining to technology as well as intellectual content: the court thereby upheld a provision of the *Broadcasting Act* that prohibits political advertising on the day before an election; but see also *Quebec (A.G.) v. Kellogg's Company of Canada*, [1978] 2 S.C.R. 211, which upheld a Quebec law that regulated cartoons aimed at children, including those on television.

cable television facilities.[130] More recently, telephone companies operating in a single province have been held to come under the federal jurisdiction because they invariably participated in the national telecommunications system.[131] In all these cases, however, the company over which federal jurisdiction was extended was a *work* or an *undertaking*, given the articulation of these terms in the *Radio Reference* case, namely, that a work is a physical thing and an undertaking, although not a physical thing, is an arrangement under which physical things are used. In other constitutional cases undertaking has been equated to organization or enterprise.[132]

Regarding the Internet, there is little doubt that the traditional carriers with respect to their traditional services, be it the telephone companies or the cable companies, come under federal jurisdiction. By contrast, what about the thousands of new content providers that will be appearing on the Internet, such as the schools, retailers, and travel agencies noted above? Are they interprovincial works or undertakings? And it is not clear that one can consider the Internet itself as an undertaking, given its anarchical, decentralized nature, as outlined in section A(6), "The Internet," in chapter 1. Nevertheless, if the federal government assumed jurisdiction over every website in Canada, is the CRTC capable of regulating thousands of new "broadcasters"? This raises the further question whether the current definitions of *broadcasting* and *program* in the *Broadcasting Act* are wide enough to capture all aspects of this new Web-based activity. The definition of program is very broad, covering sounds or visual images and excluding only visual images that consist predominantly of alphanumeric text. Thus, in its definition only text-based services, such as a stock market data feed or the cable wire news service that shows as text, are excluded from being a program. Moreover, the requirement that broadcasting involve transmission of programs "for reception by the public" is likely not an obstacle if they are made available to users of the Internet, and even if they are more tar-

---

130   *Capital Cities Communications Inc.* v. *C.R.T.C.*, [1978] 2 S.C.R. 141. In this case the Supreme Court found in favour of the federal government's continuity of regulation from off-air broadcasting to cable transmission. See also *Public Service Board* v. *Dionne*, [1978] 2 S.C.R. 191 in which it was held that a provincial agency may not exercise regulatory authority over a cable company as this field of activity is reserved exclusively to the federal government.

131   *AGT*, above note 128; *Téléphone Guèvremont Inc.* v. *Quebec (Régie des Télécommunications)*, [1994] 1 S.C.R. 878.

132   *Canadian Pacific Railway* v. *British Columbia (A.G.)*, [1950] A.C. 122 (P.C.); *A.G. for Ontario* v. *Israel Winner*, [1954] A.C. 541 (P.C.); *Reference re Validity of the Industrial Relations and Disputes Investigation Act*, [1955] S.C.R. 529.

geted in their dissemination where the quality of the "audience" did not comprise only pre-existing friends or acquaintances.[133] And in any event, even if the definitions of broadcasting or programs were too narrow to capture all aspects of broadcasting on the Internet, Parliament could amend them to be more expansive.

In the end, however, it is not statutory language that most brings into question the ability of the CRTC to regulate the Internet; rather, it is the unruly technology of the Internet as discussed in section A(6), "The Internet," in chapter 1. For example, the Internet is extremely global. A user in Canada can access websites around the world. Consider a user of a broadband Internet in the near future accessing a website resident on a computer in Florida to pull down American movies. The CRTC may be able to argue that the American website operator is carrying on a broadcasting undertaking in part in Canada, thus giving the CRTC jurisdiction under subsection 4(2) of the *Broadcasting Act*, but even if it could, to what end would this argument be made if the Florida website operator did not have assets in Canada? There is the technical option of requiring the Internet service provider in Canada, or the Canadian regulated carrier, to block access to the website, but again the practical difficulties of this sort of action become daunting when the example of this single Florida-based website is multiplied a thousand times over by the vast number of websites around the world.[134] It is almost like trying to regulate telephone conversations among individuals. In short, the Canadian government does not regulate the material carried in bookstores, music stores, and video rental stores in order to implement Canadian content rules because, quite frankly, it is an impossible task. Of course, the urge and impetus for the CRTC to regulate the Internet will be great, just as at one time all individual users of radios needed a licence from the government, but just as Ottawa eventually gave up this practice, so too will the CRTC have to be realistic about its ability to tame the unruly Internet tiger.[135]

In order to regulate, governments need effective and efficient control points that permit regulation. To date, in the broadcasting field, television and radio stations and cable companies have been extremely

---

133   See the discussion of "public" in section C(6), "Copyright and the Internet," in chapter 2 and section B(5), "Obscenity and Child Pornography," in chapter 3. See also *R. v. Continental Cablevision Inc.* (1974), 5 O.R. (2d) 523 (Prov. Ct.).

134   See the example of the court order banning publication of the Homolka trial proceedings referred to in section B(7), "Criminal Libel," in chapter 3 for a real-life case study of how difficult it is to regulate content on the Internet.

135   See *Gignac*, above note 129; *Nolan v. McAssey*, [1930] 2 D.L.R. 323 (P.E.I.S.C.).

convenient control points. Telecommunications carriers, and even larger new entrants into the Internet content business with assets in Canada, will serve as manageable regulatory control points. The Internet, however, simply has many fewer effective control points relative to the thousands and thousands of purveyors of information on the Internet. And as these unregulated entities take material market share away from the traditional broadcasters, the latter will clamour for a general deregulation. This is not to say the future of the CRTC is doomed, because there will continue to be a traditional broadcast industry. Even elements of it on the Internet will be able to be regulated by the CRTC. Nevertheless, the huge fragmentation and democratization that will occur with so much content on the Internet will simply be beyond the practical regulatory purview of the CRTC. For an "early warning" indicator of what soon will confront the CRTC, one simply has to recall the problems encountered during the last federal election by Elections Canada in enforcing, on the Internet, the rule that public opinion polls must not be published in the forty-eight-hour period prior to election day, and the rule that election results may not be released in a region until the polls have closed there.[136] Of course this prediction may prove to be somewhat off the mark or it may not come to pass for some time. Given the phenomenon of information overload, there will always be a demand for services that aggregate, edit, and present information and content in manageable portions, and arguably these types of entities are reasonably convenient regulatory control points, particularly if broadcast regulators around the world band together in some coordinated fashion to impose their collective wills globally. In any event, there is no question that the four dynamics of computer law will make the broadcasting regulator's task much more difficult.

The Canadian government and the CRTC are mindful that the Internet presents novel questions. In October 1994 the government requested the CRTC to conduct hearings and prepare a report on the regulatory issues of the Information Highway. The resulting CRTC *Convergence Report*,[137] released in May 1995, as well as the 1995 report of

---

136   See Mary Gooderham, "Officials Rushing to Plug Cyberspace Loophole" *The [Toronto] Globe and Mail* (27 March 1997). See also "Chaos Theory in Action" in the "Briefly Noted" section of *The [Toronto] Globe and Mail* (23 May 1997), which describes Election Canada's problem in enforcing another election law on the Internet. When an Ottawa-based website operator removed his material at the behest of Elections Canada, copies of it sprang up in six countries, including several sites in Canada. Regulating the Internet is like putting small fingers into huge cracks in the dyke.

137   CRTC, *Competition and Culture on Canada's Information Highway: Managing the Realities of Transition*, 19 May 1995 [*Competition and Culture*].

the government's Information Highway Advisory Council (IHAC)[138] published a few months later, and the government's official *Convergence Policy Statement*[139] issued in August 1996, contain a number of interesting observations and policies. With respect to carriage of telecommunications and broadcasting signals, the primary policy objective will be to allow for complete convergence between the telephone companies and the cable companies; that is, telephone companies will be permitted to provide broadcasting services, and cable companies and other broadcasting undertakings will be permitted to provide telecommunications services including local telephone service. As well, third-party service providers will be entitled to use the facilities of both to provide broadcasting and telecommunications services. Such convergence, and the access by third parties, will be subject to a host of rules related to interconnection, rate restructuring, and the prevention of cross-subsidies and other anticompetitive practices. In short, the liberalization process that has resulted in increased competition in the telecommunications sector will continue and will include the broadcasting sector; this policy objective is being implemented by the CRTC's decisions referred to in notes 106 and 107 above.

With respect to content issues and the ability of the *Broadcasting Act* to face the challenges posed by the Information Highway, the government's policy and the CRTC and IHAC reports are unanimous in observing that reinforcing Canadian sovereignty and cultural identity through the *Broadcasting Act* remains a paramount objective. The CRTC report is almost defiant in its tone when responding to the question whether it has sufficient regulatory tools to respond to a networked, digital world, as seen in the following excerpts from the report:

> Section 3 of the *Broadcasting Act* sets out detailed objectives for a distinctively Canadian broadcasting system. The Act is not a dusty and dated piece of legislation passed in the days of crystal sets and Victrolas. It is an expression of the will of Parliament studied, debated and passed just over four years ago. This legislation anticipated both the extraordinary pace of technological change and an explosion of broadcasting services in a competitive environment. Nevertheless, the framers

---

138 Canada, Information Highway Advisory Council, *Connection, Community, Content: The Challenge of the Information Highway, Final Report of the Information Highway Advisory Council,* (Ottawa: The Council, 1995): <http://strategis.ic.gc.ca/IHAC> and also at <http://xinfo.ic.gc.ca/info-highway/final.report/eng/>.

139 Industry Canada, *Convergence Policy Statement,* 10 July 1996. This document can be found at <http://strategis.ic.gc.ca>.

of that legislation held to the primary importance of maintaining a Canadian system that offers Canadians programming of high standard and one that, in its totality, reinforces the sovereignty of their country and their own cultural identity.

The 1991 *Broadcasting Act* is the latest in a consistent set of responses to the two central questions that have preoccupied Canadians since before the 1919 sign-on of Canada's first radio station, XWA (now CIQC) in Montréal. How can Canada create and maintain a distinctive Canadian broadcasting system, and how can that system ensure the availability of high quality and diverse Canadian programming, particularly in the face of the attractive, low-cost, popular culture spilling over our southern border? Both of these goals have rested on the conviction that "Keeping Canada on its own airwaves" could never be guaranteed by U.S.-dominated market forces, but must rely on reasonable forms of Canadian public intervention. Like Canada itself, our national broadcasting system is not an accident of the market; it is an act of will.

The challenges facing Canadians today, as we adapt to a new era of information technology, do not differ in principle from the challenges posed by radio in the 1920s and 1930s; television in the 1940s and 1950s; cable in the 1960s and 1970s; and, communications satellites in the 1970s and 1980s. In each case, attractive new services were first available from U.S. sources. With Canadians rightly demanding access to these services, government policy had to ensure that attractive and viable domestic services were also available within the system.

The Canadian broadcasting system, as it exists today, is the product of more than five decades of cooperation between public and private elements; compromise between idealism and pragmatism; balance between national identity and continentalist market forces; and concentration on the principles in section 3 of the *Broadcasting Act*.

Canadians can be justifiably proud of their broadcasting system. It is studied and emulated by nations around the world. We live beside the world's most prolific exporter of popular culture and mass media, one whose products reach us in particular abundance, and in one of our own official languages. Despite this, and in a vast and thinly-populated land, Canadians have accomplished the following:

- established publicly-funded radio and television services, educational services and community services, in both official languages;
- extended public broadcasting services to over 97% of the population;
- established private conventional radio and television services that provide Canadians with a range of choices in virtually every community;

- established multilingual radio, television and specialty services directed to Canada's multicultural population, as well as services controlled by and dedicated to the aboriginal peoples of Canada;
- developed an advanced cable distribution system that is available to 94% of Canadian homes; and
- created over 30 specialty and pay television services available to cable subscribers.[140]

The CRTC and the government perceive the current regulatory model going forward to cover new culture-delivery technologies and distribution systems in the future. Thus, both documents stipulate that new licensed distribution undertakings will be required to make financial contributions to the production of Canadian programming, as currently is the case. Similarly, these entities will be required to provide an affordable and attractive base package of services that include predominant Canadian choice. For example, licensed VOD services will be required to offer a meaningful amount of Canadian titles, and they must make use of navigational systems that give priority to Canadian programs. The CRTC considers that the tools in the *Broadcasting Act* and the *Telecommunications Act* are sufficient to ensure cultural policy objectives because it does not perceive this digital world to be a great deal different from the existing broadcasting environment. For example, the CRTC believes that VOD services will require significant financial resources to launch and market, will involve the acquisition of program rights, and generally will resemble the structure of licensed broadcasters today. This will be an accurate view for some time since currently the prime drivers behind large-scale VOD services will be telephone and cable companies that are already regulated. There is, however, the possibility that a new content distribution model will develop on the Internet involving very different entities. The CRTC, in its report, is willing to consider amending the definition of program in the *Broadcasting Act* to exclude, in addition to alphanumeric text-based services, other services that "while they likely fall within the definition of broadcasting, will not foreseeably contribute materially to the achievement of the *Broadcasting Act*'s objectives";[141] the Convergence Report then provides a non-exhaustive list of such services as including interactive courses offered by accredited instructional organizations or used by medical institutions, online commercial multimedia services, and educational multimedia materials directed to schools. The CRTC also

---

140   *Competition and Culture*, above note 137 at 27–28.
141   *Ibid.* at 30.

stated that it might be reasonable to simply issue exemption orders in respect of such activities, as it has already done in respect of home shopping.[142] Interestingly, the IHAC report and the government policy statement are not convinced that additional exemptions should be added to the definition of programs, and are willing only to concede that more study should be devoted to this issue. One is left with the impression after reading these reports and policy statements that the CRTC, the IHAC, and the government are not fully cognizant of the digital world that will be unfolding, or of the difficulty the CRTC and the government will have regulating it to achieve cultural sovereignty objectives as a result of the four dynamics of computer law.

FURTHER READINGS

Books

CAVOUKIAN, Ann, & Don TAPSCOTT, *Who Knows: Safeguarding Your Privacy in a Networked World* (New York: McGraw-Hill, 1997)

MCCARTHY TÉTRAULT (Peter S. Grant, Anthony H.A. Keenleyside, Michel Racicot & Paul Hurtubise), *1996–97 Canadian Broadcast and Cable Regulatory Handbook* (Toronto: McCarthy Tétrault, 1996)

MICHAEL, James, *Privacy and Human Rights: An International and Comparative Study* (Aldershot, U.K.: Dartmouth, 1994)

RYAN, Michael H., *Canadian Telecommunications Law and Regulation* (Toronto: Carswell, 1993) (looseleaf, updated)

WACKS, Raymond, *Personal Information: Privacy and the Law* (Oxford: Clarendon Press, 1989)

Internet Sites

Canadian Radio-television and Telecommunications Commission
<http://www.crtc.gc.ca/>

Internet Privacy Coalition
<http://www.privacy.org/ipc/>

The President's Information Infrastructure Task Force (United States)
<http://iitf.doc.gov/>

Privacy Commissioner of Canada
<http://infoweb.magi.com/~privcan/>

---

142   *Exemption Order Respecting Teleshopping Programming Service Undertakings,* Public Notice CRTC 1995-14, 26 January 1995.

COMMERCIAL LAW

The business of selling computers, software, and information-based products differs from other enterprises in a number of legally important ways. The computer industry is driven by three interrelated phenomena. Perhaps the most fundamental and far-reaching is the short product cycle in the computer business. Short product cycles also result in a unique aspect of software — it invariably has errors or bugs in it. In particular, the year 2000 millennium bug hovers ominously over the computer industry. Another result of short product cycles is that the distribution channels for much hardware, and most software and information-based products, are multitiered and complex.

These three characteristics of the computer industry raise a number of legal issues. Short product cycles and complicated product distribution channels have implications under competition law. Information-based products also tend to be licensed, rather than sold, thereby differentiating them from most other goods. Licensing products in an environment of rapid technological change can be legally challenging. Computer products also present questions under negligence law and raise issues regarding the applicability to them of sale of goods legislation. As software is critical to a company's well-being, it is not surprising that bankruptcy issues are of concern to a supplier and user of technology-oriented products. And, as in all areas of commercial endeavour, tax questions can pose intriguing problems for the suppliers and users of computer, software, and information-based products. Two other subjects are also worth mentioning: international trade law because of the global nature of the computer industry and its strategic role in the world economy; and labour law because of the profound impact that technology has had on the workplace. In most of these subareas of the law there are few statutes, or even provisions within statutes, devoted to computer and information products.[1] Rather, the analysis often involves reviewing a general commercial law rule and assessing how well (or poorly) it applies to a high-technology issue. In conducting this analysis, the dynamics of computer law should be kept in mind. Particularly relevant to this chapter is the rapid pace of technological change, and depending on the issue area (such as sales legislation and tax), the elusive nature of information, and the blurring of the national and international realms.

A. MARKETING COMPUTER AND INFORMATION-BASED PRODUCTS

1) Short Product Cycles

The incredible rate of technology development, the first dynamic of computer law, translates into a commercial environment characterized by short, and ever shortening, product cycles. In virtually all submarkets of the computer business, innovation is measured in weeks or months rather than years. Most computer software and information-based products have short shelf lives, at least for any particular version of the product. One report in the United States notes that the "extraordinarily rapid pace of technological change in information technology (IT) hardware and software . . . creates the equivalent of three to five [automotive] model changes each year."[2] Moreover, every segment of the computer market is characterized by intense competition. New entrants are continually bringing to market new products. Marketing people in the computer business talk in terms of narrow temporal windows of opportunity to get a new product or version out into the marketplace before it invariably collides with a competitor's subsequent version.

---

1   An interesting exception is Quebec's proposed Bill 40, *An Act to Amend the Charter of the French Language*, introduced in the Quebec National Assembly in 1996, that would, among other things, amend Quebec's French language law (*Charter of the French Language*, R.S.Q. 1977, c. C-11) to require that a supplier's French-language version of software (if one exists) be made available in Quebec at the same time as the English language version.

2   Cited in Margaret E. McConnell, "The Process of Procuring Information Technology" (Winter 1996) 25:2 Public Contract Law Journal 379 at 385.

The business and legal impact of short product cycles is significant. It leads, for example, to the formation of numerous alliances within the industry among different companies and organizations. These arrangements vary in terms of degree and intensity from product distribution agreements, to joint R&D agreements, to full-blown mergers. In each case, however, there is the common thread of understanding that in today's technology business it is very difficult for one firm to possess in-house all the required core competencies. Some large technology firms, such as Microsoft, Intel, and Cisco, are acquiring minority positions in smaller companies to bolster the market for products that will increase demand for these companies' core products, as well as to use these investment targets as surrogate R&D test beds.[3] All these different types of arrangements raise competition law issues. From another perspective, the short product cycles raise, often to unreasonable levels, expectations within the user community. This can result in liability claims, sounding both in contract and in negligence, if ultimately the products or services do not measure up to these expectations.

2) Imperfect Software: The Y2K Problem

The creation of software normally involves several distinct phases from the initial high-level design, through coding the instructions and statements, and finally to an exercise of testing to find and fix as many problems as possible before it is shipped to customers.[4] Although most software products undergo a significant amount of testing, it is a central fact of software development that it is virtually impossible to detect and eradicate all the bugs in advance. Bug-free software, if such a state were even attainable, would be so expensive and time-consuming as to make it impractical in a commercial setting, at least given how that environment is structured currently. Thus, suppliers of software offer support programs to users of their products, a major element of which is the correction of bugs that come to light once the customer has commenced to use the software product. Another component of the typical software support program is the provision of future versions and upgrades of the software. A prime rationale for such follow-on versions is to provide the user with new or enhanced features, but upgrades are also used to distribute to users new copies of the previous software with a number of the bugs corrected. Software and other information-based products,

---

3   "Silicon Valley's New Sugar Daddies," *The Economist*, 12 July 1997.
4   See section A(3), "Software," in chapter 1.

such as CDs based on software, are unique in the world of commerce in that they involve an ongoing relationship between the supplier and the user not seen with other products.

A computer defect that will cost suppliers and users billions of dollars over the next few years is the year 2000 problem (the Y2K problem).[5] In simple terms, the Y2K problem exists because a broad range of computer programs and hardware systems have been programmed with two-digit date fields. Thus, the year 1999 is expressed simply as "99." This practice of leaving out the first two digits of the date arose in the early days of computer programming (the 1960s and 1970s) when computers were much less powerful than they are today. It seemed a good idea at the time, given it was an easy way to save on precious capacity resources: Why use a four-digit date field when a two-digit version would suffice? As for those who thought about the longer-term implications of this design decision, they likely believed that by the year 2000 the particular computer system with the two-digit date field would be long replaced by a new system that would be Y2K compliant. And in many cases this is precisely what has happened, as old "legacy" systems have been replaced by modern, fully Y2K compliant successors.

Not all old systems, however, have been replaced. Many, many legacy systems, riddled with two-digit date fields, stubbornly continue as the workhorses of innumerable public and private organizations. The result is a panoply of problems caused by the inability of these programs to handle the Y2K. Consider a simple example from a human resources program. It is common for a computer program to calculate a person's age by deducting a person's date of birth, such as 57 (being 1957), from the then current year, say, 97 (being 1997), to give the result 40. Along comes the year 2000, and the same program will perform the following math: $00 - 57 = -57$. If the program does not recognize negative numbers it will assume the person is 57 years old, rather than 43. The impact in the real world of this software glitch, and thousands of similar Y2K computer problems, could be immense.

Date-related elements are found throughout software programs and are wired into hardware devices. There is no magic fix that effortlessly can find all these problematic portions of code and transform them into

---

5   For various materials on the Y2K problem, see <http://www.mitre.org/research/y2k/> and <http://www.year2000.com>. See also Canada, Task Force Year 2000, *A Call For Action: Report of Task Force Year 2000*, February 1998, available at <http://strategis.ic.gc.ca/sos2000>. See also: "The Millennium Bug: Please Panic Early," *The Economist*, 4 October 1997; and Ian Karleff, "Canadian Firms Ill Prepared for Millennium 'Bomb'" *The Financial Post* (3 April 1998).

a four-digit presentation. Instead, some programs will permit the retro-fitting of logic for a four-digit date field. In most cases, however, the extremely time-consuming task of finding and fixing the troublesome date references simply cannot be avoided. And while various vendors have tools to assist in this exercise, it is still an expensive proposition.[6] Original estimates of $1 per line of code to undertake Y2K conversion are constantly being revised upwards as the Y2K deadline looms and the shortage of trained personnel grows dire. Not surprisingly, many users of computer resources are contemplating replacing their mainframe leg-acy systems, some of which are about twenty-five years old, in favour of modern, fully Y2K compliant client/server solutions. Why spend money, so the logic goes, on date conversions in old, creaking systems when you have to replace them soon anyway? The answer, in some cases, is that the new systems may not meet the requirements of the tried and true legacy systems. And a switch to a major client/server application is an expensive proposition. Nonetheless, the replacement option should be considered seriously by most organizations faced with a Y2K problem, just as the designers of two-digit date field software thought it would be twenty years ago. Whether the solution is a fix or a replacement, an organization's answer to the Y2K problem will be expensive, consuming scarce dollars from the information systems bud-get. And given the facts that this conversion project has a hard deadline and that there is a shortage of good information technology personnel, the planned budget for an organization's Y2K activities will probably be revised upwards a few times as the enormity of the project seeps in. These factors suggest that many organizations will be actively looking to off-load at least some of their Y2K-related costs on some other person by means of legal recourse.[7]

---

6   For example, Bell Canada will spend $75 million on Y2K activities over the next couple of years, and the federal government will spend $1 billion: Carey French, "Banks Fear Telecom Industry Too Late to Year 2000 Problem" *The [Toronto] Globe and Mail, Technology Quarterly* (3 June 1997). It is estimated that between $300 billion and $600 billion will be spent worldwide on the Y2K problem: see Alison Rea, "Does Your Computer Need Millennium Coverage," *Business Week*, 10 March 1997 ["Millennium"]. See also: "Year Zero: The Bill for the Millennium Bug Keeps Going Up," *The Economist*, 28 March 1998. As for Y2K remediation plans, see *Year 2000 Computing Crisis: An Assessment Guide*, U.S. General Accounting Office/ AIMD-10.1.14, September 1997, available at <http://www.gao.gov/>.

7   The enormous extent of the Y2K problem can be gauged by the fact that several insurance companies have begun to sell Y2K-related insurance: see Rea, "Millennium," above note 6; and Thomas Hoffman, "CIOs Wary of Year 2000 Insurance," *Computerworld*, 3 February 1997.

3) Multiple Marketing Channels

Most industries have a rather well-defined set of procedures and mechanisms for getting products and services into the hands of the ultimate customer. Not so the computer industry. There are a myriad of ways in which computer products are distributed, and new channels are constantly being explored. Again, as with so much of the computer business, change is the only constant. Thus, in some cases, an end user can buy a computer product directly from a hardware manufacturer or software developer. However, there may be several intermediate layers of distribution and other players between the developer and the end user. There may be the general distributor, who buys from the software developer or hardware manufacturer and resells to dealers, who may resell to retailers or to companies that integrate the diverse products into particular solutions for ultimate sale to end users. Third parties, some authorized by the product's creator and some not, may also offer to provide valuable ongoing support and services. Interestingly, in many distribution models the supplier has no direct contact with the purchaser in terms of the marketing or sale of the product, but may have direct ongoing responsibilities in the area of product support and maintenance. And then there is the Internet, which shows incredible promise for helping suppliers develop one-on-one marketing and distribution strategies.

Numerous commercial law impacts result from the particular marketing structures that have developed around the computer industry. Shrink-wrap licences purport to bind the developer of mass market software to the ultimate user even though these two parties may not deal directly with one another in the initial sales process. The various intermediaries that reside between the developer and the user will be concerned about being treated unfairly vis-à-vis their competitors, and they may be able to look to competition law for redress in certain circumstances. Tax issues come to the fore as a result of the constant shifting in the nature and functions of the various participants in the diverse distribution chains. This was true even before the Internet created yet additional uncertainty as to the place and identity of the taxpayer in an international, digital environment, particularly in respect of the sale and transmission of digital-based products.

B. COMPETITION LAW

Canada's *Competition Act* contains numerous prohibitions on anticompetitive conduct.[8] This statute applies in the context of the computer

---

8   R.S.C. 1985, c. C-34, as amended.

business because of the multitiered marketing and distribution channels in the high-technology industries and because of the strategic importance of these industries in the wider economy. The purpose of the *Competition Act* is to promote efficiency within the Canadian economy and provide consumers with competitive prices and product choices.[9] The statute provides for a number of criminal offences, contained in Part VI, which typically carry penalties consisting of fines and imprisonment for officers of the company for up to five years.[10] The statute also permits a private right of action for a party that has suffered damages as a result of conduct that constitutes a violation of the statute's criminal provisions. The *Competition Act* also contains in Part VIII a number of reviewable practices, which are civil proceedings brought before the Competition Tribunal, a body better suited than a judge alone to sift through the complex economic evidence to determine if a particular practice has an anticompetitive impact in the marketplace.[11] The Competition Tribunal can make a number of remedial orders where it finds a reviewable practice to lessen competition substantially. The Competition Bureau, a unit within Industry Canada, plays a central role in investigating alleged infractions under the *Competition Act*; it negotiates consensual settlements if possible and brings cases to the Competition Tribunal, or in the case of criminal offences, to the regular court system through the Department of Justice, where a voluntary solution was unattainable. Most companies view the Competition Bureau as a type of government regulator and approach the *Competition Act* in a defensive mode, trying to avoid running afoul of it. Although such an attitude is certainly warranted, organizations should also regard the Competition Bureau in a more offensive light, as a department that can

---

9   Section 1.1 of the *Competition Act* provides:
> The purpose of this Act is to maintain and encourage competition in Canada in order to promote the efficiency and adaptability of the Canadian economy, in order to expand opportunities for Canadian participation in world markets while at the same time recognizing the role of foreign competition in Canada, in order to ensure that small and medium-sized enterprises have an equitable opportunity to participate in the Canadian economy and in order to provide consumers with competitive prices and product choices.

10 Although it is not common for individuals to be charged under the statute, in a recent case involving price fixing among driving-school operators a one-year prison term was imposed on one of the individual principals of the companies involved, and another individual was sentenced to 100 hours of community service and a fine of $10,000: see *CompAct: News From the Competition Bureau*, Issue 3, July–September 1996.

11 The Competition Tribunal is a hybrid body composed of judges and lay experts, constituted under the *Competition Tribunal Act*, R.S.C. 1985, c. 19 (2nd Supp.).

help when they are adversely affected by the anticompetitive behaviour of competitors, suppliers, or others. Laws similar to the *Competition Act* exist in other nations, notably the United States and Europe, but they can differ significantly from Canada's in terms of substance and procedure. A Canadian company doing business through non-Canadians accessing its website should review what laws apply to such activity in the foreign jurisdiction, such as local competition law that often prohibits misleading advertising.[12]

1) Criminal Offences

a) Conspiracy and Bid Rigging

The *Competition Act*, in subsection 45(1), makes it a criminal offence for two or more parties to conclude an agreement, or otherwise conspire in any manner, that would lessen competition unduly, as was the case in the early 1990s when a number of companies participated in an illegal conspiracy to fix prices in Canada and the United States for thermal fax paper.[13] Agreements that could also run afoul of the conspiracy offence include dividing up customers or markets in a manner that unduly lessened competition. Competitors in the high-technology industry, however, can collaborate for certain purposes enumerated in subsection 45(3) of the *Competition Act*, in particular to define product standards or to participate in research and development. Subsection 45(4), however, denies this exemption if, in the course of this permitted collaboration, the parties stray into the areas of pricing, production, customer, or distribution matters. Accordingly, computer and software companies involved in such collaborative research, or participating in high-tech trade shows or industry trade associations or other activities where there is contact between competitors, have to be extremely vigilant not to run afoul — or be even perceived as running afoul — of the *Competition Act*'s conspiracy provisions. Section 46 of the statute also prohibits "bid rigging," the practice of colluding on the submission of bids in response to tender calls by a government or a private sector purchaser, such tenders being a very common practice when procuring high-tech products. Interestingly, the bid-rigging provision creates a *per se* offence, thus requiring there to be no adverse impact on competition.

---

12   See section C(2), "Jurisdiction," in chapter 6 for a discussion about the Internet from the perspective of jurisdiction and regulation.

13   This case is referred to in "Enforcement: Current Activities," in *CompAct: News From the Competition Bureau*, Issue 3, July–September 1996, which publication also mentions that up to September 1996, $2.6 million in fines had been levied in this case.

b) Resale Price Maintenance

Given the plethora of multitiered distribution channels in the computer business, perhaps the single most important provision in the *Competition Act* related to this industry is subsection 61(1), which reads as follows:

> 61 (1) No person who is engaged in the business of producing or supplying a product, who extends credit by way of credit cards or is otherwise engaged in a business that relates to credit cards, or who has the exclusive rights and privileges conferred by a patent, trade-mark, copyright, registered industrial design or registered integrated circuit topography shall, directly or indirectly,
>
> (a) by agreement, threat, promise or any like means, attempt to influence upward, or to discourage the reduction of, the price at which any other person engaged in business in Canada supplies or offers to supply or advertises a product within Canada; or
>
> (b) refuse to supply a product to or otherwise discriminate against any other person engaged in business in Canada because of the low pricing policy of that other person.

The prohibition in paragraph 61(1)(a) effectively precludes an entity in the product distribution chain from engaging in resale price maintenance, namely, dictating what an entity lower down in the chain charges for a particular product, with the proviso that maximum prices can be set (so long as they do not become, by virtue of practice or an ancillary agreement, the minimum price as well!). The reference to patent, copyrights, and other intellectual property rights at the end of the lead-in paragraph in subsection 61(1) has the effect of confirming that licensing and distribution arrangements for software and related products are covered by the provision. Activity that is not direct resale price maintenance is also problematic, as illustrated by the *Epson* case, where a manufacturer was held to have violated the predecessor of paragraph 61(1)(a) by requiring dealers, through a clause in the dealer agreement, not to advertise the manufacturer's computer products for sale at a price lower than the manufacturer's suggested retail price.[14] The court concluded that this clause violated this provision of the statute, even though the evidence indicated that no dealer actually honoured the clause, and notwithstanding the expert testimony of an economics professor to the effect that such a clause is not always economically harmful. In refusing to accept this economic evidence, the court stated that resale price maintenance is *per se* criminal conduct, again not requiring

---

14   *R. v. Epson (Canada) Ltd.*, (1987) 19 C.P.R. (3d) 195 (Ont. Dist. Ct.).

any adverse impact on competition, like the bid-rigging offence. It should be noted, however, that under subsection 61(3), a supplier can suggest resale prices, but it must be made clear to the distributor, preferably in writing in the agreement between the parties, that failure to follow the suggestions will in no way adversely affect the relationship between the supplier and the distributor. The upshot of paragraph 61(1)(a) is that distribution channels in the computer industry must be carefully planned and implemented. Indeed, a software developer that considered it very important that its particular product not sell for less than a certain price to end users would likely have to change its proposed relationship with the distributor as a result of subsection 61(1). For instance, the software developer could appoint a sales representative, where the latter would drum up business for the developer, but the end user's price would be set by the developer, and the representative would receive only a sales commission from the developer once each sale is concluded.

c) Refusal to Deal

Many companies in the computer business attempt to obtain a copy of a competitor's new software product or a unit of a new hardware item as soon as it is released in order to study it and, if permitted by relevant agreements, take it apart and study its inner workings (a practice sometimes termed reverse engineering). Many suppliers comply with such a request as they believe that competition law requires them to sell to anyone who demands to buy. This is an erroneous belief. Generally, anyone can refuse to sell to anyone else, subject to a couple of important exceptions, the first one being paragraph 61(1)(b) of the *Competition Act*, which makes it an offence not to supply someone because of the low pricing policy of that person. In other words, paragraph 61(1)(b) prohibits refusing to supply product to discounters, of which there are a number in the computer business. This prohibition applies even if the supplier had never before conducted business with the discounter. Certain exceptions to this rule are contained in subsection 61(10), as where the distributor would use the supplier's products as "loss leaders," or where the distributor has shown that it is unable to provide adequate service for the relevant product, a not unimportant consideration with a high-technology product. As well, paragraph 61(1)(b) would not be triggered if the reason for refusing to supply was a rational business purpose, such as concern over the creditworthiness of the potential distributor, or simply the fact that the supplier already had a sufficient number of distributors, though in each such case real evidence should bolster the rationale. It would, for example, be difficult for a supplier to rely on the latter argument if, within a short time after refusing the discounter, the supplier appoints another distributor for the same market. In effect, great care must be taken in operationalizing the provisions of the *Competition Act*.

Several other criminal provisions in the *Competition Act* are worth mentioning. Under paragraph 50(1)(a) it is an offence to make a practice of giving a discount, rebate, allowance, or any other advantage to one customer that is not made available to all competitors of that customer with respect to sales of like quantity or quality. This prohibition on price discrimination essentially requires entities in the distribution chain to treat in a consistent manner those of their customers who are competitors with one another. Also, paragraph 50(1)(b) makes it illegal for a supplier to engage in a policy of selling products or services at prices that are unreasonably low if the intent, effect, or tendency of the policy is to lessen competition substantially or to eliminate a competitor. Although it is not entirely clear when a price is "unreasonably low," predatory pricing, as this practice is often called, probably includes a price that is not covering fixed and variable costs of the supplier.[15] The predatory pricing provisions of the *Competition Act* can be relevant to the computer industry where the practice is to give away product at low prices in certain circumstances. The intent behind the activity, however, is what is critical. If it was merely to meet the competitive pricing of another supplier then paragraph 50(1)(b) should not come into play; a different conclusion, however, may be warranted where the intent of the discounting supplier, which intent is often evidenced by incriminating memos or e-mails, is to eliminate a competitor.

d) Misleading Advertising

Under subsection 52(1) of the *Competition Act*, it is a criminal offence to make, directly or indirectly and by any means whatever, a false or misleading representation to the public, or to make a claim to the public regarding a product or service, for instance about performance, that is not based on a proper or adequate test, or to make a warranty to the public that is misleading. Misleading advertising provisions apply in the computer industry, where short product cycles, changing technology, and intense competition may tempt suppliers to make unfounded claims about their products. For example, in the United States, a company was

---

15   In the leading case, *R. v. Hoffman-La Roche Ltd.* (Nos. 1 and 2) (1981), 33 O.R. (2d) 694 (C.A.), the enterprising defence was put forward that giving away pharmaceuticals to hospitals for free did not constitute a sale, and hence the predatory pricing section should not apply, but this argument was refused by the court, which held that giving away something still implied a price, albeit an extremely low one.

convicted for advertising a product as available when it was not,[16] and another company settled a prosecution brought against it by the U.S. Federal Trade Commission (the equivalent of the Canadian Competition Bureau) for advertising that a product would increase the memory and performance of personal computers when it did not.[17] In another U.S. case, a manufacturer of computer terminals was found liable for false advertising for describing its products as "compatible" with those of another product when the evidence showed that a manual, intermediate step had to be undertaken by the user to make the two items work together, thereby leading the court to conclude that the items were not compatible as that term is understood in the computer industry.[18] Also in the United States there was a class action lawsuit brought on behalf of millions of buyers of 14-inch computer monitors when the actual measurement of the screens proved to be 7 percent smaller.[19]

Another aspect to the misleading advertising provisions relates to the use of the Internet by companies, individuals, and organizations, both in the high-tech industry as well as those in other businesses, to make claims to the public by posting material on their websites. In April 1997 the Competition Bureau announced that it had moved against a number of websites and usegroups that contained potentially misleading descriptions of business opportunities.[20] Interestingly, given the global nature of the Internet, the Competition Bureau undertook these actions in coordination with its counterpart in the United States, the Federal Trade Commission. Such joint activity is the product of an agreement signed in September 1996 between these two enforcement authorities that established a Canadian–U.S. Task Force on Cross-Border Deceptive Marketing Practices.[21] These actions indicate two important points about the Internet as a business communications medium. First, if the content is problematic in the physical

---

16   *United States* v. *Commodore Business Machines, Inc.*, 2 Computer Cases (CCH) ¶46,281 at 62,120 (E.D. Penn. 1990).

17   *Re Syncronys Softcorp et al.*, Guide to Computer Law, New Developments (CCH) ¶60,544 at 82,183 (F.T.C. 1996).

18   *Princeton Graphics Operating, L.P.* v. *NEC Home Electronics (U.S.A.), Inc.*, 732 F. Supp. 1258 (S.D.N.Y. 1990). See also *Creative Labs Inc.* v. *Cyrix Corp.*, 42 U.S.P.Q.2d 1872 (N.D. Cal. 1997).

19   "Read This and Become ($6) Richer," *The Economist*, 21 June 1997.

20   Competition Bureau, News Release, *Online Anti-competitive Behaviour Hit by Canadian Competition Bureau and U.S. Federal Trade Commission*, 24 April 1997: available at <http:strategis.ic.gc.ca/ competition>.

21   See "Bureau News," *CompAct: News From the Competition Bureau*, Issue 3, July–September 1996.

world, it is equally problematic in the online, electronic world. And second, it may be even more problematic in the electronic world because authorities in other countries are apt to take jurisdiction over a website operated on a computer located in a foreign state if the website is being accessed by its nationals.[22] Thus, even if the content of the Canadian website is acceptable under Canadian law, the operator of the website must be concerned whether the content is contrary to the laws of another country. This point illustrates well the fourth dynamic of computer law, namely, the blurring of national and international.

2) Reviewable Practices

a) Abuse of Dominant Position

A number of reviewable practices under Part VIII of the *Competition Act* can influence distribution, development, and other activities in the computer, networks, and related sectors of the economy. The abuse of dominant position provision in section 79 of the statute provides that where an entity substantially controls, alone or with others, a class of business throughout or in a region of Canada, and that entity (or entities) engages in anticompetitive acts that are likely to prevent or lessen competition substantially, the Competition Tribunal may order the entity(ies) to prohibit engaging in the anticompetitive behaviour. Section 78 sets out a non-exhaustive list of anticompetitive acts, one of which is particularly germane to the computer business, namely, adopting product specifications that are incompatible with products produced by another person and are designed to prevent that person's entry into, or eliminate them from, a market. It was under section 79 that the Competition Bureau several years ago commenced an investigation of Interac, a company owned by Canada's major banks and a few other financial institutions and that operates a network of automated banking machines and debit payment systems. The bureau took the view that several aspects of Interac's bylaws were anticompetitive by restricting, among other things, membership in the electronic network and the manner by which it charged its members for services. After lengthy negotiations and a hearing before the Competition Tribunal, in June 1996 the Competition Tribunal approved a consent order negotiated between the bureau and Interac's members that has the effect of adjusting fees and of opening up the network to other participants on a nondiscriminatory basis, provided only duly regulated financial institutions

---

22 See section C(2), "Jurisdiction," in chapter 6.

can issue cards to access the network.[23] The case, and the significant resources devoted to it by the bureau, illustrates that the Competition Bureau understands the increasingly important role of computer networks in the Canadian economy.

Companies with patented products can run afoul of the abuse of dominant position provision when, upon the expiry of their patents, they attempt to sustain their monopoly market share by having customers enter into supply contracts that implement a number of exclusionary measures vis-à-vis the competition, such as fidelity rebates.[24] At the same time, however, subsection 79(5) of the *Competition Act* provides that any act engaged in pursuant only to the exercise of any right under the *Copyright Act*, the *Patent Act,* and the other intellectual property statutes is not an anticompetitive act. In light of this provision, it is also worth noting that subsection 32(2) of the *Competition Act* gives the Federal Court of Canada the power to make remedial orders in a situation where the exclusive rights conferred by a copyright, patent, or trademark have been used in a manner that prevents or lessens competition unduly. This provision, which is neither a criminal offence nor a reviewable practice, is aimed primarily at preventing a number of potentially anticompetitive or restrictive provisions in intellectual property licences, such as the requirement that a patent licensee purchase from the patent holder/licensor all the raw materials required to produce the patented product. Where such an act lessens competition unduly, the Federal Court may order one or more of the following remedies: declare the relevant licence agreement to be void, in whole or in part; prohibit the exercise of the objectionable provision in the licence agreement; order that licences be granted to other licensees on terms the court thinks fit, and other acts to be done or omitted as the court sees fit so as to prevent future anticompetitive use of the patent or trade-mark. While these remedial provisions are very broad, this section of the *Competition Act* has been used very little. Nevertheless, section 32 of the *Act,* together with a number of other sections of the *Competition Act,* such as subsection 61(1), illustrate the tension between the intellectual prop-

---

23 For background on the Interac case, see: "Enforcement: The Interac Case," in *CompAct: News From the Competition Bureau,* Issue 2, April–June 1996. For a discussion of a U.S.-based automated banking machine network and various technical and business aspects of its operation, see *Plus System, Inc. v. New England Network, Inc.,* 804 F. Supp. 111 (D. Colo. 1992), a case referred to in section C(2), "Jurisdiction," in chapter 6.

24 See *Canada (Director of Investigation and Research) v. NutraSweet Co.* (1990), 32 C.P.R. (3d) 1 (Comp. Trib.).

erty regimes that, by their very nature, provide more or less extensive monopoly rights to holders of intellectual properties, and the *Competition Act* that attempts to curb perceived and potential abuses of such intellectual property rights.

In the recent *Tele-Direct* case, the Competition Tribunal had occasion to consider subsection 79(5) of the *Competition Act*.[25] In this proceeding the bureau sought an order requiring the owners of the registered trade-mark "Yellow Pages" to grant licences to this trade-mark to third parties who, the bureau argued, were adversely affected by not being able to use the trade-mark. The bureau argued that refusal to licence the trade-mark to certain parties but not others was an anticompetitive act under the abuse of dominant position provision. The Competition Tribunal disagreed, concluding that while there may be instances where a trade-mark is misused:

> The respondents' refusal to license their trade-marks falls squarely within their prerogative. Inherent in the very nature of the right to license a trade-mark is the right for the owner of the trade-mark to determine whether or not, and to whom, to grant a licence; selectivity in licensing is fundamental to the rationale behind protecting trade-marks. The respondents' trade-marks are valuable assets and represent considerable goodwill in the market-place. The decision to license a trade-mark — essentially, to share the goodwill vesting in the asset — is a right which rests entirely with the owner of the mark. The refusal to license a trade-mark is distinguishable from a situation where anti-competitive provisions are attached to a trade-mark licence.[26]

The Competition Tribunal also determined that a trade-mark owner's motivation for refusing to license a competitor is irrelevant, given that the *Trade-Marks Act* does not place any limits on the exercise of the right to license a trade-mark.

b) Refusal to Deal

Another reviewable practice is "refusal to deal," contained in section 75 of the *Competition Act*. Under this provision, if a customer can show that it is substantially affected in its business because of its inability to continue

---

25   *Canada (Director of Investigation and Research)* v. *Tele-Direct (Publications) Inc.* (1997), 73 C.P.R. (3d) 1 (Comp. Trib.).

26   *Ibid.* at 32. For an indication of when U.S. antitrust authorities will consider certain intellectual property licensing practices to be anticompetitive, see U.S. Department of Justice and the Federal Trade Commission, *Antitrust Guidelines for the Licensing of Intellectual Property,* 6 April 1995.

to obtain adequate supplies of a product because of insufficient competition among suppliers, the customer may be able to obtain an order from the Competition Tribunal requiring a supplier to provide it with product, provided the product is in ample supply and the customer is willing to meet the usual trade terms of the supplier. This provision can be of particular relevance to companies that provide maintenance and support services for computer products manufactured or supplied by others. For example, in the *Xerox* case, the Competition Tribunal ordered Xerox to supply a third-party service organization with spare parts as without these the third party could not continue its business of servicing Xerox machines.[27] It should be noted that the refusal to deal provision does not require that the refusal have an adverse effect on competition generally, but rather only on the particular customer affected by it. Thus, participants in the computer industry need to keep it in mind when establishing their distribution networks and appointing dealers and others who will carry their products.

c) Exclusive Dealing, Market Restriction, and Tied Selling

Three other reviewable practices under subsection 77(1) of the *Competition Act* are:

- "exclusive dealing": the practice of requiring or inducing a customer to deal only or primarily in products of the supplier;
- "market restriction": the practice of requiring a customer, as a condition of supplying him with the product, to sell a product only in a defined market area;
- "tied selling": the practice of requiring or inducing a customer as a condition of supplying him with one product (the "tying" product) to buy another of the supplier's products (the "tied" product).

These three practices are quite common in the computer industry. A hardware or software supplier will often require a distributor or dealer not to carry any products that compete with the supplier's products. When establishing a distribution system, a supplier may also require that dealers sell only in predetermined geographic areas. A supplier may also insist that in order to be supplied with a preferred product in which the supplier has competitive advantage courtesy, perhaps, of a patent or copyright, the dealer or end user must also purchase a less attractive product in which the supplier has no particular competitive advantage,

---

27 *Canada (Director of Investigation and Research)* v. *Xerox Canada Inc.* (1990), 33 C.P.R. (3d) 83 (Comp. Trib.).

such as paper sales being tied to patented computer-based document imaging equipment. These practices, however, are not in and of themselves problematic under the *Competition Act*; they only become so if they are engaged in by suppliers with significant market power and have the effect of excluding others from the marketplace or have some other substantial adverse effect on competition.[28] It should be noted, however, that the Competition Tribunal is directed under subsection 77(4) not to make an order in respect of exclusive dealing or market restriction where they are engaged in only for a reasonable period of time in order to facilitate entry of a new supplier or of a new product into a market. Similarly, the *Competition Act* provides a defence to the tied selling reviewable practice where it is reasonable having regard to the technological relationship between or among the two products at issue. This defence can be particularly relevant to participants in the computer industry where the two products at issue have a *bona fide* functional rationale for being intertwined.

The defences to exclusive dealing, market restriction, and tied selling noted above illustrate why these practices and the other reviewable practices in Part VIII of the *Competition Act* are not criminal offences but rather are reviewable practices — namely, in certain circumstances these practices can be procompetitive or at least neutral in their effect on competition; that is, the same exclusive dealing behaviour may be either beneficial or detrimental to competition, depending largely on the market share of the supplier engaging in the activity. The same observation is valid in respect of the list of anticompetitive acts set out in the abuse of dominant position provision. For example, a requirement by a software or CD-ROM product supplier with a small share of the market that an exclusive dealer not carry competitive products may be procompetitive because it causes the dealer to devote all its energies to the supplier's new product, thereby increasing the prospect for meaningful *inter*brand competition, namely, between the supplier's new product and the existing products of other suppliers. If, after time, the same product captures 90 percent of the relevant market, the same exclusive arrangement may be anticompetitive if it has the effect of precluding *intra*brand competition, namely, the ability to purchase a very popular product from more than one source. Similarly, in some cases it might be reasonable, at least for a period of time, to require customers to purchase service contracts only from the supplier of a sophisticated

---

28   For a discussion of one of the first (and one of the few) exclusive dealing cases, see George S. Takach, "Exclusive Dealing after Bombardier: The Law Is Not a Great Deal Clearer Than Before" (1983) 8 C.B.L.J. 226.

technology-based product, whereas this practice may constitute tied-selling in other cases.[29] Thus, the key in these reviewable practices matters is to understand thoroughly the dynamics and parameters of the relevant product market and the roles played by the various participants in it, and then to monitor these factors vigilantly. Some commentators believe that the robust nature of the computer industry precludes the need for intervention by competition law authorities, since the market continually self-corrects as very few participants are able to hold significant market share for very long. In some industries the Internet will permit competition law authorities to consider the relevant geographic market to be much more international, particularly with respect to digital assets that can be distributed electronically; but this also applies where the Internet is still primarily a marketing tool and shipment is overland (but much improved with next day delivery).[30] The Competition Bureau, while generally sensitive to these sorts of arguments, nonetheless looks at each case before it on its specific merits, including those involving the high-technology sector.

d) Mergers

This case-by-case approach can be seen in the bureau's handling of the computerized airline reservation case almost a decade ago. Under the merger provisions in section 92 of the *Competition Act*, the Competition Tribunal has the power to dissolve, or to order the disposal of assets related to, a merger of two or more businesses that prevents or lessens competition substantially. Since its addition to the *Competition Act* in 1986, the merger provision has been used by the bureau to block certain business combinations it viewed as anticompetitive, or more commonly, to allow them to proceed provided the parties took certain steps to alleviate the bureau's concerns, typically by divesting certain assets of the combined business that would decrease the level of its postmerger market share. It was under this merger provision that the proposed combination in 1987 of the computerized reservation systems of Air Canada and Canadian Airlines was challenged. A number of parties objected to the merger on the grounds that it would permit Air Canada and Canadian Airlines to benefit from their computer reservation system favouring the two "host airlines" over third parties. The dissolution

---

29   See Drew Fagan, "Digital Agrees to Change Its Ways: Government Alleges 'Tied Selling'" *The [Toronto] Globe and Mail* (31 October 1992).

30   See, for example, Patrick Butler *et al.*, "A Revolution in Interaction," *The McKinsey Quarterly* 1 (1997): 4, which argues that networks like the Internet dramatically decrease the transaction costs related to searching for and contracting with partners.

proceeding was settled by the merged entity agreeing to establish rules relating to the new, combined network information system that would not portray flight booking and other information of any airline in a biased manner, but would give non-discriminatory treatment to the data of all carriers, as well as give the computerized reservation system of other airlines access to all Air Canada and Canadian Airlines booking information on the same basis.[31] This case recognized the potential for anticompetitive conduct when vital information networks are operated in an exclusionary or discriminatory manner, and in a sense presaged the Interac matter some years later, discussed in subsection B(2)(a), "Abuse of Dominant Position," in this chapter.[32]

C. LICENCES FOR SOFTWARE AND CONTENT

Copies of books are sold; copies of software are licensed. There are a number of historic reasons for licensing software, as well as certain contemporary rationales for the practice. A common vehicle for licensing mass market software is the shrinkwrap licence, a form of agreement whose enforceability has been questioned by a number of courts, though recent cases seem to be more amenable to it. There is also controversy regarding the rights granted to licensees and whether they are broad enough to cover new technical delivery mechanisms and media. The following cases illustrate some of the difficulties inherent in the field of technology licensing given the first dynamic of computer law, namely, the rapid rate of technological change.

1) Why Software and Content Are Licensed

There are three ways in which the owner of the intellectual property rights — the copyright, trade secrets, and patent rights — in a software program or other information-based work could permit another entity to use those rights. First, it could assign those intellectual property rights outright, in which case it would be transferring, for example, the

---

31   *Canada (Director of Investigation and Research)* v. *Air Canada* (1989), 44 B.L.R. 154 (Comp. Trib.).

32   Airline computer reservation systems have been the subject of litigation, and regulation, in the United States as well. For a sense of the issues, see a short piece by Thomas Hoffman & Mitch Betts, "Scheduling Software Ignites Airline Battle," *Computerworld*, 28 August 1995. See also *United Air Lines, Inc.* v. *Civil Aeronautics Board*, 766 F.2d 1107 (7th Cir. 1985).

entire and exclusive right to make copies of the work under the *Copyright Act*. Given that after such an assignment the original owner of the work could no longer make copies of it or otherwise exploit it for financial gain, such an assignment is not used where a customer merely wishes to use a copy of the work, and the original owner wishes to continue to exploit it to other users. By contrast, where the owner of the work is selling the business related to the work by virtue of a sale of assets, there typically would be an outright assignment of the intellectual property rights related to the work. Incidentally, as discussed in chapter 2, any such assignment, to be legally effective, must be in writing given subsection 13(3) of the *Copyright Act*.

The second way the owner of the intellectual property rights in a work can exploit the intellectual property is to sell copies of the work, as when the owner of the copyright in a book sells copies of the book. Selling title in a copy of a book or other work is a very different proposition from selling title in the intellectual property of the work.[33] Selling title to a copy of a work merely gives the purchaser the right to use that particular copy of the work; it does not generally afford the right to make further copies of the work because the intellectual property rights granted by the *Copyright Act* are not transferred to the purchaser of the copy of the work. When the holder of the copyright in a book sells title to a copy of the book, however, it cannot control the use, resale, or other exploitation of that copy of the book, subject always to the restriction that the owner of the copy cannot make further copies of it.[34] The various rights provided to the copyright owner under the *Copyright Act* do not include a right that prohibits use or even distribution of copies of the work, and thus once a copy of a work is sold into the stream of commerce with the permission of the copyright owner, that copyright owner cannot further control the resale, distribution, or use of the work, with the exception that the copyright owner can prohibit rental of certain works if such rental is done for a motive of gain.[35] It is sometimes said the copyright owner's rights are "exhausted," subject always to the ongoing right to control further copying. Even in the United States, where that country's copyright law provides copyright owners a right of distribution, there is a "first sale doctrine" that precludes a copyright

---

33   This distinction is made clear in *Société d'informatique R.D.G. Inc.* v. *Dynabec Ltée* (1984), 6 C.P.R. (3d) 299 (Que. Sup. Ct.), aff'd (*sub nom. Dynabec Ltée.* v. *La Société d'informatique R.D.G. Inc.*) (1985), 6 C.P.R. (3d) 322 (Que. C.A.).

34   *Fetherling* v. *Boughner* (1978), 40 C.P.R. (2d) 253 (Ont. H.C.J.).

35   See section B(3), "Copyright," in chapter 2.

owner from exercising control over the use or distribution of a copy of a work once it is released into the stream of commerce.[36]

The third way to exploit intellectual property rights in a work is to license copies of the work. In intellectual property terms, a licence is a permission to a user from the owner of the work to do something that the user would not otherwise have the right to do.[37] This method allows the owner of the intellectual property to retain maximum control over it. Thus, in the case of many software-based or other information-based works, the related licence contains the restriction that the work may only be used for the benefit of the licensed user, and that it cannot be used to process the data of third parties. Similarly, the licence agreement would place restrictions on the ability of the licensee to transfer the work to a third party.[38] In this way, the owner of the intellectual property rights is better able to control the exploitation of the work and can reap greater economic returns by prohibiting a resale market for copies of the work. A licence also permits the owner of the intellectual property in software to permit copies of it to be exploited on a temporary or evaluation basis, as is the case with *shareware*, which typically allows use for a short period of time, say thirty days, after which the user must make payment or cease using the software.[39] As well, if the work contained trade secrets and confidential information, as is the case with

36 See the discussion at footnote 7 in *Step-Saver Data Systems, Inc.* v. *Wyse Technology*, 939 F.2d 91 at 96 (3d Cir. 1991) [*Step-Saver*].
37 *Electric Chain Company of Canada Limited* v. *Art Metal Works Inc.*, [1933] S.C.R. 581. In this case the court cites a passage from an earlier English decision that states that a licence confers no interest or property in a patent, but that rather a grant is required to convey an interest in property, and that a pure licence is not a grant and does not convey an interest in property.
38 *Perry Engineering Ltd.* v. *Farrage* (1989), 28 C.P.R. (3d) 221 (B.C.S.C.). In this case one party argued it should be unenforceable to have a non-transferable software licence as this would make unusable the related hardware that operated only in conjunction with the software upon a subsequent sale of the hardware, but the court did not decide this issue as the case before it involved only the licensee and the subsequent transferee and not the owner of the intellectual property in the software.
39 Shareware should be contrasted with "freeware," which is software the intellectual property rights in which are still owned by someone who gives copies of it away and "public domain software" in which there are no further intellectual property rights either through waiver or expiry: for an Australian decision that discusses shareware, see *Trumpet Software Pty. Ltd. & Another* v. *OzEmail Pty. Ltd. & Others*, [1996] ACL Rep. 240 FC 32 (Austl.). For a U.S. discussion of shareware, see *CompuServe, Incorporated* v. *Patterson*, 89 F.3d 1257 (6th Cir. 1996) [*CompuServe*], a case discussed in section C(2), "Jurisdiction," in chapter 6.

most software, the licence would also require the user to keep confidential the work and not disclose it to third parties. Without such a restriction imposed on the user, the owner of the work would be hardpressed to preserve trade secret rights in the work. The licence agreement also serves other purposes from the perspective of the developer or supplier of the software product. As discussed in sections D, "Negligence," and E, "Contracts and Sales Law," in this chapter, poorly functioning software can cause users harm, and so software companies attempt to limit their liability contractually (via a licence agreement in the case of software) by shifting to the user certain risks related to the software, as well as limiting the company's liability for certain types of damages.

Section A(4), "Data and Databases," in chapter 1 described the phenomenon of the electronic database, and section C(4), "Copyright Protection for Electronic Databases," in chapter 2 discussed the current uncertainty surrounding the legal protection afforded databases and the underlying data in them. Accordingly, creators of databases and other providers of online services that supply fact-intensive information increasingly resort to having their customers sign licence agreements that restrict the ability of the user, for example, to make the database or the underlying facts or information available to others. These sorts of restrictions were upheld in the line of *Exchange Telegraph* cases that began in England more than one hundred years ago, in which a news wire service company was successful in prohibiting subscribers from conveying news feeds to non-subscriber third parties.[40] In these cases the courts were prepared to restrict further dissemination of financial information and horse racing results by customers of the news wire service on the basis that such use and transfer of them constituted a breach of their subscriber contracts with the news wire service. It may also well be that the increasing use of CD-ROM and other digital technologies will encourage suppliers of these products to use licence agreements to prevent the development of secondary markets in their products. One rationale for not licensing paper-based products, such as books or directories, is that these items degrade with use over time, such that secondhand bookstores do not represent a serious threat to mainstream book retailers and publishers. Similarly, the resale market for vinyl records and even more recent tape-based music cassettes is limited by the deterioration these products experience on each subsequent play.

---

40   *Exchange Telegraph Company Limited* v. *Giulianotti*, [1959] Scots Law Times 293 (O.H.); *Exchange Telegraph Company* v. *Gregory & Co.*, [1896] Q.B. 147; *Exchange Telegraph Company Limited* v. *Central News, Limited*, [1897] 2 Ch. 48. These cases are discussed in section C(8), "Other Measures of Protection," in chapter 2.

By contrast, the digitized signals derived from CD-ROMs retain their initial quality regardless of the amount of use, and therefore a secondary market in CDs presents the music industry with significant economic challenges. It will be interesting to see if the music industry moves to a licensing model at some point in order to stem the resale of their products. Moreover, when content distribution systems become more common on the Internet, they may include mechanisms, such as digital metering systems, that will authorize the use of the digital content on only specific machines, or on a set number of machines, so that again limits are put on the use that the user can make of the particular item. Such systems will be a practical, technologically oriented response to the second dynamic of computer law, namely, the elusive nature of information.

2) Shrinkwrap Licences

Many licences for software are paper-based documents that are signed by representatives of both the software company and the user organization. Such signed software licences usually apply to more expensive, complex software programs where the parties have usually negotiated a number of matters within the licence agreement, such as delivery schedules, customization work and training to be performed by the software developer, and payment milestones. This kind of software, and negotiated software licence, can be contrasted with mass market software that is typically supplied to the public by retailers and which requires no customization by the software developer. Given the price of this kind of software, often less than $100 a copy, it would be too expensive in terms of transaction costs for the software supplier to enter into a signed licence agreement in respect of each purchase of a licence. Accordingly, such software typically comes with a licence statement inside the box to which reference is often made on the outside packaging of the box. Alternatively, the diskette containing the software can be in an envelope inside the box, on the cover of which is the licence statement. At one time the actual licence statement was placed on the back of the box containing the software disk, and then the box was tightly cellophane-wrapped so that the prospective user could see the licence statement before purchasing the product. It was this practice that gave rise to the term *shrinkwrap licences*.[41] The licence statement contains the usual use permissions and restrictions, some of which were discussed in section C(1), "Why Software and

---

41 For an overview of the history of the shrinkwrap licence, see Robert W. Gomulkjewicz and Mary L. Williamson, "A Brief Defense of Mass Market Software License Agreements" (1996) 22 Rutgers Computer & Technology Law Journal 335.

Content Are Licensed," in this chapter, together with warranty disclaimers and limitations on liability in favour of the software developer. There is also included, typically in bold, capital letters, the statement that if the user does not accept the various licence terms, then the user can return the software for a full refund, and that commencing to use the software confirms the user's agreement with the license terms.

a) The *Systemshops* Case

In Canada, and elsewhere, there has traditionally been uncertainty as to whether these shrinkwrap licences are enforceable. In Canada, the uncertainty was engendered by the *Systemshops* case, in which a purchaser argued that it could make and use multiple production copies of a single copy of a mass market software program because the licence statement was not brought to his attention at the time the purchaser paid for the product.[42] The court agreed with this position, noting that the licence statement was included in the back of the manual for the product, which was wrapped in cellophane, and thus the licence restrictions were not made known to the defendant at the time of purchase. The court then went on to conclude that as the licence restrictions were without effect, the defendant could do "whatever the purchaser [defendant] wished with the product,"[43] which in this case included making multiple production copies of it. Leaving aside for a moment the question as to the enforceability of the licence statement, the court's conclusion that in the absence of a licence restriction a purchaser of a copyright work can make unlimited copies of it is questionable. Rather, the *Copyright Act* would still apply such that the user would, at most, be able to make such copies as are required to reasonably use the original copy; that is, it would be reasonable to make a copy on the user's hard drive for his own subsequent ease of use of the software, but this is a far cry from the multiple additional hard drives onto which the software was copied in the *Systemshops* case. Of course, in the absence of a licence agreement, a user could resell and transfer (but not rent, as noted earlier) the original copy of the software, but again only so long as additional copies were not made.

As for the question whether shrinkwrap licences are enforceable in Canada, it is too rigid a reading of the *Systemshops* case to conclude that it requires that notice of all the terms be brought to the purchaser's attention at the time of purchase. Obviously this is the ideal scenario, but the outside surfaces of the boxes containing mass market software

---

42   *North American Systemshops Ltd. v. King* (1989), 68 Alta. L.R. (2d) 145 (Q.B.) [*Systemshops*].

43   *Ibid.* at 155.

simply do not provide enough space to contain the whole licence. Hence some software companies indicate on the outside of the box that a full licence agreement is contained within the box. This sort of notice given to the purchaser prior to or at the time of sale should be sufficient to legally bind the purchaser to the terms of the full licence inside the box. This is particularly true given that today these licences have become so standard and ubiquitous that the average user would be hard-pressed to argue that he did not know about them or the various terms contained within them. Indeed, the court in *Systemshops* acknowledged that in contrast to the practice of the plaintiff in that particular case, it had subsequently become commonplace to insert the disk in a sealed envelope that prominently displays both a warning that the disk is sold subject to licence conditions and a licence agreement. This envelope is then found in the box after the purchaser has left the store, at which point the purchaser has the option of agreeing to the licence terms or returning the software for a refund. Similarly, it should be sufficient if before using the software, and right after loading it into the computer for the first time, one of the first screens to appear on the computer contained the licence agreement, together with a clear statement that further use of the software would be deemed to be consent to the licence terms by the user. If the user did not agree to the terms, the agreement would reiterate the option of returning the software for a full refund.

b) The *ProCD* Case

In a recent U.S. case, *ProCD, Incorporated* v. *Zeidenberg*,[44] a shrinkwrap licence contained in a box, only notice of which was included on the outside of the box, was held to be enforceable by an appeals court, overturning a contrary lower court decision that had decided that all the licence terms had to be brought to the purchaser's attention at the time of sale. Distinguishing several previous cases that had essentially stood for the proposition supported by the trial court,[45] the appellate court pointed out that the practice of printing a notice of a licence on the outside of the box, and including the licence inside the box with a right of refund if the terms are unacceptable, is consistent with numerous other mass market contracting practices, such as buying theatre or airline tickets over the telephone, or buying insurance when the customer pays the premium first and agrees to the general terms (such as amount of coverage, number of years, etc.) and then the detailed policy, with the

---

44   86 F.3d 1447 (7th Cir. 1996) [*ProCD*].

45   See *Step-Saver*, above note 36; *Arizona Retail Systems, Inc.* v. *Software Link, Inc.*, 831 F. Supp. 759 (D. Ariz. 1993).

various exclusions, follows; or indeed numerous examples of the purchase of consumer goods where the customer buys, say, a radio, and then only comes across the product warranty that was inside the box containing the product later, when unpacking the radio at home. Thus, the court concluded that while a final contract can be formed at the point of purchase, a contract can also be formed subsequently when, after the user reads the licence statement accompanying the product, the user can denote acceptance by commencing to use the software.

It remains to be seen whether courts in Canada will adopt reasoning similar to that found in the *ProCD* case.[46] A recent Ontario case involving the purchase of a truck (rather than computer equipment) held that warranty limitation provisions brought to the attention of the purchaser of the vehicle several months after he purchased it were ineffective because they were not made known at the time of the purchase.[47] The court in this case held that "[t]imely notification of these clauses is especially important where they purport, as they do in this case, to extinguish or limit common law rights."[48] The court cited another Canadian case in which it was held that a limitation clause is not effective unless the party wishing to rely on it took reasonable steps to bring it to the attention of the other party at or prior to the time of making the contract.[49] Notwithstanding these decisions, a court in Canada faced with a standard shrinkwrap licence should follow the *ProCD* decision where a standard licence statement is at issue, particularly where notice of a fuller licence statement is contained on the outside of the box containing the relevant software. This would be an important result not just for suppliers selling software in boxes at retail outlets, but also for the increasingly important practice of distributing software to users over the Internet where, as the court in the *ProCD* case points out, there is no box at all but merely a stream of electrons that will include an initial screen containing the licence terms, with a statement that commencing to use the software denotes acceptance of the terms. In Internet situations, however, it is possible to create contracting processes where the

---

46   See *Beta Computers (Europe) Limited* v. *Adobe Systems (Europe) Limited*, [1996] 23 F.S.R. 367, where a Scottish court, in considering when a contract arose in the context of a shrinkwrap licence, concluded that no contract was concluded until the purchaser accepted the licence terms of the software developer, thereby echoing the holding in the *ProCD* case under Scots law.

47   *Gregorio* v. *Intrans-Corp.* (1994), 115 D.L.R. (4th) 200 (Ont. C.A.) [*Gregorio*].

48   *Ibid.* at 205.

49   *Trigg* v. *MI Movers International Transport Services Ltd.* (1991), 84 D.L.R. (4th) 504 (Ont. C.A.).

user, before being transmitted the digitized content, signifies his or her consent to the relevant licence or other agreement by sending an affirming keystroke or message. Thus, so-called clickwrap agreements concluded over the Internet should not even raise the issue discussed in the cases above, though such electronic contracting situations may, however, raise other contract formation issues in some jurisdictions with respect to "writing" and "signature" requirements, as discussed in section A "Contract Law Issues," in chapter 6. Importantly, in a recent U.S. case the court acknowledged affirmatively such a contract concluded over the Internet where one party consented to terms proposed by another party online by clicking the "AGREE" button at several points in the agreement as it scrolled over the computer screen.[50]

3) Licensing in a Digital Environment

In addition to licensing end users, creators and owners of software and content regularly grant licences to other entities in the distribution chain to market and distribute their products. The particular rights licensed in all these circumstances can give rise to disputes, particularly where technological developments occurring after the date of the licence allow the licensed content to be used or distributed in a manner that may not have been contemplated by one or both parties at the time of the original licence agreement. For example, the ability of newspapers to distribute their material in electronic form both over the Internet as part of a database type service, as well as on CD-ROM type products, has resulted in lawsuits by freelance journalists who contend that traditionally their articles were licensed for one-time use in the paper-based edition of the newspaper, and that any subsequent online or other electronic use requires the further permission of the journalists.[51] For their part, the newspapers argue, among other things, that as owners of the copyright in the newspaper, namely the compilation of the various articles when taken together, they can exploit the newspaper as they please. It will be interesting to see which side carries the day in court on this

---

50   *CompuServe*, above note 39.
51   For a discussion of class action suits brought by freelance authors against Thomson Corp. and Southam Inc., respectively, see Elizabeth Raymer, "Electronic Copyright Fight Heads to Court" *The Lawyers Weekly* (21 February 1997), and Elizabeth Raymer, "Electronic Copyright Battle Heats Up: Quebec Freelancers Launch $30 million Class Action" *The Lawyers Weekly* (27 June 1997).

issue driven by the first dynamic of computer law.[52] As more and more content from the paper-based era is scanned or otherwise transformed for use in the electronic era, it can be expected that these sorts of lawsuits will multiply as the parties review their original licence agreements and disagree as to the scope of the rights originally granted, and in particular whether electronic rights are included in the grant clauses.

These sorts of cases are not new in the content industries (such as music, books, and broadcasting), particularly in the motion picture business where, in the United States especially, there have been a number of court decisions dealing with the question whether the language of prior licence grants is broad enough to permit the distributor to exercise distribution rights in new technology platforms or environments. For example, in a number of cases courts have had to decide whether the right to exhibit motion pictures (or to use music) included the ability to exercise these rights in the context of television broadcasts, and subsequently whether television rights included the videocassette market. In one line of cases,[53] these questions are answered in the affirmative, based on a combination of the following factors: the broad, often expansive nature of the licence language; the absence of limiting language in the grant clause; the level of sophistication of the content owner, and the related inference that the new technology was at least recognized by knowledgeable people at the time of the licence grant; and a finding that the two distribution streams are linked technologically; for example, television includes videocassettes because both are still seen through the mechanism of the television. By contrast, in those cases where it has been held that motion picture exhibition rights do not include television, or that television rights do not include videocassettes, courts have focussed on: language that is narrower and where sweeping grants of rights are not present; the licensor often being less sophisticated;

---

52   In the U.S. a trial judge in *Tasini v. New York Times Co.*, 972 F. Supp 804 (S.D.N.Y. 1997), reconsideration denied 981 F. Supp 841 (S.D.N.Y. 1997), recently decided this issue in favour of the publisher of the newspaper, though the applicability of this decision to the Canadian suits referred to in above note 51 is open to question given the differences in the Canadian and American copyright statutes in several of the areas related to the allegedly infringing activity.

53   *Bartsch v. Metro-Goldwyn-Mayer, Inc.*, 391 F.2d 150 (2d Cir. 1968); *Rooney v. Columbia Pictures Industries, Inc.*, 538 F. Supp. 211 (S.D.N.Y. 1982), aff'd without reasons 714 F.2d 117 (2d Cir. 1982); *Brown v. Twentieth Century Fox Film Corporation*, 799 F. Supp. 166 (D.C.D.C. 1992), aff'd without reasons 15 F.3d 1159 (D.C. Cir. 1994); *Bourne v. Walt Disney Company*, 68 F.3d 621 (2d Cir. 1995), cert. denied 116 S. Ct. 1890 (1996); *Boosey & Hawkes Music Publishers, Ltd. v. Walt Disney Company*, 934 F. Supp. 119 (S.D.N.Y. 1996).

and an analysis of the mechanics of, for example, television and video-cassette distribution that concludes that they are very different market segments and indeed quite distinct media.[54] Frankly, reconciling some of the cases in these two lines of authorities can be difficult; one has the sneaking suspicion that in a few of them the court decided for some reason (not apparent from reading the case) who should be entitled to the unexpected windfall represented by the new technology, and then the court partook of results-oriented reasoning by parsing words and the like.

In any event, the existence of the two lines of licensing cases referred to in the previous paragraph signifies the importance of careful drafting of licence grants in an industry as dynamic as the one related to computers, networks, and information-based products. Those desiring broad rights should try to include in licence grant clauses phrases such as "through any and all media, now or hereafter known," or "by present or future methods or means," or "in any medium, manner or form," while of course content owners wishing to keep their options open with respect to new media will likely resist such broad grants of rights. Particularly in respect of the Internet, which, commercially speaking, is still in its infancy and for which the business and technological models of content distribution are still not worked out in any great detail, content owners will likely be wary for some time before they enter into long-term licence agreements. For example, it is still not clear how consumers will be most willing to pay for content delivered over the Internet.[55] Many paradigms can be envisaged, ranging from subscriber models that allow unlimited access upon payment of a monthly fee to per-byte models where the consumer pays only for what she takes, or even broadcast models where the service is free to consumers but paid for by advertisers. And during the current embryonic stage of the Internet, service providers might waffle between these and other models until they hit upon the right one. Thus, content owners will likely want to see how these various models with end users pan out before locking themselves into any particular upstream licensing arrangement with an Internet service provider or content distributor.

---

54 Cohen v. Paramount Pictures Corp., 845 F.2d 851 (9th Cir. 1988); Tele-Pac, Inc. v. Grainger, 570 N.Y.S.2d 521 (1991), leave to appeal dismissed 588 N.E.2d 99 (N.Y. 1991); Rey v. G.D. Lafferty, 990 F.2d 1379 (1st Cir. 1993).

55 See "A Survey of Electronic Commerce: In Search of the Perfect Market," The Economist, 10 May 1997.

D. NEGLIGENCE

Under the law of negligence, someone (referred to here as the defendant) who causes harm to someone else (referred to here as the plaintiff)
for failing to comply with a reasonable standard of care will be liable to
the plaintiff for the damages caused to the plaintiff provided the law
determines that the defendant owed the plaintiff a duty of care. In negligence law, courts determine what the reasonable standard of care is in
any given situation and, assuming the standard has not been met, courts
then determine who is entitled to be compensated by the defendant's
failure to adhere to the standard. The purpose of negligence law is to
compensate certain plaintiffs who are harmed by certain actions of certain defendants, and thereby also to encourage safer behaviour through
the adoption of cost-effective measures to avoid situations that cause
damage. Under negligence law, these obligations are imposed by the
courts, and hence are non-voluntary, in contrast to contract law which
deals with voluntarily assumed obligations.[56]

Given the widespread presence of computers and computer networks in our society, it is not surprising that computers raise a number
of issues under the law of negligence, some of them quite unique. There
are questions related to negligence in the creation of computer-based
products, particularly in light of ever shortening product cycles — the
alter ego of the first dynamic of computer law — and the fact that bug-
free software is, practically speaking, an unattainable goal. The year
2000 problem (Y2K problem) encompasses a virtual hornet's nest of
negligence issues. As well, computers can be used in ways that are negligent. And ironically, negligence can also arise when computers are not
used. In all these scenarios the general law of negligence will apply, but
often with particular nuances given the unique characteristics of the
computer industry. It should also be noted that in many of these scenarios contract and sales law will also be relevant, particularly in attempts
to limit exposure for negligence, and these topics are discussed in the
next part of this chapter.

---

56   This is a ridiculously short description of negligence law. For a full discussion of
this fascinating area of the law, and its development over the years, see Allen M.
Linden, *Canadian Tort Law*, 6th ed. (Toronto: Butterworths, 1997).

1) Negligence in Creation: The Y2K Problem

There are relatively few reported cases involving negligence claims brought against the developers of computers, software, and related products. This is probably attributable to several factors, including that to date, for the most part, the harm caused by malfunctioning computers has been economic loss rather than injury to persons or damage to physical property. As a result, most claims against suppliers for defective computer resources have been in contract, which is more receptive than negligence to compensating for pure economic loss. Indeed, one way that courts limit the scope of negligence law is to severely curtail the circumstances under which they will award compensation for pure economic loss, thereby reserving negligence, in a practical sense, primarily to the domain of compensation for personal injury or loss to tangible, physical property although, as can be seen in the cases in this section, negligence law can be pressed into action from time to time to compensate for pecuniary losses. As software finds its way into more and more tangible products, however, the likelihood of physical injuries resulting from substandard software will increase.[57] For example, in a pair of U.S. cases, the design and lack of repair, respectively, of computer-based devices led to automobile accidents that caused personal injury and damage to tangible property.[58] The paucity of negligent design and build cases to date should not be taken as an indicator of future expectations. For example, there will undoubtedly be numerous claims arising out of the Y2K problem. Indeed, the first Y2K-related lawsuit was recently filed in Michigan by a grocery store chain when electronic cash registers purchased by them could not process credit cards

---

57 See, for example, Barbara Wade Rose, "Fatal Dose," *Saturday Night*, June 1994, which chronicles the physical harm inflicted on cancer patients by overdoses of radiation attributable to a software glitch in a radiation therapy machine. As for property damage, see the short mention in *The Economist*, 8 June 1996, of the destruction of $500 million worth of uninsured spacecraft and scientific satellite when apparently a software glitch made the launch rocket go off course just after lift-off.

58 *Roberts v. Rich Foods, Inc.*, 654 A.2d 1365 (N.J. 1995); *Arizona State Highway Department v. Bechtold*, 460 P.2d 179 (Ariz. 1969).

expiring after the year 2000.[59] Some lawsuits will entail pure economic loss, but others will be directly linked to personal injury and even property damage, if predicted calamities involving malfunctioning traffic lights, aircraft flight-related computers, train-related control systems, etc., come to pass. Cases involving Y2K problems will set some dynamic new precedents.

A negligence case relating to the creation of a computer-based product has the potential to raise some unusual issues. Consider a computer/software system used to help doctors diagnose medical patients by analysing a patient's symptoms relative to a knowledge base contained within the program. These so-called medical expert systems often exhibit artificial intelligence by being able to store previous patient histories and diagnoses in a large database and "to learn" from these previous cases to improve the accuracy and quality of its diagnoses. A threshold issue relative to such a system is who would be liable if a doctor using such a program arrived at an incorrect diagnosis. The candidates for liability include: the doctor; the hospital that acquired the system; the supplier of the system; the developer of the system; the medical research team that provided the knowledge base for the system; the developers of the artificial intelligence inference engine that is used in the system; and some combination of all or some of the above. In essence, many computer systems and software products are the result of collaborative efforts among a number of participants, and determining the boundaries of responsibility among them for purposes of a negligence analysis can be a challenge. Nonetheless, courts engage in such delineation all the time, as in the recent decision in *A.T. Kearney v. International Business Machines Corporation*.[60] This case arose out of a lawsuit brought by a retailer against its consultant, A.T. Kearney, for proposing 100 IBM AS/400 mid-range computers that ultimately proved to be

---

59   *Produce Palace International v. TEC-America Corporation*, (Mi. Cir. Ct., complaint filed 12 June 1997), reported in *Computer & Online Industry Litigation Reporter*, 19 August 1997 at 24,466. See also Joanna Glasner, "Millennium Bug Sparks Lawsuit" *The National Law Journal* (12 August 1997). See also *Atlaz International v. Software Business Technologies Inc.*, No. 172539 (Ca. Super. Ct., Marin Cty., complaint filed 2 December 1997), reported in *Computer & Online Industry Litigation Reporter*, 16 December 1997 at 7, complaint reproduced at D1ff., a claim brought by users of Y2K non-compliant software against the software company that licensed them the software over the past few years. For another case along these lines, see *Capellan v. Symantec Corporation*, No. CV772147 (Ca. Super. Ct., Santa Clara Cty., complaint filed 19 February 1998) [unreported].

60   *A.T. Kearney, Inc. v. International Business Machines Corporation*, 867 F. Supp. 943 (D. Or. 1994), aff'd 73 F.3d 238 (9th Cir. 1995).

inadequate; instead, the retailer ended up buying an IBM mainframe computer. The retailer sued the consultant for $110 million for negligence, breach of contract, negligent misrepresentation, and breach of fiduciary duty, and they settled for a payment from the consultant to the retailer of $13.25 million. The consultant then sued IBM for negligence, for failure to disclose its doubts about the ability of the proposed system to meet the needs of the retailer. The court dismissed the consultant's claim, finding that IBM was merely a seller of goods and had no special relationship with the consultant and had no consulting or services obligations.

The Y2K problem will likely result in claims brought against numerous potential defendants, as there are a number of persons, companies, and other organizations against whom Y2K-related lawsuits might be brought in appropriate circumstances.[61] Software developers, of course, will be a prime target depending on the state of their products. Hardware manufacturers whose products are not Y2K compliant will also be likely defendants. There are then the myriad of participants in the computer industry involved in supplying, selling, or licensing products through various distribution channels. Similarly, system integrators and consultants who recommended specific sourcing decisions to customers and clients may be at risk, depending on the nature of their advice. Yet another category of potential defendant is the vendor of so-called outsourcing services who agreed to support the systems of the customer, or agreed to keep these systems at certain levels of performance, particularly where the term of the agreement extends beyond 1 January 2000. An outsourcing of even a subset of such services may also cause the service provider to attract Y2K liability. Users and operators of computer resources (which means just about every company and organization on the face of the earth today) may also find themselves subject to judicial scrutiny if their systems experience malfunctions that cause them to fail to provide adequate service to their customers or other stakeholders such as EDI trading partners; that is, while a user of such technology may have a claim in such a situation against the third party technology developer (if the system was not developed in-house), this would not preclude the user being sued in the first instance. There are a number of decided court cases in which courts have held users responsible for damages ultimately caused by their malfunctioning or poorly designed computer systems.[62] It is not difficult to contemplate these cases being cited as precedents when users are brought into the Y2K

---

61   Geoffrey Rowan, "Year 2000 Plants Liability Minefield" *The [Toronto] Globe and Mail* (4 June 1997).

62   See section D(2), "Negligence in Use," in this chapter.

legal maelstrom. Certain parties may become Y2K defendants not by virtue of their direct work with computer systems, but rather as a result of their failure to warn others about a particular company's state of affairs in light of the Y2K problem. Will, for example, directors or officers have an obligation to ensure that a company's financial statements adequately disclose prospective costs that will be attributable to the Y2K problem if these are material? Or if a company in the middle of 1999 realizes that it simply will not have enough time to make its systems Y2K compliant by 1 January 2000, is this a disclosure item, particularly in the context of a public company?[63] And what about the role and duty of auditors in this regard? Depending on the severity of the problem in a particular case, is a note to the financial statements warranted where material financial and other liabilities inevitably will arise due to the Y2K issue?

It should also be noted that the range of potential plaintiffs in the Y2K legal environment is equally diverse. Depending on the particular facts of each case, the customers of technology suppliers clearly represent a likely category of claimants. Similarly, customers of companies that use computer systems may be in a position to make claims if and when these companies fail to provide products or services to previous standards as a result of computer problems engendered by the Y2K problem. An intriguing plaintiff would be the business partner who exchanges data with the defendant company in an internetworked environment, if such exchange becomes problematic or impossible after 1 January 2000 because of Y2K problems. Many such relationships will be strong enough, and symbiotic enough, to withstand the adverse consequences of a corruption in intercompany data flows. The legal fur may fly, however, where the damages are simply too significant to ignore or where the lack of a long and deep pre-existing relationship prompts a review of legal options. An interesting variable in this analysis is intro-

---

63   See, for example, the U.S. Securities and Exchange Commission, *Report to the Congress on the Readiness of the United States Securities Industry and Public Companies to Meet the Information Processing Challenges of the Year 2000,* June 1997 [*Readiness*], which discusses disclosure issues for public companies: <http://www.sec.gov/news/studies/yr2000.htm> [*Report*]. This report, at page 1 of the Executive Summary, includes the following passage: "[I]t is important that one essential principle be understood: It is not, and will not, be possible for any single entity or collective enterprise to represent that it has achieved complete Year 2000 compliance and thus to guarantee its remediation efforts. The problem is simply too complex for such a claim to have legitimacy. Efforts to solve Year 2000 problems are best described as "risk mitigation." Success in the effort will have been achieved if the number and seriousness of any technical failures is minimized, and they are quickly identified and repaired if they do occur."

duced by the increasing ability in several Canadian provinces to bring class action claims.[64] These are lawsuits brought on behalf of a large number of claimants; each claimant's individual damages may be rather small, but when grouped procedurally with hundreds or thousands of other plaintiffs, a significant legal risk is produced for the defendant company. There are numerous requirements and hurdles that must be overcome in "certifying a class" in such litigation, but it is quite possible that the multiple users of the same Y2K non-compliant systems might litigate together, and indeed may be a central tactical move on the part of the lead plaintiff orchestrating the case.

In addition to determining who the proper parties are in a computer-related negligence claim, another difficult challenge lies in determining what standard of care to apply to the development of a computer system or software program, whether it be a medical expert system or any other application. There are, for instance, no general licensing or certification requirements for software developers. One must be a licensed engineer in order to design a bridge that will span a street or highway; no such licence is required by the software programmers designing a key network bridge along the information superhighway. Similarly, while there are a number of textbooks on software design, programming, and testing, there are no generally recognized standards as there are, for example, in the accounting profession and contained in the *CICA Handbook*. Thus, there are no widely accepted standards among software programmers as to how much testing a new product should undergo — of how many bugs per line of code can remain — before the software is released commercially. On large software development projects the user relies on express contractual provisions to address these concerns; in the mass market environment most users are content to wait for a subsequent release of the product to fix the known bugs.

With respect to the Y2K problem, the intriguing question will be what the standard of care ought to be — or will be found by a judge to be — in respect of designing Y2K compliant systems. For example, there is probably little doubt that someone selling a system over the next few years that is not Y2K compliant will have difficulty successfully defending a negligence claim (subject to contractual disclaimers, etc., discussed below) given the current level of awareness of the problem. More problematic is determining the earliest date by which system developers knew, or ought to have known, about the Y2K problem such that not making their systems Y2K compliant henceforth would constitute

---

64   In Ontario, see: *Class Proceedings Act*, 1992, S.O. 1992, c. 6.

negligence. An important article on the subject by Canadian Peter de Jaeger appeared in September 1993.[65] Is this the magic date? Or should it be earlier, given that some commentators were writing about the subject in publications with narrower audiences in the 1980s. It will also likely be relevant to a determination of the negligence issue as to when the computer industry generally began to make their systems Y2K compliant. Courts will often use as a benchmark for gauging behaviour the prevailing practice in the relevant industry. Every now and then, however, a court finds that a whole industry's behaviour is substandard, as was the case in The T.J. Hooper case.[66] Is the Y2K problem a good candidate for such a finding?

Other types of negligence may also come into play in the Y2K environment. In addition to negligent design, there can be negligence on the part of suppliers merely for failure to warn users of the system that it lacks Y2K compliance.[67] Consider the scenario where a software supplier releases in 1998 a new version of its system that, for the first time, is Y2K compliant. The new release is delivered to all customers who subscribe to the company's software support program. A number of users of earlier versions of the program, however, do not receive maintenance upgrades, or simply have not had anything to do with the supplier for a number of years. Is there, in such a situation, a positive duty on the supplier to warn such customers that their earlier versions of the software are not Y2K compliant and that they should reapply for support in order to receive the new version that is? Or, if the same company is selling a non-compliant system in 1997, does it have to disclose that the user will need to upgrade to the 1998 version if it wants to be Y2K compliant. Is there fraudulent misrepresentation, or at least negligent misrepresentation, for failure to do so? Negligence may also be the basis for claiming against a number of different persons who have disclosure obligations with respect to a company or organization. If a user organization will face extraordinary costs in becoming Y2K compliant, particularly if the organization will come under significant financial pressure in becoming Y2K compliant, then it is open to question whether, particularly in the context of a public company, the company has an obligation in its financial statements to disclose such a material liability. In the normal course, one would not expect to see financial statements make particular reference to future information technology costs, and likely most Y2K expenditures would equally not be the subject of special treat-

---

65   Peter de Jaeger, "Doomsday," *Computerworld*, 6 September 1993.
66   *The T. J. Hooper*, 60 F.2d 737 (2d Cir. 1932) [*Hooper*].
67   *Rivtow Marine Ltd.* v. *Washington Iron Works* (1973), 40 D.L.R. (3d) 530 (S.C.C.).

ment in the financial statements. If, however, the risk presented by the Y2K issue becomes material and financially significant, then some thought at least should be given to such disclosure issues. Companies preparing annual reports, prospectuses, and other such material for securities law purposes would be well advised to consider whether Y2K-related disclosures should be included in such documents.[68] In a prospectus, for example, the "risks of the investment" section might be an appropriate place to describe the issue, particularly if the company is not confident that it can be fully Y2K compliant by 1 January 2000 and this would, for securities law purposes, constitute a "material fact." An investor who bought shares of such a company in the summer of 1999 on the strength of a prospectus that was silent on the Y2K issue, only to see the share price drop dramatically as system problems led to severe operating hardships, dramatically increased costs, and drastically lower revenues in the first quarter of 2000, will likely cite the lack of a reference to Y2K in the prospectus as part of the claim.

2) Negligence in Use

a) Malfunctioning Computers
A wide variety of situations can be contemplated where users of computers are negligent in the manner in which they employ computers. In one type of case, the computer malfunctions with the result that it processes an erroneous result. In such cases, courts have generally been unwilling to let users argue as a defence to liability that the particular computer had malfunctioned. For example, in an early U.S. case, a car leasing company repossessed a customer's car for non-payment even though the customer had promptly paid the required monthly accounts.[69] The problem was that the computer would not register the payments, and therefore it issued the notice to repossess the car. The customer brought a claim for compensatory and punitive damages. The company admitted liability, but tried to explain the whole incident

---

68   See *Readiness*, above note 63. See also Canadian Securities Administrators Staff Notices 41-301 and 51-302, *The Year 2000 Challenge Disclosure Issues*, available at <http://jupiter.micromedia.on.ca/micromedia/oscbhtml/HTML2105/1_1_3.htm> and The Toronto Stock Exchange, By-law No. 685, *A By-law with Respect to Disclosure by Listed Issuers Regarding Year 2000, amending the General By-law of The Toronto Stock Exchange*, adopted on 6 January 1998 and effective on 12 January 1998, and available at <http://jupiter.micromedia.on.ca/micromedia/oscbhtml/HTML2105/C13_1_1.htm>.

69   *Ford Motor Credit Company v. Swarens*, 447 S.W.2d 53 (Ky. App. 1969).

because of a computer error. The court did not accept this excuse, and concluded:

> Men feed data to a computer and men interpret the answer the computer spews forth. In this computerized age, the law must require that men in the use of computerized data regard those with whom they are dealing as more important than a perforation on a card. Trust in the infallibility of a computer is hardly a defense, when the opportunity to avoid the error is as apparent and repeated as was here presented.[70]

In a more recent Nova Scotia case, an insurance company failed to send out a renewal notice on an insurance policy due to a computer error.[71] This caused the policy to lapse and the previously insured individual brought a claim for compensation resulting from an automobile accident. The court found the insurance company liable, and again a computer glitch was not permitted to excuse negligent behaviour. In yet another case, the computer of a lottery corporation erroneously indicated to a ticket holder that he had won $835, when in fact he really only won $5.[72] Before the error was pointed out to the ticket holder, he had spent about $400 wining and dining friends to celebrate the lottery win. When the lottery corporation refused to pay the $835, the winner

---

70   *Ibid.* at 57. A similar sentiment was expressed by a court in a later U.S. case, *Poullier v. Nacua Motors, Inc.*, 439 N.Y.S.2d 85 at 86 (N.Y. Sup. Ct. 1981) [*Poullier*]:
> At first blush, it would appear that this court must determine the guilt or innocence of a computer. But such is not the case. In our modern machine age, it's tempting to shift the ills of society onto the heartless, mechanical world of computers. Yet, responsibility cannot be so easily escaped since a computer, not unlike an infant of tender years, is totally dependent on being spoon-fed by a human world. A computer error must always relate back to a human error, whether it be the human as source of the information fed into it, the human as creator of its programming or the human as mechanic for its proper functioning.

Equally, in the American case *Re McCormack*, 203 B.R. 521 at 524 (Bankr. D.N.H. 1996) [*McCormack*], the court found that a bank should not be allowed to hide behind its computer:
> The testimony by Chase's witness that its software at the time would not accommodate separate accounting and recording of payments coming from the trustee under the plan I find amounts to the "computer did it" defense. That defense is a nonstarter in this Court's judgment since intelligent beings still control the computer and could have altered the programming appropriately . . . To paraphrase the old quote 'garbage-in' adage a version here pertinent would be 'contempt-of-court in' and 'contempt-of-court out.'

71   *Judgment Recovery (N.S.) Ltd. v. Sun Alliance Insurance Co.* (1986), 74 N.S.R. (2d) 412 (T.D.).

72   *Budai v. Ontario Lottery Corp.* (1983), 142 D.L.R. (3d) 271 (Ont. H.C.J.).

brought a claim and the court agreed with him, concluding that the corporation "in effect, invited him to depend on the computer and he had every reason to believe it was accurate."[73] The court did suggest, however, that if the prize had been greater than $835, then at some point it would have been negligence on the part of the winner not to confirm the win, and actually receive the money, before incurring significant expenses in the expectation of using the lottery winnings to pay for such expenses.

Not all malfunctioning computers, however, will result in liability being visited upon their users. In one case a customer certified a cheque for $7500 on the strength of the amount shown in a bank passbook that had not been updated, and that could not be updated at the time the cheque was drawn because the bank's computers were inoperable.[74] Once the computers came back online, and all the interim postings were made to the account, it turned out the customer was in an overdraft position of roughly $950. The customer refused to pay, ostensibly on the grounds that had he known the true balance in his account he would have reduced the amount of the certified cheque accordingly. The court, ignoring estoppel arguments and the authorities that indicate that the customer's passbook is the only record of the true state of a customer's account, found for the bank and ordered the customer to pay the $950 on the basis of unjust enrichment. In another case, a stockbroker, on the strength of a malfunctioning computer, quoted $7.00 as the price he could get for options held by the customer; in fact, the price the computer should have shown was around $2.50, and the stockbroker unknowingly sold the options for this amount, kicking up a substantial loss for the customer.[75] When the customer sued the broker for the loss, the court, interestingly, held for the broker on the basis that the price of the options deteriorated even further after their sale by the broker, such that, ironically, selling at the erroneous price nevertheless saved the customer money by reducing his potential loss. In other words, the misrepresentation by the computer did not cause the investor's damage. Ironically, however, the court did not let the broker collect any commission on the trade as the inaccuracy in the information provided by the broker had so little value to the customer.

---

73 *Ibid.* at 273.
74 *Bank of Nova Scotia v. Butt* (1978), 11 A.R. 616 (Dist. Ct.).
75 *Walwyn Stodgell Cochrane Murray Ltd. v. Ryan* (1981), 36 N.B.R. (2d) 187 (Q.B.T.D.).

b) Negligent Design

In addition to these cases where the particular computer malfunction leads to erroneous processing or computation, there are the intriguing cases where the user's fault lies in the design of the computer being used by it; that is, the computers are working the way they were programmed to work, but the particular way they work (i.e., the design programmed into them) is itself negligent. A good example of this is *Remfor Industries Ltd. v. Bank of Montreal.*[76] In this case a customer of a bank wished to stop payment on a cheque, and to this end gave the bank the date and number of the cheque, the name of the payee, and the amount of $10,800, which was $53 short of the actual amount of the cheque. The bank's computer was programmed only to register the account number and the precise amount of the cheque, and therefore the bank failed to stop payment because the number given to the bank was incorrect by $53. In the subsequent claim between the customer and the bank, the court held in favour of the customer, concluding that the customer gave a reasonably accurate description to the bank, which was all it had to do, and thereafter it was up to the bank to have an adequate system to properly act on this information:

> I am of the opinion that the learned trial Judge was correct in holding that having regard to the information given to it by the plaintiff, the bank was under a duty to inquire from its customer as to whether the cheque presented for certification was the cheque with respect to which the direction to stop payment had been given. The bank's failure to do so constituted negligence. The information given to the bank was correct in every respect other than the amount. The instructions clearly related to the cheque, the number of which had been given to the bank. The bank's internal procedure in limiting the information supplied to its computer, by reference to account number and the amount of the cheque only, cannot relieve the bank of its duty where the customer has supplied such precise additional information.[77]

In other words, a human bank clerk, faced with the same information from the customer, invariably would have called to enquire of the customer to sort out the discrepancies in the amounts at issue, and hence would have effected the stop payment. The computer program used by the bank, because it was poorly designed, required precise information and therefore was not as flexible as the human system it replaced.

---

76   (1978), 90 D.L.R. (3d) 316 (Ont. C.A.) [*Remfor*].
77   *Ibid.* at 320.

Several American cases have come to conclusions similar to that in the *Remfor* case. In one case, *Parr v. Security National Bank*, the court was faced with facts identical to those in *Remfor*, and the court also held in favour of the customer.[78] The court concluded that the customer simply had to identify the cheque on which it wished to stop payment with "reasonable accuracy," and therefore the court did not take into account the actual state of the computer program used by the bank or any other matter relating to how the bank handled stop payment orders, notwithstanding that, as the court stated, this result might place a burden on banks. In another U.S. case, however, the bank was able to shift this burden from its back and put it squarely on that of the customer by notifying the customer, in advance, that the bank needs the precise amount of the cheque given that the bank's computer is programmed in a manner to recognize only precise numbers.[79] Thus, even though the customer was out by only one digit (the plaintiff told the bank the amount was $4,287.65, when it was really $4,247.65), the court held in favour of the bank:

> Had plaintiff presented the bank with the correct amount of the check, and thereafter, the computer failed to detect the stop payment order, plaintiff would then be correct in her contention that the computer through its master, the bank, had erred. However, such is not the case. Defendant Bank's request for the exact amount was not unreasonable and is in fact mandated by a stop payment system, necessarily computerized due to the large number of branch offices where such an instrument could be negotiated. Nor is plaintiff's contention that she should not be held responsible for a mere "1 digit mistake," a valid one in that one digit can be a world of difference to a computer, who by nature, is quite finicky.[80]

A Canadian court followed a similar rationale involving a dispute regarding Ontario's computerized personal property registration system.[81] In this case, the plaintiff argued the registration system's computer failed to give it adequate information in that it did not display a second variation of a name for a particular debtor. The lower court accepted this argument, but the appellate court did not, noting that the government's computer did not give a wrong answer, rather the plaintiff

---

78   680 P.2d 648 (Okla. App. 1984).
79   *Poullier*, above note 70.
80   *Ibid.* at 86.
81   *Federal Business Development Bank v. Registrar of Personal Property Security* (1984), 45 O.R. (2d) 780 (H.C.J.).

asked the wrong question. The court noted, in a manner reminiscent of the decision in the *Poullier* case, that the precise rules dictated by the computerized registration system were made available to all users of the system, and therefore the onus was on the plaintiff to comply with its requirement for precision.

A trio of other cases are worth mentioning that echo the result in the *Remfor* case and highlight the requirement for users to ensure that their computers are adequately designed. One decision dealt with a computerized trading system developed and used by a gas pipeline operator.[82] When inputting data into this system, an employee of the company confused two entities with virtually identical names, with the result that delivery of the gas went to the wrong party. The court found both parties to the litigation 50 percent responsible for the error. With respect to the pipeline company, its negligence stemmed from, among other things, failing to design and implement a system that would avoid the kinds of errors encountered in the case. The court cited six specific elements of negligence against the pipeline company, two particularly noteworthy ones being: failure to warn the public that its trading system was not free of the types of errors it experienced in the case; and the other a failure to confirm transfers of gas early enough to allow customers to detect any mistakes. In another case, negligence was found when an electric utility disconnected power to a newly built and not yet occupied house in the middle of winter due to non-payment of the utility's bills, causing the pipes to burst and damages to the premises.[83] Again the court castigated the utility for blindly relying on the computer when it gave the order to terminate service, and for the failure to verify the situation by a human intervention, which the court concluded would have quickly led the utility to realize the new home had just been built and was unoccupied.

A final case worth noting involved a bank's failure to keep track of appropriate amounts in a bankruptcy administration where the bank was also a secured creditor.[84] The bank pleaded its computers could not handle the particular nuances of the various court awards. The court refused to accept this excuse (see note 70 above), and indeed, went on to award punitive damages against the bank:

---

82   *Shell Pipeline Corporation v. Coastal States Trading, Inc.*, 788 S.W.2d 837 (Tex. App. 1990).

83   *Pompeii Estates, Inc. v. Consolidated Edison Co. of New York, Inc.*, 397 N.Y.S.2d 577 (N.Y. City Civ. Ct. 1977).

84   *McCormack*, above note 70.

Perhaps a less knowledgeable and less sophisticated business enterprise might not be charged with punitive damages for failing to set up appropriate computer or specialized accounting procedures with appropriate instructions to employees to avoid violations of the automatic stay in this context. Be that as it may, the Court does not believe that that concept or that defense should be available to an enterprise of the nature of Chase. . . . Sophisticated commercial enterprises have a clear obligation to adjust their programming and procedures and their instruction to employees to handle complex matters correctly.[85]

The court concluded that if the bank was in fact unable to modify its computer systems appropriately, it should have adopted adequate manual procedures. Instead, much to the chagrin of the court, the bank was content to let its computer spew forth a large volume of printouts that did not meet the requirements of the situation:

The panoply of computer printouts presented to the debtor in this case bring to mind the phrase "cruelty to dumb animals" in that no borrower in my judgment should have been subjected to that barrage of incomprehensible accounting printouts in response to a simple question of what has happened to the obligations cured under the plan as opposed to post-confirmation transactions. The barrage of totally meaningless and in fact misleading printouts employed by Chase in this instance was truly outrageous and egregious conduct.[86]

In section B(6), "Intelligent Computers," in chapter 1, the question was asked whether Immanuel Kant, who exalted humans as the only species capable of moral, autonomous judgment, would be pleased by the computer revolution if he were alive today. Clearly the cases referred to in this section would distress him, but the responses of the courts would hearten him. In effect, computers are wonderful, indispensable tools, but they are only tools. They do our bidding. Therefore, it is up to people to ensure that their computers and the business or administrative processes of which they are a part are designed in a manner that is appropriate to the task. On occasion this will require that a human intervention step (or two) be factored into the business process design implemented by the computer. Third parties must be given clear and advance notice of the limitations of the computer system. Where a computer user does not do this, and the resulting computer-based business process fails to address the requirements of the particular situation

85   *Ibid.* at 525.
86   *Ibid.*

— and not just the exigencies of the computer user — courts will stick the user with liability, rather than permit them to hide behind the computer.

3) Negligent Non-Use

Although users of computers and technological devices can be negligent when they use computers in a careless manner, they can also be negligent if they fail to use computers, or more up-to-date computers. An important early U.S. case on the question of failing to use readily available and relatively inexpensive technology is *The T.J. Hooper* case, where the distinguished American jurist, Learned Hand, concluded that a tugboat owner was negligent in not fitting the vessel with a radio receiving set that could have warned the captain of the ship about an impending storm which, in the event, caused the ship to lose one of the barges it was towing.[87] The court found negligence on the basis that an adequate radio set could be purchased at a small cost and was reliable if kept maintained, and would have greatly helped avoid the kind of harm experienced in this case. Importantly, the court also determined that it was no defence to argue that not all ships had yet adopted the radio device; the court rationalized that there are times when a whole industry might lag behind in adopting new and available technology, and the court should not hesitate to set higher standards in such circumstances. In a more recent case, also in the United States, an airline was held to be negligent when its existing computer system failed to detect a forged airline ticket.[88] The court refused to accept the airline's argument that it should not be faulted for its inability to detect the alteration in the tickets due to the nature of its then current computer system. Instead, the court concluded:

> Plaintiff could have prevented the passengers from using altered tickets by maintaining a system capable of confirming which passengers are scheduled for a particular flight. In light of the advanced computer technology available today, this is not an unreasonable burden to place on the plaintiff. . . . I do not recognize Swiss Air's reliance on its computer system as a legally cognizable defense. Had Swiss Air been properly equipped with a more sophisticated computer system, it could have promptly discovered the irregularity of the defendant's ticket.[89]

87 *Hooper*, above note 66.
88 *Swiss Air Transport Company, Ltd. v. Benn*, 467 N.Y.S.2d 341 (N.Y. City Civ. Ct. 1983).
89 *Ibid.* at 344.

This reasoning is illustrative of an interesting twist on the first dynamic of computer law, namely, that in certain circumstances the law will require users to stay reasonably current with the pace of technological change.

A finding of negligence can also be made where a particular technology is installed, but then not utilized, as happened in an American case where a bank was held liable when its teller paid on a stopped cheque without consulting the computer terminal that, had it been accessed, would have indicated the stop payment order.[90] In this case, the bank argued it did not have sufficient time to act on the customer's stop payment notice as it was given at one branch and the cheque presented the next day at another branch. The court disagreed and concluded that if the bank employee at the second branch had checked the computer, the stop payment notice would have appeared. Similarly, a pharmacy was held liable in a U.S. case when it advertised its computer system as being able to detect harmful prescription interactions; in fact, the pharmacy failed to detect such an interaction which led a customer to suffer a stroke and subsequently commit suicide.[91] The failure to detect the interaction, however, was not due to a malfunction of the computer but rather was the result of the failure to use the computer system by the person at the pharmacy dispensing drugs. All these cases reaffirm the general sentiment in legal and business circles that technological progress is a positive development, and companies should strive to take advantage of it. Likewise, it is worth noting a line of case law in the United States that stands for the proposition that franchisors may lawfully terminate their relationships with franchisees that refuse to adopt new computer technology proposed by the franchisor.[92]

---

90   *Chute v. Bank One of Akron, N.A.*, 460 N.E.2d 720 (Ohio App. 1983).

91   *Baker v. Arbor Drugs, Inc.*, 544 N.W.2d 727 (Mich. App. 1996), leave to appeal denied 558 N.W. 2d 725 (Mich. App. 1997).

92   In *J.I. Case Company v. Early's, Inc.*, 721 F. Supp. 1082 (E.D. Mo. 1989), the court concluded that the new system was necessary for effective communications between franchisor and franchisees; in *Re Groseth International, Inc.*, 442 N.W.2d 229 (S.D. 1989), the court, in addition to noting that the new computer system would save the franchisor money and staff costs, found that it was an essential and reasonable requirement to impose on franchisees in order that the whole franchise system could compete in the marketplace; and in *Crim Truck & Tractor Co. v. Navistar International Transportation Corporation*, 823 S.W.2d 591 (Tex. 1992), the court upheld the franchisor's decision to terminate a franchisee partly on the strength of the franchisee's refusal to participate in a mandatory computer-based dealer communication network that would share computerized information between the manufacturer/franchisor and its dealers.

Once a computer system is installed, however, courts will not generally require an inordinately high standard of redundancy or fail safe technology, particularly if such back-up systems are quite expensive. Thus, in an American case, a bank was not considered negligent when it failed to have a back-up computer system available when its newly acquired system failed to operate.[93] The court in this case concluded that the bank had exercised adequate due care when it promptly called upon the computer maintenance company to correct the problems as quickly as possible. In a similar manner, in *Moss* v. *Richardson Greenshields of Canada Ltd.*, a cancellation of a sale order could not be communicated to the relevant office as a result of a computer network linking offices in several different cities becoming inoperable.[94] One important issue was whether the company was grossly negligent in not having a back-up system in place to deal with such a contingency. The court concluded it was not grossly negligent to forgo such a system as the main computer network had never failed previously. Just as important, if not more so, the company shifted the risk of such problems to users by means of clauses in their contracts that excluded their liability except in the case of gross negligence or wilful misconduct, thus precluding claims that were based on mere negligence. It is, of course, open to speculation whether similar facts would give rise to similar decisions today if it could be shown that technically sound back-up systems, and so-called disaster recovery services, are available to computer users on relatively reasonable financial terms.

E. CONTRACTS AND SALES LAW

Computers, software, information-based products, and related services are typically provided to users under a wide variety of written contracts. Software is typically licensed, as has been noted previously in this chapter. Hardware can be sold outright pursuant to a purchase agreement under which the user obtains title to the equipment, or leased or rented pursuant to agreements that merely permit the user to use the equipment for a period of time in return for a periodic fee. Ongoing maintenance services are typically provided for both hardware and software. Where there exists no off-the-shelf software that meets a user's require-

---

93   *Port City State Bank* v. *American National Bank*, Lawton, Oklahoma, 486 F.2d 196 (10th Cir. 1973).

94   [1988] 4 W.W.R. 15 (Man. Q.B.), aff'd [1989] 3 W.W.R. 50 (Man. C.A.).

ments, a software development firm may be retained by a user to develop custom software pursuant to a software development agreement, or perhaps the specifications are first developed for the software under a consulting agreement. Instead of acquiring hardware or software, under an outsourcing or service bureau agreement, a user may buy computer services, with the supplier operating the computer system on behalf of the user. All these arrangements present both suppliers and users of computing resource with a number of risks. As noted in section C(4), "Dependency on Computers," in chapter 1, computer system implementation projects can encounter serious technical or financial difficulties. Even if implemented, the system can exhibit tendencies to crash or malfunction on an ongoing basis. In either case, the supplier and user can accumulate significant liability. In the context of two commercial parties undertaking such activities, in the absence of a written agreement to the contrary, the implied warranties and conditions found in sale of goods legislation may apply to the transaction. In many cases, however, suppliers insist on displacing these implied provisions, which in turn results in most users insisting on the computer contract addressing certain issues expressly. In effect, a computer contract is a means of voluntarily assuming certain obligations and avoiding others. Contracts can effectively allow parties to create something of their own law in circumstances where law reform has not kept up with the rapid pace of technological change or has not adequately addressed any of the other dynamics of computer law.[95]

1) Implied Warranties and Conditions

The sale of goods statutes of the common law provinces[96] contain a number of warranties and conditions that are implied into all contracts for the sale of goods, unless they are expressly disclaimed (except, as noted below, in the case of consumer sales, where other statutes generally prohibit disclaiming these implied warranties and conditions). It

---

95 The following discussion only scratches the surface of several important issues related to computer contracts. For an overview of a range of other issues, see George S. Takach, *Contracting for Computers*, 2d ed. (Toronto: McGraw-Hill Ryerson, 1992) [*Contracting*]; for an in-depth treatment of the case law, see chapter 2 of Barry Sookman, *Sookman Computer Law: Acquiring and Protecting Information Technology* (Toronto: Carswell, 1991) (looseleaf, updated) [*Sookman Computer Law*]; and for precedent clauses together with helpful commentary, see Esther C. Roditti, *Computer Contracts: Negotiating, Drafting* (New York: Matthew Bender, 1997) (looseleaf, updated).

96 For example, Ontario's *Sale of Goods Act*, R.S.O. 1990, c. S.1.

therefore becomes important in the context of commercial sales, in situations where express disclaimers are not in place, to determine as a preliminary matter whether the sales statute applies to the particular transaction; that is, is there a sale of a good? Where the object of the transaction is a sale of hardware, it is invariably easy to answer this question in the affirmative, for an item of equipment clearly falls within the *chattels personal* definition of goods in the sales statute. Where the deal involves a bundled system consisting of hardware and software, courts also generally do not have difficulty concluding the sales statute should apply, particularly where the software component can be characterized as being *incidental* to the hardware.[97] Moreover, there is even American authority for the proposition that the supply of existing software, without any hardware, should come within sales legislation — in the case of the United States, the *Uniform Commercial Code (UCC)*, even when the software was accompanied by customization services.[98] In these cases, courts are wrestling with the second dynamic of computer law, specifically the intangible nature of software. By focussing on the fact that software is distributed on a tangible media (e.g., a disk or a tape), these courts understood pre-existing software to be a widely distributed product, and hence they concluded that the "goods aspect" dominates in the case of a software purchase, particularly where services such as training are a small or incidental part of the transaction. The court in the *Advent* case stated that by bringing software sales under the purview of the *UCC*, it would be interpreting the *UCC* in light of commercial and technological developments.

By contrast, agreements solely for the provision of custom software development services have been held not to come within the purview of the *UCC*.[99] In the *Data Processing* case, there was no sale of hardware or even a sale of pre-existing software; rather, DPS was retained to design, develop, and implement a computer system to meet the customer's specific needs.[100] The court, in concluding that the *UCC* did not apply, held that the essential purpose of the contract was to obtain skill, knowledge, and ability, and not a product, not unlike a client seeking legal advice or

---

97   *Burroughs Business Machines Ltd.* v. *Feed-Rite Mills (1962) Ltd.* (1973), 42 D.L.R. (3d) 303 (Man. C.A.), appeal dismissed without reasons (1976), 64 D.L.R. (3d) 767 (S.C.C.) [*Burroughs*].

98   *Advent Systems Limited* v. *Unisys Corporation*, 925 F.2d 670 (3d Cir. 1991). See also *RRX Industries, Inc.* v. *Lab-Con, Inc.*, 772 F.2d 543 (9th Cir. 1985).

99   *Data Processing Services, Inc.* v. *L.H. Smith Oil Corporation*, 492 N.E.2d 314 (Ind. App. 1986) [*Data Processing*]; *Micro-Managers, Inc.* v. *Gregory*, 434 N.W.2d 97 (Wis. App. 1988) [*Micro-Managers*].

100 *Data Processing*, above note 99.

a patient obtaining medical treatment. The court acknowledged that a computer disk containing software did pass from DPS to the customer, but this was merely a device utilized to deliver the results of the services. In the *Micro-Managers* case it was also found to be an important factor that the supplier was paid on a time and materials basis, again indicating a strong services rather than product orientation.[101] It should be noted, however, that in the *Data Processing* case, in the absence of the *UCC* substantive rules applying, the court found the supplier liable under common law negligence for having provided substandard services. Similarly, in a recent controversial United Kingdom case, an appeal court judge concluded that even if the U.K. sales law did not apply to a software development project, an implied warranty that the software is capable of achieving its intended purpose would nevertheless be applicable under a negligence rule governing computer programming services.[102]

If the sales legislation applies, then, in the absence of an agreement to the contrary, several implied warranties and conditions will come to bear on the particular transaction.[103] One of them provides that if the seller is a merchant, and the goods are bought from a description given by the seller who deals in goods meeting the description, the supplier's products must be of a "merchantable quality," that is, suitable for their intended purposes. The second important implied warranty and condition provides that where a purchaser relies on the skill and knowledge of the seller, the seller has specific knowledge of the purpose to which the goods will be put at the purchaser's premises, and where the purchaser relies on the skill of the seller, then the supplier must deliver goods which are fit for their purpose. To be in effect, this implied warranty and condition requires that the supplier be informed of the specific requirements of the user. Thus, in one case, a supplier of a computer system was held not to be liable for failure of the system to perform a key function as the supplier was not apprised of the need for such a function by the user; the supplier was not told that the inventory management aspect of the business included a manufacturing component, something the supplier's system did not support.[104] In another

---

101   *Micro-Managers*, above note 99.

102   *St. Albans City and District Council* v. *International Computers Ltd.*, [1997] FSR 251 (C.A.).

103   The *UCC* only has implied warranties, while Canadian sales statutes have implied warranties and conditions: see *Gregorio*, above note 47. For a case that discusses the distinction between implied warranties and implied conditions, see *Michael's Pizzeria Ltd.* v. *LP Computer Solutions Inc. et al.* (1996), 433 A.P.R. 294 (P.E.I. S.C.).

104   *Saskatoon Gold Brokers Inc.* v. *Datatec Computer Systems Ltd.* (1986), 55 Sask. R. 241 (Q.B.).

case, a supplier was not found liable under the fitness for purpose warranty and condition when its optical disk drive device did not work properly with the other computer equipment of the buyer, because the buyer failed to communicate to the supplier what it needed the device for, and there was also a question whether the defect was the fault of the supplier's device.[105] By contrast, where the customer makes known to the supplier why the customer needs a particular software product, and the supplier's employee indicates that the software can meet this specific need, then the implied warranty and condition as to fitness for purpose will apply.[106] Indeed, this implied warranty and condition can apply even where the user has employees knowledgeable in computer matters, so long as there is reliance on the expertise of the supplier.[107]

Sales statutes also address the question when a buyer of goods is deemed to have accepted the goods, in the absence of a written agreement. This is important because once an item is accepted, the user is generally limited to money damages for any subsequent malfunctions in the item, where prior to acceptance the remedy of rescinding the sale agreement and receiving a full refund is still available. Sales statutes generally provide that acceptance can occur in one of three ways: the buyer indicates to the seller it has accepted the goods; the buyer does anything in relation to the goods inconsistent with the ownership of the seller; or after a reasonable time, the buyer retains the goods without indicating to the seller that they have been rejected. The application of

---

105   *Classified Directory Publishers Inc.* v. *Image Management Technologies Inc.*, [1995] O.J. No. 36 (Gen. Div.) (QL). In this case, the supplier's device provided secondary online storage, whereas the user needed primary online storage. The supplier, however, was not responsible for this mismatch because the court concluded at para. 31:

> The plaintiff chose the defendant's equipment without fully informing the defendant of the purpose to which it would be put and without sufficient expertise on its own part and without relying upon consultants which were available to it for that purpose. It has not been established that the failure of the system can be ascribed to the equipment supplied by the defendant. There is no evidence that it would be impossible to determine the reason for such a failure. The essential elements needed to invoke the warranty protection under section 15 have therefore not been established.

106   *Western Engineering Service Ltd.* v. *Canada Malting Co.*, [1994] O.J. No. 2026 (Gen. Div.) (QL). See also *Caul (W.J.) Funeral Home Ltd.* v. *Pearce* (1997), 475 A.P.R. 252 (Nfld. S.C.).

107   *Public Utilities Commission (Waterloo)* v. *Burroughs Business Machines Ltd.* (1974), 6 O.R. (2d) 257 (C.A.) [*Waterloo*]. In this case the supplier was liable because the employees of the customer, although generally knowledgeable about computers, did not have specific knowledge concerning the supplier's system.

these provisions to sophisticated computer systems can often be difficult. In one case, a court concluded a computer system was still not accepted after seven months.[108] In another case, a court found that the system was not accepted even fourteen months after its delivery to the buyer because it never worked properly, the computer system consisted of very complicated equipment and components, the supplier knew of the problems (and was working to correct them), and the customer needed to keep the supplier's poorly functioning system until it acquired a new one in order to mitigate its damages; hence, the buyer could still reject the system.[109] In a U.S. case, however, a buyer was held to be unable to argue the same position where it used the computer for nineteen months without intimating any problems to the seller.[110]

2) Limitations on Liability

Sales statutes are, for the most part, approximately one hundred years old. The original U.K. *Sale of Goods Act*, on which the Canadian common law provinces sales statutes are modelled, was intended to codify the law of sales related to the products pouring out of England's new industrial era factories of the mid- to late 1800s. It is not surprising, therefore, that in many respects the sales statutes are not well suited to the nuances involved in computer systems.[111] In effect, these are statutes covering the sale of tangible goods, and therefore do not expressly address issues related to the licensing of intangible software and information-based products. As a result, most suppliers of computing resources, in their contracts with customers, expressly disclaim all implied warranties and conditions. Also, because computers and software can be put to so many uses by purchasers, some entailing a high

---

108   *Burroughs*, above note 97.
109   *Waterloo*, above note 107.
110   *Softa Group, Inc. v. Scarsdale Development*, 5 Computer Cases (CCH) ¶47,055 at 66,304 (Ill. App. 1993).
111   It is for this reason that in the United States there is an effort underway to codify a "new" sales law in respect of software, which would address such issues as: applicability to mass market software; confirm enforceability of shrinkwrap licences; ability to assign and relocate licensed software; and software-related warranties and disclaimers on questions such as infringement, performance, protection against viruses and disabling routines: see Raymond T. Nimmer, "Article 2B [of the *UCC*] Meeting the Information Age," in *The Law of Computer Technology: Rights, Licenses, Liabilities* (Boston, Mass.: Warren, Gorham & Lamont, 1992) (looseleaf, updated) at Appendix SC-3 to 1996 Cumulative Supplement No. 3.

amount of risk — such as when a personal computer operates a large factory's automated processes — suppliers are also keen to provide a general limitation of their liability in the contract with the user, typically by capping their responsibility for direct damages at a certain dollar amount and excluding all other damages, especially lost profits or other consequential damages.[112] Even without such contractual-based limitations on liability, courts in a wide variety of situations have expressed an unwillingness to impose unlimited liability on the providers of information-related products and services, particularly for what courts call "pure economic loss."[113] In an early Canadian telegraph case, *Kinghorne* v. *The Montreal Telegraph Company*, the court noted that in some cases telegraph companies limit their liability through contract.[114] In the *Kinghorne* case, the telegraph company did not utilize this device, and still the court was willing to severely curtail its exposure, as the court was reluctant to visit the company with "ruinous damages" that might flow to a customer for a message not being delivered even though the telegraph company stood to gain such little revenue from sending the one message. The court stated that if a particular message is so important, the customer must bring that fact expressly to the attention of the telegraph company. In a more recent American case, the similar sentiment was expressed when the court failed to hold an online information service provider strictly liable for the accuracy of the content of its messages, as this "would open the doors 'to a liability in an indeterminate amount for an indeterminate time to an indeterminate class,'" to cite a phrase used in one of the judgments referred to in this case.[115]

A recent decision from British Columbia illustrates the judicial reluctance to award economic damages, in this case specifically in the context of a computer system. In *Seaboard Life Insurance Co.* v. *Babich*, the defendant hit a hydro pole with his truck causing minimal damage to the pole — it cost only $200 to fix the pole — but dislodging some step-down conductors that caused some wires to fall, with the result that power was disrupted for ninety minutes for about 1500 customers

112   For a thoughtful discussion of the distinction between direct and consequential damages in a computer contract context, see *Applied Data Processing, Inc.* v. *Burroughs Corporation*, 394 F. Supp. 504 (D. Conn. 1975).

113   In *Ontario (A. G.)* v. *Fatehi* (1984), 15 D.L.R. (4th) 132 (S.C.C.), the Supreme Court of Canada summarized "pure economic loss" as a diminution of worth incurred without any physical injury to any asset of the plaintiff.

114   (1859), 18 U.C.Q.B.R. 60 [*Kinghorne*].

115   *Daniel* v. *Dow Jones & Company Inc.*, 520 N.Y.S.2d 334 at 338 (N.Y. City Civ. Ct. 1987). This quote is originally found in *Ultramares Corporation* v. *Touche*, 174 N.E. 441 at 444 (N.Y. 1931).

of B.C. Hydro.[116] As a result, the plaintiff insurance company's computers were inoperable for about five hours, causing some loss of data. The plaintiff sued the defendant for the downtime of its employees and their loss of productivity. In light of those cases that have awarded damages for economic loss only where there is also some property damage, the plaintiff argued that its data (that was lost) should be characterized as property. The court disagreed and concluded:

> There may be contexts in which computer data will be held, in law, to constitute property. But for the purposes of distinguishing between pure economic loss and damage to property in the law of damages, I consider that it would simply be productive of confusion to treat the loss of the data as anything other than economic loss. In this case, the loss was purely economic. Some employees had to stand by until the computers were operational. Others had to spend some time checking them and "re-inputting" data. All, essentially, a matter of increasing the cost of doing business.[117]

This finding is reminiscent of the decision of the Supreme Court of Canada in *R. v. Stewart*, where the court held that confidential information cannot constitute property for purposes of the *Criminal Code*'s theft or fraud provisions.[118] The case also illustrates, once again, the second dynamic of computer law — namely, the elusive nature of information — and demonstrates, at a practical level, how important it is for users of computers to have adequate back-up and disaster recovery plans in place, including uninterruptible power supply systems, to help deal with a power outage or some other unforeseeable event that knocks out their computer systems.

That is not to say, however, that courts do not award damages in computer-related cases, because of course they do.[119] And because they do, suppliers try to limit their exposure contractually, as a government corporate name search agency did when its computers failed to perform adequately; the trial judge found the organization liable, but the appeal court reversed on the grounds that the arrangements under which the organization provided the service disclaimed the organization's

---

116 [1995] 10 W.W.R. 756 (B.C.S.C.).
117 *Ibid.* at 760.
118 (1988), 41 C.C.C. (3d) 481 (S.C.C.). This case is discussed in section B(1), "Theft," in chapter 3.
119 For a useful list of the types of damages that courts in Canada and elsewhere have awarded in computer-related litigation, see chapter 2, section 19(c) of Sookman, *Sookman Computer Law*, above note 95.

responsibility.[120] Indeed, courts will generally enforce these provisions in agreements between businesses, provided they are set out in clear and unambiguous language.[121] Moreover, such limit of liability clauses can also be used to deflect negligence claims that might otherwise be brought against the supplier by the user, given that tort and contract claims can be sustained simultaneously by the same facts.[122] If there is any ambiguity in the wording of the limitation or disclaimer, or if the court concludes that the supplier is in fundamental breach of its obligations under the contract, then courts may decline to enforce the exclusionary clauses.[123] As well, suppliers who merely disclaim "implied warranties," typically being affiliates of U.S. entities that only have implied warranties to contend with under the American *UCC*, can be rudely surprised when a court in Canada finds them liable under the implied conditions of Canadian sales statutes, given that, in contrast to the *UCC*, the Canadian sales statutes have both implied warranties and conditions.[124] It should also be noted that the implied warranties and conditions in the sales statutes cannot be disclaimed in the context of consumer sales, such as where personal computers are purchased for home use.[125] Indeed, where computer and information-based products are being sold to "consumers" (i.e., non-businesses), the consumer protection laws of each province in which sales are made need to be reviewed as they often contain specific rules regarding consumer warranties and other matters.

---

120   *R. v. 87118 Canada Ltd.* (1981), 56 C.P.R. (2d) 209 (F.C.A.).

121   *Hunter Engineering Co. v. Syncrude Canada Ltd.* (1989), 57 D.L.R. (4th) 321 (S.C.C.) [*Hunter*]; *Group West Systems Ltd. v. Werner's Refrigeration Co. Ltd.* (1988), 85 A.R. 82 (Q.B.) [*Group West Systems*]; but note that under Article 1474 of Quebec's *Civil Code*, one cannot limit liability with respect to gross fault.

122   *BG Checo International Ltd. v. British Columbia Hydro & Power Authority*, [1993] 2 W.W.R. 321 (S.C.C.); *Kinghorne*, above note 114; *Queen v. Cognos Inc.* (1993), 99 D.L.R. (4th) 626 (S.C.C.).

123   *Listo Products Ltd. v. Phillips Electronics Ltd.*, [1983] B.C.J. No. 432 (S.C.) (QL) [*Listo*]; *Hunter*, above note 121. In a number of cases, however, courts have upheld limit of liability provisions in contracts even where there has been a fundamental breach: see *Group West Systems*, above note 121, and *Fraser Jewellers (1982) Ltd. v. Dominion Electric Protection Co.* (1977), 34 O.R. (3d) 1 (C.A.).

124   See, for example, *Gregorio*, above note 47 at 207, where the court stated: "The express terms of the Peterbilt [truck maker] Warranty do not exclude the statutory conditions of fitness for a purpose and merchantable quality in s. 15. There is a difference between a breach of warranty and a breach of condition. Words that exclude only implied warranties do not also exclude implied conditions. Although a vendor may exclude the implied conditions contained in the *Sale of Goods Act*, he must use explicit language to do so."

125   See, for example, Ontario's *Consumer Protection Act*, R.S.O. 1990, c. C.31, s. 34. As well, under Article 1474 of Quebec's *Civil Code*, one cannot contract out of liability for gross fault.

3) Express Warranties

Given the practice of suppliers in the computer industry to disclaim implied warranties and conditions, and given the difficulty of applying these warranties and conditions to computer-related transactions even if they were not disclaimed, many users of computing resources provide for express warranties in their contracts with suppliers. These are often coupled with an acceptance test provision, as well as express remedies in favour of the user if these obligations are not met by the supplier. Provisions such as these can be beneficial to both the purchaser and supplier if they are evenhanded and the performance benchmarks in them are based on reasonable, objective criteria.[126] The *Listo* case illustrates well the unfortunate fate that can befall parties that do not provide for express warranties, acceptance tests, and remedies in a contract for the supply of computer equipment.[127] In this case, the supplier and its subcontractor bungled along for five years trying to install a computer system when a court finally put an end to the miserable tale by awarding judgment for fundamental breach against the supplier. Of course, one cannot really talk of a "winner" of such a lawsuit, since the user had by this point suffered excruciatingly, largely because it did not have the contractual means to bring to a speedy end a project that clearly was in dire straits soon after it began. By contrast, in the *Hawaiian Telephones* case the user had a series of express remedies that it brought to bear quickly upon non-performance by the supplier, thereby making the best of a bad situation.[128] Users must be very careful, however, in exercising remedies that purport to terminate contracts. In a number of cases, courts have recognized that computer technology is usually sophisticated, and complicated, and therefore suppliers should be afforded a reasonable period of time to fix bugs within the system. Thus, in the *Gerber Scientific* case, the trial court stated:

> In contracts for computer systems, especially complex ones, it is reasonable to contemplate start-up problems. The defendant's position presumes that the vendors installed a perfectly functioning system. This presumption does not reflect reality. Problems in a newly installed system are inevitable.[129]

---

126 For a discussion of reasonable, win-win computer contract clauses, see Takach, *Contracting*, above note 95.

127 *Listo*, above note 123. For a more recent example of the multiple problems that can scuttle a relationship between a software developer/system integrator and a client, see *Lalese Enterprises Inc. v. Arete Technologies Inc.* (1994), 59 C.P.R. (3d) 438 (B.C.S.C.).

128 *Hawaiian Telephone Co. v. Microform Data Systems, Inc.*, 829 F.2d 919 (9th Cir. 1987).

129 *Gerber Scientific Instrument Co. v. Bell-Northern Research Ltd.* (1991), 5 B.L.R. (2d) 20 at 29 (Ont. Gen. Div.) [*Gerber Scientific*], rev'd (1994), 17 B.L.R. (2d) 21 (Ont. C.A.).

Similarly, even when a user has the right to terminate a contract, it must exercise the provision with great care and with a clear, unambiguous notice, or else a court may find in favour of the supplier on the basis that the user terminated the agreement prematurely.[130]

4) The Y2K Problem

A key legal battlefield for the Y2K issue will be the contractual paperwork existing among the various parties to the dispute. There are a number of contracts that could be relevant. The supply agreement under which the hardware was sold or the software licensed may well contain express warranties or general statements or provisions that could have material legal implications. Phrases such as "our ABC system will meet your needs today and well into the next century" could have important ramifications if included in marketing proposals that are incorporated into the legal contracts. Maintenance agreements will be another critical form of documentation. What precisely are the support obligations being assured by contract? Does the service include fixing all bugs and errors in the software? Is the Y2K problem a bug? Most users would say so if the problem caused the system to crash or even to process data erroneously commencing 1 January 2000. Outsourcing agreements present similar questions. If an outsourcing vendor has committed to maintaining a series of legacy systems at 99.9 percent uptime, but there is no express mention of Y2K in the contract, is the outsourcing vendor responsible for ensuring, and paying for, such systems becoming Y2K compliant? Users, of course, will answer this question in the affirmative, arguing that no other particular problems or errors are enumerated in the agreement either, and yet the vendor is responsible if they cause the uptime benchmark not to be met. Vendors, on the other hand, will argue that the Y2K work is beyond the reasonable expectations that the parties had at the time they entered into the contract. Court decisions on issues such as this will be interesting reading!

Where a plaintiff is suffering damages, a basic principle of both negligence and contract law requires the plaintiff to take reasonable steps to minimize those damages. Accordingly, in the Y2K context this likely means that parties who are confronted with Y2K non-compliant systems cannot simply wait until 1 January 2000 and then watch their damages begin to run. They must take steps now to reduce both the likelihood of

---

130   *M.L. Baxter Equipment Ltd. v. Geac Canada Ltd.* (1982), 133 D.L.R. (3d) 372 (Ont. H.C.J.).

those damages occurring, and then attempt to keep those damages to a minimum. This means that if a user cannot convince a supplier to make a system previously supplied by the supplier Y2K compliant, the user should take its own steps to do so (or replace the system). The user, of course, would keep a record of its costs in taking these (or other measures), and then claim for recovery of these. Potential plaintiffs in Y2K cases also need to keep in mind the general legal rules regarding so-called limitation periods that in most cases provide that contract or negligence claims must be brought within six years after the date the plaintiff knew or ought to have known of the facts which gave rise to the claim.[131] This rule exists to avoid lawsuits that would have to rely on facts, recollections, and evidence that would be more than half a dozen years old. The six-year limitation period raises some interesting issues for Y2K-related claims. When, for example, does the period begin to run? Does the clock start when the Y2K non-compliant system is delivered to the user, given that at that point the user would know that it uses a two-digit date field? Or is it only later once the user understands the legal significance of the fact of Y2K non-compliance? Or is the start date for the limitation period 1 January 2000 (or possibly an earlier date in the case of some systems, as noted above), being the date that the system defect began to manifest actual operational problems for the user? The limitations question is further compounded by the fact that limitation periods commence in contract when the breach occurs and in negligence when damage occurs. On the latter point, what is damage in this context and when is it suffered?

Given the importance of the Y2K topic, a few additional points are worthy of mention. First, prudent users and suppliers should review a number of insurance-related questions regarding systems that may not be Y2K compliant. Careful attention must be paid to the kinds of damages that may arise, covering the spectrum from physical injury (for example, where a computerized medical device causes harm to a patient) to pure economic loss. Then a review of specific business interruption, third-party liability, errors and omissions, and other insurance policies must be undertaken to ascertain if the organization's insurance coverage is adequate to address the various risks. Insurance carriers may want to review their policies from a Y2K perspective in order to revise coverage wording in policies written before 1 January 2000.

Y2K legal concerns are real and sooner or later will become pressing for many participants in the information technology industry. Accordingly,

---

131 See, for example, the Ontario *Limitations Act*, R.S.O. 1990, c. L.15.

thinking about and *acting* on Y2K legal issues today may pay significant dividends in the future. Users should begin their Y2K legal activity the same way they did a technical audit to assess the extent of the Y2K problem facing them. The legal audit should review the agreements and other arrangements in place in Y2K-sensitive areas to determine the user's contractual and legal position. These activities would be followed by letters to suppliers inquiring as to their plans if it is not clear what the supplier has in mind in terms of making the systems Y2K compliant. Of course, in current and future contracts, express warranties regarding Y2K compliance should be added. Where suppliers indicate that they are not going to make the relevant system Y2K compliant, the user must make some difficult decisions about whether to repair or replace the system, etc., as noted above. Depending on the decision, and after a careful review of relevant limitation period issues, it may be prudent to put the supplier on notice about the claim the user believes it has against the supplier, all the while taking steps to mitigate damages by using cost effective means to fix the Y2K problem. There may also be difficulties encountered in taking steps to fix the problem, such as where the user does not have access to the necessary source code for the Y2K non-compliant system. In such circumstances, again the user would be well advised to put the supplier on notice sooner rather than later. If the necessary solution for fixing the Y2K problem entails retaining a third party to help with the conversion activity, further complications may arise, such as the underlying licence agreement not permitting third parties to have access to the relevant software. There are also contracts to be drawn up with the service provider that would address, possibly, price protection and the assignment of specific people to the user's project, provisions that may prove to be useful as the rate of Y2K activity picks up in the next few months.

Suppliers should also be considering a number of possible current Y2K activities. Again, the starting point is probably an internal review of some sort to determine the extent of Y2K non-compliance within the various products of the company. And not only current releases or versions of products should come under scrutiny. What about older models or releases? If the supplier is currently fully Y2K compliant, from when has it enjoyed this status and what about products shipped before such date? From this technical/product review should flow the review of contracts, particularly maintenance agreements, as these will be especially important for determining the company's legal position vis-à-vis Y2K issues. A series of related questions will then follow naturally. Should contracts be revised going forward? Depending on the technical environment the supplier operates in, does it need to be said expressly in the contract that while the supplier's systems are Y2K compliant, the supplier takes no responsibility for users using the system with other products or data that are not so compliant? Moreover, even where a supplier is Y2K compliant there are often important details as to how this compliance is effected and tested for. Thus, the supplier may well consider it prudent to send out a standard communication to all clients informing them about Y2K issues as it affects them as users of the system. As with users, some time and effort invested in the Y2K issue up front will result in important rewards later down the road.

Finally, all companies with potential liability would do well not to create an internal record of admissions of liability. Sometimes in litigation, internal memoranda appear which seemingly admit legal liability or blame where none may exist. Courts are more likely to conclude that there is a breach of a standard of care where a defendant said so in its own records. Hence, corporate records should reflect proper concern about the Y2K issue and due diligence in response to the issue but should not admit obligation or fault. Organizations should also remember that e-mails are as durable as paper-based communications, and therefore great care and discretion should be exercised in reducing Y2K communications to e-mail or paper-based memos.

F. TECHNOLOGY LICENCES UPON BANKRUPTCY

Several questions arise when a licensee, or especially a licensor, of technology goes bankrupt. These questions are particularly important because of the nature of software licences. As noted in section C(4), "Dependency on Computers," in chapter 1, virtually all businesses, governments, and other organizations have become reliant on licensed software. It would be devastating if, upon a bankruptcy of the licensors of such software, the users were to lose the right of continued use of the software. Yet such a possibility cannot be dismissed — the question has not yet been decided in Canada. Another view, however, holds that Canadian bankruptcy law should not be interpreted to afford such a result. By contrast, the amendments to the *Bankruptcy and Insolvency Act* (*BIA Act*) in 1992 make quite clear the rights of technology licensors when their licensees file a proposal under the *BIA Act*.[132]

---

132 *Bankruptcy and Insolvency Act*, R.S.C. 1985, c. B-3, as amended. Prior to 1992, this statute was the *Bankruptcy Act*.

1) Bankruptcy of Licensor

The uncertainty in Canadian bankruptcy law as to the ability of a licensee of technology to continue to use it upon a bankruptcy of the licensor arises, ironically, because of subsection 365(a) of the U.S. Bankruptcy Code.[133] This permits a trustee who is vested with the property of the debtor upon a bankruptcy to reject "executory contracts," contracts that contain ongoing obligations of the licensor. This ability on the part of a trustee in the United States to reject executory contracts led a court to conclude in the *Lubrizol* case that the trustee for a bankrupt licensor of metal-coating process technology could disclaim all the debtor's non-exclusive licences in order to improve the terms of sale of the technology to another company from the bankrupt licensor.[134] The result in *Lubrizol* was that the licensee lost its rights to work the technology. The harsh result of the *Lubrizol* decision led to the addition of paragraph 365(1)(n) to the U.S. *Bankruptcy Act*, which provides that if a trustee disclaims an intellectual property licence, the user may nevertheless affirm the licence, in which case the user can continue to use it in return for giving up the right to sue for any damages from the bankrupt estate.[135] Some observers in Canada of the *Lubrizol* case have commented that a trustee in bankruptcy in Canada could come to the same result as in that U.S. case, with a devastating result given that no equivalent to paragraph 365(1)(n) of the U.S. statute exists in the Canadian one. Thus, some users insist that in source code escrow agreements (an arrangement whereby a neutral party, such as a trust company, holds the source code version of a supplier's product in order to make it available to a user upon the bankruptcy or other default of the supplier, but until such release keeping the important confidential information out of the hands of users), the supplier sell title in a copy of the source code to the trustee to try to get it out of the estate of the supplier upon any bankruptcy. This is a very dangerous practice for the supplier given that any related restrictions on the trustee may not be enforceable. It is open to question, however, whether the concern generated in Canada over the *Lubrizol* case is entirely warranted, for a number of reasons.

---

133   *Bankruptcy Reform Act of 1978*, 11 U.S.C.A. 101.

134   *Lubrizol Enterprises, Inc. v. Richmond Metal Finishers, Inc.*, 756 F.2d 1043 (4th Cir. 1985) [*Lubrizol*].

135   In an early case involving para. 365(1)(n) of the U.S. *Bankruptcy Act* and Ontario Hydro, the software licensee, the court held that the extent of the claims are to be determined by U.S. bankruptcy law and not Ontario law (the law provided for in the relevant software licence agreement): *Re EI International, Debtor*, 123 B.R. 64 (Bankr. D. Idaho 1991).

First, most software licences are not all that executory in nature. In *Lubrizol* the main factor that made it executory from the licensor's perspective was that, involving a licence for a metal coating product (and not a software licence), the licensor had undertaken a duty to inform the licensee if it granted a third party better licence terms, and then such more favourable terms had to be granted to the original licensee. These sorts of provisions are quite rare in commercial software arrangements involving off-the-shelf products. Similarly, the licensee's primary ongoing activity in *Lubrizol* was to pay the licensor royalties; again, most software licences involve a single, lump sum payment, so this is yet another factor by which to distinguish *Lubrizol*. Most importantly, the court in *Lubrizol* focussed on the specific wording in the U.S. bankruptcy statute to permit the disclaimer by the bankruptcy trustee. As noted below, however, the *BIA Act* does not contain such a general provision. Thus, a court in Canada, if faced with the question whether a trustee in bankruptcy can disclaim the software licences granted prior to the bankruptcy of a Canadian software company, may not follow the *Lubrizol* case and instead might follow the decision in the *Erin Features* case.[136]

In *Erin Features*, a trustee in bankruptcy brought a motion to disclaim an agreement in which the debtor had previously granted exclusive marketing rights in a film to a distributor. The court refused to grant the motion, concluding that the "property rights" conveyed to the distributor cannot subsequently be disturbed by the trustee. While the court in this case reached the right conclusion, the reasoning in the case may be open to some criticism given that it is not clear that the grant of even exclusive marketing rights conveys a property interest. Nonetheless, there are several other reasons why the same result should occur again if similar facts present themselves. First, as opposed to the U.S. and U.K.[137] bankruptcy statutes, which contain express provisions allowing trustees to disclaim executory contracts, no similar general right exists in the *BIA Act*.[138] Second, paragraph 30(1)(k) of the *BIA Act* does address when a trustee can disclaim contracts, namely, allowing a

---

136   *Re Erin Features #1 Ltd.* (1991), 8 C.B.R. (3d) 205 (B.C.S.C.) [*Erin Features*].

137   *Insolvency Act 1986* (U.K.), 1986, c. 45, s. 315.

138   For example, the Canadian case *Stead Lumber Company Limited v. Lewis* (1957), 37 C.B.R. 24 (Nfld. S.C.), cites *Halsbury's Laws of England* for authority that a trustee in bankruptcy can disclaim certain executory contracts. These references to *Halsbury's* in turn rely on provisions in the United Kingdom's then prevailing bankruptcy statute. Thus, it is open to question how relevant this case is to an analysis of the current Canadian bankruptcy legislation.

bankrupt lessee to disclaim real property leases or similar contracts. Accordingly, in Canada a correct conceptual analysis of the rights of trustees in respect of technology licences would be that, except as otherwise provided by statute, a trustee receives the same quality of title in the debtor's estate as was enjoyed by the debtor. A trustee in bankruptcy for a software company, for example, should acquire the intellectual property rights in the software subject to the licences granted prior to the bankruptcy. Incidentally, this produces an extremely just result, as the same situation would have come to pass had the assets of the software company been sold while the company was still solvent.

2) Bankruptcy of Licensee

Where a trustee for a bankrupt technology company may be interested in terminating the previous licences granted by the company, the trustee for a bankrupt company that is the licensee of various technologies has just the opposite objective. It wants to ensure that the tenure that the bankrupt estate has in the technology, such as a software licence, continues. In this regard, where the insolvent licensee wishes to make a proposal under the *BIA Act*, which then allows the company to attempt to restructure its affairs and avoid bankruptcy, section 65.1 of the *BIA Act* makes it clear that licences for intellectual property rights — such as software licences — cannot be terminated by the licensor for failure to make past payments. The licensor can, however, insist on being paid currently for future obligations, such as software maintenance services, and if there is a failure to pay these amounts then the licence can be terminated. By contrast, where there is a bankruptcy (and not just a proposal), many software licences will provide that the agreement is terminated by such an event. The enforceability of such a provision will likely turn on how the agreement is construed. Was a property right conveyed by the licence, or was it simply a bare bones licence to use the particular software?

A similar issue arises in respect of the ability of the trustee in bankruptcy to deal with the licence in a manner that was not available to the prebankrupt debtor. For example, trustees in bankruptcy often purport to sell or assign software or other intellectual properties that are licensed to the bankrupt on a non-assignable basis. In effect, however, a trustee should only acquire such rights as the debtor itself had in the licensed material. Thus, a licensor should be able to stop a trustee from transferring the intellectual property to a third party where the debtor did not have this right in the first place. Indeed, this point is buttressed by the discussion in section C(1), "Why Software and Content Are

Licensed," in this chapter that explained that a software licence generally does not convey to the licensee (and hence does not convey to the trustee in bankruptcy upon the licensee's bankruptcy) a property interest; rather, the licence is merely a contractual-based permission to do something that otherwise would not be permitted. Thus, in the absence of a specific clause in the licence agreement to the contrary, the trustee in bankruptcy for the licensee's estate should not be able to deal with the software for purposes of transferring it.

There may be an exception to this rule if the software licence is silent on assignment, in which case, depending on all the facts of the situation, it may be argued that it is an implied term of the contract that it be able to be assigned, at least to a purchaser of the assets of the original licensee's business. Of course, this raises the point that licensees, when negotiating the terms of their licence agreements, should be careful to ensure that the software can be assigned at least to an entity that purchases all or substantially all of the assets of the licensee, or at least intends to carry on the licensee's business, as discussed.[139] Where a licensee fails to achieve this flexibility, however, the bankruptcy law should not be interpreted to afford such rights to trustees in bankruptcy.

G. TAX ISSUES

The marketing, licensing, and sale of computer software and other information-based products presents the tax system with numerous challenges. The intangible nature of these items and the many ways they can be supplied to the end user often make the exercise of applying tax laws to them akin to putting the proverbial square peg in the round hole. This is illustrated by the treatment afforded software under provincial retail sales tax legislation, as well as by the manner in which the withholding tax provisions of the *Income Tax Act* (*IT Act*) have been historically applied to software licence payments.[140] Applying tax laws in the Internet environment also raises some novel questions. In each of these areas the four dynamics of computer law are quite evident. There are, of course, other tax issues germane to the computer industry, such as the important research and experimental development tax credit regime in the *IT Act* and various other tax-related measures relevant to the funding of computer-based innovation activity, but these are

---

139   See section C(1), "Why Software and Content are Licensed," in this chapter.
140   *Income Tax Act*, R.S.C. 1985, c. 1 (5th Supp.), as amended.

beyond the purview of this short section.[141] The diversity of tax issues relevant to computers and networks can also be seen from a recent case that determined that a community-based "freenet" in Vancouver could qualify for tax purposes as a charity.[142]

1) Software and Sales Tax

Most provincial sales tax statutes provide for a tax to be levied on the sale of items of tangible personal property.[143] Two immediate issues are raised by such statutory language in the context of software and other information-based assets. First, is software sold? Second, is software tangible personal property? Both questions require negative answers, at least on a liberal reading of the statute. Thus, in the *Telecheque* case, a court concluded that operating system software and application software licensed under software licences were not tangible personal property under British Columbia's *Social Service Tax Act*.[144] In this case the taxpayer, as part of a sale of its entire business, sold hardware, software, and data pursuant to a sale agreement that listed these items separately and allocated a portion of the total purchase price to each of them. The minister of finance, in a manner reminiscent of the sales legislation cases where installations of hardware and software were treated as a single "good,"[145] argued that the hardware, software, and data made up a single bundle of assets all subject to tax. The court disagreed, concluding that the data/information component represented "experience" and was separate from the computer (i.e., the business could have used this information in a manual mode), and similarly the hardware was separate from the software as the former would have value by having some other software operated on it (i.e., the software was not so intimately linked to the hardware as to constitute one object).

A provincial taxing authority wishing to realize tax revenues from the burgeoning information sector, however, may focus on the fact that

---

141   For an accessible overview of the R&D tax rules, see Karen Wensley & Irene J. David, "Income Tax and GST Considerations for Software Companies," in George S. Takach, *The Software Business*, 2d ed. (Toronto: McGraw-Hill Ryerson, 1997). It should be noted that tax rules are constantly changing, and entities affected by such rules need to stay constantly abreast of developments in these matters.

142   *Vancouver Regional FreeNet Assn.* v. *M.N.R.* (1996), 137 D.L.R. (4th) 206 (F.C.A.).

143   See, for example, Ontario's *Retail Sales Tax Act*, R.S.O. 1990, c. R.31.

144   *Continental Commercial Systems Corporation (Telecheque Canada)* v. *R.*, [1982] 5 W.W.R. 340 (B.C.C.A.) [*Telecheque*].

145   See section E(1), "Implied Warranties and Conditions," in this chapter.

most software transactions involve the supply of a physical diskette or CD-ROM on which the intangible software is resident. This would then allow them to tax the physical item, based on the value of the intangible information it contained. This was the result in the *Kia-Ora Video* case where the sale of videotapes was found to be the sale of tangible personal property, much like the sale of a book.[146] In this case the taxpayer, in reliance on the *Telecheque* decision, argued that the movie content portion of the videos was intangible and therefore should not be subject to tax. The court disagreed, holding that the price of the videos was not allocated among different components, as was the case in the *Telecheque* case. As well, the court found that each of the software and hardware in *Telecheque* could be used separately, whereas in the case of a videocassette, the physical tape and the content were one indivisible unit. In a subsequent case, the court struggled with the question whether customized application software provided to operate with telephone switching equipment should be subject to Newfoundland's retail sales tax.[147] In a confusing judgment, the court ultimately found the software to be a taxable product, though the court seemed to concede that some software may be capable of being acquired in a non-taxable form.

In an attempt to avoid questions such as these, Ontario recently amended its *Retail Sales Tax Act* to expressly cover computer programs under the definition of "tangible personal property."[148] This statutory amendment continues the previous policy of treating off-the-shelf software as a good and subject to provincial sales tax. Under the new statutory rules, custom software developed to meet the specific requirements of the initial purchaser is non-taxable as it is considered a service rather than a good. Under the previous policy, however, pre-existing software subject to a written licence agreement was also exempt from tax, but this is no longer the case under the new law.

The federal government makes a distinction between off-the-shelf software, and all other software, for purposes of various collection procedures related to the federal Goods and Services Tax.[149] Under Revenue

---

146   *Re Kia-Ora Video Ltd.* (1984), 56 B.C.L.R. 242 (Co. Ct.).

147   *Newfoundland Telephone Co. v. Newfoundland (A.G.)* (1992), 43 C.P.R. (3d) 40 (Nfld. S.C.).

148   *An Act to stimulate job growth, to reduce taxes and to implement other measures* contained in the 1997 budget (Bill 129), S.O. 1997, c. 10, subs. 30(3), received royal assent 26 June 1997.

149   See Revenue Canada, GST Technical Information Bulletin B-037R, "Imported Computer Software," 1 November 1994; and Customs Memorandum D13-11-6, "Determining Value for Duty of Computer Software," 2 July 1997.

Canada's current policy, prepackaged off-the-shelf software marketed with a shrinkwrap licence is treated as tangible personal property. If such software is delivered to the Canadian user from outside of Canada, the user acts as the importer for purposes of paying the GST at the time of importation. In contrast, all other software is treated as custom software, is categorized as the supply of intangible personal property, and is considered to be supplied to the user's premises in Canada regardless of how and where it was actually delivered, even if transmitted to the user electronically. Accessing an online computer by means of a modem is considered to be the supply of a service, not of personel property.

2) Software and Withholding Tax

The application to software-related payments of Canada's withholding tax provision in the *IT Act* represents a rich and varied tale driven by a number of seemingly unconnected factors, such as whether software is protected by copyright, whether there is a one-time payment or running royalties, the nature of the particular media on which the software is resident, and how the software is distributed in this country. The core withholding tax provision is set out in paragraph 212(1)(d)(i) of the *IT Act*, which requires persons in Canada to deduct and remit to Ottawa a 25 percent withholding tax on rental or royalty payments for the use or right to use in Canada any property, invention, trade-name, patent, or similar property right. In the *Saint John Shipbuilding* case in the mid-1970s, it was held that one-time, lump sum licence fee payments are not caught by these withholding tax provisions.[150] In this case the court found that a "rental" denoted a payment that was applicable for a limited term, and that "royalties" were payments calculated in reference to use or production from property or from profits; the court held that a lump sum payment for the right to use software for an indefinite term did not fall into either of these categories. It should be noted, however, that various bilateral tax treaties between Canada and other countries, which generally reduce the 25 percent withholding tax rate to 10 percent, have been amended over time to include language broader than that in the *IT Act* withholding tax provision, with the result that Revenue Canada now takes the view that lump sum licence fees, of the kind exempted in the *Saint John Shipbuilding* case, are covered by the 10 percent withholding tax obligation. Also, however, several of these bilateral treaties, such as those with the United States and the Netherlands, have

---

150   *R. v. Saint John Shipbuilding & Dry Dock Co. Ltd.*, 80 D.T.C. 6272 (F.C.A.) [*Saint John Shipbuilding*].

been amended to completely exclude from withholding tax payments in respect of software.

An important exemption from the withholding tax is found in paragraph 212(1)(d)(vi) of the *IT Act*, which provides that the tax is not payable in respect of the reproduction of copyright. Originally intended to cover situations such as the printing and distribution in Canada of foreign-owned books, there have always been several nagging doubts about its applicability to software. First there was the question, in the 1970s and early 1980s, whether copyright covered software. This question was resolved definitively in 1988 with the insertion of computer program into the *Copyright Act* as a protectable work. On the other hand, Revenue Canada does not allow the exemption to end users of software, taking the view that an end user's act of copying is merely incidental to its use of the product. Rather, Revenue Canada is of the view that "right to produce" means, essentially, putting the copies made by the distributor into the stream of commerce. The typical beneficiary of this provision is the distributor that is given a master copy of the product and the associated rights to produce copies in Canada for further distribution.

3) Taxing the Internet

The Internet raises several taxation issues, primarily as a result of the second and fourth dynamics of computer law. The elusive nature of information causes the Internet to pose similar tax categorization questions as discussed earlier in this section, but even more tellingly because a number of information-based products — text, sound, music, graphics, all sorts of digital content — can now be transmitted over the Internet. A key question is whether the particular transaction should be characterized as a sale of a product, a licensing of an intangible, or the provision of a service. Things are simple to define in the physical world. For example, the sale of a copy of a newspaper is a sale of a good. Accessing the same newspaper content online raises the questions whether the essence of the transaction is still the sale of a product, or is it now more reasonable to refer to the essence of the deal being the licensing of intellectual property (particularly if search software accompanies the content), or is it the provision of a service (especially if the newspaper is but one database that can be accessed from the information service supplier's website). And these characterizations matter in some jurisdictions, such as in Europe where value-added tax would apply, for example, to a purchase of a physical disk containing software, but would not if the non-European software company transmitted the software to the European customer over the Internet.[151] Most tax laws have origins in an environment of manufactured physical goods, and the digital ether created by the Internet does not mesh well with such a tax regime.

In addition to the dephysicalization challenge posed by digitization, the tax laws have to cope with the fourth dynamic of computer law, the blurring of national/international. This issue pre-dates the Internet, since the general increase in mobility and international commerce has seen capital, people, technology and even production capacity move offshore for a number of years. This issue occurs, too, in distance selling through mail-order and catalogue operations and is exacerbated by the ability of the Internet to reach customers globally. In the United States, state tax authorities are quite concerned about tax erosion. The concern arises because of the decision in the *Quill* case, in which the U.S. Supreme Court concluded that a state cannot require an out-of-state mail-order house to collect tax on its sales made to residents of the state where the vendor did not have a physical outlet or sales representatives in the state.[152] Interestingly, the court below took the opposite view, partly on the basis that given the new computer technologies used by such vendors, it would no longer be a significant burden for them to collect and remit taxes for multiple states; this was long one of the rationales for not making them subject to various tax regimes (i.e., it was simply too difficult to comply). The U.S. Supreme Court, however, did not agree. In coming to its conclusion, the court noted that the "due process" clause of the U.S. constitution no longer was an impediment to imposing sales tax on non-resident vendors, because clearly they had sufficient contacts with the state; this is consistent with the general trend in the non-tax Internet jurisdiction cases discussed in section C(2), "Jurisdiction," in chapter 6. The court, however, held that the "substantial nexus" required by the U.S. constitution's commerce clause (that bans state actions that impede or place a burden on interstate commerce) required more than the communication and other links found sufficient for the purposes of the due process clause; that is, the court decided to maintain the "physical presence" rule, largely it seems because it provides a clear demarcation line that businesses could easily understand and then factor into their operational plans.

---

151   Elaine Erickson and Michael Loten, "On-Line Transactions Blur Goods vs. Services Distinction for VAT Purposes," *High-Tech Industry*, November/December 1996.

152   *Quill Corp. v. North Dakota*, 504 U.S. 298 (1992).

The amount of physical presence in a U.S. state required to meet the *Quill* test as articulated in subsequent decisions, however, does not have to be significant. For example, in one recent case, a company that sold computers by mail order to residents of New York state also sent employees into the state on occasion to provide installation, training, and error correction services.[153] These minimal contacts were sufficient for the court to uphold the state government's right to require the company to collect and remit New York state sales tax. What has state and other tax authorities particularly worried, however, is that in an Internet environment even these services can be provided online, thereby obviating the need for any physical presence in the state that wishes to levy sales tax. Similarly, in the context of income tax, many jurisdictions have adopted, in their bilateral tax treaties, the concept that they will not consider income to be sourced in their jurisdiction, and hence will not levy tax, unless the entity has a "permanent establishment" in the jurisdiction. The permanent establishment concept, however, has always had a physical orientation, and its application in an Internet environment is made much more problematic. For instance, does a Canadian company have a permanent establishment in the United States when it contractually agrees to have a U.S. company load the Canadian company's valuable database onto a server at the U.S. company's premises, from which server the U.S. company will provide access to its subscribers around the world and pay the Canadian company a royalty in respect of such exploitation?[154]

These questions are causing a number of tax authorities to assess their legal regimes in light of the Internet.[155] There is even talk of a "bit tax," which would not tax products or services but rather the transmission of data itself. This suggestion has been criticized, but the very fact that it has been advanced indicates the degree to which certain taxing authorities consider the Internet to be a threat to critical tax revenues.[156]

---

153   *Orvis Company, Inc., v. Tax Appeals Tribunal of the State of New York*, 654 N.E.2d 954 (N.Y. 1995).

154   For a general discussion of these and related Internet tax conundrums, see James D. Cigler, Harry C. Burritt & Susan E. Stinnett, "Cyberspace: The Final Frontier for International Tax Concepts?" (1996) 7 J. of Int. Tax. 340.

155   Richard G. Cohen & Paul Terry, "Online Taxation Issues Undergo Federal Scrutiny" *The National Law Journal* (5 May 1997).

156   Organization for Economic Co-operation and Development, *Electronic Commerce: Opportunities and Challenges for Government (The "Sacher Report")* (Paris: OECD, 1997). This is a short but useful conspectus of a wide range of issues related to electronic commerce, including questions pertaining to commercial (including tax), security, infrastructure, social, and cultural questions.

Indeed, the Clinton administration, in a wide-ranging report titled *A Framework for Global Electronic Commerce*, proposed that no new taxes be imposed on Internet commerce.[157] As for existing taxes, this report notes that the U.S. government wants to ensure that any taxation of commerce over the Internet avoids double taxation, and that any taxation of Internet sales follow these principles:

- It should neither distort nor hinder commerce. No tax system should discriminate among types of commerce, nor should it create incentives that will change the nature or location of transactions.
- The system should be simple and transparent. It should be capable of capturing the overwhelming majority of appropriate revenues, be easy to implement, and minimize burdensome record keeping and costs for all parties.
- The system should be able to accommodate tax systems used by the United States and our international partners today.[158]

In the coming years it will be interesting to see just how well these principles are applied to the Internet. Frankly, given the complexity of tax rules in the physical world, it would be surprising if any "simple and transparent" system could be developed as the core tax regime for the Internet.

H. OTHER ISSUES

The foregoing discussion in this chapter has covered a broad range of commercial issues. Two more are worth noting — international trade law and labour law. Neither topic is primarily related to computing and network technologies. Nonetheless, the important economic role of computer technology and the large international market for buying and selling these products (about 10 percent of all international trade) make several legal issues relevant. In labour law, the significant impact of

---

157   President William J. Clinton & Vice President Albert Gore, Jr., *A Framework for Global Electronic Commerce* (Washington, D.C.: White House, 1997). This paper, which contains the U.S. Administration's views on a broad range of topics, such as financial (including customs, taxation, and electronic payment), legal (including a *UCC* for electronic commerce, intellectual property, privacy, and security), and market access (including telecommunications infrastructure and information technology, content, and technical standards) matters, is available at <http://www.ljx.com/internet/ecommframe.html>.

158   *Ibid.* at 4–5.

computing technologies in the workplace requires a brief survey of legal questions. And in both these areas several of the four dynamics of computer law are busily at work.

1) International Trade

One international trade issue that illustrates the first dynamic of computer law involves the customs classification process whereby new products have to be slotted into existing tariff classifications in order to determine the rate of duty to be paid upon the importation into Canada of the particular product. As with all categorization exercises involving the computer industry, the hazard here is that often the authorities are being asked to fit square pegs into round holes. In one case, computerized branch exchanges (CBX) were imported, which are small digital telephone switches that also contain a computerized call tracking function so that businesses and organizations that install these systems in their offices can keep track of calling patterns by employees.[159] The Tariff Board, the agency that heard appeals from the decisions of the Department of National Revenue, determined that the CBX product should come under the category of electric telephone apparatus because its primary function was telecommunications, and its data processing capability was only an ancillary feature. The Federal Court of Appeal overturned this decision and concluded instead that the proper tariff category was electronic data processing machines. The court reasoned that the word "telephone" related only to the transmission of sound and voices, whereas the CBX product was used to transmit data as well, and also that there was a distinction between "electronic" and "electric" that, although not apparent from the decision, favoured treating the CBX product as electronic rather than electric.[160] The decision of the court is less than satisfying, but the importer appreciated it because the tariff rate on data processing equipment (about 3.9 percent) has traditionally been lower than for telephone equipment (17.5 percent). This area of the law has witnessed a number of instances where the language in the government regulations has not kept pace with technological developments, again illustrating the first dynamic of computer law.

---

159 *IBM Canada Ltd. v. Deputy M.N.R., Customs and Excise*, [1992] 1 F.C. 663 (C.A.).

160 For a similar determination in favour of finding computerized telecommunications equipment to be data processing rather than telephone equipment, see *General Datacomm Ltd. v. Deputy M.N.R. (Customs and Excise)* (1984), 9 T.B.R. 78 (T. Bd.).

As a result of a number of international trade agreements, there is less opportunity for arbitrage among different tariff categories because the tariffs on most computer (and telecommunications) products are being reduced over time. Since the Second World War, most of the industrialized countries, and even the less developed ones, have participated in successive rounds of tariff reduction under the *General Agreement on Tariffs and Trade* (GATT), and since 1995, the World Trade Organization (WTO). Regional free trade agreements, such as the 1989 *Canada–U.S. Free Trade Agreement* (FTA) and the 1994 *North American Free Trade Agreement* among Canada, the United States, and Mexico (NAFTA), also provided for the elimination of tariffs on a wide range of goods, either immediately or during a phase-out schedule over several years.[161] For example, under the FTA, duties on computers and central office switching telephone equipment were eliminated on 1 January 1989, provided the products qualified under the FTA's complex but useful "rules of origin" as being either Canadian or American in origin. Most recently, forty countries under the auspices of the WTO have agreed to eliminate customs duties on many high-technology products by the year 2000, including computers, telecom equipment (which, interestingly in light of the *IBM* decision noted in the previous paragraph, includes switching apparatus and modems), semiconductors, semiconductor manufacturing equipment, software and scientific instruments, but not consumer electronic goods.[162] There are four stages of tariff reduction of 25 percent each, commencing on 1 July 1997 and on each January 1 thereafter until 1 January 2000. This will benefit Canadian importers of telecommunications products from certain non–North American countries and, more importantly, will be a boon to Canadian exporters of high-tech goods since tariffs are as high as 50 percent on these products in many developing countries.

Although governments have largely given up the tariff as a means of protecting domestic industry, they have discovered other mechanisms — non-tariff barriers to trade — to assist companies within their juris-

---

161   For an overview of the NAFTA generally, see Jon R. Johnson, *The North American Free Trade Agreement: A Comprehensive Guide* (Aurora, Ont.: Canada Law Book, 1994), and for a treatment of the NAFTA specifically from the perspective of the computer industry, see Barry B. Sookman, *North American Free Trade Agreement and Computers: A Summary,* presented to the Fourth Annual Significant Developments in Computer Law Conference sponsored by The University of Dayton School of Law, Program in Law and Technology, 11 June 1993.

162   WTO, "Elimination of Tariffs on Computer Products By Year 2000 Agreed," *Focus Newsletter,* No. 17, March 1997.

dictions. One such method, particularly in the high-tech sector, is government procurement, since governments purchase huge volumes of computers, software, and related services. In 1981 a number of GATT members agreed to a set of rules contained in the *Government Procurement Code* that was aimed at reducing discrimination against foreign suppliers. This agreement was augmented and superseded by the WTO's *Government Procurement Agreement*, as well as by government procurement provisions in trade agreements such as the FTA and NAFTA. For contracts above a certain dollar value, governments must put the tender out to competitive bid and cannot devise the tender criteria to favour one supplier over another. This rule is especially important in the computer sector where specifications for a tender can easily be skewed to favour a particular vendor. Sometimes, however, tender requirements that might seem unfair can be found to be reasonable, as in an American case that held that the U.S. government could specify a certain software operating system for handheld computers based on past procurements and the necessity to have interoperability.[163] And, of course, in awarding these contracts, the government cannot favour domestic suppliers, but must base its decision solely on the neutral criteria set out in the tender request. The NAFTA also implemented a bid protest mechanism whereby disgruntled parties can request the Canadian International Trade Tribunal (CITT) to investigate (but not reverse) questionable tender situations. This mechanism has been used with positive results in several high-tech procurements, but bidders wishing to use this vehicle must do so quickly; complaints must be lodged with the CITT within ten days of learning of the bases for the complaints.[164]

2) Labour Law

The computer revolution has changed the nature of the workplace. Information technology has become a fixture in the factory as well as at the office. Computers have raised a cluster of labour law issues in the contexts of union and non-union employment environments. A critic of computerization lists the labour movement's concerns with the microchip as follows:

---

163   *Integrated Systems Group, Inc.* v. *Department of the Army*, Guide to Computer Law, New Developments (CCH) ¶60,446 at 81,580 (1993).

164   The rules on government procurement bid protests before the CITT are set out in the *North American Free Trade Agreement Procurement Inquiry Regulations*, SOR/93-602, 15 December 1993.

- job loss: last century the industrial revolution's factories absorbed the displaced agricultural workers; after the second world war, the service sector absorbed the displaced factory workers; this cycle will not continue with workers displaced by the computer;
- job degradation: the computer takes over the more interesting tasks associated with a job;
- electronic monitoring: terribly stress-inducing as each keystroke is recorded by management;
- loss of job mobility: lower-level employees cannot move into middle management because the role of middle managers to collect and aggregate information is now performed by computers;
- increase in part-time work: as information is stored in computers rather than in brains, fewer full-time staff are needed to serve as the institutional memory of an organization;
- health hazards from video display terminals: carpal tunnel syndrome, pain in the hand and wrist, and musculoskeletal conditions could be added to this category;
- telecommuting: by keeping workers at home, connected to the office by computers and networks, management can facilitate the break-up of unions or prevent them from organizing;
- an adverse impact on women: many of the above concerns fall disproportionately on women.[165]

Of course, each microchip has two sides, and there is a counter-argument to most of these points. Job loss, for example, is contentious because it is not at all clear that the economy, on a macro level, is unable to generate the necessary number of new jobs; indeed, thousands of high-tech jobs are currently unfilled.[166] Nevertheless, at a micro level workers have been displaced by technology, and for many older workers made redundant by the computer it is little consolation that the firm has hired young computer programmers to maintain the overall employment level. In many unionized environments the method by which new technology is introduced into the workplace is a subject for collective bargaining and results in grievance arbitrations. For example, in a U.S. case, the arbitrator determined that a collective agreement's management rights clause allowed the employer to introduce a computerized

---

165   David Bishop Debenham, "Clipping Away at Labour Relations: Legislative Policy in the Age of the Microchip" (1988) 17 Man. L.J. 232.

166   For an evenhanded assessment of the job loss issue, see Zavis Zeman & Robert Russell, "The Chip Dole: An Overview of the Debates on Technological Unemployment," *CIPS Review* (January/February 1980): 10.

receiving system that had the effect of eliminating a clerk's job.[167] Similarly, in Canadian unionized environments joint management–labour committees address the contentious issues presented by the first dynamic of computer law, namely, the rapid pace of technological change.

New technologies in the workplace have also led to problems in non-unionized environments. For example, in one adjudication under the *Canada Labour Code*, an employee had inadvertently obtained access to the company's payroll file that listed all the staff salaries. While printing his own work on a local area network, he wondered why it was taking so long and noticed that another job in the print queue was the payroll run; "out of curiosity" he made a copy of the payroll file to see what his co-workers earned.[168] The employee was fired when senior management learned he had copied the payroll file — extremely confidential information — because as a television station it did not want the salaries of its on-air personalities known by advertisers. The employee sought redress under the *Canada Labour Code*, and the adjudicator, noting that the employee had not misused the information for any personal gain nor disclosed it to any third party, ordered reinstatement of the employee. One lesson from this case is that it is incumbent upon management to take appropriate steps to keep certain information confidential if they in fact do not want it accessed by staff generally. Thus, rather than running the payroll on the company's local area network where other users can access it, it should have been run off a stand-alone system not accessible to other staff. Management's response to the situation upon learning of the employee's access to the information was arguably also poorly handled; in effect, employers are struggling with new situations presented by computer technology.

Another case showing poor management skills when dealing with computer-related issues involved a financial institution where the computer password of one of its employees was used to steal $1850 from several dormant customer accounts.[169] The employer, assuming that the person who stole the money was the employee to whom this password was assigned, fired her on the day before she was to move from Halifax to Ottawa to take up a promotion with the company; she had already sold her car, shipped her belongings, cancelled her lease in Halifax, and entered into a new one in Ottawa. Moreover, the company gave her no

---

167 *Teamsters, Local Union No. 878 and Harvest Foods, Inc.*, Guide to Computer Law, New Developments (CCH) ¶60,386 at 81,245 (1992).

168 *Leech v. British Columbia Television Broadcasting System Ltd.* (8 April 1991) [unreported].

169 *Conrad v. Household Financial Corp.* (1992), 327 A.P.R. 56 (N.S.C.A.).

reasons for the firing. The court found that it could not be proved she stole the money, and in fact it was likely not her because on one of the occasions that money was taken the plaintiff was out of the country and could not have accessed the computer remotely. Some other employee had obtained the plaintiff's computer password and used it to steal the funds, and the plaintiff was exonerated. The court found the employer terminated the employee wrongfully and awarded punitive damages against the employer for its callous treatment of the plaintiff.

A final employment case worth noting is *Russell v. Nova Scotia Power Inc.*[170] The plaintiff, a long-time employee in the financial information systems group of a large company, had completed overseeing the implementation of a major new software application when a new controller was appointed to whom the plaintiff reported. The plaintiff and the controller did not get along well, and the company eventually dismissed the plaintiff for incompetence. To make matters worse, the controller sent an e-mail to hundreds of the plaintiff's co-workers indicating not only that he was no longer in the information systems department (which the court found would be a legitimate purpose for such an e-mail), but also that he was terminated for incompetence. The court found that there was no evidence supporting the claim of incompetence (i.e., many of the "problems" the controller attributed to the difficulties with the new software application were not the fault of the plaintiff), and that the plaintiff was wrongfully terminated and entitled to eighteen months' notice or pay in lieu of such notice. Moreover, while not finding the employer deserving of punitive damages, the court did award $40,000 in aggravated damages because the e-mail message was sent in order to embarrass the plaintiff and make an example of him and led to a serious aggravation of a pre-existing anxiety disorder. The court dismissed the plaintiff's claim for defamation, largely because it might result in double compensation in light of the award of aggravated damages for many of the same factors that underpinned the defamation claim. This is another example of an employer behaving badly in light of new computer technology and then using the new technology to make matters even worse.

---

170   (1996), 436 A.P.R. 271 (N.S.S.C.).

FURTHER READINGS

Books

AFFLECK, Donald K., & K. Wayne MCCRACKEN, *Canadian Competition Law* (Toronto: R. DeBoo Publishers, 1998) (updated)

NIMMER, Raymond T., *The Law of Computer Technology: Rights, Licenses, Liabilities* (Boston, Mass.: Warren, Gorham & Lamont, 1992) (looseleaf, updated)

RODITTI, Esther C., *Computer Contracts: Negotiating, Drafting* (New York: Matthew Bender, 1997) (looseleaf, updated)

SOOKMAN, Barry B., *Sookman Computer Law* (Toronto: Carswell, 1991) (updated)

TAKACH, George S., *Contracting for Computers*, 2d ed. (Toronto: McGraw-Hill Ryerson, 1992)

TAKACH, George S., *The Software Business: Financing, Protecting and Marketing Software*, 2d ed. (Toronto: McGraw-Hill Ryerson, 1997)

Internet Sites

Canadian Competition Bureau
<http://strategis.ic.gc.ca/competition>

Software Industry site
<http://www.softwareindustry.org/>

U.S. Federal Trade Commission

Year 2000 issues
<http://www.mitre.org/research/y2k/>
<http://www.year2000.com>

CHAPTER 6

ELECTRONIC COMMERCE AND INTERNET LEGAL ISSUES

For the past few hundred years, paper-based documents — in the form of contracts, purchase orders, invoices, and bills of lading — have been the predominant means to record and share commercial information. With the advent of the telegraph, commercial information was communicated electronically without paper. The telex and fax continued this trend, as did direct computer-to-computer communications, often referred to as electronic data interchange (EDI), an important means for transmitting commercial information in certain industries. Today, the Internet is poised to become the most important means of doing business electronically, both in the context of the one-on-one transactions of early electronic communications, as well as in the online environment of many-on-many. As well, data are often stored electronically; even previously paper-based documents are scanned and their contents stored electronically through imaging systems to save money and to improve access through indexing and retrieval systems. This shift from a paper-based to an electronic-based environment raises numerous legal issues — contract formation, evidence law, records retention, libel, jurisdiction, and regulation. The legal system has had several hundred years to craft rules, through statutes as well as judge-made common law, to address the risks and problems presented by paper. Although a number of legal rules have been created for the electronic environment, the newness of EDI and the Internet means that many legal challenges are still to be addressed. This is not surprising given that the four dynamics of computer law, namely, the rapid rate of technological change, the elusive nature of information, and the blurring of private/public and national/international, are very much in evidence vis-à-vis doing business electronically.

A. CONTRACT LAW ISSUES

Contract law facilitates the efficient operation of markets by establishing rules for concluding contracts and making payment under them. To this end, contract law has developed a number of principles and doctrines intended to promote certainty among business people in their commercial relations. In particular, the law has promulgated several rules related to the formation of contracts, addressing such questions as what formalities need to be observed, and when and where contracts arise. With respect to contracts and other commercial documents that are paper-based, these rules are quite elaborate and well developed, as might be expected from a body of law that has matured over several hundred years. Less developed are the rules relating to contracts that arise in an electronic environment. Since the advent of the telegraph, commercial relations effected through electronic means have presented the law with a number of challenges, primarily because of the first and second dynamics of computer law; that is, courts have been confronted by technologies that have obviated the need for paper, and once free of a paper-based medium, judges have had to contend with the truly ephemeral nature of information. Generally, however, courts have been receptive to the new technologies, have taken pains to understand them and the risks and opportunities they represent, and have assisted business people in adopting them by recognizing their legal legitimacy. Nevertheless, as the economy approaches the commencement of a new era in which Internet-based commerce will explode, there are still several nagging issues that are in need of resolution by the courts or legislators.

1) The Writing Requirement

a) The *Statute of Frauds*

Contract law has for several hundred years frowned upon the practice, once widespread, of entering into oral contracts for certain types of agreements, in which two or more parties do not reduce their oral agreement to any fixed form of record. Some three hundred years ago, the problems presented by oral contracts and the rules of civil procedure and evidence were so acute — and the number of disputes over oral contracts brought before the local magistrates so numerous — that post-

Cromwellian England passed the *Statute of Frauds*.[1] This legislation, which should really be called the *Statute against Frauds*, established the requirement that certain contracts, in order to be enforceable, must be in "writing." The statute, whose purpose was to reduce the likelihood of fraud and fabrication and to promote certainty in commercial relations, was repealed in England in 1954, but survives to this day in the common law provinces, such as in Ontario's version of the statute that still requires a number of agreements related to land transactions to be in writing.[2] Moreover, the concept that particular contracts must be reduced to writing has been imported from the *Statute of Frauds* into literally scores of other statutes and regulations.[3] Accordingly, while the following discusses the writing requirement and related issues generally, it is always important to understand what, if any, statutory rules apply in a given situation, and then to approach the particular rule from the context of the purpose of the applicable statute. Nevertheless, the general principles articulated here should assist in any such specific exercise.

b) Telegraph Cases

In all likelihood the English Parliament in 1677 contemplated a "writing" to be words and figures written in ink on paper, given that this was the predominant method of recording commercial information at the time (having superseded stone tablets, clay tablets, metal papers, papyrus, and parchment used by earlier civilizations). With the introduction of the telegraph some 150 years ago, the question arose whether telegraphic messages would satisfy the writing requirement in the *Statute of Frauds*. For the most part, this question was answered in the affirmative in Canada,[4] England,[5] and the United States.[6] In some cases, courts simply

---

1   The original *Statute of Frauds* was passed in 1677, as 29 Charles II C.3, "An act for the prevention of frauds and perjuries." For a discussion of the historic context for this legislation, see Douglas Stollery, "Statute of Frauds" (1976) 14 Alberta Law Review 222 ["Frauds"].

2   *Statute of Frauds*, R.S.O. 1990, c. S.19.

3   For example, subs. 13(4) of the *Copyright Act*, R.S.C. 1985, c. C-42, as amended, requires any copyright assignment to be in writing.

4   *Kinghorne v. The Montreal Telegraph Co.* (1859), 18 U.C.Q.B.R. 60 [*Kinghorne*].

5   *McBlain v. Cross* (1871), 25 L.T. 804; *Coupland v. Arrowsmith* (1868), 18 L.T. 755 [*Coupland*]. See also Evelyn G.M. Carmichael, *The Law Relating to the Telegraph, the Telephone and the Submarine Cable* (London: Knight & Co., 1904).

6   See the various telegraph cases in S. Walter Jones, *A Treatise on the Law of Telegraph and Telephone Companies*, 2d ed. (Kansas City: Vernon Law Book Company, 1916).

assumed that a telegram constituted a writing. In other cases, the courts took the view that the "original" writing is the paper-based message provided to the telegraph company by the sender and that the message sent by the telegraph company is merely a transcript confirming the original writing.[7] Courts even were able to overcome a break in the paper trail when they were confronted with the practice of clients of telegraph companies telephoning their messages to the telegraph office, sometimes (but not always) relying on the legal construct that the telegraph clerk, for this narrow purpose, was the agent of the client. Thus, in the *Selma Sav. Bank* case,[8] the court, following this approach, concluded that the writing requirement of the applicable statute was met by the telegraph clerk transcribing the signature on behalf of the customer as fully as if the customer's own staff had written out and signed the message, because the "mechanical means of making and signing the writing are not important," in view of the definition of writing in the applicable law "providing that 'written' includes printed, and 'writing' includes print." In coming to this conclusion, the court cited in full the following passage from an earlier American case:

> So when a contract is made by telegraph, which must be in writing by the statute of frauds, if the parties authorize their agents either in writing or by parol, to make a proposition on one side and the other party accepts it through the telegraph, that constitutes a contract in writing under the statute of frauds; because each party authorizes his agents, the company or the company's operator, to write for him; and it makes no difference whether that operator writes the offer or the acceptance in the presence of his principal and by his express direction, with a steel pen an inch long attached to an ordinary penholder, or whether his pen be a copper wire a thousand miles long. In either case the thought is communicated to the paper by the use of the finger resting upon the pen; nor does it make any difference that in one case common record ink is used, while in the other case a more subtle fluid, known as electricity, performs the same office.[9]

This case is indicative of a predilection on the part of judges to sensibly accommodate new developments in technology. In short, in the area of contract formation courts have been able to cope successfully with the first dynamic of computer law — the rapid pace of change in technology and the equally constant advances in business practices engendered thereby.

---

7   *Kinghorne*, above note 4; *Howley v. Whipple*, 48 N.H. 487 (1869) [*Howley*].
8   *Selma Sav. Bank v. Webster County Bank*, 206 S.W. 870 at 872 (Ky. App. 1918).
9   *Ibid.* at 872 from *Howley*, above note 7 at 488.

c) Fax Cases

More recently, courts have had to determine whether fax communications satisfy the writing requirement. In the British Columbia case of *Beatty* v. *First Explor. Fund 1987 & Co.*,[10] a partner argued that proxies for a special meeting of the partners that were sent by telecopier should be declared invalid, on the basis that the partnership agreement required proxies to be "written" and "signed by the appointer." The court disagreed, stating that

> the law has endeavoured to take cognizance of, and to be receptive to, technological advances in the means of communication. . . . The conduct of business has for many years been enhanced by technological improvements in communication. Those improvements should not be rejected automatically when attempts are made to apply them to matters involving the law. They should be considered and, unless there are compelling reasons for rejection, they should be encouraged, applied and approved.[11]

The Ontario Court of Appeal, in *Rolling* v. *Willann Investments Ltd.*, came to a similar conclusion when it held that a fax transmission of an offer was valid:

> Where technological advances have been made which facilitate communications and expedite the transmission of documents we see no reason why they should not be utilized. Indeed, they should be encouraged and approved.[12]

The sentiments in the *Beatty* and *Rolling* cases encapsulate the common-sense, practical approach taken by Canadian judges to new technologies and related business practices in the area of contract formation legal issues. Similarly, in an English case a court held that service of certain legal documents could be effected by fax, with the judge stating that he could see no reason why "advantage should not be taken of the progress in technology which fax represents to enable documents to be served by fax."[13] Interestingly, the party arguing against use of fax in this case made the point that the paper quality from the fax was poor, and that if the fax was left on a radiator the writing would come off. The court responded to this concern by stating that in practice this technological shortcoming can be dealt with by making a photocopy of the fax.

---

10 (1988), 25 B.C.L.R. (2d) 377 (S.C.) [*Beatty*].
11 *Ibid.* at 383 and 385.
12 (1989), 70 O.R. (2d) 578 at 581 (C.A.) [*Rolling*].
13 *Hastie & Jenkerson* v. *McMahon*, [1991] 1 All E.R. 255 at 259 (C.A.).

In the United States there are also fax cases that have adopted reasoning commensurate with that articulated in the *Beatty* and *Rolling* cases. For example, in one decision a court held that a fax of a certified copy of a court judgment is admissible as evidence.[14] In another case, a court concluded that where a statute required that a particular document be under seal, a fax copy of the seal satisfied the statutory condition.[15]

In the *Beatty* and *Rolling* cases, the respective judges took comfort from the fact that the faxed document was a copy of an original document, and that underlying the faxes were paper-based originals with human autographs for signatures. These cases reflect a particular type of fax technology where original, paper-based documents are reproduced by a system akin to photocopying and then transmitted. More modern fax technology, however, allows a sender of a message to transmit directly from a computer, without first creating a paper document. Similarly, EDI involves direct computer-to-computer transmission of data, without the creation of paper-based records at either the sender's or recipient's end. The older fax cases illustrate an important legal side effect of the first dynamic of computer law; the rapid pace of technological change means that great care and sensitivity must be exhibited when "classifying" a decision for jurisprudential, precedential purposes. One should not, for example, say that the *Beatty* case stands for the proposition that *all* fax technology has been held to satisfy the writing requirement. Rather, forms of fax technology other than those at issue in the *Beatty* and *Rolling* cases should be approached from the perspective of a functional analysis of the purpose of the writing requirement and the underlying technical and business process aspects of the communication in issue. Even the technology underpinning photocopying is shifting from one based on a process of optical and mechanical "dry photography" to one that involves digital scanning, printing, and transmission all in one.[16]

d) Electronic Messages

In the context of electronic-based fax and EDI messages, which would include e-mail and other messages over the Internet, courts have not yet entertained a case that has given them an opportunity to come to the same conclusions as in the telegraph and fax cases noted in this chapter in sections A(1)(b), "Telegraph Cases," and A(1)(c), "Fax Cases,"

---

14 *Englund v. State*, 907 S.W.2d 937 (Tex. App. 1995).

15 *State v. Smith*, 832 P.2d 1366 (Wash. App. 1992).

16 Kevin Marron, "Digital Copiers Save Time and Shoe Leather" *The [Toronto] Globe and Mail, Technology Quarterly* (3 June 1997).

respectively,[17] although the *Re a Debtor*[18] case discussed in section A(2), "Signatures," in this chapter contains some useful language regarding electronically transmitted documents. One possible concern in Ontario (and jurisdictions with *Interpretation Acts* similar to Ontario's) regarding electronic messages and the writing requirement is the definition of *writing* in the Ontario *Interpretation Act* that provides: "'writing,' 'written,' or any term of like import, includes words printed, painted, engraved, lithographed, photographed, or represented or reproduced by any other mode in a visible form."[19] The question is whether this definition requires the writing to be visible to the *unaided* eye, or whether the use of technical intermediaries, such as a computer monitor, would be accommodated under the definition. Without making reference to any case law, a pair of English commentators, considering a similarly worded definition in their *Interpretation Act*, have concerns regarding EDI messages that are passed between computers and that are not normally viewed by humans: one has expressed the view that the "reference to 'visible form' might militate against the characterisation of a purely electronic document as a writing,"[20] and the other has taken an even harder line, being of the opinion contracts will not be enforceable using EDI until the writing definition in the *Interpretation Act* is amended.[21] These assessments, particularly the latter, are not warranted, having regard to the purpose and wording of the writing definition in the context of modern day computer-based communications.

Where the electronic message is displayed on a computer monitor, the *Interpretation Act* definition of writing is satisfied because words are directly represented in a visible form. Even where a monitor is not used in each case, however, the writing definition should be satisfied for a

---

17   It has been reported, however, that a court in the United Kingdom approved a law firm serving a writ by means of the Internet for a libel action: see "Libel Writ Served by E-mail," *Electronic Telegraph*, Issue 374, 1 May 1996, at < http://www.telegraph.co.uk/index.html>.

18   *Re a Debtor (No. 2021 of 1995)*, [1996] 2 All E.R. 345 (Ch. D.) [*Debtor*].

19   *Interpretation Act* (Ontario), R.S.O. 1990 c. I.11, subs. 29(1). Generally this type of language is used in the other common law provinces. Slightly different wording is used in the federal *Interpretation Act*, R.S.C. 1985, c. I-21.

20   Christopher Millard, "Contractual Issues of EDI," in *EDI and the Law*, ed. Ian Walden (London: Blenheim Online Publications, 1989) at 47 [*EDI and the Law*]. In this same book another British author argues that the *Interpretation Act* definition of writing arguably is wide enough to cover EDI messages: Rob Bradgate, "Evidential Issues of EDI," in Walden, *EDI and the Law*.

21   Chris Reed, "EDI — Contractual and Liability Issues" (1989) 6(2) Computer Law and Practice 36.

couple of reasons. Consider, for example, an EDI system where the computers of both users participate in the creation of the electronic contract and both retain an electronic version of the various EDI messages, all of which can be printed out on paper if desired. Or consider an Internet-based transaction where two parties, through their computers, satisfy the requirements of offer and acceptance by means of transmitting electronic e-mail messages, each of which is retained by both computers and susceptible to being reproduced in a paper-based form if so desired. In these cases, the judicial focus on reliability of records, which at base is the purpose of the *Statute of Frauds'* writing requirement, should shift from a document-specific enquiry to a systemic analysis of the various technological devices and business processes that gave rise to the contract. In the case of these examples, indicia of trustworthiness include the fact that both parties actively participated in the creation of the contract, and that from the time of creation and thereafter each party can access the contract in both electronic mode through computer terminals or by printing out a hard copy. Thus, these examples should satisfy the writing definition in the *Interpretation Act* for two reasons. The definition is not exhaustive, and therefore the definition should not be limited to a paper-based environment when, as in the above-noted examples, reliable forms of writing have been created. As well, these examples should also satisfy the visible form requirement given that at all relevant times a version of the contract was and continues to be available in a visible form, whether displayed on a computer screen or by being printed out. In other words, in an electronic contracting environment the writing requirement should be interpreted as admitting of more than one legally relevant version of the contract. This would be consistent with the decisions in several cases discussed in this chapter in section B(2)(b), "Old Evidence Statutes and the Common Law," and section B(2)(c), "Multiple Originals."

The approach to the writing requirement noted in the previous paragraph is echoed by an American court that had to determine whether a computer disk (or more precisely, the information contained electronically on it) provided to an insurance agent would constitute "written notice."[22] The court noted that no previous case had dealt with this issue in the context of a computer disk, although various cases had held that videotapes and tape recordings constituted a "writing" for various statutory purposes. In coming to its conclusion that the computer disk did satisfy the writing requirement, the court stated:

---

22 *Clyburn v. Allstate Insurance Company,* 826 F. Supp. 955 (D.S.C. 1993).

Although, as noted, these cases [related to videotapes and tape recordings] arise in entirely different contexts and stem from different statutes or rules, the cases do suggest that other media forms are recognized as "writings." The storage of information on tape recordings and video-tapes is not that much different from that on floppy diskettes for computers, but rather is more a difference in the devices used to read the information. The information can be retrieved and printed as "hardcopy" on paper. In today's "paperless" society of computer generated information, the court is not prepared, in the absence of some legislative provision or otherwise, to find that a computer floppy diskette would not constitute a "writing" within the meaning of [the relevant statute].[23]

Bolstering the court's finding were the facts that (a) there was no evidence to suggest that the insurance agent did not have the necessary equipment to access or read the computerized document, and (b) the sending of such computer disks was a standard method for the insurance company to communicate with its agent. This case, and the ones mentioned previously, should lead courts to find that electronic fax and EDI messages satisfy any relevant writing requirements. And such a result would accord with the public policy rationale underlying the writing requirement, namely, to ensure reliable records of contracts. These electronic messages are the same ones that huge organizations rely on in order to operate on a day-to-day basis; a court could not hope for more trustworthy documents.

In approaching the writing issue, particularly in the context of sales transactions, courts should also be wary of the context in which many of these cases arise. Typically, an agreement is struck for the future delivery of a product, and between the time of concluding the contract and making delivery the price of the product fluctuates such that the seller could sell the same product for more to another buyer, or the buyer could obtain the product for less from another source. Thus, one or other party brings a claim under the writing requirement as a pretext for extricating itself from the initial bargain. In one such Ontario case during the telegraph era, where the plaintiff argued that a service of letters and telegrams did not constitute an agreement in writing for the purpose of the *Statute of Frauds*, the court was unpersuaded and upheld the contract, using the following language:

---

23   *Ibid.* at 956–57.

The fact that the price of leather had increased, and the unwilling-ness of the defendants to deliver it after such increase at the price they had named for it in their first letter, and at which the plaintiff had offered to take it, suggest that the view of the contract now con-tended for by the defendants is an attempt to get rid of a bargain by an ingenious interpretation of the correspondence, rather than frankly carrying out what they had really agreed to, and what both parties at the time understood.[24]

Such judicial sentiment and conclusions are consistent with and sup-portive of the rule that the *Statute of Frauds* should not be used to per-petrate a fraud.[25]

e) Law Reform

Until a court confirms the approach to the definition of writing in the *Interpretation Act* outlined above, legislators could consider several solutions to deal with the writing requirement in the context of elec-tronic messages. One methodology is to statutorily deem electronic and related messages to be writings. Another approach is the "functional equivalent" method. This approach has been taken by the United Nations Commission on International Trade Law (UNCITRAL) in its Working Group on EDI, which has prepared a set of model provisions for uniform rules on the legal aspects of EDI.[26] Article 6 of the UNCI-TRAL Model Law, for example, provides that whenever a rule of law requires a writing, that rule is satisfied by an electronic data message having certain characteristics. Illustrating yet another approach to law reform is the most recent version of the U.K.'s copyright law that con-tains a broad definition of writing: "any form of notation or code, whether by hand or otherwise and regardless of the method by which, or medium in or on which, it is recorded."[27] More simply, Ontario's *Hos-pital Management Regulation* was amended to provide that "writing includes an entry in a computer."[28] In the early 1990s, such a solution on a large scale was proposed to the Ontario government, namely, to expand the definition of *writing* in the *Interpretation Act* to include

---

24 *Thorne v. Barwick* (1866), 16 U.C.C.P. 369 at 377 [*Thorne*].
25 For cases that discuss the rule that the *Statute of Frauds* should not be used to perpetrate frauds, see Stollery, "Frauds," above note 1.
26 See the UNCITRAL Model Law on Electronic Commerce, adopted in 1996, available at <http://ra.irv.uit.no/trade_law/doc/ UN.Electronic.Commerce.Model. Law.1996.html>.
27 *Copyright, Designs and Patents Act 1988* (U.K.), 1988, c. 48, s. 178.
28 Hospital Management, R.R.O. 1990, Reg. 965, subs. 1(1).

information recorded by electronic, magnetic, or optical means. The government chose not to implement this approach because at the time the Ontario statutes contained over 2000 references to writing, many of which were to consumer notices where the government believed it inappropriate to permit electronic communications. The government's concern was somewhat misplaced. There should not be a problem deeming electronic messages to satisfy the writing requirement. The real problem is ensuring the delivery of the notice, whether it is in paper-based or electronic form. Thus, someone should be entitled to give a consumer notice electronically so long as the sender can show that it was given (i.e., that the recipient had adequate computer technology, etc.). And, of course, occasionally it may be more difficult to give the notice electronically, as in the situation where a landlord and tenant statute requires the posting of a message in a lobby of an apartment building. However, this would be a snap electronically if a lobby is outfitted with a digital display device that carries all sorts of tenant programming, including official notices. This is not such a far-fetched idea — the author's office elevators have recently been equipped with compact computer monitors that display news, weather, information, and advertising — to help pass the thirty-second ride to the fiftieth floor.

For an interesting twist on the writing definition, the court in the *Ellis Canning* case in the United States had to decide whether a tape of a telephone conversation comprised a writing under the *Uniform Commercial Code (UCC)*.[29] The court answered this question in the affirmative, because in the *UCC* the definition of *writing* includes "printing, typewriting *or any other intentional reduction to tangible form*"(italics in original). The court found that the tape recording of the oral contract was a reduction in tangible form, but that "probably the opposite result would be required under historical statutes of frauds which do not contain the tangible form language of this somewhat unusual definition of the word 'written.'"[30] In order to comfortably accommodate an electronic environment any reference to tangible form should be avoided in writing definitions, unless it is made clear that the tangible form may be printed out as a second or indirect step.

A second approach to the writing requirement has been simply to delete the particular requirement altogether. For example, a *Statute of Frauds* writing requirement has historically been part of sale of goods legislation in the common law provinces (e.g., Ontario's *Sale of Goods*

---

29   *Ellis Canning Company v. Bernstein*, 348 F. Supp. 1212 (D. Colo. 1972) [*Ellis Canning*].
30   *Ibid.* at 1228.

Act prior to December 1994 contained a provision that contracts for the sale of goods to be delivered in the future having a value of over $40 must be in writing).[31] England repealed the equivalent provision in its *Sale of Goods Act* in the 1950s, and, in keeping with the general trend over the past few decades to reduce formal requirements for contracts, British Columbia, Manitoba, and New Brunswick have also repealed the provision in their sales statutes. As well, Ontario and most other provinces effectively repealed this provision in May 1992 for international sales contracts given that the *United Nations Convention on Contracts for the International Sale of Goods* provides that a contract of sale need not be evidenced in writing (though a signatory to this convention could derogate from this provision, thus continuing to require certain formal requirements for contracts).[32] This results in the perverse situation where two parties conducting EDI or some other form of electronic commerce within a province that still has a writing requirement in its *Sale of Goods* statute, do so with less certainty than if either of them contracted electronically with an entity in the United States, given that in the latter case the U.N. International Sales Convention, to which the United States is also a signatory, effectively repeals the writing requirement. This ironic state of affairs was rectified in Ontario in December 1994 when that jurisdiction finally repealed section 5 of its *Sale of Goods Act*,[33] but the bizarre situation still exists in those provinces that have not taken this step. Indeed, even in provinces that have repealed the writing provision in their sales statutes applicable to commercial sales, a similar writing provision in respect of consumer sales may continue to exist in another statute.[34]

f) Contractual Measures

Yet another approach to the writing requirement involves parties to electronic commerce transactions dealing with the issue contractually. For example, the EDI Council of Canada has published a *Model Form of*

---

31   *Sale of Goods Act*, R.S.O. 1990, c. S.1.
32   Each province and the federal government implemented this U.N. Convention by passing enabling legislation; for Ontario's see *International Sale of Goods Act*, R.S.O. 1990, c. I.10.
33   The repeal was effected by s. 54 of the *Statute Law Amendment Act (Government Management and Services), 1994*, S.O. 1994, c. 27.
34   For Ontario, for example, see s. 19 of the *Consumer Protection Act*, R.S.O. 1990, c. C.31, which provides that "executory contracts" must be in writing; an executory contract is a sale of goods or services to a consumer worth more than $50 where delivery of the goods or performance of the services is to be made after the agreement is entered into.

Electronic Data Interchange Trading Partner Agreement and Commentary (*Model TPA*).[35] The *Model TPA* is intended to be used by organizations engaging in EDI. The *Model TPA*, which has numerous counterparts around the world, addresses a number of the technical, operational, contractual, and legal issues that arise in EDI relationships.[36] With respect to the writing requirement, section 6.04 of the *Model TPA*, titled "Enforceability," provides as follows:

> The parties agree that as between them each Document [being an electronic message] that is received by the Receiver shall be deemed to constitute a memorandum in writing signed and delivered by or on behalf of the Sender thereof for the purposes of any statute or rule of law that requires a Contract to be evidenced by a written memorandum or be in writing, or requires any such written memorandum to be signed and/or delivered. Each party acknowledges that in any legal proceedings between them respecting or in any way related to a Contract it hereby expressly waives any right to raise any defence or waiver of liability based upon the absence of a memorandum in writing or of a signature.

It is open to question, however, as the commentary to the *Model TPA* points out, whether parties can "contract out" of a writing requirement, or whether such a provision would be void as against public policy. Accordingly, if possible, parties should choose to have their EDI contract governed by the laws of a jurisdiction that no longer contains a writing requirement; for example, it would be wise to have an EDI agreement between parties in Alberta and British Columbia governed by British Columbia law, given that British Columbia's *Sale of Goods Act* does not contain a writing requirement. It should also be noted that such contractual measures to address the writing requirement and other issues need not be restricted to EDI situations. Organizations doing business over the Internet could implement the same type of provision in agreements with subscribers or other parties.

---

35   Legal and Audit Issues Committee of the Electronic Data Interchange Council of Canada, *Model Form of Electronic Data Interchange Trading Partner Agreement and Commentary, 1990* [*Model TPA*].

36   For the version developed by the American Bar Association, see: ABA Electronic Messaging Services Task Force, "Model Electronic Data Interchange Trading Partner Agreement and Commentary" (1990) 45 Bus. L. 1717.

2) Signatures

Many of the statutes that call for certain types of contracts or notices to be in writing also stipulate that the writing be "signed" by the party against whom the writing is being enforced. As with the writing issue discussed above, the question arises whether the signature requirement can be met in an environment of electronic messages. In 1677, when the first *Statute of Frauds* was promulgated, the predominant form of signature would have arguably been the human autograph.[37] In a number of cases, however, courts have taken a purposive approach to the signature requirement and have concluded that various means will suffice in addition to the human autograph. In a Quebec case, a court had to decide whether the then current rule of civil procedure requiring legal documents to be signed by a lawyer would permit the lawyer's name to be stamped on a relevant document.[38] The court noted an early French definition for signature that described an individual writing his name by his hand at the end of a document, but then went on to discuss and adopt more liberal interpretations of signature that included stamping and other means of inscription, so long as no prejudice can be shown to the contesting party, and hence the court held that the legal document under consideration with only a stamp of the lawyer's name satisfied the particular writing requirement. More recently, the English Court of Appeal also found that solicitors could sign their accounts by stamping them in addition to signing them by hand.[39] These cases show that the rapid pace of technological change, and the novel business practices engendered by it, will not distract courts from understanding that the true function of the signature requirement is to authenticate a document, and from concluding that this purpose can be satisfied in a number of ways in addition to the use of the human autograph.

---

37   In earlier times, the Bible tells how a merchant would authenticate a commercial transaction by giving one of his sandals to another trader; subsequently, the trader could verify the party he was dealing with by comparing the comparative wear on the soles of the pair of sandals: Ruth 4:7. This example leads to the conclusion that what we are striving for in modern times is not the electronic signature, but the "electronic sandal"!

38   *Grondin* v. *Tisi & Turner* (1912), 4 D.L.R. 819 (Que. Ct. Rev.).

39   *Goodman* v. *J. Eban, Ltd.*, [1954] 1 All E.R. 763 (C.A.). In this case Lord Denning registered a dissenting view, stating at 769: "This is such common knowledge that a rubber stamp is contemptuously used to denote the thoughtless impress of an automaton in contrast to the reasoned attention of a sensible person." The point that Lord Denning missed, but that the majority understood, and that courts in virtually all other cases in this area have grasped, is that automated systems and business processes can, in fact, be extremely sensible, reliable, and trustworthy.

a) Telegraph and Fax Cases

In an early case, a party argued that a telegram cannot be a document for *Statute of Frauds* purposes because it was not signed.[40] The court disagreed, and held that telegrams, together with previous correspondence, did constitute a binding contract. In an American telegraph case, a court held that a typed signature, effected by the telegraph company on behalf of a customer, satisfied the relevant signature requirement; the court stated that "[i]n view of the way in which business is done nowadays, any other view would be unrealistic and would produce pernicious consequences, impeding the conduct of business transactions."[41] In another American case, the court was confronted by the teletype form of telegraphy, where machines took the place of the transmission/receiver clerks.[42] In this case the court "conceded that these teletype messages do not bear the signature in writing of the party to be charged in the sense that they were not literally signed with pen and ink in the ordinary signature of the sender."[43] Nevertheless, the court noted that each party was readily identifiable and known to the other by the symbols and code letters used. In approaching the question what constitutes a signature in order to satisfy the California *Statute of Frauds*, the court stated it must "take a realistic view of modern business practices, and can probably take judicial notice of the extensive use to which the teletype machine is being used today among business firms, particularly brokers, in the expeditious transmission of typewritten messages."[44] The court, not being able to find any other case on point with respect to teletype machines, nevertheless held teletype messages to satisfy its jurisdiction's *Statute of Frauds*. In a later U.S. case, a court decided that a taped telephone conversation satisfied the signature requirement, given that the purpose of this requirement is to identify the contracting party, and this was effected through the audio tape, as both parties admitted and did not contest.[45]

Courts are willing to look at the purpose of the signature requirement, which they have determined to be to connect a person to a document in order to denote authenticity and consent; that is, to make it attributable to the author and to signify the author's approval of the doc-

---

40   *Coupland*, above note 5.

41   *La Mar Hosiery Mills, Inc. v. Credit and Commodity Corporation*, 216 N.Y.S.2d 186 at 190 (City Ct. of N.Y. 1961).

42   *Joseph Denunzio Fruit Co. v. Crane*, 79 F. Supp. 117 (S.D. Cal. 1948).

43   *Ibid.* at 128.

44   *Ibid.* at 128–29.

45   *Ellis Canning*, above note 29.

ument in order to give it legal effect. By focussing on this functional analysis, courts have avoided stumbling over the various technological obstacles seemingly thrown up by the first dynamic of computer law. Instead, like Olympic hurdlers, courts jump over these different and successive challenges, apparently without effort, but in fact thankful for the diligent conditioning undergone by the common law with all previous technologies. In this regard, it is useful to note that *Interpretation Acts* do not generally contain a definition for signature, thus permitting a very flexible environment in which the term can operate. Of course, for certain documents the human autograph remains a useful signature. And sometimes the legislature will expressly require a signature by hand, as in one U.S. case where a faxed version of a document was held not to conform to the strict signature requirements of the regulations.[46] This case, however, is not in conflict with the others noted above. Indeed, it may be taken to support them indirectly in the sense that it can be said to stand for the proposition that today, with fax technology as ubiquitous as it is, the judicial presumption ought to be for its acceptance in meeting formal writing and signature requirements, and the onus should be on Parliament to expressly exclude it or other similar communications technologies from satisfying such requirements in the rare circumstances where this is thought to be necessary.

Moreover, the human autograph is not foolproof, even for paper-based documents. Indeed, the entire field of handwriting analysis developed from the legal challenges to the authenticity and genuineness of autographs. A similar sentiment was presciently pointed out in the recent *Debtor* case in the United Kingdom that considered whether a faxed proxy was valid for a meeting of creditors where the relevant rules required the proxy to be "signed."[47] The court, approaching the question from first principles, noted that the purpose of the signing requirement is to provide some measure of authentication to the proxy form. In this regard the court pointed out:

---

46   *Gilmore v. Lujan*, 947 F.2d 1409 (9th Cir. 1991). While upholding the ability of the government department to reject the fax based on its regulations, the court commented on how this rule served no sensible purpose, effectively encouraging the agency to revise its finicky, counterproductive, and unfair procedures. Indeed, to illustrate how out of date this agency's policy was, consider that in Ontario a contract, to be under "seal," no longer requires a wax impression or even a paper wafer, but merely a party's signature over the words "seal" in the signature area of the document: see *872899 Ontario Inc. v. Iacovoni* (1997), 33 O.R. (3d) 561 (Gen. Div.).

47   *Debtor*, above note 18.

> Of course even if the rule were strictly limited to signature by direct manual marking of the form, the authentication is not perfect. Signatures are not difficult to forge. Furthermore, in the overwhelming majority of cases in which the chairman of a creditors' meeting receives a proxy form, the form will bear a signature which he does not recognise and may well be illegible. Authenticity could only be enhanced if the creditor carrying suitable identification signed the form in person in the presence of the chairman. Even there the possibility of deception exists.[48]

This observation is important because it usefully reminds anyone considering the actual or potential shortcomings of electronic messaging systems, from the perspective of security and alterability, that modern technology systems and business practices should not be compared to some nirvana-like method of perfection, but rather to a paper-based environment that also has its weaknesses. When a court is being asked to judge the trustworthiness of some new computer or network-based technology or business practice, it should not demand that the system be 100 percent accurate or foolproof, because, of course, perfection is a status that no system — whether paper-based or electronic — can hope to achieve. Rather, the standard should be whether organizations in the real economy entrust their daily operations to the particular technology or administrative mechanism. If so, the procedure that meets the everyday needs of thousands of enterprises should meet the requirements of the law, insofar as contract formalities are concerned.

In the *Debtor* case, the court concluded that the faxed proxy did satisfy the signature requirement. In doing so the court noted that the fax method of transmitting the proxy was superior to sending it by post (which the party also did in this case):

> When a creditor faxes a proxy form to the chairman of a creditors' meeting he transmits two things at the same time, the contents of the form and the signature applied to it. The receiving fax is in effect instructed by the transmitting creditor to reproduce his signature on the proxy form which is itself being created at the receiving station. It follows that, in my view, the received fax is a proxy form signed by the principal or by someone authorised by him. The view which I have reached appears to me to be consistent with the realities of modern technology. If it is legitimate to send by post a proxy form signed with a rubber stamp, why should it not be at least as authentic to send the form by fax?

---

48   *Ibid.* at 351.

The facts of the present case illustrates [*sic*] the point well. Here the proxy form was sent both by post and by fax. Such being the nature of postal delivery, the creditor could not be certain whether his proxy was received at all or on time. On the other hand, when the fax is transmitted he knows that it has been received because, first, he obtains an answerback code and, secondly, an activity report is normally printed out. From the chairman's point of view, there is nothing about a received fax which puts him in a worse position to detect forgeries than when he receives through the post or by hand delivery a document signed by hand by a person whose signature he has never seen before or one signed by stamping. The reality is that fax transmission is likely to be a more reliable and certainly is a more speedy method of communication than post.[49]

The court in the *Debtor* case made another important point when it stated that the chairman who receives a proxy by fax is entitled to treat it as authentic unless there are surrounding circumstances that indicate otherwise. The presumption ought to be that messages sent by fax are authentic (for contract law purposes) and admissible (for evidence law purposes), but of course this presumption can always be rebutted. This same approach was taken in *R. v. Kapoor*, in which the accused challenged the validity of an information, the official document issued by a justice of the peace that contained the charges against the accused, on the basis that the signature of the justice of the peace was unintelligible.[50] The signature was in fact unintelligible, and there was no printing of the name to indicate who the signature belonged to (illustrating another shortcoming of the human autograph — it is often a very messy and incomprehensible example of penmanship!). Nonetheless, the court turned down the challenge to the official document on the basis of the legal dictum *omnia praesumuntur rite et solemniter esse acta donec probetur in contrarium*, which, as all Latin scholars know, means "everything is presumed to be rightly and duly performed until the contrary is shown." It is suggested that this is a sensible rule to apply to all formal and evidentiary matters related to computer-generated documents, and not just to those emanating from a public office.

b) The Authentication Function

A final important point worth noting in the *Debtor* case is that the court, based on its salutary "first principles" approach, went on to

---

49   *Ibid.* at 351–52.
50   *R. v. Kapoor* (1989), 52 C.C.C. (3d) 41 (Ont. H.C.J.).

consider messages in a form beyond the fax immediately before the court and concluded:

> Once it is accepted that the close physical linkage of hand, pen and paper is not necessary for the form to be signed, it is difficult to see why some forms of non-human agency for impressing the mark on the paper should be acceptable while others are not.
>
> For example, it is possible to instruct a printing machine to print a signature by electronic signal sent over a network or via a modem. Similarly, it is now possible with standard personal computer equipment and readily available popular word processing software to compose, say, a letter on a computer screen, incorporate within it the author's signature which has been scanned into the computer and is stored in electronic form, and to send the whole document including the signature by fax modem to a remote fax. The fax received at the remote station may well be the only hard copy of the document. It seems to me that such a document has been "signed" by the author.[51]

Although this passage relates to a hypothetical example raised by the court, its analysis is unassailable. The fact is the technical and business foundations of these electronic messages make them hugely reliable. This explains why, in contrast to the telegraph technology of the last century that spawned an epidemic of litigation, courts in Canada, the United States, and elsewhere are witnessing so few contract formation disputes arising out of the new computer and network technologies.

To the trenchant and helpful analysis in the *Debtor* case can be added the point that in today's commercial environment there are many ways of authenticating particularly sensitive documents and messages. We see payroll or mass-produced cheques and bank notes mechanically stamped or printed with a copy of a human autograph — quite a silly practice if one considers that the whole point of a human autograph is that it be done by a human; there are other much more effective ways to authenticate mass-produced documents, such as the thin film reflective patches used on certain Canadian bank notes. Moreover, even more sophisticated electronic authentication mechanisms can be deployed to meet signature requirements for particularly sensitive documents. Token-based devices, such as smart cards or credit cards with magnetic strips containing security functionality are used in many electronic environments, such as automated cash dispenser machines. Biometric devices, such as retina scans or finger-

---

51 *Debtor*, above note 18 at 351.

prints, are also growing in popularity.[52] With these biometric systems, a central registry logs an authentic version of the fingerprint or signature, and then subsequent usage of the particular vehicle is compared to the master version kept on file electronically. By one estimate, police, computer firms, and other corporations spent more than $500 million on fingerprint and other biometric devices in 1995, with sales projected to grow 40 percent annually.[53] Indeed, with the growing use of electronic pads that can record signatures, the oldest of biometric mechanisms — the signature — will find new applications in the electronic environment. Other types of authentication in the computer and network environment draw on knowledge-based systems involving passwords and/or personal identification numbers. For particularly sensitive transactions or documents, mathematic encryption systems can be used. Some jurisdictions are supporting the use of encryption systems by enacting digital signature statutes.[54] These laws provide that if parties use encryption technology and encrypted message certification authorities approved or licensed under the statute, the resulting signatures *and* messages of the parties will be deemed to be originals and enforceable under applicable law.

Of course, persons have to use all such authentication and communications systems in a manner that convinces a court (if challenged) that the person truly intended to be bound by the specific electronic transmission. For example, there are two lines of U.S. authorities on the point whether a company's paper-based letterhead, with the name of the company printed on top of the page, satisfies the signature requirement

---

52   See Ann Davis, "The Body as Password," *Wired*, July 1997, which mentions the "traditional" biometric technologies of retina scans, as well as less-known ones such as hand contours involving the knuckles, voice modulation, and head resonances.

53   Estimate by the Yankee Group, a U.S. consultancy, reported in Tom Abate, "New Chip Can Verify Fingerprints" *The [Toronto] Globe and Mail, Technology Quarterly* (3 June 1997). This article refers to a company with a new postage stamp–sized fingerprint pad and related chip and software that can read and verify fingerprints. Another company mentioned in the article uses optical technology to verify fingerprints, apparently with the competitive advantage that it can detect when a live finger is used, to differentiate from one that has been chopped off to gain access to the restricted area. See also David Berman, "Mytec's Secret Identity," *Canadian Business*, September 1997.

54   For example, Utah's *Digital Signature Act*, 46 Utah Code Ann. ch 3, Utah Administrative Code RI 54-2- 101. For a review of the Canadian legal environment for digital signatures and public key infrastructure systems, see Industry Canada, *Final Report of the Legal Issues Working Group of the Information Technology Security Strategy Steering Committee*, 8 October 1977 (Ottawa: Industry Canada, 1997).

where no actual autograph or other mark is left by the person sending the document. One line is evident in a leading decision, when Justice Cardozo explained that in such cases the court must assess all the relevant facts to ascertain whether the party sending the letterhead intended to be bound, or was simply using the letterhead as a non-binding "scratch pad."[55] A similar question was asked in a recent American case where a document alleged to be a financial guarantee was sent by fax without a human signature but contained the name of the sender company on the top of the page because the sender's fax machine imprinted this corporate name automatically on each page that was faxed by the machine. The lower court concluded there was no question but that the sender intended to be bound by the faxed guarantee, and that the plaintiff acted in reliance upon it, and that the guarantor "should not be permitted to evade its obligation because of the current and extensive use of electronic transmissions in modern business transactions."[56] A second line of reasoning was shown when the appellate court reversed this finding (although for reasons that are not altogether apparent from the judgment), and instead treated the corporate name imprinted by the fax machine as insufficient to denote intent on the part of the defendant to authenticate the document.[57] In effect, this case illustrates that all the fancy computer and communications paraphernalia in the world still do not obviate the need for sensible and sound business processes, which can then be implemented by the newfangled technology. As with the negligence cases reviewed in section D(2), "Negligence in Use," in chapter 5, computer technology in these contexts should be viewed as a means to an end, rather than as an end in itself.

Accordingly, out of an abundance of caution, as with the writing requirement, parties to EDI and other agreements that contemplate electronic messages are also stipulating contractually in their EDI TPAs that the various electronic messages constitute *signed* writings.[58] Even in the absence of such contractual confirmation, the signature requirement in *Statute of Frauds* provisions should be satisfied by messages produced by those electronic-based systems that implement a trustworthy system for the exchange and recording of information where the identity of the sender of the message is conveyed by a reasonably secure technical

55   *Mesibov, Glinert & Levy v. Cohen Bros. Mfg. Co.*, 157 N.E. 148 (N.Y. 1927).
56   *Parma Tile Mosaic & Marble Co., Inc. v. Estate of Short*, 590 N.Y.S.2d 1019 at 1021 (N.Y. Sup. Ct. 1992).
57   *Parma Tile Mosaic & Marble Co., Inc. v. Estate of Short*, 663 N.E.2d 633 (N.Y. 1996).
58   See s. 6.04 of the *Model TPA*, above note 35, which covers the signature as well as the writing issue.

means. The cases show that courts will not block the use by business people of new technologies that are accepted by them to provide the signature requirement where the underlying rationale of the signature requirement can be achieved through one or more technological devices or business processes. Courts should continue this approach when considering documents and messages emanating from new communication networks, always focussing their analysis on the underlying functions of the relevant technological devices and business processes.

3) Offer and Acceptance

A contract arises when, in response to an offer made by an offeror, the offeree's acceptance is received by the offeror. Where parties conclude a contract in face-to-face, simultaneous communications, the existence of an offer and an acceptance is usually clear. Where parties negotiate a contract and they are distant from one another, and if they are not communicating in real time but through a telecommunications mechanism, it may not be clear what communications actually constitute an offer or an acceptance. In a number of cases involving telegraphed messages, disputes arose as a result of the differing conclusions that could be drawn from the various words and phrases used in the (often many) telegrams that passed to and fro between the parties; each telegram added ambiguity to the core question as to whether the parties had come to a meeting of the minds on quantity and price (in a sale of goods context).[59] Indeed, in an early Canadian telegraph case, the court noted that the fee for telegrams was charged by the word and was expensive, so senders limited the number of words used and this increased the likelihood of misunderstanding and dispute.[60] Conflicts about offer and acceptance can arise in the context of more recent technology as well, and one such falling out involving a computerized telephone ordering system led to the decision in the U.S. case *Corinthian Pharmaceutical Systems, Inc. v. Lederle Laboratories*.[61] In this case, a drug wholesaler ordered a large quantity of a particular product the day before a large price increase was to take effect. The wholesaler used the manufacturer's automated telephone order system, and after placing the order message with the computer, was issued a "tracking number" by the manufacturer's computer system. No human representative of the manufacturer participated in taking the order. Subsequently, the manufacturer did not wish to supply the large quantity of product to the wholesaler at the

---

59   For a discussion of some of these cases, see *Thorne*, above note 24.
60   *Kinghorne*, above note 4.
61   724 F Supp. 605 (S.D. Ind. 1989) [*Corinthian*].

lower price, and therefore argued that the tracking number issued by its computer was not an acceptance of the wholesaler's order, but merely an acknowledgment of receipt of the order (which, the manufacturer argued, was the offer in contract law terms). The court agreed, concluding that no contract had been consummated, with the result that the wholesaler was denied the lower price for the manufacturer's products.[62]

In order to avoid misunderstandings of the kind that arose in the *Corinthian* case, the EDI Council of Canada's *Model TPA* encourages parties to be extremely precise as to what electronic messages constitute a purchase order, a functional acknowledgment (the equivalent of the non-binding tracking number in the *Corinthian* case), and a purchase order acknowledgment. Indeed, EDI if properly utilized can help avoid the problems encountered in the cases referred to in the previous paragraph because it is a system based on a structured protocol of standard electronic messages, the meaning of each of which is well settled. Again, it is worth asking why there is a lack of case law involving contract formation disputes in an EDI environment. The answer, quite simply, is that the current computer-based technologies are more effective than previous technologies at permitting parties to come to a meeting of the minds in an unambiguous manner. In effect, the pace of technological change, articulated as the first dynamic of computer law, presents the law with numerous challenges, but at the same time technical progress assists the law by devising even more reliable means of communication. EDI messages, however, only address core contract formation issues, such as quantity, price, and time of shipment, and generally do not cover secondary matters such as warranty terms, interest on overdue payments, etc. Thus, the *Model TPA* addresses another fertile source of conflict that arises in the traditional paper-based commercial environment, namely the so-called battle of the forms regarding these secondary contract conditions. This is the term given to the phenomenon of the various commercial documents of trading partners containing differing, and often conflicting, terms and conditions regarding warranty, etc. The price list of a manufacturer, generally considered not an offer but an invitation to treat, will contain certain product warranty terms, which may be different from the warranty terms contained in the buyer's purchase order, and which may differ from the warranty terms of the manufacturer's purchase order acknowledgment. In Canada, this

---

62   It is interesting to speculate, in light of the negligence cases referred to in section D(1), "Negligence in Creation: The Y2K Problem," in chapter 5, involving the design of computer-based systems, whether the plaintiff in the *Corinthian* case might not have had a reasonable negligence claim arising out of the facts of the case.

battle is usually won by the party taking the last shot; for example, the manufacturer if the goods are shipped after it sent its own form of purchase order acknowledgment.[63] In contrast, the manufacturer can lose the battle if it ships product in a situation where the last paper to cross the trenches is the buyer's purchase order (which is accepted by the shipping of the goods).

Recreating the battle of the paper-based forms in an EDI trading environment is quite difficult because the standard messages used for EDI, or transaction sets as they are called, do not include legal terms and conditions. Therefore, the *Model TPA* stipulates that the parties attach a mutually agreeable set of terms and conditions to the TPA, which will then govern the various sales of product made under the agreement. This is an eminently sensible approach, but it does require trading partners to negotiate terms and conditions they normally would not in a paper-based environment (where they rely instead on the hope that their particular standard form will win the battle of the forms if a dispute ever crops up). Accordingly, not wishing to spend time negotiating terms and conditions, some EDI trading partners perversely attach their various paper-based forms to the TPA and stipulate that the terms in these forms will apply as if the forms were actually being used (which, of course, they are not). The result may well be that the whole arrangement is void for uncertainty. Of course, parties not wishing to spend the time negotiating items such as warranties could remain silent on the issue and simply let the various implied warranties and conditions of sales legislation, either domestic or international, apply to the transactions. This is a risky approach, however, as the scope, coverage, and meaning of these implied warranties can be extremely uncertain.[64] There is, therefore, really no better course of action vis-à-vis the battle of the forms problem than to take the time to negotiate a mutually acceptable set of warranties and other terms that will govern the relationship between the parties; and of course the time spent on such negotiations will decrease dramatically if both sides take a sensible, middle-ground approach right from the beginning instead of spinning their wheels in interminable discussions of mutually unreasonable positions.

---

63 The United States *Uniform Commercial Code* has different rules for dealing with inconsistent standard form contract terms: see the decisions in *Step-Saver Data Systems, Inc. v. Wyse Technology*, 939 F.2d 91 (3d Cir. 1991) and *Arizona Retail Systems, Inc. v. Software Link, Inc.*, 831 F. Supp. 759 (D. Ariz. 1993); these cases are referred to in section C(2), "Shrinkwrap Licences," in chapter 5.

64 See section E(1), "Implied Warranties and Conditions," in chapter 5.

4) Garbled Messages

Where contracts are not negotiated in a face-to-face environment, but by means of a telecommunications device, there is always the risk that the messages intending to create contractual obligations do not reach their destination or, perhaps more dangerously, are received by the recipient but not in precisely the form sent by the sender. The telegraph was notoriously susceptible to errors, particularly at the various points where human actors were involved in the process of dictating, transcribing, transmitting, receiving, or deciphering a telegraphic message. So many different things could go wrong in the transmission of a telegram. In *Henckel* v. *Pape*, for example, two commercial parties had exchanged several messages regarding the possible purchase of up to fifty rifles, the number that the plaintiff had available for sale.[65] The defendant finally wrote out a telegram ordering three rifles. By mistake, the telegraph clerk telegraphed "the" for "three," with the result that the plaintiff sent all fifty rifles. In the ensuing action by the seller against the purchaser, the court held that the purchaser should not be responsible for the error of the telegraph clerk, that there was no contract between the parties, and thus the defendant was not responsible to pay for the rifles. A similar result was arrived at in an American telegraph case, with the court concluding that no contract came into existence when the telegraph company understated the price actually quoted by the sender of the telegram.[66] Another American case gives a good example of the dangers inherent in the telegraph system; the seller wired a quotation of a particular commodity at $1.70, but it was delivered to the buyer at $1.07.[67] In addition to the very common problem illustrated in these cases, numerous other inherent weaknesses in the telegraph system caused a flood of litigation surrounding this technology in the last century.[68] For starters, the Morse code system was terribly susceptible to error — there is not much difference between a dot and a dash, and really only very experienced telegraph operators could send messages with consistent accuracy. Often a telegraph message had to be relayed through multiple telegraph companies, multiplying the risks all around, as well as introducing the opportunity for the message to fall between the cracks during

---

65   (1870), 23 L.T. 419 [*Henckel*].

66   *Harper* v. *Western Union Telegraph Co.*, 130 S.E. 119 (S.C. 1925).

67   *Postal Tel. Cable Co.* v. *Schaefer*, 62 S.W. 1119 (Ky. App. 1901).

68   For a review of many of these cases, see William L. Scott & Milton P. Jarnagin, *A Treatise upon the Law of Telegraphs* (Boston: Little, Brown, 1868), as well as the books in above notes 5 and 6.

the stages where typically boys delivered the message on foot between the offices of different telegraph companies in the same city.[69] The telegraph technology effecting the transmission was also extremely prone to malfunction. Poorly insulated telegram wires disrupted many transmissions, and perhaps not surprisingly, given that many early insulators were made of cowhorns or cloth soaked in beeswax. Electrical storms played havoc with early telegraph transmission systems. In short, it is no wonder that in the *Kinghorne* decision the court stated in respect of telegraphic messages:

> We must look, I think, in the case of each communication, at the papers delivered by the party who sent the message, not at the transcript of the message taken through the wire at the other end of the wire, with all the chances of mistakes in apprehending and noting the signals, and in transcribing for delivery.[70]

Compared to early telegraph systems that caused numerous misadventures, current telecommunications networks are much more reliable and trustworthy. This is one reason why today, notwithstanding the huge increase in telecommunications traffic over the last twenty years, there is a relative dearth of litigation over garbled messages and the like. Another reason, of course, is that in certain jurisdictions the telephone companies operate under tariffs and limitations of liability that restrict the claims that can be brought against them. Also helping to reduce basic communication mix-ups in today's computerized networked environments are technologies that permit the testing of certain parameters of an electronic message to ensure it accords with past practice and the anticipated relationship between the parties.[71] A contract provision that reflects this is section 5.04 of the EDI Council of Canada's *Model TPA* that requires each party to undertake reasonableness testing on messages received so that a recipient does not act upon erroneous messages, such as where a million units of a product are ordered by a single electronic purchase order when, historically, no more than 1000 were

---

69 In *Kinghorne*, above note 4, the telegraph message was sent from Kingston to Ogdensburg, where the recipient telegraph company was to send the message by hand to another company's office in Ogdensburg for onward transmission to its office in Oswego. The message never did arrive in Oswego, and the lawsuit against the initial telegraph company ensued.

70 *Ibid.* at 66.

71 Of course, this does not mean electronic systems are infallible: see *Shell Pipeline Corporation v. Coastal States Trading, Inc.*, 788 S.W.2d 837 (Tex. App. 1990), referred to in section D(2), "Negligence in Use," in chapter 5.

ordered at a time, probably indicating that three zeros were mistakenly added to the electronic purchase order. Such verification procedures were available to persons using, for example, the telegraph, but they were time-consuming and cumbersome. For example, in the *Henckel* case, it was noted that on the back of the preprinted form that a customer used to write down the contents of the telegram, there was offered for an additional fee a procedure whereby, if the sender desired to adopt an "extra security against risk of error," it could have the telegram, as prepared by the telegraph clerk from the originator's handwritten message, delivered to the sender by a messenger for a confirmation check, only after which it would be transmitted by the telegraph company.[72] Of course such "repetition," as it was called, took extra time and was charged as an additional service. One doubts if it was used very often. By contrast, in an EDI or other electronic environment, a party agreeing to undertake reasonableness testing in, for example, an EDI Trading Partner Agreement, can do so because it has software that carries out this function, thereby illustrating yet another example of how sophisticated technology can assist parties in bringing greater precision to their contract formation activities. This is an important point. All too often the first dynamic of computer law is viewed merely as a challenge to the law, indeed often as an adversary, as in the criminal law area discussed in chapter 3, where the law has a difficult time keeping up with new technological means of causing harm. In other areas, however, the first dynamic of computer law means a rash of new products, such as encryption programs, authentication mechanisms (such as biometric devices), and more stable transmission technologies, to help promote stability and certainty. Contract formation processes are getting better, and the evidence for this is the relative scarcity of lawsuits in this area of the law.

5) Time and Place of Contract

When parties sign a contract simultaneously in a face-to-face setting, there is no doubt as to when and where the contract came into being. When either an offer, or an acceptance, or both, are sent by telegraph, telex, fax, EDI, e-mail, or via the Internet, or are communicated by telephone, it is often not a trivial legal task to determine when and where the contract arose. The uncertainty began even before the advent of the telegraph, with the mail delivery system. The general contract law rule is that an offer is not considered accepted until the acceptance of the offer is received by the offeror. In the 1800s in England an exception to

---

72 *Henckel*, above note 65 at 420.

this rule was developed by judges for offers and acceptances sent by the mail. The so-called post box rule holds that where an offer is made by the mail, the contract is made immediately at the time acceptance is posted in the mail (rather than when the acceptance is actually received by the offeror) where use of the mail is reasonable in the circumstances or expressly contemplated by the parties. This rule effectively operates to place the burden of uncertainty of the waiting period on the offeror; that is, the offeror does not know that it has earlier concluded a binding contract until it receives the offeree's acceptance in the mail, whereas the offeree knew the contract came into existence the moment it posted its reply letter. Shifting this risk to the offeror, and giving the concomitant comfort to the offeree, was reasonable because of the increased reliability of the Royal Mail in the 1800s, to the point where multiple deliveries a day in larger urban centres were the norm. The post box rule is a good example of a legal doctrine being firmly grounded in the communication environment and business processes of its day.

As the telegraph, telephone, and each other new communications technology came into widespread use, cases developed as to when and where contracts were consummated. Thorny inconsistencies in the case law appeared. In *Carow Towing*, an early Canadian telephone case, it was held that a contract entered into by telephone should be treated like a letter and should follow the post box rule, with acceptance occurring at the place the acceptance is spoken and not where the offeror hears the acceptance.[73] By contrast, in the *Entores* case, a later British decision, Lord Denning concluded that for simultaneous communications like the telephone, the place where the contract is entered into is where the offeror hears the acceptance, and thus, if the line goes dead during the telephone conversation, the onus is upon the offeree to ring back the offeror to ensure the words of acceptance had gotten through to the offeror.[74] Subsequent cases in Canada have followed the decision in *Entores* rather than the approach in *Carow Towing*,[75] with the exception of Quebec where, up until recently, the preponderance of cases have followed the rule that telephone contracts arise when and where the offeree speaks its acceptance;[76] since the enactment of the current *Civil Code* in

---

73 *Carow Towing Co. v. The "Ed. McWilliams"* (1919), 46 D.L.R. 506 (Ex. Ct.).

74 *Entores, Ltd. v. Miles Far East Corporation*, [1955] 2 All E.R. 493 (C.A.) [*Entores*].

75 See, for example, *McDonald & Sons Ltd. v. Export Packers Co. Ltd.* (1979), 95 D.L.R. (3d) 174 (B.C.S.C.) [*Export Packers*]. See also *Re Viscount Supply Co. Ltd.* (1963), 40 D.L.R. (2d) 501 (Ont. S. C.); and *National Bank of Canada v. Clifford Chance* (1996), 30 O.R. (3d) 746 (Gen. Div.) [*Clifford Chance*].

76 *Rosenthal & Rosenthal Inc. v. Bonavista Fabrics Ltd.*, [1984] C.A. 52 (Que. C.A.).

January 1994, Article 1387 makes it clear that in respect of telephone contracts acceptance occurs when and where the acceptance is received. The *Entores* decision was also followed in a pair of fax cases, one in Nova Scotia[77] and one in New Zealand,[78] that each held that a contract made by fax arises when the offeror receives by fax the acceptance of the offeree.

The *Entores* decision also held that telex technology results in instantaneous communications with the result that acceptance occurs when the message is received by the offeror. This approach was confirmed in a useful and insightful decision by the House of Lords in the *Brinkibon* case.[79] In this decision the court determined that although telex communications should be categorized as simultaneous, in each case the specific constituent elements and factors in the communications system need to be carefully considered, such as the following:

> The senders and recipients may not be the principals to the contemplated contract. They may be servants or agents with limited authority. The message may not reach, or be intended to reach, the designated recipient immediately: messages may be sent out of office hours, or at night, with the intention, or on the assumption, that they will be read at a later time. There may be some error or default at the recipient's end which prevents receipt at the time contemplated and believed in by the sender. The message may have been sent and/or received through machines operated by third persons. And many other variations may occur. No universal rule can cover all such cases; they must be resolved by reference to the intentions of the parties, by sound business practice and in some cases by a judgment where the risks should lie.[80]

These factors articulated in the *Brinkibon* case raise a number of questions in respect of EDI, e-mail, and Internet communications. Certain EDI transmissions, for example, will fall into the simultaneous communications category. A good deal of EDI is effected not between the trading principals, however, but by use of intermediaries, so-called value-added networks (VAN) or service providers. An EDI message could likely route through the message sender's VAN, then through the recipient's VAN, and finally to the recipient. Similarly, e-mail messages over the Internet may be sent to electronic mailboxes from which an intended recipient has to then download the message. In such circumstances it may be more

---

77   *Balcom (Joan) Sales Inc. v. Poirier* (1991), 288 A.P.R. 377 (N. S. Co. Ct.).

78   *Gunac Hawkes Bay (1986) Ltd. v. Palmer*, [1991] 3 N.Z.L.R. 297 (H. Ct.).

79   *Brinkibon Ltd. v. Stahag Stahl and Stahlwarenhandelsgesellschaft mbH*, [1982] 1 All E.R. 293 (H.L.) [*Brinkibon*].

80   *Ibid.* at 296.

difficult to conclude that the simultaneous communication rules should apply. Or, it may be difficult to discern when exactly an electronic message has arrived at the recipient's location for purposes of being legally effective. For instance, there is an old British case that held that a paper-based letter sent in a sealed envelope is not considered received until it is opened by the addressee personally.[81] Should such a rule apply in the case of e-mail, or should an e-mail message be deemed received when it is available to be viewed by the intended recipient, regardless of the time at which the recipient actually reads the message? Or when should a telex or fax be deemed to have arrived at a workplace? In one case,[82] the answer was when the message is received by the recipient's machine (on a Friday after business hours and not three days later on a Monday morning when a person actually read the telex).

Given these uncertainties, prudent users of electronic commerce should try to avoid having to refer these sorts of questions to a judge by providing, in their EDI Trading Partner Agreement or other similar document, precisely what electronic message must be received by which computer (i.e., the recipient's or the recipient's VAN) in order for a contract to arise, thereby bringing certainty to the dual questions of when and where the electronic contract arose. Indeed, as to the "where" question, the parties to the TPA would do well to select a governing law in advance, and to make sure the VAN agreements contain the same jurisdiction, so that there is no question which law would apply if resort to the courts were ever required. This is particularly true for EDI and Internet transactions where each trading party's VAN, or internet service provider, may be in a jurisdiction separate from the customer, with the result that possibly the laws of four different jurisdictions may come into play if the parties remain silent on the governing law question. In such circumstances, as Lord Denning noted in the *Entores* case dealing with simply two parties in different jurisdictions, the problems arise because the laws of the respective jurisdictions are different. Therefore, predicting a court's probable response is difficult, given that the court will invariably try to do the just thing under the circumstances, but in some cases this is truly a difficult task. Consider, for example, the court's commentary in the *Export Packers* case where the judge advocated that the various rules developed by the law over the years, such as the simultaneous communication rule in the *Entores* case, should not be applied in a dogmatic fashion:

---

81   *Arrowsmith v. Ingle* (1810), 3 Taunt. 234.
82   The *"Pendrecht,"* [1980] 2 Lloyd's Rep. 56 (Q.B.).

When the common law rules relating to offer and acceptance were under development the telephone did not exist. At that time agreements were made by two or more persons getting together and reaching a common understanding. As the postal system came into being elaborate rules were made by the Courts covering the mechanics of reaching a bargain by mail. Today a person ordinarily resident in British Columbia may telephone from Japan where he is on a business trip to a person ordinarily resident in Ontario but who is also then visiting Italy. They may agree to the same kind of contract which is the subject-matter of this writ. It does not necessarily follow the place where the contract was made was Japan and that Japanese law governs its interpretation. Alternatively, it would be hard to argue the place where the contract was made was Italy and the law of that country ought to apply to its interpretation.[83]

A passage such as this clearly confirms the benefit in users of electronic commerce crafting their own rules for dealing with contract formation issues. Making commercial relationships more secure and predictable through contract, however, can be a costly and time-consuming exercise. Therefore, this may be an area ripe for law reform. Thus, in the United States, the National Conference of Commissioners of Uniform State Law are working toward establishing new rules under the *Uniform Commercial Code* that would take the view that Internet communications are instantaneous in nature and that therefore a contract comes into existence when the sender of the offer receives an electronic message signifying acceptance. This does not, however, answer the question when the acceptance is effective if the offeror was not present before the computer; in other words, does receipt require a human acknowledgment. In determining this question regard should be had, in each case, to: the purpose and function of the rule; who would be prejudiced by a particular holding; what are the reasonable expectations of the parties; and on whom is it reasonable to place a burden for helping to "fix" the system if indeed it needs it.

B. EVIDENCE LAW

Evidence law strives to ensure that only reliable evidence is permitted to be provided to judicial and other decision makers in legal, administrative, and related proceedings. To this end, a number of evidence law

---

83   *Export Packers*, above note 75 at 178.

rules have been developed, initially in the context of oral testimony and, more recently, documents and records. Statutory records retention rules also attempt to ensure that companies and other organizations maintain trustworthy information in order to permit the relevant government agency to carry out its regulatory and other functions properly. These evidence law and records retention rules, for the most part, were created in an era that pre-dates the collection, storage, and dissemination of information electronically. Of all the federal and provincial *Evidence Acts*, for example, only a few deal expressly with computer-generated records. In the jurisdictions that do not address computer-generated records directly, questions from time to time can be raised as to whether the traditional rules of evidence are adequate to deal with the economy's shift from paper-based to electronic record keeping. The first two dynamics of computer law — the rapid pace of technological change and the elusive nature of information — have presented a number of challenges to the laws of evidence. Nonetheless, as in the contract law area, the judiciary's approach to computer-generated records has generally been adequate to deal with these challenges. Courts have endeavoured to understand the technology underpinning the computer-generated record, and then have sensibly applied the common law or statutory evidence law rule, almost invariably with the result that a copy of the computer generated record has been admitted into evidence. Notwithstanding the generally positive track record, however, there are some questions and uncertainties in the law of evidence as it relates to computer-generated records which probably warrant some law reform initiatives.

1) Admissibility of Business Records

Traditionally, the form of evidence preferred by judges was oral testimony given by live witnesses, in order that the veracity of the witnesses, and their credibility, might be tested by rigorous, and sometimes withering, cross-examination. Moreover, a live witness would only be allowed to testify as to matters of which he or she had personal knowledge; information that the witness heard someone else say — referred to as "hearsay" — would be excluded, given that such other person should be compelled to testify firsthand so that, again, the reliability testing mechanism of cross-examination could be brought to bear.[84] Under such a hearsay rule, documents were also frowned upon as evidence because, strictly speaking, they constituted hearsay; again, the

---

84 See *R. v. O'Brien*, [1978] 1 S.C.R. 591 for an articulation of the hearsay rule.

theory was that the actual author of the document should also have to appear personally in court. By the early 1800s, however, business records were becoming such a prevalent means of storing information it was no longer practical to bring to court the author of every single document in the company. As important, judges took comfort in the trustworthiness of these business records because they were the very same documents that were used to organize and operate in some cases vast and impressive corporate or financial empires; if they were good enough for the business, they were good enough for the legal system. Thus developed an important exception to the common law hearsay rule: business records created in the ordinary course of business could be admitted into evidence.[85] Accompanying the common law business records exception to the hearsay rule was the "best evidence" rule, which required that the best evidence possible be provided to the court. In the context of documents, this meant, for example, that original documents were to be preferred to copies.[86] This best evidence rule can be seen operating, for example, in some of the old telegraph cases referred to in the previous part of this chapter, where courts preferred to see before them the actual paper-based message written out by the customer rather than the transcript of this message produced by the telegraph company.[87]

Over time, the business records common law exception to the hearsay rule became enshrined in many of Canada's evidence law statutes. For example, in respect of bank records, the *Canada Evidence Act* provides in section 29:[88]

> 29 (1) Subject to this section, a copy of any entry in any book or record kept in any financial institution shall in all legal proceedings be admitted in evidence as proof, in the absence of evidence to the contrary, of the entry and of the matters, transactions and accounts therein recorded.
>
> (2) A copy of an entry in the book or record described in subsection (1) shall not be admitted in evidence under this section unless it is first proved that the book or record was, at the time of the making of the entry, one of the ordinary books or records of the financial institution, that the entry was made in the usual and ordinary course of business, that the book or record is in the custody or control of the financial

---

85   *Ares v. Venner* (1970), 73 W.W.R. 347 (S.C.C.) [*Ares*]; *R. v. Monkhouse*, [1988] 1 W.W.R. 725 (Alta. C.A.).

86   *R. v. Cotroni* (1979), 45 C.C.C. (2d) 1 (S.C.C.).

87   See *Kinghorne*, above note 4, and *Howley*, above note 7.

88   *Canada Evidence Act*, R.S.C. 1985, c. C-5.

institution and that the copy is a true copy of it, and such proof may be given by any person employed by the financial institution who has knowledge of the book or record or the manager or accountant of the financial institution, and may be given orally or by affidavit sworn before any commissioner or other person authorized to take affidavits.

The earliest predecessor of section 29 was added to the *Canada Evidence Act* in 1927, illustrating that quite early on Parliament was comfortable with the circumstantial trustworthiness that resulted from the well-kept records of Canada's banks, this confidence being fostered no doubt in part by the close government regulation of these financial institutions and the fact that customers relied on these records as well. Forty years later, a general business records provision was added, now section 30 of the *Canada Evidence Act*:

30 (1) Where oral evidence in respect of a matter would be admissible in a legal proceeding, a record made in the usual and ordinary course of business that contains information in respect of that matter is admissible in evidence under this section in the legal proceeding on production of the record.

. . .

(6) For the purpose of determining whether any provision of this section applies, or for the purpose of determining the probative value, if any, to be given to information contained in any record admitted in evidence under this section, the court may, on production of any record, examine the record, admit any evidence in respect thereof given orally or by affidavit including evidence as to the circumstances in which the information contained in the record was written, recorded, stored or reproduced, and draw any reasonable inference from the form or content of the record.

The essential scheme created by sections 29 and 30 is to admit the bank or business record subject to the court's ability to probe the so-called foundation evidence relating to the process that created the record to ensure its trustworthiness.

Section 31 of the *Canada Evidence Act* also contains provisions providing for the admissibility of microfilm copies:

(2) A print, whether enlarged or not, from any photographic film of
   (a) an entry in any book or record kept by any government or corporation and destroyed, lost or delivered to a customer after the film was taken,
   (b) any bill of exchange, promissory note, cheque, receipt, instrument or document held by any government or corporation

and destroyed, lost or delivered to a customer after the film was taken, or

(c) any record, document, plan, book or paper belonging to or deposited with any government or corporation,

is admissible in evidence in all cases in which and for all purposes for which the object photographed would have been admitted on proof that

(d) while the book, record, bill of exchange, promissory note, cheque, receipt, instrument or document, plan, book or paper was in the custody or control of the government or corporation, the photographic film was taken thereof in order to keep a permanent record thereof, and

(e) the object photographed was subsequently destroyed by or in the presence of one or more of the employees of the government or corporation, or was lost or was delivered to a customer.[89]

To complete the picture, it should be noted that section 26 of the *Canada Evidence Act* provides for the admission of certain government documents, including material in government books in subsection 26(1):

26(1) A copy of any entry in any book kept in any office or department of the Government of Canada, or in any commission, board or other branch of the public service of Canada, shall be admitted as evidence of that entry, and of the matters, transactions and accounts therein recorded, if it is proved by the oath or affidavit of an officer of the office or department, commission, board or other branch of the public service of Canada that the book was, at the time of the making of the entry, one of the ordinary books kept in the office, department, commission, board or other branch of the public service of Canada, that the entry was made in the usual and ordinary course of business of the office, department, commission, board or other branch of the public service of Canada and that the copy is a true copy thereof.

A number of the provincial evidence statutes, but not all of them, contain provisions similar to these and those in the previous paragraph. Moreover, although animated by the same general principles, the specific bank, general business records, microfilm, and government document provisions in the various provincial and federal evidence statutes are by no means uniform, and important differences exist between them.

---

89   Subsection 31(1) defines "photographic film" to include "any photographic plate, microphotographic film and photostatic negative."

2) Admissibility of Computer-generated Evidence

a) New Evidence Statutes

Quebec and New Brunswick have expressly taken cognizance of computer-generated evidence in their evidence law statutes. Article 2837 of the Quebec *Civil Code* recognizes data stored in a computer, so long as the document reproducing the data is intelligible and its reliability is sufficiently guaranteed. Moreover, article 2838 provides that reliability is presumed in respect of computers when the data entry is carried out systematically and without gaps and the computerized data is protected against alterations. In 1996, the *Evidence Act* of New Brunswick was amended by adding thereto the following provision:[90]

> 47.2(1) Where, in the normal course of business or affairs, a document that was created in electronic form by a person is recorded or stored electronically in order to keep a permanent record of the document, a printout of the document generated by or produced from a computer record or other electronic medium is admissible in evidence in all cases and for all purposes for which the document would have been admissible had it been created in a tangible form.
>
> 47.2(2) A printout described in subsection (1) is not admissible in evidence unless
>
> (a) the document was recorded or stored electronically in the normal course of business or affairs, and
> (b) the contents of the document being tendered are as originally recorded and stored and have not been altered.

A further provision was also added to this statute that recognizes the practice of electronic imaging, a process whereby paper-based documents are scanned and stored electronically:

> 47.1(2) Where a document kept or held by a person is copied by a process of electronic imaging or similar process and is recorded or stored electronically in the course of an established practice in order to keep a permanent record of the document, a printout of the document generated by or produced from a computer record or other electronic medium is admissible in evidence in all cases and for all purposes for which the original document would have been admissible.

---

90 R.S.N.B., 1973, c. E-11. The amendments are found in *An Act to Amend the Evidence Act*, S.N.B. 1996, c. 52.

47.1(3) A printout described in subsection (2) is not admissible in evidence unless

    (a) the original document was copied by a process of electronic imaging or similar process and was recorded or stored electronically in the course of an established practice in order to keep a permanent record of it,

    (b) the original document was destroyed after being copied and recorded or stored in accordance with paragraph (a), and

    (c) the printout is a true copy of the original document.

Interestingly, this provision does not reference the relatively recent national standard for imaging that has been published by the Canada General Standards Board (CGSB).[91] This standard sets out a number of practices and procedures recommended for imaging systems. Usefully, the lack of a reference to this standard in subsection 47.1(2) of the New Brunswick statute ostensibly will permit imaging systems to comply with it that fall below the rather rigorous processes set out in the CGSB standard. On the other hand, it is unfortunate that paragraph 47.1(3)(b) requires the original of the document to be destroyed; while many users of imaging systems may well do this, it really should not be a statutory requirement. As well, it would have been useful if the New Brunswick statute would have made it clear that with respect to paragraph 47.1(3)(c), one could prove that a printout is a copy of the original by relying on the reliability of the system that produced the printout.

b) Old Evidence Statutes and the Common Law

In those jurisdictions that have to date not implemented, or in the future do not implement evidence law provisions similar to those noted in the previous paragraph, parties arguing for the admissibility of computer-generated records tend to rely on either the statutory business records rules in the various evidence acts or on the common law business records exception to the hearsay rule. Generally, courts have expressed very little reluctance to admit computer-generated records. In an early case, the British Columbia Court of Appeal concluded, without any discussion, that printouts from a computerized accounting system were clearly admissible under section 30 of the *Canada Evidence Act.*[92] A

---

91   Canadian General Standards Board, *Microfilm and Electronic Images as Documentary Evidence*, CAN/CGSB-72.11-93 [*Microfilm*].

92   *R. v. Vanlerberghe* (1976), 6 C.R. (3d) 222 (B.C.C.A.). See also *R. v. Sanghi* (1971), 6 C.C.C. (2d) 123 (N.S.C.A.), where computer-related evidence was admitted without a discussion of reliability issues.

dozen years later the same court confirmed this position, again without any substantive discussion.[93] And where an evidence statute is found to be unavailable because one of its conditions is not met, the common law principle has been used to admit the computer-based record.[94] Thus, in *Kinsella* v. *Logan*,[95] a 1995 New Brunswick case that pre-dates the amendments to the New Brunswick evidence statute referred to above, the court determined that the business records provision of this statute did not apply to computer-generated credit reports because of the statutory requirement (not found in the *Canada Evidence Act*) that the business record be made at or near the time of the acts or events recorded. The credit report, which is produced by the computers of the credit reporting agency by sorting and processing data provided by the computers from many merchants and financial institutions, is constantly being updated, and hence did not fit the contemporaneity requirement in the statute. Undaunted, the court reviewed the recent Supreme Court of Canada decisions on the common law hearsay rule,[96] which essentially permit the admission of any document that is reliable, and admitted the credit report on the strength of the fact that such credit reports are extensively used in banking and business, and hence the court ought to consider them to be reliable as well.

The *Kinsella* case exhibited an eminently sensible approach to computer-generated evidence. The computer-based record at issue in this case was the lifeblood of the company that generated it. In almost all organizations today, computer-based records and the printouts derived from them, serve as the informational bricks and mortar that support the whole infrastructure and operations of the entity. Indeed, as noted in section C(4), "Dependency on Computers," in chapter 1, this phenomenon has led to a large number of business and other organizations becoming entirely dependent on the computer. In some respects this can be a risky situation, and even an unfavourable state of affairs, as when a new project to upgrade all or some of the computer system fails to come to fruition, as discussed in section E(3), "Express Warranties," in chapter 5. From an evidentiary perspective, however, this inordinate reliance on computers is a reassuring fact. It means that judges should defer to the computer-generated document, given its tremendous degree of circumstantial trustworthiness.

---

93   *R.* v. *Bicknell* (1988), 41 C.C.C. (3d) 545 (B.C.C.A.).
94   See; for example, *R.* v. *Sunila and Solayman* (1986), 26 C.C.C. (3d) 331 (N.S.S.C.) [*Sunila*].
95   (1995), 163 N.B.R. 1 (N.B.Q.B.) [*Kinsella*].
96   *R.* v. *Khan*, [1990] 2 S.C.R. 531; *R.* v. *Seaboyer*, [1991] 2 S.C.R. 577.

From time to time, however, the evidence law statutes have raised questions since their wording pre-dates computer concepts. Thus, in *R. v. McMullen* the trial judge excluded a computer printout related to an accused's account at a bank branch on the basis that the branch itself had no written record other than the printouts, and the printouts were generated from information obtained from other locations through computer connections.[97] Thus, given that no person in the particular branch could be said to be in charge of the operation of the computer system in terms of overall input, processing, and output, the trial judge concluded that section 29 of the *Canada Evidence Act* does not apply to computer-type evidence, and specifically the word "record" in section 29 does not include computer-generated evidence. On appeal, Linden J. disagreed with the trial judge and held that a computer printout is a copy of a record kept by a financial institution. In reaching this conclusion he stated in a passage reproduced in the Court of Appeal decision:

> The types of records that have been kept have varied through the ages. Human beings have used stone tablets, papyrus, quill pen entries in dusty old books, typewritten material on paper, primitive mechanical devices and now sophisticated electronic computer systems. All, however, serve the same function of recording and this had been recognized by the American authorities that were cited to me. Parliament has indicated its faith in the reliability of the records of financial institutions in whatever form they may have been kept through the years. I conclude, therefore, that the language used by Parliament in the *Canada Evidence Act* includes records kept in computers.
>
> Methods of copying have also changed much over the years. At one time, copies were done by scribes by hand. Then printing was invented. Eventually, primitive copying machines were designed. Now the sophisticated xeroxing equipment can produce copies that can hardly be distinguished from the original. In my view, a computer print-out is a copy of what is contained within that computer, whether it be on tape or disc, though it is in a different form than the original record. It is merely a new type of copy made from a new type of record. Though the technology changes, the underlying principles are the same.[98]

On a further appeal, the Ontario Court of Appeal upheld Linden J.'s decision, and then went on to discuss the type of foundation evidence

---

97   (1978), 42 C.C.C. (2d) 67 (Ont. H.C.J.) [*McMullen*].
98   *Ibid.* at 69.

regarding the relevant computer system the court believed necessary in the case of computer-generated evidence:

> I accept that the demonstration of reliability of computer evidence is a more complex process than proving the reliability of written records. I further accept that as a matter of principle a Court should carefully scrutinize the foundation put before it to support a finding of reliability, as a condition of admissibility . . . The nature and quality of the evidence put before the Court has to reflect the facts of the complete record keeping process — in the case of computer records, the procedures and processes relating to the input of entries, storage of information, and its retrieval and presentation . . . If such evidence be beyond the ken of the manager, accountant or the officer responsible for the records . . . then a failure to comply with s.29(2) must result and the print-out evidence would be inadmissible.[99]

With respect to the question of foundation evidence, it is worth noting that in a case that pre-dates the decision in *McMullen*, the court refused to admit a computer printout because the human witness of the party wishing to introduce it did not know where the documents came from, how they were created, the origin of the data, and the processes used to produce them.[100] In the later *R. v. Bell and Bruce* case noted in the next paragraph, however, a much more sensible approach to foundation evidence was exhibited — it was simply not an issue.[101]

c) Multiple Originals

A few years after the *McMullen* decision, a further peculiarity of computer-based records came under scrutiny in the *Bell and Bruce* case.[102] In this case, the Crown wished to introduce copies of the paper-based monthly records of a bank account that were generated by the bank's computer. This particular computer stored electronically all the deposits and withdrawals that occurred in a month, but at the end of the month printed out a paper-based cumulative record, and then the electronic memory was wiped clean, leaving the monthly paper-based account statement as the sole record. The defence argued that the *Canada Evidence Act* only permits the admission of a copy of the original record, that the electronically stored data was the original record in this case, and therefore a copy of the paper-based record was inadmissible as

---

99   *R. v. McMullen* (1979), 100 D.L.R. (3d) 671 at 678–79 (Ont. C.A.).

100   *R. v. Rowbotham* (1977), 33 C.C.C. 411 (Ont. Gen. Sess.).

101   *R. v. Bell and Bruce* (1982), 35 O.R. (2d) 164 (C.A.) [*Bell and Bruce*].

102   *Ibid.*

it was not a copy of the original record. The trial judge accepted this argument and acquitted the accused. The Ontario Court of Appeal, however, disagreed with the argument. In a manner reminiscent of the decisions in the *Beatty* and *Brinkibon*[103] cases, the appellate court in *Bell and Bruce* indicated that "[b]ecause of the rapidly changing nature of the technology, it would be impossible to lay down general rules to govern every case"[104] involving computer-generated evidence. Nonetheless, the court went on to stipulate several general propositions, including the following: a record may be in any form, even an illegible one; and the form in which information is recorded may change from time to time, and the new form is equally a record of that kind of information. Based on these principles, the court held that the information in the bank's computer changed its form when it was printed out as a paper-based monthly statement, and that this hard copy thereupon became the record that was kept by the financial institution, and hence a copy of it was admissible.

Interestingly, there is in the *Bell and Bruce* case no extended discussion of foundation evidence the way there was in the *McMullen* decision. This is indicative of the attitude of most judges when considering computer-generated evidence emanating from financial institutions in particular. For example, in a U.S. case an appellate court stated:

> In this case, there was no error in admitting the evidence without requiring that technical information be supplied. Certainly when the computer-generated evidence is provided by a well-established national banking institution, maintaining numerous branches in the state, it is reasonable for a court to assume that the "electronic-computer" equipment is reliable.[105]

The court in this case noted that perhaps a stronger foundation could have been laid if the prosecutor had provided information regarding the type of data in the computer and other matters, but even without this foundation evidence the court was comfortable admitting the computer-generated evidence from the bank. And this comfort was not misplaced. It is not clear what foundation evidence regarding the computer is really intended to achieve. Suppose, for a moment, that the foundation evidence shows that the computer did experience some downtime, as all computers are wont to do on occasion. So what? In order for the business to run, and survive, the reason for the downtime was fixed. If

---

103   *Beatty*, above note 10; *Brinkibon*, above note 79.
104   *Bell and Bruce*, above note 101 at 166.
105   *State v. Kane*, 594 P.2d 1357 at 1361 (Wash. App. 1979).

information was lost, it was recovered. If files were corrupted, they were redone. In short, probably the only meaningful foundation evidence would be the admission that the company went bankrupt as a result of its computer system not working. Short of this, the only foundation question that really needs to be asked is, quite simply, "Does the organization rely on this computerized information on a daily basis either directly or indirectly as data for other reports and records that the organization relies on directly?" If the answer to this question is affirmative (as it invariably will be, unless the organization has superfluous computer systems on its premises), then the document containing such data should be viewed as being sufficiently reliable to permit its introduction as evidence.

The cases above illustrate that courts have had little difficulty applying the existing rules of evidence to computer-generated records. By focussing on the purpose of these rules, and understanding the technologies and business processes involved in the fact situations before them, courts have arrived at sensible decisions when confronted with computer-generated evidence, invariably by admitting the computer-generated record where they have direct or circumstantial confidence in the reliability of the computer system that generated them. At the risk of stating the obvious, it should be noted that this process is only called into play on those rare occasions when one party challenges the admissibility of computer-generated evidence; that is, for the most part litigators do not feel the need to fight this battle. Where, however, courts are asked to pass on this matter, the process noted above has been assisted by the fact that many of the cases involved computer-generated records held by a person unconnected with the particular matter being litigated, that is, a disinterested third party, and this added to the sense of trustworthiness of the records at issue. Nevertheless, in other cases the computer-based records of a party to the litigation were at issue, and a similar positive approach to admissibility was displayed by the court.[106] In a case

---

106 *Tecoglas, Inc.* v. *Domglas, Inc.* (1985), 51 O.R. (2d) 196 (H.C.J.). In this case the court permitted a construction company's own computer printouts, containing expenditure data, to be admitted, and concluded at 205:

>The complexity of this type of construction project has increased substantially even since the decision of *Ares* v. *Venner* . . . in 1970 [see *Ares*, above note 85]. There are not many large enterprises operating successfully today who do not use computers in connection with their record-keeping. It would be almost impossible and certainly impractical to prove expenditures of the nature of those in this case without admitting the computer records or documents based on the computer print-out. Accordingly, both documents will be admitted as exhibits and as evidence in support of the claim that the expenditures shown are the actual expenditures to the date in question.

not involving computer-generated evidence, it was held that any records of a business, and not just those related to its routine business activities, could be admitted under the business records rule of Ontario's evidence statute.[107] This decision is particularly useful in the context of imaging technologies where a company may be scanning and storing records that do not relate to its core business functions. This is not to say, however, that electronic-based material cannot present problems from time to time. There is no doubt that, in one sense, electronically stored material is more volatile, changeable, and at the very least prone to updating and, more ominously, alteration and even deterioration.[108] For example, academic journals that are available only online on the Internet in an electronic format without any paper-based version being published raise concerns if, say, the journal's website is discontinued; that is, how does one prove what the official version of the article was? There are, of course, several ways of dealing with these exigencies, such as lodging electronic copies with deposit libraries or other trusted third parties.

Another factor arguing in favour of trustworthiness of electronic documents is that while they may be more volatile, they are also more numerous from the perspective of the number of copies made and maintained of all the different versions of the material, because storage capacity is no longer an issue for electronic documents. Indeed, it is difficult to destroy electronic documents. Thus, in one U.S. case a felon thought he had deleted the copy of the ransom note used in the crime, but electronic retrieval measures allowed the note to be recovered from the computer's hard drive.[109] Simply pressing the delete keystroke on a computer does not completely destroy the relevant information; rather, it is posted to an area of the hard drive waiting to be overwritten, but can be recovered with certain software utilities if it has not yet been overwritten. The defendants in the *Prism* software copyright case learned this lesson when their denial of accessing the plaintiff's source code was disproved by such a "smoking gun" electronic retrieval.[110] In this regard it should also be noted that in Ontario a case has held that a computer disk must be produced for discovery in litigation, and not just

---

107   *Setak Computer Services Corporation Ltd.* v. *Burroughs Business Machines Ltd.* (1977), 76 D.L.R. (3d) 641 (Ont. H.C.J.).

108   Marcia Stepanek, "From Digits to Dust: Surprise — Computerized Data Can Decay before You Know It," *Business Week*, 20 April 1998.

109   *Commonwealth* v. *Copenhefer*, 587 A.2d 1353 (Pa. 1991).

110   *Prism Hospital Software Inc.* v. *Hospital Medical Records Institute* (1994), 57 C.P.R. (3d) 129 (B.C.S.C.). See also Linda Himelstein, "The Snitch in the System: Old Data Are Showing Up in Court — and Winning Cases," *Business Week*, 17 April 1995.

the information contained on it, given that the old authorities defining "document" spoke in terms of "any matter expressed or described upon any substance by means of letters, figures, or marks."[111] There has even been a case in the United States where e-mail messages, never before printed out until the trial, were admitted even though they arose in a completely paperless environment.[112] The court in this case acknowledged that messages in the e-mail system could be erased or altered, but the court was satisfied that the various password and other controls in place for the system reduced the likelihood that the message was modified. In effect, the ability of courts to handle the peculiar dynamics of computer-generated evidence under the general business records rules and the common law — that is, their facility in handling the first two dynamics of computer law when it comes to evidence law issues — have led some commentators to question the need for special computer-related statutory provisions.[113]

d) Prospective Law Reform

Nonetheless, the provisions of the *Canada Evidence Act* do contain some shortcomings. For example, in one case the term *book* in subsection 26(1) was held not to include a computer.[114] It probably would make sense, therefore, to at least add the concept of "record" to subsection 26(1) so as to capture electronic-based materials, given the broad definition of "record" in subsection 29(12). As well, while cases such as *McMullen, Bell and Bruce,* and *Kinsella* are indeed helpful and demonstrate the flexibility inherent in the current legal regime, they also illustrate some of the limitations of the present statutory rules. First, the inconsistency in the coverage of the statutory provisions across the country can be a problem, particularly for organizations with operations in more than one province. Then there is the simple fact that the words in the statutes, given the first dynamic of computer law, simply do not reflect computer-related reality that well. Of course appellate courts in *McMullen* and *Bell and Bruce* have managed to over-

---

111 *Reichmann v. Toronto Life Publishing Co.* (1988), 66 O.R. (2d) 65 at 67 (H.C.J.).

112 *United States v. Poindexter,* 951 F.2d 369 (D.C. Cir. 1991).

113 J. Douglas Ewart, *Documentary Evidence in Canada* (Toronto: Carswell, 1984).

114 *Sunila,* above note 94. In this decision, the court, after noting that in an earlier case the term *book* was held to apply to files loosely fastened together, concluded at 336: "[W]hile it is one thing to stretch the meaning of a well-known word used in a statute within a certain context, to equate book with computer would be to ignore completely the common and accepted meaning of the word 'book.' It would be tantamount to legislating a new word into the statute. That is the sole responsibility of our legislators, not of judges."

come this language problem, but it should not be forgotten that in both cases the judges at first instance went in the other direction. Indeed, two cases that came after *Bell and Bruce* illustrate that some courts are still having difficulty dealing with computer-generated records.[115] Accordingly, it would be useful to fine-tune some of the statutory shortcomings and uncertainties of the present legal regime related to computer-generated evidence.

As a result, the Uniform Law Conference of Canada (ULCC), which comprises representatives of all the offices of attorneys general in the Canadian provinces, the federal government, and the two territories, in the summer of 1997 published a draft *Uniform Electronic Evidence Act*.[116] A key objective of the draft statute is to provide that the best evidence rule is satisfied in respect of electronic records by proof of the integrity of the electronic records system by which the data was recorded or preserved. Moreover, the draft statute would allow the integrity of the record-keeping system to be implied from the operation of the underlying computer. This proposal for a uniform electronic evidence statute would usefully achieve a number of objectives. It would support the admissibility of electronic evidence, while still permitting a party to challenge it if the reliability of the computer system or network that produced it can be put into question. Perhaps most importantly, the proposal would effectively resolve the issue of what constitutes the "original" record in the context of the creation, storage, and communication of electronic information by effectively abandoning the concept of original in an electronic environment. This would serve as a useful recognition of a trend articulated by decisions such as *Bell and Bruce*. The concept of original is paper-based — it applies where a person types or writes directly onto a piece of paper, thereby clearly creating an original of the letter. Where computers send messages electronically, the second dynamic of computer law kicks in and it is no longer meaningful to talk in terms of which is the original — the copy of the message in the sender's or recipient's computer — and which is a reproduction. The thrust of the ULCC proposals would be to shift the analysis from an assessment of a particular electronic document to the computer-based system that produced it, and then to take comfort about this system based on its operational track record. The ephemeral nature of information should lead to an enquiry at the systemic level of the processes that pro-

---

115   See *R. v. Hanlon* (1985), 69 N.S.R. 266 (N. S. Co. Ct.); and *R. v. Cordell* (1982), 39 A.R. 281 (C.A.), where ultimately the computer printout was admitted by the appellate court, but only after being excluded by the trial judge.

116   Uniform Law Conference of Canada, *Uniform Electronic Evidence Act*, August 1997, available at <http://www.law.ualberta.ca/alri/ulc/current/eueea.htm>.

ducèd the information, rather than focussing on any particular manifestation of that information. Of course, it would always be possible for a party to object to the admission of any particular item based on evidence of tampering or alteration, but it would be the rare situation indeed where this would occur. The general rule ought to be along the lines of a variation on the adage "I think, therefore I am" transcribed as "the document is produced in the normal course of business (whether electronically or in any other mode) and relied upon by the business, and therefore it should be admitted."

Until a statute like the one proposed by the ULCC comes into effect, private parties may wish to bolster the admissibility of electronically generated evidence through contract. It is, for instance, quite common for EDI trading partners to stipulate contractually how records of their electronic messages are to be kept. Moreover, just as EDI trading partners will often deem these electronic messages to be writings for contract law purposes (as noted above), so too does the EDI Council of Canada's *Model TPA*, in section 7.04, contain a similar provision addressing evidence law issues:

> Each party hereby acknowledges that a copy of the permanent record of the Transaction Log certified in the manner contemplated by this Agreement shall be admissible in any legal, administrative or other proceedings between them as *prima facie* evidence of the accuracy and completeness of its contents in the same manner as an original document in writing, and each party hereby expressly waives any right to object to the introduction of a duly certified permanent copy of the Transaction Log in evidence.[117]

The transaction log referred to in this provision refers to the electronically stored summary or index of messages sent between the EDI trading partners.[118] As with the equivalent provision dealing with the "writing" issue, it is open to question whether such a provision is enforceable; nonetheless, it is still a useful provision to include in TPAs today. The ULCC proposal, if implemented, would obviate the need for such contractual provisions.

Law reform through statutory amendment is no panacea. Even new legislative provisions have to be monitored to ensure they remain up to

---

117   *Model TPA*, above note 35.

118   In *Roberts v. United States*, 508 A.2d 110 (D. C. 1986), a similar electronic-based log was admitted into evidence, in that case being summaries of the transactions of automated teller machines which were compiled from the bank's computerized transaction records.

date, given the relentless effect of the first dynamic of computer law. This need for legislators to stay vigilant can be seen in the amendment in 1968 of the U.K. civil evidence statute to provide that any "document produced by a computer" is admissible.[119] A commentator writing about this section has suggested that the U.K. government, indirectly, has put into question whether this provision is broad enough to cover EDI or other electronic messages where, in effect, the record in one computer has been created by and sent by another computer.[120] Thus, the ULCC, and others, contemplating statutory amendments in this area should be careful to use language that encompasses a wide spectrum of technologies and potential business practices, such as where documents arise out of the interconnected collaboration of different parties over the Internet or other networks. And the ULCC should not consider its task complete upon the presentation of its proposed amendments.

3) Records Retention Rules

A similar issue to the one of evidence law arises in connection with the records retention requirements stipulated by numerous statutes in many jurisdictions. A large number of laws require companies, organizations, and individuals to maintain certain books and records in order that a particular government department be able to have access to the information contained therein for regulatory and other purposes. In most cases, the records retention provisions of various statutes either expressly, or impliedly, contemplate paper-based documents as the manner in which information must be retained. Over time, some of these provisions have been amended to include the recording and storage of information in electronic form. As with the writing requirement caveat given above, however, it must be understood that there are a multitude of these record retention provisions and the specific ones relevant to any entity's situation must be reviewed in detail. Nevertheless, in order to illustrate the phenomenon by way of an example, consider the records retention rules under the *Income Tax Act*, contained in an *Information Circular*,[121] which provide that Revenue Canada recognizes several types of books and records: the traditional books of account with supporting

---

119   *Civil Evidence Act 1968* (U.K.), 1968, c. 64, subs. 5(1).

120   Rob Bradgate, "Evidential Issues of EDI," in *EDI and the Law*, above note 20.

121   *Income Tax Act* (Canada), R.S.C. 1985, c. 1 (5th Supp.). The *Income Tax Act's* record retention rules are contained in *Income Tax Information Circular No. 78-10R2, Books and Records Retention/Destruction*, 14 July 1989, which cancelled and replaced *Income Tax Information Circular No. 78-10R*, 17 January 1983.

source documents; records maintained in a machine-sensible data medium that can be related back to the supporting source documents and which is supported by a system capable of producing accessible and readable copy; and microfilm reproductions of books of original entry and source documents, if the microfilming process complies with the Canada General Standards Board microfilm standard.[122] In 1995 Revenue Canada amended this policy to expressly provide that imaging is also an acceptable method of keeping records, provided the imaging methodology employed complies with the CGSB imaging standard described earlier.[123] The Revenue Canada policy provides that each imaging program should include the following:

a) someone in the organization has confirmed in writing that the program will be part of the usual and ordinary activity of the organization's business;

b) systems and procedures are established and documented;

c) a log book is kept showing:
   (i)   the date of imaging;
   (ii)   the signatures of the persons authorizing and performing the imaging;
   (iii) a description of the records imaged; and
   (iv)   whether source documents are destroyed or disposed of after imaging, and the date a source document was destroyed or disposed of;

d) the imaging software maintains an index to permit the immediate location of any record, and the software inscribes the imaging date and the name of the person who does the imaging;

e) the images are of commercial quality, and are legible and readable when displayed on a computer screen or reproduced on paper;

f) a system of inspection and quality control is established to ensure that c), d) and e) above are maintained; and

g) after reasonable notification, equipment in good working order is available to view, or where feasible, to reproduce a hard copy of the image.

Revenue Canada's decision to recognize imaging as an acceptable method of records retention has been well received by the Canadian business community, given the increasingly rapid diffusion of imaging technology throughout the country. Unfortunately, other aspects of

---

122   See *Microfilm*, above note 91.
123   *Ibid.*; and see *Income Tax Information Circular No. 78-10R2 SR, Books and Records Retention/Destruction*, 10 February 1995.

Revenue Canada's records retention policy remain vague and unhelpful. For example, what does "traditional" books of account and supporting source documents mean? How many years of use of computerized books of account are required before the new process is considered "traditional"? Moreover, the only recognition of computerized documents refers to a "machine-sensible data medium that can be related back to the supporting source documents." This covers a computer-based spreadsheet or other accounting program to serve as the company's general ledger, but do the supporting source documents have to be in paper form, or can they be data in a computer's long-term memory? What about electronic EDI messages where the electronic message *is* the source document? Having clarified its position regarding imaging, it would be extremely useful if Revenue Canada gave similar assurance for direct computer-to-computer messages. Moreover, from a conceptual perspective, it can be asked whether it would make sense to more closely align the records retention rules with the existing and especially any revised evidence law provisions so that businesses, other organizations, and individuals can approach their computer-based business practices with more certainty.

Several examples exist of how the computer and network technologies might be addressed from a records retention perspective. Ontario's *Vital Statistics Act*, the statute under which the government registers and stores documents relating to births, marriages, deaths, and other similar events, has been amended to permit it to accommodate new data storage technologies.[124] Thus, subsection 4(1) of this statute now provides that the registrar may cause registrations and other documents to be accurately recorded by any technology, so long as an accurate and easily readable paper copy of the registration or other document can be made from the record. Moreover, the statute provides in subsection 46(1) that a certified copy of a registration signed by the registrar general or deputy registrar general or on which the signature of either of them is reproduced by any method is admissible as evidence in any Ontario court as proof of the facts so certified, in the absence of evidence to the contrary. Similarly, the statute also provides in subsection 46(3) that a paper copy made from the record of a document, other than a registration, that is made under section 4 is admissible in evidence to the same extent as an original document. The result is a statutory regime of certification and document storage that is malleable enough to accommodate a wide range of new technologies. Equally, the provision in the *Canada Business Corporations Act* specifying how certain records are to be maintained contains a flexible computer-related option at the end of it:

---

124   R.S.O. 1990, c. V.4.

All registers and other records required by this Act to be prepared and maintained may be in a bound or loose-leaf form or in a photographic film form, or may be entered or recorded by any system of mechanical or electronic data processing or any other information storage device that is capable of reproducing any required information in intelligible written form within a reasonable time.[125]

C. INTERNET LEGAL ISSUES

There has already been much discussion in this book of the Internet and the legal issues engendered by this network of computer networks.[126] This book, however, has consciously not devoted a separate chapter to the Internet, nor has it opted to treat the Internet as an altogether novel or unique phenomenon. Rather, approaching the Internet as another

---

125   *Canada Business Corporations Act*, R.S.C. 1985, c. C-44, subs. 22(1). Section 139 of Ontario's *Business Corporations Act*, R.S.O. 1990, c. B.16 provides a similar regime, though somewhat more onerous from the perspective of the record keeper, but still sensibly flexible and electronically friendly:

> 139. (1) [**Records**] Where this Act requires a record to be kept by a corporation, it may be kept in a bound or looseleaf book or may be entered or recorded by any system of mechanical or electronic data processing or any other information storage device.
> (2) [**Guard against falsification of records**] The corporation shall,
>> (a) take adequate precautions, appropriate to the means used, for guarding against the risk of falsifying the information recorded; and
>> (b) provide means for making the information available in an accurate and intelligible form within a reasonable time to any person lawfully entitled to examine the records.
> (3) [**Admissibility of records in evidence**] The bound or looseleaf book or, where the record is not kept in a bound or looseleaf book, the information in the form in which it is made available under clause (2)(b) is admissible in evidence as proof, in the absence of evidence to the contrary, of all facts stated therein, before and after dissolution of the corporation.

126   A brief description of the Internet was offered in section A(6), "The Internet," in chapter 1; intellectual property issues related to it were canvassed in chapter 2, particularly in section C(6), "Copyright and the Internet" and section C(7), "Trade-marks and the Internet"; the impact of it on criminal law was discussed in chapter 3; the issues related to possible regulation of it by the CRTC were a subtopic in section C(3), "Regulating the Internet," in chapter 4; licensing and tax issues germane to it were discussed in section C(3), "Licensing in a Digital Environment" and section G(3), "Taxing the Internet," respectively, in chapter 5; and earlier in this chapter several questions related to doing business on it electronically were discussed.

step along the steady path of the evolution of computers and networks, this book has attempted to integrate the analysis of Internet issues into the technologies and business processes that were its predecessors, such as telegraphy, telephony and broadcasting. Indeed, the four dynamics of computer law that have driven these industries are currently driving the Internet as well; moreover, the Internet may well be the phenomenon that best exemplifies the active and sustained operation of the rapid pace of technological change, the elusive nature of information, and the blurring of private/public and national/international. Nonetheless, while there are some truly revolutionary characteristics of the Internet, the legal issues presented by it are best understood in their historic context, drawing on existing and prior analogies and metaphors; that is, in approaching the Internet it is sensible not to overreact (and, for example, to be "overwhelmed" by its novelty), but neither to underreact (and, for example, to be lulled into a sense of *déjà vu* by its sameness with what has come before). Thus, the following discussions of libel, jurisdiction, and Internet regulation are firmly rooted in the principles and analyses developed by the law in response to a series of pre-Internet technologies and business practices.

1) Cyber Libel

a) Libel Law and the Internet
The Internet provides unprecedented opportunities for local, regional, national, and global communications of text and other content. Chapter 1 described the technology that makes the e-mail, website, usegroups, and other features of the Internet an important advance in the history of message passing among humans.[127] Included in such messages, of course, will be defamatory ones. Defamation is a published false or derogatory statement that discredits a person, or impugns that person's honesty or integrity, or brings into doubt the person's financial solvency,

---

127   As mentioned in section A(6), "The Internet," in chapter 1, *American Civil Liberties Union v. Reno*, 929 F. Supp. 824 (E.D. Pa. 1996) [*ACLU*] provides a solid analysis of how the Internet works and also how it differs from other electronic communication media. While the *ACLU* case dealt with the constitutionality of U.S. legislation aimed at certain pornography, its observations about the Internet are also relevant to formulating sensible and practical libel rules for the Internet.

provided the statement is made known to a third party and is not excused because it is the truth or fair comment or protected by privilege.[128] In the recent *Hill* case, the Supreme Court of Canada spoke eloquently about the danger of defamation, and the laudatory objective of protecting a person's reputation, being the essential purpose of the law of libel:

> Although much has very properly been said and written about the importance of freedom of expression, little has been written of the importance of reputation. Yet, to most people, their good reputation is to be cherished above all. A good reputation is closely related to the innate worthiness and dignity of the individual. It is an attribute that must, just as much as freedom of expression, be protected by society's laws. . . .
>
> Democracy has always recognized and cherished the fundamental importance of an individual. That importance must, in turn, be based upon the good repute of a person. It is that good repute which enhances an individual's sense of worth and value. False allegations can so very quickly and completely destroy a good reputation. A reputation tarnished by libel can seldom regain its former lustre. A democratic society, therefore, has an interest in ensuring that its members can enjoy and protect their good reputation so long as it is merited.[129]

The court in the *Hill* case also gives a brief historic overview of the libel law to the present day, including its important role in the age of the Star Chamber in seventeenth-century England to replace duelling and blood feuds. The civil law of Quebec also provides for the protection of reputation by enshrining the principle in both the Quebec *Civil Code* and the Quebec *Charter of Human Rights and Freedoms*.[130] Defamation may also be criminal in its nature; see the discussion of criminal libel in section B(7), "Criminal Libel," in chapter 3.

---

128   For a good discussion of the intricacies of defamation law, see Raymond E. Brown, *The Law of Defamation in Canada*, 2d ed. (Toronto: Carswell, 1994) (looseleaf, updated) [*Defamation*].

129   *Hill v. Church of Scientology of Toronto*, [1995] 2 S.C.R. 1130 at 1175 [*Hill*].

130   Article 3 of the *Civil Code of Québec* provides: "Every person is the holder of personality rights, such as the right to life, the right to the inviolability and integrity of his person, and the right to the respect of his name, reputation and privacy. These rights are inalienable." Section 4 of the Quebec *Charter of Human Rights and Freedoms*, R.S.Q. c. C-12 states: "Every person has a right to the safeguard of his dignity, honour and reputation."

The law of defamation is extremely relevant to the Internet because just as the Internet is the ultimate vehicle developed to date to effect copyright infringement, a subject discussed in section C(6), "Copyright and the Internet," in chapter 2, so too does the Internet promise to be the supreme mechanism for perpetrating libellous statements. Indeed, it is truly unique in that it is the only means of mass communication where the author of the disseminated material is generally not subject to an editorial filter prior to publication, at least at the point of initial publication. Contrast this with broadcasting, newspapers, or book publishing, where a producer, editor, or some similarly stationed person vets an author's content before it hits the airwaves, newsstands, or the bookstore. The Internet makes each user — all 60 million and counting — a publisher in his or her own right, at least from the perspective of launching the libellous statement into cyberspace.[131] Of course, the Internet does not represent a fundamental departure from certain communications technologies and practices with respect to all activities on it. As emphasized in the other analyses of the Internet provided earlier in the context of copyright and criminal law, it must always be remembered that the Internet comprises a myriad of communication and related activities, undertaken by a broad range of actors. Thus, the multifarious nature of the Internet must be kept in mind as the various scenarios for liability for libel on it are discussed below.

An intriguing threshold question about defamatory statements on the Internet is whether they are libel or slander, the two subcategories of defamation. The distinction matters, at least in those provinces where the two have not been combined in defamation statutes.[132] Slander, which is an oral defamation, generally attracts smaller monetary damage awards and requires the proof of financial loss on the part of the plaintiff. Libel, which is a written defamation, requires no actual damages, and is generally considered the more serious of the two, given the assumption that a written statement is more deliberate and premeditated, and is also more permanent in its longevity. Most messages on the Internet are text-based and are characterized as libel. Many spontaneous messages, however, also contain libellous sentiments. As well, many

---

131   This was also seen, for example, in R. v. Pecciarich (1995), 22 O.R. (3d) 748 (Prov. Ct.), discussed in section B(5)(b), "Intermediary Liability," in chapter 3, where the accused single-handedly created and disseminated child pornography over the Internet.

132   Such as Ontario's Libel and Slander Act, R.S.O. 1990, c. L.12. In some libel statutes, the distinction between libel and slander is almost completely eliminated: see, for example, Manitoba's The Defamation Act, R.S.M. 1987, c. D20.

areas of the Internet are not permanent. Messages on bulletin boards and usegroups are regularly purged and content is deleted as websites are updated. But telephony and radio broadcasting over the Internet raise the possibility of slander. And voice recognition systems where data is entered into a computer orally and then transmitted in a text-based format truly blur the distinction between libel and slander. In provinces like Ontario that have a *Libel and Slander Act*, these distinctions may well be moot since the legislation provides that defamatory words in a "broadcast" are deemed to be a libel[133] and *broadcasting* is broadly defined and would capture most Internet-based messages.

While the definition of *broadcasting* in Ontario's *Libel and Slander Act* is quite technology-neutral,[134] the definition of *newspaper*, the other key concept in the statute, is quite closely aligned to the traditional paper-based journal.[135] This raises the question whether a journal published in an online environment would be a broadcast or a newspaper, an important distinction. For example, subsection 8(1) of the statute provides that certain other provisions of the statute that are of benefit to newspapers by providing for short limitation periods are only available to the newspaper if the name of the proprietor and publisher and address of the publication are stated either at the head of the editorials or on the front page of the newspaper. In a recent case an appellate court construed this provision very strictly, holding that placing of the editorial information at the bottom of the editorial page did not comply with

---

133 See, for example, *Libel and Slander Act*, R.S.O. 1990, c. L.12, s. 2.

134 *Ibid.*, s. 1:

> "broadcasting" means the dissemination of writing, signs, signals, pictures and sounds of all kinds, intended to be received by the public either directly or through the medium of relay stations, by means of,
>
> > (a) any form of wireless radioelectric communication utilizing Hertzian waves, including radiotelegraph and radiotelephone, or
> >
> > (b) cables, wires, fibre-optic linkages or laser beams, and "broadcast" has a corresponding meaning;
>
> Note that this definition of *broadcasting* is different than the one in the *Broadcasting Act*, S.C. 1991, c. 11, discussed in section C(2), "Regulating Broadcasting," in chapter 4.

135 *Ibid.*, s. 1:

> "newspaper" means a paper containing public news, intelligence, or occurrences, or remarks or observations thereon, or containing only, or principally, advertisements, printed for distribution to the public and published periodically, or in parts or numbers, at least twelve times a year.

subsection 8(1).[136] In the context of a newspaper put up on a website, for example, what constitutes "the head of the editorials" or the "front page of the newspaper"? In the case of the latter, is it the absolutely first screen of the website? Or what if an icon on this screen, once clicked, brings up the editorial information; is this sufficient? Or what if another screen from another service of the publisher hotlinks the viewer directly into the editorials, bypassing the first page? This practice may also raise copyright and trade-mark issues.[137] In the non-linear environment of the Web, and the Internet generally, how does one apply concepts like "the head of" and the "front page"? Somewhat more broadly, what if the electronic forum in which the libel appeared offers a particularly effective and timely method for a rejoinder by the subject of the libel?

Questions not unlike these were addressed in a recent U.S. decision, *It's In the Cards, Inc.* v. *Fuschetto*.[138] In this case the court concluded that messages by subscribers to an electronic bulletin board on the Internet were not "periodicals" for purposes of a Wisconsin statute similar to Ontario's *Libel and Slander Act*.[139] The court held that posting a message to the bulletin board was a random communication of a computerized message analogous to posting a written notice on a public bulletin board, and not a publication that appears at regular intervals. Moreover, the court offered the view that the Wisconsin statute, by using the words "magazines, newspapers, and periodicals" contemplated paper-based writings involving the print media; the court stated the electronic bulletin board postings could not be classified as print. In coming to this conclusion the court referred to an earlier case, *Hucko* v. *Jos. Schlitz Brewing Co.*, where it had held that the particular Wisconsin provision did not apply to broadcast media; ostensibly the court in the *Fuschetto*

---

136   *Hermiston* v. *Robert Axford Holdings Inc.* (1994), 120 D.L.R. (4th) 283 (Ont. Div. Ct.); but see also *Elliott* v. *Freisen* (1984), 6 D.L.R. (4th) 338 at 343 (Ont. C.A.), where "some attempted compliance at the head of the editorial page" was found to be sufficient by the court.

137   See section C(6), "Copyright and the Internet" and section C(7), "Trade-marks and the Internet," in chapter 2.

138   535 N.W.2d 11 (Wis. App. 1995) [*Fuschetto*].

139   The Wisconsin statute provided that any party claiming to be defamed in a "newspaper, magazine or periodical" must provide the other party an opportunity to retract the alleged libel: see *ibid.* at 12, footnote 1. While the Ontario statute refers only to "newspaper," the definition of *newspaper* in s. 297 in the *Criminal Code*, with respect to the criminal libel provisions, refers to "paper, magazine or periodical" that are "printed." The reference to "printed" is in the Ontario statute as well, but interestingly, given the court's view on the matter referred to below, not in the Wisconsin statute.

case was unwilling to accept a third type of media between paper-based and broadcast, that is, the Internet.[140] The court in the *Fuschetto* case justified its conservative approach on the following basis:

> Additionally, subsec. (2) of [the Wisconsin statute] was repealed in 1951 and reenacted in its present form, years before cyberspace was envisioned. The magnitude of computer networks and the consequent communications possibilities were non-existent at the time this statute was enacted. Applying the present libel laws to cyberspace or computer networks entails rewriting statutes that were written to manage physical, printed objects, not computer networks or services. Consequently, it is for the legislature to address the increasingly common phenomenon of libel and defamation on the information superhighway.
>
> The rate at which technological developments are growing coupled with the complexity of technology is beyond many laypersons' ken. A uniform system of managing information technology and computer networks is needed to cope with the impact of the information age. It is the responsibility of the legislature to manage this technology and to change or amend the statutes as needed. Therefore, we conclude that extending the definition of "periodical" under [the Wisconsin statute] to include network bulletin board communications on the SportsNet computer service is judicial legislation in which we will not indulge.[141]

In this regard, however, it should be noted that in the *Chuckleberry* case discussed in section C(2)(b), "Internet Cases," in this chapter, the court concluded that the words *magazine* and *periodical* in a 1981 injunction order could include a website containing text and pictures of the defendant.[142] The court found that the word *magazine* meant a "storehouse of information," and that the word *periodical* was appropriate because the material on the website was updated from time to time. Readers are also directed to the discussion of criminal libel in section B(7), "Criminal Libel," in chapter 3, which discusses a case that was willing to view

---

140 In *Hucko v. Jos. Schlitz Brewing Company*, 302 N.W.2d 68 at 72 (Wis. App. 1981), the court concluded that it was obvious from the unambiguous language of the Wisconsin statute that by referring only to magazines, newspapers, and periodicals, the statute did not cover radio or television because it did not refer to these means of communication expressly. Although this may be a reasonable conclusion, for the *Fuschetto* court to draw the inference from this that magazines, newspapers, and periodicals might not find some form of existence on the Internet in other than the traditional paper-based format is less convincing.

141 *Fuschetto*, above note 138 at 14–15.

142 *Playboy Enterprises, Inc. v. Chuckleberry Publishing, Inc.*, 939 F. Supp. 1032 (S.D.N.Y. 1996) [*Chuckleberry*].

"printed" as including photocopied, thereby supporting as well the position that the court in *Fuschetto* took too narrow an approach.[143] Nonetheless, as suggested by the court in *Fuschetto* in respect of its own libel law, and in light of the first dynamic of computer law — namely, the rapid pace of technological change — governments with statutes such as Ontario's *Libel and Slander Act* should consider updating them to capture issues germane to the Internet. In short, libel statutes were enacted to implement desirable policy objectives with respect to certain important channels of communication, some of which apply in an Internet environment. Accordingly, this statutory regime needs to be brought current with today's online technologies and business practices.

b) Intermediary Liability

There is little doubt that the author of a libellous statement can commit the act of defamation by transmitting it to third parties over the Internet or other electronic networks. In the *Finucan* case, a court in Ontario found that a professor's defamation claim was a separate and distinct cause of action from his wrongful termination claim when his superior's highly critical performance evaluation and termination letter were distributed to all professors in the college via an internal e-mail network.[144] In an Australian case, a professor was awarded A$40,000 in damages when a libel was communicated over a bulletin board available to thousands of students and academics.[145] In many cases, however, it is not worth proceeding against the author of the libellous message because they are either judgment-proof by virtue of having no meaningful assets, or they are out of the defendant's jurisdiction and hence difficult or expensive to pursue (for a discussion of jurisdiction in the context of the Internet, see the next part of this chapter). In other cases, the author's identity is simply not known, given the ability of a person to communicate on the Internet in an anonymous manner by using a name, or handle, other than his real name.[146] In such circumstances plaintiffs may well want to pursue other persons who, although not involved in the actual writing of the defamatory message, participated in its transmission in some way. Are the various intermediaries who provide Internet services

---

143   *Xerox of Canada Ltd.* v. *IBM Canada Ltd.* (1977), 33 C.P.R. (2d) 24 (F.C.T.D.).

144   *Egerton* v. *Finucan*, [1995] O.J. No. 1653 (Gen. Div.) (QL). See also *Russell* v. *Nova Scotia Power Inc.* (1996), 436 A.P.R. 271 (N.S.S.C.), discussed in section H(2), "Labour Law," in chapter 5.

145   *Rindos* v. *Hardwick*, [1994] ACL Rep. 145 WA 4 (Sup. Ct.).

146   The state of Georgia has passed a law prohibiting users of the Internet from operating anonymously: see section C(3)(c), "Consumer Protection Laws," in this chapter.

liable for the part they play in the transmission of libellous messages? These issues are similar to those discussed regarding the liability of Internet intermediaries for copyright infringement or criminal law offences (see section C(6), "Copyright and the Internet," in chapter 2 and section B(5), "Obscenity and Child Pornography," in chapter 3).

Defamation law has long recognized that in addition to the author of the libellous statement, third parties involved in its publication are also to be held responsible. The publisher of a book is liable for any libel contained in it, given that through the exercise of the editorial function the publisher has thorough knowledge of the contents of the book and the ability to excise the offending libel. Newspapers are similarly liable for defamatory statements contained in them, and indeed they are responsible for any republications that are a "natural and probable consequence of the original publication," as in the *Holt* case, when a Toronto newspaper was held liable for defamatory remarks republished by another newspaper in British Columbia.[147] This rule, coupled with the principle that each republication is a separate libel, may hold serious adverse ramifications for persons who transmit libellous e-mail over the Internet. Given its electronic make-up, and the ease with which e-mail can be retransmitted by its recipient, it would not be surprising for a court, in the appropriate circumstances, to find that the original sender of an e-mail message is responsible for its subsequent transmission, as this was a natural and probable consequence of the original e-mail transmission. E-mail raises several other issues in respect of libel. A libellous message sent in a sealed envelope through the mail will not be deemed published until it is opened after being delivered by the postal service. By contrast, a postcard is deemed to be published to the post office as well, given the ease with which it can be read.[148] As noted in section B(10), "Interception of Communications," in chapter 3 with respect to the application of the *Criminal Code*'s interception of communications provisions to e-mail, this question will be determined by the characteristics of the type of e-mail message in question, such as whether it is encrypted or not. Another important factor will be whether the ultimate destination of the message was to be posted to a public message board, such as one belonging to a usegroup.

In this regard, another line of non-electronic libel cases that may be relevant to crafting statutory or judge-made rules for third-party liability are those that have addressed liability for failure to remove derogatory statements from physical premises. For example, in *Byrne* v. *Deane*,

---

147 *Chinese Cultural Centre of Vancouver* v. *Holt* (1978), 7 B.C.L.R. 81 (S.C.).
148 See s. 7.12(1) of Brown, *Defamation*, above note 128.

a golf club was held to be liable for participating in the publication of a defamatory statement when it did not remove from its interior walls such a statement about the plaintiff after the club acquired knowledge of the statement.[149] Similarly, in *Hellar* v. *Bianco*, a court in a preliminary proceeding held that an owner of a bar could be held to participate in a republication of an offending message about the plaintiff in the men's room if it failed to remove it promptly enough after being notified of it; the court decided to leave up to the jury whether the plaintiff gave sufficient time to the defendant (in this case, about thirty minutes), given all the surrounding circumstances (i.e., the bartender was busy when the plaintiff initially called to complain).[150]

In an earlier U.S. case, the proprietor of an office was held to have ratified the libel in a newspaper article when he posted the article on a bulletin board in his office for a period of forty days and declined to remove it even after notified of its libellous nature.[151] In *Scott* v. *Hull* a proprietor of a building was not found responsible for offensive graffiti on an exterior wall, based on the rationale (and the distinguishing fact from the preceding cases) that the defendant did not invite the public onto the premises where the offending material was situated;[152] that is, in the other cases, the libellous material was posted by invitees (or the proprietor in the *Fogg* case) and viewed by invitees. If these cases are cited as analogous in an Internet case, it will be necessary to understand, for example, whether the forum where the libel took place online was a "public place," such as an open-to-all-the-public usegroup, or whether it was a "private" gathering of selected e-mailers. In determining such questions involving the third dynamic of computer law, see the discussion of the cases regarding "distribution to the public," "public place," and "exposure to the public" in sections B(5)(c), "Internet Distribution," and B(6), "Illegal Speech," in chapter 3.

---

149   [1937] 1 K.B. 818 (C.A.).

150   244 P.2d 757 (Cal. App. 1952). The "shocking" matter complained of, and that led the court to conclude at 759 that a "[r]epublication occurs when the proprietor has knowledge of the defamatory matter and allows it to remain after a reasonable opportunity to remove it," indicated to the court at 758 that the "appellant was an unchaste woman who indulged in illicit amatory ventures." See also *Tacket* v. *General Motors Corporation*, 836 F.2d 1042 (7th Cir. 1987), where an employer was held liable for failing to remove a defamatory sign on its wall painted by an unknown third party.

151   *Fogg* v. *Boston & L.R. Co.*, 20 N.E. 109 (Mass. 1889) [*Fogg*].

152   259 N.E.2d 160 (Ohio App. 1970).

c) Pre-Internet Innocent Dissemination

With respect to the various intermediaries that operate on the Internet, it is important that in contrast to the book and magazine publisher, defamation law does not hold liable the so-called "innocent disseminator," such as bookstores, news vendors, and libraries, provided that (a) they do not know of the libel contained in the work disseminated by them, (b) there are no circumstances that ought to have led them to suppose it contained a libel, *and* (c) it was not negligence on their part that they did not know it contained a libel.[153] Interestingly, something akin to this test has been codified recently in the U.K. *Defamation Act 1996*, one of the purposes of which was to modernize the defences in the law of defamation having regard to the current and future technologies of communications.[154] Key provisions in this statute relevant to the present analysis read as follows:

s.1(1) In defamation proceedings a person has a defence if he shows that
    (a) he was not the author, editor or publisher of the statement complained of,
    (b) he took reasonable care in relation to its publication, and
    (c) he did not know, and had no reason to believe, that what he did caused or contributed to the publication of a defamatory statement.
. . .
(3) A person shall not be considered the author, editor or publisher of a statement if he is only involved
    (a) in printing, producing, distributing or selling printed material containing the statement;
    (b) in processing, making copies of, distributing, exhibiting or selling a film or sound recording (as defined in Part I of the Copyright, Designs and Patents Act 1988) containing the statement;
    (c) in processing, making copies of, distributing or selling any electronic medium in or on which the statement is recorded, or in operating or providing any equipment, system or service by means of which the statement is retrieved, copied, distributed or made available in electronic form;

---

153 *Menear v. Miguna* (1996), 30 O.R. (3d) 602 (Gen. Div.), reversed for other reasons (1997), 33 O.R. 223 (C.A.) [*Menear*]; *Newton v. Vancouver* (1932), 46 B.C.R. 67 (S.C.); in this case a municipality and a hospital were denied the innocent disseminator defence, and became liable as publishers, when they supervised the printing and circulation of a report containing defamatory statements.

154 *Defamation Act 1996* (U.K.), 1996, c. 31.

(d) as the broadcaster of a live programme containing the statement in circumstances in which he has no effective control
over the maker of the statement;

(e) as the operator of or provider of access to a communications
system by means of which the statement is transmitted, or made
available, by a person over whom he has no effective control.

In a case not within paragraphs (a) to (e) the court may have regard to
those provisions by way of analogy in deciding whether a person is to
be considered the author, editor or publisher of a statement.

. . .

(5) In determining for the purposes of this section whether a person
took reasonable care, or had reason to believe that what he did
caused or contributed to the publication of a defamatory statement, regard shall be had to

(a) the extent of his responsibility for the content of the statement
or the decision to publish it,

(b) the nature or circumstances of the publication, and

(c) the previous conduct or character of the author, editor or
publisher.

Stating the test for innocent dissemination is relatively simple — the
intermediary will only be liable if it knew or ought to have known of the
libel — but its application can be a challenge, particularly as new technologies and business practices present novel fact patterns. In crafting
sensible rules for Internet-based libel, it is worth having regard to the
pre-Internet case law. In *Emmens* v. *Pottle* the modern concept of innocent disseminator was first propounded, and in that case a news vendor
was held not to be liable because he did not have knowledge of the libel
among the materials he sold.[155] By contrast, the innocent disseminator
defence was denied a book retailer where it was given clear notice of the
libel and the retailer continued to sell the offending work.[156] In two British cases, however, the duty to act reasonably (effectively the requirement of the second two prongs of the test articulated at the beginning
of the previous paragraph) was held not to require a bookseller to
review each title in its shop. Thus, in one case the bookseller was able
to rely on the fact that the libel was in scholarly publications by authors
of high character,[157] and in the other case a large chain of stores that dis-

---

155   (1885), 16 Q.B. 354 (C.A.).

156   *Lambert* v. *Roberts Drug Stores Ltd.*, [1933] 4 D.L.R. 193 (Man. C.A.).

157   *Weldon* v. *"The Times" Book Company (Limited)* (1911), 28 T.L.R. 143 (C.A.).

tributed 400 to 500 different magazine titles, for a total of 50,000 copies a week, was exonerated because there was nothing in the nature of the particular magazine that contained the libel that should have led them to suppose it contained a libel.[158] However, in two other British cases intermediaries were found liable. In one case, the operator of a circulating library claimed the defence should apply given the large number of books it handled, but then went on to admit that it made a conscious decision not to hire anyone to screen books because this was too expensive, and that it preferred to run the risk of having to defend the odd claim in court, an admission found to be particularly damning by the court.[159] In the other case, a large book retailer argued that its throughput of books and other materials at head office was so great that it did not have the ability to screen materials, thereby not catching a libellous advertising poster from one of its suppliers that went out to its bookstall locations.[160] The court found, however, that the managers of the bookstalls did read the posters as they were being put up or soon thereafter, and that they should have been instructed to screen for libel, or the company should have had someone at head office do so. In short, the court found the company liable because the company's "system" was faulty and negligent in this regard. These cases, and the ones referred to in the next few paragraphs, emanate from circumstances that present several useful analogies to a number of situations found on the Internet.

A number of libel cases have examined whether printers should be entitled to the innocent disseminator defence. Traditionally the answer has been negative, given the knowledge that the printer gained of the libellous work through the activity of typesetting. Indeed, in one case the officers of a printing company were found liable for allowing their employees to use the company's presses to put into circulation defamatory statements.[161] In a recent case, however, a printer was entitled to the innocent disseminator defence because the particular technology used by the printer did not require the printer to compose type nor in any other way read or learn of the contents of the work being printed.[162]

---

158   *Bottomly v. F.W. Woolworth and Co. Limited* (1932), 48 T.L.R. 521 (C.A.).

159   *Vizetelly v. Mudie's Select Library, Limited*, [1900] 2 Q.B. 170 (C.A.).

160   *Sun Life Assurance Co. of Canada v. W.H. Smith & Son Ltd.*, [1933] All E.R. 432 (C.A.).

161   *Lobay v. Workers and Farmers Publishing Association Limited*, [1939] 1 W.W.R. 220 (Man. K.B.).

162   *Menear*, above note 153. It should be noted, however, that the lower court decision in this case was set aside, not for substantive reasons, but because the Ontario Court of Appeal concluded that matters in dispute in the case were not properly the subject of a summary judgment proceeding, which is how the lower court dealt with the matter.

In this decision the court was cognizant of the impact of new technology and its ability to relieve the printer from liability. It is interesting to note that subsection 1(3) of the U.K. *Defamation Act* now excludes from liability someone only involved in printing printed material containing the defamatory statement.

d) Telegraphy and Broadcasting

Several pre-Internet communication technologies have presented vexing dilemmas in the application of the innocent disseminator rule. For example, courts in Canada and elsewhere have had to wrestle with whether telegraph companies should come within the defence. In one decision the court permitted an action to proceed against the telegraph company, but at the same time was mindful of the difficult position this puts the company in because of, among other things, the large volume of messages transmitted by it:

> The question raised by the motion is of extreme importance. It is manifestly not desirable that any person may, by going to a telegraph office and filing a message with libellous matter in it, make the company liable to an action for libel and put it to the expense of defending an action. On the other hand, it is not desirable that irresponsible persons should make the telegraph company the instrument for libelling innocent persons. One cannot easily conceive how the law could intend that every telegraph operator should be a judge of whether any particular message is or is not a libel.[163]

In an earlier telegraph case, the Supreme Court of Canada wrestled with the same Gordian knot.[164] In the *Dominion Telegraph* case, a telegraph company was sued for its role in transmitting a libellous story from Halifax to a newspaper in Saint John, which subsequently reprinted it. Of the six Supreme Court judges who heard the case, two expressed no views on the liability issue. Another pair held that a common carrier such as the telegraph company should not be immunized from defamation actions. Chief Justice Ritchie, expressing this position, believed that exempting telegraph companies from liability for defamation would give them the power to perpetrate injustices and wrongs of all manner. Nevertheless, the Chief Justice recognized the difficult upshot of holding telegraph companies liable for all messages:

---

163   *Kahn v. Great Northwestern Telegraph Co. of Canada* (1930), 39 O.W.N. 11 at 11–12, aff'd (1930), 39 O.W.N. 143 (First Div. Ct.).

164   *Dominion Telegraph Co. v. Silver* (1881), 10 S.C.R. 238 [*Dominion Telegraph*].

In the transmission of messages for publication, especially letters and news for the public newspapers, it would seem that telegraph companies assume a responsibility similar to that of the publishers. By this agency libellous matter would be necessarily brought to the knowledge of operators who otherwise would not have cognizance of it. By their immediate and indispensable agency, "press despatches" and the like are brought before the public. In communications specially designed for the press, we see no reason why they should not stand on the same footing with publishers. But in strictly private messages the reason for so stringent a rule does not obtain, perhaps should not be applied at all.[165]

It should be noted that a factor that seemed to colour Chief Justice Ritchie's finding of liability for the news despatch was the fact that it appeared that the telegraph company not only transmitted the libellous news from Halifax to Saint John, but collected the news in Halifax as well. Thus, in an Internet context, the telegraph company may have been more than a passive conduit, but an information provider as well.

In the *Dominion Telegraph* case, two judges took a view contrary to that of Chief Justice Ritchie and expressed the following view:

I do not see how this verdict can be sustained, nor how the defendants can be held responsible for the publication in the *St.* [sic] *John Daily Telegraph*, which is the publication complained of, unless they are responsible in all cases for the use which the receivers of telegraphic messages transmitted over the defendants' line may make of such messages when received, and so to hold would, as it appears to me, be subversive of the telegraphic system and destructive of the benefits conferred upon the public by an invention without which it would be impossible that the affairs of the world could in the present age be conducted. The company by their charter are bound to transmit all despatches received by them for transmission in the order in which they are received, (subject to certain specific exceptions,) under heavy pecuniary penalties. It would be impossible for them to comply with this provision of the statute if they should be compelled, or it was a duty imposed upon them by law in order to their own protection [sic], to enquire into the truth of matter stated in the despatches delivered to them for transmission at the peril, in case of neglect to do so, of being responsible in damages if such matter should be libellous.[166]

---

165 *Ibid.* at 261–62.
166 *Ibid.* at 265–66.

American courts wrestled with the same conundrum presented by the telegraph business process; given that human telegraph operators read each message in the course of sending it, it was tempting to place an onus on them to be responsible for transmitting libellous ones; on the other hand, to hold them to such a duty would slow down the service immeasurably. Thus, in the United States, the compromise was articulated that the telegraph company should not be responsible for messages where, knowing nothing of the parties or their circumstances, a person of ordinary intelligence and acting in good faith would conclude that defamation was not the object of the message.[167] In other words, the telegraph company would only be responsible if the message was libellous on its face.

This test was applied in an early Canadian telegraph libel case where a telegraph company transmitted to the office of a news service a message that impugned the character of a federal politician.[168] All five judges agreed with the chief justice that the message was "libellous on its face,"[169] and therefore, although they recognized they were dealing with a novel action without much precedent, they had no trouble finding the telegraph company liable, citing by analogy the news vendor who sells a newspaper knowing it to contain a libel. While unanimous on the issue of liability, the justices disagreed on the appropriate quantum of damages. Two of them thought the trial judge's award of $50 was sufficient since there was no malice, the telegraph company's employees erroneously believed they were under an obligation to send every message, and as the two judges put it, the plaintiff did not suffer "one cent of damage"[170] and "there is very little in the terms of the telegram itself that is injurious."[171] The three judges in the majority disagreed. Finding the telegram to constitute a libellous defamation, and noting that the telegraph company did not reveal to the plaintiff the identity of its

---

167 *Nye v. Western Union Tel. Co.*, 104 F.R. 628 (D. Minn 1900). In articulating this "libellous on its face test," the court in this case concluded at 631:

>   Any rule imposing a stricter responsibility upon telegraph companies in respect to the character of messages transmitted than is above indicated would be productive of such embarrassment and delays, and make necessary such annoying inquiries, as to greatly diminish the efficiency of the service, and subject telegraph companies on the one hand to danger of prosecutions and suits for refusal to transmit messages or to transmit them promptly, and on the other to vexatious actions for fancied injuries, and even to conspiracies between senders and addressees to mulct these supposedly wealthy corporations.

168 *Archambault v. The Great North Western Telegraph Co.* (1886), M.L.R. 4 Q.B. 122.
169 *Ibid.* at 131.
170 *Ibid.* at 133.
171 *Ibid.*

sender, they increased the libel award from $50 to $500, a substantial sum in 1886. This case illustrates that standards such as "libellous on its face," even if they can be operationalized for purposes of liability determination, still present a challenge in calculating damages, an issue extremely relevant in the Internet environment. Nevertheless, these telegraphy cases, and the broadcasting ones referred to in the next paragraph, address a number of the central issues that are germane to the Internet libel analysis.

Another pre-Internet communications technology worth noting is broadcasting. Broadcasters traditionally have been responsible for libellous statements emanating from the shows they produce, for much the same reason as book publishers or newspaper editors. In a recent Australian case, a television company was even held liable when it was merely retransmitting a program that it relayed from another broadcaster.[172] In this case, the broadcast was a current affairs program where the broadcaster producing the show knew what the guest was going to say and that it would be controversial. Nevertheless, the rebroadcaster did not know any of this, and thus it is not surprising that a strong dissent was lodged in this case in favour of finding that the innocent disseminator defence should apply on the basis that the rebroadcaster was just the conduit in the channel of distribution. Consistent with this minority decision is a U.S. case which held that a local broadcaster that serves as a "mere conduit" does not republish a libel contained in an unedited feed.[173] Interestingly, the court in this case cited as authority for this proposition the *Cubby, Inc. v. CompuServe Inc.*[174] Internet case discussed in section C(1)(e), "Internet Intermediaries," in this chapter. One type of broadcasting that has several analogues in the Internet world is the radio talk show. In one case, a radio station was held liable for adopting the defamatory statements of a call-in guest when the host of the show agreed with the guest's statements.[175] In another case, however, the station was not liable as it did not have knowledge of the defamatory nature of the statement.[176] In the United States several states have addressed the issue of the "outside speaker" by legislating that radio stations are not liable for such statements so long as they took due care to prevent the statement and were not guilty of negligence or malice.

172   *Thompson v. Australian Capital Television Pty. Ltd.* (1994), 127 A.L.R. 317 (Austl. Fed. Ct.).
173   *Auvil v. CBS "60 Minutes,"* 800 F. Supp. 928 (E.D. Wash. 1992).
174   776 F. Supp. 135 (S.D.N.Y. 1991) [*Cubby*].
175   *Lawson v. Burns,* [1976] 6 W.W.R. 362 (B.C.S.C.).
176   *Smith v. Matsqui (Dist.)* (1986), 4 B.C.L.R. (2d) 342 (S.C.).

e) Internet Intermediaries

The Internet raises a host of issues related to libel. For example, one intriguing question is whether a party can be liable merely for having HTML links from her website to another website that contains libellous material. Pre-Internet cases have held that a publication of a libel occurs where the defendant, in addition to showing the libellous letter herself, requested third parties visit a place where the defamatory material was available to be read;[177] or where a defendant's letter to a newspaper simply made reference to a speech that included the defamation which was reported in another publication;[178] or where the defendant, without saying anything, sat by a placard containing libel and directed attention to it.[179] In another U.S. case, however, no responsibility was visited upon a radio commentator who made an on-air reference to a libellous article that appeared in a magazine because, the court concluded, the commentator did not repeat the libel verbatim or in substance, and the words actually broadcast were not themselves libellous.[180]

In Canada, no cases have yet considered the liability of Internet-related disseminators of defamatory statements, but a couple have been brought in the United States. In the *Cubby* case, an online services company, CompuServe, made available some 150 special interest fora and newsletters, one of which was the "Journalism Forum," which in turn contained a daily newsletter entitled "Rumourville USA."[181] CompuServe contracted with a third party, Cameron Communications, Inc. (CCI) to create and run this forum, and the newsletter was contracted for by CCI from the newsletter's publisher, Don Fitzpatrick Associates (DFA). The contract between CCI and DFA provided that all editorial responsibility for the contents of the newsletter resided with DFA, and CompuServe had no opportunity to view the newsletter's contents before DFA made it available to CompuServe subscribers by means of the "Journalism Forum." When an issue of the newsletter contained defamatory statements, the plaintiff brought an action against DFA and CompuServe. CompuServe argued it should not be visited with liability because it was only a distributor and not a publisher, and the court agreed:

> CompuServe has no more editorial control over such a publication than does a public library, book store, or newsstand, and it would be no more feasible for CompuServe to examine every publication it carries for

177   *Lindley v. Delman*, 26 P.2d 751 (Okla. 1933).
178   *Lawrence v. Newberry* (1891), 64 L.T. 797 (Q.B.).
179   *Hird v. Wood* (1894), 38 S.J. 234 (C.A.).
180   *MacFadden v. Anthony*, 117 N.Y.S.2d 520 (Sup. Ct. N.Y. 1952).
181   *Cubby*, above note 174.

potential defamatory statements than it would be for any other distributor to do so. . . . Technology is rapidly transforming the information
industry. A computerized database is the functional equivalent of a more
traditional news vendor, and the inconsistent application of a lower standard of liability to an electronic news distributor such as CompuServe
than that which is applied to a public library, book store, or newsstand
would impose an undue burden on the free flow of information.[182]

The court also found that CompuServe did not know, nor had reason to
know, of the defamatory statements in the newsletter, and so the court,
influenced to an important degree by U.S. First Amendment (which
provides constitutional protection for free speech) protection of distributors considerations, found in favour of CompuServe's motion for summary judgment. This finding is similar to the decision in *Daniel* v. *Dow
Jones & Company, Inc.*, where a non-interactive online service was held
not to be liable for erroneous data if it simply distributed it and did not
have knowledge of the inaccuracy in it.[183] The important fact that CompuServe shifted editorial control to a third party over the particular
forum also is somewhat analogous to the situation contemplated in subsection 303(2) of the *Criminal Code*, in the criminal libel provisions,
where a proprietor of a newspaper gives to another person the authority
for the editorial affairs of the paper.

The other important American Internet libel case, *Stratton Oakmount,
Inc.* v. *Prodigy Services Company*,[184] declined to follow the *Cubby* case as
a result of the very different facts found by the court in the *Prodigy* case.
Prodigy, an online service provider like CompuServe, distinguished itself
from other service providers by presenting itself as a family-oriented service that screened its public message areas for offensive messages. One
such area was "Money Talk," where subscribers could post messages
regarding financial matters, investment views, and the like. One such
message was a defamatory one, and the plaintiff, after being unable to
find the message's originator, sued Prodigy. The court reviewed
whether Prodigy was a publisher or a distributor, and found it to be the
former on the strength of Prodigy's own statements that it exercised
content guidelines, had employed board leaders to moderate the online
discussions, and implemented a software-based screening program. On
appeal, Prodigy argued that while it did exercise screening techniques,
these were only to exclude certain key offensive words and could not

---

182   *Ibid.* at 140.
183   520 N.Y.S.2d 334 (N.Y. City Civ. Ct. 1987) [*Daniel*].
184   5 Computer Cases (CCH) ¶47,291 at 67,772 (N.Y. Sup. Ct. 1995) [*Prodigy*].

possibly screen for libellous statements. The case was never heard on appeal as the parties settled in the meantime. Nevertheless, in order to counteract the decision in the *Prodigy* case, section 230 was added to the U.S. *Telecommunications Act of 1996*, which provision stipulates that no provider or user of an interactive computer service shall be treated as the publisher of any information provided by another information content provider just because the provider took steps to screen the information.[185] In two cases to date this provision has been used by an Internet online service provider to shield itself from liability.[186]

It is too early to tell what influence the *Cubby* and *Prodigy* cases will have in Canada. In the United States a number of commentators view these two cases as standing for the proposition that an online service provider improves its chances of avoiding liability by not screening content or otherwise exercising any editorial control over the public message space on its network. Whatever the merits of this position in the United States, it would appear to be a dangerous approach in Canada given that if a network operator does nothing in this country it could still be found liable, even if it did not have actual knowledge of the libel. In order for a participant on the Internet in Canada to argue successfully the innocent disseminator defence it must show it did not have knowledge of the libel *and* that there are no conditions that would lead it to suspect libel *and* the entity was not negligent in failing to know about the libel. Therefore, the first step in analysing an intermediary's liability for libel publication over the Internet should begin with a detailed assessment of the defendant's role and activities on the Internet as they specifically and actually pertain to the alleged libel. This requires going beyond labelling the defendant an Internet service provider, or an online content supplier, or a bulletin board service operator, or a common carrier, or a discussion forum or usegroup moderator, or one of any number of other labels. Similarly, the urge to label the defendant by analogy to a news vendor, library, newspaper, broadcaster, or one of any number of other pre-Internet categories should be avoided. Rather, a functional assessment of the defendant's specific activities related to the alleged libel should be undertaken, focussing on the degree of knowledge and control (if any of either) that the defendant had of the libel. Similarly, to the extent that pre-Internet cases are drawn upon for jurisprudential support, such cases must also be analysed from the perspec-

---

185   *Telecommunications Act of 1996*, 47 U.S.C.A. §230. This statute is also discussed in section B(5)(d), "Legislative Responses," in chapter 3.

186   *Zeran v. America Online, Inc.*, 958 F. Supp. 1124 (E.D. Va. 1997) [*Zeran*]; *Doe v. America Online, Inc.*, 1997 WL 374223 (Fla. Cir. Ct.) (Westlaw).

tive not of "labels," but rather the degree of knowledge and control exercised by the relevant defendant.

Armed with this information, the court must then approach the defendant by being cognizant of the competing policy positions at issue in Internet libel cases. On the one hand, the law must be mindful of the admonition of the Supreme Court of Canada in the *Hill* case as to the great importance and value of a person's unsullied reputation, and how it would be unfortunate indeed if the Internet became a medium where libellous statements went unchecked.[187] On the other hand, it would be equally extreme to take the position that disseminators of other people's messages over the Internet were absolutely liable for their content, regardless of the actual measures taken by the defendant. Clearly, justice and practicality lie somewhere in between. Thus, where the defendant has knowledge of the libel, and the ability to control its further dissemination or storage, liability should follow if, within a reasonable period of time after being notified of it, the defendant does not take measures to delete the libellous material or block access to it. In this regard, where the defendant is involved in some form of forum moderation and has the opportunity to review messages prior to their posting on a public message board or soon after, the test of "libellous on its face" might usefully be employed to determine, in the context of a time-sensitive service, whether the defendant was negligent in letting libellous material through its screen.

Actual knowledge, however, should not be the sole test for libel liability in respect of Internet intermediaries; rather, the second and third prongs of the innocent disseminator defence should apply equally in cyberspace. Thus, where actual knowledge of the libel is absent, the court should also ask whether there are circumstances that ought to have led the defendant to suppose that, for example, the online discussion forum would contain a libel, or whether the defendant was negligent in letting it happen. This should not mean, however, that the defendant must screen every message of every type. In most cases this simply will not be practical. A large online service provider like America Online currently delivers some 11,000,000 messages a day. At some point in the future software may well be intelligent enough to screen all this traffic for libel, but it certainly cannot be done today. Nor should the defendant be made to do so, as this would bring the fast-flow, low-cost, ease-of-use aspects of the Internet communications model into serious question. A defendant should be expected, however, to monitor a bulletin board that is notorious for its ability to attract defamatory

---

187   *Hill*, above note 129.

statements. Or a defendant should be expected to monitor closely the messages sent by persons known to participate in abusive or offensive behaviour. In effect, the Internet is a fabulous information resource of immense help. The Internet will not, however, be able to maintain or develop this role if it becomes a cesspool of defamation. All intermediaries on the Internet have to take reasonable measures to deter, or neutralize the effects of, persons who would make defamatory statements on the Internet. The standards and approaches noted above will ensure that the various participants on the Internet do their fair share in preserving and enhancing the value of the Internet.

2) Jurisdiction

a) Pre-Internet Law

As a general proposition, the jurisdiction of a government to pass and enforce laws is limited, in terms of physical proximity, to the land mass comprising the particular country, province, state, municipality, or other substate entity under the control of such government. This principle is based on the fundamental tenet of international law, namely, that all countries are independent and sovereign, and that for reasons of international comity, no state will exceed its inherent jurisdiction.[188] Thus, the general rule is that law is based on geographic communities, and that the law takes jurisdiction over an entity and its actions when they are both in the physical jurisdiction. The Internet presents a fundamental challenge to such a physically based legal system. In terms of function, the Internet has no physical boundaries, and its communities are virtual rather than physical in nature. Cyberspace appears to have no geographic borders. On reflection, however, it is clear that the Internet has not wiped away borders, but that it allows borders to be crossed with great ease. The fourth dynamic of computer law postulates a blurring of domestic and international frontiers, rather than the elimination of national ones.

The ability of communications technologies and business practices to breach national boundaries pre-dates the Internet. As transnational activities increased through the acceleration of international trade and travel and the transmission of information across national frontiers by means of the mail, telegraph, telex, phone, and fax, a number of exceptions to the strict territorial principle of legal jurisdiction began to develop. Courts in Canada today are prepared to assume jurisdiction in a number of situations where domestic actors have an impact on per-

---

188   Ruth Sullivan, ed., *Driedger on the Construction of Statutes*, 3d ed. (Toronto: Butterworths, 1994).

sons outside of Canada, and conversely where foreign actors affect persons within Canada. Numerous hybrid situations, involving both domestic and foreign parties, can also be envisaged. For example, the rules of some Canadian courts will permit jurisdiction to be exercised when the parties themselves have agreed contractually to be bound by the laws of a province of Canada.[189] In the context of tort law, Canadian courts, following well-established conflicts of laws principles, will assert jurisdiction if there is a real and substantial connection between the wrongdoing and the Canadian jurisdiction.[190] In a libel case, for example, the plaintiff brought a claim in Ontario against a U.S. broadcaster for a radio broadcast by the defendant's station in the United States and heard across the border in Canada.[191] The defendant brought a motion to dismiss the action, arguing that the Ontario court had no jurisdiction to entertain the matter. The Ontario court disagreed, holding that the U.S. broadcasts were so transmitted as to be published in Ontario, and in its reasons stated the following:

> A person may utter all the defamatory words he wishes without incurring any civil liability unless they are heard and understood by a third person. I think it a "startling proposition" to say that one may, while standing south of the border or cruising in an aeroplane south of the border, through the medium of modern sound amplification, utter defamatory matter which is heard in a Province in Canada north of the border, and not be said to have published a slander in the Province in which it is heard and understood. I cannot see what difference it makes whether the person is made to understand by means of the written word, sound-waves or ether-waves in so far as the matter of proof of publication is concerned. The tort consists in making a third person understand actionable defamatory matter.[192]

A similar conclusion was reached in a later Ontario libel case with respect to a television broadcast that originated in the United States and was received in Canada either directly via U.S. television stations or indirectly after being retransmitted by Canadian-based cable companies.[193]

189 See, for example, Ontario *Rules of Civil Procedure*, Rule 17.02.
190 See, for example, *Hunt v. T&N plc* (1993), 109 D.L.R. (4th) 16 (S.C.C.) [*Hunt*], where the court concluded that some of the traditional rules on enforcement of foreign judgments that emphasized sovereignty are no longer reasonable in the new international environment of the constant flow of products, wealth, and people across the globe.
191 *Jenner v. Sun Oil Co. Ltd.* (1952), 16 C.P.R. 87 (Ont. H.C.J.).
192 *Ibid.* at 98–99.
193 *Pindling v. National Broadcasting Corp.* (1984), 49 O.R. (2d) 58 (H.C.J.).

This latter case may also be said to illustrate "forum shopping" in the modern world of transnational communications and business, given that the plaintiff, the prime minister of the Bahamas, decided to bring his suit in Canada instead of the United States, which he was clearly entitled to do.

Where, however, a court believes it would be unreasonable for a plaintiff to bring a claim in a certain case, it could steer the plaintiff away on grounds of *forum non conveniens*, the rule that some other jurisdiction is better placed to entertain the matter because of, for instance, the location of witnesses. For example, in a recent case involving allegations of negligence by a U.K.-based law firm, the court decided that the contract by a Toronto-based party to retain the U.K. firm was concluded in Toronto because the offer emanated from Toronto over the telephone and hence the contract arose in Toronto when the offeror received the U.K. firm's acceptance over the phone.[194] Nevertheless, because the opinion was rendered by U.K. lawyers in the United Kingdom, on matters of U.K. law, involving a U.K.-based project, and for other similar reasons involving the U.K., the court held that the litigation should be moved to the United Kingdom under the doctrine of *forum non conveniens*. The determination in these cases is whether it is inherently reasonable for a court to take jurisdiction over a person not resident within the court's physical territorial boundary.[195] In making this determination courts should not consider a mechanical counting of contacts and connections, but instead should focus on what promotes order and fairness in the given situation.[196]

With respect to criminal matters, the Supreme Court of Canada in the *Libman* case provided a thorough review of the U.K. and Canadian law as to when a court should take jurisdiction where a foreign actor or action is relevant.[197] The court concluded that "all that is necessary to make an offence subject to the jurisdiction of our courts is that a significant portion of the activities constituting that offence took place in Canada . . . it is sufficient that there be a 'real and substantial link' between an offence and this country."[198] The court found that even in the late nineteenth century, with the invention and development of modern communications, courts in England exercised criminal jurisdiction over transnational transactions so long as a significant part of

---

194   *Clifford Chance*, above note 75. This decision is consistent with the current trend in determining the place of contracts effected by telephone as noted in section A(5), "Time and Place of Contract," in this chapter.

195   *Moran v. Pyle National (Canada) Ltd.* (1973), 43 D.L.R. (3d) 239 (S.C.C.) [*Moran*].

196   *Hunt*, above note 190.

197   *Libman v. R.* (1985), 21 D.L.R. (4th) 174 (S.C.C.) [*Libman*].

198   *Ibid.* at 200.

the chain of action occurred in the United Kingdom. Since that time, the court noted the "means of communications have proliferated at an accelerating pace"[199] and therefore the interests of states in continuing this judicial trend, as well as being "our brothers' keepers" in a shrinking world, have only increased, even if this means that many countries may be able to take jurisdiction (a development the court stated can be handled by the doctrines of *autrefois acquit* and *convict*). The *Criminal Code* addresses a number of circumstances where it might not otherwise be clear which territorial division within Canada (which province or smaller judicial division) is to have control over a particular offence.[200] For example, paragraph 476(d) of the *Criminal Code* provides that where an offence is committed in an aircraft in the course of a flight, the offence can be said to have been committed where the flight commenced or ended or in any jurisdiction over which it passed. Similarly, paragraph 476(e) provides that where an offence is committed in respect of the mail in the course of its door-to-door delivery, the offence shall be deemed to have been committed in any jurisdiction through which the mail was carried on that delivery. With respect to the offence of defamatory libel, subsection 478(2) of the *Criminal Code* provides that anyone charged with this offence in respect of a newspaper be tried where he resides or where the newspaper is published.

Cases such as *Hunt, Moran,* and *Libman* raise the question what connections or links, in an Internet context, are sufficient to make the initiator of a particular Internet activity subject to the jurisdiction of a Canadian court? While there are no Canadian cases in this area yet, a number of U.S. judicial decisions have begun to address these points.[201] These U.S. cases are particularly germane to Canadians involved in Internet activities because they address when a non-U.S. entity or individual will become subject to the jurisdiction of a U.S. court. It is worth mentioning

---

199 *Ibid.* at 201.

200 R.S.C. 1985, c. C-46.

201 A decision on this point in Canada may be forthcoming soon in a matter involving the jurisdiction of the Canadian Human Rights Commission over the effect on Canada of a website located on a computer in the United States but accessible to Canadians: see Donn Downey, "Rights Panel's Jurisdiction over 'Zundelsite' Disputed" *The [Toronto] Globe and Mail* (27 May 1997). In a somewhat related case, a judge in British Columbia found a B.C. resident in contempt of court when the resident, following the issuance of an earlier injunction against the resident's telephone service that contained pre-recorded hateful and racist propaganda, moved the recordings to the United States but left a message on the Canadian number directing callers to the U.S. number; *Canada (Human Rights Commission)* v. *Canadian Liberty Net*, [1996] S.C.C.A. No. 157 (QL), [1996] 1 F.C. 787 (C.A.), [1992] 3 F.C. 504 (T.D.).

that each U.S. state has a statute (a "long arm statute") that extends the jurisdiction of the courts of that state beyond its own physical boundaries. These statutes typically permit "general jurisdiction" to be exercised over a person (or other entity) if it is resident in the state or has some permanence or continuity of presence in the state. The statutes also allow for "specific jurisdiction" (sometimes called "personal jurisdiction") to be exercised where the non-resident makes some "purposeful availment" of doing business or conducting transactions in the state or commits some tortious act in the state or outside the state that has an effect in the state, provided the taking of jurisdiction does not offend notions of fair play or substantial justice and there are no *forum non conveniens* reasons for declining jurisdiction.[202] In effect, the U.S. rules are like the Canadian rules, with courts essentially asking whether there is sufficient connection between the non-resident defendant and the forum state for the court to reasonably take jurisdiction.

In pre-Internet cases in the United States, as is the situation in Canada, the trend has been for courts to more readily allow an out-of-jurisdiction resident to be brought into the courts of the forum state. In a case some forty years ago, a Texas-based insurance company was held to be subject to California's jurisdiction on the basis of issuing a single insurance contract through the mails.[203] In a leading U.S. Supreme Court decision, which (like the Supreme Court of Canada in the *Hunt* and *Moran* cases) rejected any "talismanic jurisdictional formula" (i.e., there is no mechanical system of approaching the "contacts with the jurisdiction" issue), the court, echoing the fourth dynamic of computer law, made it clear that physical presence in the jurisdiction is not necessary to a finding of jurisdiction:

> Jurisdiction in these circumstances may not be avoided merely because the defendant did not *physically* enter the forum State. Although territorial presence frequently will enhance a potential defendant's affiliation with a State and reinforce the reasonable foreseeability of suit

---

202 *Burger King Corp.* v. *Rudzewicz*, 471 U.S. 462 (1985) [*Burger King*].

203 *McGee* v. *International Life Insurance Co.*, 355 U.S. 220 (1957). In this case, the court observed at 222–23:

> Looking back over this long history of litigation a trend is clearly discernible toward expanding the permissible scope of state jurisdiction over foreign corporations and other nonresidents. In part this is attributable to the fundamental transformation of our national economy over the years. Today many commercial transactions touch two or more States and may involve parties separated by the full continent. With this increasing nationalization of commerce has come a great increase in the amount of business conducted by mail across state lines.

there, it is an inescapable fact of modern commercial life that a substantial amount of business is transacted solely by mail and wire communications across state lines, thus obviating the need for physical presence within a State in which business is conducted. So long as a commercial actor's efforts are "purposefully directed" toward residents of another State, we have consistently rejected the notion that an absence of physical contacts can defeat personal jurisdiction there.[204]

Pre-Internet, Canadians have been subject to U.S. jurisdiction based on, for example, trade-marked products and mail-order sales effected in the United States[205] and in one libel case on a single telephone call.[206] In several of the U.S. pre-Internet cases, listings and advertisements in telephone directories in the forum state did not result in a finding of jurisdiction,[207] but something more such as posting a message to a pre-Internet computer-based bulletin board did.[208] In coming to this conclusion, the court in this latter case stated:

> Through the use of computers, corporations can now transact business and communicate with individuals in several states simultaneously. Unlike communication by mail or telephone, messages sent through computers are available to the recipient and anyone else who may be watching. Thus, while modern technology has made nationwide commercial transactions simpler and more feasible, even for small businesses, it must broaden correspondingly the permissible scope of jurisdiction exercisable by the courts.[209]

b) Internet Cases

Although it is still early days in the United States on the Internet jurisdiction issue, two lines of authorities are beginning to emerge. In one,

---

204 *Burger King*, above note 202 at 476.

205 *Vanity Fair Mills, Inc. v. T. Eaton Co. Limited*, 234 F.2d 633 (2d Cir. 1956).

206 *Brainerd* v. *Governors of the University of Alberta*, 873 F.2d 1257 (9th Cir. 1989). Typically, in these cases the Canadian company is resisting being haled into the U.S. court. On occasion, however, the shoe is on the other foot and the Canadian company is vying to achieve jurisdiction in the United States because the relevant U.S. law is more favourable than its Canadian counterpart: see *Nowsco Well Service, Ltd. v. Home Insurance Company*, 799 F. Supp. 602 (S.D. W. Va. 1991) where the Canadian company tried to achieve jurisdiction in the United States but was sent back to Alberta for reasons of *forum non conveniens*.

207 See, for example, *Baird* v. *Day & Zimmerman, Inc.*, 390 F. Supp. 883 (S.D.N.Y. 1974); *Ziperman* v. *Frontier Hotel of Las Vegas*, 374 N.Y.S.2d 697 (Sup. Ct. App. N.Y. 1975).

208 *California Software Incorporated v. Reliability Research, Inc.*, 631 F. Supp. 1356 (C.D. Cal. 1986).

209 *Ibid.* at 1363.

courts are refusing to find access to a website or the creation of a website sufficient to bring the out-of-state person into the jurisdiction of the forum court. For example, in the *Pres-Kap* case, the court refused to take jurisdiction in Florida over a New York user of a Florida-based online information network service when the non-resident used the service simply to gain access to a database.[210] The relevant contract between the parties was negotiated and signed in New York, and the customer was serviced by the Florida company in New York; these findings make the court's conclusion more understandable, in light of the following cases. In another case, the Blue Note jazz club in Missouri established a website where it advertised.[211] Persons wishing to frequent this club, however, had to call to order tickets and had to pick them up at the club. The website contained a disclaimer that this club was not associated with the well-known New York jazz club of the same name. When the New York club brought a trade-mark infringement proceeding against its Missouri namesake, the court refused to find infringement, concluding that the website was intended to give information and was not the equivalent of advertising, promoting, or selling in New York City; a clubgoer could not order tickets over the Internet, but had to go to Missouri for them. The court also found it important that 99 percent of the patrons of the Missouri club were local residents; the club serviced the local university and the website took the place of putting posters up on the walls of university buildings. Similarly, the court in the *SunAmerica* case refused to find jurisdiction in a trade-mark case solely on the basis of the defendant's operation of a general access website, and concluded:

> Plaintiffs ask this court to hold that any defendant who advertises nationally or on the Internet is subject to its jurisdiction. It cannot plausibly be argued that any defendant who advertises nationally could expect to be haled into court in *any* state, for a cause of action that does not relate to the advertisements. Such general advertising is not the type of "purposeful activity related to the forum that would make the exercise of jurisdiction fair, just or reasonable."[212]

---

210   *Pres-Kap, Inc. v. System One, Direct Access, Inc.*, 636 So. 2d 1351 (Fla. App. 1994). For a similar holding, see *Cook v. Holzberger*, 3 Computer Cases (CCH) ¶46,736 at 64,613 (S.D. Ohio 1992).

211   *Bensusan Restaurant Corporation v. King*, 937 F. Supp. 295 (S.D.N.Y. 1996), aff'd 126 F.3d 25 (2d Cir. 1997).

212   *IDS Life Insurance Co. v. SunAmerica, Inc.*, 958 F. Supp. 1258 at 1268 (N.D. Ill. 1997), aff'd in part, vacated in part, 1998 WL 51350 (7th Cir.) (Westlaw).

Similar decisions were given in the *Goldberger*[213] and *McDonough*[214] cases, with equivalent sentiments expressed by the respective courts, the sole activity in each case being the operation of a "passive" general access website. At issue in the *McDonough* case was the question of general jurisdiction, and U.S. courts to date have declined to find general website access sufficient for the purposes of finding general jurisdiction, even in those cases that find it sufficient for personal jurisdiction;[215] though in *McDonough* the court also found it did not have personal jurisdiction. The *Goldberger* decision, however, was based on only personal or specific jurisdiction, and the court in that case considered, but refused to follow, the *Inset* and *Maritz* decisions.[216]

In a second line of U.S. judicial authority, courts are taking jurisdiction over non-resident defendants on the basis that their Internet-related activities have progressed beyond interactivity or advertising. Thus, in *CompuServe, Incorporated* v. *Patterson*, the court held a Texas-based computer programmer subject to Ohio law given the nature of this person's dealings with CompuServe, the Ohio-based online service that had contracted to distribute and sell copies of the programmer's software.[217] The Texas-based individual had never visited Ohio during their dealings, yet Ohio jurisdiction was established given that an electronic contract was concluded (that was governed by Ohio law) and CompuServe

---

213 *Hearst Corporation* v. *Goldberger*, 1997 WL 97097 (S.D.N.Y.) (Westlaw). In this case the court stated at para. 1:

> Where, as here, defendant has not contracted to sell or actually sold any goods or services to New Yorkers, a finding of personal jurisdiction in New York based on an Internet web site would mean that there would be nationwide (indeed, worldwide) personal jurisdiction over anyone and everyone who establishes an Internet web site. Such nationwide jurisdiction is not consistent with traditional personal jurisdiction case law nor acceptable to the Court as a matter of policy.

For a similar result see: *Cybersell, Inc.* v. *Cybersell, Inc.*, 44 U.S.P.Q.2d 1928 (9th Cir. 1997); and *Blackburn* v. *Walker Oriental Rug Galleries*, No. 97-5704 (E.D. Pa., 7 April 1998), reported in *Computer & Online Industry Litigation Reporter*, 21 April 1998 at 4.

214 *McDonough* v. *Fallon McElligott Inc.*, 40 U.S.P.Q. 2d 1826 (S.D. Cal. 1996). In this case the court stated at 1828:

> Because the Web enables easy world-wide access, allowing computer interaction via the Web to supply sufficient contacts to establish jurisdiction would eviscerate the personal jurisdiction requirement as it currently exists; the Court is not willing to take this step. Thus, the fact that Fallon has a Web site used by Californians cannot establish jurisdiction by itself.

215 See, for example, *Panavision International, L.P.* v. *Toeppen*, 938 F. Supp. 616 (C.D. Cal. 1996) [*Panavision*], where general jurisdiction was declined, but personal jurisdiction was found in an Internet-related trade-mark/domain name dispute.

216 See below note 222.

217 89 F.3d 1257 (6th Cir. 1996).

was distributing the product from Ohio. Similarly, in other cases courts have taken jurisdiction on the basis of sales made to customers through the defendant's website,[218] or based on soliciting donations,[219] or based on subscribers signed up by the defendant for services delivered over the Internet,[220] or for having follow-on contacts, negotiations, and other dealings in addition to, and often as a result of, the initial Internet-based communication.[221] The common sentiment expressed by courts in these cases is that parties who avail themselves of technology in order to do business in a distant place should not then be able to escape that place's legal jurisdiction. These cases run the gamut from contract breach claims to tort, including trade libel; in several cases, courts have even found jurisdiction in trade-mark infringement matters merely on the basis of a defendant's general access website,[222] or linking to a national

---

218   *Digital Equipment Corporation* v. *AltaVista Technology, Inc.*, 960 F. Supp. 456 (D. Mass. 1997). See also *Cody* v. *Ward*, 954 F. Supp. 43 (D. Conn. 1997), where a court took jurisdiction based on telephone and e-mail communications that consummated a business relationship begun over *Prodigy*'s "Money Talk" discussion forum for financial matters. In partially justifying this decision, the court noted that the use of fax technology, and even live telephone conferences, can greatly reduce the burden of litigating out-of-state.

219   *Heroes, Inc.* v. *Heroes Foundation*, 958 F. Supp. 1 (D.D.C. 1996).

220   *Zippo Manufacturing Company* v. *Zippo Dot Com, Inc.*, 952 F. Supp. 1119 (W.D. Pa. 1997).

221   *Resuscitation Technologies, Inc.* v. *Continental Health Care Corp.*, 1997 WL 148567 (S.D. Ind.) (Westlaw). The court in this case was not concerned that the defendants had never visited the forum state in person and concluded at para. 5: "Neither is the matter disposed of by the fact that no defendant ever set foot in Indiana. The 'footfalls' were not physical, they were electronic. They were, nonetheless, footfalls. The level of Internet activity in this case was significant." See also *EDIAS Software International, L.L.C.* v. *BASIS International Ltd.*, 947 F. Supp. 413 (D. Ariz. 1996). In this case the court summed up the essence of many of the Internet jurisdiction cases by stating at 420: "BASIS [the defendant] should not be permitted to take advantage of modern technology through an Internet Web page and forum and simultaneously escape traditional notions of jurisdiction." See also *Gary Scott International, Inc.* v. *Baroudi*, 981 F. Supp. 714 (D. Mass. 1997).

222   *Panavision*, above note 215; *Maritz, Inc.* v. *CyberGold, Inc.*, 947 F. Supp. 1328 (E.D. Mo. 1996); *Inset Systems, Inc.* v. *Instruction Set, Inc.*, 937 F. Supp. 161 (D. Conn. 1996). In the latter case the court observed at 165:
   In the present case, Instruction has directed its advertising activities via the Internet and its toll-free number toward not only the state of Connecticut, but to all states. The Internet as well as toll-free numbers are designed to communicate with people and their businesses in every state. Advertisement on the Internet can reach as many as 10,000 Internet users within Connecticut alone. Further, once posted on the Internet, unlike television and radio advertising, the advertisement is available continuously to any Internet user. ISI has therefore, purposefully availed itself of the privilege of doing business within Connecticut.

ATM network through a telephone line indirectly through an independent data processor in a third state.[223]

An overall assessment of the U.S. civil cases noted above would conclude that while the general trend is for courts to assert jurisdiction over non-residents based on their Internet activities, there are still a few situations where some courts may not take jurisdiction. On the criminal side, no such bifurcation of authority seems to be developing. Instead, the criminal and quasi-criminal cases illustrate a dogged determination of courts, governments, and law enforcement authorities to retain control over harmful activities they perceive to be occurring in their jurisdiction. For example, in the *Chan* case, the court was confronted with evidence of a complicated, multinational fraud and money laundering scheme with funds flowing from a bank in Macau to Nigeria through a New York–based bank.[224] There were extensive wire transfers of funds effected through the accused's bank account in the New York bank, but the accused was never physically in New York. When the victim sued in New York to recover its monies, the defendant argued the courts of New York should not take jurisdiction over the matter as he was never present in New York. The court declined to hold that physical presence was required for purposes of New York's long arm statute and concluded:

> [T]o allow a defendant to conspire and direct tortious activities in New York, in furtherance of that conspiracy, and then avoid jurisdiction because it directs those activities from outside the state or country, is to ignore the reality of modern banking and computer technology in the end of the twentieth century! A defendant with access to computers, fax machines, etc., no longer has to physically enter New York to perform a financial transaction which may be criminal or tortious, i.e., conversion. He may secrete himself and/or direct activities from locations where jurisdiction may be impossible to acquire, including a boat beyond the three mile limit. Thus, the emphasis should be on the locus of the tort, not whether defendant was physically here when the tortious act occurred. Once the court finds that the tort occurred *within* the state, it should look at the totality of the circumstances, to determine if jurisdiction should be exercised. . . . Having found that the tort occurred within New York the court concludes that defendant's bodily presence is not an indispensable requirement for long-arm jurisdiction. It would be a travesty to permit the use of our institutions to channel stolen funds and/or the proceeds from heroin sales by those who

---

223 *Plus System, Inc. v. New England Network, Inc.*, 804 F. Supp. 111 (D. Colo. 1992).
224 *Banco Nacional Ultramarino, S.A. v. Chan*, 641 N.Y.S.2d 1006 (Sup. 1996).

impudently claim they are beyond our borders! It would be a gross violation of common sense and reality to shelter such activities.[225]

Another case worth considering in some detail arises out of a 1981 injunction that was granted in favour of *Playboy* magazine prohibiting the importation into the United States by an Italian publisher of a publication titled *Playmen* on the grounds of trade-mark infringement (the *Chuckleberry* case).[226] Fifteen years later, the Italian publisher established a website in Italy on the Internet that carried the Playmen trademark. Users visiting the site could become subscribers to the electronic magazine by paying the requisite fee, after which a password would be issued. The court in the 1996 contempt proceeding found that this activity, in respect of U.S. subscribers, violated the 1981 injunction order. The court was not swayed by the defendant's argument that as the Internet did not exist in 1981, the injunction could not possibly have contemplated, nor should it apply, to defendant's Internet-based activities. The court disagreed, stating:

> The Injunction's failure to refer to the Internet by name does not limit its applicability to this new medium. Injunctions entered before the recent explosion of computer technology must continue to have meaning.[227]

The court also did not accept the defendant's argument that when someone in the United States accessed the Italian website, it was essentially the same as that person getting on a plane and flying to Italy. Rather, the court found that merely uploading the material onto the website in contemplation of Internet users downloading the material in the United States constituted distribution of the material in the United States. Accordingly, the court concluded that sufficient contacts were made with the United States when would-be subscribers faxed completed application forms to Italy and were issued passwords in return. The court found the Italian publisher advertising and distributing material in the United States through this Internet site, and it was not important to the analysis whether the actual activity was characterized as a subscriber pulling down the infringing material or the publisher sending it down to the subscriber. With respect to the resulting remedial order, the court required the Italian publisher to either shut down the Internet site or cease to accept new subscribers from the United States, indicate on the

---

225   *Ibid.* at 1009–10.
226   *Chuckleberry*, above note 142.
227   *Ibid.* at 1037.

site that no new subscriptions will be offered to U.S. residents, to invalidate existing U.S. users and refund them the remaining portions of their subscriptions, and to pay damages to the U.S. plaintiff in respect of past sales to U.S. customers.

In the *Granite Gate* case, the attorney general of Minnesota brought a consumer protection action against the operator of a sports betting website on the Internet.[228] The attorney general's claim of consumer fraud, deceptive trade practices, and false advertising was based on U.S. federal law that prohibits betting by telephone, wire, or facsimile, as well as on Minnesota state law that prohibits sports betting. The defendant was not resident in Minnesota, being based in Nevada with the computer for the website being in Belize, and argued that the Minnesota courts lacked jurisdiction over him and his operation. The court disagreed, finding that the website's ability to be accessed by Minnesota residents was sufficient to find jurisdiction. The court analysed the quantity and quality of contacts, the connection between these contacts and the cause of action, the interest of the state in providing a forum, and the convenience of the parties. The court concluded that the website operator was conducting a direct marketing campaign in Minnesota, and that by advertising in Minnesota he was purposefully availing himself of the privilege of conducting business in the state. Interestingly, the judge noted that Internet advertising through a website is more sustained than traditional paper-based advertising that is often discarded and reaches fewer people. The court also noted the defendant's tracking technology that could tell him in which state a user of the website was resident; indeed, the defendant knew that a specific number of its customers were Minnesota residents. A final factor relevant to the court was the defendant's own statement on the website that customers who were delinquent in payment would be sued either in Belize or in the customer's home state. The court concluded it was impossible for the defendant to argue inconvenience once it had itself made the offer of using the Minnesota jurisdiction for this particular purpose.

A final U.S. criminal case worth noting is *United States* v. *Thomas*.[229] In this case, the accused operated a subscription bulletin board system from a computer in California that permitted subscribers to download sexually explicit material. Instead of bringing an obscenity case in the San Francisco area where the accused lived and operated the system,

---

228   *State of Minnesota* v. *Granite Gate Resorts, Inc.*, 1996 WL 767431 (D. Minn.) (Westlaw) [*Granite Gate*]. See also the Minnesota Attorney General's *"Warning to All Internet Users and Providers,"* at <http://www.state.mn.us/ ebranch/ag/memo.txt>.

229   74 F.3d 701 (6th Cir. 1996).

law enforcement authorities deliberately brought it in Tennessee where a postal inspector had downloaded some materials from the service. The accused was convicted for transmitting obscenity and appealed on several grounds, including that the venue of Tennessee was improper. The appellate court dismissed the appeal, concluding that the prosecution can be brought where the material originates or where it is received. Indeed, the court felt that the community standard for obscenity in Memphis (which would be more conservative than in San Francisco), was preferred because it was the community affected by the distribution. Not surprisingly, the court denied the accused's argument that a cyberspace community standard for judging obscenity among like-minded users was more important than a physical place's standards.

Based on the foregoing U.S. cases, it can be concluded at this early stage of the development of the Internet jurisdiction jurisprudence, that American courts will generally take a rather expansive view of their jurisdiction in both civil and criminal matters and will permit plaintiffs to pursue claims in their own jurisdiction based on the plaintiff having contact with the out-of-state defendant over or by means of the Internet. Where such contact only involves accessing a general access website or minor interactivity with such a site, some judges may find insufficient contact for taking jurisdiction, but some have taken jurisdiction even in these circumstances. Courts will not hesitate to take jurisdiction, however, where the defendant conducted some sort of business through the Internet or through follow-on activities initiated via the Internet. Given the decisions in the Canadian *Hunt, Moran, Libman, Jenner* and *Pindling* cases, together with *R. v. McKenzie Securities Ltd.*,[230] it is likely that Canadian courts will take a similar approach to jurisdiction questions.

The foregoing American cases do not, of course, answer all the questions posed by Internet jurisdiction issues. There is also the enforcement issue. In the civil context, a decision like *Bachchan* v. *India Abroad Publications Incorporated* should be noted.[231] In this case the plaintiff, a national of India, brought a libel claim in the United Kingdom against a New York publisher because England's libel laws were more plaintiff-friendly than those in the United States. The plaintiff was successful in England, but when it came to execute on his judgment in New York (the defendant had no assets in the United Kingdom), the New York court declined to enforce the judgment in New York on the basis that the lack of a U.S. First Amendment free speech law in the United Kingdom made

230   (1966), 56 D.L.R. (2d) 56 (Man. C.A.) [*McKenzie*]. See the discussion of this case in section C(3)(a), "Securities Law," in this chapter.
231   585 N.Y.S.2d 661 (Sup. 1992).

it contrary to public policy to enforce the judgment in the United States. Also with respect to enforcement, it can reasonably be asked how a court would take effective steps to enforce a judgment against a foreign website operator. How would, for example, the court in the *Chuckleberry* case enforce its order against the Italian website operator if the latter refused to comply with it? Does it commence extradition proceedings against the principals behind it? Can it require Internet service providers to block their subscribers from accessing the site? These and other practical issues still need to be sorted out.

In any event, based on these cases to date, operators of websites would be well advised to consider the following measures if they wish to decrease the likelihood of their being haled into a particular jurisdiction's court. Through express contracts with subscribers, website operators should try to choose a governing law for the relationship, together with the forum in which any disputes would be settled. Written disclaimers should also be used if the website operator wishes to control with whom it does business. So, if a website operator puts a promotional contest online that is accessible by residents in all provinces and the operator does not find it cost-effective to comply with the contest rules of one or another province (or of the United States or other jurisdictions), then the site should clearly state that the contest is open only to persons from a particular province(s).[232] The website operator should employ technology and business procedures to ensure that contestants for the contest, or subscribers for other purposes, do not come from prohibited jurisdictions. It will be interesting to see how these targeting mechanisms, if applied in a *bona fide* manner, stand up to judicial scrutiny in future cases. Based on the *Granite Gate, Chuckleberry,* and *Bensusan* cases (in the first case the attorney general of Minnesota asked that the website clearly state that its services were void in Minnesota; in the second case the Italian website was permitted to operate so long as it precluded access by Americans; and in the third case the Columbia,

---

232   The previous discussion of jurisdiction has focussed on Canada and its largest trading partner, the United States. The Internet, of course, is supremely global and so Canadians must also consider the ramifications of their Web and other Internet activities in the context of non–North American jurisdictions. For example, an American university learned this lesson recently when it was hauled into a Paris courtroom because its website (accessible around the world, including in France), which offered information about the university's courses conducted in France, was not in the French language, thereby violating a French law that information offering goods and services in France must be in French: see Wendy R. Leibowitz, "National Laws Entangle the Net: It's a Small, Small, Litigious Web" *The National Law Journal* (30 June 1997) also available at <http://www.ljx.com/internet/0630natlaw.html>.

Missouri, defendant's website stated it was for Columbia residents only), such measures to "localize" the reach of a particular website should be met with a positive judicial reception. Nonetheless, given the fourth dynamic of computer law — namely, the blurring of national and international — people who use the Internet to do business in foreign countries should be prepared to become subject to the laws of those countries, and therefore should review related issues pertaining to tax, insurance, legal compliance, trade-marks, misleading advertising, etc., just as if they were establishing offices in the foreign jurisdictions. The huge benefits of the Internet must be cultivated prudently.

3) Regulating Cyberspace

Governments in Canada and around the world have implemented many regulations to protect the public from nefarious activities. Previous chapters have already dealt with misleading advertising and criminal law. Other laws with similar objectives involve securities regulation and consumer protection statutes. In all these areas the Internet poses a number of challenges. Of course the phenomenon of responding to new, technologically driven issues and activities is nothing new in this area of the law. Fraudsters have long used the mails and telephone to bilk unsuspecting members of the public from a distance.[233] The Internet is just another stage in the evolution of technology and business environments where the rules of consumer protection and industry regulation need to be applied; but is the existing legal regime adequate to deal with some of its novel aspects?

a) Securities Law

In the area of securities regulation, the investment community, long a leading user of computers and networks, has discovered the many advantages of the Internet.[234] For example, securities law administrators in Canada have implemented an automated system for the receipt, processing, and distribution of disclosure documents, known as SEDAR (System for Electronic Document Analysis and Retrieval).[235] SEDAR reduces the time, effort, and cost involved in filing disclosure documents required of public companies, and it should also enhance the efficiency of the securities market by allowing for a more rapid distribution

---

233   For example, in *Libman*, above note 197, the telephone was used by persons resident in Canada to perpetrate securities fraud on victims outside of Canada.

234   A decade ago, for example, the *Daniel* case, above note 183, resulted from an investor utilizing an online financial information service.

235   The SEDAR system was established by *National Instrument 13-101, System For Electronic Document Analysis and Retrieval (SEDAR)* of the Canadian Securities Administrators.

of information in electronic form. Interestingly, although all documents are to be filed electronically under the SEDAR system, those that call for signatures require handwritten ones on certificates of authentication to be filed in a paper-based format soon after the electronic version is submitted. With the ongoing improvement and diffusion into the business world of biometric and related authentication devices,[236] it may be that at some point soon adequate systems can be developed to replace this last vestige of paper in the SEDAR process.

As well as communicating with regulators, computers and networks are increasingly being used to assist companies, investment dealers, and others in the investment community to communicate with investors and members of the public. This has prompted securities law regulators to review their rules. How well do they apply in an electronic environment? Is there any new functionality that may be problematic and that was not addressed in the former rules? To take one example, rules related to the delivery of a prospectus looked at putting paper-based versions of the document in the mail. When a prospectus is put on a website, many of these rules no longer work and must be updated to reflect the new technology.[237]

With the Internet's ability to transmit a large volume of material to a large number of people at low cost, companies are exploring it as a vehicle for attracting investment capital. An early effort was the raising of approximately $1.6 million by Spring Street Brewing, a U.S. company, in early 1996 by use of an online prospectus.[238] Indeed, software is now available that assists in compiling a prospectus, again helping the smaller firm raise money over the Internet.[239] "Road shows," in which companies raising money by a prospectus give presentations to prospective investors, can now be done by video transmissions.[240] Retail investors have for some time used the Internet to buy and sell stocks — it is estimated that in the United States about 800,000 individual investors use

---

236   See section A(2), "Signatures," in this chapter.

237   For a useful discussion of these sorts of issues, see Securities and Exchange Commission, *Use of Electronic Media for Delivery Purposes*, Release No. 33-7233, 6 October 1995, available at <http://www.sec.gov/rules/concept/33-7233.txt>. This is an interpretive document requesting comments; the final rules are set out in *Use of Electronic Media for Delivery Purposes*, Release No. 33- 7289, 9 May 1996, available on the SEC's website at <http://www.sec.gov/rules/final/33-7289.txt>.

238   After issuing these shares, Spring Street Brewing then established an "off-the-grid" securities trading system using its website: see Richard Raysman & Peter Brown, "Securities Offerings Over the Internet" *The New York Law Journal* (10 June 1997) ["Securities"].

239   "On-line Capitalism," *The Economist*, 23 November 1996.

240   "Securities," above note 238.

Internet discount brokers — but the move by larger companies and their financial advisers into underwriting and distribution is new.[241] Securities regulators will have to update rules promulgated for a different environment. For example, the ability of a company to offer shares to the public in British Columbia using only the Internet is restricted by the requirement in that province that a person cannot trade in a security unless the person is registered as a securities dealer.[242] Thus, a company considering using the Internet to raise investment capital must carefully consider what rules apply to it in its home jurisdiction, as well as in any other jurisdiction where the company intends to have investors.

The need to carefully scrutinize the securities law ramifications of Internet-based investment activities is illustrated by the first enforcement action by the Ontario Securities Commission (OSC) against a website that occurred when it contacted the operator of the Federal Bureau of Investments site to cease operation.[243] This site, by giving detailed advice about stocks, led the OSC to conclude that it ran afoul of the requirement that the operator of it be a registered adviser under Ontario securities law, which the operator was not. Apparently, the operator of the site did not know that the site's activities required him to be registered. This highlights a dimension of the Internet that has been referred to in previous chapters — the technology and communication infrastructure is so accessible to persons of even modest means that regulators will see more contravention of, for example, the unregistered investment adviser. There is also a strong element of the third dynamic of computer law at play here, namely, the blurring of private/public by means of Internet technology; for example, a "hobby" investment club among a few close friends can turn into a serious regulatory concern if the club's activities are posted on an Internet home page.

Of course, the Web is crawling with more nefarious characters who view the Internet as an ideal communications vehicle for "pump and dump" schemes where they heavily promote a thinly traded stock so that the price of it rises and then they sell their positions, often causing the price to collapse.[244] One press report on this phenomenon quotes a

---

241 Linda Himelstein & Leah Nathans Spiro, "The Net Hits the Big Game," *Business Week*, 28 October 1996. This article describes the marketing of a $500 million bond issue by General Motors Acceptance Corporation through a brokerage that uses a website from which the prospectus can be downloaded.

242 See the British Columbia *Securities Act*, R.S.B.C. 1996, c. 418, s. 34.

243 Janet McFarland, "OSC Shuts Investment Web Site" *The [Toronto] Globe and Mail* (21 June 1997).

244 Peter Morton, "Net Scams Leave Investors Burned: Old-Fashioned Stock Fraud Thrives on High-Tech Internet" *The Financial Post* (15 June 1996).

representative of a U.S. self-regulatory organization in the brokerage industry as commenting: "I think the Internet is a wonderful tool because it's inexpensive, because it's easily accessed, because it provides massive amounts of information to people at virtually no cost. . . . And for those very same reasons, it is a wonderful vehicle to perpetrate a fraud."[245] However, if the activity is illegal in the physical world it is invariably illegal in cyberspace as well; thus, by early 1997 the Securities and Exchange Commission in the United States had brought nine enforcement actions against persons selling unregistered securities over the Internet and it had also halted trading in a number of stocks that were the subject of pump and dump schemes.[246]

One issue that complicates enforcement in respect of the Internet is the fact that the perpetrators of the illegal act may be resident outside the geographic confines of a regulator's jurisdiction. As noted in section C(2), "Jurisdiction," in this chapter, however, public authorities will not be deterred from asserting regulatory oversight simply because the offender is not physically present in its jurisdiction, so long as the links between the perpetrator and the victim are meaningful. And this is not a new regulatory approach. In the *McKenzie* case, two persons resident in Toronto were charged in Manitoba for selling securities without being registered when they sold stocks to a resident of Manitoba pursuant to contacts made by mail and by telephone.[247] The accused were registered in Ontario, but the court found this did not cure their unregistered status in Manitoba. In response to the argument that the accused did not trade in securities in Manitoba because they were never personally in that province, the court concluded:

> The sole point to be determined is whether the accused Dubros and the accused West, both of whom were unlicensed here, traded in securities in Manitoba. That they did not physically enter the borders of the Province is not conclusive of the matter. A person may, from outside the borders of a Province, do certain acts within the Province so as to make himself liable to the provisions of this statute. . . . Although offences are local, the nature of some offences is such that they can properly be described as occurring in more than one place. This is peculiarly the case where a transaction is carried on by mail from one territorial jurisdiction to another, or indeed by telephone from one

---

245 Janet McFarland & Paul Waldie, "Hype Artists Spin Stocks on the Web" *The [Toronto] Globe and Mail* (9 August 1997).

246 Christopher Wolf & Scott Shorr, "Cybercops Are Cracking Down on Internet Fraud" *The National Law Journal* (13 January 1997); also available at <http://www.ljx.com/internet/0113cops.html> ["Cybercops"].

247 *McKenzie*, above note 230.

such jurisdiction to another. This has been recognized by the common law for centuries. Thus, where a threatening letter was written and posted in London, and delivered in Middlesex, it was held by the Court that the writer could properly be tried in Middlesex.[248]

By the same token, today if the operator of a website solicits purchasers of securities from foreign jurisdictions it should be prepared to comply with the laws of those countries. Where this is impractical or uneconomic, the operator should attempt to limit the geographic range of its customers by stating clearly at the beginning of the site those jurisdictions from which it will not accept customers; or it should list only those jurisdictions from which it will accept customers. For example, the British Columbia Securities Commission has indicated that such notices, which have the effect of keeping B.C. residents from using a particular website subject to certain conditions, would be sufficient to remove the communication from the registration and prospectus requirements of the B.C. securities law.[249]

b) Banking

Internet sites and other forms of network technology are also being used by banks and financial institutions to conduct banking and to provide financial services. Computers and chip technologies are also finding their way into electronic payment systems, from well-established, large-volume clearing systems to debit card systems to stored value card systems ("smart cards") that are still in their infancy.[250] Statutes that regulate banks and financial services companies are dealing with new issues, such as privacy (discussed in section A, "Privacy and Data Protection," in chapter 4) and cryptography (discussed in section B(3), "Regulating Encryption Technologies," in chapter 4). Another is the legal nature of "electronic money.[251] And another is "money laundering" — the term used to describe the criminal practice, especially of drug traffickers, to "cleanse" the proceeds from their criminal acts by running them

---

248   *Ibid.*, above note 230 at 63.

249   Douglas M. Hyndman, Chair, B.C. Securities Commission, "Notice: Trading Securities and Providing Advice Respecting Securities on the Internet," NIN 97/9, 3 March 1997.

250   Smart cards are essentially credit card-like devices fitted with a chip that can store "value" electronically, as well as intelligence, with the value being drawn down as purchases are made: see Shameela Chinoy, "Electronic Money in Electronic Purses and Wallets" (1996–1997) 12 B.F.L.R. 15.

251   See Bradley Crawford, "Is Electronic Money Really Money?" (1996–1997) 12 B.F.L.R. 399.

through a series of financial institutions so they cannot be traced to the illegal source.[252]

The primary law against money laundering in Canada is subsection 462.31(1) of the *Criminal Code*.[253] To assist in the enforcement of this law, in 1991 the government enacted the *Proceeds of Crime (Money Laundering) Act*,[254] which requires banks and other financial institutions to keep certain records to facilitate investigations under subsection 462.31(1) of the *Criminal Code* and several other money laundering provisions in federal statutes. The record-keeping requirements are set out in a regulation and require the financial institution to verify the identity of individuals who open accounts and to keep track of cash transactions of $10,000 or more.[255] Specifically, the regulation requires banks and other deposit-taking institutions to have persons complete a signature card when they open an account and to ascertain the identity of the person who signs this card by reference to the person's "birth certificate, driver's licence or passport, or to any similar document."[256] These requirements present interesting challenges in the age of the Internet and high-tech smart cards. For example, the identification regime assumes a face-to-face encounter between a representative of the financial institution and the new customer, and therefore poses a problem for some aspects of Internet banking. New technologies, however, such as biometric devices (retina scans, fingerprints) and videoconferencing, may permit the identification process to occur in a remote, online mode. Similarly, if the cardholder is anonymous, it may become difficult to keep records of money exchanges done through smart cards. But technologies that feature less anonymity would increase privacy concerns, although they would assist money laundering

---

252   It is estimated that between $300 billion and $500 billion of such funds are cycled through the United States each year: Steven Solomon, "Know Your Customer — Or Else," *Business Week*, 21 July 1997.

253   *Criminal Code*, R.S.C. 1985, c. C-46, subs. 462.31(1):

Every one commits an offence who uses, transfers the possession of, sends or delivers to any person or place, transports, transmits, alters, disposes of or otherwise deals with, in any manner and by any means, any property or any proceeds of any property with intent to conceal or convert that property or those proceeds, knowing or believing that all or a part of that property or of those proceeds was obtained or derived directly or indirectly as a result of

(a)   the commission in Canada of an enterprise crime offence or a designated substance offence; or

(b)   an act or omission anywhere that, if it had occurred in Canada, would have constituted an enterprise crime offence or a designated substance offence.

254   S.C. 1991, c. 26.

255   *Proceeds of Crime (Money Laundering) Regulations*, SOR/93-75, 11 February 1993.

256   *Ibid.*, subs. 11(2).

enforcement. Clearly, these new technologies will require some creative thinking by regulators, business people, and technologists to integrate them into existing regulatory regimes.

c) Consumer Protection Laws

Ontario's *Business Practices Act*, which prohibits certain forms of false representations and other unfair business practices, is drafted in a relatively technology-neutral manner such that its application to the Internet presents little difficulty.[257] In contrast, Ontario's *Consumer Protection Act* requires that certain consumer "executory contracts" be "in writing," raising the question whether agreements concluded electronically over the Internet meet this requirement.[258] As well, this statute allows a consumer to rescind such a contract within two days if it is negotiated, solicited, or signed by the buyer at a place other than the seller's permanent place of business. Although this provision was primarily intended to capture itinerant salespeople (e.g., the door-to-door seller), would a website constitute a company's permanent place of business?[259] These sorts of questions need attention by regulators, legislators, and business people.

Other consumer protection laws (both in Ontario and the other provinces), while arguably not requiring amendment as a result of the Internet, do require review. For example, promotional contests must not require contestants to pay any consideration (or must be based on an element of skill) in order not to be considered an illegal lottery under section 206 of the *Criminal Code*.[260] In this regard, certain online requirements of a vendor's website (e.g., that the contestant fill out a survey, etc.), if made part of the contest, could be considered to constitute consideration. In other respects, however, the online contest might be made more regulatory-friendly if contestants signify their agreement to the rules by typing and transmitting an acknowledgment in conjunction with the screen that displays the rules.[261] And where the operator

---

257 R.S.O. 1990, c. B.18.

258 R.S.O. 1990, c. C.31, subs. 19(1). Though, see the discussion in section A(1)(d), "Electronic Messages," in this chapter that concludes that electronic messages satisfy general writing requirements.

259 Issues not dissimilar to this one are discussed in section B(6), "Illegal Speech," in chapter 3 and section G(3), "Taxing the Internet," in chapter 5.

260 R.S.C. 1985, c. C-46; see section B(8), "Gaming and Betting," in chapter 3 for a brief discussion of gaming issues as they apply to the Internet. Note that s. 59 of the *Competition Act*, R.S.C. 1985, c. C-34, also contains requirements for a legal promotional contest.

261 For a discussion of this sort of "clickwrap" agreement, see section C(2), "Shrinkwrap Licences," in chapter 5.

of the contest does not wish to comply with the requirements of any particular jurisdiction, it should be made clear at the beginning of the site that the contest is open to players from certain jurisdictions only or, conversely, that it is not open to persons from certain jurisdictions.

Many consumer protection laws in Canada and in other countries will require little or no modification to apply to the Internet, so U.S. authorities, for example, have been quite active in applying their laws to Internet-related mischiefs. By January 1997, the U.S. Federal Trade Commission had brought at least eight enforcement actions against companies in respect of their false claims in Internet communications.[262] The activities of Canada's Bureau of Competition Policy to combat Internet-related misleading advertising are discussed in section B(1), "Criminal Offences," in chapter 5. In a recent case, the attorney general of New York state was held to be able to proceed against an online business that used false testimonials from fictitious consumers to promote a magazine subscription service; attempts to trace the authors of these testimonials were unsuccessful because they did not exist.[263] Interestingly, in an attempt to reduce such frauds, the state of Georgia recently enacted a statute that prohibits the use of false names when communicating over the Internet.[264] Soon after its enactment, this statute attracted a constitutional challenge from a number of parties who argued that communicating anonymously and pseudonymously over the Internet served many legitimate functions and that banning all such activity is an overreaction to the problem.[265] The court agreed and, in a judgment reminiscent of the U.S. Supreme Court's opinion in the *ACLU* case,[266] found the statute vague and constitutionally overbroad.[267] This

---

262   "Cybercops," above note 246.

263   *People v. Lipsitz*, 663 N.Y.S.2d 468 (Sup. Ct. 1997).

264   Act No. 1029, Ga. Laws 1996, codified at O.C.G.A. §16-9-93.1 which amends the *Georgia Computer Systems Protection Act*, Article 6, Chapter 9, Title 16 of the Official Code of Georgia. For a disturbing example of the mischief at which this statute is aimed, see *Zeran*, above note 186, where a subscriber of America Online received multiple harassing and threatening calls, including death threats, after a third party anonymously affixed the plaintiff's name and telephone number to an America Online bulletin board advertising T-shirts and other items with slogans glorifying the Oklahoma City bombing in which 168 people died.

265   For a copy of the complaint in this case, *American Civil Liberties Union of Georgia v. Miller*, 977 F. Supp. 1228 (N.D. Ga. 1977) [*Miller*], see <http://www.aclu.org/issues/cyber/censor/GACOMPLT. html>.

266   *ACLU*, above note 127, (*sub nom. Reno v. American Civil Liberties Union*) 117 S. Ct. 2329 (1997). This case is discussed at the end of section B(5)(d), "Legislative Responses," in chapter 3.

267   *Miller*, above note 265.

case illustrates, once again, the unruly nature of the Internet and the difficulties in controlling it.[268]

FURTHER READINGS

Books

BROWN, Raymond, *The Law of Defamation in Canada*, 2d ed. (Toronto: Carswell, 1994) (looseleaf, updated)

HORNING, Richard Allan, "The Statute of Frauds in Cyberspace," in *Commercial Alliances in the Information Age*, ed. D. Campbell (Chichester: John Wiley & Sons, 1996)

JOHNSTON, David, Sunny HANDA & Charles MORGAN, *Cyber Law: What You Need to Know about Doing Business on Line* (Toronto: Stoddart, 1998)

SMEDINGHOFF, Thomas J., ed., *OnLine Law* (Reading, Mass.: Addison-Wesley, 1996)

WRIGHT, Benjamin, *The Law of Electronic Commerce EDI, FAX and E-mail: Technology, Proof and Liability* (Boston: Little, Brown, 1991) (supplemented)

Internet Sites

Canadian Association of Internet Providers
<http://www.caip.ca/>

Law of the Internet
<http://www.ljx.com/internet/irjuris.html>

Organization for Economic Co-operation and Development
<http://www.oecd.org/>

Uncitral materials
<http://ra.irv.uit.no/trade_law/doc/UN.Electronic.Commerce.Model.Law.1996.html>

U.S. Securities and Exchange Commission
<http://www.sec.gov>

World Trade Organization
<http://www.wto.org/>

---

268   In this regard, the discussion of the *ACLU* case in section B(5)(d), "Legislative Responses," in chapter 3, and the discussion of the CRTC's prospects for regulating the Internet in section C(3), "Regulating the Internet," in chapter 4, are relevant.

COMPUTER LAW: DYNAMICS, THEMES, AND SKILL SETS

This book presents a wide-ranging analysis of intellectual property law, criminal law, regulatory legal regimes, commercial law, and electronic commerce and Internet legal issues in terms of four principal dynamics. First, there is the impact on the law of rapid technological change and the law's response to this. A second dynamic is the elusive nature of information, particularly in its digital form, and how the law is coping with the challenges posed by this. A third dynamic is the increasing fusion of the public and private spheres in many computer law matters. Finally, there is a blurring of the dividing line that has traditionally separated that which is national and that which is international in computer law. Each of these dynamics presents computer law and its practitioners with several fundamental challenges.

In meeting these challenges, the legal system can consider four themes, the elements of which weave through this book. First, there is the need for consistency in computer laws. Then one needs to understand something about regulatory control points and the law. A third theme recurs around the liability of intermediaries; and finally, the law must consider the dangers of mischievous metaphors. Armed with an appreciation of the aforementioned dynamics and themes, the legal practitioner can approach virtually any present or future legal problem by employing one or more skill sets: the common law, by which reliance is placed on judge-made interpretations of the current law; contract, by which persons, companies, and organizations craft their own rules, particularly in the absence of meaningful judicial precedent;

technology, which involves using technical measures to overcome perceived weaknesses in the law; and law reform, which entails changes in statute-based law to solve a problem in the previous state of statute or judge-made law and, in certain cases, to reduce the need for contractual and technological solutions.

A. COMPUTER LAW: DYNAMICS

1) The Rapid Pace of Technological Change

The first and most important driving force in the computer law field is the relentless pace of technological change. The computer industry rides a roller coaster that appears — and in fact is — out of control. No other industry produces new products and services at such a dizzying pace. Each new product that is launched engenders other products, some competitive, some complementary. There are also continual developments in the formats, methodologies, and technologies for delivering traditional content — such as music, images, and text. Relatively recent developments include multimedia products on CD-ROM, and most recently, of course, there is the use of the Internet for commercial purposes. In a word, developments in the computer field are breathtaking, especially when considered in light of the fact that the microchip is only twenty-five years old. It is, without a doubt, an extremely exhilarating time for this vibrant industry. While the cadence of technological change has perhaps never been as peripatetic as it is today, the phenomenon of one technology-driven device leapfrogging the other to produce an intensively competitive and dynamic environment is not entirely new. The thrust and parry between the telegraph and the telephone created an analogous situation, and later devices such as the radio, teletype, telex, television, cable transmission, and other technologies all added to the mix, each leaving new legal challenges in its wake. With the microchip and the computer revolution, however, this process has been accelerated, with enormous implications for the law.

The dynamic of rapid technological change is evident in the area of intellectual property law. Developers of new technologies and information-based products are constantly agitating for intellectual property protection for the fruits of their labour. The *Copyright Act*, for example, has been amended on numerous occasions to recognize new works resulting from new technologies. In 1988, computer programs were included as protected literary works. Today, defining the contours of protection for software under copyright and patent, determining the scope of protection for electronic databases, and wrestling with the impact of the Internet are difficult technolgically induced challenges to intellectual property laws. The problems are not new, but the current breakneck pace with which the issues are arising is unprecedented.

Technological changes have also been a constant driver of the amendments over the years to the *Criminal Code*. Courts in Canada have been reluctant to interpret the provisions in the *Criminal Code* in a technologically expansive manner, thereby resulting in numerous acquittals when the law was challenged by the rapid pace of technological change. Indeed, it seems that the *Criminal Code* has been one or two technologies behind the latest mischief-causing development. The *Criminal Code* was brought somewhat up to date in the mid-1980s with the addition of the computer abuse and data abuse provisions. Nevertheless, the first dynamic of computer law continues to present a fundamental challenge to the criminal law.

In the regulatory arena, the law and policy surrounding data protection and the privacy of personal information is being affected by the first dynamic of computer law. Given the development of technologies that collect huge volumes of data (such as point of sale systems in retail stores), and gargantuan databases that aggregate, sort, and profile the data and then transmit them instantaneously to the four corners of the globe, should the data protection laws covering the government sectors be extended to the private sector, as has already been done in Quebec? Although the federal government has committed itself to implementing data protection in the federally regulated private sector by the year 2000, it remains to be seen if this can be done in a manner that produces consistent regimes across the country, assuming provinces follow suit. There is also the possibility that the new law will harness technological progress to assist in the preservation of privacy; that is, in addition to presenting the law with questions, the first dynamic of computer law may also hold within itself certain solutions.

The need to keep pace with technology is particularly telling in the area of export control. There is, of course, the requirement to stay current with new technological developments so as to know when to add a new item to the Export Control List. Just as important, however, is to be able to remove an item from the ECL promptly after it is widely available on the world market. Not doing so will adversely affect Canadians who, because of anachronistic export controls, will be disadvantaged in pursuing sales or other commercial opportunities abroad. In effect, there is a danger in underregulating when some new technology appears that provides Canada and its allies with some strategic military benefits. On the other hand, with the rapid pace of technology diffusion around the world even without a breach of export control rules, the ECL should be pruned regularly.

The CRTC also faces fundamental regulatory challenges from the onslaught of technology. Of course the CRTC, and its predecessors, have been confronted with new technologies and services before, such as the introduction of cable distribution in the 1960s. On the telecommunications front, since the early 1980s the CRTC's work has become more complicated as technological advances permitted telephone sets and other terminal equipment supplied by businesses other than the phone company to be connected to the main telephone network. Regulatory complexity increased as the technical means developed to permit competition in long distance telephone services. Similarly, the most complex regulatory environment will arise when competition in local telephone service is instituted, again a regulatory option made possible by new technologies. From a regulatory perspective, however, all these technologically driven new developments have been manageable because they all involve relatively substantial companies, each with a physical presence in Canada, and therefore the CRTC can effectively assert jurisdiction over them pursuant to the *Telecommunications Act* and the *Broadcasting Act*. In contrast, several newer technologies do not fit comfortably within the traditional regulatory models, and they will prove to be far more difficult to regulate. Direct to home satellite transmissions from foreign service providers is one such technology. Already an estimated 250,000 Canadian homes have satellite dishes that receive these unauthorized signals. Similarly, in a few years an Internet with broadband capacity will allow computer users in Canada to access literally thousands of sites around the world in order to obtain a wide variety of programming. Indeed, the Internet poses squarely the question whether there are certain technologies that the CRTC should simply not even attempt to regulate?

The relentless march of technology is keenly felt in the commercial law area. New technology-oriented products and technology-based distribution structures for old and new products and services often have implications, both positive and negative, under the *Competition Act*. Technology also drives the evolution of the various licensing models used in the computer industry and with information-based products. Rapid technological developments raise a host of negligence questions, including the perennial conundrum of when it is negligent not to adopt new technology. It is also a challenge to determine appropriate standards of care for the creation and use of new technology-based products, such as software, precisely because they are new and ever changing.

Developments in technology can also wreak havoc on established tax rules, particularly where the rule is intended to cover a specific activity; then a new technology appears that reflects the previous activity but in a new manner. In the context of electronic commerce/Internet issues, new technologies are also constantly challenging the core principles of contract and evidence law. Much of the law of contract contemplates a paper-based written agreement, signed by the parties simultaneously in a face-to-face setting. Since the advent of the telegraph, however, more and more contracts have been effected at a distance using means other than paper. Thus, each new technological trend, from the telegraph to the Internet, has prompted the law of contract to reassess when and where offer and acceptance occurred and the time and place of the contract. Computers and related technologies, such as imaging, optical disks, and even direct output from computer to microfilm, have also raised questions as to the admissibility of evidence that is collected, stored, or altered by a computer. In the libel area, a completely new legal dynamic in the law of defamation has been created in a few short years as a result of the Internet connection of millions of personal computers to the vast global computer network. Today, untold numbers of "publishers" can access communication vehicles without editorial filters to monitor or control them. The first dynamic of computer law continues to churn up a host of legal issues in its wake.

2) The Elusive Nature of Information

The second dynamic of computer law is the elusive nature of information. Information is intangible. Unlike land and goods, which both have tangible, physical properties, information is ephemeral, and only begins to take on a physical presentation when it is reproduced on a medium such as paper. Intangible information, however, should not be confused with the physical vessels it tends to be carried in. Indeed, now that information in its electronic state has been freed from the constraints of paper, it can fully reveal its fluid, plastic nature. The dephysicalization of information has set it free. It is not only its intangibility, however, that makes information elusive. Another unusual aspect of this malleable asset is that it takes its value from its context. Traditional assets sometimes exhibit this, for example, when agricultural land is rezoned for residential or industrial use, but usually the purpose to which a particular plot of real estate is put is unchanging for a lengthy period of time. Similarly, tangible, moveable goods, like chairs, retain their single purpose throughout their existence. Information, in contrast, can gain or lose value and regain it again, for reasons completely extraneous to itself. Yet another aspect of elusiveness is that much information is incomplete, and therefore is continually in a state of becoming. Fact-intensive information (imagine a stock market feed) and scientific knowledge, even software, is constantly being improved and updated, like a service rather than a commodity. To define the parameters of information-based assets from a legal perspective or to regulate the use, reproduction, and movement of information-based assets is fiendishly difficult.

Intellectual property regimes face difficult challenges when confronted by the elusive nature of software and information-based products. While a court can easily delimit the contours of a parcel of land or the physical outlines of a chair, it cannot easily formulate sensible ownership regimes for information-based assets. It is no simple task to determine where the line between the protected and unprotected should be drawn, for example, with respect to facts contained in electronic databases. And even if the data were to be protected in some manner, would higher levels of aggregation based on the underlying data also be protected? Dissemination of ephemeral information over the Internet also raises a number of challenges for intellectual property law. The Supreme Court's decision in the *Stewart* case to not protect confidential information under the *Criminal Code*'s theft provision illustrates a similar difficulty caused by the second dynamic of computer law, and this lacuna in the criminal law has not been rectified with a statutory amendment. As well, the wire-tap cases in the criminal law area that recognize only the contents of conversations as deserving of protection and deny protection to seemingly peripheral information, such as the number of calls and their duration, again show the difficulty the legal system has with the ephemeral nature of data. The proponents of data protection legislation note that the intangible nature of personal information makes it so easy to disseminate it that it should be protected before the data begin their travels around the vast computer and telecommunications networks of the world. In certain commercial law contexts, such as the sale of goods and tax statutes, the challenge is to determine whether software is a good or a service. The dephysicalization of information — primarily through the substitution of electronic networks for stand-alone paper-based communications — also has important ramifications for contract and evidence law. In all these areas the second dynamic of computer law is hard at work.

3) The Blurring of Private/Public

A third theme in the computer law area is the blurring of the dividing line between the public and private spheres. This phenomenon is being driven largely by technological developments that permit individuals to assume greater powers of creation, storage, and dissemination of information-based works. In the past, the function of creating content-based works was restricted to businesses or organizations that could amass the financial and technical resources required to publish a book or produce a music record. Although these major content developers and distributors continue to exist, a multitude of smaller players now participate in the content creation business, aided by inexpensive personal computers, image scanners, and related technology. And the Internet will permit these players to bypass the traditional distribution infrastructures in order to market and transmit their content products directly to end users. Similarly, the Internet and CD-ROMs, for example, permit individuals to receive content in their homes or offices (which are increasingly partly or wholly at home). The same dynamic applies to data, especially personal information, which is now being recorded in many ways, as people sit in the privacy of their homes but broadcast data about themselves to the whole world on the Internet. All these developments fuse the public and private realms of human activity into one seamless, interconnected medium.

This third dynamic of computer law confronts intellectual property laws in several ways. Traditionally, infringers were businesses that sold their illegal wares to the public. This was dictated largely by technological constraints; a large printing press was required in order to make unauthorized copies of a book and sophisticated technology was required to make bootleg copies of films and vinyl long-playing records. Recently, since high-quality photocopiers are still beyond the means of individuals, most legal cases of unauthorized photocopying still involve larger defendants, such as companies, governments, or educational institutions. Current technologies, however, bring to the fore a whole new category of infringer, the private individual. Cheap handheld scanners, inexpensive computers, small and affordable photocopiers, and a raft of similar devices have permitted individuals to get into the reproduction business. And not just for their personal use. Machines that can produce copies of CD-ROMs are now within easy reach of an individual's budget. Most importantly, the Internet represents an extremely low-cost distribution mechanism for information-based products. Whether these trends are viewed as the extension of the public sphere into the private, or vice versa, the upshot for intellectual property owners is that the battlefield on which they will defend their assets will increasingly be private homes and offices. This is an uncomfortable venue for intellectual property law. It also raises very relevant questions about the practicalities of dealing with a multitude of infringers.

The third dynamic of computer law also has important ramifications for criminal law. The home and other private places like a person's automobile were considered by the law to be important sanctuaries, zealously protected from outside interference. Then homes began to be wired and otherwise connected to the outside world. In came the mail, radio, and television, each more forceful but still passive in nature. The telephone was the first interactive device, and now, of course, there is the Internet that brings the world to the desktop in an immediate and sustained manner. The physical membrane separating the private home from the public world is in tatters, and its penetration will have a profound impact on the law. The criminal law protections against search and seizure have been expanded to extend beyond the home, to cover the person, and in some cases to apply to information as well, though the *Fegan* and *Plant* cases illustrate that this process still requires some development. This may be the ironic result of the public intruding into the private; the private person in the comfort of her private study can perpetrate crime in the public sphere by connecting to the multitude of networks and computers accessible to her personal computer.

The proponents of a legal regime for data protection argue that a prime rationale for such a law is to prevent the fusion of public and private in the realm of personal information. Similarly, in the traditional world of export control the border was a relevant place at which to stop the export from Canada of items that cannot legally be shipped out of the country. However, software and technical data that are controlled items under the ECL can now be transmitted from an office or private home; indeed, even taking them out of the country by more traditional means is facilitated by putting the information on a small tape or CD-ROM or loading them into a laptop computer, which would be far more difficult to detect than a sheaf of blue prints. Satellite signals and electrical impulses sent over the Internet are extremely difficult to control, let alone block completely. Moreover, since they are received by private individuals, there are precious few intermediaries that the regulatory apparatus could use to help implement its goals. The "push" model of public broadcasting is far more amenable to CRTC regulatory oversight than the "pull" model of narrowcasting over the Internet; the blurring of private/public will present significant challenges to the CRTC over the coming years.

Libel on the Internet provides a compelling example of the fusion of private and public. There are no editorial filters or controlling intermediaries in the Internet environment, with the result that the border between private and public is erased and in its place is seamless cyberspace. E-mail is a trenchant example of the third dynamic of computer law; the same electronic message that can be sent seemingly privately to one recipient can, with the push of a few keystrokes, be distributed to millions. Courts and legislatures will have to respond creatively in order to deal with the challenges posed by the third dynamic of computer law.

4) The Blurring of National/International

A final dynamic involves another blurring, this time between the national and the international boundaries. The computer business is probably the most global industry in the world. Computers, software, and other information-based products are traded around the world at a frenzied pace. Since the invention of the telegraph, information has been flowing between countries at an increasing rate, to the point where today, with the Internet and other international private and public networks, enormous volumes of data, information, and content are transmitted over geographic frontiers every minute. These networks ignore geography in an increasing number of areas of human endeavour.

This dynamic is being felt keenly by the owner of intellectual property. There was a time when the business responsible for the infringement was located in the same jurisdiction as the content creator, when the authority of the intellectual property law clearly applied, and when the assistance of the local police could be called upon for large-scale infringement. Intellectual property was a national affair, since production centres were close to their markets. As international trade in books and other content-based product increased, Canadian content owners could still rely on customs officers to help keep out infringing products. These options began to erode once paper, vinyl, and celluloid were no longer the primary media for the carriage and presentation of content. Today, computer disks and CD-ROMs are much more difficult to control, and the Internet and other networks, which allow the digital bits and bytes themselves to be sent across the border, make it extremely difficult for national border guards to assist the domestic content creators. It's a very small world after all the technological advances of the last decade. At a conceptual level, international intellectual property treaties are making progress. Achieving redress for piracy in the real world, however, is an expensive, time-consuming, and imperfect exercise. It would also seem, at first blush, that the fusion of the national with the international would not cause too many conceptual concerns for the criminal law, given that extraditing criminals from abroad and gathering evidence in foreign lands has been a traditional activity in the criminal law realm. Nevertheless, the volume and sophistication of harmful computer-based conduct effected in one state adversely affecting persons, businesses, and organizations in another is unprecedented. For example, child pornography flows into Canada over the Internet, all but ignoring the electronically porous border. Most police forces are slowly beginning to grapple with the consequences of Internet crime. The evidentiary and enforcement issues will tax to the limit the current structures in place for international cooperation in crime prevention.

The supporters of data protection legislation for the private sector are well aware of the international dimensions of the issue. With huge amounts of personal data being transmitted around the world, there is the need for some mechanism to ensure consistent data protection globally. Otherwise, countries or substate jurisdictions will appear that are willing to ignore data protection laws in order to become "data havens." And just as data protection laws fight valiantly to keep alive the distinction between private and public, so too the export control laws endeavour to enforce the separateness of the national and the international. Nevertheless, the technological developments noted above, culminating in an Internet that ignores borders with impunity, make it more and more difficult to stand on guard at the border. The sources of many of the transmissions that the CRTC will find problematic lie outside of Canada. Regulation works best when there are intermediate control points, or choke points, within Canada where the regulator, by exercising control over a larger entity relatively high up in the distribution chain, can efficiently dictate the options available to the millions of individuals lower down in the chain. Radio and television stations, cable companies and telephone companies, each with significant operations and physical plant in Canada, have served admirably as control points in the past and will continue to do so for the foreseeable future as their product offerings continue to find a market in this country. Foreign satellite and Internet transmissions effectively bypass these control points and, for the most part, are requested and received directly by the end user in the privacy of his or her home. Although Internet transmissions are carried by Internet service providers, they generally act simply as conduits, and attempting to regulate content through them would be an enormous task for the CRTC. Such an effort, however, pales in comparison with regulating individual Internet users who access websites around the world in order to receive the new broadcasting programming. In short, the new technologies pose fundamental challenges to the manner in which the CRTC carries out its mandate.

The theme of national/international fusion also permeates electronic commerce/Internet issues. Initially, in the contractual setting, the focus was on determining which jurisdiction's law applies given that the electronic contractors were in different countries. More recently, the Internet has challenged the very concept of the nation state by eliminating geography as a factor in its use. Courts, governments, and regulators, sensing a profound threat, are responding in a manner that they hope will maintain national sovereignty in a networked world. Thus, foreign actors are being made subject to the jurisdiction of the United States when their conduct over the Internet has an impact on Americans. It is a small world, courtesy of the new technology, but one still consisting of separate and distinct countries. Therefore, users of the new technologies should not forget that the fourth dynamic of computer law speaks not in terms of the elimination of the national, but of its fusion with the international. Travellers on the Internet should not forget that when they extend their presence through the Internet into other countries, the laws of those countries may well come into play to regulate their activities.

B. COMPUTER LAW: THEMES

In addition to approaching computer law issues from the perspective of the four dynamics, four themes run throughout the legal subtopics that have been discussed in this book. The first is consistency. This theme emphasizes that legal rules for the computer industries should be consistent with the best jurisprudence applied to earlier technologies. As well, they should be consistent in different jurisdictions and in different subdisciplines of the law. A second theme relates to what may be termed *regulatory control points*, to order and enforce behaviour. The upshot of this theme is that in an electronic world the traditional control points are under pressure and new ones may have to be devised. A third theme relates to the rules of liability applicable to intermediaries. Entities that indirectly facilitate infringing, criminal, or libellous activities in a computer and networked environment, but who do not initiate the offending activity themselves, pose some difficult questions for the law, particularly in the Internet setting. A final theme concerns what may be termed *mischievous metaphors*. The legal system tends to analyse current activities, and persons or entities associated with them, in terms of categories developed in the past. This is a useful approach, but one fraught with dangers as it risks trapping its participant in out-dated and ill-fitting legal paradigms.

1) Consistency in Computer Laws

Consistency should play a role in computer law in at least three distinct but interrelated ways. First there is the objective of striving for historic consistency in the jurisprudence. This means, for example, that the preferred analytical approach to the Internet is an evenhanded, measured one. The Internet should not be viewed as a completely revolutionary and "never-seen-before" communication vehicle that "breaks all the rules." Nor should it be seen as representing "business as usual." The ideal approach is to see the Internet as another stage in the evolution of communications technologies that consist of mail, the telegraph, the telephone, radio, telex, fax, television, and the like. The new statutes and case law should be consistent with that of the past. Of course, this will not always be possible or even desirable, but in a surprising number of cases it will be, much to the delight of today's legal and business communities who are searching for sensible and predictable rules to order relations in the Information Age.

Consistency should also be an objective in national (i.e., among the Canadian provinces) and international contexts. In an industry as global as the computer business, countries can benefit from similar legal solutions in other countries. Thus, Canadian courts should regularly read the decisions of courts in the United States, Europe, Asia, and elsewhere, particularly where a point appears to be new in Canada. Where the foreign decision displays sound judgment and a sensible resolution of a thorny problem, the Canadian court should not hesitate to draw heavily on it.

Law makers should also not be averse to drawing generously on another jurisdiction's law, if it is well done and the jurisprudence under it appears sound. The tendency in some jurisdictions to insert unusual provisions solely to differentiate a law from its predecessors in other countries ought to be discouraged; indeed, uniform law exercises within a country (i.e., among the various provinces and the federal government) and between countries should be the norm for moving ahead with new legislative initiatives. Legislators should realize that the nation state cannot resolve some of the world's more intractable problems alone.

There is also a need for achieving consistency among the different subdisciplines of computer law. It is common for two or more areas of computer law to consider the same issue, albeit from a different perspective (which should never be forgotten). Both the civil law of intellectual property and the criminal law have had to wrestle with the contours of what constitutes confidential information. Sales statutes and tax statutes have had to wrestle with the intangible properties of software. The concepts of public and private are germane to copyright, criminal law, and privacy laws. Originality is a concept native both to intellectual property law and evidence law. On these and other points there has been some cross-fertilization among different areas of the law, but not nearly enough. Obviously, this should not be done unthinkingly, but there is no reason why, for example, the concepts of public and private should not be the same across all the laws that utilize these words, particularly where use on the Internet is concerned.

2) Control Points and the Law

The law has traditionally relied heavily on several regulatory control points to help enforce its rules. One important control point used to be geography and its various physical derivatives and associated principles. Historically, most intellectual property enforcement focussed on the businesses that made or distributed infringing copies of protected works. The retail establishment on the street sold the illegal music records produced by the infringing pressing plant in the industrial park. Illegal goods crossing the border could be intercepted by customs authorities. These geographic control points continue to exist, but they are handling fewer and fewer information-based products because they are being bypassed altogether by consumers who can obtain digital content directly, on disk, by mail order, or over the Internet. And regulating the individual in the comfort of his or her own home is onerous and not politically popular, hence the change in the copyright law to permit private copying of music in exchange for a levy on blank tapes.

Another important control point has been the physical identity of an individual. In a number of contexts, such as pornography, gaming, and even with some contract/evidence law issues, the ability of a gatekeeper or ticket taker to look at a person and to judge their age or other physical characteristics was a key part of the legal regime regulating that activity. With the move to electronic environments that no longer require physical presence, the law is confronted with either banning non-physical access to the computer-based environment or striving to recreate the same security of identity but in an online context. While this will be a challenging task, there are new biometric and other authentication technologies being developed that may assist.

Paper has traditionally been an important control point for information. In many areas the existence of paper, and the process leading up to the creation of the particular paper-based document, served as an important legal ordering function. Putting "pen to paper" usually meant a single author, or a small subset of authors, could clearly identify their discrete contributions to the work. In contract and evidence law, a signed paper document gives comfort, not just because the signatory put her autograph on it, but because the very process of signing most documents usually entails being present, physically, with the document, and therefore probably reading it (or at least discussing it with someone else). These factors cannot be taken for granted in a non–paper-based environment. That is not to say new control points cannot be created in a digital environment. Their focus, however, may not be on a particular letter or document, but on whether the system creating them is working properly, in which case the authenticity and veracity of the information will simply be assumed.

3) Intermediary Liability

A recurring theme in computer law is that the direct protagonist of a particular mischief is unavailable to the person harmed. Thus, the infringer of a copyright work, or the creator of the obscene material, or the author of the libellous statement, cannot be found, or is impecunious, or is otherwise not worth pursuing. In each case, however, one or more parties providing one or more services is associated with some technology or business practice that in some way assists the perpetrator of the blameworthy conduct. The question in such a context is straightforward: Should the intermediary be liable for the harm?

While the question may be put simply, the answer is complicated. The first step in responding to it is to understand the intermediary's precise role in the allegedly harmful activity. Then the analysis should focus on what knowledge and control the intermediary had on either the creation or dissemination of the problematic message. And by knowledge, more is meant than actual knowledge. Negligence might also suffice if the entity had reason to know that the perpetrator was a "regular" on the network, and the entity took no steps to minimize the harm. Or, in a criminal context, a similar standard is referred to by the term *wilful blindness*; that is, the operator of the service suspected a problem but consciously decided not to look further. In these and related sorts of situations, visiting the intermediary with liability will be appropriate. And again, the law ought to strive for consistency in the various subareas that deal with intermediary liability.

4) Mischievous Metaphors

There are many situations in computer law where the lawyer, judge, academic, or legislator is confronted with what seems to be a novel situation and, in order to make sense of it, a similar example — a metaphor — for the new activity is found in past experience. When determining an Internet participant's liability for libel, for example, there is a strong urge to categorize the participant as "publisher," "news vendor," "bookstore," "library," "broadcaster," etc., because the entire legal schema associated with the category can be utilized without having to expend too much time and effort. This tendency to use metaphor, incidentally, is not unique to lawyers. The etymology of the Internet is full of it. One "surfs the Web," although one wonders just how many spiders can ride the real wooden boards of Southern California. Or one uses a "bookmark" to save the location of a site. Metaphors are used elsewhere in computing: one "cuts and pastes" text in a word processing program. And, of course, outside the computer industry, car engines are still measured in "horsepower," a holdover from the days when cars and buggies shared the same road.

Metaphors can help the novice quickly grasp something new by putting it in the context of something old. They can also, however, become substitutes for vigorous, independent thought and analysis. Lawyers often have problems explaining what something is; rather, they describe what it is like. After a point, metaphors can do as much harm as good. Similarly, legal classification systems can also be counterproductive if not approached with great care. Consider one author's assessment of the predilection of scientists to slot phenomena into pigeon-holes:

> Early zoologists classified as mammals those that suckle their young and as reptiles those that lay eggs. Then a duck-billed platypus was discovered in Australia laying eggs like a perfect reptile and then, when they hatched, suckling the infant platypi like a perfect mammal.
>
> The discovery created quite a sensation. What an enigma! it was exclaimed. What a mystery! What a marvel of nature! When the first stuffed specimens reached England from Australia around the end of the eighteenth century they were thought to be fakes made by sticking together bits of different animals. Even today you still see occasional articles in nature magazines asking, "Why does this paradox of nature exist?"
>
> The answer is: it doesn't. The platypus isn't doing anything paradoxical at all. It isn't having any problems. Platypi have been laying their eggs and suckling their young for millions of years before there were any zoologists to come along and declare it illegal. The real mystery, the real enigma, is how mature, objective, trained scientific observers can blame their own goof on a poor innocent platypus.
>
> Zoologists, to cover up their problem, had to invent a patch. They created a new order, monotremata, that includes the platypus, the spiny anteater, and that's it. This is like a nation consisting of two people.[1]

Like good scientists, lawyers must not allow their classification systems to become confining straightjackets. So, in assessing the liability of an Internet participant, the focus should be on function rather than status. Then a very careful assessment of the participant and technology involved in the cases being compared should be undertaken. Again, function should be the hallmark. For example, it is not enough to say

---

1   Robert M. Pirsig, *Lila: An Inquiry into Morals* (New York: Bantam, 1991) at 101–2.

that a particular case stands for the proposition that a fax can be used to deliver a message in writing, or that a cellular phone message comes under the wire-tap prohibition of the *Criminal Code*; in both cases a detailed understanding of the particular kind of fax and cellular technology is required as this will have enormous impact on their jurisprudential value. And where there is a dearth of applicable metaphors — where we are confronted by a legal platypus — courts and legislators should not hesitate to carve out new categories, essentially the monotremata of computer law.

C. COMPUTER LAW: SKILL SETS

The dynamics inherent in computer law, and in the technological trends driving it, present lawyers and other participants in the legal system with a number of daunting challenges. In tackling these challenges, four primary skill sets, or approaches, can be contemplated. Recourse can be had to the common law by relying on judge-made decisions to address the various novel and pressing legal issues presented by the computer and information-based assets. A second skill set centres on contract law, and the ability of entities, when confronted with new or uncertain situations, to craft their own laws, as it were, for use between the private parties. Technology can also be employed to fill gaps and fissures in the law by channelling behaviour through the use of specific technological devices contained within computers, networks, and software programs. The fourth skill set relates to law reform, which involves shepherding through the parliamentary process legislation that will address the specific needs of participants in the computer, networking, and information-based industries. This book concludes with a discussion of the parameters of these four skill sets.

1) Common Law

The genius of the common law lies in its tremendously flexible nature. It would appear, therefore, that the common law would be extremely well suited to coping with the four dynamics of the computer industry. Through the good offices of a presiding judge, the common law can quickly accommodate existing rules to apply to a new technology or product. Judges should also be able to assess the economic differences between tangible assets, on the one hand, and information, on the other hand. As for the public/private dimension, judges act as guardians of the private sphere of human existence, just as they can delineate national boundaries to ensure that the international nature of the computer business does not defeat the protective objectives of various national laws, though the common law regularly falls short in achieving this goal.

In the intellectual property area, several decisions, such as in the American *Altai* and Canadian *Delrina* and *Prism* cases, craft tests for infringement that, while not satisfying everyone with their precise contours, nevertheless indicate an effective understanding of the relevant technology. Moreover, the reduction in the scope of protection between the *Whelan* and *Altai* cases illustrates the common law's ability to recalibrate itself where a consensus begins to emerge that the previous standard is either incorrect, dysfunctional, or merely dated. In the area of electronic commerce, again judges have shown their willingness to adapt the law of contract and evidence to new technological conditions. In a host of situations judges have shown a receptiveness to new technology, and an ability to tackle the four dynamics of computer law. Accordingly, a participant in the computer industry, when confronted with a new legal problem, should be willing to consider making use of the common law skill set, at least in certain circumstances.

Not in all circumstances, however. For all the court decisions that are made with a sensitivity to the new technologies and with a willingness to wade into new fact situations armed only with analogies from a low-tech past, there are other decisions that show the court's aversion to tackling technological subject matter. In some cases, there is an admitted lack of understanding of the technical material presented by the parties. In the criminal law area, there is an unwillingness on the part of judges to perform a role they believe rightfully rests with Parliament, namely, keeping the *Criminal Code* abreast of new technological developments. In other areas such as data protection, there is not a relevant statutory regime, and judges are reluctant to create a new branch of the law when the jurisprudential underpinnings are so weak. Moreover, even where a particular judge decides to venture forth boldly and to tackle a new technological conundrum confronting the law, there is always the problem that the decision will stand alone for some time, while participants in the computer industry wait anxiously to see if it will be adopted in their own jurisdiction. This was the situation Canadians faced in the trial judgment in the *Tele-Direct* case that considered the scope of protection for material in a yellow pages telephone directory. The U.S. *Feist* case was briefed before the trial judge in this case, but the court declined to decide whether the principles animating *Feist* were directly applicable, or not, in Canada. Unfortunately, the result was that Canadian database developers did not know precisely what degree of protection they had for their products on the two sides of the

Canada–U.S. border. Put another way, the common law, because of its very nature as a vehicle that is national in scope, is often poorly equipped to deal with the fourth dynamic of computer law, namely, its international dimension. Fortunately, the Federal Court of Appeal cleared up this uncertainty in the *Tele-Direct* case by indicating that Canadian and U.S. copyright laws provided a similar degree of protection for fact-based compilations.

2) Contract

Contracts are another skill set, or approach, that address the dynamics in computer law. In the intellectual property area, contracts can be harnessed in many ways. For example, where electronic databases are not protected, the particular property can be exploited pursuant to a licence agreement that requires the user to agree to a certain set of rules, including, most importantly, not transferring the information to third parties. In effect, a result not afforded by intellectual property law is achieved through contract. Even with information-based assets that are clearly protected by intellectual property law, such as software, contracts are still used to regulate the dissemination of the asset. Software licence agreements restrict the use that can be made of the software, such as to process only the data of the user and not of third parties, and also prohibit a user from transferring the software to a third party. A contract requiring the user to maintain the confidentiality of the information is central to the very preservation of the trade secrecy status of software.

Contracts are also used to clarify the relationship between two parties. In the commercial context, for example, contracts between the users and suppliers of computers and services might specify such matters as when the particular computer system is to be considered accepted by the user. In a similar vein, the parties will override the generic implied warranties and conditions provided in sale of goods statutes so that the reasonable expectations of the parties can be managed, and met, with a greater likelihood of success. Achieving greater certainty than the general law is also a prime rationale for the use of contracts in the field of electronic commerce. Parties desiring their electronic messages to constitute binding agreements can provide, in a master written agreement, precisely which messages, when transmitted to specific computers, will give rise to irrevocable contracts. Similarly, they can stipulate what records of these messages will be admissible as evidence. In short, parties endeavour to make their own law by means of contracts. The result has been the development of a wide variety of contracts for the computer industry, including shrinkwrap licences for software and trading partner agreements for electronic data interchange. Indeed, by opting for arbitration over the court system as a means of dispute resolution, the parties can also, again through contract, deal privately and precisely with the rules they wish to have applied if they have a falling out with one another.

If the number and variety of contracts were not proof enough of their important role in the computer industry, consider how well the contract vehicle responds to the four dynamics of computer law. Private parties can agree to stay current with technological change, as when the parties to an EDI trading partner agreement determine, in the contract, how they will keep their system updated. Contracts can also handle the unique indicia of information-based, intangible assets, such as when a software licence, or database exploitation agreement, defines with precision what does, and what does not, constitute the protected material of each party. Similarly, contracting parties can undertake to keep certain information confidential, thus attempting to keep from becoming public that which is private. Finally, contracts travel well across borders, thereby allowing a seamless welding of the domestic with the international, fusing two different domestic legal systems (each party's "international" is invariably the other party's "national"). Indeed, the contract vehicle is so useful in bridging the gap between different nations that international arbitration conducted in a third country is often used to move the legal venue of any dispute out of either party's jurisdiction. Contracts have proven themselves, time and again, to be an essential skill set for the legal practitioner seeking to implement secure, lasting solutions in the computer law field.

Contracts, however, are not panaceas. They involve a number of specific costs and disadvantages that should be weighed at the outset. Transaction costs for negotiating and drafting contracts for high-tech goods can be quite high, when calculated as a percentage of the total value of the deal. There is much risk for both buyer and seller and much time and effort can be expended on larger deals. For simpler transactions, the computer industry has developed the shrinkwrap licence that is enclosed with the mass marketed product; it is read but not signed by the user who consents by commencing to use the software. Although this type of contract is increasingly being used across the computer industry, there are concerns about unfair bargaining power on the side of the supplier and even unconscionability.

Contracts, however, lead to another concern, which might be called the privatization of the legal system. Consider the use of arbitration as a dispute resolution mechanism. The parties, in their contract, provide for private, speedy arbitration if ever a claim arises between them. One day the arbitration provision is invoked, and the privately appointed arbitrator quietly settles a thorny point of fact and law, perhaps in the area of electronic commerce. From a private perspective this has been an efficient episode of dispute resolution. From a public perspective, however, the jurisprudence of computer law has been denied a reported case that could serve to educate others. Contrary to popular wisdom, the objective is not to learn from your own mistakes, but to learn from the mistakes of others. The private arbitration model does not have a pedagogical aspect, which is provided by the common law in the publicly available decisions of trial and appeal courts that canvass the facts of the cases they decide. At a micro level the parties are better off, but at a macro level the legal system is disadvantaged. The same problem is encountered wherever the general statutory rules are abandoned in favour of private ordering through contract.

3) Technical Solutions

The privatization of computer law through the use of contracts stands to be assisted by another skill set, namely, the use of technical devices to control the dissemination and use of software and other information-based products. Put another way, content creators and owners who perceive there to be serious shortcomings in the common law, or in the current statute-based law, as they apply to the protection and exploitation of high-tech goods and services, are likely to gravitate towards technologically oriented solutions to make up for shortcomings in the law. Some software is already distributed in a copy-protected format; this software is activated in a manner that will make it operate only on a specific computer of the user, thereby deterring the making of unauthorized copies of the program. Although not in widespread use because users find it too cumbersome and most suppliers of mass market software do not want to put obstacles in the way of the use of their products, the full potential of such copy protection devices will be achieved in the context of protecting the dissemination of content over the Internet. Several forms of digital metering are also being developed that will track authorized transmissions of content over networks and restrict unauthorized distribution of the content. Coupled with sophisticated but inexpensive and user-friendly encryption technologies, such digital metering devices will permit content owners to capture 100 percent of the potential returns derived from the use of their products.

Such digital metering technologies and other devices that permit the content owner to control the distribution and use of his or her material have implications for the various intellectual property law regimes. Most pressing, perhaps, is the possibility that such technologies could lead to a complete displacement of the *Copyright Act*. The *Copyright Act* represents a carefully measured set of compromises between content creator and user. For example, when a book is purchased from an authorized dealer, the purchaser can resell it or lend it, but cannot make copies of it except in the context of fair dealing for the personal research or study of the user. Moreover, the *Copyright Act* permits potential book buyers to browse through the work at the bookseller before deciding whether to buy it. Libraries can do even more by lending books to patrons on a temporary basis. Important questions arise from proposed widespread digital metering that will restrict all forms of use of the work except those specifically authorized by the content owner. Will practices such as the resale of content, or the lending of content by libraries, or the browsing of content in a retail environment be permitted and at what cost? If these activities are completely curtailed, or made too expensive for the average person, then what would have been achieved is an end run around the *Copyright Act* — a finessing of the public policy tradeoffs inherent in the statute. Such a private ordering system would turn the information highway into a toll road of mammoth proportions. People of modest means may not be able to access it at all.

It would appear, then, that the technical skill set responds favourably to the four dynamics of computer law noted above. It positively glows from the perspective of the rapid rate of technological change, because this skill set is of technology itself. By being integrated into the content, digital metering and related devices can adapt as the product or delivery mechanism changes. In this regard, the technology skill set is superior to even the contract one. Similarly, the ephemeral nature of software and information-based assets can also be easily accommodated because technology, particularly in the form of encryption devices, is used to respond to the very fact that makes intangible information so elusive. Encryption and other security measures can also be used to keep private information from leaking into the public realm, and so one can anticipate that technological solutions will play an important role in addressing privacy and data protection legal issues. And, of course, the technology can be made to operate globally, so that the technical skill set can be made effective around the world.

Yet the technical skill set carries with it nagging concerns. The fact that it operates outside of established legal regimes raises the problems of uniformity of treatment, cost of access, lack of transparency, and transaction costs. Coupled with the contract skill set, nothing less than a wholesale sidestepping of the current legal system is being proposed. Those who do not relish such a result can respond in one of two ways. First, they can focus on the contract/technical skill sets and attempt to ameliorate their most objectionable aspects by regulating, for example, access to certain groups such as libraries and schools. The other approach is to focus on the fourth skill set, law reform, in order to convince content owners and other participants in the computer industry not to abandon the public legal systems in favour of private solutions.

4) Law Reform

Law reform is the fourth skill set available to participants in the computer industry. The law has adapted often to the Information Age, such as with the repeal of the writing requirement in Ontario's sales statute to remove doubt as to the enforceability of contracts concluded electronically for the sale of goods. Many other areas, however, need a review from the perspective of possible law reform, including intellectual property (such as the protection of databases and the implementation of intellectual property principles on the Internet), data protection, and the privacy of personal information, evidence law and record retention rules, commercial law issues, and Internet issues such as the liability of service providers for libel and copyright infringement initiated by others. Law reform can play a vital role in alleviating shortcomings in the common law and can obviate the need to rely on contractual and technical mechanisms. Law reform is sometimes required because certain judges, when confronted with a new technology, are unwilling to create a new category of rights, calling instead upon the legislature to do so if they think it appropriate. To achieve such lofty ambitions, however, the particular law reform initiative must respond to the four dynamics of computer law.

First, and perhaps foremost, the process of law reform must stay current with technological developments. To this end, an Institute for the Study of Computer Law could be established, either as a stand-alone entity or as part of an existing organization. The institute's mandate would be to conduct, on an ongoing basis, studies of existing and new technologies and their impact on the legal system and on the information society more broadly. Such an institute would be multidisciplinary, drawing on expertise in all the legal subdisciplines.

The second element in the effort to keep current with the raging pace of technology would be a Parliamentary standing committee (or a subcommittee of one of the current standing committees) that would have as its entire or partial mandate the monitoring of developments in the information society and an assessment, on a continuous and sustained basis, of whether Canadian law is adequate to deal with the new issues and conundrums. Again, as with the institute, one objective would be to build up expertise and develop a rigorous approach to enquiry, as opposed to the *ad hoc* manner in which current efforts are undertaken. For example, several years ago there was a flurry of research activity surrounding the information highway, and several reports were released. Although this was valuable work and there has been some follow-up, an ongoing commitment to review issues — some identified, some not — is missing

The process of introducing proposed legislation is also *ad hoc*. The history of legislative amendments to the *Copyright Act* is a telling case in point. The amendments in 1988 and the Bill C-32 amendments in April 1997 each proceeded on the basis of trying to make a large number of changes to the law because copyright law reform was seen as an extremely rare occurrence. Consequently, huge lobbying efforts were mobilized in both cases, leading to a number of unsatisfactory provisions in the 1988 amendments. In effect, law reform in the areas discussed by this book all too often become gut-wrenching, pitched battles between vehemently opposed interests, with the result that even relatively uncontroversial proposals are held up, and often get caught up in the crossfire of the larger truly divisive issues. Arguably better and more effective law reform would result from a cadence of proposed amendments that were less ambitious but more frequent.

These proposals should not be taken to favour a particularly active law reform agenda. The study of issues and new technologies should be ongoing and vigorous; proposing legislative solutions should be a more circumspect exercise. In most cases, Parliament should allow the common law a reasonable period of time to see if it can adequately handle the new challenge. Often it will, possibly assisted by scholarship emanating from the institute or the Parliamentary committee. Where the judicial decisions are inconsistent or in conflict, or where the issues are too numerous and the interests too diverse, or where the common law is too inefficient, or where the courts specifically seek Parliament's assistance — in these cases the law reform process will be prepared to craft more timely and more sensible solutions.

In terms of the actual law reforms, care should be taken to regulate function or behaviour, and not form. Artificial categories with seemingly handy, but ultimately counterproductive, labels should be avoided. Thus, in the age of convergence in the broadcasting and telecommunications areas, references to telephone companies and cable companies need to be increasingly replaced by reference to what a particular entity does, not what it generally calls itself. In the tax area a similar heed should be paid to the underlying business activity, rather than to the formal categories established by the *Income Tax Act*, when dealing with topics such as withholding tax. As well, drafters of new laws should usually strive for technologically neutral legislative provisions so that the resulting law stands a better chance of withstanding the onslaught of the first dynamic of computer law, namely, the rapid pace of technological change.

Law reform needs to be global or at least to involve Canada's primary trading partners. Thus, the institute and the Parliamentary committees should endeavour to monitor international developments so that Canada's initiatives line up with similar moves abroad. If there are no such international counterparts, then an important role in Canadian law reform will be to help stimulate them, particularly through international bodies such as WIPO. And, of course, law reform in Canada should be consistent across the provinces; therefore, the Uniform Law Conference of Canada exercises are important. A law reform skill set that is animated by such considerations will serve an extremely useful purpose. It will help fill gaps left by the common law, and may relieve some of the intense pressure to rely overly on contract and technical solutions. Of course, in all likelihood resort to all four skill sets will be required over time, depending on the particular issue confronting computer law.

TABLE OF CASES

INDEX

ABOUT THE AUTHOR

George S. Takach is a Toronto-based partner of McCarthy Tétrault, Canada's national law firm, where he is head of the High Tech Law Group. Mr. Takach practises business law, with an emphasis on software, computers, technology, and related matters. A recent nationwide survey conducted by Lexpert, a law directory publisher, ranked Mr. Takach among a handful of leading lawyers in Canada in the computer law field. This survey also found McCarthy Tétrault to have the strongest computer law practice in Canada.

Mr. Takach previously taught a course in computer law at the University of Toronto's Faculty of Law, and currently (since 1990) teaches "Computers, Information, and the Law" at Osgoode Hall Law School. Mr. Takach has a B.A. (Hons.) in political economy from the University of Toronto; the third year of this degree was completed at the Institut d'Études Politique, Université d'Aix-Marseilles, France. He also has an M.A. in international relations from the Norman Paterson School of International Affairs, Carleton University in Ottawa. He earned his LL.B. from the Faculty of Law, University of Toronto, where he graduated on the Dean's List.

What spare time George has he spends with the two women in his life: his wife, Janis, and their daughter, Natalie. They especially enjoy skiing and travelling together.

McCarthy Tétrault (prior to 1991, McCarthy & McCarthy) is Canada's largest law firm with over 600 lawyers in offices in Vancouver, Surrey, Calgary, London, Toronto, Ottawa, Montreal, Quebec, and London, England. The firm provides Canadian and international clients with a wide range of legal services, including business law, litigation, and numerous specialty areas. The firm's High Tech Law Group has extensive experience serving a wide variety of Canadian and international technology companies and organizations marketing or acquiring various computing and other technology resources.

George S. Takach
Phone: (416) 601-7662
Fax: (416) 868-1891
Internet: gtakach@mccarthy.ca